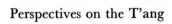

Perspectives on the T'ang

Perspectives on the T'ang

edited by Arthur F. Wright and Denis Twitchett

New Haven and London, Yale University Press

1973

Designed by John O. C. McCrillis
and set in Baskerville type.
Printed in the United States of America by
The Murray Printing Co., Forge Village, Massachusetts.

Published in Great Britain, Europe, and Africa by
Yale University Press, Ltd., London.
Distributed in Latin America by Kaiman & Polon,
Inc., New York City; in Australasia and Southeast
Asia by John Wiley & Sons Australasia Pty. Ltd.,
Sydney; in India by UBS Publishers' Distributors Pvt.,
Ltd., Delhi; in Japan by John Weatherhill, Inc., Tokyo.

Contents

v

Maps

Acknowledgments

The editors have many to thank for enabling them to organize the first research conference on T'ang studies ever held in the West, and for assistance in turning the conference papers into a volume. We wish first of all to thank the American Council of Learned Societies which, through its Committee on Studies of Chinese Civilization, sponsored the conference. The hospitality of Cambridge University and of Sidney Sussex College provided excellent amenities for the meeting. To these were added the private showing of Chinese antiquities arranged for the conferees by Cheng Te-k'un and the evening of T'ang music reconstructed and played by the noted musicologist Laurence Picken.

The rapporteurs were extremely conscientious and wrote up a wonderfully coherent account of the proceedings. They were Hilary Beattie of Newnham College, Cambridge; Michael Dalby now of the Society of Fellows, Harvard; and Robert Somers of Yale University. Mr. Somers also helped with the editing of several of the papers and prepared the glossary-index. We are deeply in his debt.

Finally we wish to thank the editors' secretaries, who did much of the essential work for the conference and the volume, especially Janis Cochran of the Yale history department and Joan Howlett of Cambridge University.

Abbreviations

CKCY	Chen-kuan cheng-yao
Code	Ku T'ang-lü shu-i
CTP	Sui T'ien-t'ai Chih-che Ta-shih pieh-chuan
CTS	Chiu T'ang-shu
CTShih	Ch'üan T'ang shih
CTW	Ch'üan T'ang-wen
CWTS	Chiu Wu-tai Shih
FTTC	Fo-tsu t'ung-chi
FTTT	Fo-tsu li-tai t'ung-tsai
HJAS	Harvard Journal of Asiatic Studies
HKSC	Hsü-kao-seng-chuan
HTS	Hsin T'ang-shu
HWTS	Hsin Wu-tai Shih
HYISIS	Harvard-Yenching Institute Sinological Index Series
KCPL	Kuo-ch'ing po-lu
KHMC	Kuang Hung-ming chi
RGG	Ryō no gige
RSG	Ryō no shūge
SKCC	Shih-kuo ch'un-ch'iu
SKSC	Sung-kao-seng-chuan
SPPY	Ssu-pu pei-yao
SPTK	Ssu-pu ts'ung-k'an
T	Taishō shinshū Daizōkyō
TCTC	Tzu-chih t'ung-chien
TFYK	Ts'e-fu yüan-kuei
THY	T'ang hui-yao
TLT	T'ang liu-tien
TT	T'ung-tien
TTCLC	T'ang ta-chao-ling chi

1. Introduction

Denis Twitchett and Arthur F. Wright

In the millennial history of the Chinese Empire the T'ang, 618–907, is one of the great ages. It was a time of unprecedented material prosperity, of institutional growth, of new departures in thought and religion, of creativity in all the arts. What accounts for its tremendous vitality? First was its eclecticism—the way the T'ang drew together the many cultural strands from the tumultuous history of the preceding four hundred years. Second was its cosmopolitanism—its openness to foreign influences of all kinds. These qualities of T'ang civilization gave it a universal appeal. From T'ang China neighboring peoples drew the elements which transformed for all time their own cultures. And to T'ang China came people from all over Asia: students and Buddhist monks from Korea and Japan; tribal leaders and warriors from among the Turks, the Khitans, the Uighurs; emissaries, artists, and musicians from the oasis kingdoms of Central Asia; merchants from many lands— Samarkand, Bokhara, India, Persia, Syria, and Arabia among others. The T'ang capital at Ch'ang-an was more than the functioning capital of a great empire: it was a cosmopolis, the greatest city in the world; it was the radiating center of civilization for the whole of Eastern Asia; from it came the latest in Buddhist doctrine, the latest in poetical modes, authoritative models for institutions, and so on, down to the newest in *haute couture* and hair styles.

If we are to understand the universal or cosmopolitan quality of T'ang civilization, we must look briefly at its heritage from the past. In the distant past the men of T'ang saw their political model: the great empire of Han, which had disintegrated in the second century A.D. They saw this model across a great reach of time during which Han institutions had largely given way to militarism and hereditary privilege. From the Han the T'ang had inherited, over centuries during

1

which the tradition had barely survived, the moral and ideological system of imperial Confucianism.

However, the effects of the intervening Age of Disunion (c. 180–581), when invaders from the steppe displaced the Chinese from the ancient centers of their culture in North China, were to be seen in almost every aspect of T'ang life. In the north the culture of the invaders mingled with that of the subject Chinese. In the south the Chinese legitimists imbibed over the centuries more and more of the ancient southern regional cultures. Below the Yangtse the outward push of Chinese agricultural settlement wrested the land from the aborigines and started the process that would eventually turn the area into the richest part of China. The Age of Disunion was also the time of the Buddhist invasion of both North and South China, first the transplantation of basically Indian ideas and institutions, followed by their transformation into Chinese adaptations in almost infinite variations of those ideas and institutions. Buddhist temples and monasteries were to be seen across the land—in the cities and towns, in remote mountain areas, on eminences along the great rivers. With the growth of Buddhism and its spreading power came the emergence of a new variety of the Chinese tradition of Taoism, which, from the fifth century onward, began to compete with Buddhism for the minds of Chinese of all classes.

If the T'ang had been the *direct* heirs of the complex legacy of the Age of Disunion, their history would have been quite different. But many of the tasks of reuniting these diverse and often discordant elements into a workable cultural and political system had been accomplished for them by their immediate predecessors, the short-lived dynasty of Sui (581–617). We should therefore say a word about the Sui accomplishment, which laid so many of the foundations of T'ang civilization.

Sui Wen-ti (reigned 581–604) was a typical northern aristocrat of the sixth century, whose family had intermarried advantageously with families of the dominant foreign peoples. Tough and ruthless, he was a formidable strategist and a hard-driving admininstrator. He was heir to the mighty war machine of the last of the purely Northern Dynasties, which he used, first, to crush resistance in the great Yellow River plain and then, in 589, to destory the last of the "legitimate" Chinese dynasties in the south. After these military victories, he proceeded to create a centralized imperial system for the whole reunited empire and took steps to limit hereditary privilege as a qualification for public office and to establish an examination system. In addition to reorganizing central and local administration and demilitarizing to a large degree the practices and the ethos of government, he established a code of law, which drew on several legal traditions from the Age of Disunion. He began the process, completed by his son, of building an empire-wide system of canals and roads. He ordered the design and the building of what was to be the T'ang capital of Ch'ang-an, while his son saw to the construction of what was to be the T'ang's eastern and secondary capital at Loyang. The building of a granary system for the empire was likewise begun by the father and completed by the son. In all the areas surrounding China, the Sui made its power felt: Japan and Formosa, Indochina, Central Asia, Mongolia, and Manchuria. Although the Sui met defeat and consequent domestic rebellions in their effort to conquer the Manchurian-Korean kingdom of Koguryŏ, their many expeditions, their repair and renovations of the Great Wall, and their setting up of garrison posts and military colonies undoubtedly left the people of the periphery with a new sense of a reunited and formidable Chinese power.

In the civil war that followed the failure of the Sui forces in the northeast, there arose a great variety of contending parties—bandit groups, fleeing conscripts, regional dissidents—but it is significant that the most formidable armies that rose against Sui rule were commanded and officered by disaffected members of the Sui elite. The first of these was Yang Hsüan-kan, son of the *éminence grise* of the Sui court and, at the time of his revolt in June of 613, president of the Board of Ritual. He was crushed, but in the next few years other members of the Sui elite also defected. Li Mi, who came from a line of noted officials, led the armies that broke the back of Sui power. In 617 there rose in revolt the experienced Sui commander at Taiyuan, Li Yüan. His mother had been a sister of the first Sui empress, and his ancestors for generations had held office under the non-Chinese dynasties of the north. Li Yüan was thus no bandit chief or proletarian rebel, but a member of the favored elite of the Sui empire who might be expected to bring about, not a revolution, but a restoration of order by a new dynasty. This is exactly what he did. He took the Sui capital late in 617, and six months later he proclaimed the new dynasty of T'ang.

Li Yüan (posthumously T'ang Kao-tsu) reigned for nine years, most of which were spent crushing the remaining contenders for power and restoring peace and order throughout the land. Li Yüan's second son, Li Shih-min, led a series of hard-fought but victorious campaigns against formidable rivals in the great plain, and by 624 peace had been restored. In 626, Shih-min, whose successes had made him the object of deadly plots by his brother the crown prince, ambushed the crown prince and his party (including another brother) outside the north gate of Ch'ang-an. He killed the principals and a few weeks later forced his father to abdicate. He ascended the throne and proclaimed the era name Chen-kuan.

The reign of Li Shih-min (T'ang T'ai-tsung) from 627 to 649 has been viewed by men of later times as a period of enlightened rule during which a gifted emperor worked in perfect harmony with the talented officials who surrounded him. T'ai-tsung was indeed a brilliant man, but during the early part of his reign he had everything to learn from his officials about the conduct of civil government. He learned very fast, and his instinct for choosing the right men was unerring. During his reign the predominance of the mixed-blood aristocracy of the northwest, which had been a feature of all the Northern Dynasties for more than two centuries, slowly began to decline, and a higher proportion of officialdom came from the great plain and from the south. An increasing, though still small, number of officials without strong official family backing were moving into positions of importance in the T'ang bureaucracy on the basis of merit alone. The emergence of a more diversified elite was symptomatic of the full unification of the empire—a process the Sui had only begun.

There were no striking innovations in the structure of government or the exercise of power under T'ai-tsung. Domestically, he refined the centralized governmental machinery set up by Sui Wen-ti, accomplishing, for example: improvements in the quality of local officials, reduction and rationalization of the units of provincial and local government, stepped up support for schools, recodification of the laws, revival of the relief granaries (i-tsang) that had been part of the Sui system, and improvement of the canal system. In foreign policy T'ai-tsung had notable successes: the breaking of the power of the Western Turks and the assertion of Chinese control over the Tarim Basin and the oasis kingdoms along the main routes to the West all the way to the Pamirs. As a result, trade with Central Asia and with India grew. The Chinese court received embassies from Sassanid Persia and the Byzantine Empire. Ch'ang-an was thronged with merchants, emissaries, foreign monks, and it had a variety of foreign communities—a pan-Asian cosmopolitanism reflected in exotic goods in the markets, foreign styles of clothing and dance, and the temples of Zoroastrianism, Manicheanism, and Nestorianism, which now were added to the magnificent Buddhist and Taoist establishments. T'ai-tsung's boast in 639 reflects the extent of his accomplishments and some of the complacency this engendered: "In times past those who have thoroughly unified the empire and conquered the barbarians of the four quarters were only Ch'in Shih Huang-ti and Han Wu-ti. I, with my three-foot sword, have pacified all within the four seas, and the barbarians from distant places have come to submit, one after the other. In this accomplishment I yield nothing to those two monarchs."

The last years of his reign were marred by a disastrous and divisive struggle over the succession. The man who succeeded him—known in history as Kao-tsung (reigned 650–83)—is generally and rightly regarded as a weak successor to his great and effective father. His first years were dominated by the surviving great statesmen who had served his father, but the emperor came more and more under the domination of Wu Chao, one of his late father's concubines who, by incessant intrigue, had the reigning empress deposed and herself elevated to replace her. But this exalted role did not satisfy her; she purged the court of the last of T'ai-tsung's ministers and had the former empress and another favorite brutally murdered. After 660, when Kao-tsung suffered a stroke, Empress Wu moved into effective administrative control of court and empire.

Wu Chao was not of the old northwestern aristocracy, but of a good family from Shansi, and had considerable support among the aristocracy and lesser gentry of the eastern plain. During her reign the court frequently moved east for long periods to Loyang, which she embellished with palaces and public buildings appropriate to a great capital. Under her rule, the size of the bureaucracy was greatly increased, and many of the new posts were filled by graduates of the examination system—new men, more malleable to her will than the grandees of the northwest; as a corollary she sought to reduce the powers of chief ministers as spokesmen of the court. She had her own "Scholars of the Northern Gate" who carried on much of the business of government outside the usual channels and under her direct scrutiny. In 690, after a carefully planned series of favorable portents, she proclaimed a new dynasty with herself as "emperor" (the only female emperor in Chinese history). Like every usurper, she appealed to supernatural forces for legitimation. The Buddhist monks interpreted the sutra *Ta-yün ching* to show that she was the incarnation of the Buddha Maitreya, and each prefecture was ordered to establish a special temple where the sutra would be expounded. Loyang was named the "holy capital" *(shen-tu)* and became the center of the state cult as well as the seat of power. Naturally, Empress Wu receives harsh treatment at the hands of Confucian historians, but there is little evidence of any general deterioration in the empire under her reign. The capital bureaucracy and the court were wracked by fear of her disfavor; local officials suffered under her purges and counterpurges, yet she retained the loyalty of a number of distinguished officials of high rank. Until about 700, when she fell more and more under the influence of worthless sycophants, she was a strong and effective ruler.

By 705 serious domestic problems had accumulated, particularly in the realm of state finance and taxation; the empress was now eighty, and her favorites committed increasingly outrageous excesses. Finally the bureaucrats at court carried out a coup and forced her to abdicate. The T'ang house was restored to power. After an abortive attempt of yet another empress to establish herself in power and a short sharp struggle among those who wrested power from her, the emperor Hsüan-tsung won out and in 713 assumed full control of the empire. His reign, which lasted until 756, is generally regarded as the height of the T'ang: a period of great prosperity and relative peace, of important institutional changes, of tremendous flowering of all the arts. To list the works of art and the notable poets or to describe the cosmopolitan opulence of the great cities would still not evoke the splendor of the "high T'ang," either as it existed in time or in the nostalgic memories of later men. A contemporary poet evokes a moment—a *fête champêtre*—near its end:

> Third day of the third month
> The very air seems new
> In Ch'ang-an along the water
> Many beautiful girls . . .
> Firm, plump contours,
> Flesh and bone proportioned.
> Dresses of gauze brocade
> Mirror the end of spring
> Peacocks crimped in thread of gold
> Unicorns in silver. . . .
> Some are kin to the imperial favorite
> Among them the Lady of Kuo and the Lady of Ch'in.
> Camel-humps of purple meat
> Brought in shining pans
> The white meat of raw fish
> Served on crystal platters
> Don't tempt the sated palate.
> All that is cut with fancy and
> Prepared with care—left untouched.

Eunuchs, reins a-flying
Disturb no dust
Bring the "eight chef d'oeuvres"
From the palace kitchens.
Music of strings and pipes . . .
Accompanying the feasting
Moving the many guests
All of rank and importance.
Last comes a horseman
See him haughtily
Dismount near the screen
And step on the flowery carpet. . . .
The chancellor is so powerful
His mere touch will scorch
Watch you don't come near
Lest you displease him.[1]

Politically Hsüan-tsung began his reign by carefully excluding members of the imperial clan and of the empresses' families from positions of influence, and for a time the bureaucrats recruited by Empress Wu continued in high office. But gradually members of the great aristocratic clans returned to the arena of power, and after Hsüan-tsung used a sequence of aristocratic specialists to reform the empire's finances—often in the face of bureaucratic opposition—a polarization developed between the two groups. New commissions, set up to carry through the reform of coinage, transport, land registration, and so on, became centers of aristocratic influence. So did the censorate. At the very epicenter of power, the chief ministers came to exercise far more policy-making and administrative authority than they had in the earlier years of the dynasty. From 736 on an aristocratic chief minister, Li Lin-fu, established himself as virtual dictator, while the emperor withdrew to enjoy the pleasures of the inner palace and the study of Taoism. Ironically, Hsüan-tsung, who had initially taken careful precautions against "woman power" at court, came under the influence of the most famous *femme fatale* of Chinese history, Yang Kuei-fei, and she—true to type—began to forward the careers of her relatives and friends. Her second cousin Yang Kuo-chung (the "chancellor" in the last lines of the quoted poem) rose rapidly and in 752 succeeded Li Lin-fu as chief minister and de facto dictator. But

---

1. I have rendered this famous poem of Tu Fu rather freely. Whatever felicities it may have I owe to William Hung's version or to David Lattimore's.—A.F.W.

he lacked Li's experience and political skill. The new commissions, kept in check by Li, expanded their powers outside the regular bureaucratic structure. The morale and effectiveness of central power was increasingly weakened, and serious troubles were not long in developing.

Hsüan-tsung's reign had been troubled by serious threats along the western and northern frontiers. Conflicts with the Turks disturbed the northwestern frontiers from the time of his accession until 736, when the Turkish power disintegrated. In the struggles that followed, the Uighur people emerged as the dominant power in the steppe, and they followed a policy of peaceful coexistence, indeed of alliance, with the T'ang, much to the latter's benefit. The Tibetans, newly unified in the seventh century, had become increasingly warlike, and they invaded the northwest almost annually from 714 onward. There were abortive peace efforts, but in 752 the Tibetans allied themselves with the southwestern kingdom of Nan-chao and thus could threaten the full length of China's western frontiers.

In the face of continuous external threats and a series of military reverses, Hsüan-tsung organized a ring of military provinces under military governors (*Chieh-tu-shih*) all along the frontier from Szechwan in the southwest to Manchuria in the northeast. These governors were initially appointed from the roster of active officials, but they were given ever-wider responsibilities for logistics, for the support of their troops, and so on. They then began, very gradually, to encroach on the jurisdiction of civil officials in frontier areas. As the total number of troops under their commands rose to more than half a million, they clearly became a potential threat to the central government. This threat was even more dangerous, since once-powerful armies in the capital area had been weakened by intrigue, inanition, and neglect.

An Lu-shan, a general of Sogdian origins, profited from the favor of Li Lin-fu to gain control of all three of the northeastern commands, and his armies eventually numbered 160,000. When Chief Minister Li Lin-fu died and was succeeded in 752 by the hostile, ambitious, but far less competent Yang Kuo-chung, a confrontation between the central power and An Lu-shan was almost inevitable. In spite of a long period of peace and prosperity, the last years of Hsüan-tsung's reign found the T'ang state in serious jeopardy: the emperor in virtual retirement; a weak chief minister in his post not by merit but by favoritism; the functioning organs of government divided uneasily between the regular apparatus, staffed by career bureaucrats, and the imperial commissions, staffed for the most part by aristocrats; military power as weak at the center as it was strong on the periphery.

When in 755 An Lu-shan saw his chance and rose in open revolt, he met initially with spectacular success. He took the northeastern province easily, captured the eastern capital at Loyang early in 756, the main capital of Ch'ang-an in July of the same year. Hsüan-tsung took the difficult mountain road to Szechwan and, in his flight, was forced to have his favorite Yang Kuei-fei and members of her faction put to death. Hsüan-tsung's heir fled to the northwest where he proclaimed himself emperor in place of his father. But the new monarch (Su-tsung, reigned 756–62) faced desperately difficult problems. An Lu-shan's rebels occupied the imperial capitals and controlled most of the North China plain. An Lu-shan himself was murdered early in 757, but his son and then his subordinates continued the rebellion until 763 when it was finally suppressed. Meanwhile the rich area of Honan had been devastated, millions of peasants had been uprooted, and tens of thousands had perished. Victory over the rebels was made possible partly by the use of Uighur mercenaries and partly by the failure of rebel leadership. Yet the emperor was obliged, partly by Tibetan pressure from the west, to make a very compromising peace; he was beholden to the Uighurs who had helped him to victory, and they exacted a heavy price; to restore a semblance of order he was obliged to exercise clemency toward the rebels; many leaders were pardoned and some were appointed military governors in the areas where they had surrendered. In Hopei and Shantung the governors and their armies entrenched themselves; they exercised a great deal of autonomy, posed a constant threat to the central government, and deprived it of a major source of revenue and manpower. In addition to these northeastern provinces, the system of military governors also became entrenched in the area west of Ch'ang-an; in the vital areas of Honan, which protected both the eastern capital and the grand canal links to the Huai and the Yangtse; and in Szechwan where Tibetan threats continued. The centrifugal movement of power was reflected in the southern provinces, as well, where civil governors, especially in large and self-sufficient provinces, exercised far more policy-making and administrative powers than they had before the rebellion. Thus one legacy of the rebellion and its suppression was a vastly altered polity, one in which the central government had much diminished powers. Most of the political history of post-rebellion T'ang is the story of the successive emperors' efforts to reclaim, in one way or another, a measure of the fiscal and territorial control exercised by their predecessors.

Under the weak Tai-tsung (reigned 762–79), the court was dominated by his favorite Yüan Tsai whose appointments of *his* favorites to office eroded still further the regular administration. In Tai-tsung's reign eunuchs came to rival the powers of the high-ranking ministers as advisers to the throne, and lesser eunuchs spread their influence to the military high command, to the various secretariats of the central government, and to the emperor's private treasury, which they came to dominate. Some fiscal reforms were put through: the salt monopoly and the salt tax, by the end of Tai-tsung's reign, were producing a major part of the central government's revenue and financing; and a reconstructed canal and transport system brought tax goods from the areas still under the capital's control—central China, the Huai Valley, and the lower Yangtse. The salt and transport system was managed by an independent commission with headquarters near Yang-chou, which gradually took over the entire financial administration of southern and central China.

In 779 Tai-tsung was succeeded by a young, forceful, and ambitious successor, Te-tsung (reigned 780–805). He immediately put in train a series of administrative reforms designed to restore the authority of the throne, to revive the regular bureaucratic processes of Hsüan-tsung's time, and to reduce the authority of the provinces. The central bureaucracy was reformed and the Salt Commission slashed in an attempt to place control of the empire's revenues firmly in the hands of the court.

Before Te-tsung had had time to consolidate his position, events forced him into a showdown with the provincial governors of Hopei, where he attempted to exercise his right to appoint new governors. In 781 the northeastern provinces rose in rebellion, and a wave of revolts paralyzed the empire for the next five years, bringing the T'ang even nearer to extinction than during the An Lu-shan Rebellion. The dynasty survived largely through dissension among the rebels and because, as in the time of An Lu-shan, the south remained loyal to the throne.

Te-tsung's activist policies were thus a failure, but his reign nonetheless saw a great improvement in almost every field of government. In foreign affairs the Tibetans, who had overrun the northwest during An Lu-shan's uprising and even had briefly occupied Ch'ang-an, were contained. The frontier defenses were progressively strengthened, and in 791 the alliance of Tibet with Nan-chao, which threatened the entire western frontier, was broken. At home, although Te-tsung made no further attempt to curb his provincial governors, the dominance of the regular bureaucracy was steadily reasserted. In spite of the ruinous cost of the rebellions of 781–85, by the end of Te-tsung's reign the state's finances were in a sound state for the first time since the 750s. In addition, Te-tsung gradually built up a new palace army, which provided the central government with a striking force more than the equal of any of the provincial armies.

This revival of central authority, however, had its negative side. Te-tsung became increasingly suspicious of his ministers and increasingly intent on retaining a close personal grasp on affairs. He began to delegate many of the powers that were properly the prerogative of his ministers to members of his personal secretariat, the Han-lin yüan; and his new armies were placed under the command of eunuchs. The military power base that this gave the eunuchs was to prove a grave threat to stability under weak later emperors.

Te-tsung was succeeded by Shun-tsung, who was physically incapable of ruling, and under whom power was dominated by a small clique led by Wang Shu-wen. This whole episode is likely to remain obscure, but it is clear that an abortive attempt was made to oust the eunuchs from their military commands. The survivors of Wang Shu-wen's group, which included several of the best young minds of the day, were ruthlessly hounded into obscurity, and this seems to have ushered in a period when partisan politics at court became intensified.

Hsien-tsung (reigned 806–20), another forceful personality on Te-tsung's model, devoted much of his reign to the restoration of imperial authority over the provinces. Like Te-tsung he began actively intervening in provincial affairs, but with the difference that he had inherited both a sound financial position and a well-trained military establishment. Rebellions in Szechwan (806) and the lower Yangtse (807) were quickly suppressed. In 809–10 a campaign in the northeast was badly handled by an incompetent eunuch general, and once more the court was forced to accept the status quo in Hopei. Later in his reign a rebellion in Huai-hsi province threatened to cut the court's transport links with the south. After three years of fighting, this rebellion was crushed and the province carved up among its neighbors. A similar fate met the province of P'ing-lu in Shantung in 819. By 821 provincial separatism had been confined to a small area in the northeast, and the rest of the empire was firmly under central control.

Simple military conquest of recalcitrant provinces was backed, as is shown in Charles A. Peterson's chapter, by a series of institutional reforms designed to restore the prefectures and counties as the chief centers of local power. Local appointments were once again filled by the court; the governorships of provinces were used, as Wang Gungwu demonstrates, as lucrative appointments for great ministers who had temporarily fallen from favor. The unity of the bureaucratic service, badly shaken in the late eighth century, was restored.

The long-term success achieved by Hsien-tsung in restoring central authority over the provinces was not, however, accomplished without cost. The eunuchs, already in command of the largest armies, began to provide the emperor with a personal secretariat in the Palace Council (Shu-mi-yüan) and to interfere in policy decisions. This continued the trend established under Te-tsung to shift authority from the regularly constituted court offices to bodies personally dependent upon the emperor.

Under a powerful monarch like Te-tsung or Hsien-tsung this trend was kept in check. But the later T'ang emperors were not of the same caliber. Hsien-tsung himself was murdered by some of his eunuchs, and under his successors their power grew rapidly. After 820 the eunuch generals and the eunuch members of the Palace Council intervened in almost every succession to the throne. Holding the affairs of the palace and the imperial household in their hands, they could control the emperor's knowledge of affairs and began to interfere seriously in politics.

The bureaucracy was to some extent demoralized by the encroachments of eunuch power and riven by deep-seated and violent factional dissension. Each faction attempted to secure alliances with one eunuch group or another and to gain the support of the armies. The factional strife persisted for some forty years and produced great bitterness. During this period many people, realizing that real power was no longer embodied in the bureaucracy, became disillusioned with the whole business of court politics.

Disillusionment reached a low point when in 835 Wen-tsung, who had chafed under the growing influence of his eunuchs for years, attempted to engineer a coup against them, which failed disastrously and led to the execution of many of his most prominent ministers. But the peak of eunuch power did not last long. Wu-tsung, who succeeded to the throne in 840 with eunuch backing, nevertheless kept them well in check and under his able minister Li Te-Yü did much to restore the position of the bureaucracy. Even under his weak successors, although individual eunuchs acquired great influence and exercised political patronage, there was no longer a well-organized eunuch "establishment" with such ramifications of power as in the 820s and 830s.

Under Wu-tsung (reigned 840–47) the dynasty went through a period of crisis. A new situation in foreign affairs was brought about with the fall of the Uighur Empire, which had dominated the northern border since Hsüan-tsung's last years. Tibet too began to lose its strong political cohesion. A Sino-Tibetan treaty of peace had been signed in 821–22. In 838 the Tibetan king died, and under his successors internal strife rapidly destroyed all semblance of central power. Chinese authority once again spread into the lost territories of the northwest. While foreign affairs were still in the balance, Wu-tsung faced yet another major internal rebellion, this time in southern Shensi, and the culmination of a financial crisis, which had been building up during the preceding reigns.

Like Te-tsung and Hsien-tsung before him, Wu-tsung was a deeply committed Taoist and decided to solve his problems by suppressing the Buddhist monasteries and sequestering their wealth on a vast scale. All but a handful of the empire's monasteries were suppressed; their monks and nuns returned to lay life, their lands sold, their slaves and dependents freed, their vast accumulations of wealth confiscated. At the same time other foreign religions, in particular Manicheanism, suffered the same fate. Wu-tsung's successor swiftly rescinded these measures, but their impact both on Buddhism and on Chinese society, which had been so completely permeated with Buddhist influence, was profound.

Under Wu-tsung's successor, Hsüan-tsung (reigned 847–59), some effort was made at reform, particularly in the field of finance, and a halfhearted attempt at a new codification of law was carried through. But the power of the dynasty was slowly ebbing, and the first signs of discontent and rebellion began to appear in the Yangtse Valley and in the south, upon which the court relied increasingly for revenue. In Chekiang an uprising led by a local brigand, Ch'iu Fu, disrupted a wide area in 859–60, sparked off in part by levies of seamen and troops required in the defense of the southern protectorate of Annam (North Vietnam) against a large-scale invasion from Nan-chao.

This war spread rapidly to Nan-chao's border with Szechwan and dragged on painfully from 858 to 866, at great cost in lives and wealth. No sooner had the invasion been finally beaten off, than some of the troops who had been drafted many years before for the defense of the Canton area mutinied. Under their general, P'ang Hsün, they fought and pillaged their way through South China and back to their homes in Honan. Here throughout 868 and 869 they kept large government forces at bay and completely disrupted the canal traffic, which ordinarily brought much-needed revenues and grain supplies to the loyalist armies and the capital. No sooner was this rebellion quelled, than war broke out again with Nan-chao, whose forces now overran much of Szechwan.

After the suppression of P'ang Hsün's rebellion, Honan had suffered a succession of disastrous floods. In 874 these were followed by a prolonged drought. The government, its resources exhausted by years of warfare, proved unable to give relief to the starving population, and a series of peasant uprisings spread through Honan. The most serious of these was led by Wang Hsien-chih. After his death in battle the rebellion came under the control of Huang Ch'ao, whose armies swept through southern China as far as Canton, which was sacked. Defeated by government troops, the rebels then turned north and in 880 captured Loyang. Ch'ang-an fell to them in the next year. Ch'ao's forces were eventually driven from the capital with the aid of the Sha-t'o Turks, but from this time onward the court was powerless, the emperors mere puppets manipulated by the generals. Political chaos, the progressive fragmentation of territorial authority, and the utter collapse of the civil administration ensued, and although the dynasty lingered on until 907, the division of China into local regimes, which characterizes the Five Dynasties period, had become an accomplished fact a quarter of a century before.

The Perspective of Thought and Religion

The age of T'ang was heir to three major traditions of religious and moral ideas, and each of these traditions was used and developed by the men of T'ang so that each was deeply transformed.

Confucianism, during the long period of disunion, had suffered an eclipse of its authority. Its Classics were preserved and studied in well-to-do households, and its moral norms were as pervasive as any standards of secular conduct. Confucianism continued to have a monopoly of the symbolism, ritual procedures, and nomenclature of legitimation so that even the northern rulers fresh from the steppe and speaking no Chinese were obliged to invoke them. But its intellectual vitality had waned, and in only a few circles were Confucian ideas seriously discussed. A violent age, an age of military domination, made an inhospitable climate for Confucian studies. Wei Cheng, writing in the early T'ang, looking back on this long period of neglect, says: "It is now nearly three hundred years since new year's days ceased being the same (i.e. the Northern and Southern dynasties proclaimed different calendars). The theories of the various Confucian masters are contradictory, and there is no way of choosing what is correct."

Both the Sui and the T'ang consciously sought their model in the unified empire of Han which had fallen four centuries earlier. They assembled fragments of lost Confucian texts, resuscitated half-moribund traditions, and deliberately reenacted the great ritual observances associated with imperial Confucianism. This highly eclectic body of belief and practice—the seasonal sacrifices; the solemnities of the cult of imperial ancestors; the music, symbolism, and impedimenta of court ceremonies; the rhetoric of imperial pronouncements—conferred legitimacy and linked the T'ang to the great Han and thence to the shadowy sage emperors of remote antiquity. It provided the outward and visible signs of the emperor's cosmic rule and his role as father of his people and guardian of their welfare. Let us describe one of the many seasonal observances to suggest how it may have appeared to a resident of Ch'ang-an. An important ceremony occurred in the first lunar month and symbolized the opening of the agricultural year. Long before dawn on the appointed day the emperor—having prepared himself by a period of abstinence—left his palace in a special six-horse chariot, on which was mounted a ceremonial plow. Accompanied by guards, officials, and a numerous retinue, he moved in stately procession to a ceremonial area outside the south wall of the city. There, assisted by ranking nobles, officials from the board of agriculture, musicians, ritualists, and other functionaries, he solemnly took the plow in his hands and proceeded to make a furrow that signaled the beginning of the planting season. He was followed by other dignitaries who took their turns at the plow. Often at the close of the ceremony the emperor would take further steps to ensure a harmonious concord between nature and his people: an empire-wide amnesty, gifts to the officials, a change of the era name to suggest the opening of a new and auspicious sequence of years. Such were the symbolic and ceremonial aspects of state Confucianism, rituals performed in the capitals and provincial centers so that all might see and be inspired with awe. But there were many further aspects of Confucianism at the heart of T'ang civilization.

The Sui and T'ang emperors were intent on establishing a common set of moral values for the whole reunited empire, and here too they turned to Confucianism and to traditional enactments and procedures: imperial exhortations to virtue and conspicuous rewards or public monuments to exemplars of such virtues as filial submissiveness, chastity in widows, official probity, honesty, studiousness in the young, valor and loyalty in warfare.

In the first year of the T'ang, the emperor ordered the establishment of an empire-wide hierarchy of schools; there were to be, after the Sui model, three schools in the capital with a total complement of 342 students eligible according to the official ranks of their fathers or grandfathers. In the following year seasonal sacrifices to Confucius were ordered at the most prestigious of these schools. At the prefectural and county levels, according to the decree of 618, schools were to be opened

with relatively small complements of students. We know nothing about
the actual working of such local schools, although there is one report
that an instructor in an early T'ang prefectural school drank day and
night and that his lectures were uninspired! But the T'ang developed
and maintained throughout its long life an elaborate network of schools;
in 738 it was extended even to the village level. The less prestigious
among the schools were those devoted to practical subjects: mathe-
matics, medicine, law, practical calligraphy. The three capital academies each offered a four-year course with a curriculum of the Confucian Classics. Distinguished scholars of high official rank were
appointed to teach, and they usually specialized in one of the Classics.

Since nearly four hundred years of chaos and instability had preceded
reunification, there was the question of which Classics and whose interpretations should be taught. T'ai-tsung, in 633, appointed a distinguished commission to establish the standard texts and interpretations.
This resulted in the *Wu-ching cheng-i* [The Five Classics with Orthodox
Interpretations]. The Classics were the *Book of Changes,* the *Book of
Documents,* the *Odes,* the *Ch'un-ch'iu* with the *Tso-chuan* and the ritual
compendium known as the *Li-chi.* The commentaries chosen as authoritative represented both northern and southern traditions, Han and
post-Han interpretations that had developed along different lines
during the Age of Disunion. Thus the interpretation of the Classics
was another deliberate effort to reunify divergent traditions. It was
also, in the Han manner, a way of assuring that a uniform official
orthodoxy was the basis of all schooling and that this orthodoxy in
turn became the basis of a common moral outlook among the elite.

The civil service examinations were, with minor exceptions, based
on this same body of texts, and, as these examinations became an ever
more prestigious route to office, status, and privilege, family and clan
pressure upon the young to master them increased. However, there is
ample evidence that boredom, irritation, and occasional rebelliousness
among the youth also increased. Throughout the T'ang, there were
complaints that mere mastery of the proper forms and parroting of the
appropriate classical phrases gained high places for careerists, while
those with intellectual interests in one or more Classic failed. Han Yü
(768–824) described the examinations of his day in scathing terms and
remarked that if the great sages of the past—Mencius, the poet Ch'ü
Yüan, the great historian Ssu-ma Ch'ien, and others—had been put
forward for such examinations, they would certainly have been filled
with shame and would have refused to take them. Despite the sterility
of the curriculum and the writhings and complaints of successive gener-

ations of young men, these men did take their places in the elite with the common moral outlook and common body of traditional knowledge that made them cohere as a group and made them play out their public roles with awareness of the Confucian norms. They drew on this knowledge, this learned vocabulary and body of historical allusions, whenever they wrote letters to one another, engaged in policy arguments, drafted imperial edicts, composed tomb inscriptions or commemorative odes. This knowledge of the Classics, which they acquired under social and political pressure, both repelled and attracted. It repelled because much of it was dry, scholastic, and often impenetrable and especially because it was imposed. It attracted because it encompassed a great deal of China's past and formulated—often in terms that must have seemed stilted and archaic, but often in pithy and unforgettable phrases—many of the great and perennial problems of man and society.

This second, more positive appeal of Confucianism gradually began to be felt in the centuries after the An Lu-shan Rebellion. The five intellectuals discussed in David McMullen's chapter came from diverse though uniformly aristocratic backgrounds, and in their private lives they were drawn to Buddhism or Taoism. They all began work under official auspices before this great upheaval, during the high tide of prosperity under Hsüan-tsung when official scholars led long, quiet, and productive lives with generous stipends and access to public and private libraries. In these years there were controversies and debates over history and literary theory, yet—interesting as they were—they strike us as extremely conservative, moving within a circumscribed and conventional *Problematik*. During and after the rebellion, this comfortable mode of life was violently disrupted. In the following years a semblance of the previous life was pieced together and some libraries were rebuilt, but McMullen's five protagonists wrote under conditions of uncertainty, and they wrote shorter, sharper literary pieces, informed by a more critical spirit than their pre-rebellion work. They turned to history in the same mood. Still, the classical authorities, the classical vocabulary, and the events of the distant past limited what they talked about and ultimately what they wrote. These post-rebellion thinkers, therefore, may be viewed as a transitional generation deeply shaken and trying to say something fresh but nonetheless limited by the weight of their intellectual inheritance and by their conception of their roles.

Thereafter, change proceeded on all levels of T'ang life, and what people did with their required Confucian learning also changed. In his polemics Han Yü reasserted the philosophical primacy of Confucianism—an attitude that would have been inconceivable in the eighth century—and struck a xenophobic note—equally inconceivable in the high T'ang. Li Ao, writing at the very end of the eighth century or early in the ninth, took up many of the basic themes of Chinese speculative thought; his borrowings from Buddhism and Taoism are apparent in his essays. Both he and his master Han Yü, with their sense of problem sharpened by Buddhism, began to wring out of the "Chung-yung" chapter of the *Li-chi* (usually translated "Doctrine of the Mean") the elements of a modernized Confucian metaphysic. Yet the serious writings of the late T'ang Confucians, interesting in what they pre-figure, are few and intellectually thin. Compared to the great flowering of creative thought in the third and fourth centuries or to the discursive speculative flights that were to characterize Sung Confucianism, they seem indeed pale, full of suggestions but unimaginative and unsystem-atic. The reason lies in the primacy of Buddhism, which preempted system building and dominated so many other areas of T'ang thought and belief, even after the first stirrings of a Confucian revival had begun to appear.

It is obvious to the most casually interested that during the T'ang dynasty Buddhism suffused T'ang life, penetrated every segment of Chinese society to a degree that it had not done before and was never to do again. The reunifying dynasty of Sui had recognized Buddhism as one of the vital threads common to north and south in the Age of Disunion, which could now be used to knit together a uniform culture for the whole empire. The Sui and many of the T'ang emperors were brought up as Buddhists, but whatever their personal views the usual policy, at least until 845, was to tolerate lay and monastic Buddhism and to shore up the Confucian ideology of empire with Buddhist elements. Stanley Weinstein's chapter, in analyzing the background of T'ang schools of Buddhism, gives a vivid account of the beginnings of the most independently Chinese of the Buddhist schools, the T'ien-t'ai. Its founder, Chih-i (538–97), was the son of a prominent official of the last of the Southern Dynasties; and his personality, his new doctrines, and his power as a preacher had won him a wide following in the Ch'en capital. When in 589 the Ch'en fell to the Sui, the con-querors quickly sought to use Chih-i's great prestige to win over the Buddhists of the south. The viceroy of the south (later Emperor Yang-ti) took the Bodhisattva vows from Chih-i, showered him with favors, and repeatedly urged him to teach in the viceregal capital at Yang-chou, where a group of distinguished southern monks was being brought together. After Chih-i's death the Sui maintained its links with T'ien-t'ai, and when the future Yang-ti was elevated to crown prince, he took his southern clerics north to live in a newly built monastery in the capital. The three-way relationship—among the emperor as symbol and person, the politics of empire, and the interests of Buddhist believers, lay and clerical—was a constant in T'ang life; it was a delicate relationship where clashes of values and interests lay just below the surface.

The manipulation of this delicate balance in the first two reigns of the T'ang is discussed by Arthur Wright in chapter 7. He advances the hypothesis that T'ang Kao-tsu, generally a cautious and prudent man, was driven by the financial demands of his long campaigns against his rivals (and the cost of buying off some of them) to order, in 626, a drastic purge of the Buddhist clergy and a massive confiscation of the wealth accumulated by Buddhist establishments. There shortly ensued a struggle between the future T'ai-tsung and his brother for the T'ang throne. In this struggle it seems that the issue of Buddhism figured more than has been previously noted. The faction of the future T'ai-tsung came out strongly against the purge, and, indeed, when T'ai-tsung had murdered his brothers and forced his father into retirement, one of his first acts as emperor was to rescind the anti-Buddhist order. Thus T'ai-tsung in a desperate moment had used the Buddhist interest part of the three-way relationship and had won. Did this then mean that for the balance of his reign he showed the Buddhists extraordinary favor? By no means.

The texts show that T'ai-tsung knew his three-part equation well. He built battlefield temples where masses were to be said for those who died in the civil war; he endowed a splendid temple in honor of his mother; he attended the colorful public ceremonies of the Buddhist faith, gave maigre feasts for the monks, had his crown prince receive the Bodhisattva vows for laymen, and so on. Yet he and his officials (many of whom were personally Buddhist) kept Buddhist practices under close watch and detailed control; an imperial edict even described current abuses and forbade profiteering from the sale of holy images. Buddhist clergy were invited to the palace on set occasions for sutra readings or discourses, but the suggestion that a group of them appear every morning for religious services was met by protest from a ranking minister and quickly vetoed by the emperor. Again, by his order for the copying and circulation of the very strict *Sutra of the Testamentary Teachings*, T'ai-tsung clearly intended to keep the monks and nuns under stringent discipline and no doubt to curb the irregular monks of the country villages. Thus, if Wright's hypothesis is correct, T'ai-tsung used the Buddhist community in his bid for power but thereafter behaved as an evenhanded ruler of a predominantly Buddhist populace, but a ruler intent above all on preserving the structure of the civil state with himself at its apex. His treatment of the great traveler and translator monk Hsüan-tsang underscores this attitude. T'ai-tsung received him with great courtesy, expressed no interest in doctrinal trends in India and elsewhere, but tried first of all to get Hsüan-tsang to break his religious vows and become an official consultant on the inner-Asian relations of the T'ang Empire. That approach having failed, the emperor ordered him to write a full descriptive account of the countries he had visited and to translate the *Tao-te ching* into Sanskrit with a view to impressing the Indian world with the greatness of Chinese thought. As this last order of T'ai-tsung illustrates, there emerged in the first two reigns a fourth element in the equation or balance of interest—religious Taoism, which we shall consider briefly at the end of this section.

The strength of the Buddhist community was dramatically demonstrated during the reign of Kao-tsung, when an order that the clergy should pay homage to their ruler and their parents was aborted by the organized efforts of the monks and Buddhist laymen in the capital. We have noted in the preceding section that Empress Wu, in her search for reassurance and legitimation, summoned Buddhist monks of easy conscience to interpret a scripture in such a way as to establish her supernatural rights to supreme power and then ordered that interpretation spread by imperial order. Empress Wu, nevertheless, was no blind supporter of the Buddhists and their interests. Like any other effective ruler she sought to maintain a balance of forces and interests. Yet the continuous flow of donations—of land, houses, money, and treasure—created Buddhist establishments with great economic and social power in many regions of China. This omnipresent institutional power went contrary to Chinese ideas of political economy and invited the suppression that was eventually decreed.

It is clear from Weinstein's chapter that the individual emperors' preferences—whether for a doctrine or a particular exponent of that doctrine—had a direct bearing on a school's success or failure. For example, the Fa-hsiang school, introduced from India by Hsüan-tsang and developed by his disciple Tz'u-en, found no imperial sponsor and few followers after Tz'u-en's death in 682. Again, it would seem that the Hua-yen school prospered greatly during the thirty-five years of Empress Wu's patronage of its leading systematizer, Fa-tsang, when it became established as one of the major traditions of Chinese Buddhism. Weinstein demonstrates that the various philosophical schools, such as T'ien-t'ai, Fa-hsiang, and Hua-yen, did not develop out of an isolated doctrinal dialectic but in close relationship to the tastes and political interests of their imperial patrons.

With the diffusion of political power after the An Lu-shan Rebellion, the military governors came to share with the imperial court the patronage of Buddhism. The governors and the men around them were attracted to the ideas of the school of meditation (Ch'an), and this school flourished in many provincial centers. At the same time impassioned preachers spread the teachings of the Pure Land schools—which promised salvation by invoking the name of a Buddha or the title of a sutra—first among the common people in the countryside and then in provincial cities and in the imperial capital itself. The disruptions of the rebellion and the spread of ideas of an imminent apocalypse *(mo-fa)* intensified religious emotions, which were manifested in countless ways at all levels of society and in all parts of the country.

Let us look at some of the practices of popular Buddhism, since they are characteristic of T'ang life and are not dealt with by any of the authors in this volume. So rich and varied are the accounts of Buddhist activities that it is difficult indeed to select a representative sample. Here is an account of festivities on the occasion of the Buddha's birthday in the year 872.

> On the eighth day of the fourth moon . . . a bone of the Buddha was brought to Ch'ang-an. From the K'ai-yüan gate to the An-fu tower Buddhist music being played along both sides of the street fairly shook the earth. The emperor himself went to the An-fu temple and personally made obeisance to it. The great houses of the Yen-shou ward and the adjacent West Market combined to give in its honor a great vegetarian feast and religious gathering open to all. They rivaled one another in assembling the clergy and in erecting Buddha-images on a grand scale. The blowing of conches, the clashing of cymbals, the flickering of lanterns were unceasing, and the Yen-shou ward became a place of festive assembly.[2]

Such festivities combine many motifs of T'ang popular Buddhism: the adoration of holy relics; the celebration of religious holidays, here

---

2. *Tu-yang tsa-pien* as quoted in Hsü Sung, *T'ang liang-ching ch'eng-fang k'ao* (Kyoto facsimile edition), 4.11b. One should note that the author of this description was friendly to neither Buddhism nor Taoism and that the scene he describes occurred a generation after the persecution of 841–45.

the Buddha's birthday; the vegetarian feast combined with prayers, chanting, and the intoning of scriptures; the mingling of social classes, here plebians, upper-class families, and the clergy, in common religious observances; lavish expenditures on the part of the well-to-do, which, in the Buddhist faith, would add to their capital store of spiritual goods.

The pilgrimage was another Buddhist innovation that became a feature of T'ang life. Sites of special Buddhist sanctity were often places long venerated in Chinese folk religion. The great mountains, the seats of tutelary divinities, had now become the sites of Buddhist monasteries and shrines. Thanks to the diaries of the Japanese pilgrim Ennin (and to his gifted translator Edwin Reischauer), we get a glimpse of the pilgrims on their way to a great shrine, of pious or venal hostel keepers along the way, of the peddlers of holy relics, of the solemn silence of the great temples where the Buddhist divinities and their avatars were thought to dwell. Thousands of ordinary people moved across the land to one holy place or another, and the elite made trips into the mountains where they might see impressive groups of holy images and pay a visit to some monk famous for his miraculous powers or his learning.

Confucians of earlier centuries admitted that their teachings had little color and little popular appeal, and some of them had used Buddhist ceremonies as one of their colonization strategies to beguile the aborigines of the south. Just as temples, monasteries, and shrines added color and variety to their streets, ceremonies of countless varieties now punctuated the life of the capitals and the great cities. Most impressive were the grand ordinations conducted under state supervision with great pomp and solemnity, the ceremonies dedicating a new temple or a new image such as the one T'ai-tsung attended in 634 to "open the eyes of the Buddha" image at the temple he had built in memory of his mother. But the lesser ones were equally full of color: the installation of a new abbot marked by a solemn procession of chanting monks, the waving of censers, the sound of cymbals and conch-horns; similar processions moving along the avenues bearing a new imperially written name plaque for a new temple; the solemn funeral processions; the masses said on the death anniversaries of the great; prolonged public chanting of magical formulas to drive away a plague or end a drought. Han Yü, writing about 820, describes the scene in the capital:

> In the eastern streets, in the western streets
> They preach the Buddhist sutras
> They embroider and exaggerate tales of retribution and reward
> The listening crowd shoves and pushes

> Jostling each other like clotted water-plants
> A yellow robed Taoist monk
> Also preaches his theories
> But below his platform
> The listeners are few
> Like a few bright stars in an empty sky.

Han Yü goes on to describe the appearance in the capital of a Taoist priestess, and tells us of her intention to drive out the foreign teachings of Buddhism and return peoples' faith to the native gods and spirits. Word got out that she would perform mysterious rituals behind closed doors and for a moment, or a day or two perhaps,

> The Buddhist temples were swept clean of their crowds
> And not a human trace remained.
> Splendid horses blocked the streets
> Unbroken lines of covered carriages . . .

This was one level of the competition between Buddhism and religious Taoism, and we turn now to this last of the three strands of thought and belief that were woven into the fabric of T'ang life.

Religious Taoism had its roots in the Age of Disunion when those who perpetuated a variety of Chinese cults, folk beliefs and practices, and the subterranean but important traditions of the heavenly masters (T'ien-shih) began to rally against the onslaught of Buddhism. By T'ang times religious Taoism had become the focus of defense and of counterattack. It had developed a pantheon, monastic orders for men and women, a body of scripture, liturgies, and sacred rituals. It also had a considerable popular following, some of it centered in particular localities of which Szechwan was one. At the height of the T'ang's glory, the Taoist religion was flourishing. In the official figures for the empire of about that time the Taoists had 1,687 monasteries and nunneries as against 5,358 for the Buddhists. In Ch'ang-an itself the Taoists had, in 722, sixteen establishments as against ninety-one Buddhist.

Taoism enjoyed a favored position under the T'ang. The ruling house was persuaded that it was descended from Lao-tzu, the supposed author of the *Tao-te ching* who long before this time had been apotheosized into one of the central divinities of religious Taoism. The T'ang examination system included an examination on the *Tao-te ching* and even one on the *Chuang-tzu*. Although we know little of those who took these examinations or what it availed them to pass, we do know these

books had a profound influence on the T'ang elite. The Taoist clergy
claimed precedence over the Buddhist at public functions, and T'ang
emperors found it difficult to deny the claim. The great emperor Hsüan-
tsung, who presided over the golden years of the T'ang, wrote a
commentary to the *Tao-te ching;* and he and nearly all his immediate
successors were personally attracted to Taoism and practiced one or
another of its esoteric techniques. (Hsüan-tsung, however, is also known
to have written commentaries to the Buddhist *Vajrachedikā-sutra* and to
the Confucian *Hsiao-ching* [Classic of Filial Submission]). Despite the
favor they enjoyed, the Taoists could not claim a monopoly of imperial
favors. The emergence of their monastic orders, the proliferation of
their temples and estates, and the personal influence of their great
clerics presented the T'ang state with just the problems of regulation
and control that the growth of Buddhism had. The measures which
had been developed earlier to control Buddhism were applied under
the T'ang to religious Taoism. Metropolitan temples of the two faiths,
built as centers of control, faced each other across the main north-south
street of the imperial capital. Revolts that broke out in T'ang times
were less often fueled by elements of the Taoist faith (after all, the ruling
house was descended from Lao-tzu!) than by the Buddhist, although
the unordained country "priests" of both religions were always potential leaders of the hungry and disaffected.

Rivalry between Buddhism and religious Taoism, as we have suggested, extended from the imperial court and capital to the countryside.
It expressed itself most formally in the scheduled debates held at the
palace among distinguished spokesmen of Confucianism, Buddhism,
and Taoism; these were often held on the emperor's birthday. The
most virulent polemics developed, of course, between Buddhism and
Taoism, for they were rival religions with parallel appeals to similar
clienteles and similar desires for imperial and upper-class favor. For
most of the T'ang, the advantage was clearly with Buddhism, but in
the years 841–45, the emperor Wu-tsung, who had some personal
preference for Taoism out of complex personal, political, and economic
motives, carried out a massive persecution of Buddhism, which is said to
have resulted in the destruction of 46,600 temples and shrines and the
laicization of 410,000 clergy and their slaves. Included in the persecution were Manicheans, Zoroastrians, and Nestorian Christians, whose
clergy were few in number but clearly derived their teaching from
outside China. The virulent tone of the imperial edict of 845 makes it
plain that the emperor not only coveted (as he desperately needed) the
vast wealth of the Buddhist church but also that he desired to put an

end to the long-existing equation by which his predecessors had balanced imperial interests, in the context of domestic politics, against the interests of the community of Buddhist believers. The tone of the edict is not only virulent, it is xenophobic. The edict and its drastic effects on the entire empire marked the end of T'ang cosmopolitanism, a tendency to draw back into the particularism of strictly Chinese traditions. Although the T'ang dynasty lingered on in deepening crisis for another fifty years, the brilliance of its religious and intellectual life had passed into history.

The Institutional Perspective

Institutionally the T'ang straddles two very different periods. When the Sui had reunified China, it did so as the successor to the Northern Dynasties, the series of sinicized non-Chinese regimes beginning with the Northern (Toba) Wei, which had restored some semblance of stability and order to North China after the anarchy and political fragmentation which followed the foreign invasions of the third and fourth centuries. The Wei had already formulated what were to become the basic military, financial, and administrative policies adopted by the empires of the Sui and the T'ang. In this sense, the early T'ang was not so much a period of radical institutional development and innovation as the culmination of a long process of prior growth and the adaptation of existing institutions to the needs of a unified empire and a changing social order. The T'ang is thus a great period of codification, when confidence in the permanence of central control inclined the government to think in terms of everlasting norms—an attitude that limited its flexibility in dealing with current problems.

The reign of T'ai-tsung, for example, celebrated for its good and orderly government, is noteworthy not so much for the emergence of any completely new institutions or any major swing in government policy, as for the consolidation of dynastic power and the personal style of T'ai-tsung's rule, particularly his establishment of firm ascendancy over the various powerful aristocratic groups at his court. Historians acclaim his achievement not only for having consolidated the T'ang, but also as an example of a highly personal exercise of power by a forceful, impulsive, yet fundamentally wise and benevolent sovereign, one always willing to heed the advice of an unusually gifted group of counselors. This type of government conformed nicely to the ethical-moral and anti-institutional prejudices of Confucian historiography. Much of the stress and strain involved in the renewal of imperial institutions had been taken by the Sui, and the first two emperors of the T'ang had the primary task of making these institutions and these innovations acceptable and of accommodating them both to the conflicting interests at the center of power and to a variety of partisan interests in the country as a whole.

This theme is examined in detail in Howard J. Wechsler's chapter, which provides an analysis of the various regionally centered aristocratic power groups who remained influential during T'ai-tsung's reign and of the measures that were taken first to balance these against each other and then to control them. Here again the fundamental problem for the early T'ang—recentralizing the state and reestablishing the unquestioned authority of the imperial house after centuries of aristocratic dominance—was solved not by the sudden imposition of novel institutions, but by a lengthy process of manipulation and accommodation to the status quo.

The Sui and early T'ang emperors faced two fundamental problems of great complexity: first, how to impose a unified set of institutions upon North China and upon the south, where different modes of life had evolved and differentials of other kinds had emerged. For example, while the north had developed a powerful military organization, the south had, in some respects, more advanced economic and fiscal policies. Second, besides being heirs to two distinct systems of institutions, emperors in north and south alike had to exercise power through a far from unified ruling class. In both regions, the pre-Sui period had been one of dominance by a comparatively small elite of powerful aristocratic clans, who not only dominated local government, but who also monopolized on a hereditary basis the highest offices of state. The T'ang imperial house itself came from this aristocracy, in which it had occupied a comparatively low rank. The entire T'ang period can be seen as a struggle between the state attempting to retain effective control over their appointment of individuals to office, to strengthen centralized institutions, and to keep effective executive power in the hands of the emperor, on the one hand, and the great aristocratic clans continually fighting a rearguard action to retain their privileges and prestige against the encroachment of centralized government, on the other. The composition of this "aristocracy" was itself far from simple, and Denis Twitchett's chapter attempts to analyze the various components of the aristocratic interest and the efficacy of the measures taken by the state to limit their influence.

The long-term solution to the problem of elite recruitment was the institution of the system of state examinations, which allowed entry into the bureaucracy on the basis of talent. Examination entry, which in Sung times was to replace the old aristocracy by a meritocracy and to lead to the emergence of the professional bureaucracy as the dominant social elite, remained a comparatively minor means of recruitment in Sui and early T'ang times. It was not until the empress Wu usurped the throne and needed the support of a large cadre of officials not too closely tied to the T'ang imperial house or to the great aristocratic clans that the examinations began to be used on a large scale. Even after this, when examination candidates gradually became the elite group within the bureaucracy, their numbers remained comparatively small. It is difficult to set up any simple polarization of political interest between the professional bureaucrats recruited through the examinations and the members of the long-established aristocracy recruited by hereditary privilege. The two groups overlap very considerably, and to differentiate between their interests is a very complex matter. In sum, the achievement of the T'ang in broadening the elite has perhaps been exaggerated. Until late in the ninth century the bulk of the bureaucrats, whether recruited by hereditary privilege or by examination, still came from a comparatively restricted social background. This elite of locally prominent and powerful clans was only finally dismembered during the civil wars, political chaos, and social anarchy following the fall of the T'ang.

Institutionally, the importance of the examination system was great, for it broke the monopoly of the greatest clans on the highest offices of state by giving an opportunity of accelerated promotion to men of relatively lowly families, and it gave the state a means of controlling the ability of its servants. Already under the T'ang, too, this system had begun to exercise a strong influence on the content and aims of upper-class education, but it still contained sufficient variety of options and concern with practical affairs to prevent its becoming the stultifying blanket on intellectual life which it became in later dynasties.

One major achievement of the early T'ang was the gradual growth of the concept of the bureaucracy as a single unified body with a powerful esprit de corps and a sense of corporate identity. The gradual integration of local government posts into the general career structure of the bureaucracy and the constant attempts to limit tenure of provincial appointments, to prevent men from serving for long terms in their home districts, to enforce the system of regular and systematic review and assessment of officials' in-service achievement all helped to bring this about.

In fact one of the cornerstones of the early T'ang government was its successful establishment of an acceptable balance of power between central government and its local representatives. No longer, as had been the case under the Northern and Southern dynasties, were prefectural and county administrations dominated by the members of prominent local clans. These were replaced by central appointees, and locally recruited men were no longer employed except in lowly positions. Both the personnel and the methods of local government were thus brought firmly under central control.

But at the same time, strict limitations were placed on the direct intervention of central government in local affairs. Early T'ang local administration was certainly characterized by strong central influence and by centralized policies and procedures, but this centralized influence was restricted to limited areas of activity—essentially to the maintenance of law and order, to tax collection and the allied problems of the census and land allocation, to the mobilization of manpower for corvée and military service. Even in these fields, as Ikeda On shows clearly in the case of the registration and taxation systems, effective execution of central policy depended not so much upon active interventionist policies enforced by the local prefects as upon the smooth operation of a set of accepted compromises between centrally formulated policy and the needs of the local situation—compromises that were perpetuated by a sub-bureaucracy of local headmen and minor functionaries who were at one and the same time representatives of the local population and its interests and also minor employees of the state.

The early T'ang, like all their predecessors, worked upon the assumption that the administrative ideal was an empire in which a common uniform system of laws and institutions obtained everywhere, irrespective of local conditions and environmental differences. This desire for standardization in fact put a severe limit on the exercise of strong centralizing policies, since measures practicable for employment throughout China were inevitably measures of a very generalized type adaptable to a subcontinental range of environmental and social situations.

Local administration, moreover, was spread very thinly, and during T'ai-tsung's reign there was a marked reduction at the lowest levels in the number of county (*hsien*) units. It was at these low levels that provincial clan influence had been strongest in the pre-T'ang period, and this measure was in part designed to reduce or eliminate such local influences. But the county magistrate, with no more than a handful of colleagues drawn like himself from the career bureaucracy, worked

through a staff the great majority of which were permanent office
employees drawn from the local population. He was thus obliged at all
times to aim at compromise, accommodation, and peaceful arbitration,
rather than at an interventionist imposition of central policy. Officials
who attempted a too rigorous legalistic imposition of the letter of the
law were in fact as often liable to censure as to praise. An active administrator had no coercive force at his disposal. If he aroused widespread popular resentment and trouble broke out, he could call upon
central government forces, but this was considered proof of the failure of
his administration and would lead to a serious setback in his career.
A local government's effectiveness depended, then, on establishing
strict limits of action while maintaining strong authority within this
carefully delineated field of activity.

Within this predetermined limitation the early T'ang was one of the
great periods of codification of law and of administrative practice.
Not for nothing has T'ang law been compared with Roman law. Not
only did T'ang law provide models for the government structure and
practice and for the criminal law of later dynasties, it also proved to be
a rich tradition, which was successfully adapted and modified to meet
the needs of the other states within the Chinese cultural sphere. T'ang
law and institutions provided the models for the emergent Japanese
state of the Nara and Heian periods, for the Koreans, and for the
Vietnamese. In less direct forms its influence was felt among the non-
Chinese peoples of the southwestern Nan-chao state, among the Tanguts
and their successors the Hsi-Hsia, and among the Central Asian Uighurs.

In China itself, from 618 until 737, the entire corpus of codified laws
was under constant revision with the aim, first, of producing in the Code
(Lü) a system of fundamental laws which would hold good for all time,
and second, of keeping administrative law in line with the demands of
changing conditions by the constant codification and amendment
of the secondary kinds of law. Even local variations from the norm
were supposed to be codified, normalized, and regularized under the
scrutiny of the central authorities. Here again T'ang codified law was
neither revolutionary nor innovative—it inherited much from the
codification of Sui Wen-ti, and like the administrative structure of the
empire it was the perfected end-product of centuries of development.

Striking evidence of the relative effectiveness of this centralized
codified control over the local administration, within its self-imposed
limitations, is to be found in the documents from Tunhuang, on the far
northwestern border, and Turfan, a Chinese outpost in the desert of

Turkestan. Even here, far from the central authorities of the capital, in an area with a large non-Chinese minority and an ecology radically different from China proper, with a very strong military presence, which must have placed great pressures upon the functioning of local government, routine administration proceeded smoothly along the standardized lines prescribed from the capital and followed closely the letter of the law. Ikeda shows how rigorously the *forms* of administrative procedure were observed, not only by the career officials of the prefectural offices but also by the substructure of clerks and local employees who carried on day-to-day routine business.

Ikeda's chapter also deals with the T'ang administrative practice of household registration designed to produce a direct chain of control between the government and the head of each of the households, which were the irreducible social units in T'ang China. The fiscal system of the early T'ang, like that of its predecessors, assumed that each local government would closely and regularly supervise the allocation of lands; the registration of household members; the assessment of taxes, corvée, and military services on each household. To maintain this supervision demanded a detailed and continuing process of registration and classification of households and their members. The early eighth century, as Ikeda shows, was a period when registration was highly effective, and the local populations were under careful detailed supervision. Until 737 the central government each year assessed afresh every county's quota of taxes and labor services and of allowable expenditures. The files of the Board of Finance contained—in theory, at least—details of the age, status, land, and tax liability of every household and every individual in the empire. Even though a fairly large proportion of the population remained unregistered, and although there were many shortcomings in the actual operation of the system, there was a remarkable degree of central control over these aspects of local administration. Thus, in some key areas of administration, uniformity of practice was most efficiently imposed.

The keynotes of early T'ang government were straightforwardness and simplicity. The failure of the Sui regime—after the achievement of a high degree of stability—as a result of the precipitate imposition of centralizing policies was constantly in the minds of early T'ang statesmen. For all the great achievements of the seventh century, and in spite of the centralizing, standardizing, and codifying tendencies of the time, government remained simple, relatively cheap, and relatively close to Confucian ideals of frugality and non-intervention. But simplicity and standardization in government, however well they accorded with such ideals, were not well suited to deal with the ever-growing complexity of government in the seventh and eighth centuries.

The fundamental tension in T'ang administrative history arose from the fact that the institutions inherited from the relatively backward Northern Dynasties were now called upon to deal with a far more highly developed social situation. For example, the *chün-t'ien* system of land allocation, developed under the Toba Wei to encourage the maximum cultivation of land in a situation of underpopulation, now had to be employed in many regions to ensure an equitable distribution of land that was in short supply and to restrict the emergence of a free market in land. The *tsu-yung-tiao* tax system, which assumed such an equitable distribution of land and strict control over its allocation, had also been designed for a comparatively primitive economy. It depended upon taxes levied in grain and cloth, envisaged the minimum use of money, and made no attempt to derive revenue from the non-agricultural sectors of the economy. Imposed on a nationwide scale under the T'ang, this system posed immense logistic problems in transporting the vast revenues in grain and other commodities, prevented the government from deriving revenue from some of the most prosperous segments of the economy, and inhibited it from taking steps to develop an adequate currency. Similarly, the *fu-ping* militia system, which was supposed to provide the government with a self-supporting army of farmer-soldiers annually performing short terms of military service, proved inadequate to provide the standing professional armies that were necessary both to guard the frontiers and to engage in campaigns across most of Eastern Asia.

The machinery of central government also proved inflexible. Even before the An Lu-shan Rebellion there was a steady trend toward specialization and professionalism, at first in military affairs, with the growth of permanent army organizations and regional command zones *(Chieh-tu-shih)*, and then in finance, with the development of specialized commissions outside the normal bureaucracy to deal with land registration and allocation, taxation, transportation, currency, and military colonies.

In other respects the detailed control of routine business in the prefectures proved impossibly difficult to keep up. During the early eighth century increasing use was made of provincial inspecting commissioners *(An-ch'a-shih)*. In the latter years of Hsüan-tsung's reign the central calculation of a detailed annual budget of expected revenue and permitted expenditure for every prefecture in the empire became too great a task for the central ministries, and considerable powers were delegated to the local authorities in this field. Thus as government became increasingly complex, as the bureaucracy and the military establishment multiplied, as the extent of government intervention widened, the strains on the simple administrative structures of the seventh century grew, and the old sources of revenue became insufficient to bear the new burdens. But until 755 the T'ang state remained a strongly centralized empire in which the emperor and his executive ministries at the capital exercised real direct authority over local government, and in which the codified laws and administrative procedures laid out at the capital were strictly enforced throughout the empire. But by this time it was becoming apparent that the government of a vast and varied empire by the old institutions was no longer practicable. The simple non-interventionist state with all effective power concentrated in the emperor's hands, the uniform systems of land allocation, taxation, labor service, and military service remained ideals. Political writings continued to look backward to the dynasties of antiquity for models. But from this time onward these ideals were recognized as models of perfection, unattainable in the present; never again was there any systematic attempt to turn them into reality.

The immediate cause of the breakdown of the early T'ang system of government was the outbreak of the An Lu-shan Rebellion. An Lu-shan, an immensely powerful frontier general, owed his power to the system of regional military commands on the northern frontiers set up in the early eighth century. Primarily set up for strategic reasons, these commands, as we have noted, grew rapidly into semi-independent provinces. An's rebellion, and the series of secondary uprisings which followed it, threw the empire into confusion for seven years. The emperor was driven from Ch'ang-an; the capitals were taken by the rebels; great areas in the heart of China were ravaged and depopulated.

As we saw in the first part of this introduction, the suppression of rebellion was followed by a centrifugal movement of power to the provinces in a variety of independent and semi-independent governorships. Everywhere, the province appeared as an intermediate unit of administration between the central government and the local prefectures, and the provinces tended both to take over many of the former functions of central government and to encroach upon the freedom of action of the prefects and county magistrates within their boundaries.

The years following 755 saw central government struggling for survival. Not only did its power over the local organs of administration decline and the area of its own authority contract, but the whole fabric of central government was torn apart. Many of the old ministries and offices at the capital became sinecures. Others simply decayed, their buildings falling into disrepair, their vacancies unfilled.

Central government precariously survived largely by the working of the Salt Commission, which ensured a regular flow of revenues from the comparatively passive southern and central provinces and which was able to derive some revenue even from the semi-autonomous areas through its new salt monopoly. This extremely powerful new organization introduced a new degree of specialization and professionalism into government and was completely independent of the established organs of government.

A parallel development was the emergence of new organs of government to take over many of the policy-making functions once exercised by the old ministries. Typically, these organs were entirely dependent on the emperor, and they advised and formulated policy without regard to the regular machinery of the court and central administration. On the one hand, the scholars of the Chi-hsien yüan and later the Han-lin yüan developed into personal secretariats which could draft documents and work out detailed policy for the emperor. On the other hand, the eunuchs, who apart from one or two prominent individuals had played little part in the politics of early T'ang times, now became increasingly influential. During the 770s they temporarily dominated the empire's treasuries. Later they provided the emperor with a personal secretariat within the palace, controlled the machinery for the transmission of documents and commands, exercised supervisory powers in the provinces, and also came to dominate and command the emperor's palace armies, the most powerful military forces in the empire. Later, in the ninth century, they began to exercise real political power, dominating certain of the weaker emperors, intervening in factional struggles, and determining the succession to the throne.

Although the facade of government in the late T'ang appeared little different from that of the early eighth century, the centers of authority had shifted elsewhere. Under the shrewd and ambitious emperor Te-tsung the central government began to win back much of the authority lost in the aftermath of the An Lu-shan Rebellion. The new tax system of 780 incorporated an agreed compromise with each province by which tax quotas were set up for each local unit, but the local officials were given great latitude in the means by which they raised the revenue. This and an attempt to exert control over the appointment to key governorships was followed by an armed confrontation between Te-tsung and the most recalcitrant governors of the northeast, which ended after years of destructive fighting in stalemate and in the recognition by the central government of the status quo, and which again brought the dynasty close to extinction. But after this setback Te-tsung continued slowly to strengthen central power particularly in the military sphere. Under Hsien-tsung a further restoration of dynastic power was achieved. Peterson's paper outlines the policies by which he achieved a more satisfactory modus vivendi with the provincial governors. A series of military campaigns enabled Hsien-tsung eventually to bring all but a few autonomous provinces under central control and to dismember or reduce in size those provinces that had posed a serious threat. The central government thus reestablished its right to control appointments to provincial posts, which were brought back into the general line of civil service promotions. A series of reforms also strengthened the power of the prefectures over military and financial matters at the expense of the provincial governments.

By 820 the immediate threat from the provinces had largely passed. But regionalism remained a powerful force in late T'ang times and reemerged in a more extreme form after the almost complete breakdown of central power after Huang Ch'ao's rebellion in the 880s. Wang Gungwu's detailed case study of the central Yangtse region shows how the forces of local regional autonomy interacted with the demands of political centralization, both in the late T'ang and in the Five Dynasties period when the area was on the border between a number of independent regimes. Paradoxically, it was during the Five Dynasties, an era when China was divided up among ten or more rival states, that the provincial system was finally broken down into units too small to form viable autonomous entities, so that the Sung in the years after 960 was able to reestablish the prefectural system of local government comparatively easily.

Institutionally, the developments after the An Lu-shan Rebellion had other far-reaching effects on succeeding dynasties, and a few of them may be mentioned here. The tax system—with its allowance for local variation and its use of indirect and monopoly taxes—lasted into the Ming dynasty and beyond. Professionalism and specialization, characteristic of the late T'ang, can be traced well into the Sung. The examination system, which had produced an elite within the bureaucracy in the late T'ang, by the eleventh century was producing nearly the whole of officialdom and many surplus graduates as well. This in turn helped bring about a massive change in the character of the social elite; so great was the change that one eleventh-century scholar—looking back upon the early T'ang—felt it to be so different from the society he knew that he compared it to a totally alien model: the caste society of India. The vastly increased social mobility of Sung times was, however, not simply the result of the examination system; perhaps more important was the large-scale introduction of new blood into the elite of the late T'ang and Five Dynasties via the specialized commissions, the provincial governments, and the military service. Men of humble backgrounds had an unprecedented opportunity to gain office, enrich themselves, and acquire property. The great aristocratic clans which had survived the upheavals of the pre-Sui period, thanks to their local power bases on great estates with numerous client families and tenants, had lost these bases by late T'ang times and had become part of a metropolitan elite, dependent on the fortunes of one dynasty or another. It was symptomatic of their decline that none of the regional regimes of the Five Dynasties period—even the southern ones organized on the T'ang model—was ruled by one of these once-great clans.

The preceding summary has suggested the scale and the reach of social and political change generated in the second half of the T'ang. One dimension of change that has not been mentioned and is not dealt with in any of the papers is economic change, and we might note some of its features here.

Since the Sui there had been a steady growth in the population of the Yangtse-Huai area and thus in its productivity relative to the older settled areas of Hopei and Honan. Although the interpretation of the surviving statistics is difficult, it appears that in the pre-rebellion period the area of steadiest increase was in the Huai and lower Yangtse basins. After the rebellion this trend was greatly accelerated, and settlement also proceeded rapidly in the modern provinces of Kiangsi, Hunan, and Hupei. Lastly, in late T'ang the serious Chinese settlement of Fukien at last began. By the middle of the eleventh century, the south of China had become not only more productive but more populous than the north.

The shift of population to the south had important general economic effects. After the initial period of clearing, reclamation, and settlement, southern agriculture was considerably more productive and more varied than that of the north. Under the late T'ang the center of economic power in China already had begun to shift from the great plain to the Yangtse Valley.

The breakdown of the intricate system of population and land registration after the rebellion also had far-reaching results. We have noted that from the fifth century onward successive administrations had attempted, with varying degrees of success, to impose systems of state land allocation. These systems all granted the right of use to a household for a limited period and reserved to the state the rights to free disposal. Lands were allotted to the individual, who in return had the duty to pay tax and to perform labor services for the state. The objectives of the system were a productive peasantry, the maximum cultivation of land, and at the same time a check upon excessive accumulations of land. This system did not function perfectly—it is not even certain whether it was ever enforced at all in much of central and southern China, even at the zenith of Sui and T'ang power—but it was certainly taken seriously as the legal system governing the tenure of land.

After An Lu-shan's time, there was never again any possibility of reimposing such a system on a national scale. By degrees, de facto recognition was given to the rights of individual landholders to the possession and free disposal of their lands, and although theoretically all land remained the emperor's land, in practice a free market in land was established. The tendency was for the great landed estate worked by tenant cultivators to become more and more widespread. Great estates had always existed, usually in the hands of the state, the imperial clan, the great aristocratic clans, high officials, or religious foundations, who could claim exemption from the legal limitations on landed property. After An Lu-shan there was a free-for-all in which all sorts of wealthy persons joined.

In connection with this shift from public to private ownerhip of land there was also a change in the nature of tenancy. Where in early T'ang times tenancy usually involved a short-term purely economic contract between equals, by the late ninth century long-term agreements implying a degree of personal subordination of the tenant to the landlord were normal, and this development led into the system of semi-servile tenancy common in some parts of China under the Sung. This new order of tenancy was not simply the result of economic pressures, for the peasant also sought security in times of civil disturbance under the protection of a powerful patron. This phenomenon was in turn a part of a general tendency toward highly personalized relationships throughout society: relations between master and retainer, patron and client, and even pseudokinship relationships, as when some ninth-century governors adopted their subordinates as sons. In short, there was a reemergence of small-scale, closely knit social groupings that would replace the lost empire-wide hierarchy of rank. The last effort to define the standing of recognized aristocratic clans throughout the empire, described by Twitchett, may be interpreted as a last, and ultimately futile, effort to reestablish an aristocratic elite as a substitute for the vanished authority of the central government.

The decentralization of political power after the mid-T'ang had many economic repercussions: the development of regional markets centered on the new provincial capitals, the increasing density of small towns and market centers, the rapid increase in trade and the circulation of commodities, the government's inability to continue its Confucian-inspired restriction of merchants and mercantile life. Freed from the strict institutional checks of early T'ang times, the merchant class began to develop as a self-conscious urban bourgeoisie, which by Sung times had its own subculture and its own life-style and was capable of breaking the hitherto impenetrable social barrier between itself and the scholar-official elite.

The general increase in productivity and the circulation of goods led gradually to a fundamental change in government economic attitudes; this change again marks the eighth and ninth centuries as the end of an era. The old stress on agriculture and the peasantry as the source of prosperity and revenue remains; but from this time onward the Chinese government was always closely involved with commerce, both by direct intervention in profitable sectors of industry—by the management of state monopolies and by the increasing use of taxes on trade—and by policies designed to draw revenue from the urban population. In response to these changes the government abandoned its time-honored policy of using silk as a form of commodity money. Although there was no dramatic change, the creation of a more adequate coinage, the emergence of credit institutions and primitive forms of banking, and the steady decline of interest rates all contributed to the spectacular growth of urban prosperity under the Sung.

In sum, the attempt to control the economy from the center in accord with a model that had come down from the third century B.C. broke down at every level. Centralized land allocation and the control of commerce were abandoned and were never reimposed by any later dynasty. The economy, freed from these constraints, grew rapidly for the next four centuries at such a rate that serious historians have proposed that the society that grew on late T'ang foundations had by the twelfth century all the prerequisites for the emergence of a modern capitalist economy.

The Perspective of Poetry

To the average educated Chinese the automatic association conjured up by the word *T'ang* is unlikely to be either social or institutional change or new trends in thought or religious doctrine. It would be rather an image of a high point in Chinese culture and the arts, and would quite probably be simply "poetry." For the T'ang was the golden age of poetry, the age in which poetry achieved its unchallenged standing as the preeminent genre of Chinese literature, the age when it began to play such a vital role in formal education that every educated man became, if not a poet, at least capable of writing verse. Even today a Chinese schoolboy's first encounter with his own poetic tradition is likely to be the standard anthology of three hundred T'ang poems *T'ang shih san-pai shou*. And even if only a few scholars know the *Complete Poetry of the T'ang*, with its forty-eight thousand surviving poems, the oeuvre of the T'ang masters remains to provide the central core of the poetic tradition and to establish the canons of taste and sensibility, the models against which all later writing came to be measured.

It may at first sight seem strange that we have included studies of poetry in a volume of essays devoted to topics which, in Western terms, would be the normal subject matter for the historian. But there are powerful reasons compelling the historian of the T'ang to grapple with the poetry of the period.

The historical sources produced by the orthodox tradition, our major source of information, are predominantly court-centered political narratives, concerned above all to explore the exercise of power and the functioning of governmental institutions. They provide us with rich biographical material on a wide range of T'ang personalities, but these biographies are so concentrated on the individuals' exercise of specific functions that one gets no feeling for the relationship between the individual and his broader milieu or for the quality and texture of life in society as a whole.

Prose literature is almost equally disappointing for the modern historian of the T'ang. Fiction, which for later periods provides us with colorful detail and a feel for ordinary life, was still in its infancy. The extensive prose writings of individual authors which survive in the *Complete T'ang Prose* are overwhelmingly either documents written in the context of their authors' official careers or commemorative inscriptions and formulaic *pièces d'occasion*. There is a singular lack of extended reflective writing, such as characterizes the Sung. For any real insight into the personal attitudes and beliefs of the men of T'ang our main resources are personal correspondence, a good deal of which survives from the latter half of the eighth century on, and the reflective essays *(lun)* which became common in the same period.

But even in the case of an individual who has extensive official biographical records and has left a substantial body of prose writings, it is rarely possible to gain a view of his personal reactions to everyday life, of his emotional responses, of his feelings toward things other than his official career and formal role. For these we can turn only to poetry, and it is surely not accidental that the only modern biographies of T'ang figures are biographies of poets. Poetry is thus an indispensable source for the T'ang historian, for it is through poetry that he can bring his dramatis personae alive and grope toward a feel for the quality of T'ang life. Its subject matter, too, ranges over many everyday subjects beneath the notice of the Confucian historian, but of absorbing interest today.

Poetry, in any culture, has its dangers as historical material. Only too often one finds a flight of fancy taken for fact; Li Po offers a thousand pieces of gold for a cup of rare wine, and the economic historians reach to plot another price on their graphs. But the dangers and difficulties of using poetry as history are far more subtle than such lapses of common sense and imagination.

Chinese poetry tended always to deal with events in terms of timeless and universal themes and to express them by conventions that the reader must constantly bear in mind. Hans H. Frankel's chapter, for example, explores the various ways in which images of the past were used by some T'ang poets. Since history constituted a large element in a conventional classical education, all Chinese writing in the old literary tradition was steeped in a sense of the past, and historical examples were automatically cited to justify present policies, institutions, and even personal actions—to validate the present from the lessons of past experience. In prose and poetry alike, the past provided both an endless source of models and ideals and a yardstick against which to measure present performance in politics and personal behavior.

In a curious way, the past was also viewed as undifferentiated from the present, a sort of backward extension of the present world. There was a basic assumption that in spite of the ups and downs of political history there was a universality of institutions, a constant quality of human life. Frankel shows the indirect and evocative ways in which poets could use the symbols of the past, a past held up for comparison with a present which it both resembles and stands in contrast to. The poetic response to this comparison is more subtle, more indirect than that of the historian or political adviser making a specific historical analogy, but the underlying assumption of a continuity of human affairs is shared by both.

This overwhelming feeling for history as a continuum of which one forms a part underlies one feature of Chinese historiography that the modern Western historian finds so perplexing: the almost total lack of a "sense of period" or of the immediate feeling for anachronism that we have in relation to our own past. When the Chinese poet mentions some image evocative of the past, it will be heavy with historical associations—the grave mounds of emperors long dead, the ruins of a city wall—but will give no sense of the shape and reality of a time different in quality, atmosphere, and appearance from the present. Ironically enough, thanks to archaeology we today have a far better idea of what Han China looked like than did the literati of T'ang times. The T'ang artist would depict the sage emperors of antiquity in the familiar court dress and surroundings of his own day, for the identity and continuity of past and present were assumed without question.

In many areas of belief and attitude, as in the image of the past, poetry enables us to explore the subtle variations of response aroused in contemporary minds by events we know of in a more general sense from our historical reading.

The tradition of classical exegesis, followed avidly by later poetic commentators, had accustomed the Chinese reader to approach poetry at several levels of meaning and to seek ambiguities and concealed allusions—the half-spoken thought, messages in a sort of emotional code—in the most apparently transparent verse. This was possible only in a society whose elite was extraordinarily homogeneous, and perhaps the most important single insight that T'ang poetry affords to the historian is the understanding it gives us of the inner life of the T'ang elite. The picture that emerges is of a community of educated and intelligent men bound together by a common education, by commitment to a complex cultural and literary tradition, and by the common pursuit of "letters" in the broadest sense, to a degree which has never been approached in the West, except perhaps in the medieval Church.

David Lattimore explores this common world of the mind and spirit, in which poetic communication was facilitated and enriched by the constant availability of this tradition, which any poet could assume was shared to a surprising depth by all his readers. This was a world in which, to the fastidious writer, every word had a wealth of association, in which he could assume—thanks to the common education and experience that he and his readers shared—an appropriate range of response not only to specific allusions to the literature of the past, but to a wide spectrum of more intangible aesthetic stimuli. The subtlety and variety of poetic technique, which made these allusions possible, is explored both by Lattimore and by Elling O. Eide, in his essay on some of Li Po's poems. These studies show how a web of allusion and reference, direct and indirect, found its expression in terms of a prosodic and formal complexity, which reached a new level of refinement in T'ang times. These new techniques, moreover, not only made possible a new technical variety in verse forms, but offered an additional element of poetic communication.

To speak of T'ang poetry, however, as though it were a single genre is surely misleading. Traditional literary historians long ago subdivided the T'ang poets into five periods and into various schools, but for us it is perhaps enough to underline the fact that in this field, as in all others, the An Lu-shan uprising marks a major change. The mid-eighth century is at once a culmination of a poetic tradition in the work of the great masters Li Po and Tu Fu and an era of change, as the political events of the post-rebellion period produced new trends. On the one hand some poets, such as those involved in the new *yüeh-fu* movement, began to write on social, satirical themes—a well-established poetic tradition and one in which Tu Fu had written many of his most famous pieces, but one to which the new poets brought simplicity, directness of utterance, and use of commonplace, deliberately "unpoetic" diction. On the other hand there was a tendency toward an introspective and highly personal, in part escapist, poetry, exploring the realms of fantasy and imagination, pressing literary sensibility and sensual response to the limit. These new trends were not so much separate schools (the same poets were often involved in both types of writing at one time or another) but were rather new extensions of the appropriate matter of poetry, based on the revival in each case of trends to be found in the earlier Chinese poetic tradition. And it is clear that they each arose in response to external factors—to the reformist ambition to restore the stability of society and to the realization by the educated elite, including the poets, that political developments had left them powerless to effect any lasting change, As the ninth century progressed, more and more writers withdrew from active commitment to the world of affairs and retreated into a personal world of self-exploration and introspection.

T'ang poetry did not come to flower in total isolation. The Sui and T'ang were periods of dazzling achievements in all the arts. From city-planning and architecture through sculpture and painting down to ceramics, metalwork, and textiles, the visual arts all show new peaks of technical accomplishment and a vitality and realism that were seldom achieved in later dynasties. The arts highlight an aspect of T'ang life that sharply marks it off from later ages—its cosmopolitanism. Under

the T'ang, China was subject to foreign influences as never before or
since. Poets and young scholars, drunk with Western grape wine,
celebrated the charms of Central Asian courtesans in poems set to
foreign tunes. The music of popular entertainment was Central Asian
music, performed on Western instruments, and accompanying exotic
foreign dances. To the disgust of conservative Confucian scholars, even
the solemn ritual music of the court and of the imperial ancestral
temple was gradually replaced by foreign music, traces of which are
still clearly discernible in the court music which the Japanese adopted
from T'ang China. Poetry was not written for the eye alone. It was
sung, and the foreign tunes of the popular entertainers introduced new
and strange melodic shapes, rhythms, and forms into poetry, some of
which are identified by Eide.

But the foreign influence on poetry was not simply the influence of
the musical milieu in which poetry flourished. Men were fascinated by
the exotic, by the strange products and stranger tales that came into
China from Central Asia, from the Indies, and from the far south. A
new awareness of the sense of place, a consciousness of the "feel" of
distant regions, of the variety of environment and human life, brought
to poetry a new richness of imagery, a wider range of reference. T'ang
poets, many of whom in the course of their official careers themselves
served in the distant border provinces, could hardly escape these influences. One of the major contrasts between the T'ang historical
record and T'ang poetry is between the purely Chinese political scene
given in the histories, where foreign peoples appear only as peripheral
rivals to the Chinese Empire, and the broader world depicted by the
poets, in which foreigners, foreign ideas, and foreign products appear so
frequently as to be taken for granted.

Moreover, in some cases we get a glimpse, through a poet like Li Po,
of what it actually meant to be a member of the aristocracy with its
mixture of Chinese and foreign blood, which from the historical records
seems to be only a matter of pedigree. As Eide's study of Li Po shows,
his poetry is haunted by strange symbolism deriving from a totally
non-Chinese culture and by atavistic echoes of the virile life of the
T'ang's powerful nomadic neighbors.

Here again, poetry enables us to form an impression of the distinctive
life-style of this period, so different from the scholarly self-image reflected by Chinese scholars of later generations and by their Western imita-
tors. The T'ang elite were far more active and led far less bookish lives
than their successors. They were horsemen and hunters who practiced
archery and falconry and played polo. And unlike their successors, their

womenfolk led equally active lives. Traditionally, Chinese scholars
have accounted for this by the assumption that there was something
freakish and unnatural about such a society—the effects of Turkish or
other non-Chinese blood. But it is surely more. This was a continuation
of the Chinese past: the T'ang was the last dynasty when a member of
the elite was expected to have learned the basic martial arts; the last
dynasty when military and civil careers were not sharply separate; the
last when the predominance of the civil virtues was not absolute; and it
was certainly the last dynasty in which one could conceive of an
imperial emissary come to seek the hand of a high-born lady on behalf
of a royal prince being kept waiting because the young lady was out
hunting.

Such impressions give an important new dimension to our picture of
a closely knit T'ang literate elite. For all the subtleties of their diction,
for all the level of literary scholarship that was *de rigeur* among them,
this was no inward-looking, ineffectual literary clique, no bookish group
of intellectuals. They were essentially practical men, living active lives
for the most part as busy public servants. Many of the most prominent
writers held very high offices. Even if they failed to achieve office,
public service was their almost universal ambition. And the poetry
they wrote is important to us not merely because of the extraordinary
literary heights it achieved, but also because it is the closest we can
get to the lives and personalities of its writers and to the ambience of
their society.

Part I
Institutions and Politics

2. The Composition of the T'ang Ruling Class: New Evidence from Tunhuang

Denis Twitchett

It is common ground among all serious historians of China, whatever their political complexion, that the period from about 700 to 1000 was one of profound and radical social change, although the interpretations placed upon this social change have been almost as various as the authors who have written about it. To some it marks the transition to a "modern" period of Chinese history; to others, the first stirrings of capitalism and urbanization; and to still others, the transition from a society based upon slavery to a stage of "feudalism."

I do not propose here, however, to touch upon these larger problems of periodization, which are in any case more often treated as articles of faith than as practical historical issues. Instead, I attempt to deal with only a single aspect of this general transformation of society, which I believe to have had the most profound effects upon the later course of Chinese history, the radical change in the structure and composition of the Chinese ruling class.

Ever since Naitō Torajirō, in his *Shina Ron* of 1914, first formulated his well-known hypothesis that the late T'ang, Wu-tai, and early Sung periods mark the transition form the "medieval" to the "modern" period of Chinese history, it has been widely accepted that during this period the "aristocratic" form of government which had emerged at the end of the Han dynasty was gradually replaced by a "bureaucratic" system. During the pre-T'ang period there had been a sharp and formal distinction in status between commoner *(shu-min)* and scholar-official *(shih ta-fu)* families. The latter, and in particular a comparatively small group of extremely powerful lineages who formed the elite among

For a discussion of source materials referred to, see the Bibliographical Note at the end of the chapter.

them, had completely dominated the political scene; they produced
the ruling houses of many of the succession of short-lived dynasties
in both northern and southern China and monopolized the highest
offices of state through their rights to hereditary employment and their
dominant social standing. In this system the emperor himself had been
only *primus inter pares*. His ministers considered themselves his social
equals, sometimes indeed as his social superiors, and their primary
loyalty was directed toward their own class and to the existing social
order rather than toward the ruling dynastic house.

When the Sui and the T'ang once again reunified the whole of China,
they gradually came to realize that such a social system was unfavorable to political stability and to strong centralized authority. Through
their newly established structure of state examinations they began to
recruit a professional bureaucracy, the members of which were selected
by the state, on individual merit, from a far broader social spectrum
than the old aristocracy. Unlike the old aristocracy, these new bureaucrats owed their primary allegiance to the state, which had given them
office, rather than to their own social group. This change had many
repercussions. Whereas the new system greatly increased the opportunities for social mobility—at least for the members of the educated
elite—at the same time, from the Sung period onward the emperor
was never again on the same terms of comparatively easy intimacy
with his chief ministers. And, being the sole source of political authority,
he came to exercise ever more arbitrary power over the officials of the
bureaucracy through which he ruled. While the power of the throne
became more and more autocratic and despotic, the emperor, socially
isolated and cut off from easy personal relations with his chief ministers
and the great officials, was forced increasingly to rely upon members of
his personal secretariat and upon the eunuchs of his household for the
intimate everyday discussion of state affairs.

These changes, however, did not come about overnight, but rather
took several centuries. Until the end of the T'ang period the old aristocracy remained comparatively powerful, hereditary privilege survived,
and the principle of the recruitment of officials solely on the basis of
their education and literary talent by no means went unchallenged. It
has been customary, at least since the brilliantly perceptive studies of
T'ang politics published during World War II by Ch'en Yin-k'o, to see
the T'ang as a transitional period and to interpret its political history
in terms of a continuing basic tension between the members of the old
aristocracy and the new class of professional bureaucrats who had been
selected through the examination system and who came from relatively

humble origins. A great deal of extremely interesting work developing this basic interpretation has already been published, and this conception of a fundamental political polarity between the two interest groups has obviously proved a fertile and productive point of departure.

It is therefore somewhat surprising that no serious attempt has yet been made to define more precisely the composition of the "aristocracy" of the pre-T'ang period or to specify in more than vague general terms who should be considered to have been members of the aristocratic interest in T'ang times.

If we look at the society of the pre-T'ang period of division between north and south, it seems to be distinguished from Chinese society in later times by two features, each of which is relevant to the concept of an "aristocratic" society. First, at the highest level, the position of emperor and the control of office in the upper echelons of central government were dominated—almost monopolized—by the members of a comparatively small number of immensely powerful clans. Second, at a rather lower level, there was a rigid and formal distinction in legal status between scholar-official (shih ta-fu) and commoner (shu-min, han-men) lineages. This distinction was expressed in legal terms by scholar-official households being listed in household registers entirely separate from those of commoner families. Scholar-officials registered in this way were accorded the privilege of exemption from corvée labor, military service, land tax, and market tolls; were not liable to corporal punishment; and were entitled to commutate punishments either to money fines, or to a proportionate reduction in rank or official status, or to a setback in their official career. Even more important, marriage between members of scholar-official families and commoners was forbidden, and even within the scholar-official class there was a complex hierarchy of lineages and families, some of which also practiced group endogamy.

The historians who have dealt with the aristocracy of T'ang times have devoted their attention almost exclusively to the first of these questions, the dominance of the great aristocratic clans in court politics and the central government. Virtually all of the analytical studies of the social background and origins of T'ang officials and of the composition of the ruling class as a whole have been concentrated upon those persons who reached the highest posts in central government, the chief ministers and presidents and vice-presidents of the executive boards. This means that the samples employed have by no means been typical for the ruling class as a whole, for these posts were not only of outstanding importance and prestige, but their incumbents worked closely with the emperor himself, and thus personal considerations, which would have been inoperative at somewhat less exalted levels of the bureaucracy, must have entered into their selection. However, it is impossible to carry a systematic analysis much further than this, owing to the sparseness and limitations of the sources for the T'ang period, which are in no way comparable with the immensely rich materials at the disposal of the historians who have recently made such significant advances in our understanding of social mobility in Ming and Ch'ing society. The T'ang official histories, encyclopedias, and compilations of official documents are overwhelmingly concerned with the history of the court and the exercise of power through the central administration at the capital, and it is only for the employees of these central ministries that we can reconstruct a continuous record full enough for any sort of systematic or statistical analysis.[1]

Even at this highest level of political life, however, it seems an over-simplification to speak of a single coherent aristocratic faction. Among the comparatively restricted group of preeminently powerful clans whose members regularly achieved the highest ranks and who held nationwide prestige, it is clear that there was not one single "aristocracy," even though in given circumstances all the clans concerned might act together out of common interest. There were rather at least four regionally based aristocratic groups, each with its separate historical roots in the pre-Sui period of political division between north and south. The most powerful and prestigious of these groups were the four great clans of East of the Mountains (i.e. modern Hopei), who claimed to be the representatives of the purest Chinese cultural tradition, who married only among themselves (unless heavily bribed to do otherwise), and who looked down upon even the T'ang imperial house as social upstarts. Successive T'ang emperors made repeated efforts to break down their exclusiveness and to deflate their social pretensions, but with little success. Equally powerful, and only slightly less proud, were the great clans of Kuan-chung in the northwest, of which the T'ang royal house was one. These clans had risen to eminence under the succession of barbarian dynasties of conquest which had ruled northern China during the fifth and sixth centuries. They had con-

1. The only surviving systematic materials as to the personnel of offices are (1) for the chief ministers, (2) for the principal offices of the Six Boards under the Department of State, (3) for the censorate, (4) for the Han-lin Academy. Apart from these the only materials available for analysis are the entries on examination candidates included in the *Teng-k'o chi-k'ao.*

stantly intermarried with the non-Chinese ruling families and nobility of these dynasties and had close ties by marriage with the peoples of Central Asia and the steppes, many aspects of whose cultures they had adopted. Somewhat less powerful were the great clans of northern Shansi (Tai-pei), the area which had served as the power base for the T'ang's initial rise to power. These clans had many of the characteristics of the Kuan-chung aristocracy, with a still stronger admixture of foreign blood. Lastly there were the immensely wealthy aristocratic clans of the Yangtse Valley, who had risen to power during the Southern Dynasties.[2]

At the highest level of political life members of these great aristocratic clans remained a tremendously important force in early T'ang government. The policies of the first two emperors at least seem to have been designed more to preserve a balance of power between the rival regional aristocratic groups and to prevent the complete dominance of any one faction among them than to challenge the power of the aristocracy as a whole.[3] This was clearly felt by historians writing in the late eighth and early ninth centuries, who were very conscious of the radical changes which had by then taken place in the composition of the ruling elite. Su Mien in the *Hui-yao*, his administrative encyclopedia completed in 804–05, comments that "all of the chief ministers who assisted in the founding of the present dynasty came from the great aristocratic clans *(kuei-tsu)*. Ever since the three dynasties of antiquity there has never been any dynasty so [aristocratic in its origins] as our own T'ang house."[4]

But even though the power and influence of these great clans had waned by the time of Su Mien, they remained a force to be reckoned with in politics until their final destruction and disappearance during the military disorders, social chaos, and political anarchy of the late ninth and early tenth centuries.[5]

Their gradual eclipse and eventual disappearance certainly had a great influence upon the course of China's subsequent history. Nearly three centuries before Natiō produced his hypothesis on the social transformation of the late T'ang and Wu-tai period, the great seventeenth-century historian Ku Yen-wu had already clearly pointed out some of the social and political results of the extinction of the aristo-

2. On this point, see the essay on genealogy of Liu Fang, "Hsing-hsi lun," in *HTS* (Po-na edition) 199.10b–13a; *CTW* (Kuang-ya shu-chü edition, 1901) 372.7a–11b.

3. See Howard J. Wechsler's paper later in this volume and the authorities cited there.

4. *THY* (Kuo-hsüeh chi-pen ts'ung-shu edition, 1935) 36.663–64.

5. See Sun Kuo-tung, "Tang Sung chih chi she-hui."

cratic clans at the end of the T'ang. For Ku Yen-wu, writing in the shadow of the fall of the Ming, the T'ang represented a period of monumental stability, and to him it was no mere coincidence that the T'ang had also been the apogee of the power of the great aristocratic clans. Their final decay during the ninth and tenth centuries, in his view, had removed not only an all-important and irreplaceable element in the political continuity and stability of the court, but also an essential focus of local power and influence in their home provinces, which had provided a rallying point and a nucleus for local political and social stability and continuity in times of crisis. Ku Yen-wu contrasted the T'ang aristocrats with the great ministers of his own troubled times, whose authority no longer rested upon a solid basis of personal and family power and influence in the provinces, but depended merely upon the "empty titles conferred upon them by a failing dynasty." Ku Yen-wu's essay, entitled "P'ei-ts'un chi" [The record of the P'ei family village] reads as follows:

> Alas! From the time when the way of government began to deteriorate more and more the state has been without powerful lineages. Being without powerful lineages, there has been no solid foundation upon which to erect the state. Without such a solid foundation for the state there has been disorder within and rebellion without so that in the end we have arrived at a state of collapse. This being the case, is not the preservation of the system of powerful lineages the means by which to support the regulation of the people and to extend the power of the state?
>
> I arrived at the P'ei village in Wen-hsi county. I paid my respects at the shrine to the Duke of Chin (i.e. P'ei Tu, 764–839) and inquired after his descendants. There were still one or two hundred men who left their plowing to come and pay their respects together. When I left and came to the public highway, I read a memorial stele dating from the T'ang, which recorded their genealogy and lineage. I climbed onto a bank and gazing around could see that for a distance of 10 *li* grave mounds and tombs were ranged one after the other. A hundred and several tens of these were the graves of persons whose names, styles, offices, and noble ranks could still be ascertained.
>
> Now in recent antiquity the influence of the noble lineages was at its peak under the T'ang, and the Ho-chung area was in T'ang times in the vicinity of the court. The territory was thus of prime importance, and its clans were most powerful. Such clans as the

Liu of Chieh-hsien and the P'ei of Wen-hsi were all continuously employed as officials for several hundreds of years, with an unbroken record of members in official service. The Hsüeh clan of Fen-yin took advantage of the Yellow River to defend themselves against Shih Hu (of the Later Chao). When Fu Chien (of the Former Ch'in) was carving out a territory for himself, not a single one of their members took service with his dynasty. The Fan and Wang clans of I-shih raised troops to resist Kao Huan (of the Northern Ch'i). If it had not been that the worthies among them had not led them in the correct way of preserving their families and strengthening their clans, how could they possibly have lasted as long as they did without falling into a decline? From the fall of the T'ang their genealogies all come to a complete stop. Yet even so, some six or seven men of P'ei Shu's party were still a source of envy for Chu Ch'üan-chung, who had to wait until he had had them murdered at the Pai-ma post station before he could usurp the T'ang throne. The interrelationship between the powerful clans and the state was as close as this.

But by the end of the Five Dynasties the emperor was little more than a chess picee, while the great clans and eminent families had sunk to becoming yamen runners. Thus when the Northern Sung fell, there was not a single family able to assist the commander-in-chief or to defend themselves. The entire Ssu-ma clan of Hsia-hsien took refuge in the south, and only returned to their native place less than a century ago.

Alas! When this is the reason why the way of government deteriorates day by day, is it not inevitable that when one morning a crisis arises the ruler will have no great ministers on whom he may rely, while the common people will have no great families in whom they can trust so that all of them will flee like scuttling rats, putting aside all consideration of right or wrong to seek their own mean interest?

It was for this reason that the T'ang emperors honored the official clans and placed great weight on family privilege. They did so because they realized that the feudal system *(feng-chien)* could not be restored and thus embodied the same idea in the great official clans *(shih ta-fu)* so as to guard themselves against any sudden emergency. This was certainly a policy which later rulers have proved unable to comprehend! . . .

To expect one's great ministers to take command of the safety or peril of the state, furnished only with the empty title of a petty chief minister, is a policy that cannot possibly end successfully. The *Chou kuan* says, "The T'ai-hsiang attaches the people of the state by means of the nine relationships. . . . The fifth says, 'The clan *(tsung)* obtains control of the people through its lineages *(tsu)*.' " This can be clearly perceived in general terms by examining the relationship between the P'ei clan and the survival and fall of the T'ang dynasty.

Since it is impossible to restore the form of government of feudal times, if one wishes to establish one's state by depending instead upon the power of the great official families, all will depend upon giving due importance to the great clans and lineages! All will depend upon giving importance to the great clans and lineages![6]

Ku Yen-wu thus clearly perceived the widespread political consequences of the disappearance of the small number of very powerful clans whose members had dominated court politics while at the same time retaining a territorial power base in the provinces. But, like Ch'en Yin-k'o and his followers among modern scholars, he saw the aristocratic clans primarily as a source of social and political stability and as a factor in central government and national politics and concerned himself only with the most powerful among them.

Far earlier still, however, a much broader concept of the nature of the social changes during late T'ang times had been put forward by the great Sung polymath Shen Kua (1031–95) in one of the essays in his *Meng-ch'i pi-t'an* completed in 1086. Shen Kua clearly recognized that not only the social origins of the political elite, but the whole structure of society during the Six Dynasties, the Sui, and the T'ang, had been quite different from the social order of his own day. This difference he characterized by the existence in the earlier period of unusually rigid and precise hierarchical distinctions between various social groups. He compared these distinctions with the Indian caste system, a type of social organization which he apparently believed to be common to all non-Chinese peoples, and which he thought had been introduced into China by the Toba Turks during the Northern Wei period.

Although differences of standing among the families of scholar-officials have existed since antiquity, these had never been of any particular significance. Beginning with the Wei (i.e. Three Kingdoms), when the government had come to select men for office, they had been ranked in accordance with the standing of their

6. See Ku Yen-wu, "P'ei-ts'un chi," *Ku T'ing-lin shin-wen-chi* 5 (Peking, 1959): 106–07.

families. But men were still not selected for employment solely on the basis of their descent *(men-ti)*.

It is only among the four barbarians that noble and base are distinguished purely on the basis of their family. Thus for example in India only the two surnames Ksatriya and Brahmin are noble, while all others such as Vaisya and Sudra are the surnames of commoners. Beneath these again are the four poor surnames: Kung, Ch'iao, Ch'un and T'o. All foreign countries have a system like this, with the rulers and great officials having their own sorts of surname, so that if a man is not of noble descent, none of the people are willing to give obeisance to him. Those bearing common surnames, no matter how industrious or able they may be, are perfectly happy to live as the inferiors of these great families. Such a state of affairs has persisted down until the present time.

From the time when the Later [Toba] Wei gained possession of the central plain, this sort of custom began to flourish in China as well. Thus we see the emergence of such groups as the "eight clans" *(pa-shih)* the "ten surnames" *(shih-hsing)*, the "thirty-six lineages" *(san-shih-liu tsu)*, and the "ninety-two surnames" *(chiu-shih-erh hsing)*. Those whose forebears had for three generations held the rank of one of the Three Dukes *(San Kung)* were entitled *Kao-liang*. Those whose members had been [*Shang-shu*] *Ling* or *P'u-ye* were entitled *Hua-yü*. Those whose members had been Presidents of Boards *(Shang-shu)* or *Ling-[chün]* or *Hou-[chün]* or above were styled "Surnames of the First Rank" *(Chia-hsing)*. Those whose members had been presidents of the nine courts or prefects *(Fang-po)* were styled "Surnames of the Second Rank" *(I-hsing)*. Those whose members had been *San-ch'i ch'ang-shih* or *Ta-chung tai-fu* were styled "Surnames of the Third Rank" *(Ping-hsing)*. Those whose members had been *Li-pu* [*lang-chung*] or *Cheng-yüan lang* were styled "Surnames of the Fourth Rank" *(Ting-hsing)*. All those families which were eligible for membership of any of these groups were known as the "Four [Categories of] Surnames" *(Ssu-hsing)*.[7]

Later on this rigid system was altered and fell into confusion, so that it became no longer possible to define the ranks of families precisely. Eventually, taking the registers of officials from previous generations as a basis, the Ts'ui clan of Po-ling, the Lu clan of Fan-yang, the Li clan of Lung-hsi, and the Cheng clan of Jung-yang were designated as the "Lineages of the First Class" *(Chia-*

7. This interpretation of *Ssu-hsing* was already obscured by the seventh century, when the great clans of Hopei claimed to be the "four families" (i.e. four surnames).

tsu). During the reign of Kao-tsung under the T'ang (650–84) the Wang clan of Taiyuan, the Ts'ui clan of Ch'ing-ho, and the Li clan of Chao-chün were added to them to form the "Seven Great Surnames" *(Ch'i-hsing)*.

But there were some tens of [other] clans which used their local influence to overthrow one another, who pushed and disparaged one another, wrote books and increasingly compiled records. It reached the point where the court established offices for them and made special provision for them. This change spread everywhere and was fanned up until it became customary, and even the power of the state was unable to dispel it. Speaking in general terms these [locally prominent] clans formed five degrees of rank and totaled in all some hundred families all of whom were entitled "scholar-official lineages" *(shih-tsu)*. All families outside this group were considered to be "commoner surnames" *(shu-hsing)*, and none of them dared class themselves with these hundred [scholar-official] lineages in contracting marriages or in serving in office. Even though the Li clan of Lung-hsi were the imperial house, they still only ranked third, the importance placed on the relative standing of clans being so immense. In the very first rank were such lineages as the Lu clan of Kang-t'ou, the Ts'ui clan of T'u-men, the Li clan of Che-ti, and the Yang clan of Ching-kung who styled themselves the "Tripod Lineages" *(Ting-tsu)*.

At the end of the T'ang period, these customs fell by degrees into decline and disuse.[8]

Shen Kua thus believed that while lineage, descent, and recognized family standing had played a major role in the recruitment of potential officials since the third century, under the foreign influences which reached their peak under the Toba Wei dynasty the existing system of relative family standing was rigidly institutionalized into a strict status hierarchy of clans and lineages. Although the resulting precise correlation between family status and the office held by family members decayed at the end of the period of division in the late sixth century, a super-elite of extremely powerful clans emerged, which survived, with some changes and additions, into the T'ang dynasty. This super-elite may be roughly equated with the eminent aristocratic clans discussed by Ch'en Yin-k'o and by Ku Yen-wu before him. Shen Kua, however, adds a totally new factor to this problem in his mention of the emergence by early T'ang times of a larger, lower-grade, locally rather than

8. Shen Kua, *Meng-ch'i pi-t'an chiao-cheng*, ed. Hu Tao-ching (Shanghai, 1956), 24: 772–73.

nationally prominent group of a hundred or more lineages calling themselves "scholar-official lineages." These too were an exclusive group who married only among themselves and claimed favorable treatment in seeking official employment.

What Shen Kua suggests, then, is not merely the existence of a small closed aristocratic super-elite, such as we can easily infer to have existed from the evidence in the Standard Histories, but rather a hierarchy of such castelike and exclusive social groups, with the great Hopei clans at the top and the very much larger group of locally prominent lineages at the bottom, who in turn were rigidly distinguished from the commoners.

Some very interesting evidence supporting such a view and adding further refinement to it was recently published by the late Niida Noboru and by Takeda Ryūji. This evidence is incorporated in a number of Ming and Ch'ing clan genealogies. It is not generally appreciated that the genealogical works known as *chia-p'u* and *tsung-p'u*, even of comparatively recent date, frequently cite prefaces, inscriptions, and official documents allegedly of Sung, T'ang, and even occasionally of Chin date. Niida[9] and Takeda[10] have made considerable use of these, and they have also been noted by Makino Tatsumi in his work upon Ming and Ch'ing genealogical writings.[11] I myself have come across several further examples, and a systematic search through the genealogies in the larger collections would probably yield a great many more.[12] The late dates of the works in which these documents are quoted naturally renders them suspect, but does not *necessarily* cast doubt upon their authenticity, since many recent genealogies are merely the end product of a continuous process of compilation going back at least to the Sung period. But the authentication of such documents is by no means straightforward, especially when, as in the present case, there is no confirmatory evidence of more nearly contemporary date, and when it

9. See Niida Noboru, "Ton-kō hakken no *Ten-ka sei-bō shizoku hō:* Tōdai no mibun-teki naikonsei wo megutte," reprinted with additions and corrections in *Chūgoku hōsei shi kenkyū: Dorei, nōdo hō; Kazoku, sonraku hō* (Tokyo, 1962), pp. 656–60.

10. See Takeda Ryūji, "*Jōgan shizokushi* no hensan ni kansuru ichi kōsatsu," *Shigaku* 25, no. 4 (1952): 23–41.

11. Makino Tatsumi, *Kinsei Chūgoku, sōzoku kenkyū* (Tokyo, 1949), pp. 40–120.

12. One especially interesting example is the *Lu-shih Feng-men chih-p'u,* dated 1881; Taga Akigoro, *Sōfu no kenkyū* (Tokyo, 1960) (hereafter cited as Taga) bibliography no. 812, in the Diet Library, Tokyo. This contains a number of T'ang documents: the preface to a branch genealogy dated 741, the rules of revision for the genealogy dated 755, a preface to a revision of the old genealogy written by the Sung poet Lu Yu, and documents connected with the official recognition and registration of no less than forty-nine branch lineages by the court in 812 (see ibid., 15. la-28b, 16.5a–12a).

is apparent that the texts themselves, if genuine, must have suffered severely in the course of transmission.

The principal document relevant to the point under discussion purports to be an "Edict" dated K'ai-yüan 5 (717). This edict, which is not mentioned in any T'ang historical source, defines the social standing of the lineages of the empire. It says that in 655 it had been decided that twenty-six surnames were to be considered as distinct from all the other surnames of the empire. This list had been reexamined in 666, and the status of the clans included confirmed. It goes on to list the twenty-six clans, which are divided into two groups, ten described as "Pillars of the State" *(Kuo-chih-chu)* and sixteen described as "Cross-beams of the State" *(Kuo-chih-liang)*. It ends by prescribing a punishment of two years hard labor in cases of marriage between unequal partners, presumably referring to marriages between members of these restricted groups of lineages and ordinary commoners.

The earliest known citation of this edict is in the *Hsin-an Wang-shih Pa-kung p'u,* the genealogy of a branch of the Wang lineage in Hsin-an, Anhwei, the preface to which is dated 1535. This genealogy, however, includes prefaces to earlier recensions of the genealogy going back to one written by Chu Hsi,[13] and there is ample evidence both that Hsin-an was an area in which genealogical studies were unusually well developed from an early period and that the Wangs' history was known in considerable detail.[14] There is thus a reasonable chance that the edict in question *may* have derived from an earlier genealogy written in late Sung times. It is also quoted in a later genealogy of another branch of the Wang clan, the *Wu-yüeh Wang-shih chih-p'u* of 1897.[15] This and a later edition of the same genealogy published in 1909[16] also include a further ostensibly T'ang document, a memorial by Wang Hua, prefect of She-chou (the T'ang name for Hsin-an), dated 632 or 633, which was supposed to have been presented to the throne together with the clan's genealogy to lay claim to its recognition as a prominent lineage. This memorial, however, is almost certainly spurious.[17] The edict

13. This genealogy is not listed in Taga under this title. It is probably identical with Taga 312, entitled *Hsiu-ning Hsi-men Wang-shih tsu-p'u.*

14. See the immense detail accumulated in the *Hsin-an ming-tsu chih,* an attempt to list genealogical details of all the prominent clans of the area, among which the Wang clan features very importantly. This work was first compiled in late Yüan times, and two versions survive, one from very early Ming times (among the rare books in Peking National Library and in the Tōyō Bunkō) and another from the early seventeenth century (in Tōyō Bunka Kenkyūjo).

15. Taga 320.

16. Taga 321; Takeda, "*Jōgan shizokushi,*" p. 34.

17. See Takeda, "*Jōgan shizokushi,*" pp. 36–38.

itself, with very minor variants, is also cited by other genealogies, the *Yeh-shih tsung-p'u* of 1873, in which it is noted as having been "taken from the former genealogy,"[18] and the *Lu-chiang chün Ho-shih ta-t'ung tsung-p'u* of 1921, a general genealogy of all the Ho lineages of central and southern China.[19]

The last-named genealogy also makes an apparently independent reference to the "twenty-six eminent lineages" specified in the edict, by saying: "When during the Yung-hui period (650–56) of the T'ang the social standing of clans and lineages were defined, they were placed in order in accordance with the official rank which their members had achieved under the T'ang. The most eminent surnames, twenty-six families in all, were singled out."

Yet another apparently independent mention of these twenty-six preeminent lineages appears in the *Fang-shih lien-tsung t'ung-p'u*, the genealogy of the Fang clan of Huang-kang in Hupei, published in 1924 but deriving from an edition originally compiled in 1820.[20] This claims that the Fang clan of Honan, from which the Hupei clan claimed to have been descended, had been one of the twenty-six Pillars of the State in T'ang times. The Fang do not, however, appear among the lineages which are listed together with the edict in the Wang and Yeh genealogies.

The lineages included in this list, as Niida pointed out,[21] are in any case very difficult to reconcile with historical facts. To begin with, of the seven great surnames mentioned in Shen Kua's essay quoted above, who were recognized by an edict of 659[22] to be an aristocratic elite which intermarried only among themselves, only one lineage, the Cheng clan of Jung-yang, is included. If, on the other hand, the list was a newly made one, designed as a blow to the excessive pretensions of these preeminent clans, which would fit in with what we know of the circumstances surrounding the compilation of the *Hsing-shih lu* in 659, it is difficult to explain why the Cheng clan was left in. Moreover, if as the above quotation from the Ho clan genealogy says, these twenty-six lineages were specially designated because of the outstanding achievements of their members in office under the T'ang, which again agrees with what we know of the compilation of the *Hsing-shih lu*, how is it that the lineages included bear not the slightest discernible rela-

18. Taga 939.
19. Ibid. 196.
20. Ibid. 12.
21. Niida, "*Ten-ka sei-bō shizoku hō*" (see note 9), pp. 657ff.
22. *THY* 83.1528–29.

tionship with the families whose members held the highest offices under the first three T'ang emperors? In addition, Kao-tsung is said to have rearranged the relative standing of the great lineages in 659 specifically because the existing lists omitted the kin of his favorite who later became the empress Wu.[23] Her lineage too is missing from these lists. Several of those lineages which are mentioned, on the other hand, are elsewhere considered as comparatively obscure, while no less than six are otherwise totally unknown.

In view of these doubts about the various lineages included in the list, coupled with considerable misgivings about the literary style of the document and the late date and uncertain provenance of the materials as a whole, I am very skeptical about the authenticity of the edict of 717 and the related passages from genealogies.

However, even if as seems likely this edict is in fact a fabrication of Ming date, it is still interesting to see that as late as the sixteenth century, and in a region where the sense of genealogical continuity was particularly highly developed, there survived a strong tradition that under the T'ang not only had the relative social standing of the great lineages been a matter of such importance that it was defined by the state, as might be inferred from the Standard Histories, but also that society had been formally organized in a hierarchy of exclusive groups of lineages which had intermarried only among themselves.

That such a tradition had solid grounding in historical fact is not difficult to prove. There is ample evidence in the standard historical sources of the compilation of family records, genealogies, lists of eminent lineages, and genealogical works on a larger scale which categorized and ranked in their relative order of social standing the great lineages of the empire. The compilation of such works, as might be expected, had been widespread during the pre-T'ang period when the official endorsement and recognition of a clan's status had had all-important effects upon the lives and careers of its members. The bibliographical chapters of the *Sui Shu* and the two T'ang histories list a very large number of genealogical works dating from pre-T'ang times, which range from genealogies of single lineages, the precursors of modern *chia-p'u* and *tsung-p'u,* to works dealing with all the prominent lineages of a specific region, and to mammoth compilations made on a national scale. The compilation of such works reached its climax under the emperor Wu-ti of the southern Liang dynasty, when Wang Seng-ju compiled a massive genealogical work extending to almost seven hundred chapters and listing all the eminent clans of the Liang empire.

23. Ibid. 36.665n.

All of these works listed in the Sui and T'ang histories were lost long ago, many of them before the eighth century. Apart from some fragmentary quotations the only surviving pre-T'ang and T'ang works representative of this genre are manuscripts from Tunhuang, an area whose inhabitants had a strong tradition of local historical writing.[24] They also seem to have had a genealogical tradition, for the Imperial Library of Hsüan-tsung's time included an extensive genealogy in twenty chapters of the locally prominent Chang lineage, the *Tun-huang Chang-shih chia-chuan*.[25] Among the Tunhuang documents in the British Museum is a considerable fragment of a smaller work of the same genre, dealing with the locally prominent Fan clan, entitled *Tun-huang Fan-shih chia-chuan*.[26] This work, the authorship and date of composition of which are not clear, but which is certainly pre-T'ang, is not a detailed genealogy like the *chia-p'u* of recent centuries, listing the precise family relationship of all male descendants. It begins instead with a short account of the descent of the Fans, who are traced back to a mythical origin in Chi, younger brother of the great Yao, down to their first settlement in Tunhuang in 28 B.C. This is followed by a rhymed eulogy and then by a series of short biographical sketches of exemplary members of the clan, only the first ten or so of which are preserved. These biographies deal with members of the local clan only, not of the more famous parent clan from Chi-pei in Hopei, from which the introduction traces their descent during Han times. The work is thus precisely what its title would lead us to expect, an account of the localized lineage, making no extraordinary claims to national importance, and its contents almost certainly derive in large part from the local history *Tun-huang shih-lu* by the fifth-century author Liu Ping. It seems probable that many other of the *Chia-chuan* listed in the Sui and T'ang histories, most of which were works in a single chapter, were of a similar type, rather than genealogies on the modern pattern.

The second Tunhuang manuscript, in the Bibliothèque Nationale, was first published in 1924 by Pelliot and Haneda, who gave it the provisional title *Tun-huang ming-tsu chih*.[27] It is much more fragmentary than the *Fan-shih chia-chuan*, lacking both its beginning and its title. In a recent study of this document Ikeda has shown that it was written

24. For example, the earliest known work with the title "Veritable Record" *(Shih-lu)* was produced in this area is the fifth century.

25. *CTS* (Po-na edition) 46.28b.

26. See Ikeda On, "*Tonkō Hanshi kaden* zankan ni tsuite," *Tōhōgaku* 24 (1962): 14–29; the original MS is numbered S. 1889.

27. First published in Paul Pelliot and Haneda Tōru, *Tun-huang I-shu* (Shanghai, 1926), 7: 29–34.

about 710 and possibly had some connection with the compilation of
the vast *Hsing-tsu hsi-lu* compiled by imperial order and completed in
713.[28] The Tunhuang manuscript is a fragment of a work dealing with
the prominent clans of a single locality, a genre that seems to have
been widespread in the pre-T'ang period, to judge from the number of
titles mentioned in the histories, but which later became very uncommon. The only well-known example in recent times is the *Hsin-an
ming-tsu chih* dealing with the prominent lineages of the Hsin-an district in Anhwei, which went through a number of editions during Yüan
and Ming times.[29] The Tunhuang example preserves the complete
entry on only one lineage and small fragments of two others. But there
is enough to show clearly that this too was not a full and systematic
genealogy, but simply a list of the more prominent members of each
lineage with the chief offices which they had filled.

Although no extended fragments of other T'ang genealogical works
survive, we know that the compilation of all types of genealogy, both
by private individuals and by the state, continued throughout the T'ang
period. The object behind such compilation varied—the individual
works normally aimed to preserve the pretensions of the aristocratic
clans, while the official compilations were designed primarily to check
upon and eventually to control aristocratic claims to preeminent status
and influence both in politics and in social life.[30]

The first three T'ang emperors, reigning as they did through a court
which continued to be dominated by members of the older aristocratic
lineages, were very self-conscious about their own ancestry and may well
have falsified their own line of descent in order to lay claim to membership of the Li clan of Lung-hsi.[31] Whatever the truth in this claim,
however, it did not protect them from the arrogance of the four great
surnames—the four premier clans of Shantung (i.e. modern Hopei).
This problem appears to have come to a head early in the reign of
T'ai-tsung, whose response was to appoint a committee of very high
ranking officials to draw up a large-scale genealogical work covering the
whole empire, which would define the relative importance and social
standing of all the great lineages. It was to be based upon the contents
of genealogical works collected from all parts of the empire and to
incorporate the advice of local officials upon this material. It was then

28. See Ikeda On, "Tōchō shizokushi no ichi kōsatsu: iwayuru '*Tonkō meizokushi*' zankan
o megutte," *Hokkaidō daigaku bungakubu kiyō* 13 (1965): 3–64. This is a most important study
of the attempts to define the aristocracy.

29. See note 14.

30. See Ikeda, "Tōchō shizokushi no ichi kōsatsu," and Takeda, "*Jōgan shizokushi*."

31. See Ch'en Yin-k'o, *T'ang-tai cheng-chih shih shu lun kao*.

to be checked against the historical record to ensure its accuracy. After T'ai-tsung had rejected a first draft and ordered the reduction in status of one of the great Hopei clans, the work was eventually completed and presented to the throne in 638 under the title *Chen-kuan Shih-tsu chih*. It was a very extensive work in one hundred chapters, listing 1,651 separate lineages from 293 surnames, all of which were graded in nine degrees of social importance, "rewarding and promoting the loyal and sage, and demoting the rebellious and refractory." The emperor approved it, and it was promulgated to the empire.[32]

Modern genealogies include a number of documents which are allegedly connected with this compilation, several of which were published some years ago by Takeda Ryūji. The *Wu-yüeh Wang-shih chih-p'u* of 1897, already mentioned as citing the so-called edict of 717, also includes what purports to be the memorial written by Wang Hua, the founder of the Hsin-an branch of the Wang clan, when he submitted their genealogy for inspection in 632.[33] The *Ou-yang-shih liu-tsung t'ung-p'u*, published in 1937, includes what is represented to be the official certification of the status of various branches of the Ou-yang clan issued in 632. But this is so full of anomalies that it is certainly a fabrication.[34] The *An-ch'ang Hsü-shih tsung-p'u*, a genealogy of a Chekiang lineage of the Hsü published in 1884, includes a rather similar document, somewhat less obviously spurious but still extremely dubious, and also what is claimed to be a eulogy written by T'ai-tsung himself for the clan's genealogy.[35] As Professor Takeda has shown, all these documents are at best highly suspect and cannot be accepted as genuine or contemporary. But it is nonetheless interesting that it should have been considered worthwhile as late as Ming and Ch'ing times, when these forgeries were probably written, to fabricate documents claiming an association of the ancestors of the clan with the compilation of the *Chen-kuan Shih-tsu chih*. Although the *Chen-kuan Shih-tsu chih* was soon replaced by newer official compilations, it retained its high reputation not only throughout the T'ang, but beyond.

In 659 Kao-tsung decided to replace it with a new work on an even grander scale. He is said to have done so because he felt dissatisfied that the *Chen-kuan Shih-tsu chih* had not included the lineage of his favorite, the empress Wu. Kao-tsung himself wrote the preface and rules of compilation for the new work, which was entitled *Hsing-shih lu*. It

32. On this, see Takeda, "*Jōgan shizokushi*."
33. Taga 320; Takeda, "*Jōgan shizokushi*," pp. 36–37.
34. Taga 1044; Takeda, "*Jōgan shizokushi*," pp. 38–39.
35. Taga 559; Takeda, "*Jōgan shizokushi*," pp. 35–36.

consisted of two hundred chapters and included 2,287 lineages from 245 surnames. Unlike the earlier compilation, which was based upon existing genealogies and upon long-recognized social standing, the *Hsing-shih lu* ranked all families strictly in accordance with the official rank or noble title achieved by the heads of the families under the reigning dynasty and restricted the resulting family status exclusively to the direct descendants of the holder of this office, denying equivalent status to collateral and distant relatives.[36]

The period during which Empress Wu dominated the court (660–705) is generally considered to have been a period of rather marked social change, and it was during these years that the professional bureaucrats recruited through the examination system first began to play a really significant part in politics.[37] It is therefore not surprising that the compilation of 659 stressed office and personal achievement rather than birth, or that on the restoration of the dynasty after her death it was felt necessary to produce a revised list of eminent lineages.

This was undertaken following a memorial from Liu Chung, a member of the Bureau of Historiography, who was himself from a very prominent noble lineage of southern Ho-tung. It is certain that this call for a revision of the lists of prominent clans and lineages coincided with the beginning of the revival of the power of the aristocratic interest in politics, which continued throughout Hsüan-tsung's reign. It was perhaps for this reason that Liu Chung requested the revision not of Kao-tsung's *Hsing-shih lu*—since such a revision would have conferred status upon the descendants of the many persons of comparatively humble origins who had held high rank under the empress Wu—but of the *Chen-kuan Shih-tsu chih*. The new work, however, was nonetheless to take due note of social changes. "The *Chen-kuan Shih-tsu chih* had been compiled so as to distinguish between the scholar-official families and the commoners. But by now almost a century had elapsed. Among the various surnames some had risen, and others had changed their status in the meanwhile."

It is perhaps significant that the suggestion for a new listing of eminent families originated on this occasion not from the emperor himself, as in previous instances, but from a high official who was himself a member of an old aristocratic lineage. It is just possible that this indicates a shift of emphasis away from the former preoccupation with the definition of the standing of lineages relative to that of the royal

36. See Ikeda, "Tōchō shizokushi no ichi kōsatsu."

37. See the works of Ch'en Yin-k'o, Hu Ju-lei, and Yokota Shigeru mentioned in the Bibliographical Note at the end of this chapter.

house—as in T'ai-tsung's time—toward a restatement, on behalf of the aristocratic clans, of their traditional status, in the face of the political challenge of men from comparatively humble origins.[38]

The new compilation differed from its predecessors in another important respect. Liu Chung was not only an official and a member of a noble lineage; he was also a professional historian, employed in the Historiographical Office, to which the compilation of the new work was entrusted. The problems involved in the compilation of genealogies had aroused considerable interest among historians in the latter part of the seventh century. Under Empress Wu the official historian Lu Ching-shun had devoted himself to the writing of genealogical works and had acquired such a high reputation that later genealogists claimed him as the founder of their branch of scholarship.[39] Liu Chung himself is said to have been his follower.[40] In 704 the great historical theorist Liu Chih-chi had caused a considerable stir by the publication of a critical genealogy of the various Liu lineages which, by the application of the strictest criteria of historical criticism, had demolished several widely accepted claims to very distinguished ancestry.[41] So conscious was he of the importance of this branch of historical studies that in his *Shih t'ung* he later advocated the inclusion in the standard dynastic histories of special monographs devoted to the great clans.[42] Liu Chih-chi became one of Liu Chung's collaborators in the compilation of the new list of eminent lineages.

Liu Chung's work was eventually completed and presented to the throne in 713. It is variously entitled *Hsing-tsu hsi lu* or *Hsing-tsu lu* and comprised two hundred chapters. In the next year, after Hsüan-tsung's accession to the throne, Liu Chung, Liu Chih-chi, and Hsüeh Nan-chin were ordered to correct and update it, and it was promulgated to the empire.[43] The fragmentary *Tun-huang ming-tsu chih* mentioned above

38. See Liu Chung's biographies, *CTS* 189B.8a–b; *HTS* 199.10a–13b. On the compilation of the *Hsing-tsu hsi-lu* see the extremely full documentation in the article by Ikeda, "Tōchō shizokushi no ichi kōsatsu," particularly pp. 30–46, which gives copious details on the various persons engaged in the compilation, showing (p. 45) that most of them were members of families of prominent T'ang officials or related to the imperial house by marriage, although none were members of the greatest aristocratic clans.

39. See *HTS* 199.4a–b; *CTS* 189B.3a.

40. See *HTS* 199.4b;11a–b.

41. See *THY* 36.665. Liu Chih-chi, however, was not the first to cast doubts on the Liu claims to exalted ancestry. K'ung Ying-ta had already done so in his standard commentary to the *Tso Chuan*, *Tso Chuan Cheng-i* (under Duke Wen 13, Duke Hsiang 24). See Chang Hsi-t'ang, *T'ang-jen pien wei chi-yü* (Hong Kong, 1963), pp. 17–18.

42. See E. G. Pulleyblank, "Chinese Historical Criticism: Liu Chih-chi and Ssu-ma Kuang," in *Historians of China and Japan,* ed. Beasley and Pulleyblank (London, 1961), p. 145.

43. See *TFYK* (edition of Li Ssu-ching, 1642) 560.20a–21b; *THY* 36.665; *CTS* 189B.8a; *TFYK* 554.33b; *CTS* 7.4b; *CTS* 8.6b, etc.

is suggested by Ikeda to have been compiled in connection with the gathering of material for this work.[44]

Between 723 and 726 the great historian Wei Shu, who was then a young man employed in the Imperial Library *(Pi-shu sheng)*, privately compiled a large supplement to Liu Chung's work, which was published in twenty chapters under the title *K'ai-yüan p'u*.[45] Wei Shu had a considerable name as a genealogist among his contemporaries.[46]

During Hsüan-tsung's reign a great deal of work seems to have been done in the field of genealogy. Besides Wei Shu, the essayist Hsiao Ying-shih was well known for his expertise in this type of work.[47] Another well-known genealogist was K'ung Chih who in 753–54 compiled a work entitled *Pai-chia lei-li*, which achieved notoriety by omitting the lineage of the great minister Chang Yüeh in spite of the fact that his son, who was married to one of the daughters of Hsüan-tsung, was currently the emperor's favorite. K'ung Chih is also said to have been the author of yet another genealogical study entitled *Hsing-shih tsa-lu*.[48]

In addition to these privately compiled genealogical works there were two official compilations, both very short lists, issued toward the end of Hsüan-tsung's reign. The first of these, the *T'ien-pao hsin-p'u* in a single chapter, was issued under the emperor's name and may have been a genealogy of the imperial clan.[49] The second, another official list in a single chapter, which bore the title *T'ien-hsia chün-wang hsing-shih tsu-p'u*, was published in 749 under the name of Li Lin-fu at a date when the victory of the aristocratic party at court was assured. We are told, though by a late source, that on the official promulgation of this list families not included were declared ineligible for marriage with members of the listed lineages.[50]

After the social upheaval caused by the An Lu-shan Rebellion and its aftermath, the remarkable activity in the field of scholarly genealogy

44. Ikeda, "Tōchō shizokushi no ichi kōsatsu," pp. 36–38.
45. See *HTS* 58.17a–b. To fit the account in Wei Shu's biography, *CTS* 102.13a–b and *HTS* 132.5b, the *K'ai-yüan p'u* must have been compiled in 723–26. See also *Yü-hai* (edition of 1806) 50.31a.
46. *CTS* 102.13a–b; *HTS* 132.5b.
47. See *HTS* 202.12a–13b and his long letter to Wei Shu, *CTW* 323.6b–17b. On his reputation as a genealogist see also *HTS* 199.11b. In *TFYK* 560.21b; *THY* 36.666, his name is wrongly given as Chia Chih.
48. See *HTS* 199.15b; *T'ang Yü-lin* (Chung-kuo wen-hsüeh ts'an-k'ao tzu-liao ts'ung-shu edition [Shanghai, 1956–57]) 2.47–48; *Feng-shih wen-chien chi chiao-chu* (Shanghai, 1956–57) 10.88. On his standing as a genealogist see also *HTS* 199.11b.
49. See Utsunomiya Kiyoshi, "Tōdai kijin ni tsuite no ichi kōsatsu," *Shirin* 19, no. 3 (1934): 61. This work is not mentioned in any T'ang source.
50. *Yü Hai* 50.31b.

seems to have died down.[51] The only notable scholar active in this field seems to have been the official historian Liu Fang, who completed the *National History (Kuo-shih)* in 759 after the death of Wei Shu and is thus the ultimate source of most of our material on the early T'ang, particularly on Hsüan-tsung's reign.[52] Among the few surviving writings by Liu Fang is a long and interesting essay on clans and lineages, which is the only extended contemporary T'ang period discussion of the subject.[53] This work is extremely important in the context of the genealogical compilations discussed here, since Liu Fang makes the point that true genealogical study would place a check upon the more excessive claims of the greatest noble lineages, rather than bolster them up. This is doubly interesting, since Liu Fang was descended from the same lineages as Liu Chung, and it would appear that there was a strong family tradition of genealogical expertise. Among his many other assignments in the Historiographical Office, Liu Fang was entrusted with the compilation of the official genealogy of the imperial house, the *Yung-t'ai hsin-p'u* in twenty chapters, which was presented to the throne in 766.[54] When a continuation of this was commissioned in 839, its compilation was undertaken by the Han-lin scholar Liu Ching, who was Liu Fang's grandson.[55]

A last attempt to produce a grand official genealogical work surveying all the prominent lineages of the empire came early in the ninth century, when under Hsien-tsung the T'ang experienced a temporary revival of central authority. The resulting work was the *Yüan-ho hsing-tsüan,* compiled in ten chapters by Lin Pao and presented to the throne accompanied by a postface written by the Han-lin draftsman Wang Yai in 812.[56] This work was, however, different from its predecessors both in arrangement and purpose. It no longer arranged lineages in any strict order of their social and political eminence, but simply listed them in rough order of importance under each rhyme, and thus had more in common with the later scholarly works on surnames than with its politically motivated forerunners.

Of the works which I have mentioned none survives in its original form. A few tiny fragments of the *Chen-kuan shih-tsu chih* are quoted in

51. On this, see the paper in this volume by David McMullen.

52. On Liu Fang, see D. C. Twitchett, "Liu Fang: A Forgotten T'ang Historian," *Asia Major* 17 (1972).

53. *HTS* 199.10b–13a; *CTW* 372.7a–11b. A full translation and notes are included in Twitchett, "Liu Fang." See also *THY* 36.666n for a mention of its completion.

54. On Liu Fang's ancestry, see *HTS* 73A.5a. On the imperial genealogy see *THY* 36.666, *TFYK* 560.21b, *Yü Hai* 50.32b–33b.

55. *TFYK* 560.22a; *THY* 36.666.

56. See *Yü Hai* 50.33b–34b, *THY* 36.666, *TFYK* 560.21b–22a.

rhyme dictionaries and in the Sung compilation of surnames *Ku-chin Hsing-shih shu pien-cheng*, but these are too short to give us any idea of the work's style, arrangement, or content.[57] Only of the *Yüan-ho hsing-tsuan* do substantial fragments survive. But although these were painstakingly reassembled from quotations by a number of Ch'ing scholars, the result is still too incomplete to give anything but a very imprecise picture of the original[58] and far too fragmentary to give us what we so badly require, a full listing of the lineages that were considered outstandingly important by contemporary T'ang scholars.

To sum up what we can say on the basis of the printed sources: it is clear that the T'ang government, at least until the An Lu-shan Rebellion, regularly compiled lists of notable lineages and clans, that genealogical claims were subjected to official scrutiny, and that the compilation of such official lists was commonly entrusted to the official historiographers, several of the most prominent of whom were also notable as genealogists. We know too that this was not an isolated activity, for the Board of Civil Office and the Board of Rites checked for accuracy not only family genealogies but also all commemorative writings destined for use in the family cult, to eliminate any false claims to preeminent ancestry.

This care over genealogical claims served two quite distinct, and often incompatible, purposes. On the one hand, the state was anxious to limit the pretensions of the great lineages and to prevent false claims to exalted descent in a society where ancestry was still a matter of paramount social importance. In this sense the genealogies may be seen as one aspect of the attempt to limit intermarriage among the greatest lineages and the continuing policy of cutting away the power and authority of the great Hopei clans. On the other hand, however, we are told that the object of compiling these lists was also to define the social hierarchy among the prominent lineages and to distinguish between scholar-official and commoner families. In other words, while attempting to limit the power of the highest levels of the aristocracy, the government still maintained the distinction in standing between officially recognized scholar-official families and commoners at a lower level of society. But it remains far from clear just what such a distinction was supposed to mean in actual practice. Certainly, official employment no longer depended upon family standing, as in the pre-Sui period. At least in the *Hsing-shih lu* of 659 and the *Hsing-tsu hsi-lu* of 713

57. These are included in Ikeda On, "Tōdai no 'gumbō hyō': kyūju seiki no Tonkō shahon wo chūshin toshite," *Tōyō Gakuhō* 42, no. 3 (1959): 94–95.

58. See the enormously painstaking work of Ts'en Chung-mien, *Yüan-ho hsing-tsuan ssu-chiao-chi*, 3 vols. (Shanghai, 1948), Preface.

the opposite was the case, and the compilation was designed to bring the record of family standings into line with the actual achievements of members and with the results of current social change. Only in the case of Li Lin-fu's *T'ien-hsia chün-wang hsing-shih tsu-p'u* of 749, a short work obviously far different both in nature and scope from the great earlier compilations, is there any specific indication (and that from a very late source) that intermarriage was to be restricted among a group of designated lineages and that the list was thus designed to define a closed castelike social group.

So far the picture I have given differs only in precision and in details from that given by the great Ch'ing historian Chao I in the eighteenth century.[59] It is into this background picture that I shall now try to fit the Tunhuang manuscripts, which give us unique evidence—complex as its interpretation may be—as to the exact membership of the social elite of prominent clans which was defined by these long-lost compilations.

The first of these documents to be published, and the only one which has attracted any attention in the scholarly world, outside a small circle of Japanese specialists, is a manuscript in the Peking National Library, catalogue number *wei* 67. This document was first published by Hsiang Ta in 1930, and it has since been discussed and reedited by many scholars,[60] most recently by Ikeda On, who has meticulously collated the former transcriptions.[61]

59. Chao I, *Kai-yü ts'ung-k'ao* (Shanghai, 1937; reprinted 1959), 17: 315–22.

60. Hsing Ta's original publication, "Tun-huang Ts'ung-ch'ao," in *Kuo-li Pei-p'ing T'u-shu-kuan kuan-k'an* 5 (1931): 53–80; 6 (1932): 57–62. See the later studies of Utsunomiya Kiyoshi, "Tōdai kijin ni tsuite no ichi kōsatsu," *Shirin* 19, no. 3 (1934): 50–106; Naba Toshisada, "Zui Tō Godai Sō shakai shi," in *Shina chiri-rekishi taikei* (Tokyo, 1941); Niida Noboru, *Chūgoku hōseishi kenkyū: Dorei nōdohō; kazoku sonraku hō* (Tokyo, 1962); Moriya Mitsuo, *Rikuchō mombatsu no ichi kenkyū* (Tokyo, 1951), pp. 131–35; Mou Jun-sun, "Tun-huang T'ang hsieh-pen *Hsing-shih lu* ts'an-chüan k'ao," *Wen shih-che hsüeh-pao* 3 (1952): 61; Takeda Ryūji, "Tōdai shijin no gumbō ni tsuite," *Shigaku* 24, no. 4 (1951): 26–53; and Wolfram Eberhard, *Conquerors and Rulers: Social Forces in Medieval China* (London, 1952); idem, "Additional Notes on Chinese 'Gentry Society,'" *Bulletin of the School of Oriental and African Studies* 17 (1955): 317–18; and idem, "The Leading Families of Ancient Tun-huang," *Sinologica* 4 (1956), all of which deal with this document. All of these depended upon transcriptions. The most generally used was that included in Hsü Kuo-lin's *Tun-huang Tsa-lu, hsia*, pp. 153a–154b.

61. See Ikeda, "Tōdai no gumbō hyō," *Tōyō Gakuhō* 42 (1959): 293–331; 42 (1960): 412–30. This article meticulously collates the earlier transcriptions of the manuscript. None of the scholars since Hsü Kuo-lin (see note 60) had actually seen the document or a facsimile, and the MS was not included among those parts of the Peking Tunhuang collection microfilmed in the 1950s. Hsü Kuo-lin's transcription, which was used by Niida and by Eberhard, is, like much of this author's *Tun-huang Tsa-lu*, extremely careless and inaccurate. Since then a much-reduced and barely legible photograph has appeared in Fan Wen-lan's *Chung-kuo t'ung-shih chien-pien* (Peking, 1965), 3: 93.

The manuscript is incomplete; it lacks the beginning and the title. The body of the document lists in succession the commanderies of the empire, with a note of the T'ang prefecture to which the commandery name referred, followed by the number of prominent clans from the area and a list of their surnames. After this list follows the text of an edict dated 634 mentioning the name of Kao Shih-lien.

The latter is known to have been one of the principal compilers of the *Chen-kuan shih-tsu chih* of 638, and on the basis of this fact Hsiang Ta identified the manuscript as a part of the *Chen-kuan shih-tsu chih*.[62] Niida accepted this general interpretation but preferred to relate the manuscript not to the finished work presented to the throne in 638, but to an earlier draft list presented to the throne in 632. This view was upheld by Utsunomiya Kiyoshi in an article published in 1934.[63] Later Naba Toshisada suggested that this manuscript was rather a résumé or list of contents of the *Chen-kuan shih-tsu chih*.[64] Niida suggested that the primary purpose of the list was to define once and for all an acceptable group of prominent lineages whose members married only within their own group of social equals. A somewhat similar interpretation was placed upon it by Wolfram Eberhard who believed this list to be a sort of *Almanach de Gotha* of a noble class of distinguished clans (which he calls the "gentry," thus introducing yet another element of confusion into the picture) whose social position and economic and social power remained stable, permanent, and impervious to the effects of frequent changes of dynasty from the Late Han until the Five Dynasties.[65]

Whether or not this document was based upon an official normative compilation, it is certainly not an official copy. It was copied in 836 by a monk called Wu-chen, a minor scholar with a local reputation,[66] and it is a careless copy liberally sprinkled with vulgar abbreviations, wrong characters, and inconsistencies between the total number of surnames given for each commandery and the surnames actually listed. By 836, when this copy was made, not only was Tunhuang under Tibetan domination, so that the list can have had no possible legal significance there, but even in metropolitan China the *Chen-kuan shih-*

---

62. Hsiang Ta, "Tun-huang Ts'ung-ch'ao."

63. Utsunomiya, "Tōdai kijin ni tsuite no ichi kōsatsu."

64. Naba, "Zui Tō Godai Sō shakai shi," pp. 124–35.

65. Eberhard, *Conquerors and Rulers;* see also Pulleyblank's review article on this, "Gentry Society: Some Remarks on a Recent Work by W. Eberhard," *Bulletin of the School of Oriental and African Studies* 15 (1953): 588–97; and Eberhard's rejoinder "Additional Notes on Chinese 'Gentry Society' " (see note 60); see also Eberhard's later article "The Leading Families of Ancient Tun-huang."

66. On Wu Chen see Chen Tsu-lung, *La vie et les oeuvres de Wou-tchen (816–895) : contribution à l'histoire culturelle de Touen-houang* (Paris, 1960). On this document see pp. 9–10.

tsu chih was completely obsolete, having been several times replaced by later compilations.

The first dissenting voice objecting to the linking of the manuscript with the *Chen-kuan shih-tsu chih* came with the publication in 1951 of a short but important critical discussion of the document by Mou Jun-sun,[67] who demonstrated that the manuscript was quite substantially different in content, form, and layout from the known quoted fragments of the *Chen-kuan shih-tsu chih*. He also showed that the so-called edict appended to the list is so ill written, full of stylistic infelicities, and plain mistakes that it cannot possibly be accepted as an official document publicly promulgated after a memorial by a famous scholar-official such as Kao Shih-lien. He also objects to it on the grounds that the edict, which attempts to forbid marriage between members of the designated clans and outsiders and thus to perpetuate the castelike exclusiveness of the aristocracy, is thus diametrically opposite to T'ai-tsung's known intention to put a limit upon the aristocracy's power and pretensions. Mou's argument was further strengthened by the publication in 1958 of a long note upon this manuscript written by Wang Chung-min, who draws attention to a formidable list of further errors and inconsistencies and also shows that the cyclical date given to the edict is incorrect and that the total number of surnames mentioned in the edict (398) does not agree with that known to have been included in the *Chen-kuan shih-tsu chih* (293).[68] It is clear that the theory that this manuscript bears any close relationship with the *Chen-kuan* list is untenable. The problem has been further complicated, however, by the subsequent discovery of several other manuscripts of a similar nature in the London and Paris collections of Tunhuang documents.

The first of these, a short and mutilated fragment of some twenty lines, was discovered in Paris by Naba Toshisada and published in 1941.[69] It lists the prominent clans of four commanderies in Kuan-chung, arranged in much the same way as in the Peking manuscript, but additionally including a note of the first ancestor claimed by each clan. Unfortunately it is impossible to collate or compare its contents with the Peking manuscript, which lacks the section listing the prominent clans of this region.

The second group of newly discovered material comprises five fragments. One of them was also published by Naba Toshisada in 1941.[70] The other four fragments form S. 5861 in the Stein Collection in the

67. Mou Jun-sun, "Tun-huang T'ang hsieh-pen *Hsing-shih-lu* ts'an-chüan k'ao."
68. Wang Chung-min, *Tun-huang ku-chi hsü-lu* (Peking, 1958), pp. 101–04.
69. Fonds Pelliot Touen-houang, P. 3421. See Naba, "Zui Tō Godai Sō shakai shi."
70. Fonds Pelliot Touen-houang, P. 3191. See Naba, "Zui Tō Godai Sō shakai shi."

British Museum and were first published by Niida in 1958.[71] Both Niida and Ikeda have taken these to form parts of a single document.[72] All five short fragments are very badly mutilated, and it is difficult to reach a firm conclusion, but in my opinion one of these fragments, Niida's S. 5861a, is an example of a quite different type of list, in which all the prominent clans with a given surname are listed together. The form of this fragment, of which portions of only eight lines covering four surnames are preserved, is identical with that of certain citations from the *Shih-tsu chih* in the *Kuang-yün* and other rhyme dictionaries.

The other four fragments, which are almost certainly mutilated pieces of a single manuscript, are clearly very closely related to the Peking manuscript. Three of them, P. 3191 and S. 5861b,c correspond closely in form to the body of the Peking manuscript, the only difference being that the commanderies are broken up into separate sections for each province *(tao)*. The commanderies included overlap to a considerable degree with those of the Peking list, and the clans listed are much the same, though not exactly identical. These do little to modify our view of the longer Peking manuscript.

The last fragment, S. 5861d, does however raise the possibility of a new interpretation. This small mutilated fragment of a few characters from six lines of text is obviously a part of the same edict which is appended to the Peking manuscript. It mentions the same total of 398 surnames, the same families "which are not recorded in the historical sources," and what at first appears to be the same date, although the reign title is missing. As far as one can judge from the few characters preserved, the wording is virtually identical. There are, however, two very significant differences. First, the date of the edict, although it does not include a reign title, is written eighth year, fifth month, tenth day, employing the character *tsai* for year instead of the normal *nien*, a practice confined to the T'ien-pao period (742–56). The date is thus 749. In addition, where the Peking list has the name of Kao Shih-lien, here only a single character survives. But this character *fu* is the last part of the name of Li Lin-fu, the chief minister who, as we have seen, was responsible for the promulgation of a list of eminent clans in the eighth year of T'ien-pao (i.e. 749).

It seems then that the Peking manuscript and these fragments derive from a common original, which the compiler of the Peking document attempted to associate with the compilation of the more prestigious

71. Niida, *Chūgoku hōseishi kenkyū: Dorei nōdohō; kazoku sonraku hō* (Tokyo, 1962), pp. 622–60.

72. Ibid.; Ikeda, "Tōdai no gumbō hyō."

Chen-kuan shih-tsu chih and with the name of Kao Shih-lien, but which the writer of the S. 5861 fragment associated with the list compiled more than a century later in 749 by Li Lin-fu.

It would seem to me that the most likely origin of these lists is not the massive *Chen-kuan shih-tsu chih* of 638, but rather Li Lin-fu's single chapter list drawn up in 749, the following description of which in *Yü-hai* fits these fragments rather well:

> *T'ien-hsia chün-wang hsing-shih tsu-p'u* in one chapter, compiled by Li Lin-fu. Records the places of origin of the eminent clans of each commandery. Lists in all 398 surnames. Promulgated in the T'ien-pao period (742–56). Those whose line of descent is not listed in it were forbidden to intermarry [with those who were].[73]

These particulars meet all the major objections raised by Mou Jun-sun and Wang Chung-min. Obviously, however, the reservations expressed by Mou on the grounds of style apply equally whether the list is supposed to date from 638 or 749, and it is most unlikely that the Peking manuscript is an exact copy of Li Lin-fu's work. What I would rather suggest is that both the Peking and London lists are popular corrupt derivatives from Li Lin-fu's list, and that in the case of the Peking manuscript the compiler has clumsily falsified the date and given the name of Kao Shih-lien rather than that of Li Lin-fu so as to give the list a spurious age and authority by associating it with what remained the most authoritative and widely quoted of the early T'ang genealogical compilations, the *Chen-kuan shih-tsu chih*.

There remains a body of literary material that is clearly connected with the actual contents of the Tunhuang lists and needs to be fitted into this picture. I have already mentioned the considerable number of very short fragments of *Chen-kuan shih-tsu chih* cited in *Kuang-yün* and other lexical sources and in the various Sung handbooks on surnames. Much the most important material, however, if only because of its almost complete coverage of China, are the lists of eminent clans given under each prefecture in the great early Sung geography *T'ai-p'ing huan-yü chi*.[74] Since the latter was an important official publication, intended to be authoritative, its lists of eminent clans almost certainly were taken from an accepted official source. Clearly these lists were not freshly compiled, since the social changes which had taken place in the century before *T'ai-p'ing huan-yü chi*'s compilation had rendered this

73. *Yü Hai* 50.31b.

74. These materials are carefully collected and collated in Ikeda, "Tōdai no gumbō hyō," pp. 78–87.

type of grouping completely obsolete. Since the information was thus of mainly antiquarian interest, the editors would certainly have used some existing list. Li Lin-fu's simple work would have been perfectly adequate for their needs and was, in addition, the most recent officially promulgated work of its type.

The clans included in *T'ai-p'ing huan-yü chi*, and for that matter those in the rhyme dictionaries, are closely similar to those in the Tunhuang fragmentary lists, even to those fragments which are cast in a variant form (P. 3421, S. 5861a); and I would like to suggest that all these lists derive from a single grouping of locally prominent lineages, the most likely source of which is Li Lin-fu's work of 749.

There is, however, yet another body of evidence which complicates the picture still further, in the shape of another Tunhuang manuscript in the British Museum, S. 2025, which was also published by Niida in 1958.[75] Unlike the other manuscripts I have described, this is not a fragment but a complete copy, including both title and preface. It bears no date or name of its compiler, but it is written in a rather crude ninth-century hand, and internal evidence provided by place names proves that it cannot have been written before the mid-790s. It is entitled *Hsin-chi T'ien-hsia hsing-wang shih-tsu p'u* and is in a single chapter. This title is otherwise unknown, but it is suggestively similar to that of Li Lin-fu's list, and it may well be that since the title begins "Newly revised . . . ," it is, or purports to be, a reedition of that work. But if this is so, it had undergone a drastic revision indeed, for in place of the 398 surnames of Li Lin-fu's list this manuscript lists no fewer than 791, many of which are extremely uncommon and difficult to associate with clans of established reputation. Moreover, the order in which the clans of any given commandery are listed—and all the scholars who have studied these manuscripts have assumed that the clans were listed in order of importance and social standing—is entirely at variance with the other sources, extremely well-known and influential clans sometimes being ranked only third or fourth in their commandery.

The numerous anachronisms in the use of place-names alone rule out the possibility that this was any sort of official document. Moreover, its short preface makes none of the pretensions to authority which the attachment of the so-called edict and the names of Kao Shih-lien or of Li Lin-fu gave to the Peking and London manuscripts I have already described. There can be little doubt that, far from being an authoritative official compilation, this was a semipopular work dating from the

75. This is transcribed and subjected to close critical scrutiny in Niida, *Chūgoku hōseishi kenkyū: Dorei nōdohō; kazoku sonraku hō* (see note 71), pp. 640–56.

early ninth century. It cannot, moreover, have been a popular compilation made in Tunhuang itself, since curiously enough the names of the various prominent clans from Tunhuang which are listed in the *Kuang-yün* and attested elsewhere do not appear at all in this manuscript.

It seems clear then that in the early ninth century, even while Tunhuang was under Tibetan occupation, there were circulating a variety of lists of prominent clans, some of which were connected, if only at second hand, with the official lists of prominent lineages compiled by the government during the seventh and early eighth centuries; others of them were almost certainly semipopular compilations made at a rather later date. The political circumstances under which they circulated—even in central China the government had long ago ceased to revise and recompile their massive authoritative genealogical lists and the Tunhuang area itself was under alien control—together with the fact that *all* these lists, with their very different contents, were apparently being copied and circulated at the same period, show conclusively that they cannot be taken at their face value as definitive authoritative lists of ranking families with any rigorous social implications. Far from being the formal official manifestation of a castelike division of society, laid down by decree by a government still dominated by an aristocracy in full flower, they seem much more likely to be a later reflection of such an attempt to define the social order, compiled partly out of nostalgia for the past, partly out of a desire to revive and bolster up the remnants of a hierarchical social order whose foundations were already crumbling under the impact of political, economic, and social change.

If then we cannot accept these lists at their face value as an official listing of eminent clans or as the *Almanach de Gotha* of a semi-permanent medieval Chinese aristocracy; if the original purpose behind the compilation of the vast official lists upon which these documents were based had long become irrelevant, what is the significance of these manuscripts for the modern historian?

Whatever their precise provenance, for whatever reason they were originally compiled and continued to be copied, these lists provide us with the membership of a series of groups of prominent clans which, at the time of compilation, were commonly considered to have formed the social elite in each commandery of the empire. Although it is impossible to date either of these groupings precisely, comparison with the surviving literature would suggest that the group of manuscripts *wei* 67 (Peking), P. 3421, P. 3191 (Paris), and S. 5861a-d (London), together with the list of clans included in the *T'ai-p'ing huan-yü chi* and the material in the *Kuang-yün*, are all derived from the list compiled in 749 under Hsüan-tsung and are in some way intimately bound up with the last stages of the T'ang government's attempt to exercise strict control over the designation of eminent lineages; while the manuscript S. 2025 (London) dates from the first half of the ninth century. We have then, in one case unfortunately only in fragmentary form, the detailed membership of two groups of lineages generally acknowledged in their period to have held superior social standing. The first group is closely related to the official classifications of clans carried out by the early T'ang government; the second is a very much larger group representing those lineages popularly recognized early in the ninth century in northern China, probably in Kuan-chung, as holding a position of social preeminence.

Even the earlier and smaller of these groups is of course very much broader than the small exclusive super-aristocratic groups which Ch'en Yin-k'o and other modern scholars identify as the focal points of court factions at the pinnacles of political power during the early T'ang, although these preeminent clans are included. What these documents enable us to do is not to be more precise in our definition of this super-aristocracy, but to place this relatively small group in its social context as the highest level of a much wider social stratum, corresponding roughly with the broader but nonetheless still exclusive groups of *locally* prominent scholar-official clans who formed such an important factor in Shen Kua's analysis of early T'ang society. It is certainly significant that to Shen Kua, writing in the late eleventh century, the existence of this clearly defined local social elite—the prefectural aristocracy whose membership we can now at least roughly identify—differentiated the society of T'ang times from that of his own day just as surely as did the political dominance at court level of the much smaller super-elite of outstandingly powerful clans.[76]

To the modern social historian this is a matter of great importance. The most obvious result of the decline of official recruitment through hereditary privilege and membership of a delimited superior stratum of society, and its replacement by recruitment on the basis of education and ability through a system of open examinations, is clearly the increased opportunity for upward social mobility thus afforded to the

---

76. The following articles attempt to define the function, mode of life, social role, and ethos of the locally prominent clans *(chün-wang)*. Takeda, "Tōdai shijin no gumbō ni tsuite," *Shigaku* 24, no.4 (1951): 26–53; idem, "Tōdai shizoku no kahō ni tsuite"; *Shigaku* 28, no. 1 (1955), pp. 84–105; Imahori Seiji, "Tōdai shizoku no seikaku sobyō," *Rekishigaku kenkyū* 9, no. 11 (1939): 59–80; 10, no. 2 (1940): 46–81.

educated members of relatively humble families. But the discussion of social mobility during any period of Chinese history is set around with most formidable problems of interpretation. Even in the study of the Ming and Ch'ing periods, where there is a superabundance of source material, the almost complete absence of precise information about the economic circumstances of individuals and their lineages as a whole, coupled with the very wide and inclusive legal status categories which defined the individual's standing vis-à-vis the state, and which had only the most generalized correlation with his and his lineage's actual social standing and condition of life, help render this type of analysis less precise than we would wish. For the T'ang, when biographical and genealogical material is comparatively very sparse, any precise, indeed, any really meaningful statement on social mobility is impossible. To begin with, our available material—essentially the biographies in the histories and the commemorative inscriptions available in epigraphical collections and in authors' collected works—is preselected, in that such writings were composed only for the successsful and prominent. We have no resources like the later *chia-p'u* and *tsung-p'u* through which we can get a picture of the lineage as a whole, compare the successful with the less successful members, and observe the rise and fall of the whole lineage's fortunes through many successive generations. The only extant evidence of this type, the genealogical tables of clans producing chief ministers included in the *Hsin T'ang shu*, is still highly selective and has been demonstrated to be defective and highly inaccurate in specific cases.[77] Similarly, we know virtually nothing about local history in T'ang times, so that we are totally ignorant, save in the most generalized terms, of the local societies in which the various lineages operated.

So far the attention of historians interested in social mobility and cognate problems under the T'ang has been focused exclusively upon one type of problem, the correlation of an individual's social origins with his achievement within the bureaucracy.[78] To define an individual's social origins only two criteria have been readily available. First there has been proven membership of the very small group of super-elite aristocratic clans which can be unmistakably identified through the dominant political roles which they can be seen to have played in the

77. See the preface by Chou I-liang to the Harvard-Yenching Index to the Tables, No. 16 *Hsin T'ang-shu Tsai-hsiang shih-hsi piao yin-te* (1934), pp. i–xix. Moriya Mitsuo's study of the Wang clan of Taiyuan, *Riku-chō mombatsu no ichi kenkyū*, also shows clearly the deficiencies of these tables.

78. See, for example, Wittfogel and Feng, *History of Chinese Society: Liao* (New York, 1949), pp. 450–63; D. C. Twitchett, "The Salt Commissioners after the Rebellion of An Lu-shan," *Asia Major* 4 (1954): 60–89; and E. G. Pulleyblank's analysis of political factions.

dynastic histories. Second, there has been the method by which the individual entered official service, whether through the examination system or through the exercise of hereditary privilege *(yin)*. This latter criterion has been widely and somewhat indiscriminately employed, on the assumption that an examination entrant was probably from a comparatively humble background and a *yin* candidate from an aristocratic family, but it is one which must be used only with the greatest caution.[79] Examination candidates probably still filled only a small fraction of the total posts in the bureaucracy, even in late T'ang times.[80] But in any case many members of even the most influential aristocratic clans gained office through success at the examinations, while *yin* privilege of hereditary employment was *not* a blanket privilege granted to all male members of designated noble clans, but was granted solely on the basis of the father's *official rank,* regardless of his clan or social origins. Thus the sons of a bureaucrat from humble origins who had reached high rank had precisely the same claim to hereditary privilege as the sons of an aristocrat of equal official rank.[81]

It has been widely assumed that the men who, although not members of the great aristocratic clans, nevertheless attained the highest office through the examination system were "new men." In a sense this is certainly true, since they were clearly more dependent upon the emperor and his dynasty and were more committed bureaucrats than their aristocratic colleagues, committed to the existing *political* order, rather than to the stability of their own social group. But it does *not* follow that they were men of comparatively lowly origins—and certainly not, as some contemporary Chinese scholars have claimed, that they were predominantly of petty landowner and merchant origin. Although I have not made the necessary systematic analysis of the available evidence, my general impression is that many of these "examination-entrant bureaucrats," far from being parvenus from unknown and lowly origins, were, although not aristocratic in the sense of belonging to one of the handful of preeminent clans, nevertheless members of the provincial elite of prominent clans found in the Tunhuang lists, many of which

79. On these see D. C. Twitchett, "The Government of T'ang in the Mid-eighth Century," *Bulletin of the School of Oriental and African Studies* 18 (1956) : 322–30.

80. These are no statistics for the *ming-ching* degree. The *chin-shih* examination produced a steady twenty to thirty-five graduates per year throughout the dynasty. See *WHTK* (Shih T'ung edition [Shanghai, 1936]) 29.276–80. It seems doubtful if as many as one hundred graduated altogether in any given year.

81. On the employment of *yin* privilege see *THY* 81.1498–1507; *CTS* 42.13b. Wittfogel and Feng, *History of Chinese Society,* p. 459, claims that the beneficiaries were limited to one or two persons. But there are many cases where several sons, and sometimes nephews and grandsons, received *yin* privilege.

could claim as long a record of official service and recognized social standing as could the greatest clans of Hopei. I would hazard the guess that although the examinations did indeed open a career in government service to some talented young men whose descent would previously have barred them, the really new element of mobility which emerged through the examination system in early T'ang times was the possibility for members of these comparatively minor locally prominent clans to secure accelerated promotion and to rise to the very highest offices which had previously been more or less monopolized by the greatest aristocratic clans.

The real breakthrough in social mobility for the ordinary provincial commoner families seems to me to have come not so much with the development of the examination system in the late seventh century, as with the greatly increased and diversified possibilities for employment in provincial governments or specialized government agencies, which followed the decay of central civil authority and the transfer of effective political and military authority from the central government to the provinces a century or more later. Having said this, it is most essential to try and define as closely as possible just what sort of locally based social elite the Tunhuang documents and the official listings of eminent clans were meant to delimit.

First of all, in spite of Shen Kua's imaginative analogy, there is no question here of an unchanging permanent castelike group of scholar-official clans, a sort of Chinese Brahmin caste differentiated from the rest of society by legal distinctions and privileges and by formal difference of status. The T'ang administrative Statutes *(Ling)* of 719 incorporated the classical division of society into the four social classes *(ssu-min)*—scholar-officials, farmers, artisans, and merchants.[82] But the rule is given only in the most general terms; it simply forbids officials from competing for profit with their inferiors and prohibits merchants and artisans from associating with officials. There is no suggestion that membership in any of these occupational categories was castelike, hereditary, or immutable. There is also no question that members of all four groups were considered as free *(liang)* commoners. Admittedly members of the bureaucracy and holders of official titles enjoyed considerable privileges, both legal and financial; but these privileges, like the right to official employment by heredity *(yin)*, arose from the individual's tenure of office and were restricted to the officeholder and his immediate family. His wider lineage was not benefited except indi-

82. See *TLT* (edition of Konoe Iehiro [1724], together with Tamai Zehaku's complete collation with the fragmentary Sung print, in his *Shina shakai-keizai-shi kenkyū* [1942]) 3.31a–b.

rectly through the prestige which relationship with an official gave them in local society. All commoners had the right of entry for the examinations and to official employment, with the exception of merchants and artisans. But even this rule seems not to have been strictly observed, and there is evidence that not only did individuals from merchant backgrounds successfully compete in the examinations, but that it was possible for a family that wished one of its members to enter for the examinations to renounce its status as artisans or as merchants.[83]

The T'ang Code, which spends much time on the careful definition of the distinctions in legal status between free men *(liang-min)* and the various categories of bondsmen *(chien-min)*, and upon the privileges accorded to holders of office or official titles, has absolutely nothing to say about any similar distinctions between the ordinary free commoners and the members of any specially designated group of scholar-official lineages or of any restricted aristocratic class. In particular, whereas the Code lays down the most stringent regulations on intermarriage between free men and bondsmen, there is no suggestion anywhere that there was any state-imposed legal restriction upon marriage between members of the different social groups within the free population.

In fact, even if the so-called edict banning marriage between members of the aristocratic clans and ordinary commoner families which are cited in the Tunhuang lists *wei* 67 and S. 5861 and in the various Ming and Ch'ing genealogies or the prohibition mentioned by *Yü-hai* in connection with Li Lin-fu's list of 749 ever existed in authentic form, their ruling on this subject was never embodied in the Code. Since the Code was considered to embody those laws which provided unchanging and immutable norms of social conduct, if such a fundamental law was enacted before 737, the date of the extant last recension of the Code, it must have been considered to have been of a temporary or provisional nature and either remained as an edict or was incorporated as a clause in the subsidiary Regulations *(Ko)*. Not a single trace of it remains, either in the histories or in the extensive collections of official documents from T'ang times, although these do include an edict *banning* such intermarriages among the great aristocratic clans of Hopei.[84] If such laws were in fact ever enacted, which I myself strongly doubt, it seems most likely that they were unsuccessful short-lived attempts on the part of the aristocratic interest to bolster their increasingly vulnerable position.

83. See D. C. Twitchett, "Merchant, Trade and Government in Late T'ang," *Asia Major* 14, no. 1 (1968): 63–95.
84. See *THY* 83.1527–30.

This is not of course to deny that members of these various groups did in fact intermarry. A most meticulous study by Saitō Aiko of the principal aristocratic clans of Hopei shows conclusively how exclusive their marriage circle remained until the very end of the T'ang period.[85] And it would go counter to everything we know of Chinese society in later and better-documented periods to suggest that the lineages of the educated elite in the provinces did not tend to intermarry. What I find impossible to accept in the case of the T'ang period is the suggestion that the limits of such intermarrying groups were formally and rigidly defined by the state and that intermarriage across the borders of these restricted groups was legally prohibited. Unless some new and extremely powerful evidence is forthcoming to prove the contrary, we should, in my opinion, be wiser to accept that such matters were largely settled by custom and local usage, rather than by orders of the central government, defined by law and maintained by the exercise of state authority.

A second general point, which deserves a separate study, is that the prominent lineages with which I have been concerned did not form a homogeneous economic class or function as an economic elite. Like the "gentry" lineages of recent centuries, probably only a small minority of their members actually became officials, and there was certainly a wide range of economic status and of occupation among their members. There is evidence of persons from the most exalted aristocratic clans living in poverty or working their own lands. There is equally ample evidence that it was possible for persons of humble origins to amass vast fortunes in trade and that members of the official class engaged in trade in order to better their economic position. Nonetheless, the prominent lineages of T'ang times still seem to have been far more successful than lineages of more recent times in maintaining their power, influence, and wealth through many successive generations, and they undoubtedly enjoyed a nationwide prestige and social standing which only one or two lineages in Ch'ing times could equal.

A further important general point is that the "places of origin" of these prominent lineages express membership of a particular line of descent and do not necessarily imply any actual connection with a person's place of birth or residence. Many of the members of the great Hopei clans, for example, are known actually to have resided in Ch'ang-an. Some other lineages, on the other hand, retained very close links with a provincial home base; for example, the P'ei clan mentioned in the essay by Ku Yen-wu translated above. Moreover, the sources are frequently at variance over an individual's "place of family origin,"

85. M. A. diss., Tokyo University, 1964.

and it is probable that such variations result from the practice of being more or less precise about one's ancestral line in differing social contexts, for example, as between one's ancestry as stated for official purposes, for marriage, or for use in the ancestral cult of one's lineage. Thus a statement that "so-and-so was a man from such-and-such" means that he was descended from the prominent lineage bearing his surname, which was traditionally linked with that place. It *may* also mean that he was a native of the same place, but this cannot be assumed unless we have other evidence to support it.[86]

This means that, except in the case of a few clearly defined groups which can be shown to have consistently acted in common—for example, the great Hopei clans and the so-called Wu surnames from the Su-chou area—it is very dangerous to postulate the existence of a genuine regional faction based upon actual local interests simply on the basis of the common "origin" of the individuals and lineages concerned, for some of these might well have been cut off completely from their "place of origin" for several generations, or even centuries. It cannot be stressed too often that what are needed above all in this particular field are detailed studies of individual lineages, which would provide the concrete data without which our theorizations lack a solid foundation.

What we *may* confidently assert at the present time, even on our present meager evidence, is that T'ang society at its higher levels was far more distinctly stratified and hierarchical than Chinese society has been during any subsequent period. There existed a small and still extremely influential super-elite of old, established aristocratic clans whose roots were entangled in the complex political history of the period of division in the fifth and sixth centuries. There also existed at the same time a much larger and more fluid group of lineages whose origins often went back at least as far, but whose social and political influence was essentially provincial rather than national. Their standing, nonetheless, was recognized as superior both by the state and by society at large. Each of these groups was socially exclusive, though not to the extent of its forming a self-contained caste, and they were collectively considered superior to the ordinary commoner in status. These were

86. Takeda, "Tōdai shijin no gumbō ni tsuite," gives, with many striking examples, an able picture of the complexity of this situation and attempts to analyze claims to noble kinship in the context of the specific social situation in which such claims were made. He lists (pp. 42–43) many examples of men whose "origins" are given differently in their own epitaphs or funerary inscriptions and in the two T'ang histories. The question was still further complicated by fraudulent claims to kinship with the great clans as shown in Liu Chih-chi's *Shih-t'ung* 5; section 19, "*I-li.*"

matters of which the state took cognizance, and over which it attempted to exercise some measure of control.

Clearly, when compared with their predecessors in the pre-Sui period, both the greatest aristocratic clans and the provincial prominent lineages alike were far weaker under the T'ang. Stripped of their fiscal and legal privileges, which were now accorded only to individual members by the state when they achieved office, not granted by birthright; deprived of their separate registration and their monopoly of hereditary office, which had been the foundation of their authority, their influence now depended on their inherited wealth and local influence, on their political and social cohesiveness, and on the strength of their inherited traditions and education. They survived remarkably well. But at least from the late seventh century onward they were on the defensive.

I interpret the listings of lineages, the scholarly pursuit of genealogy, the preoccupation with descent and precedence which I have described as evidence of a struggle between these groups and the growing power of the bureaucratized state in whose interest it was to curb their power and pretensions. While the state attempted to define, delimit, and regularize noble descent by careful scrutiny of genealogical claims, the noble families themselves used genealogy as a weapon in an essentially rearguard action, a belated attempt to shore up the remains of the old social political order as they saw their power and social preeminence being eroded by political and social change. Perhaps we may see in the greatly increased number of socially prominent lineages in the ninth-century *Hsin-chi T'ien-hsia hsing-wang shih-tsu p'u* from Tunhuang a last-minute attempt to adjust traditional social pretensions to contemporary social reality, made after the An Lu-shan Rebellion had set in motion the ever-accelerating process of radical social change, which was, by the end of the tenth century, to have swept the last remnants of the old aristocratic order into final oblivion.

However, much detailed analysis of late T'ang society is necessary to test these hypotheses. In making these further studies, the Tunhuang evidence I have described may, so long as it is used in full awareness of the complex problems surrounding its provenance, prove a most valuable aid.

BIBLIOGRAPHICAL NOTE

For Ch'en Yin-k'o's studies of T'ang politics see *T'ang-tai cheng-chih shih shu-lun kao* (Chungking, 1944; reprinted Shanghai, 1947, Peking, 1956); and for further details

Ch'en Yin-k'o, *Sui T'ang chih-tu yüan-yüan lüeh lun kao* (Chungking, 1944; reprinted Shang-hai, 1946, Peking, 1954). Ch'en Yin-k'o returned to this subject in his studies "Lun Sui-mo T'ang-ch'u so-wei Shan-tung hao-chieh," *Ling-nan hsüeh-pao* 12 (1952): 1–14; and "Chi T'ang-tai chih Li, Wu, Wei, Yang hun-yin chi-t'uan," *Li-shih yen-chiu*, 1954, no. 1, pp. 33–51. A much refined version of Ch'en's theory, which remains the most important single study of the problem, is E. G. Pulleyblank, *The Background of the Rebellion of An Lu-shan* (London, 1955). See also the review article dealing with this problem, D. C. Twitchett, "The Government of T'ang in the Mid-Eighth Century," *Bulletin of the School of Oriental and African Studies* 18 (1956): 322–30.

In addition to the purely political attacks to which Ch'en was subjected after 1958, beginning with "Kuan-yü Sui-T'ang shih yen-chiu chung ti i-ko li-lun wen-t'i" and "P'ing Ch'en Yin-k'o hsien-sheng ti 'chung-tsu wen-hua lun' kuan-tien," *Li-shih yen-chiu*, 1958, no. 12, pp. 37–52, his theories have been criticized by various Chinese scholars, such as Ts'en Chung-mien, who in his *Sui-T'ang shih* (Peking, 1957), pp. 397–405, takes Ch'en to task for his faulty analysis of ninth-century factional alignments. In general, however, Ch'en's basic theory of a polarization between aristocracy and the new bureaucrats has remained unchallenged.

In 1956 Tanigawa Michio, in his "Bu-kō-chō matsunen yori Genso-chō shonen ni itaru seisō ni tsuite: Tōdai kizokusei kenkyū e no ichi shikaku," *Tōyōshi kenkyū* 14 (1956): 295–318, strongly criticized both Ch'en and Pulleyblank, saying that the examination-recruited bureaucrats were not, in the eighth century, yet sufficiently powerful to rival the aristocracy and asserting that political conflict remained largely conflict between rival aristocratic groups.

The role of Empress Wu's reign in the growth of the bureaucratic interest is also stressed by Yokota Shigeru in "Bu-shū seiken seiritsu no zentei," *Tōyōshi kenkyū* 14 (1956): 273–94; and by Hu Ju-lei, who in "Lun Wu-Chou ti she-hui chi-ch'u," *Li-shih yen-chiu*, 1954, no. 1, pp. 85–96, reasserted that examination-recruited bureaucrats had provided the political foundation of her regime. This view, however, has been challenged by Chang Ch'ün, who in his "Lun T'ang K'ai-yüan-ch'ien ti cheng-chih chi-t'uan," *Hsin-ya hsüeh-pao* 1, no. 2 (1957): 281–303, claimed that the introduction of new blood through the examination system can be traced back to T'ai-tsung's reign and should not be too closely associated with the empress Wu.

The only work focusing on the precise composition of the pre-T'ang aristocracy is the study by Sun Kuo-tung, "T'ang Sung chih chi she-hui men-ti chih hsiao-jung," *Hsin-ya hsüeh-pao* 4, no. 1 (1959): 211–304.

There is an enormous secondary literature on the aristocracy of the pre-Sui period, particularly in Japanese. The only general account available in a Western language is in Henri Maspero and Etienne Balazs, *Histoire et institutions de la Chine ancienne* (Paris, 1967), pp. 95ff., particularly pp. 101–05, but this is very out of date in matters of detail. General studies on the political and legal situation of the aristocracy may be found in Okazaki Fumio, "Nanchō kizoku-sei no kigen narabi-ni sono seiritsu ni itarishi made no keika ni tsuite no jakkan no kōsatsu," *Shirin* 14, no. 2 (1929): 179–94; Hamaguchi Shigekuni, "Gi Shin Nan-boku-chō Zui-Tō-shi gaisetsu" (an article first published in 1942), in *Shin Kan Zui Tō shi no kenkyū* (Tokyo, 1967), 2: 832–96; Yano Chikara, *Mombatsu shakai shi* (Nagasaki, 1965); Miyakawa Hisayuki, *Riku-chō shi kenkyū* (Tokyo, 1956); Ochi Shigeaki, *Gi Shin Nan-chō no seiji to shakai* (Tokyo, 1963). A basic study of the intermarriage and social structure of the great aristocratic clans is Niida Noboru's "Riku-chō oyobi Tō-sho no mibun-teki naikonsei," originally in *Rekishigaku Kenkyū* 9, no. 8 (1939) and reprinted in his *Chūgoku hōsei-shi kenkyū:*

Dorei nōdo sei: Kazoku sonraku sei (Tokyo, 1962), pp. 600–21. A recent summary, which attempts a statistical analysis of officeholding and the functions exercised by members of the aristocracy, is Mao Han-kuang, *Liang-Chin Nan-Pei Ch'ao shih-tsu cheng-chih chih yen-chiu,* 2 vols. (Taipei, 1966).

Studies of the systems of recommendation, Recommending Legates, and the classification of clans *(chung-cheng; chiu-p'in),* upon which the continuing power of the aristocratic families was based, are to be found in Miyazaki Ichisada, *Kyūhin kanjin hō no kenkyū* (Kyoto, 1956); and in the shorter article by Donald Holzman, "Les débuts du système médiéval de choix et de classement des fonctionnaires; les Neuf Categories et l'Impartial et Juste," *Mélanges publiées par l'Institut des Hautes Etudes Chinoises* 1 (1957): 387–414.

There are two important large-scale attempts to establish genealogies of the principal clans during this period. Yano Chikara, *Gi Shin hyakkan seikei-hyō,* 2 vols. (Nagasaki, 1960); and the more sophisticated study of Wang I-t'ung, *Wu-ch'ao men-ti* (Chengtu, 1943), which deals only with the southern aristocracy. There is only one really systematic study of a single clan, which shows how much critical work remains to be done in this field, the late Moriya Mitsuo's *Riku-chō mombatsu no ichi kenkyū* (Tokyo, 1951), a study of the Wang clan of Taiyuan.

There are several extremely interesting studies by Ochi Shigeaki, particularly his "Gi Shin Nan-chō no saika-kyū kanryō-sō ni tsuite," *Shigaku Zasshi* 74, no. 7 (1965): 1–37, on the lowest ranks of official service, which show that by the sixth century the rigid application of the aristocratic system already had broken down. T'ang Ch'ang-ju, in his "Men-fa ti hsing-ch'eng chi ch'i shuai lo," *Wu-han Ta-hsüeh jen-wen k'o-hsüeh hsüeh-yao,* 1958–59, pp. 53–68; and 1959, pp. 81–109, gives a very perceptive study of the decline of the aristocracy, and in his *Wei-Chin Nan-pei-chao shih lun-ts'ung hsü-pien* (Peking, 1959), pp. 93–123, he also deals with the widespread rise to office under the late Southern Dynasties of members of comparatively lowly families and with the beginnings of examinations (ibid., pp. 124–31).

While these studies suggest that the rigorous application of the aristocratic system was already in decay before the Sui unification, a series of articles on the early T'ang aristocracy by Nunome Chōfu, beginning with "Tōsho no kizoku," *Tōyōshi kenkyū* 10, no. 3 (1950): 24–34, claims that even at the beginning of T'ang, aristocracy as it had flourished in the Nan-pei ch'ao period was already virtually extinct. This view, however, was vigorously attacked by Yano Chikara in "Tōsho no kizoku-seiji ni tsuite," *Tohōgaku* 9 (1954): 12–18; and in his later studies Nunome is not quite so extreme in his view. See Nunome Chōfu, *Zui-Tō shi kenkyū* (Kyoto, 1968).

3. Factionalism in Early T'ang Government

Howard J. Wechsler

Let us begin with a brief definition of a faction as it is used in this study: a subgroup in a decision-making body working for the advancement of certain policies or people; its members have common interests that bring them together initially and common objectives that serve to keep them together afterward. Although a faction lacks the permanence of a political party, it is nevertheless organized around long-term interests rather than around a single, specific issue—such as a policy decision—and thus forms an alignment of significant duration within a decision-making body. Members of a faction are identifiable persons who are conscious of the special nature of their political ties.[1]

In the West, as far back as Roman times, the term *faction* has generally been pejorative, applied by one group against another in order to stigmatize its activities.[2] In imperial China, factions (*tang* or *p'eng-tang*) were also regarded with great disfavor. Early in the development of Chinese political thought Confucius admonished that the superior man *(chün-tzu)* "allies himself with individuals, but not with parties *(tang)*."[3] Subsequently, Chinese rulers came to believe that officials who formed factions did not display a requisite undivided loyalty to the throne and that their goals were selfish and detrimental to the broader interests of the state. Equally important, factionalism reflected poorly on the ruler's moral perfection, by which he was supposed to bring about universal harmony.[4] The Chinese attitude toward factionalism can well be

1. See Harold D. Lasswell and Abraham Kaplan, *Power and Society* (New Haven, Conn., 1950), pp. 171–73; and Julius Gould and William L. Kolb, *A Dictionary of the Social Sciences* (Glencoe, Ill., 1964), p. 255.
2. Harold D. Lasswell, "Faction," *Encyclopaedia of the Social Sciences* (New York, 1930), 6: 51.
3. Arthur Waley, *The Analects of Confucius* (London, 1938), 15.21, p. 197.
4. See David S. Nivison, "Ho Shen and His Accusers," in *Confucianism in Action*, ed. David S. Nivison and Arthur F. Wright (Stanford, Calif., 1959), pp. 219–22.

gauged by the fact that officials often employed charges of faction building against those at court whom they sought to discredit politically.
Demotion, banishment to provincial posts, or worse fates awaited those
found guilty of such a crime.

The emperors of the early T'ang dynasty viewed factions with the
usual antipathy. The second emperor, T'ai-tsung, for example,
thought that factions were formed by flatterers who deluded their rulers
and helped to bring about their downfall.[5] From time to time charges
were aired at court that T'ai-tsung's own officials—even some of the
most eminent ministers of the age, such as Fang Hsüan-ling[6] and Wei
Cheng[7]—were engaging in faction building. But such accusations usually could not be substantiated and came to nothing.

The question remains, just how extensive were factions during the
formative years of the T'ang, under the first two emperors, Kao-tsu
(reigned 618–26) and T'ai-tsung (reigned 627–49)? On the whole, we
lack concrete information relating to this problem, although there is
some dubious evidence in the form of the politically motivated attempts
at character assassination noted above; and it is probable that factions
were formed during the struggle for succession between the future T'ai-
tsung and his brother Li Chien-ch'eng in the 620s. But it is only late in
T'ai-tsung's own reign, in another succession dispute involving the
crown prince Li Ch'eng-ch'ien and his brothers, that the sources confirm the formation of factions by supporters of each candidate.[8] Otherwise, the rampant factionalism characteristic of the period in which
Empress Wu controlled the government (c. 660–705), as well as of the
second half of the dynasty, seems to have been absent from the early
T'ang.

The paucity of evidence on factions during the early T'ang has not
deterred scholars from seeking possible bases upon which these factions
might have been built. One of the most persuasive of these scholars
has been the late Ch'en Yin-k'o.[9] Since the publication of his study on
the split at court in 655 over the establishment of Empress Wu, Ch'en's

5. *CKCY* (*Ssu-pu pei-yao* ed., reprinted Taipei, 1967) 6.15a–16a.

6. *CTS* (Photolithographic Ch'ien-lung Palace ed., 1884) 63.8b; *HTS* (Photolithographic
Ch'ien-lung Palace ed.) 101.3b.

7. *CTS* 71.3b; *HTS* 97.2a.

8. *CTS* 76.9a. See Sun Kuo-tung, "T'ang Chen-kuan Yung-hui chien tang-cheng shih-
shih" [An explication of factional strife from Chen-kuan through Yung-hui], *Hsin-ya shu-
yüan hsüeh-shu nien-k'an* 7 (1965): 39–54, for a treatment of relations between the members of
the various factions.

9. Ch'en Yin-k'o, "Chi T'ang-tai chih Li, Wu, Wei, Yang hun-yin chi-t'uan" [The Li,
Wu, Wei, and Yang marriage blocs of the T'ang dynasty], *Li-shih yen-chiu*, 1954, no. 1, pp.
33–51.

hypothesis that the early T'ang court was divided into two blocs *(chi-t'uan)* based on the geographical origins of their members has been widely accepted.

According to this hypothesis, the supporters of Kao-tsung's first consort, Empress Wang, whom Kao-tsung wanted to demote in favor of his concubine Wu Chao, were representatives of the so-called Kuan-lung bloc. This bloc was centered on the northwest, that is, the capital Ch'ang-an and the area comprising modern Shensi and Kansu provinces. The Kuan-lung bloc was comprised of the descendants of the aristocratic families that had been in control of political power in China since the Western Wei, Northern Chou, and Sui dynasties (535–618) and that still dominated the court during the early T'ang. Over the years these families had intermarried and had established a network of loyalties that manifested itself at such crucial moments as when Kao-tsung attempted to depose a member of the bloc, Empress Wang, and replace her with a nonmember, Wu Chao. The supporters of Wu Chao, on the other hand, were representatives of the so-called Shan-tung bloc, centered on northeastern China, an area coextensive with the former Northern Ch'i state, that is, modern Shansi, Hopei, Honan, and Shantung provinces.[10] Members of the Shan-tung bloc were predominantly literati of modest backgrounds, many of whom had entered officialdom via the examination system. They opposed the dominance of the entrenched northwestern aristocrats and their hereditary privileges and hoped to reduce their authority in government by supporting Wu Chao, a northeasterner of relatively humble origins. The struggle over the appointment of Wu Chao was, according to Ch'en, not merely an internecine war of the harem and court, but a battle for supremacy between the Kuan-lung and Shan-tung blocs.

There are serious weaknesses in this theory. Ch'en places several of those officials involved in the Wu-Wang struggle in one or another of his blocs according to their "native place" *(pen-kuan)*, that is, the family seat recorded in each official's biographies in the two T'ang Standard Histories. But he rejects native place as the criterion for inclusion in these blocs in the cases of three officials, Chang-sun Wu-chi, Ch'u Sui-liang, and Hsü Ching-tsung. With some reason, despite the fact that Chang-sun Wu-chi's native place was Shantung (Ho-nan *tao*), he assigns him to the Kuan-lung bloc because of his relationship by marriage

10. On p. 1 of *Sui-T'ang chih-tu yüan-yüan lüeh-lun kao* [Draft outline of the origins of Sui and T'ang institutions] (Chungking, 1944; Shanghai, 1946), Ch'en Yin-k'o equates the "Shantung" region with the Northern Ch'i state. To my knowledge, he does not define the area more precisely in his other writings.

to the imperial house (he was T'ai-tsung's brother-in-law). And although Ch'u Sui-liang and Hsü Ching-tsung both were from regions in southern China, Ch'en maintains that after the Northern Dynasties conquered the Southern Dynasties in the middle of the sixth century, southern elements in the bureaucracy assumed the characteristics of "captive house" *(fu-lu chia)* officials and could not be politically independent. He therefore concludes that since Ch'u supported Empress Wang, he had to be a member of the Kuan-lung bloc, and because Hsü supported Wu Chao, he had to be a member of the Shan-tung bloc.[11] In the middle of his analysis he thus alters the criterion for membership in his two blocs from the geographical to the political.

Recently, new evidence has been presented that casts further doubt on the degree of geographic and social homogeneity in Ch'en's two blocs. Matsui Shūichi has traced the origins of Han Yüan, a supporter of Empress Wang, to northeastern China (Honan and Hopei) and makes the case that the forebears of Li I-fu, a Wu supporter, were not from the northeast but rather from Shu (Szechwan). In addition, he shows that Lai Chi, an alleged member of the Kuan-lung bloc, was a degree holder and that Li Shih-chi, allegedly of the Shan-tung bloc, may well have been from a family with a history of producing petty aristocrats.[12]

If the Kuan-lung and Shan-tung blocs operated as factions that influenced the play of politics at the early T'ang court, we should expect their influence to be noticeable in the settlement of other issues prior to Kao-tsung's reign as well. Unfortunately, the sources generally yield only meager data concerning the decision-making process at court, and seldom do we learn how a fairly large number of officials divided over any given issue. But during the reign of T'ai-tsung we have half a dozen cases in which the opinions or actions of a number of officials concerning a given issue were recorded. By using this group of cases we may be able to obtain at least an impressionistic view of whether factions were formed on the basis of geography during this period.

The six issues and the dates they were debated or acted upon at T'ai-tsung's court are as follows: (1) whether to reestablish a feudal *(feng-chien)* or modified feudal system, 628–37; (2) whether to resettle the vanquished Eastern Turks inside the borders of China, 630; (3)

11. Ch'en, "Li, Wu, Wei, Yang hun-yin chi-t'uan," p. 38.

12. Matsui Shūichi, "Sokuten Bukō no yōritsu o megutte" [The establishment of Empress Wu Tse-t'ien], *Hokudai Shigaku* 11 (September 1966): 1–8; idem, "Tōdai zenki no kizoku" [Aristocracy during the early T'ang dynasty], *Rekishi Kyōiku* 14 (May 1966): 41–42.

whether T'ai-tsung should perform the elaborate Feng and Shan rites, 631–47; (4) whether the brothers as well as the sons of those who had revolted against the throne should be executed, 642; (5) whom to establish as T'ai-tsung's successor, 643; and (6) whether the T'ang should launch an attack on the Kingdom of Koguryō, 643–45. These issues, encompassing a broad spectrum of problems dealing with basic governmental institutions, relations with China's neighbors, rites, penal law, the monarchy, and war, should reflect more accurately than the single issue examined in Ch'en's study the political responses of members of the early T'ang court.

Tables 3.1–3.6 list the subject matter of the six issues under examination; the positions, pro or con, taken by officials concerning each issue; the sources yielding this information; the native place (according to the T'ang dynasty system of *tao*) of each official based on information

Table 3.1. Issue: Should the T'ang reestablish a feudal or modified feudal system?

Name	Sources	Native Place	Bloc
	Pro		
Hsiao Yü	*THY*[a]46.824 *HTS* 101.2b	Shan-nan	South
Yen Shih-ku	*THY* 46.826 *TCTC*[b]193.6089	Kuan-nei	Kuan-lung
	Con		
Wei Cheng	*THY* 46.826–27 *TCTC* 193.6089	Ho-pei	Shan-tung
Chang-sun Wu-chi	*THY* 47.829 *CTS* 65.10b–11b *HTS* 105.3a *TCTC* 195.6145–46	Imperial family relative (Ho-nan)	Kuan-lung (Shan-tung)
Ma Chou	*THY* 46.827 *TCTC* 195.6145 *CTS* 74.8a–b	Ho-pei	Shan-tung
Yü Chih-ning	*THY* 47.830 *TCTC* 195.6145 *CTS* 78.1b *HTS* 104.1b	Kuan-nei	Kuan-lung
Li Pai-yao	*TCTC* 193.6089 *THY* 46.824–26 *CTS* 72.9a–13a	Ho-pei	Shan-tung

[a]Reprinted in Taipei, 1963.
[b]Reprinted in Taipei, 1962.

derived from his biographies in the two T'ang Standard Histories; and
the name of the bloc, according to Ch'en Yin-k'o's scheme, to which
the official belonged. In these tables, officials whose native places are
in Kuan-nei or Lung-yu *tao* belong to the northwestern Kuan-lung bloc;
officials whose native places are in Ho-nan, Ho-pei, or Ho-tung *tao*
belong to the northeastern Shan-tung bloc. Some objections may be
raised as to the propriety of including Ho-tung *tao* (modern Shansi
province) in "Shan-tung." The traditional definition of Shan-tung is,
after all, "east of the T'ai-hang mountains," which would exclude
much of Shansi. But Ch'en never defines the boundaries of Shan-tung
more precisely than those of the state of Northern Ch'i; and Yamazaki
Hiroshi, whose data on the Sui dynasty bureaucracy is examined
further on, places Ho-tung *tao* in the region he calls northeast. In order
to correlate our data, I have also followed this scheme. In cases where
officials are brothers or brothers-in-law of the emperor, sons or sons-
in-law of the emperor, or grandsons of the emperor, they are considered
members or relatives of the imperial family and are automatically placed
in the Kuan-lung bloc. However, their actual native places and bloc
affiliations, if non-Kuan-lung, appear in parentheses. Officials whose
native places are in Huai-nan, Shan-nan, Chiang-nan, Chien-nan, or
Ling-nan *tao* are shown as belonging to neither of Ch'en's blocs but to
the south. The question of the existence of a southern bloc will be
discussed later.

Table 3.2. Issue: Should the Eastern Turks be resettled inside the borders of China?

Name	Sources	Native Place	Bloc
	Pro		
Wen Yen-po	*THY* 73.1313–14	Ho-tung	Shan-tung
	CKCY 9.14a–15a		
	Con		
Yen Shih-ku	*THY* 73.1312	Kuan-nei	Kuan-lung
	CTW[a]147.25a		
Tou Ching	*THY* 73.1312	Imperial	
	CTS 61.11a–b	family relative	Kuan-lung
		(Kuan-nei)	
Li Pai-yao	*THY* 73.1313	Ho-pei	Shan-tung
	CTW 142.11a–b		
Wei Cheng	*THY* 73.1313	Ho-pei	Shan-tung
	CKCY 9.14a–b		
Tu Ch'u-k'o	*THY* 73.1312–13	Kuan-nei	Kuan-lung
	CKCY 9.15a–b		

[a]Reprinted in Taipei, 1965.

Table 3.3. Issue: Should T'ai-tsung perform the Feng and Shan rites?

Name	Sources	Native Place	Bloc
	Pro		
Li Hsiao-kung	*TCTC* 193.6086 *THY* 7.79	Imperial family member	Kuan-lung
Li Yüan-ching	*TCTC* 195.6156 *THY* 7.86–87	Imperial family member	Kuan-lung
Wu Shih-huo	*THY* 7.79–80 *TCTC* 193.6090	Ho-tung	Shan-tung
Chu Tzu-she	*CTW* 135.5a–b	Chiang-nan	South
Li Pai-yao	*CTW* 142.10b	Ho-pei	Shan-tung
Ts'en Wen-pen	*CTW* 150.10b–11a	Shan-nan	South
Kao Jo-ssu	*CTW* 156.23b	?	?
Chang-sun Wu-chi	*THY* 7.89–92 *CTW* 136.4a–7a	Imperial family relative (Ho-nan)	Kuan-lung (Shan-tung)
	Con		
Wei Cheng	*TCTC* 194.6093–94 *THY* 7.80–81	Ho-pei	Shan-tung
Ch'u Sui-liang	*THY* 7.88	Chiang-nan	South

Table 3.4. Issue: Should brothers of those who revolted be executed with them?

Name	Sources	Native Place	Bloc
	Pro		
Kao Shih-lien	*CTS* 74.15a–b	Ho-pei	Shan-tung
Hou Chün-chi	*CTS* 74.15a–b	Kuan-nei	Kuan-lung
Li Shih-chi	*CTS* 74.15a–b	Ho-nan	Shan-tung
	Con		
T'ang Chien	*CTS* 74.15b	Ho-tung	Shan-tung
Li Tao-tsung	*CTS* 74.15b	Imperial family member	Kuan-lung
Tu Ch'u-k'o	*CTS* 74.15b	Kuan-nei	Kuan-lung
Fang Hsüan-ling	*HTS* 99.14a	Ho-nan	Shan-tung
Ts'ui Jen-shih	*CTS* 74.15b–16a *HTS* 99.14a	Ho-pei	Shan-tung

Table 3.5. Issue: Who should be established as T'ai-tsung's successor?

Name	Sources	Native Place	Bloc
Supporters of Li Ch'eng-ch'ien			
Li Yüan-ch'ang	*CTS* 76.2b *HTS* 80.2b *TCTC* 196.6192	Imperial family member	Kuan-lung
Hou Chün-chi	*CTS* 76.2b *HTS* 80.2b	Kuan-nei	Kuan-lung
Li An-yen	*CTS* 76.2b *HTS* 80.2b	?	?
Chao Chieh	*CTS* 76.2b *HTS* 80.2b *TCTC* 196.6192	Imperial family relative (?)	Kuan-lung (?)
Tu Ho	*CTS* 76.2b *HTS* 80.2b *TCTC* 196.6192	Imperial family relative (Kuan-nei)	Kuan-lung (Kuan-lung)
Wang Ching-chih	*CTS* 70.5a *HTS* 98.4a	Ho-tung	Shan-tung
Supporters of Li T'ai			
Tu Ch'u-k'o	*CTS* 76.9a *TCTC* 196.6191 *HTS* 80.7b	Kuan-nei	Kuan-lung
Wei T'ing	*CTS* 76.9a *TCTC* 196.6191 *HTS* 80.7b	Kuan-nei	Kuan-lung
Ts'ui Jen-shih	*CTS* 74.16a *TCTC* 197.6198 *HTS* 99.14a	Ho-pei	Shan-tung
Fang I-ai	*CTS* 76.9a *HTS* 80.7b	Imperial family relative (Ho-nan)	Kuan-lung (Shan-tung)
Ts'en Wen-pen	*TCTC* 197.6195 *HTS* 80.7b	Shan-nan	South
Liu Chi	*TCTC* 197.6195 *HTS* 80.7b	Shan-nan	South
Chai Ling-wu	*CTS* 76.9a *HTS* 80.7b	Imperial family relative (Ho-tung)	Kuan-lung (Shan-tung)

Supporters of Li Chih

Chang-sun Wu-chi	TCTC 197.6196 HTS 105.3b HTS 105.10b	Imperial family relative (Ho-nan)	Kuan-lung (Shan-tung)
Ch'u Sui-liang	TCTC 197.6195–96 HTS 105.10b	Chiang-nan	South
Fang Hsüan-ling	TCTC 197.6196 HTS 105.10b	Ho-nan	Shan-tung
Li Shih-chi	TCTC 197.6196 HTS 105.10b	Ho-nan	Shan-tung

Table 3.6.   Issue: Should the T'ang attack the Kingdom of Koguryŏ?

Name	Sources	Native Place	Bloc
	Pro	Ho-nan	Shan-tung
Li Shih-chi	THY 95.1705		
	Con		
Chang Liang	CTS 69.8a HTS 94.5a	Ho-nan	Shan-tung
Ch'u Sui-liang	THY 95.1705 CTW 149.12b	Chiang-nan	South
Li Ta-liang	TCTC 197.6215 HTS 99.6a	Kuan-nei	Kuan-lung
Fang Hsüan-ling	TCTC 199.6260 THY 95.1706–07 CTS 66.7a–9a	Ho-nan	Shan-tung
Hsü Ch'ung-jung	THY 95.1707–08	?	?
Chiang Hsing-pen	CTS 59.16a HTS 91.11b	Shan-nan[a]	South

[a]But located in modern Shensi province.

It is readily observable from tables 3.1–3.6 that in each of the six cases there is no correlation between the native places of officials, or the so-called blocs to which they belonged, and the views they held. In every case, men from the Kuan-lung and Shan-tung blocs found themselves on the same side of an issue, opposing members of their own bloc on the other side. Thus, over a broad spectrum of issues, Ch'en's hypothetical blocs break down.

That this is true is further demonstrated by an examination of patterns of recommendation during the first two reigns of the T'ang.

Table 3.7.   Patterns of Recommendation

Recommendor	Bloc	Recommendee	Bloc	Sources
Wei Cheng	Shan-tung	Tu Cheng-lun	Shan-tung	*CTS* 70.15b *HTS* 106.1a *TCTC* 197.6202
Li Kang	Shan-tung	Wang Kuei	Shan-tung	*CTS* 70.1b
Wei Cheng	Shan-tung	Hou Chün-chi	Kuan-lung	*HTS* 97.15b *TCTC* 197.6202
Wang Kuei	Shan-tung	Wei T'ing	Kuan-lung	*CTS* 77.1b
Ch'en Shu-ta	South	Ts'ui Jen-shih	Shan-tung	*CTS* 74.14a *HTS* 99.13a
Li Ching	Kuan-lung	Ts'en Wen-pen	South	*CTS* 70.10a *HTS* 102.1b
Hsiao Yü	South	Feng Te-i	Shan-tung	*CTS* 63.3a *HTS* 100.6a *TCTC* 192.6024
Tu Yen	Kuan-lung	Chih Huai-tao	?	*CTS* 66.13b *HTS* 96.9b
Li Shih-min (T'ai-tsung)	Kuan-lung	Kao Shih-lien	Shan-tung	*HTS* 95.1b

Table 3.7, based on the biographies of almost one hundred early T'ang officials and other sources, lists cases where one official formally recommended *(chien)* another person or official to the emperor for either appointment or promotion. The bloc, according to Ch'en Yin-k'o's scheme, to which both recommendor and recommendee belonged, is also listed.

The sampling illustrated in table 3.7 is small despite the fact that early in the T'ang dynasty recommendation was one of the key paths to officialdom and the examination system was as yet of minor importance. But it is nevertheless clear that patterns of cooperation existed between members of opposing blocs and also between each of the two blocs and officials whose native places lay south of the North China plain.

Indeed, the presence of a third force, the southern bloc, must be taken into account. Ch'en Yin-k'o and Nunome Chōfu have claimed that southerners serving as officials in the early T'ang dynasty should no longer be considered independent parties because their families had previously become "captives" of the Northern Dynasties and the Sui.[13] Nevertheless, men like Hsiao Yü and Ch'en Shu-ta, scions of

13. Ch'en, "Li, Wu, Wei, Yang hun-yin chi-t'uan," p. 38; Nunome Chōfū, "Tōchō sōgyōki no ichikōsatsu" [An examination of the founding period of the T'ang dynasty], *Tōyōshi kenkyū* 25 (June 1966): 37.

defunct southern royal houses, were inheritors of strong family traditions that were intimately linked to geography and to a distinctive
southern culture. Similarly, it is unlikely that southerners, or people
from any other region in China, could so sharply cut themselves off
from their regional and family roots; in T'ang China there was an
intimate link between a family and its geographical identification. The
potency of this identification is underlined by the very nature of the
concept of *chün-wang* ("eminent clans of a locality"). For, even though
a clan might relocate, long afterward it still identified itself with its
chün, that is, the locality from which its social status, economic power,
and political influence originally derived.

That southerners were recognized as a distinct entity separate from
either the Kuan-lung or Shan-tung blocs is suggested by the pattern of
appointments of officials from different geographical regions in China
who shared posts in the Three Departments *(san-sheng)* during the
first two T'ang reigns, Wu-te (618–26) and Chen-kuan (627–49).
Tables 3.8, 3.9, and 3.10 show that officials who held shared posts as
the left and right vice-presidents of the Department of Affairs of State
(tso- and *yu-p'u-yeh)*, the two presidents of the Department of the
Imperial Chancellery *(shih-chung)*, and the two presidents of the Department of the Imperial Secretariat *(chung-shu-ling)* were almost
always balanced according to their native places among the Kuan-
lung, Shan-tung, and southern regions.[14] Equally significant is that in
this balance officials from the south were always utilized as counter-
weights to officials from Kuan-lung and Shan-tung. Moreover, just as
officials from Kuan-lung and Shan-tung balanced each other in these
shared posts, never did two southerners occupy both parts of a shared
office.

Table 3.9 reveals that there was a perfect balance struck among the
three regions—Kuan-lung, Shan-tung, and the south—for every year
during both Wu-te and Chen-kuan. In other words, there was no year
in which both presidents of the Imperial Chancellery represented the
same geographical region. Table 3.8 shows a balance every year except
two, and table 3.10 shows a balance every year except one and part of

14. Based on data in Yen Kang-wang, *T'ang p'u-shang-ch'eng-lang piao* [Tables of high officials in the Department of Affairs of State during the T'ang dynasty] (Taipei, 1956), 1:21–26;
and Wan Ssu-t'ung, "T'ang chiang-hsiang-ta-ch'en nien-piao" [Chronological tables of high
officials, chief ministers, and generals of the T'ang dynasty], in *K'ai-ming erh-shih-wu shih
pu-pien* [Supplements to the K'ai-ming Twenty-five Histories], 5: 7217–21. See also Chang
Ch'ün, "Lun T'ang K'ai-yüan ch'ien ti cheng-chih chi-t'uan" [On the political groups existing before and during the reign of K'ai-yüan], *Hsin-ya hsüeh-pao* 1 (February 1956): 286–87,
for an early but somewhat imprecise formulation of this idea.

Table 3.8.   Native Places of the Left and Right Vice-Presidents of
the Department of Affairs of State (5/618–5/649)[a]

Year	Left Vice-President	Right Vice-President
618	*	P'ei Chi, Shan-tung
619	*	P'ei Chi, Shan-tung
620	*	P'ei Chi, Shan-tung
621	*	P'ei Chi, Shan-tung
622	*	P'ei Chi, Shan-tung
623	*	P'ei Chi, Shan-tung
	P'ei Chi, Shan-tung	Hsiao Yü, South
624	P'ei Chi, Shan-tung	Hsiao Yü, South
625	P'ei Chi, Shan-tung	Hsiao Yü, South
626	P'ei Chi, Shan-tung	Hsiao Yü, South
	Hsiao Yü, South	Feng Te-i, Shan-tung
627	Hsiao Yü, South	Feng Te-i, Shan-tung
		Chang-sun Wu-chi, Kuan-lung
628	*	Chang-sun Wu-chi, Kuan-lung
629	Fang Hsüan-ling, Shan-tung	Tu Ju-hui, Kuan-lung
630	Fang Hsüan-ling, Shan-tung	Li Ching, Kuan-lung
631	Fang Hsüan-ling, Shan-tung	Li Ching, Kuan-lung
632	Fang Hsüan-ling, Shan-tung	Li Ching, Kuan-lung
633	Fang Hsüan-ling, Shan-tung	Li Ching, Kuan-lung
634	Fang Hsüan-ling, Shan-tung	Li Ching, Kuan-lung
635	Fang Hsüan-ling, Shan-tung	*
636**	Fang Hsüan-ling, Shan-tung	Wen Yen-po, Shan-tung
637**	Fang Hsüan-ling, Shan-tung	Wen Yen-po, Shan-tung
638	Fang Hsüan-ling, Shan-tung	Kao Shih-lien, Kuan-lung
639	Fang Hsüan-ling, Shan-tung	Kao Shih-lien, Kuan-lung
640	Fang Hsüan-ling, Shan-tung	Kao Shih-lien, Kuan-lung
641	Fang Hsüan-ling, Shan-tung	Kao Shih-lien, Kuan-lung
642	Fang Hsüan-ling, Shan-tung	Kao Shih-lien, Kuan-lung
643	*	Kao Shih-lien, Kuan-lung
644	*	*
645	*	*
646	*	*
647	*	*
648	Chang-sun Wu-chi, Kuan-lung	*
649	Chang-sun Wu-chi, Kuan-lung	*

[a]The period from the accession of Kao-tsu to the accession of Kao-tsung.
*No appointment this year.
**Year in which there was a geographical imbalance.

another. Over the period as a whole, balancing officials by geographical origins appears to have been a policy of both early T'ang emperors. This policy is illustrated particularly well in the year 626, when T'ai-tsung seized power. At this time he brought an end to the terms of all

Table 3.9.   Native Places of the Two Presidents of the Department
of the Imperial Chancellery (5/618–5/649)

618	Liu Wen-ching, Shan-tung[a]	Ch'en Shu-ta, South
	Tou Kang, Kuan-lung	
619	Yang Kung-jen, Kuan-lung	Ch'en Shu-ta, South
620	Yang Kung-jen, Kuan-lung	Ch'en Shu-ta, South
621	Yang Kung-jen, Kuan-lung	Ch'en Shu-ta, South
622	Yang Kung-jen, Kuan-lung	Ch'en Shu-ta, South
623	Yang Kung-jen, Kuan-lung	Ch'en Shu-ta, South
624	P'ei Chü, Shan-tung	Ch'en Shu-ta, South
625	P'ei Chü, Shan-tung	Ch'en Shu-ta, South
	Yü-wen Shih-chi, Kuan-lung	
626	Yü-wen Shih-chi, Kuan-lung	Ch'en Shu-ta, South
	Kao Shih-lien, Kuan-lung	
627	Kao Shih-lien, Kuan-lung	*
628	Tu Ju-hui, Kuan-lung	Wang Kuei, Shan-tung
629	Tu Ju-hui, Kuan-lung	Wang Kuei, Shan-tung
630	*	Wang Kuei, Shan-tung
631	*	Wang Kuei, Shan-tung
632	*	Wang Kuei, Shan-tung
633	Yang Kung-jen, Kuan-lung	Wang Kuei, Shan-tung
		Wei Cheng, Shan-tung
634	Yang Kung-jen, Kuan-lung	Wei Cheng, Shan-tung
635	Yang Kung-jen, Kuan-lung	Wei Cheng, Shan-tung
636	Yang Shih-tao, Kuan-lung	Wei Cheng, Shan-tung
637	Yang Shih-tao, Kuan-lung	Wei Cheng, Shan-tung
638	Yang Shih-tao, Kuan-lung	Wei Cheng, Shan-tung
639	Yang Shih-tao, Kuan-lung	Wei Cheng, Shan-tung
640	*	Wei Cheng, Shan-tung
641	*	Wei Cheng, Shan-tung
642	*	Wei Cheng, Shan-tung
643	*	*
644	Liu Chi, South	*
645	Liu Chi, South	*
646	*	Chang-sun Wu-chi, Kuan-lung
647	*	Chang-sun Wu-chi, Kuan-lung
648	*	Chang-sun Wu-chi, Kuan-lung
649	Yü Chih-ning, Kuan-lung	Chang Hsing-ch'eng, Shan-tung

[a]According to Liu Wen-ching's two biographies, he called himself a P'eng-ch'eng person
(Ho-nan *tao*), but for generations his family had lived in the capital area (Kuan-nei
tao). Since Liu is consciously identifying himself with Ho-nan, I have considered him as
belonging to the Shan-tung bloc.
*No appointment this year.

incumbents in the three offices we have been examining and appointed
new officials to replace them. A look at the tables reveals that all the
new appointees were again balanced geographically and, even more

Table 3.10.   Native Places of the Two Presidents of the Department of the Imperial Secretariat (5/618–5/649)

Year	President 1	President 2
618	Hsiao Yü, South	Tou Wei, Kuan-lung
619	Hsiao Yü, South	*
620	Hsiao Yü, South	Feng Te-i, Shan-tung
621	Hsiao Yü, South	Feng Te-i, Shan-tung
622	Hsiao Yü, South	*
623	Hsiao Yü, South	*
	Feng Te-i, Shan-tung	Yang Kung-jen, Kuan-lung
624	Feng Te-i, Shan-tung	Yang Kung-jen, Kuan-lung
625	Feng Te-i, Shan-tung	Yang Kung-jen, Kuan-lung
626	Feng Te-i, Shan-tung	Yang Kung-jen, Kuan-lung
	Fang Hsüan-ling, Shan-tung	Yü-wen Shih-chi, Kuan-lung
627	Fang Hsüan-ling, Shan-tung	Yü-wen Shih-chi, Kuan-lung
628	Fang Hsüan-ling, Shan-tung	Li Ching, Kuan-lung
629	Fang Hsüan-ling, Shan-tung	*
630	Wen Yen-po, Shan-tung	*
631	Wen Yen-po, Shan-tung	*
632	Wen Yen-po, Shan-tung	*
633	Wen Yen-po, Shan-tung	*
634	Wen Yen-po, Shan-tung	*
635	Wen Yen-po, Shan-tung	*
636	Wen Yen-po, Shan-tung	*
637	*	*
638	*	*
639	*	Yang Shih-tao, Kuan-lung
640	*	Yang Shih-tao, Kuan-lung
641	*	Yang Shih-tao, Kuan-lung
642	*	Yang Shih-tao, Kuan-lung
643	*	Yang Shih-tao, Kuan-lung
644**	Ts'en Wen-pen, Shan-tung	Ma Chou, Shan-tung
645**	Ts'en Wen-pen, Shan-tung	Ma Chou, Shan-tung
	Yang Shih-tao, Kuan-lung	
646	*	Ma Chou, Shan-tung
647	*	Ma Chou, Shan-tung
648	Ch'u Sui-liang, South	Ma Chou, Shan-tung
		Chang-sun Wu-chi, Kuan-lung
649	Ch'u Sui-liang, South	Chang-sun Wu-chi, Kuan-lung

*No appointment this year.
**Year in which there was a geographical imbalance.

significant, that the precise character of the geographical balance established by Kao-tsu was reaffirmed by his son. During many other years vacancies were filled so as to maintain prior geographical balances.

Although we have been speaking of three regional groups, this

picture may be too simplified. Liu Fang, the late-eighth-century genealogist, for one, speaks of four regions—Shan-tung, Chiang-tso, Kuan-
chung, and Tai-pei—each of whose people, he believed, had distinct
regional characteristics.[15] Regional configurations at the early T'ang
court might have been even more complex, in a political sense, than
this. Nevertheless, as we have seen previously, despite the fact that
officials belonged to loose regional groupings that were recognized
by both Kao-tsu and T'ai-tsung in their appointment patterns, regional
origin does not appear to have played a dominant role in determining
the political stands taken by officials.

One of the basic assumptions underlying Ch'en Yin-k'o's theory of
blocs at the early T'ang court is that the preponderance of power was
in the hands of bureaucrats from the northwest. This was the result,
Ch'en believes, of a policy he calls the *Kuan-chung pen-wei cheng-ts'e,* or
"Kuan-chung first policy," begun by Yü-wen T'ai, founder of the
Western Wei dynasty, in the middle of the sixth century. This policy
allegedly sought to develop and concentrate the primary political,
economic, and social elements of the Chinese Empire in the northwestern region of China, and Ch'en maintains that it continued during
the early T'ang until the reign of Empress Wu. Thus, according to
Ch'en, during the entire period from the beginning of Kao-tsu's reign
to the end of the reign of Kao-tsung (618–83), China's civil and military bureaucracy continued to be composed predominantly of members
of the Kuan-lung bloc. After this time, Ch'en maintains, Empress Wu
was able to utilize the examination system to bring to the fore the
literati families of the northeast and south at the expense of the northwestern aristocracy, and the Kuan-chung first policy was effectively
destroyed. The balance of power in T'ang government consequently
shifted away from the northwest to the northeast and south.[16]

After my own study of the problem, I have come to the conclusion
that the shift in the geographical center of gravity in the T'ang *civil*
bureaucracy, at least, which Ch'en dates from the reign of Empress
Wu, actually began much earlier—virtually at the beginning of the
T'ang dynasty—and became even more pronounced during Chen-
kuan.

The research of Yamazaki Hiroshi on Sui officialdom has made

---

15. *HTS* 199.20a.

16. Ch'en Yin-k'o, *T'ang-tai cheng-chih shih shu-lun kao* [Draft discussion of the political
history of the T'ang dynasty] (Chungking, 1944), p. 14. An English summary of Ch'en's
argument appears in E. G. Pulleyblank, *The Background of the Rebellion of An Lu-shan* (London,
1955), pp. 47–48.

Table 3.11.   Native Places of Heads of the Three Departments during
the Sui and Early T'ang Dynasties

Period	Northwest	Northeast	South	Total
Sui	13 (72.2%)	4 (22.2%)	1 (5.6%)	18
Early T'ang	7 (30.4%)	11 (47.8%)	5 (21.8%)	23
	Northwest	Northeast and South		
Sui	72.2%	27.8%		
Early T'ang	30.4%	69.6%		

SOURCES: Yamazaki, "Zuichō kanryō," pp. 15–17; Yen, *T'ang p'u-shang*, pp. 21–26; and Wan, "T'ang chiang-hsiang," p. 7217.

possible direct comparisons of the geographical origins of equivalent groups of Sui and early T'ang (Wu-te and Chen-kuan) civil officials.[17] According to Yamazaki's figures, during the Sui a total of eighteen different officials occupied the top offices in the Three Departments, as the president[18] and left and right vice-presidents of the Department of Affairs of State, the two presidents of the Department of the Imperial Chancellery, and the two presidents of the Department of the Imperial Secretariat, some of the most powerful offices in the government. According to my figures, there was a total of twenty-three such officials during the early T'ang. Table 3.11 shows the native places of officials filling these posts during the Sui and early T'ang (5/618–5/649) dynasties. Yamazaki's study of the Sui was based only on the actual native place of an official and did not take into consideration such factors as marriage alliances, which could have caused officials to shift their allegiances to other geographical regions. Data for T'ang officials are, therefore, similarly based only on native place.

It is apparent that nothing less than a major shift occurred from the Sui to the early T'ang, a virtual reversal in the ratio of officials whose native places were in the northwest to those whose native places were in the northeast and the south. Utilizing a more detailed breakdown of the data in table 3.12, we can observe that the shift, which began during Wu-te, was intensified during Chen-kuan.

Yamazaki also traced the geographical origins of Sui officials who served as the presidents of the Six Boards in the Department of Affairs

17. Yamazaki Hiroshi, "Zuichō kanryō no seikaku" [Characteristics of Sui dynasty officials], *Tōkyō Kyōikudaigaku Bungakubu Kiyō* 6 (1956): 1–59.

18. Generally, there was no president of the Department of Affairs of State. During the Sui only one official filled this office, and after 607 it was always vacant (Yamazaki, "Zuichō kanryō," p. 18). During the T'ang the office was generally left vacant out of respect to T'ai-tsung, who occupied it from 618 to 626; Yen Keng-wang, *T'ang p'u-shang-ch'eng-lang piao*, p. 15.

Table 3.12.   Native Places of Heads of the Three Departments during
Sui, Wu-te, and Chen-kuan

Period	Northwest	Northeast	South	Total
Sui	13 (72.2%)	4 (22.2%)	1 (5.6%)	18
Wu-te[a]	4 (40.0%)	4 (40.0%)	2 (20.0%)	10
Chen-kuan[b]	5 (29.5%)	8 (47.0%)	4 (23.5%)	17

	Northwest	Northeast and South
Sui	72.2%	27.8%
Wu-te	40.0%	60.0%
Chen-kuan	29.5%	70.5%

SOURCE: Yamazaki, "Zuichō kanryō," pp. 15–17; Yen, *T'ang p'u-shang*, pp. 21–26; and
Wan, "T'ang chiang-hsiang," pp. 7217–21.
[a]Up to T'ai-tsung's seizure of power in 6/626.
[b]Including the period from 6/626 to 627, and up to the accession of Kao-tsung in 5/649.

Table 3.13.   Native Places of the Presidents of the Six Boards
during the Sui, Wu-te, and Chen-kuan Periods.

Period	Northwest	Northeast	South	Unclear	Total
Sui	38 (56.7%)	28 (41.8%)	1 (1.5%)	0	67
Wu-te[a]	6 (42.9%)	7 (50.0%)	1 (7.1%)	3	17 (14)*
Chen-kuan[b]	16 (50.0%)	14 (43.8%)	2 (6.2%)	3	35 (32)*

	Northwest	Northeast and South
Sui	56.7%	43.3%
Wu-te	42.9%	57.1%
Chen-kuan	50.0%	50.0%

SOURCE: Yamazaki "Zuichō kanryō," pp. 26–33; Yen, *T'ang p'u-shang*, pp. 81–88, 223–29.
*Percentages are based not on grand totals, but on totals of officials with known and
  unambiguous geographical origins. These latter totals are given in ( ) in the table.
[a]Up to T'ai-tsung's seizure of power in 6/626.
[b]Including the period from 6/626 to 627, and up to the accession of Kao-tsung in 5/649.

of State. Although his data are not comprehensive, since he excluded
certain officials for whom there was conflicting information in the
sources, his findings are nevertheless useful for our purposes. Table 3.13
shows the native places of the presidents of the Six Boards during the
Sui, Wu-te, and Chen-kuan periods.

It will be observed that the shift to the northeast and south is not as
marked for table 3.13 as it was for table 3.11. At the same time, the
original disparity between northwestern and northeastern-plus-southern
elements was not as great either. There is actually a decrease in the
ratio of northwestern to northeastern-plus-southern elements from

Wu-te to Chen-kuan, the result of T'ai-tsung's employment of imperial family members in greater numbers than usual. Still, there is no doubt that with the commencement of the T'ang dynasty the pattern of appointment of personnel at the top level of the civil bureaucracy was altered significantly.

Additional evidence of the favor T'ai-tsung accorded northeasterners and southerners is to be found in the composition of a body of officials known as the Wen-hsüeh-kuan (College of Literary Studies). This was a private council that was founded by T'ai-tsung in 621 when he was still the prince of Ch'in and lasted until he ascended the throne in 626. At that time the Wen-hsüeh-kuan was replaced by an analogous organization known as the Hung-wen-kuan (College for Literary Development). Since the Wen-hsüeh-kuan was a private political organization with no recognized status in the formal administrative apparatus of the T'ang, and since its members were recruited solely by the order of the prince of Ch'in, it may serve as a reflection of T'ai-tsung's attitude toward the various geographical regions of China.

Biographical information exists for nineteen of the twenty scholars of the Wen-hsüeh-kuan. Of this number, six (31.6 percent) were from the northwest, six (31.6 percent) were from the northeast, and seven (36.8 percent) were from the south.[19] The ratio of northwest to northeast-plus-south is therefore 32:68. It is clearly evident that both before and after T'ai-tsung's accession he possessed a marked disposition to appoint non-northwestern elements to positions of power and influence.

What, we may well ask, was the cause of the shift away from the northwest as the native place of upper-level civil bureaucrats during the period from the Sui to the early T'ang? I believe that the answer to this question lies in the nature of the T'ang conquest of the empire. This was, it may be argued, a double seizure of the Chinese throne from strongholds located in the northeast, first by Kao-tsu from Taiyuan in 618 and then again by T'ai-tsung from Loyang in 626.

The Li-T'ang family was related by marriage to the Yang-Sui house and for several generations had maintained an estate in Shensi province. It was, therefore, a Kuan-lung element according to Ch'en Yin-k'o's classification. T'ang Kao-tsu began his official career in the Sui capital as a palace guard, and afterward served in several posts in both the capital and the provinces. But the most significant phase of his career took place in the region to the east of Kuan-lung. In 615 he was

19. According to data provided by Fukusawa Sōkichi, "Bungakukan gakushi ni tsuite" [The scholars of the Wen-hsüeh kuan], *Kumamoto Daigaku Kyōikugakubu Kiyō* 1 (March 1953): 40–41.

given special powers by Sui Yang-ti to combat banditry and Turkish incursions of the border in the region of modern Shansi province, what became known during the T'ang as Ho-tung *tao*. Then, in 617, Yang-ti appointed him garrison commander *(liu-shou)* of Taiyuan, also located in Shansi. It was in Taiyuan that Kao-tsu raised his standard of revolt against the Sui, and from there that he began his conquest of the empire in 617.

Nunome Chōfū has analyzed the body of chief supporters of Kao-tsu at the time of the T'ang uprising and during the subsequent march on the Sui capital, which fell to Kao-tsu later that year. He shows that during this period the executive body of Kao-tsu's organization, called the Administration of the Grand General *(ta-chiang-chün fu)*, was overwhelmingly composed of Sui civil and military officials who either (1) currently held offices in the vicinity of Taiyuan, (2) had previously resigned or retired from their posts and returned to their native places in the Taiyuan region, or (3) had fled from their duties as Sui officials and were now in exile in Taiyuan.[20] Of the twenty-nine men Nunome found serving as officials in the Administration of the Grand General, information relating to geographical origins was available for twenty-three. Of these, eight (34.8 percent) were from the northwest, and fifteen (65.2 percent) were from the northeast.[21]

The preponderance of adherents from the northeast is certainly a result of the fact that Kao-tsu's base, Taiyuan, was located in the northeast. We might have expected to find a more broadly based geographical distribution among his followers, especially in light of the more evenly balanced composition of the Wu-te bureaucracy examined in tables 3.12 and 3.13. It appears, then, that Kao-tsu struck a better balance among geographical regions in the Wu-te civil bureaucracy than in his military organization in Taiyuan. This was because in recruiting his bureaucracy after his accession, Kao-tsu drew on the wide circle of friends and acquaintances made prior to his revolt and, especially, on relatives of the imperial house.[22] But, in the last analysis, it was the conquest of the empire from Taiyuan that provided the high percentage of Wu-te officials with native places in the northeast.

T'ai-tsung's relationship to the northeast was even stronger than his father's. He had been with Kao-tsu in Taiyuan at the time of the T'ang

20. Nunome Chōfū, "Ri En shūdan no kōzō" [The structure of Li Yüan's organization], *Ritsumeikan Bungaku* 243 (September 1965): 3–4.

21. These figures are based on information derived from Nunome, "Ri En," pp. 14–15.

22. Tsukiyama Chisaburō, *Tōdai seiji seido no kenkyū* [The political system of the T'ang dynasty] (Osaka, 1967), pp. 29–30.

uprising and there had become friendly with several northeasterners who subsequently joined his staff. Later, during the period 618 to 621, T'ai-tsung was almost constantly engaged in campaigns of pacification, many of them on the northeastern plain, where he defeated two of the T'ang's most powerful rivals, Tou Chien-te of Hopei and Wang Shih-ch'ung of Loyang. At the same time, he began assiduously recruiting men for his own staff from among the officer corps of his vanquished enemies as well as from among former Sui officials in the Loyang region. These men later formed the nucleus of the Chen-kuan civil and military bureaucracies. Northeasterners on T'ai-tsung's staff became so numerous that in 626 when Kao-tsu, hoping to reduce the friction that had developed between T'ai-tsung and his two brothers, Li Chien-ch'eng and Li Yüan-chi, attempted to send T'ai-tsung away from the capital to Loyang, the two brothers were able to stop the plan by having people at court charge that T'ai-tsung's associates were all Shan-tung people and that if he were sent to Loyang he would never return.[23]

Loyang itself was a base of power from which T'ai-tsung wrested the succession from his elder brother, the crown prince Li Chien-ch'eng. To quote Ch'en Yin-k'o, "T'ang T'ai-tsung's real strength lay in his ability to gain possession of Loyang, pacify and use its organizational personnel, and secure the fruits of their aid." Although Wang Shih-ch'ung surrendered Loyang to T'ai-tsung in the fifth month of 621, T'ai-tsung did not return to Ch'ang-an with his prisoner until two months later. During this time the future emperor was ingratiating himself with the local elite in an attempt to gain their allegiance. This would explain, for example, why he blocked a move by his father to burn certain structures in the city that symbolized its status under the Sui as the eastern capital.[24] It is also evident that, from the first, T'ai-tsung jealously guarded his personal prerogatives and interests in Loyang against outside interference. Soon after the fall of the city, Kao-tsu sent several of his high-ranking concubines to pick and choose among the Sui treasures stored there. When the concubines began clamoring for valuables for themselves and offices in the metropolitan administration for their relatives, T'ai-tsung turned a deaf ear to all their demands.[25] Shortly afterward, Kao-tsu appointed T'ai-tsung as president

23. *HTS* 79.5b.

24. See *CTS* 69.7a, 75.14b–15a; Ch'en Yin-k'o, "Lun Sui-mo T'ang-ch'u so-wei Shan-tung hao-chieh" [The so-called *Shan-tung hao-chieh* at the end of the Sui and the beginning of the T'ang], *Ling-nan hsüeh-pao* 12 (June 1952): 6; Li Shu-t'ung, *T'ang-shih k'ao-pien* [An examination of T'ang history] (Taipei, 1965), pp. 134–35.

25. *CTS* 64.3a–b; *TCTC* (Taipei, 1962 ed.) 190.5958–59; *HTS* 79.2b–3a; Li, *T'ang-shih k'ao-pien*, p. 135.

of the Department of Affairs of State of the Shan-tung Circuit on Grand Mobile Assignment *(Shan-tung tao ta-hsing-t'ai shang-shu-ling)*, with headquarters at Loyang. The appointment merely served to accelerate T'ai-tsung's attempts to build a personal dominion in the Loyang region.

As the struggle over the succession intensified, Loyang assumed an ever larger place in T'ai-tsung's overall strategy against his elder brother. Shortly before the climax of this struggle, T'ai-tsung ordered his subordinate Wen Ta-ya "to garrison Loyang and await developments. On several occasions Ta-ya made secret plans and received handsome rewards in great measure." About the same time, T'ai-tsung dispatched his official Chang Liang from Ch'ang-an to Loyang with one thousand men to protect the city and to rally the military leaders *(hao-chieh)* of the region to his side by distributing among them great quantities of gold and silk.[26]

Lastly, T'ai-tsung emerged victorious against the crown prince by gaining military control of the Hsüan-wu Gate in the northern wall of the palace city of Ch'ang-an. It was at the Hsüan-wu Gate that T'ai-tsung and nine of his supporters ambushed and killed Li Chien-ch'eng and Li Yüan-chi at dawn on the fourth day of the sixth month, 626. T'ai-tsung had gained control of the gate by bribing the commander of the guards stationed there into allowing him to replace the guards with his own hand-picked men. This commander was Ch'ang Ho, a northeasterner.[27]

Although geography does not appear to have been a key factor in contributing to the formation of political factions during the early T'ang, it is possible to suggest other factors that may have had this effect. The first of these is the career background of each official prior to his service under the T'ang. Because the T'ang had only recently come to power, the Wu-te and Chen-kuan bureaucracies were unusual with respect to the exceptionally diverse career backgrounds of their members. Many early T'ang officials had previously served together under, or were members of the royal houses of, the Liang, Ch'en, Northern Chou, Northern Ch'i, and Sui dynasties, or had served together under former rebel enemies of the T'ang, such as Hsiao Hsien, Hsüeh Chü, Tou Chien-te, Yü-wen Hua-chi, Li Mi, Wang Shih-ch'ung,

---

26. *CTS* 61.1b, 69.7a; *HTS* 94.4a–b.

27. Ch'en, *T'ang-tai cheng-chih*, p. 41; idem, "Shan-tung hao-chieh," pp. 6–7; Woodbridge Bingham, "Li Shih-min's Coup in A.D. 626," *Journal of the American Oriental Society* 70 (1950): 93.

Shen Fa-hsing, and Tu Fu-wei. Such backgrounds might well have formed the bases for factions at the early T'ang court.

Moreover, not all officials had joined the T'ang at the same time, and distinctions arose between (1) those who had been with Kao-tsu in Taiyuan at the time of the T'ang uprising or had joined him during his campaign against the Sui capital and (2) those who threw their lot in with the T'ang sometime later. Members of the first group were singled out as "meritorious officials" *(kung-ch'en)* soon after Kao-tsu ascended the throne. The accession of T'ai-tsung further complicated matters. Some officials who had previously been on the staff of the crown prince Chien-ch'eng became members of T'ai-tsung's staff after the Hsüan-wu Gate incident. Others had been his supporters since the beginning of the dynasty and thus constituted a group of his own meritorious officials. The distinction between ordinary and meritorious officials was more than nominal. Kao-tsu's meritorious officials were given preferential treatment when titles of nobility were distributed, and T'ai-tsung ennobled his meritorious officials as dukes and furnished them with the taxes of households on the land of their nominal fiefs.[28] Since meritorious officials often came to wield great power in the early T'ang administrations, they may well have comprised a political faction opposed by other, less powerful elements at court.

Another factor potentially leading to the formation of factions is family background. Factions could have been formed by descendants of families that had a long history of providing men for government service and by descendants of nonofficial families. Factions could also have been formed, as they often were in Chinese history, on the basis of the offices held by court members. Rivalries might have existed among various branches of the government, which would have pitted, for example, members of the Secretariat against those of the Chancellery. Or, officials of low rank, regardless of the branch of government to which they were attached, may have customarily united against their higher-placed colleagues. Lastly, factions might well have been formed among those at court who were related by either blood or marriage, or among officials related to the imperial Li-T'ang family.

The highly complex problem of marriage relationships at the early T'ang court merits an entire study by itself. But tables 3.14–3.19 illustrate how the following factors influenced the political responses of officials to the same six issues we examined earlier in conjunction with native place: (1) career record, that is (a) the prior dynasty or rebel under which the official served and (b) whether the official was

28. *THY* (Taipei, 1963 ed.) 45.799–800; *HTS* 88.7a–8a.

Table 3.14. Issue: Should the T'ang reestablish a feudal or modified feudal system?

Name	Career Record		Meritorious Official?	Office Family?	Imperial Relative?	Current Office	Branch	Degree/ Class	Biographies
	Dynasty/Rebel								
Pro									
Hsiao Yü	Sui/		yes	yes	no	shang-shu yu-p'u-yeh	State	2/2	*CTS* 63 *HTS* 101
Yen Shih-ku	Sui/		no	yes	no	chung-shu shih-lang	Sec't.	3/1	*CTS* 73 *HTS* 198
Con									
Wei Cheng	/Li Mi		no	yes	no	t'e-chin	State	2/1	*CTS* 71 *HTS* 97
Chang-sun Wu-chi			yes		yes	ssu-k'ung		1/1	*CTS* 65 *HTS* 105
Ma Chou			no	no	no	chien-ch'a yü-shih	Court	6/2	*CTS* 74 *HTS* 98
Yü Chih-ning	Sui/		no	yes	no	t'ai-tzu tso-shu-tzu		4/1	*CTS* 78 *HTS* 104
Li Pai-yao	/Shen Fa-hsing Sui/Tu Fu-wei		no	yes	no	li-pu shih-lang	State	4/2	*CTS* 72 *HTS* 102

Table 3.15. Issue: Should the Eastern Turks be resettled inside the borders of China?

| Name | Career Record | | | | Current Office | Branch | Degree/Class | Biographies |
	Dynasty/Rebel	Meritorious Official?	Official Family?	Imperial Relative?				
Wen Yen-po	Sui/Lo I	no	*Pro* yes	no	chung-shu-ling	Sec't.	2/1	CTS 61 HTS 91
Yen Shih-ku	Sui/	no	*Con* yes	no	chung-shu shih-lang	Sec't.	3/1	CTS 73 HTS 198
Tou Ching		no	yes	no	Hsia-chou tu-tu		2/1–3/2[a]	CTS 61 HTS 95
Li Pai-yao	/Shen Fa-hsing Sui/Tu Fu-wei	no	yes	no	li-pu shih-lang	State	4/2	CTS 72 HTS 102
Wei Cheng	/Li Mi	no	yes	no	pi-shu-chien	Chanc'y.	3/2	CTS 71 HTS 97
Tu Ch'u-k'o		no	yes	no	chi-shih-chung	Chanc'y.	5/1	CTS 66 HTS 96

[a]Degree and class are dependent on the status of the locality, that is, either *shang*, *chung*, or *hsia*.

designated a meritorious official or not; (2) official family background, that is, whether the official's father or grandfather had served in previous administrations; (3) blood relationship or close relationship by marriage to the emperor (i.e. father-in-law, son-in-law, or brother-in-law); (4) current official post; (5) the branch of government to which the post belonged, that is, the Department of Affairs of State (State), the Department of the Imperial Secretariat (Sec't.) or the Chancellery (Chanc'y.), the directorates, courts, and so on; and (6) the degree and class of that post in the T'ang nine-degree thirty-class ranking system.

As was the case with native place, it appears that, in general, no significant correlation exists between the responses made by early T'ang officials and the six factors examined in tables 3.14–3.19. Two possible exceptions to this conclusion appear in table 3.18, which lists the various contenders for T'ai-tsung's throne and their supporters. Although Li Ch'eng-ch'ien was initially appointed crown prince, he was removed from this position in 643 by means of the intrigues of his brother Li T'ai. It was not Li T'ai who eventually succeeded T'ai-tsung, however, but another brother, Li Chih, who became the third T'ang emperor, Kao-tsung. It will be observed from table 3.18 that the supporters of Li T'ai were, on the whole, of lower rank than the supporters of either Li Ch'eng-ch'ien or Li Chih. This may have been at least partially a function of youth, for among T'ai's supporters numbered the sons and younger brothers of some of T'ai-tsung's most powerful officials.[29] Also, three out of the four supporters of Li Chih, but none of T'ai's supporters, were meritorious officials. What is the significance of this?

T'ai's two biographies[30] list him as the fourth son of the Wen-te empress, T'ai-tsung's consort. But according to the biographies of the empress's first son, the crown prince Ch'eng-ch'ien, and those of T'ai, the former was born in 619 and the latter in 618.[31] Thus, T'ai would have been older than his "elder" brother by the same mother. There is, in fact, some evidence in the sources to suggest that T'ai may not have been the son of the Wen-te empress, but rather the son of a concubine.[32] If this is true, it may be that when Ch'eng-ch'ien was demoted

29. Matsui, "Sokuten Bukō," p. 12.

30. CTS 76.1a–b; HTS 80.1a.

31. According to HTS 80.8b, T'ai died at the age of thirty-four (thirty-five sui). This was in the twelfth month of 652 (January, 653) according to HTS 3.3b. CTS 76.1b notes that Ch'eng-ch'ien was seven years old (eight sui) at the time T'ai-tsung came to the throne in 626. On this question, see also Ts'en Chung-mien, T'ang-shih yü-shen [Marginalia on T'ang history] (Shanghai, 1960), pp. 10–11; and Matsui, "Sokuten Bukō," p. 16n48.

32. The evidence is summarized by C. P. Fitzgerald, The Empress Wu (London, 1968), p. 215n9.

Table 3.16. Issue: Should T'ai-tsung perform the Feng and Shan rites?

| | Career Record | | | | | | | |
Name	Dynasty/Rebel	Meritorious Official?	Official Family?	Imperial Relative?	Current Office	Branch	Degree/Class	Biographies
			Pro					
Li Hsiao-kung		no		yes	wang		1/2	CTS 60 HTS 78
Li Yüan-ching		no		yes	wang		1/2	CTS 64 HTS 79
Wu Shih-huo		yes	no	no	Li-chou tu-tu		2/2–3/2[a]	CTS 58 HTS 206
Chu Tzu-she	Sui/Tu Fu-wei	no	no	no	?	?	?	CTS 189A HTS 198
Li Pai-yao	/Shen Fa-hsing Sui/Tu Fu-wei	no	yes	no	?	?	?	CTS 72 HTS 102
Ts'en Wen-pen	/Hsiao Hsien	no	yes	no	?	?	?	CTS 70 HTS 102
Kao Jo-ssu	?	no	?	?	?	?	?	—
Chang-sun Wu-chi		yes	yes	yes	ssu-t'u		1/1	CTS 65 HTS 105
			Con					
Wei Cheng	/Li Mi	no	yes	no	pi-shu-chien	Chanc'y.	3/2	CTS 71 HTS 97
Ch'u Sui-liang	Sui/	no	yes	no	ch'i-chü-lang	Chanc'y.	6/3	CTS 80 HTS 105

[a] Degree and class are dependent on the status of the locality, that is, either *shang*, *chung*, or *hsia*.

Table 3.17. Issue: Should brothers of those who revolted be executed with them?

Name	Career Record				Current Office	Branch	Degree/ Class	Biogra- phies
	Dynasty/Rebel	Meritorious Official?	Official Family?	Imperial Relative?				
Pro								
Kao Shih-lien	Sui/Hsiao Hsien	yes	yes	no	shang-shu yu-p'u-yeh	State	2/2	CTS 65 HTS 95
Hou Chün-chi	/Chai Jang	yes	no	no	li-pu shang-shu	State	3/1	CTS 69 HTS 94
Li Shih-chi	/Chai Jang	yes	no	no	ping-pu shang-shu	State	3/1	CTS 67 HTS 93
Con								
T'ang Chien		yes	yes	no	min-pu shang-shu	State	3/1	CTS 58 HTS 89
Li Tao-tsung		no		yes	li-pu shang-shu wang	State	3/1 1/2	CTS 60 HTS 78
Tu Ch'u-k'o		no	yes	no	kung-pu shang-shu	State	3/1	CTS 66 HTS 96
Fang Hsüan-ling	Sui/	yes	yes	no	shang-shu tso-p'u-yeh	State	2/2	CTS 66 HTS 96
Ts'ui Jen-shih		no	no	no	chi-shih-chung	Chanc'y.	5/1	CTS 74 HTS 99

Table 3.18. Issue: Who should be established as T'ai-tsung's successor?

Name	Career Record				Current Office	Branch	Degree/ Class	Biographies
	Dynasty/Rebel	Meritorious Official?	Official Family?	Imperial Relative?				
Supporters of Li Ch'eng-ch'ien								
Li Yüan-ch'ang		no	yes	yes	wang		1/1	CTS 64 / HTS 79
Hou Chün-chi		yes	no	no	li-pu shang-shu	State	3/1	CTS 69 / HTS 94
Li An-yen		no	?	?	chung-lang-chiang		4/2	——
Chao Chieh		no	?	yes	Yang-chou tz'u-shih		3/2–4/2a	——
Tu Ho		no	yes	yes	fu-ma tu-wei		5/4	——
Wang Ching-chih		no	yes	no	fu-ma tu-wei		5/4	——
Supporters of Li T'ai								
Tu Ch'u-k'o		no	yes	no	kung-pu shang-shu	State	3/1	CTS 66 / HTS 96
Wei T'ing		no	yes	no	huang-men shih-lang	Chanc'y.	4/1	CTS 77 / HTS 98
Ts'ui Jen-shih		no	no	no	chi-shih-chung	Chanc'y.	5/1	CTS 74 / HTS 99
Fang I-ai		no	yes	yes	fu-ma tu-wei		5/4	CTS 66 / HTS 96
Ts'en Wen-pen /Hsiao Hsien		no	yes	no	chung-shu shih-lang	Sec't.	3/1	CTS 70 / HTS 102

Liu Chi	/Hsiao Hsien	no	no	no	huang-men shih-lang	Chanc'y.	4/1	CTS 74 HTS 99
Chai Ling-wu		no	yes	yes	fu-ma tu-wei		5/4	CTS 58 HTS 90
Supporters of Li Chih								
Chang-sun Wu-chi		yes	yes	yes	ssu-t'u		1/1	CTS 65 HTS 105
Ch'u Sui-liang	Sui/	no	yes	no	chien-i ta-fu	Chanc'y.	4/2	CTS 80 HTS 105
Fang Hsüan-ling	Sui/	yes	yes	no	ssu-k'ung		1/1	CTS 66 HTS 96
Li Shih-chi	/Chai Jang	yes	no	no	ping-pu shang-shu	State	3/1	CTS 67 HTS 93

[a]Degree and class are dependent on the status of the locality, that is, *shang, chung,* or *hsia.*

Table 3.19. Issue: Should the T'ang attack the Kingdom of Koguryō?

Name	Career Record				Current Office	Branch	Degree/ Class	Biographies
	Dynasty/Rebel	Meritorious Official?	Official Family?	Imperial Relative?				
Pro								
Li Shih-chi	/Chai Jang	yes	no	no	ping-pu shang-shu	State	3/1	CTS 67 HTS 93
Con								
Chang Liang	/Li Mi /Li Shih-chi	yes	no	no	hsing-pu shang-shu	State	3/1	CTS 69 HTS 94
Ch'u Sui-liang	Sui/Hsüeh Chü	no	yes	no	chien-i ta-fu	Chanc'y.	4/2	CTS 80 HTS 105
Li Ta-liang	Sui/	no	yes	no	kung-pu shang-shu	State	3/1	CTS 62 HTS 99
Fang Hsüan-ling	Sui/	yes	yes	no	ssu-k'ung		1/1	CTS 66 HTS 96
Hsü Ch'ung-jung		no	?	?	?	?	?	—
Chiang Hsing-pen		no	yes	no	unclear	?	?	CTS 59 HTS 91

from his position as crown prince, and the candidates were reduced to Li T'ai and Li Chih, the meritorious officials, who were intimately linked with the founding of the dynasty and the imperial house, favored the succession of a legitimate son and so rallied around Li Chih. More will be said later about Chang-sun Wu-chi's role in this succession dispute.

The data we have examined so far suggest that during the Chen-kuan period factions based on common factors—geographical or otherwise—in the backgrounds of officials who comprised them did not exist. Perhaps this was because the backgrounds of early T'ang officials were so complex—the result of the historical circumstances surrounding the founding of the dynasty—that the court was fragmented along too many different lines for factions to have been formed around any one of them. Yet the recognition by both Kao-tsu and T'ai-tsung of the potential for the creation of durable regional power groups is well documented. Indeed, it was precisely to prevent any such formations that the two emperors were careful to see that the various regions were represented and balanced in the highest organs of government.

The early T'ang bureaucracy was, however, not without its petty jealousies, rivalries, and, even deep-seated animosities. The biographies of officials who served under Kao-tsu and T'ai-tsung occasionally reveal that so-and-so had a falling out with (yu hsi), so-and-so bore a grudge against (pu hsieh), or so-and-so slandered a colleague, and so on. And just as often we read of attacks made on certain officials whose authors are not recorded. I have gathered cases in which the names of officials undergoing strained relationships are known and have listed them in table 3.20 along with their native places, their regional blocs according to Ch'en Yin-k'o's scheme, and the sources of this information. Unsurprisingly, the table lends further support to the earlier conclusion that geographical origins in no way determined political animosities. Rather, a close reading of the sources shows that the reasons for political rivalries were almost as numerous as the specific cases themselves.

For example, in the case of Hsiao Yü a stubborn and cantankerous personality appears to have been at least partially responsible for arraying him against other officials at court. In the case of Liu Wen-ching an inflated ego and jealousy of the rewards bestowed on his friend, P'ei Chi, led to his split with P'ei. Ma Chou blocked the appointment of Wei T'ing to a high post because Wei had been rude to him earlier. The falling out of Chang-sun Wu-chi and Tu Yen is merely noted but not explained in the Old T'ang History, but another source tells us that it came about when Tu supported an official who had

Table 3.20. Strained Relationships among Early T'ang Officials

Name	Native Place	vs.	Name	Native Place	Sources
Liu Wen-ching	Kuan-chung (Kuan-lung)		P'ei Chi	Ho-tung (Shan-tung)	CTS 57.9b HTS 88.3b
Huang-fu Wu-i	Kuan-chung (Kuan-lung)		Tou Chin	Kuan-chung (Kuan-lung)	CTS 62.13b HTS 91.8b
Ma Chou	Ho-pei (Shan-tung)		Wei T'ing	Kuan-chung (Kuan-lung)	CTS 77.2a
Hsiao Yü	Shan-nan (South)		Yang Tsuan	Kuan-chung (Kuan-lung)	CTS 77.5a
Hsiao Yü	Shan-nan (South)		Feng Te-i	Ho-pei (Shan-tung)	CTS 63.3b HTS 100.6a
Ch'u Sui-liang	Chiang-nan (South)		Liu Chi	Shan-nan (South)	CTS 74.6a HTS 99.12b
Ch'u Sui-liang	Chiang-nan (South)		Ts'ui Jen-shih	Ho-pei (Shan-tung)	HTS 99.14b
Ch'u Sui-liang	Chiang-nan (South)		Li Ch'ien-yu	Kuan-chung (Kuan-lung)	CTS 87.11b
Tou Kuei	Kuan-chung (Kuan-lung)		Kuo Hsing-fang	?	HTS 95.7b
Tou Kuei	Kuan-chung (Kuan-lung)		Wei Yün-ch'i	Kuan-chung (Kuan-lung)	CTS 75.7a–7b HTS 95.7b
Chang-sun Wu-chi	Ho-nan (imperial relative)		Tu Yen	Ho-pei (Shan-tung)	CTS 66.14b

made accusations against Chang-sun Wu-chi's close friend, the general Hou Chün-chi.[33]

Chang-sun Wu-chi, T'ai-tsung's brother-in-law and the most powerful official at court during much of the Chen-kuan period, appears often to have been the focal point of political rivalries. Early in T'ai-tsung's reign charges were already being leveled by Chang-sun's enemies that he wielded excessive power. There may well be some connection between these charges and the split that occurred early in Chen-kuan between Chang-sun Wu-chi and Tu Yen over the Hou Chün-chi affair noted above. Since Tu died in the tenth month of 628, the split could not have been far removed in time from the attack made on Chang-sun in the first month of the same year.[34] Later in Chen-kuan, as table 3.5 indicates, Chang-sun Wu-chi became a partisan in the dispute over the succession. Chinese commentators have long suggested that he supported a weak Li Chih (the future Kao-tsung) in the hope of dominating the new emperor. A recent study has illuminated the efforts of one of Chang-sun Wu-chi's supporters in the succession dispute, Ch'u Sui-liang, to discredit Liu Chi and Ts'ui Jen-shih, two officials who had championed the candidacy of Li Chih's rival, Li T'ai (see tables 3.5 and 3.20).[35] Following Li Chih's accession in 649, Chang-sun Wu-chi appears to have continued his vendetta against those who had backed T'ai.[36]

There is little doubt, then, that with the commencement of a second internal struggle for the T'ang throne in 643, factional groups were formed that influenced court politics not only during the years until T'ai-tsung's death but even afterward. The character *tang* is used in the Standard History narratives of the dispute, and on one occasion in 644, T'ai-tsung, apparently with some regret was moved to praise one of his officials with the observation that "while he was in office, there were no factions" (*tang-kuan wu p'eng-tang*).[37]

Yet friction between officials, when it did occur during the early T'ang, was typically the result of personality conflicts and petty jealousies, not factional politics. Prior to 643 there were no groups of officials who saw eye to eye over a wide range of policy decisions or who joined together to realize a consistent set of goals; political divisions had not yet become rigid, and political allegiances were in a highly fluid

33. See *TCTC* 192.6025, note of Hu San-hsing; the specific cases listed in table 3.20; and *CTW* (Taipei, 1965 ed.) 161.2b.
34. *CTS* 65.7b; *HTS* 105.2a; *TCTC* 192.6046–47, 193.6058.
35. Sun Kuo-tung, "Tang-cheng shih-shih," pp. 43–45.
36. Ibid., pp. 49–50.
37. *TCTC* 197.6210.

state. Thus, political groups with any degree of cohesiveness and structure, that is, with identifiable leaders and members, had not yet emerged. The T'ang Standard Histories and other sources, such as Wu Ching's *Essentials of Government of the Chen-kuan Period (Chen-kuan cheng-yao)* (c. 707–09), celebrate T'ai-tsung's reign as a time of great harmony in government, characterized by ideal ruler-minister *(chün-ch'en)* relationships and the absence of partisan politics. The data in this paper suggest that, for at least much of the period under consideration, we have an unusual convergence of historiographical bias and historical fact.

4. T'ang Household Registers and Related Documents

Ikeda On

The Chinese system of population registration was a crucial administrative function in the operation of the government of traditional China. From the Ch'in and Han periods onward, successive governments maintained well-integrated systems of household registration and attempted to register the entire population that was under their control. In every prefecture and county of the empire multiple copies of household registers *(hu-chi)* were drawn up; these were kept in the government offices and were used as basic data for administration—in particular, for financial administration. Chinese population statistics, enormous by comparison with the rest of the world and running into tens and hundreds of millions of persons, are known only because of the existence of this system of household registration.

Under the Northern Dynasties and the early T'ang the implementation of the *chün-t'ien* ("equal field") system of land allocation and the related *tsu-yung-tiao* tax and labor service system made it imperative that the state should register every household and individual and oversee the allocation of every parcel of land. According to the formal provisions of this system, a rather substantial holding of land was given to every adult male in the country; they were in turn required to pay taxes in grain and cloth and to perform certain labor services. Whereas in later periods the government came to rely heavily on revenue from trade imposts and monopolies, they now depended almost exclusively on taxes in grain and cloth. It was therefore imperative that they keep an accurate account of every taxpaying family.

Although the constantly revised household registers were essential

For a discussion of source materials referred to, see the Bibliographical Note at the end of the chapter.

to the operation of the government in the early T'ang, they were of no importance to later officials, who could hardly be concerned with the administrative details of another time; nor were they valued by traditional Chinese scholars, whose well-defined concern with the moral lessons of the past did not encourage an interest in detailed studies of local administrative history. The great bulk of these documents are thus naturally and irretrievably lost. However, modern scholars have been presented, by chance, with a collection of these documents which have been preserved for reasons quite extraneous to their original purpose. Most of these were found late in the last century among a much larger collection of manuscripts which had been sealed for nearly a thousand years behind a wall in one of the Buddhist cave temples near Tunhuang, a community in the far northwestern corner of China on the trade route between China and the West. They had originally been preserved only because paper was scarce in that remote area and the reverse sides of the documents were valuable writing surfaces, often used to copy out Buddhist sutras. The other documents were found later in the Turfan Basin, even further north and west of Tunhuang. They were discovered, among other places, in the excavation of a cemetery, the paper having been used for funerary purposes. Though badly mutilated, they are rare and precious historical materials.

Word of the discoveries at Tunhuang spread quickly, and expeditions from several countries went to the scene. The first of these, in 1907, was headed by Aurel Stein, an English scholar and adventurer who had no idea just what had been found, but knew by instinct that he was onto a valuable cache. He bribed the Taoist monk in charge of the monastary to part with a selection of the documents, which were sent back to England. Stein's expedition was followed by that of the great French Sinologist Paul Pelliot, who was in a far better position to select with discrimination, and he too bribed the monk to part with a portion of the manuscripts. Other expeditions to Tunhuang, and to several sites in the Turfan Basin, followed; primary documents from these expedition can now be found in London, Paris, Berlin, Leningrad, Kyoto, and, most appropriately, in Peking.

For the last half century, a number of scholars have devoted themselves to the publication of household registers (hu-chi) from these finds. The contents of the household registers have been carefully scrutinized by scholars who recognized the value of these documents for historians interested in the actual functioning of local government, albeit in a rather remote and untypical area of China. Without these materials, we would be almost entirely uninformed about the implementation of government policy at the local level, where the normative institutions described in standard sources encountered the realities of local society.

In part because of the lack of documentation, it was once possible to suspect that the "equal-field" system of the T'ang had no more historical reality than the idealized "well-field" system of antiquity. Studies of the household registers have corrected this skepticism, proving that the household, personal status, age-category, and land allocation systems that are described in contemporary historical sources were in fact put into operation. While also paying attention to the differences between the systems as designed in theory and their actual implementation, these studies were thus able to correct and emend the historical image of the period, which had been formed on the basis of the traditional literature alone. In addition, by detecting instances of inaccuracy and deliberate falsification in the *hu-chi* fragments, they recognized that there was a limit to the reliability of these documents as historical evidence.

Besides the household registers, several other kinds of documents relating to population and land registration have come to light. There are, for example, "registers of selective impositions" *(ch'ai-k'o pu)*,[1] land allocation documents and documents relating to the reversion of lands to the authorities under the *chün-t'ien* land allocation system,[2] application documents submitted by heads of irrigation sectors *(yen-t'ou)* relating to cultivated lands,[3] nominal lists of monks and nuns,[4]

---

1. Published by Naba Toshisada, "Seishi ni kisai seraretaru Dai Tō Tempō-jidai no kosū to kōsū to no kankei ni tsukite" (see Bibliographical Note), and Nishimura Genyū, "Tōdai Tonkō sakabo no kenkyū," *Monumenta Serindica* 3 [*Tonkō Torohan shakai keizai shiryō*, II] (Kyōto, 1960), pp. 375–464, also included with several addenda and corrigenda under the title "Tōdai Tonkō sakabo o tsūjite mita Tō kindensei jidai no yōeki seido," in his recent *Chūgoku keizaishi kenkyū: kindenseido hen* (Kyoto, 1968), pp. 467–706.

2. Published by Nishijima Sadao, "Torohan shutsudo monjo yori mitaru kindensei no sekō jōtai," *Monumenta Serindica* 2 [*Tonkō Torohan shakai keizai shiryō*, I] (Kyoto, 1959), pp. 151–250, plates 13–33; and supplements and corrections to this in "Torohan shutsudo monjo yori mitaru kindensei no sekō jōtai; hoi, hosei," *Monumenta Serindica* 3, pp. 467–80, plates 39–40, which are included with few additional addenda and corrigenda in his collection *Chūgoku keizai shi kenkyū* (Tokyo, 1966), pp. 431–726. See also Nishimura Genyū, "Tōdai Torohan ni okeru kindensei no igi," *Monumenta Serindica* 2, pp. 293–353, plates 35–40, included with a few addenda and corrigenda under the title "Todai kinden-seido ni okeru handen no jittai" in his collection (see note 1), pp. 302–406.

3. Published by Sutō Yoshiyuki, "Dennin monjo no kenkyū," *Monumenta Serindica* 2, pp. 91–132, plates 3–11, also included with a few addenda and corrigenda under the title "Torohan shutsudo no dennin monjo kenkyū: Tōdai zenki no denninsei," in his collected volume *Tō-Sō shakai-keizai shi kenkyū* (Tokyo, 1965), pp. 1–104. See also Sutō's further article "Dennin monjo kenkyū hokō; toku ni kyōmei no ryokugō kisai ni tsuite," also in this collection, pp. 105–46.

4. Published by Fujieda Akira, "Tonkō no sōni-seki," *Tōhō gakuhō* (Kyoto) 29 (1959): 285–338; a few corrections to this article are found in his later "Toban shihaiki no Tonkō," *Tōhō gakuhō* (Kyoto) 31 (1961): 199–292, at 238, 264–66.

and various other types of population and land registers from the ninth and tenth centuries.[5] Even today, however, not all the documents which were discovered have been edited and published, and work is continuing.[6] But although we may expect various new discoveries in the years to come, it is well worthwhile at the present time to attempt a general summary of the problem, centering upon those surviving fragments of the Tunhuang household registers.

I will discuss first the formal provisions for a system of household registration. I will also describe the implementation of these provisions and how they were applied to the general population and to special groups. Then I will consider the physical condition of the surviving manuscripts and the information they contain about the size and makeup of the families of the region. I will also summarize the evidence from the registers concerning the presence of slaves *(nu-pi)* and bondsmen *(pu-ch'ü)* and their distribution among the families of the region. After noting the signs of the declining efficiency of the whole system of registration in the later years of Hsüan-tsung's reign (713–56), I will consider the information in the documents about the tax liability of the people of the area. Finally, I will present in brief some findings about local patterns of landholding.

The basic legal provisions concerning the household registers were incorporated in the Household Statutes *(hu-ling)*.[7]

> The household registers *(hu-chi)* are to be drawn up every three years. One copy is to be retained in the county, one sent to the prefecture, and one copy sent to the Board of Finance. Provision for the necessary writing materials—paper, brushes, colored wrappers, and rollers for the scrolls—should be provided by charging one cash per individual member included in a given register.

5. Published by Tamai, Naba, and Yamamoto (see Bibliographical Note) and by Thomas Thilo, "Fragmente chinesischer Haushaltsregister aus Tunhuang in der Berliner Turfan-Sammlung," *Mitteilungen des Instituts für Orientforschung* 14, no. 2 (1968): 303–13.

6. For an outline of postwar progress in this field, see Yamamoto Tatsurō's report in the *Proceedings of the Twenty-fifth International Congress of Orientalists in Moscow, 1960,* vol. 5 (Moscow, 1963), pp. 16–17; and D. C. Twitchett, *Financial Administration under the T'ang Dynasty* (Cambridge, 1963), pp. 6–9. A bibliography concerning work on household registers and related documents (done before 1963) is included in *Saiiki shutsudo kanbun-bunken bunrui-mokuroku shokō,* vol. 1, *Komonjo-rui* (Tokyo, 1964), pp. 155–99. After the Moscow conference there appeared a detailed article by Dohi Yoshikazu, "Tō-rei yori mitaru genson Tōdai koseki no kiso-teki kenkyū," *Tōyō gakuhō* 52, nos. 1, 2 (1969): 90–125, 213–64.

7. Reconstructed by Niida in his *Tōryō shūi* (Tokyo, 1933), pp. 239–44. For an excellent translation of the T'ang Household Statutes see D. C. Twitchett, *Financial Administration,* pp. 318–19.

The prefectural authorities should also annotate it as a "declaration" *(shou-shih)* or "register" *(chi)*.

The tax registers *(chi-chang)* should be compiled annually. The village headman *(li-cheng)* should scrutinize the declarations *(shou-shih)* from the people under his jurisdiction and enter in them the ages of household members.

The Japanese Yōrō Statutes, which were almost identical with the Taihō Statutes of 701, contain five articles dealing with registration: (1) on drawing up the tax registers *(keichō,* i.e. *chi-chang),* (2) on drawing up the household registers *(koseki,* i.e. *hu-chi),* (3) on the personal inspection by the local officials of the age and physical status of individuals, (4) on the dispatch of registers to the central government, and (5) on the periods for retention of registers on file in local and central government offices.[8] These, with a few modifications to suit the Japanese situation, followed the T'ang system very closely.

It has now been shown that a somewhat fuller reconstruction is possible from material included in edicts issued in 694, 708, and 730, which also show that the earliest version of these statutes, which had been closely similar to the Japanese Yōrō Statutes, underwent some degree of revision through subsequent edicts and codified regulations *(ko).*[9]

The provisions which can be extracted from these edicts read as follows:

The household registers *(hu-chi)* are to be compiled every third year. Beginning in the first ten days of the first month, the county authorities should examine the declarations *(shou-shih)* and tax registers *(chi-chang)* and take them to the prefecture. In accordance with the Ordinances *(shih)* a separate scroll should be compiled for each locality *(hsiang).* All should be made up in triplicate and the joins between the individual sheets of paper inscribed "Register of——County——Prefecture——year." The prefectural seal should be stamped over the name of the prefecture, and the county seal over that of the county. Their presentation should be completed by the thirtieth day of the third month. One copy should always be mounted with a yellow wrapper and sent to the Department of State Affairs. The prefecture and county

---

8. *Ryō-no-gige* (Shintei zōhō Kokushi taikei edition), pp. 96–98. For a translation of these provisions in full see Hans Adalbert Dettmer, *Die Steuergesetzgebung der Nara-Zeit* (Wiesbaden, 1959), pp. 86–90.

9. The further reconstruction was by Niida in his *Tō-Sō hōritsu monjo no kenkyū,* pp. 654–61.

should each keep one copy. The paper, brushes, and colored wrappers required should be paid for by charging one cash for each person included in a given register. Each of the households should have already had its household category fixed the year before the year of compilation, and this should be entered at the foot of the register. Where there are any new households formed by dividing households which are to be newly appended, these must be entered in appropriate order after the old households.

All the registers due for dispatch to the Department of State Affairs should be sent in together with the cloth for the *yung* and *tiao* taxes from the prefecture concerned. If the *yung* and *tiao* from the prefecture are not paid in to the capital, carriers may be hired *(ku-chüeh)* to transport them, the necessary costs of carriage *(chüeh-chih)* being provided from official funds.

All household registers, tax registers, and declarations at the prefectures and counties should be kept on file until five subsequent ones have been compiled. The registers sent to the Department of State Affairs should be preserved until nine subsequent ones have been sent in.[10]

The corresponding articles of the Japanese Yōrō Statutes show some modifications to bring them into line with the rather different structure of local and central administration in Japan, but in general these sections of the Japanese statutes were a faithful copy of the provisions in Chinese codified law.[11] There is thus every reason to suppose that those sections, the corresponding parts to which in the T'ang statutes have not been reconstructed—for example, the section referring to the reexamination and checking of the contents of the registers after they had been sent to the capital—were also almost certainly included in the original seventh-century T'ang statutes.

As we have seen above, the tax registers *(chi-chang)* were compiled annually and sent to the capital, where they were used as the basic data for the coming year's financial calculations by the Department of Public Revenue *(Tu-chih)* of the Board of Finance. As the basic material for the compilation of the tax registers, it was the rule for the headman of each *li (li cheng)* to demand a "declaration" *(shou-shih)* or statement from the head of each household under his jurisdiction. Thus the actual basis of the tax registers was the factual information reported to

10. Ibid., pp. 239–44; Twitchett, *Financial Administration*, pp. 318–19.

11. For example, registration, carried out at three-year intervals in China, was carried out only every six years in Japan, to coincide with the six-yearly redistribution of lands under the *handen* system.

the authorities by each individual head of household, and in the case of any household within the *li* which was absent, the headman would simply recopy the entry in the former register, adding an annotation giving the reason for their absence.

This of course was merely the letter of the law. But as the vast majority of the farming population was illiterate, we may suppose that the declarations were not actually written out by the household head, but copied down on his behalf either by the *li* headman or by a clerk from the county yamen. The household registers, which were supposed to be compiled by every prefectural administration in the whole empire every third year between the first and third months, were also compiled upon the basis of these declarations and tax registers.

Many points remain unclear concerning the precise differences between the three types of registers and their exact interrelationship. If we examine the surviving registers, there are several that are inscribed "register *(chi)* of such and such a year"; there is a single example that is inscribed as a declaration, but not a single example of a tax register. According to the edict of 708, which probably incorporates a ruling from the statutes, the household registers, tax registers, and declarations were to be retained on file by the county and prefecture until five subsequent registers had been compiled, that is, fifteen years for the household registers and five years for the tax registers and declarations. Since all three documents were made in succession, the one from the other, their contents must have been very intimately connected. The surviving declaration, which bears the seals of a government-general *(tu-tu-fu)* and a county, is certainly not the original declaration made by the heads of households, but is a clean copy made later by the clerks at the prefectural yamen. If, however, we examine its contents, they correspond exactly with those of the household registers. We may suppose then that the declarations, the contents of which were virtually identical with those of the household registers, were compiled annually by the local authorities of the prefecture and county, who made up the *hu-chi* household registers on the basis of these declarations for dispatch to the central government (with copies retained by the prefectural and county yamens).

The "locality register" *(hsiang-chang)* is described in the following passage from the "Financial Monograph" of the *New T'ang History:* "In the village *(li)* they had the declaration *(shou-shih)*. At the end of each year they reported the ages of all individuals and the extent of their land and compiled a 'locality register'. . . "[12] The "locality

12. *HTS* (Po–na edition) 51.2a.

register" would thus appear to have been a popular term for the declarations described above.

The tax registers, on the other hand, were compiled annually and played a vital role as the basis upon which all taxes and impositions were collected and reported to the Department of Public Revenue. The latter totaled the information which they contained on population, numbers of taxable adults, expected quotas of *tsu, yung*, and *tiao* taxes, and so on, this information being of crucial importance for the financial calculations of the central government.[13]

At one time it was thought that those registration documents that recorded liability to taxes were tax registers *(chi-chang)*, while those that listed only each household's individual members and its lands were household registers *(hu-chi)*. But the register dated 701, which is clearly inscribed as a household register, contains entries on liability to *tsu* and *tiao* taxes, so that it is not possible to differentiate between *hu-chi* and *chi-chang* solely on the grounds that one included entries on tax liability and the other did not.[14]

It was the rule that the household registers were to be made up into a single scroll for each locality *(hsiang,* i.e. an administrative and fiscal unit of five hundred households), and the surviving registers down to the K'ai-yüan period (713–42) bear the inscription "Register of such-and-such *hsiang.*" But the household registers and *shou-shih* from the T'ien-pao period (742–52) onward are inscribed "such-and-such *hsiang,* such-and-such *li*" and it seems possible that it became the practice also for the registers to be made into a separate scroll for each *li* (i.e. a smaller unit of one hundred households).[15]

Preliminary to the drawing up of the household registers, two detailed procedures were carried out, the personal inspection of the age and physical condition of individuals *(mao-ting)* and the settlement of

13. The contemporary Japanese *keichō,* which were the equivalent of the T'ang *chi-chang,* incorporated two types of documents, one giving the total sums and numbers involved for the district as a whole, the other *(keichō rekimei)* listing all individual households and their members. Very probably, in the case of the T'ang *chi-chang,* too, there were two types of documents, the one in a formal format identical with the household register and the *shou-shih* declaration, and the other totaling up the required information contained in these registers for dispatch by the local authorities to the Department of Public Revenue.

14. Yamamoto Tatsurō, "Tonkō hakken no Daisoku gannen seki to *Kan-sho keihōshi,*" in *Suzuki Shun kyōju kanreki kinen Tōyōshi ronsō* (Tokyo, 1964), pp. 713–32, at p. 718.

15. Since the *hu-chi* were kept on file in three separate places—in the Board of Finance at the Capital, in the prefecture, and in the county—it was a rule that they should be compiled in triplicate. But on three occasions, in 744, 747, and 750, they were compiled with an extra fourth copy to be retained in the branch of the Board of Finance in Loyang. See *THY* (Kuo-hsüeh chi-pen ts'ung-shu edition) 85.1560, *CTS* (Po-na edition) 48.3b, *TFYK* (Ming edition of 1642) 486.17a, 18b.

household categories *(ting-hu)*. The personal inspection of individuals was the responsibility of the county magistrate and was carried out in groups. (The procedure was called *t'uan-mao* or *mao-yüeh*.) The laws concerning registration with regard to age were better developed under the Sui and T'ang than they had been under the Southern Dynasties, and it is clear that the number of persons inscribed in the registers increased greatly.[16]

Under the T'ang the personal inspection was carried out annually, although for a few years after 741 it was restricted to once in three years.[17] The established convention regarding the ages which were to receive special attention in the inspection specified the "five nines" (i.e. for men, 19, 49, 59, 79, 89, and for women, 79 and 89).[18] But particularly careful attention was paid to young men of between fifteen and twenty. When a man became an adolescent *(chung-nan)* at sixteen or an adult *(ting-nan)* at twenty or twenty-one, this affected his liability for taxation, corvée service, military service, and the right to receive an allocation of land. Thus decision of these age categories was particularly important. When one reached the age of fifty there were some cases in which one was released from military service and so on, while when one reached the age of sixty, as an old man *(lao-nan)* he lost the greater part of the rights and obligations of an adult male. Eighty and ninety were ages at which one became entitled to a tax-exempt attendant adult and thus entailed the granting of tax exemption to another member of the household. That attention was concentrated upon young men in the fifteen-to-twenty age group is confirmed by the cases of revision of age that appear in the extant fragments of registers, seven out of eight of which are concerned with men aged from sixteen to twenty-one.[19]

In addition to fixing the age category and ascertaining the actual age of persons, the personal inspection was also used as an opportunity to determine the various grades of disability *(ts'an-chi,* "partially disabled"; *fei-chi,* "seriously disabled"; *tu-chi,* "totally disabled"), each of which gave entitlement to a reduction in or even total exemption from taxation and other liabilities.

Under the T'ang, household categories *(hu-teng)* were established

16. *Sui-shu* (Po-na edition) 24.11b–12a. Cf. Etienne Balazs, *Le traité économique du Souei-chou* (Leiden, 1953), p. 154, notes 139–40.

17. *THY* 85.1555; *TFYK* 486.16b.

18. *TLT* (Konoe edition) 30.34b.

19. Cf. Ikeda, "Tonkō hakken Tō Taireki yonnen shujitsu zankan ni tsuite" (see Bibliographical Note), pp. 182, 186; other examples are found in *Tun-huang tzu-liao,* I (see Bibliographical Note), pp. 17, 23.

from 636 onward to divide all households into nine grades, which were determined by the county magistrate on the basis of each household's property, in advance of the compilation of the household registers.

The household category which one held determined the amount of household levy *(hu-shui)* to which he was liable and had an effect upon the selective impositions *(ch'ai-k'o)*, which determined both the load of corvée service and military service which one had to bear, and the order in which one was called upon to serve. Fixing the household categories was thus a matter of crucial importance. During the T'ang, many edicts prohibited locally influential people and merchants from offering bribes to the local officers so as to have their household category fixed low in their own interest.[20] In the period 741–45 the system was simplified by a special edict.[21] This measure, like the cutting down of the personal inspection to once in three years, is evidence of the general relaxation of administrative policies in the last years of Hsüan-tsung.[22]

If we look for evidence of this in the surviving household registers, we find that households of the ninth grade *(hsia-hsia-hu)* are by far the most numerous, followed by those of the eighth *(hsia-chung-hu)*. Households of the seventh and higher categories are very rare. It also appears that there was a change in the method of entering the household category in the registers in the first years of the eighth century because there is no notation whatever of household category in the registers dating from 701 and before, whereas this is always noted in the registers dating from 713 and later.

Once the tax register was compiled, it was taken to the capital in the fifth month of each year by a special envoy, the *chi-chang shih*. The totals of registered households and individuals memorialized to the throne by the Board of Finance on the twenty-sixth day of the fifth month 725, for example, are based upon the tax registers that had arrived for that year.[23] The *hu-chi* household registers were sent to the capital in the carts carrying the cloth paid in for the *yung* and *tiao* taxes. In those prefectures of southern China that did not pay *yung* and *tiao* to the capital it was permitted to hire special couriers to transport the registers to the capital, the cost being met out of official funds.

The above is a general account of the system of registration in so far

20. *THY* 85.1557, an edict of 730; *TFYK* 486.15a.

21. *TTCLC* (Commercial Press edition) 113.589.

22. See a memorial by Yang Yen in *CTS* 18.8a, *THY* 83.1535, *TFYK* 488.2a, *HTS* 52.1a. See also Twitchett, *Financial Administration*, p. 157.

23. *CTS* 8.14a.

as it affected the population as a whole. Some categories of persons, however, were registered in special ways. The registers of the imperial clan were kept in the Court of Imperial Family Affairs (*Tsung-cheng-ssu*).[24] In the case of officially owned slaves, the office to which they were attached drew up two copies of a register each year, one of which was retained by the office and the other sent to the Department of State Affairs.[25] The household registers of *kuan-hu* official bondsmen, who performed recurring turns of duty for the office to which they were attached, were naturally compiled and kept by that office.

The most important group of people falling outside the normal state system were the Taoist and Buddhist monks and nuns who, having left their lay families and secular society, were listed on special registers. This had long been a problem. In the Western Chin period (317–420) the story had circulated among Buddhists that Huan Hsüan, who had made an attempt to round up those who had taken refuge in the monasteries to evade corvée, showed his special veneration for Hui-yüan's community on Lu-shan by exempting them from his investigation.[26] In the sutra *Jen-wang Po-jo-ching*, popular under the Southern Dynasties, it says, "Anyone who compiles his own official register or who performs service (corvée) for the officials, is not one of our disciples. These are laws for soldiers or slaves."[27] And in the Buddhist community regulations which were practiced under the Northern Dynasties it says, "The compilation of official registers for monks and nuns is from the very outset contrary to the correct law. From now on you are not to continue this practice."[28] Although the Buddhists objected to being registered by the temporal authorities, we can assume from the fact that such orders were issued to the Buddhist community that the monks had in fact been registered by the authorities.

In T'ang times the system of registration for monks was designed to catch still more strictly those who had left lay life. The basic rule was that every third year the prefecture and county were to produce a register of monks and nuns, of which they were to keep one copy, the second copy going to the Court of Diplomatic Reception (*Hung-lu-ssu*) and the third copy going to the Department of National Sacrifices

24. *TLT* 16.2b.

25. Cf. a memorial from the Department of Convicts under the Board of Justice dated 779, *THY* 86.1570.

26. *Hung-ming chi* (*SPTK* edition) 12.34a; *T* 52.85a.

27. *T* 8.833c.

28. Tsukamoto Zenryū, "Tonkō-bon Shina Bukkyō kyōdan seiki," *Ishihama sensei koki kinen Tōyōgaku ronsō* (Osaka, 1958), pp. 301–324, at p. 310.

(Tz'u-pu) of the Board of Rites.[29] It was also a rule that Korean or Japanese monks who had resided in China for nine years were to be entered in these registers,[30] which shows how thorough-going the registration of monks was. However, in 749 an edict was promulgated under which every prefecture or government-general was to register Taoist and Buddhist monks and nuns only at ten-year intervals,[31] after which the policy was no longer strictly enforced, and the reporting of monks and nuns to the central authorities fell into disuse. Because of this abuse, in 830, following a memorial from the Department of National Sacrifices, it was ordered that the registers of monks should once again be compiled every five years and reported as before.[32]

After the An Lu-shan Rebellion the entire local administrative machinery of early T'ang times became more and more lax, and the rules concerning registration were certainly no exception.[33] The rules for special types of registration, such as those for monks and nuns also fell into decay.

As we noted earlier the basic financial structure of the early T'ang was that a piece of land was distributed to every adult male, who in return paid a fixed amount of *tsu, yung,* and *tiao* taxes. From the end of the seventh century, however, this system slowly came to a standstill, and after the An Lu-shan and subsequent rebellions of the mid-eighth century, the whole system had reached such a state of decay that nothing could be done to retrieve the situation. As a result of the new independence of the provincial governors, the establishment of the *liang-shui* tax system, the spread of the use of professional paid troops, and the development of the monopolies in salt, tea, and so on, the whole machinery of government of the earlier period, which was based on the strict control that the central government was able to exercise over the individual, was transformed in every respect; and the great importance of the registration system was diminished. The reason for this was that

29. *TLT* 4.46b. Concerning the census registration of Buddhist monks and nuns in the T'ang, see Michihata Ryōshū, *Tōdai Bukkyōshi no kenkyū* (Kyoto, 1957), pp. 73–80; Kenneth Ch'en, *Buddhism in China: A Historical Survey* (Princeton, N.J., 1964), pp. 244–45. In the early T'ang period the Court of Reception *(Hung-lu-ssu)* kept the registers of Buddhist and Taoist monks and nuns. After an edict of 737, registers of Taoist monks and nuns in the capitals belonged to the Court of Imperial Family Affairs *(Tsung-cheng-ssu)*, and those of the Buddhists to the Department of National Sacrifices *(Tz'u-pu)*. See *TLT* 16.24b–25a.

30. *THY* 49.863.

31. *TT* (Shih T'ung edition) 23.136a.

32. *TFYK* 474.14b–15b.

33. In a letter to a Chief Minister, sent (before 796) by a high official, Lu Ch'ang-yüan, it says, "The Board of Finance *(Hu-pu)* has no census registers and maps (at the present time)." See *T'ang wen-ts'ui (SPTK* edition) 79.4a; *CTW* (Imperial edition) 510.3a.

there was no longer any necessity to increase or decrease tax liability in response to each change in an individual's circumstances, for the overall quota of tax for each prefecture was fixed in advance by the central government and was apportioned out by the prefecture or county over the population under their jurisdiction. This paralleled the tendency for the part played in the overall pattern of revenues by direct taxation, which had previously been levied upon every household, to be reduced and replaced by ever increasing revenues derived either from monopoly taxes or by taxes on trade, which taxed the individual only indirectly, through the circulation of commodities.[34]

The most powerful of the provincial governors, at the same time, never reported their population figures at all, and although the Household Statutes and the associated sections of the Regulations and Ordinances remained nominally in effect, they were in reality dead letters. Thus, after the latter half of the eighth century the previous strictly centralized registration system fell into decay, and there evolved various new forms of registers, of both land and population, which were more appropriate to the new administrative situation.

Following this general description of the T'ang system of financial administration, the importance of the household registers in this system, and the changes brought about by major developments and great military events in the early seventh century, I want to turn to a discussion of the surviving household registers and the information they yield about local society in the T'ang.

More than ten T'ang household registers were among the enormous collection of religious scriptures and various other types of literature and documents discovered at Tunhuang. Most of these are now in the Stein Collection of the British Museum and the Fonds Pelliot Touen-houang in the Bibliothèque Nationale. In addition to these household registers many other types of documents connected with the registration of land and of population, and dating for the most part from the eighth to the tenth centuries, have been found among the Tunhuang manuscripts. All these documents are connected, naturally enough, with the prefectural administration of Sha-chou, under whose jurisdiction the Tunhuang area came during T'ang and early Sung times.

In addition to these, several dozen more fragments of household registers were excavated from the ruins of temples or from burial sites

34. On the transitional character of the period after the An Lu-shan Rebellion, especially concerning financial administration, see the discussion by Twitchett, *Financial Administration*, pp. 34–65, 109–20.

at various places in the Turfan Depression. Those found by the Stein, von le Coq, and Otani expeditions are now in London, Berlin, and Kyoto respectively. These documents from Turfan, unlike the Tun-huang manuscripts which had been deliberately stored away, are for the most part very small fragments dug up in the course of excavations. They date mostly from the late seventh and first half of the eighth centuries and are almost all connected with the local administration of Hsi-chou (Chiao-ho chün), which governed the Turfan area. An ex-ception is a register of requests for land *(ch'ing-t'ien pu)* from Sha-chou (i.e. Tunhuang), which was among the manuscript fragments discovered at Yarchoto in the Turfan Basin.[35] Thus, although there are a few minor exceptions to the rule that the extant documents were discovered in the place to which their contents refer,[36] all the household registers and related documents discovered down to the present time are from Sha-chou or from Hsi-chou. Not a single item referring to any other area has yet been discovered. When we consider the vast size of the T'ang empire, with its roughly three hundred prefectures, the limitation of the extant material to two small border prefectures on the northwestern frontier is a factor that must continually be borne in mind. Further-more, none of the household registers that have been discovered are preserved in their complete form. The ones from Hsi-chou are tiny fragments of paper, mostly of a few lines or only of a few characters, only the register of 716 from Liu-chung county being a comparatively large document. Many of the others are practically impossible to identify, and many may be small pieces of the same document.

Before discussing the contents of the registers, we must again em-phasize that these documents are of very limited extent. Not only are they confined to the two prefectures of Sha-chou and Hsi-chou, but even the largest document, that of 747 from Tunhuang, contains the entries for no more than fifteen complete households. Thus when we employ these registers as evidence of the actual state of the contem-porary household and family systems, we must never lose sight of the strict limitations imposed both by the fact that they are such a small sample and by their very nature.[37]

35. See Thilo, "Fragmente chinesischer Haushaltsregister" (note 5), p. 308.

36. There are also two small fragments of household registers from Hsi-chou among the Tunhuang manuscripts in the Stein Collection, but it has not yet been ascertained whether these were in fact discovered in Tunhuang, or whether they too were excavated in the Turfan area and were later included among the Tunhuang documents by mistake.

37. Many years ago, for example, Naba Toshisada concluded, basing himself on the fact that the average number of members in the households included in the 747 register from Tun-huang is as much as ten persons, that the overall national population statistics included in the Geographical Monographs *(Ti-li-chih)* of the two T'ang Standard Histories and other sources,

According to the data that we can extract from the nearly contemporary registers of selective service from Sha-chou, which list the male members of several hundred households, the average household included slightly less than two adult male members, from which it would be reasonable to infer that the average total number of household members was between five and six, and that there is thus generally no contradiction between the average household size as shown in these types of registration document and that which can be calculated from the statistics preserved in the Standard Histories.

If we take an overall view of the various types of register surviving from the Western Liang, Western Wei, and the T'ang, although these have only a limited statistical value on account of the smallness of the sample, we can still clearly perceive that the basic form of family they portray is identical with the small, peasant "nuclear family" that was already almost universal in the Han period. The "extended household" including collateral kin was, however, by no means rare, and there are households listed in which uncles and aunts, the spouses of brothers and sisters together with their children, or the close kin of the wife or the head of household, and so on are entered in the same register.

The provisions on households and marriage in the T'ang Code forbade the children to divide the household during the lifetime of either of their parents, and this ban also included the mandatory period of mourning after their parents' death.[38] Within the limits of the evidence in the extant registers, there are no instances where the children or grandchildren had divided the household while either parent was still living. After the death of the parents there are cases both of splitting the household and also of grown-up brothers and their families living together, but it seems likely that it was the normal general tendency for the household to be divided into separate nuclear family units.

Of the 388 households listed in the registers of selective service from the T'ien-pao period (742–56), leaving aside four the size of which is unknown, 45 percent (176 households) included only one male adult; 32 percent (124 households), two; 14 percent (55 households), three; and only 8 percent (29 households), four or more adult male members.

which give an average household size of roughly five persons, are far too small and that their value as historical material is therefore dubious. But this view does not take into account such factors as the inclusion in these registers of large numbers of females who did not actually reside with the family and the fact that this particular fragment happens to include the registers of the households of a number of influential persons, including some holding honorific rank, whose households were abnormally large. See Naba, "Seishi ni kisai seraretaru Dai Tō Tempō-jidai no kosū to kōsū to no kankei ni tsukite," pp. 324–29.

38. *Code* (Kuo-hsüeh chi-pen ts'ung-shu edition), *ch.* 12, Art. 155, 156, p. 108.

On this evidence we can see that slightly less than half of the people lived in simple nuclear households with a single adult male member. Of the 124 households with two adult male members, 63 were households in which the father and an adult son lived together, 52 were households in which brothers lived together, and 9 show other combinations. Of the 55 households with three male adults living together, 27 consisted of a father and his sons, 14 were households in which brothers lived together, and 14 represent other combinations. If we examine the kin included within the households listed in these registers of selective services, households which include collateral relatives in addition to brothers form barely 10 percent of the total. These data thus reflect the actual condition of the small nuclear family as it existed under the legal system which forbade division of the household during the lifetime of the parents.

Another fact that deserves attention is the existence of a correlation between the actual category of the household *(hu-teng)* and the size of the household. If we again examine the data in the same registers of selective service, the number of adult male members in each household may be analyzed as follows:

Household Category	Average Male Members
Sixth grade *(chung-hsia-hu)*	4.25
Seventh grade *(hsia-shang-hu)*	2.90
Eighth grade *(hsia-chung-hu)*	2.40
Ninth grade *(hsia-hsia-hu)*	1.77

The distribution of these categories of household, as they appear in the same registers of selective services, shows that more than half were in the ninth grade; those in the eighth and seventh grades were only a half and a quarter respectively as numerous, while sixth-grade households were only about 1 percent of the total.[39]

Households of the fifth and higher grades were mostly those of serving ranking officials *(p'in-kuan)*, which were excluded from liability to selective service and selective impositions. Such high-ranking households thus would not figure at all in these registers. But, even so, their numbers certainly cannot have been great.

Consequently, we may see that while in the households of the lowest grade there was a striking predominance of small nuclear families, the form of family in the households of the eighth and higher grades, and

39. See Nishimura, "Tōdai Tonkō sakabo o tsūjite mita Tō kindensei jidai no yōeki seido," pp. 642–48; Ikeda On, "Hasseki chūyō ni okeru Tonkō no Sogudo-jin shūraku," *Yūrajia bunka kenkyū* 1 (1965): 49–92, at pp. 70–72.

particularly in the "medium-grade" (fourth to sixth grades, *chung-teng*) and "higher-grade" (first to third grades, *shang-teng*) households, which were predominantly households of officials or members of the wealthier classes, was still quite frequently the extended family including collateral relatives. This evidence conforms closely with what we may infer from other materials.[40]

The source materials which give us the least distorted data upon the actual state of the family during this period are perhaps the registers of grants of grain made by the Commissioner for Revenue and Public Lands of Ho-hsi province *(Ho-hsi chih-tu ying-t'ien shih)* during the latter half of the eighth century.[41] The surviving portion includes only twenty-nine households totaling 166 individuals, but nevertheless includes *all* family members, irrespective of age and sex, including newly born children who are noted as "newly entered" *(hsin)* and slaves. In practically every instance it gives the individual's relationship with the head of household, his name, and his age. Since this document was drawn up in order to make an actual grant of a specified quantity of grain to every individual in accordance with his age, sex, and personal status (i.e. free or bondsman), we may assume that it contains practically no deliberate omissions or false entries. I have tabulated the data in tables 4.1 and 4.2.

If we take an overall view of tables 4.1 and 4.2, we can get a rough idea of the standard form of family structure among the common people of this period, which does not conflict with the evidence that we can derive from the numbers of male adults listed in the households of the lowest grades in the registers of selective service. But one fact shown by these documents is certainly quite abnormal: there are extremely few females and almost no males in the age group sixteen to thirty. This may show either the influence of a drastic reduction in the birth rate for a decade or more (possibly the result of war or perhaps of an epidemic) or perhaps that the households headed by persons in this age category were included in those parts of the register that do not survive. I personally feel the latter explanation is the more probable. However, in spite of the fact that its material shows a striking distortion of the age-distribution curve, this manuscript certainly provides basic data of the greatest importance on the structure of the family.

There is no space here to pursue in detail the very important data on family structure, marriage, average age, and so on, which are contained

40. Moriya Mitsuo, *Rikuchō monbatsu no ichi kenkyū* (Tokyo, 1951), pp. 143–48.

41. These are in the possession of the Shanghai Wen-wu kuan-li wei-yüan-hui. See *Tun-huang tzu-liao*, I, pp. 114–19, and the review by Ikeda (see Bibliographical Note), p. 120.

Table 4.1. Family Details in Grain-Distribution Registers Compiled by the Commissioner for Revenue and Public Lands of Ho-hsi Province

Head of Family	Wife	Father	Mother	Son	Daughter	Wife of Son	Younger Brother	Wife of Younger Brother	Nephew	Sister	Grandson	Slave		Total Number in Family
												Male	Female	
T'ang Ting-hsing	1													2
An T'ing-hui	1			4	1									7
So Wen-tuan	1				2									4
Li Kuang-chün	1			5	2							2	2	13
Lo Yüan-chün	1													2
Ch'en Ch'ung-chih	1				3									5
Ma Chiu-niang (female)				2	2									5
Ts'ao Chin-yü	1				3		1	1						7
Wang Tzu-chin	1		1				1			2		1	1	8
Chang Yüan-hsing	1			1		2					4			9
K'ang Ching-hsien	1			2	4					1				9
Fêng Mao-nu	1			4	1									7
Ts'ao Tien-ch'ang	1													2
Chiang Chung-hsü	1		1	1										4
Hsü Yu-yen	1		1				1	1						5
Kao Chia-fu	1			1	1									4
Chang Ch'in	1			1	2									5
Liang Sheng-yün	1													2
Sung Kuang-hua	1			4	1	1						2	2	12
Wu T'ing-kuang	1		1	4	4	1	1	1	1		1	1	1	18
Ts'ao Feng-chin	1													2
Chang Feng-chang	1			1	1									4
Shih Hsiu-lin	1				2		1	1						6
Chang K'ung (female)				1	2									4
Kuo Huai-te	1			2	1									5
An T'ing-yü	1			1	1									4
Chang Ling-chiao	1			1	1									4
Shih Hsiu-chin	1			1										3
Ling-hu Ssu-chung	1	1					1							4
Total 29 families (2 female)	27	1	4	36	34	4	6	4	1	3	5	6	6	166

in the household registers and similar documents. But something should be said about the slaves and other bondsmen who played a significant role in the social history of the period. It was long ago discovered that, among various types of private slaves and bondsmen, male and female "retainers" (pu-ch'ü) appear in the household registers.[42] Pu-ch'ü

42. See Niida, Tō-Sō hōritsu monjo no kenkyū, pp. 738-44.

Table 4.2. Numbers of Age Groups in the Same Register

Age	1–5	6–10	11–15	16–20	21–25	26–30	31–35	36–40	41–45	46–50	51–55	56–60	61–65	66–70	71–75	76–80	81–85	Total
Male	22	8	10	2	0	1	8	6	9	5		1	1			1	1	75
Female	16	12	7	4	5	1	12	10	5	1		2	2			1		78
Slave {Male	3	3																6
Slave {Female	1						3		1			1						6
Total	42	23	17	6	5	2	23	16	15	6	0	4	3	0	0	2	1	165

appear in a fragmentary household register of 728 from Hsi-chou. Slaves *(nu-pi)* appear in the declaration *(shou-shih)* of 769 from Sha-chou and in household registers dating from the K'ai-yüan and T'ien-pao periods from Hsi-chou. The proportions of slaves to free men in the various registers are as follows: in the Western Wei tax register there is only a single slave in a total of more than 50 persons; in the 747 register from Sha-chou, not a single slave in a total of 163 persons; and in the 769 declaration *(shou-shih)*, four slaves out of a total of 87 persons. In all the surviving registers from Hsi-chou there are five slaves (in addition to seven *pu-ch'ü*) out of 65 persons; in the grain-distribution registers mentioned above there are twelve slaves out of a total of 166 persons. Thus if we look through the material from Sha-chou, it appears that throughout the period slaves accounted for only an insignificant percentage of the population, while in the more remote area of Hsi-chou the proportion of nonfree persons was much higher, probably nearly 20 percent. The data are very scanty, but the surviving fragments of registers from Hsi-chou are comparatively numerous, and it seems reasonable to conclude that slaves and other bondsmen were more numerous in Turfan than in Sha-chou, which was far more a part of China proper. In Hsi-chou, which was more exclusively dependent upon trade and commerce, it would appear that class-differentiation was more highly developed.

Generally speaking, most of the peasant population held no slaves at all, but where slaves were held it is most common for a household to have not one single slave but rather two, three, or more. Consequently, it is significant from the socioeconomic viewpoint that there was a clear-cut distinction between the ordinary peasant household on the one hand, and a more prosperous slaveholding stratum on the other. This is borne out by the fact that the slave-owning group tended to consist of households with more family members and a more complex structure.

Another matter that deserves some mention is whether the household registers are trustworthy evidence of actual changes in population.

In the draft register *(ts'ao-an)* of 722 a note is appended to the entry
of one family, comprising a wife, two sons, and a daughter, to the effect
that, in accordance with an official order *(fu)* dated 719, xii, 13, it
had been entered in conjunction with the register of their ancestral
head of household. Was this a case of a family that had been residing
separately and had been entered on a separate household register being
put back in or appended to the register of its original household? Or
was it a case of legitimizing the position of a family that had been illegally entered on a separate register while in fact residing together with
the parent household? The truth of the matter is not clear, but in any
case it tells us clearly that the household register was carefully kept up
to date by the prefectural and county authorities. Similarly, in a
fragment from Hsi-chou there is a note that in accordance with an edict
of 722, names of deceased persons should be removed from the registers.

Table 4.3. Sex Distribution of Individuals in Sha-chou Registers

Register[a]	Date	Households	Males	Females	Males: Females	Average Size of Household
1	701	5	6	7	1:1.2	2.6
2	716	7	8	10	1:1.2	2.5
3	722	7	15	17	1:1.1	4.5
4	744	1	1	3	1:3	4.0
5	747	1	2	7	1:3.5	9.0
6	747	15	39	124	1:3.2	9.9
7	769	16	22	17	1:0.8	2.8

[a]For typeset versions of these registers, see Ikeda On, "Chūgoku kodai sekichō shūroku"
(see Bibliographical Note), as follows: no. 1, pp. 85–90; no, 2, pp. 94–100; no. 3, pp. 100–
08; no. 4, pp. 113–15; no. 5, pp. 115–16; no. 6, pp. 116–47; no. 7 (a *shou-shih*), pp. 147–67.

It is of course well known that Yü-wen Jung's policy of reregistering
vagrant households, which was begun in 721, endeavored to correct
the existing deficiencies in the household registers and to bring the
vagrant households *(t'ao-hu, etc.)* into account.[43] Even in the register of
715 from Sha-chou there are signs of the disorder in the earlier household registers persisting into the early K'ai-yüan period (713–42)
in the form of such annotations as "fell into hands of foreign tribes
699," "entire household fled 707," "entire household fled 712." The
above-mentioned readjustment and removal of dead entries was of
course carried out to bring the registers into line with the actual situation; and this proves the continued vigor of the state authority, which

43. See Suzuki Shun, "Ubun Yū no kakko ni tsuite," *Wada Hakase kanreki kinen Tōyōshi
ronsō* (Tokyo, 1951), pp. 329–44; Twitchett, *Financial Administration,* pp. 14–15, 27, 107–09,
221–24; Tonami Mamoru, "Tō no ritsuryō-taisei to Ubun Yū no kakko," *Tōhō gakuhō*
(Kyoto) 41 (1970): 263–88.

was able to control the population closely through the medium of the household registration system, both at the prefectural and county levels.

In contrast to this, from the last years of the K'ai-yüan period onward the registration system became more and more lax. Striking evidence of this is the appearance of excessive numbers of women in the registers from the T'ien-pao period (see table 4.3). Because the register of 747 from Lung-le hsiang, with its 163 individuals (of whom no less than 124 are women), is the largest extant continuous register, there has been considerable discussion on the problem of the excess proportion of women it contains. This phenomenon has been explained as the result of falsely reporting males as females in order to evade taxation.[44] Another suggested interpretation is that the men left their actual families to live in the towns to pursue commerce and trade, leaving their womenfolk to reside in the villages.[45]

However, if we compare these figures with the data from the registers of selective service with their very numerous entries and with the very reliable registers of grain distribution, the abnormal and unnatural nature of the 747 register from Sha-chou becomes apparent. If we examine the entries in all the household registers from the Western Liang and Western Wei down to 722, the numbers of males and females are roughly equal. Again, in the registers after 758 there is no sign of an excessive proportion of females.

The notes in the 747 register on new entries and changes of entries made in the three years preceding are as follows:

			Total	Male	Female
Entered in	a)	newly born	17	8	9
Register	b)	registered as previously omitted	16	4 (of whom 1 boy)	12 (of whom 3 girls, 8 wives, 1 widow)
Removed from Register		by decease	13	11 (of whom 6 boys, 3 youths, 1 adult, 1 guardsman)	2 (both widows)

---

44. Niida, *Tō-Sō hōritsu monjo no kenkyū*, pp. 750–52; Suzuki Shun, "Tō no kindensei to sōyō-chōsei to no kankei ni tsuite," *Tōa* 8, no. 4 (1935): at p. 105.

45. Koga Noboru, "Tonkō koseki no ichi-dan jū-jo ni tsuite," *Kodaigaku* 12, no. 2/3 (1966): 109–23.

We can thus see that there was a very special trend here, a tendency for boys and youths to be removed from the register as soon as they died, while at the same time wives and other women who had previously remained unregistered were being entered in the registers. As a result, over the three-year period 744–47 the proportion of men to women in this register decreased from 1:2.76 to 1:3.2. If we extend this trend backward over the previous decade or more, it would have produced the excessive disproportion in favor of women that is shown in the 747 registers, even if there had been an equal sex distribution at the beginning of the period.

The situation in 760, which we can infer from the date in the *shou-shih* of 769, shows a slight persistence of the imbalance of women in excess of men. But, in general, the strikingly excessive proportion of women in the 747 registers from Sha-chou must be considered a special phenomenon restricted to the later years of Hsüan-tsung's reign, the period from about 735 to 756. Thus the phenomenon cannot be explained as being due either to false registration to evade tax or to male household members being absent to engage in commerce, for these causes were not limited to the T'ien-pao period (742–56). My own view is that we must seek the fundamental cause in the substantial relaxation and decay of the procedures for drawing up the registers which occurred from the end of the K'ai-yüan period (741) onward.[46] As I have already mentioned, from the end of the K'ai-yüan period Hsüan-tsung allowed the relaxation of the registration system as part of the general relaxation of administrative procedures.[47] While on the one hand population steadily increased, the money for the production of the registers was misapplied to decorate the buildings of the Board of Finance.[48] While the registers became more and more elegantly produced, the accuracy of their contents underwent a progressive deterioration. For example, in the register of 747, in striking contrast to the large numbers of women entered in the register who had "formerly been omitted," and to the conspicuous cases of one man with two or three wives, there is not a single instance of a woman *removed* from her original register through being married into another household. This meant that married women might well appear in the registers both of their original families *and* of the households into which they

46. See Ikeda, "Tonkō hakken Tō Taireki yonnen shujitsu zankan ni tsuite," pp. 177–87.

47. In his famous memorial of 780 (*CTS* 118.8a, *THY* 83.1535, *TFYK* 488.2a, *HTS* 52.1a), Yang Yen specifically relates this administrative relaxation to Hsüan-tsung's infatuation with Taoism.

48. See *THY* 59.1018–19; *HTS* 223A.9b (biography of Li Lin-fu).

were married, and there can be no explanation of this other than the
negligence and irresponsibility of local officials who had failed to
remove them from their original registers as should have been done.
If we again compare the 747 registers with other and more reliable
data, the large number of wives shown in some households should
probably not be taken at its face value but should rather be explained
by the retention in the registers of former wives whose names should
have been removed through death, divorce, or other causes. Alongside
this increase in sheer administrative negligence there was clearly an
increase in false registration motivated by the desire to evade taxation.
This led to the exclusion from the registers of boys and youths who
would in the near future become liable to the burden of taxation and
labor services.

It is well known that the increase of population and the growing
wealth and prosperity of the T'ien-pao period was in fact only a
superficial appearance concealing a state of social and political decay
and that the state's authority over the people was badly eroded. We
can perhaps perceive in the household registers symptoms of this
decay that was attacking every cell in the whole state structure.

After the An Lu-shan and subsequent rebellions the further deterioration of the T'ang government was inevitable, and the circumstances
in Sha-chou as shown in the *shou-shih* of 769—with newly born children
left unregistered, women, youths and old men collectively excluded
from registration, the exclusive concentration upon adult and adolescent males of taxable age and status—tell of a situation in regard to
registration completely different from that of T'ien-pao times. In the
nine years from 760–69 the number of households covered by the 769
shou-shih had fallen sharply from twenty to fourteen, and their registered
individual members from eighty-seven to thirty-nine. In contrast to
this, however, the proportion of adult males among the total registered
population rose from 13.5 percent in the 747 register, to 20.7 percent
in the 760 register, and to 35.9 percent in the 769 *shou-shih* itself.
Although with the recession of state authority the stage had been
reached when the rapid decline of registered population could no
longer be halted, we can see that the situation was still such that *some*
attempt was made to keep a firm control at least on adult males of taxable status.

The decay of the registration system was not restricted to the northwest. After the An Lu-shan Rebellion it is equally clear even in the
metropolitan region of China. Of six monks from the capital district
whom the Tantric master Amoghavajra requested permission to ordain

in 763 three were unregistered; of those for whom permission was
sought in 768 three out of four were unregistered, and later in the same
year in three out of four cases of persons for whom permission for ordination was requested, although their lay family had a register the individual concerned was not entered in it.[49] Thus even in the environs of
the capital itself unregistered persons existed in large numbers, and
perhaps even more significant, we see that such persons could be reported to the authorities without fear of punishment.

Of course, even before Hsüan-tsung's reign there had been individuals omitted from their registers, but their numbers were comparatively
small. There is an interesting anecdote about one Ch'en Chang-fu,
who passed the palace examination during the K'ai-yüan period but
was found to have been unregistered and was therefore failed. Ch'en
then sent a letter to the undersecretary of the Board of Personnel, in
which he emphasized that the household registers were established to
control petty people and to levy taxes upon them, not to be a hindrance
to great sages like himself; eventually his failure was revoked.[50] In the
very society in which the household registers were of great importance
to the government this behavior of Ch'en Chang-fu seems to have been
widely talked about, although it was blatantly illegal.

In the latter half of the T'ang period it seems that registration was
considered to have been the most thorough during the T'ien-pao
period. Tu Yu sees the 8.9 million households listed in the 755 household registers as the peak of registered population under the T'ang and
says that only half of the former total of prefectures reported their
household registers in 760, when the number of registered households
fell to 2.9 million. In the Ta-li period (766–79) they fell still further to
1.3 million. Even those households that were brought under government control in the financial reform of 780–81 totaled only 1.8 million
resident households *(t'u-hu)* and 1.3 million migrant settlers' households *(k'o-hu)*, a total of only 3.1 million.[51] Although later on the total
registered population rose and fell, and the number of prefectures
reporting their registers increased and decreased, the total registered
population under the T'ang never again reached 5 million households.[52]

No ninth-century registers have been discovered, however, so that we
cannot investigate a sample of the documents themselves. But for the

49. *T* 52.831a–b, 836a–b.
50. *Feng-shih wen-chien-chi* (HYISIS edition), 3.11a *(chih-k'o)*; *T'ang wen-ts'ui* 89. 10b–11a.
51. *TT* 7.41c.
52. *THY* 84.1551–52; *TFYK* 486.19a–21b.

earlier period, thanks to the registers from Sha-chou, we can trace in considerable detail the actual way in which the T'ang government maintained control over population figures from the late seventh to the mid-eighth centuries.

We have already examined the information contained in the household registers relating to the makeup of the local society of Tunhuang and Turfan. We have also seen what these documents reveal about the declining efficiency of financial administration during the seventh century. I would now like to consider the information in these documents concerning the tax liability of the people of the region.

According to the T'ang Household Statutes any household including a taxable individual was a taxable household *(k'o-hu)*, and one containing no taxable individuals was a nontaxable household *(pu-k'o-hu)*. In the 737 statutes, officials of the ninth rank *(p'in)* and above "within the current" *(liu-nei)*, males under twenty years, old men (of sixty and above), disabled persons, wives, concubines, male and female retainers *(pu-ch'ü, k'o-nu)*, and slaves were defined as nontaxable individuals.[53] Generally speaking, male adults of free status from the age of twenty-one to fifty-nine who had no physical disability and did not hold rank within the current of promotion were taxable individuals *(k'o-k'ou)*.

To the state the importance of these taxable individuals was incomparably greater than that of nontaxable individuals.[54] In the drawing up of the household registers the greatest attention was naturally devoted to taxable individuals, and the checking of persons' ages by personal inspection *(mao-ting)* was concentrated on males of around twenty years of age who were about to become fully liable to tax and labor service. Again in the 747 register, the avoidance of registration by youths and boys is a striking phenomenon, and clear conflict of interest can be seen between the state, which had a strict interest in anyone bearing tax liability, and the people themselves. Even if they were classed as taxable individuals, *shih-ting* (individuals designated as attendants on aged persons), children of officials *(p'in-tzu)*, and persons liable to military service or to various types of public duty were given exemption from paying taxes, and they were classed as persons who,

---

53. *TT* 7.42a.

54. In the section of the *Code* on households and marriage, in the case of individuals omitted from the registers, four nontaxable individuals are taken as equivalent to a single taxable individual (*Code* 12, Art. 151, p. 105), while in the statute regarding the increase and decrease of registered population, five nontaxable individuals are taken as the equivalent of a single taxable individual (*TT* 15.87b).

Table 4.4. Distribution of Taxable and Nontaxable Households
in T'ang Household Registers

| Register[a] | Date | House-holds | Taxable | | | | Percentage Actually Contri-buting |
			Actually Contri-buting	Not Currently Contri-buting	Not Taxable	Not Clear	
1	701	5	1	3	1		20%
2	716	7	2	2	2	1	33%
3	722	7	3	2	2		43%
4	722	2	2	0	0		100%
5	744	1	0	0	1		0%
6	747	1	0	0	1		0%
7	747	15	5	3	7		33%
8	769	16	7	0	9		44%
9	716	6	0	1	4	1	0%
Total		60	20	11	27	2	33%

[a]For typeset versions of these registers, see Ikeda On, "Chūgoku kodai sekichō shūroku" (see Bibliographical Note), as follows: no. 1, pp. 85–90; no. 2, pp. 94–100; no. 3, pp. 100–08; no. 4, pp. 108–10; no. 5, pp. 113–15; no. 6, pp. 115–16; no. 7, pp. 116–47; no. 8 (a shou-shih), pp. 147–67; no. 9, pp. 175–83.

although taxable, were not currently contributing *(k'o-k'ou pu shu)*. In the surviving household registers the numbers of taxable and non-taxable persons were as in table 4.4.

Taxable households *(k'o-hu)* were roughly half of the total number of households listed, but those actually contributing *(hsien-shu)* were no more than one-third of the whole. If we compare these figures with the sixth-century Western Wei tax register, in which twenty-six out of thirty-three listed households were taxable, while five more households were entitled *"t'ai-tzu,"* the equivalent to the T'ang category of *pu-shu*—theoretically taxable persons who for some legitimate reason never actually paid taxes—it is obvious that there had been a remark-able relaxation of the state's control over taxable individuals. Thus it is clear that a change in the balance of taxable individuals had occurred in response to changes in the overall economic structure of society. But the fact that, even when those not currently contributing are included, the technically taxable households are only about half of the total probably shows a slackness in drawing up the registers special to Sha-chou. According to the national statistics for 775 cited by Tu Yu,[55] taxable households accounted for roughly 60 percent of the total. Even in the Sha-chou registers, in the draft registers of K'ai-yüan times the proportion of taxable households was 70 percent or above. This had

55. *TT* 7.41c.

declined to 47 percent in the T'ien-pao registers, and we may perhaps see from this too the decay suffered by the system of registration in the later years of Hsüan-tsung.

One scholar has pointed out that in comparison to the Western Wei document, the space for the entries on taxation in the T'ang registers had dwindled, and their importance had diminished.[56] Whereas in the register of 701 there is an entry covering hemp cloth, hemp, and grain tax, in the registers of 716 and 722 only the entry on grain tax remains, while in the T'ien-pao and later registers there is not even an entry on grain tax, and all entries on tax liability are lacking. This shows that in the household register, which unlike the tax register *(chi-chang)* was not made with the recording of tax liability as its prime direct object, the importance of tax liability declined, and the officials, becoming indifferent to this matter, ceased to make the former entries connected with it.

In the registers from Hsi-chou, the entries relating to taxation survive only in the most fragmentary form, but we can see some of the ways in which the formal, normative requirments of the tax system were accommodated to local conditions.

By an examination of several fragments from Turfan,[57] we know that at Hsi-chou the quota for the *tiao* (textile) tax was two *chang* of cotton cloth *(t'ieh-pu)*,[58] while the quota for the *tsu* (grain) tax was fixed at six *tou*. According to the Taxation Statutes, the quota for *tiao* was fixed at two *chang* of silk (of the grades *ling, chüan,* or *shih*) and two *chang* five *ch'ih* of hemp cloth *(pu)*,[59] but in Hsi-chou, where there was neither silk nor hempen linen, *tiao* was paid in cotton cloth, which was a special local product. Its quota was two *chang,* the same as for silk. There does not seem to have existed any local special cotton product equivalent to the silk thread which was paid in together with silk cloth, or to the linen thread paid in together with hemp cloth. Again, whereas the quota for the grain tax *(tsu)* was fixed at two *shih* in the Taxation Statutes, in

56. Yamamoto, "Tonkō hakken kosei densei kankei monjo jūgo shu" (see Bibliographical Note), pp. 197–98, 201–02, 222–24; Dohi, "Tō-rei yori mitaru genson Tōdai koseki no kisoteki kenkyū" (see note 6), pp. 106–11.

57. In one fragment, the date of which is unclear, there is the notation "Total. . . " directly before the entry on lands received, which can thus be inferred to relate to *tsu* tax; in another MS there is the following fragmentary entry: "Total 2 *chang* of cotton cloth; [total] 6 *tou* [of grain tax]." Although there is some later writing on both sides of this fragment, the paper is of the type used in household registers, and from the format it was almost certainly the tax-entry portion of a household register. See Ikeda, "Chūgoku kodai sekichō no shūroku" (see Bibliographical Note), pp. 183–84 and *Monumenta Serinidica* 3, plate 32.

58. The famous cotton cloth produced in Turfan was known as *po-t'ieh;* certain rare characters were used in T'ang documents to designate cotton. Cf. *Monumenta Serindica* 2, plates 5–6.

59. Twitchett, *Financial Administration,* p. 140.

Hsi-chou it was very much less—only six *tou*. This was probably because of the actual conditions in Hsi-chou, where agricultural land was very scarce and the average household held only about ten *mou*.[60] In this respect, too, Hsi-chou—even more than Tunhuang—was a very special area. The existence of such local variations in the quotas for the grain and textile taxes are known only from these fragments, which are thus of great interest in understanding the actual operation of the tax system.

I hope to publish in English a detailed study of the evidence of land ownership as revealed in the household registers of Sha-chou and Hsi-chou. The detailed inquiries of many scholars have shown that the reallocation of lands under the *chün-t'ien* system was actually being carried out as late as the T'ien-pao period. From these studies we can discern the relationships between the provisions of the Land Statutes and the actual operation of the system at the local level; the special character of the system as it operated in Hsi-chou has been revealed. There are many questions still unsolved, but more work on the household registers will no doubt help to solve them.

The registration documents preserved from Tunhuang and from Central Asia have a double importance for modern historians. On the one hand they show the operation of the system of personal registration essential to the functioning of the strongly centralizing state of early T'ang times, a state whose institutions demanded direct control by the state over each individual household as a basis for the empire-wide application of common policies on taxation, labor service, military service, and local control of the population. The decay of the system, already beginning in the last half of Hsüan-tsung's reign, and finally accomplished in the aftermath of the An Lu-shan Rebellion, made new institutional arrangements in all these fields a necessity, and when these changes were accomplished in the late eighth century, they were designed specifically to operate without the same basis of a detailed registration of the population as had existed before. In this respect the mid-T'ang is a most important watershed in Chinese administrative history, as the end of the attempt, universal down to this time, to impose uniform administrative practices throughout the empire. From this time onward, administration of fiscal and labor service policies became more and more locally fragmented, more and more subject to regional quotas, with wide variations from one district to the next.

60. Nishijima, "Torohan shutsudo monjo yori mitaru kindensei no sekō jōtai" (see note 2), pp. 647–57.

The beginning of this change can already be seen in the T'ang household registers which survive. They show us a system which was still observed as a legal and institutional norm, but which was already subject to wide variation and modification in actual practice. But perhaps more important they give us a unique insight into the actual implementation of policies. Our knowledge of the actual operation of the taxation and labor service systems is greatly enhanced by the unique evidence they provide, and they also provide evidence on the land allocation system, which has not been included in this essay.

Lastly, they provide evidence, in conjunction with other administrative documents from the same area, on the actual composition of society; on the size and organization of the household, which formed the basic unit of social organization; on the incidence of slavery; and on the range of social and economic differences that can be found even in such a small and untypical community. In these documents we get closer than is possible with any other corpus of source material from medieval China to an understanding of actual living communities, which we can contrast with the social norms specified by the legal and administrative codes.

BIBLIOGRAPHICAL NOTE

Publication of the fragments of household registers found at Tunhuang has been undertaken by a number of scholars, beginning with Lionel Giles, "A Census of Tunhuang," *T'oung Pao* 16 (1915): 468–88. Kano Naoki copied several rolls of the Stein Collection of the British Museum, and the brothers Lo Chen-yü and Lo Fu-ch'ang included these materials together with their father's personal collection in their *Sha-chou wen-lu pu-yi* (1924), pp. 9a–16a. Other important work includes Hamada Kōsaku, "Stein-shi hakkutsuhin kaganroku (B)," *Tōyō gakuhō* 8, no. 3 (1918): 427–34, also in his collected papers *Tōa kōkokugaku kenkyū* (Kyoto, 1930; reprinted 1943), pp. 319–22; Lo Chen-yü and Lo Fu-ch'ang, *Chen-sung-t'ang ts'ang hsi-ch'ui pi-chi ts'ung-ts'an* (1939), vol. 2 (in facsimile); Liu Fu, *Tun-huang to-so*, Middle Series, no. 49 (Peking, 1925), pp. 217–18; Naba Toshisada, "Seishi ni kisai seraretaru Dai Tō Tempō-jidai no kosū to kōsū to no kankei ni tsukite," *Rekishi to chiri* 33, nos. 1, 2, 3, 4 (1934): 47–82, 122–52, 208–42, 303–35. Niida Noboru has published "Tonkō-to hakken Tō-Sō koseki no kenkyū," *Kokka gakkai zasshi* 48, no. 7 (1934): 885–914; "Stein tanken-tai Tonkō hakken hōritsu shiryō sūshu," *Shigaku zasshi* 47, no. 10 (1936): 1236–40; and *Tō-Sō hōritsu monjo no kenkyū* (Tokyo, 1937; reprinted 1967), pp. 650–792. Important works published by Tamai Zehaku are "Tonkō koseki zankan ni tsuite," *Tōyō gakuhō* 16, no. 2 (1927): 231–46; "Futatabi Tonkō koseki zankan ni tsuite," *Tōyō gakuhō* 24, no. 4 (1937): 536–60; these articles are included in the author's collection *Shina shakai-keizai shi kenkyū* (Tokyo, 1942), pp. 245–90. Yamamoto Tatsurō has published "Tonkō hakken keichō-yō monjo zankan," *Tōyō gakuhō* 37, nos. 2, 3 (1954): 139–98, 361–76; "A Tunhuang Manuscript of the Sixth Century

A.D. Concerning the Chün-t'ien Land System (Part I)," *Memoirs of the Research Department of the Tōyō Bunko* 18 (1959): 141–52; "Tonkō hakken kosei densei kankei monjo jūgo shu," *Tōyōbunka kenkyūjo kiyō* 10 (1956): 179–228, plates I-V, reprinted in *Tochi shoyū no shiteki kenkyū* (Tokyo, 1956), pp. 179–228, plus five plates; and "Tonkō hakken Oldenburg shōrai densei kankei monjo go shu," *Ishida Hakase shōjo kinen Tōyōshi ronsō* (Tokyō, 1965), pp. 519–34. In addition to the present article, see by Ikeda On, "Tonkō hakken Tō Taireki yonnen shujitsu zankan ni tsuite," *Tōyō gakuhō* 40, nos. 2, 3 (1957): 151–93, 262–85; and, for a recent summary of the subject, including typeset versions of all available household registers and related documents, see by the same author, "Chūgoku kodai sekichō shūroku," *Hokkaidō daigaku bungakubu kiyō* 19, no. 4 (1971): 25–242.

Collections of relevant historical documents have also been compiled by Chinese scholars who appreciated the importance of the fragments of the household registers as historical evidence. See T'ao Hsi-sheng's "T'ang hu-chi pu ts'ung-chi," *Shih-huo* 4, no. 5 (1936): 1–38, and the volume *Tun-huang tzu-liao*, I, compiled by the Historical Research Institute of the Academia Sinica (Peking, 1961; reprinted Tokyo, 1963). But unfortunately these compilations contain so many deficiencies and errors that one cannot use them without collating them carefully with more reliable studies; cf. my review in *Tōyō gakuhō* 46, no. 1 (1963): 114–33.

For critical discussion of these documents see the works by Giles, Tamai, and Naba cited above. See, in addition, Wang Kuo-wei, "T'ang hsieh-pen Tun-huang hsien hu-chi pa," "Sung-ch'u hsieh-pen Tun-huang hsien hu-chi pa," in *Kuan-t'ing chi-lin* vol. 17 (1922), posthumous edition (1959), vol. 21, pp. 1027–33. The following works by Suzuki Shun are also noteworthy: "Tō no koseki to zeisei to no kankei ni tsuite," *Tōa* 7, no. 9 (1934): 113–33; "Tōdai no koseki ni tsuite," *Rekishi kyōiku* 10, no. 2 (1935): 152–57; "Tonkō hakken Tōdai koseki to kindensei," *Shigaku zasshi* 47, no. 7 (1936): 819–79; "Koseki sakusei no nenji to Tō-rei," *Chūō daigaku bungakubu kiyō* 9 (1957): 81–90. The publication in 1937 of Niida Noboru's *Tō-Sō hōritsu monjo no kenkyū*, a lengthy chapter of which is devoted to the registration system, brought the study of the T'ang household registers to a new level of historical synthesis, by giving both a comprehensive collection of the information relating to the system in the traditional historical literature, and at the same time examining comprehensively those of the *hu-chi* fragments from the northwestern frontier region which were known at that time.

5. The Restoration Completed:
Emperor Hsien-tsung and the Provinces

Charles A. Peterson

Late in 755 the domestic calm of the T'ang empire at its apogee was abruptly and spectacularly shattered by the outbreak of the An Lu-shan Rebellion. Of major significance in both T'ang and more broadly Chinese history, the rebellion ground on for over seven years before being beaten back if not entirely suppressed. The cost however, was, enormous. With its borders seriously contracted, the empire lay in a precarious position vis-à-vis its powerful Tibetan and Uighur neighbors. The entire northeastern corner of the empire, left under the direction of former rebels, remained largely independent of central control. Much of the interior of the country was devastated, causing severe social and economic dislocation including serious depopulation in many areas. As a consequence, the state's financial machinery fell into such complete ruin as to become unsalvageable in its old form. Not least, much of the empire was under the immediate sway of military governors who were only imperfectly controlled by the central government. The appointment in the interior of governors with wide powers was an emergency measure in a time of rebellion. Though it led to the development of a new and lasting provincial structure, by the end of rebellion in 763 institutional links between center and province were still weak, and power was exerted in the provinces on a highly personal basis.

Such was the condition of the T'ang empire upon the termination of the long struggle. The T'ang's preservation of the throne under these circumstances has been regarded as one of the classic dynastic "restorations" in Chinese history.[1] In the eyes of the traditional historian there is an essentially moral quality to such restorations; they are

1. See Mary C. Wright, *The Last Stand of Chinese Conservatism* (Stanford, Calif., 1957), pp. 44–48, for a characterization of this and other restorations.

regarded as a renewal of the Divine Mandate by which a dynasty claims its right to rule. But what is the true content of such restorations? In the T'ang case, for example, the former bases of rule had collapsed so thoroughly that the restoration seems on the surface little more than ritualistic. Without their total or partial replacement, one would be hard put to explain the survival of the dynasty for nearly another century and a half. Therefore, we must be wary of regarding restorations as a mere duplication of the old order. Further, the histories of restoration regimes seem hardly to follow a common pattern. If others reached a new plateau of power and prestige within a decade or two of their return to rule and thereafter showed diminishing powers of regeneration,[2] the T'ang, on the contrary, attained this plateau only following a half-century of painful struggle and succeeded in remaining there some decades beyond that. To be meaningful, the idea of a T'ang dynastic restoration must, in short, be regarded as an extended process rather than a single event.

The architect of this "restoration completed" was the emperor Hsien-tsung (reigned 805–20). We know less than we should about this monarch, for various reasons. Certainly he has been victimized by Chinese historiography, both old and recent. The two official T'ang histories are reluctant to give serious consideration to any reign subsequent to that of Hsüan-tsung (reigned 712–56), when things are seen to have assumed their normative pattern for the T'ang.[3] Sung historians such as Sun Fu, Fan Tsu-yü, and Ssu-ma Kuang had a high respect for Hsien-tsung's achievements,[4] but already in the Sung we find the view taking shape which will predominate down to our own day. This view, as reflected in the remarks of Ho Ch'ü-fei, first, appraises those achievements in purely military terms, and second, attributes no lasting effect to them.[5] Subsequent historical writing shows little deviation from this assessment. Despite the fact that he devotes a treatise to the subject, the Ming historian Chang Tuan-ling sees the provincial problem as unalleviated throughout the second half of the dynasty.[6] And, whereas the noted eighteenth-century historian Chao I presents a reasonable

2. Cf. ibid., p. 45, where a restoration *(chung-hsing)* is defined as a time of arrested decline in the dynastic cycle "between a successfully surmounted crisis and a final catastrophe."

3. This is particularly true of the monographs, which are sometimes of very limited value for the second half of the T'ang. Fortunately, the documentary collections, the *Ts'e-fu yüan-kuei*, the *T'ang-hui-yao*, and the *T'ang ta-chao-ling-chi*, do not share this disability.

4. See Sun Fu, *T'ang-shih lun-tuan*, chap. 3 (of course, in a collection of notes such as this there is no systematic treatment); Fan Tsu-yü, *T'ang-chien*, chap. 19; and Ssu-ma Kuang's great *Tzu-chih t'ung-chien*, chaps. 236–41.

5. See Ho Ch'ü-fei's discussion under "T'ang-lun" in his military treatise *Ho-po-shih pei-lun*.

6. See Chang Tuan-ling's *T'ang fan-chen chih-chang*, esp. "Tsung-lun san-tse."

sketch of the development of a provincial system prior to the An Lu-shan Rebellion, he summarily treats matters in the provinces as going from bad to worse thereafter. Hsien-tsung is not even mentioned.[7] Recent surveys of T'ang history in Chinese largely continue this negative tradition, though Hsien-tsung's reign is on occasion characterized as a "restoration."[8] Only in Japan has this phase of T'ang history been studied in depth, but the pioneer in this effort, Professor Hino Kaizaburō, published his first important research on the subject some three decades ago and even in Japan has had dismayingly few followers.[9] One need hardly be astonished, therefore, at the fact that this emperor and reign are, save for matters of literary interest, virtually unknown in the West.[10]

It would, however, be misleading to stress the accomplishments of Hsien-tsung alone. The ground was well prepared by his predecessors, particularly by the emperor Te-tsung (reigned 779–805). This unfortunate monarch all but lost his throne in the great provincial revolts of 781–86, sparked by his own activist policies toward the provinces, and in some respects he spent the remainder of his reign recovering from the experience. Unwilling under any circumstances to risk another rebellion, he nevertheless strengthened the government's hold on important segments of the empire.[11] By augmenting the size of the Palace Armies (the *Shen-ts'e chün*) and establishing a network of central

7. Chao I, *Nien-erh-shih cha-chi*, chap. 20. Also note the treatment given by Ku Tsu-yü in his *Tu-shih fang-yü chi-yao* (1678), chap. 6, where Hsien-tsung's achievements are minimized because of the government's alleged failure to retain control over the principal Hopei provinces.

8. Surveys by Chang Chün, Fu Lo-ch'eng, Liu Po-chi, Yang Chih-chiu, and one on institutions by Yang Shu-fan demonstrate this. For example, Chang, in his *T'ang-shih* (Taipei, 1958), chap. 9, seems unwilling to believe his own demonstration of T'ang recovery. Only Lü Ssu-mien, in his *Sui-T'ang-Wu-tai shih* (Peking, 1959), vol. 1, chap. 7, exhibits a good grasp of the significance of this reign and of how it accomplished its main tasks. However, Lü's approach to history writing hardly permits him to arrive at a real synthesis.

9. Hino Kaizaburō's first major study, "Tōdai hanchin no bakko to chinshō," *Tōyō gakuhō* 26 and 27 (1939–40), was followed by his more complete, though undocumented, *Shina chūsei no gunbatsu* (Tokyo, 1942). A number of relevant articles from his hand have appeared since. Little in this present paper has not been touched upon in one respect or another by Hino.

10. The fullest narrative in a Western language, Otto Franke's *Geschichte des chinesichen Reiches*, 5 vols. (Berlin, 1930–52), finds Hsien-tsung's death, presumably murder, the only real point of interest in his reign (2: 485). In the most widely used American textbook on Chinese history, E. O. Reischauer and J. K. Fairbank's *East Asia: The Great Tradition* (Boston, 1960), the fall of the T'ang follows within paragraphs of the An Lu-shan Rebellion (see pp. 191–94).

11. The government's close grip on the Yangtse provinces, as shown in the *Yüan-ho kuo-chi-pu* of 807 (*THY* [Kuo-hsüeh chi-pen ts'ung shu edition] 84.1552–53), probably dates in post-rebellion times from Te-tsung's reign.

agents attached to the provincial administrations (the *chien-chün shih* system),[12] he created the means for a reassertion of central authority. Also, irregular though his methods may have been—for example, encouraging unregulated tribute contributions—he did bring about a marked recovery of central finances.[13] In short, Te-tsung left the empire far stronger than he had found it, and, when Hsien-tsung ascended the throne, the possibility had been created of adopting a forceful, active policy.

The brief reign of Shun-tsung in 805 had no significant impact on the situation.[14] The energies of his administration were entirely absorbed by the political struggle at court which gave rise to factionalism and dissension. Quick resolution of this state of affairs then became Hsien-tsung's first order of business. This may not have been very difficult. Whatever the truth about Shun-tsung's reign, apparently placed permanently beyond our reach by the uniformly biased and hostile surviving records, its leadership was without doubt an unorthodox one, which had alienated virtually the entire ruling elite. In consequence Hsien-tsung's first step to bring about a complete changing of the guard, found immediate and widespread approval.

Once the problem at court was dealt with, the overriding issue facing Hsien-tsung was control of the provinces. This was a nuclear problem on which much else hinged—internal and external security, finances, the material condition of the populace, the morale of officialdom. Furthermore, it was not a homologous problem, as it might have been under the centralized prefectural system of the early T'ang, but rather a set of problems varying according to the particular status of each individual province. Aside from the frontier provinces on the north and northwest, thinly populated, heavily armed, and economically dependent upon the central government, there were broadly two kinds of provinces. The vast majority were administered by court-appointed officials and

12. The figure of 150,000 given in *HTS* (Po-na edition) 50.8b, for the size of the Palace Armies in this period is certainly too low (see T'ang Chang-ju, *T'ang-shu ping-chih chien-cheng* [Peking, 1962], p. 103). The bulk of this manpower was in fact stationed on the frontiers, but the number of Palace Army troops at the immediate disposition of the court must still have been considerable. On the *chien-chün-shih* system see pp. 142–43 of the present article.

13. Save for indications of large grain reserves and transport, hard figures to demonstrate this seem to be lacking. *HTS* 52.6a states explicitly that, by the end of the reign, the treasury was full. On Te-tsung's irregular methods see *CTS* (Po-na edition) 48. 2a–b; *HTS* 52.5a–b.

14. Shun-tsung reigned from the first to the eighth lunar months of *Yung-chen* 1 (805). See B. S. Solomon, *The Veritable Record of the T'ang Emperor Shun-tsung* (Cambridge, 1955). Mainland historians have made some attempt, not altogether convincing, at a positive reevaluation of this reign. See Wang I-sheng's article in *Li-shih yen-chiu* 3 (1963): 105–30; and Hou Wai-lu, *Chung-kuo ssu-hsiang t'ung-shih* (Peking, 1959), vol. 4, pt. 1, pp. 390–96.

tended to follow court directives to a greater or lesser degree.[15] Some in this category, predominantly military in function and character, were headed by military governors, but most were little more than large units of civil administration. A much smaller number, ranging from five to seven at this time, were altogether autonomous. The five major ones, with their approximate contemporary locations, were (see map) :[16]

Yu-chou, northern Hopei
Ch'eng-te, west-central Hopei, centering on Chengting
Wei-po, southern Hopei
P'ing-lu, Shantung and a portion of eastern Honan
Huai-hsi, southeastern Honan, bordering on Anhwei and Hupei

These were military regimes whose direction and civil functions lay entirely in the hands of soldiers, Their leaders were determined locally, usually gaining subsequent approval by the throne, and they frequently succeeded to command by hereditary claim.

The problems posed by these two kinds of provinces varied. With their large armies and ample resources, the autonomous provinces presented an immediate danger and a potential challenge to the dynasty. By contrast, the problem with regard to the subordinate provinces was essentially that of maintaining routine administrative control. Lacking this control, especially in the fiscal sphere, central authority ran the risk of progressive, if only gradual, erosion.[17] Clearly, solutions to these two sets of problems would have to take entirely different forms. To the first the solution had to be political and military, to the second, institutional.

It will be useful to maintain this division as we examine Hsien-tsung's provincial policy. Nevertheless, the two kinds of problem—military-political and administrative—were interrelated. Solution of the one depended ultimately on successful management of the other: until the empire was made basically secure within, orders issued by the

15. The total number of provinces averaged forty-six to forty-seven throughout this period (see Ts'en Chung-mien, *Sui-T'ang shih* [Peking, 1957], pp. 272–73).

16. Two smaller Hopei provinces, I-wu to the northwest and Heng-hai to the east, were likewise largely autonomous at this time. The nomenclature for T'ang provinces from 755 onward is none too neat or consistent. Of the examples we have before us, all but two derive from formal titles conferred by the throne on the main garrison force, or army, in the province. The two exceptions are Yu-chou, which takes its name from its chief prefecture (and which is also known by its army title Lu-lung), and Wei-po, simply a compound formed by the names of two of the principal prefectures. P'ing-lu here is not to be confused with the pre-rebellion frontier command of the same name in southern Manchuria.

17. Garrison mutinies, endemic since the rebellion, were also a problem in the subordinate prefectures.

court would be ineffective in the provinces; while, until a viable administrative relationship between central and provincial authorities had been developed, military success alone could not be lasting.

HSIEN-TSUNG'S POLITICAL STRATEGY AND ITS EXECUTION

Centralization set the tone for Hsien-tsung's reign, but the quality and scope of his centralizing measures were, to be sure, very much circumscribed by existing conditions. To revert abruptly to the centralized order of the pre-755 period was out of the question; the provincial administrations had largely taken over the local functions of the central government, and any sweeping moves toward recentralization would almost certainly have been met by armed resistance. For the central government, demilitarization of the interior was obviously desirable. But some half-million and more men-in-arms would not gracefully see themselves put out of business, and a military force was indispensable for some of the primary tasks ahead.[18] It is in terms of these dilemmas that the strategy of Hsien-tsung must be viewed; and if he was not completely successful, it was because the weight of the immediate past lay against him.

Hsien-tsung's strategy aimed first at replacing the present leadership in the autonomous or would-be autonomous provinces with centrally appointed officials tied by loyalty and professional ambition to the court. If this could be done and hitherto separatist territories returned to the central government, greater security would prevail in the empire and a political climate would be created which would be conducive to new, centralizing measures. All this, of course, was predicated on the use of military means. Without the display and possible use of military muscle, the central government could not hope to reassert its authority. The first challenge Hsien-tsung faced, therefore, was military, and perhaps his achievement is primarily to be characterized as military. But unlike such great martial emperors as Han Wu-ti or his own ancestor T'ai-tsung, his efforts were perforce directed inward rather than to the frontiers, where deeds were more glorious and have been better remembered.

The occasion for taking action against a province was usually provided by a change in its leadership. Good arguments could be, and often were, made for not disturbing the personal modus vivendi with the

18. I refer to the number in the interior of the country. Several sources set the total number of troops in the empire at 800,000 and more (cf. *TFYK* [Chung-hua reprint of 1642 edition] 486.21a–b).

central government which had been worked out during the term of a particular governor. Such arguments, however, normally ceased to apply where new men were taking over and a new modus vivendi had to be established. The rhythm of operations undertaken by the government against individual provinces was therefore determined by developments within those provinces. The government, in other words, had no precise master plan which it could systematically pursue; it had rather to proceed piecemeal.

Tactical considerations aside, there was perhaps one strategic factor which predominated in the thinking at court throughout this period. This was simply that the T'ang lifeline to the productive and heavily taxed Yangtse provinces must be preserved at all costs.[19] This meant that provinces bordering on the canal system had to be handled with extreme caution and, further, that not the slightest sign of autonomy could be permitted in the Yangtse provinces themselves. This fundamental consideration explains, on the one hand, the great toleration and lengthy delay in dealing with the dangerous province of P'ing-lu and, on the other, the rapidity with which the first sparks of local autonomy were snuffed out in the lower Yangtse province of Che-hsi in 807.

Whatever Hsien-tsung's own schedule for action in the provinces might have been, his hand was forced immediately following his accession by developments in Szechwan. There in Chien-nan West the longtime governor Wei Kao died in the summer of 805, and his seat was immediately seized by one of his subordinates, Liu P'i, who left no doubt as to his ambitions to retain it.[20] This was not without precedent, though, contrary to the impression left by most of the historiography on the subject, it was common in only a small minority of provinces.[21] The case of Chien-nan West under Wei Kao was, moreover, a peculiar one. In his twenty-one years as governor, Wei had become one of the great viceroys of the empire. He had enjoyed complete autonomy in running the province, appropriating taxes, appointing his own officials, and, in effect, conducting his own foreign policy. If this had been all

19. On this point see in particular Ch'üan Han-sheng, *T'ang-Sung ti-kuo yü yün-ho* (Chungking, 1944), passim; and Ch'en Yin-k'o, *T'ang-tai cheng-chih shih shu-lun kao* (Chungking, 1944), p. 20.

20. *TCTC*(1956) 236.7620; also see biographies of both in *CTS* 140 and *HTS* 158. Liu, incidentally, was a *chin-shih* of high standing. Matsui Shūichi has dealt with this period in the history of Szechwan in his article "Tōdai zenpanki no Shisen," *Shizaku Zasshi* 71 (1962): 1178–214. See esp. pp. 1200–10 for treatment of the period from the An Lu-shan Rebellion to Hsien-tsung's reign.

21. See discussion on appointments later in this chapter.

there was to it, he would have differed little from the infamous governors
of the Hopei provinces, P'ing-lu or Huai-hsi. On the contrary, however,
he served as a close ally of the throne. He was a frequent adviser to the
emperor on affairs of state; he contributed heavily to imperial coffers,
though in the form of tribute rather than regular tax quotas; and,
above all, he secured China's southwestern frontier, drawing Nan-
chao into an alliance and turning back repeated Tibetan attempts to
advance.[22] Clearly, however, this cooperative attitude toward the court
was a personal affair, one which could hardly be taken for granted in a
self-appointed successor.

Hsien-tsung showed an initial toughness in this first challenge from
the provinces and refused to sanction Liu's seizure of power.[23] However,
when it became clear that Liu would resist by force any attempt to
replace him, the emperor backed down, making him assistant governor
of the province but with full powers of command.[24] This contrasts with
most subsequent occasions when Hsien-tsung exhibited little inclination
toward compromise. For the moment it was decisive that he felt himself too new and insecure on the throne to initiate a difficult military
venture.[25] Lack of military readiness must also have been a factor.[26]
Liu soon left the government no choice but military action when he
sent his own troops to seize Chien-nan East.[27] Even then there was
wavering at court, and it took the vigorous counsel of Tu Huang-
shang, the dominant minister at this time, to turn the tide.[28]

22. See *TCTC* 235.7592; *HTS* 214.3a; sources in notes 20 and 96. Wei is treated as one of
the most notorious of those officials who contributed heavily to the emperor's personal
coffers at the expense of the local populace. On Wei's administration generally see Matsui,
"Tōdai zenpanki no Shisen," which treats Wei's administration on pp. 1205–07. Matsui is
probably correct in seeing Wei's rule as bureaucratizing the administration of this province
once again after the domination by the military since the rebellion—even though direct
control by the central government remained limited.

23. *CTS* 14.5b; *TCTC* 236.7622.

24. *TCTC* 236.7623.

25. *TCTC* 236.7624. It might nevertheless be worth noting that Hsien-tsung was twenty-
seven years old upon his accession, rather older than some of his successors.

26. Commitment for a campaign against Liu was made in the first month of Yüan-ho, 1/
806, but no serious fighting seems to have occurred before the fifth month.

27. Chien-nan East lay approximately in central Szechwan. Liu is supposed to have done
this in retaliation for the court's failure to appoint him governor over both Chien-nan provinces (*CTS* 140.4b; *TCTC* 237.7626). However that may be, he surely staked his chances
on being able to hold off loyalist forces until he could win a pardon, something that was far
from unprecedented. Liu would also not have known what to expect from the new emperor.

28. Tu has biographies in *CTS* 147 and *HTS* 169. On this decision see *CTS* 147.1a-b; and
TCTC 237.7626. Lü, *Sui-T'ang-Wu-tai shih*, p. 341, calls attention to the account in the
biographies of Li Chi-fu (*CTS* 148; *HTS* 146), attributing this policy line to the latter and also
to the large bribe which Tu supposedly received from the general soon to be named com-

Tu's arguments themselves provide us with something of a policy statement for this early Yüan-ho period.[29]

> Once having passed through the grievous troubles [of his first years], Te-tsung strove [only] to be accommodating. He would not seek to replace any governor in his lifetime. [On the contrary] when a governor died, he would send a palace official (i.e. a eunuch) to learn the sentiments of the garrison before making the appointment. Occasionally eunuchs would accept bribes from top generals and return to court singing their praises. Thus when the insignias of office were conferred [on a new appointee], it was never a case of expressing the court's decision on the matter.
>
> As Your Majesty most certainly wishes to restore to vigor the basic principles of our land, He must bring the provinces under the rule of law. Only then can proper order be restored to the realm.[30]

Henceforth this was the basic outlook of the regime as it set itself a critical task.

Once government forces were mobilized, the campaign against Liu P'i was short and decisive. By the fall of 806, only four months after the beginning of actual hostilities, Liu was captured (and soon after executed) and Chien-nan West was entirely recovered.[31] It is significant that the government sent units of the Palace Army to do the bulk of the fighting and then appointed their commander to be the new governor of the province.[32] The very next year, however, this general was himself replaced by a regular career bureaucrat, indeed an outgoing chief minister.[33]

No punitive measures were taken against local officials or the populace, all of whom were declared to have been "coerced" into rebelling. The new governor was even urged, circumstances permitting, to reduce tax rates for the year.[34] There was concern, to be sure, that the province might again slip into the hands of wayward leaders; as a result, six

---

mander-in-chief of the campaign. The fact nevertheless remains that Tu was a chief minister at the time, with the primary responsibility this implies, whereas Li was not. Also, the passing of funds under the table to obtain choice appointments was by no means uncommon in this period.

29. This reign title covers virtually all of Hsien-tsung's reign, specifically, the years 806–20, and serves as a useful shorthand reference to his reign.

30. *TCTC* 237.7627; *CTS* 147.1b.

31. *CTS* 14.9a; *TCTC* 237.7636.

32. This was Kao Ts'ung-wen, who has biographies in *CTS* 150 and *HTS* 170.

33. Wu Yüan-heng, who has biographies in *CTS* 158 and *HTS* 152 and who later in the reign played an important role at court.

34. *TTCLC* (Peking, 1959) 124.665.

prefectures were withdrawn from it and placed under the jurisdiction of Chien-nan East.[35] These measures were clearly moderate and aimed at defusing this region as a potential political threat. In view of its frontier position, the province could hardly have been disarmed, nor could it have been turned into an important revenue producer as far as central needs were concerned.

Although the court under Hsien-tsung thus began by reducing one effectively autonomous province, it was nevertheless obliged in the course of this effort to sanction hereditary succession in another. In mid-806, when the governor of P'ing-lu (in Shantung) died, his stepbrother Li Shih-tao assumed control. The court initially delayed granting him official recognition, evidently out of indecision over the best course to adopt. This delay caused a good deal of anxiety within the province, as a consequence of which Li offered a bargain: in return for his confirmation in office he would pay taxes, accept central appointment of subordinate offiicals, and maintain the regulations of the salt monopoly. Tu Huang-shang again advocated a hard line in court counsels, but there seems to have been general agreement that, with one campaign underway, it would have been folly to launch another, especially against such a powerful adversary.[36] Li Shih-tao was therefore given a formal appointment, but there is no evidence to suggest that he fulfilled any of his promises to the court.

It was, we can see, hardly unusual for the government to acquiesce in internal changes in those provinces outside its sphere of control. What it would not permit was any suggestion of separatism in those provinces in the Yangtse Valley which were its economic mainstay. Such a danger had by this time taken shape in the province of Che-hsi. Li Ch'i, who had been governor of the province since 799 and until 805 concurrently head of the Salt and Transportation Commission, which virtually controlled the collection of revenue in southern China, was clearly attempting to build up an independent power base. With rich resources available from agriculture, salt production, and trade, Li was able both to nurture a high quality military force of his own and yet to maintain favor at court by sizable tribute contributions.[37]

Though our sources do not satisfactorily account for his split with the court in the fall of 807, it was at least in part a consequence of the

35. *TCTC* 237.7637. The *HTS* tables, chaps. 67 and 68, omit this transfer. Three years later two prefectures, Tzu and Chien, were returned to Chien-nan West.

36. Li has biographies in *CTS* 124 and *HTS* 213. On these developments see *CTS* 124.8b, and *TCTC* 237.7635.

37. See his biographies in *CTS* 112 and *HTS* 224a; also see *TCTC* 236.7596–97; *CTS* 48.2b.

government's success in Szechwan and of its newly gained prestige. Now solicitous of their positions, governors began to honor more conscientiously their commitment to appear periodically at court. Pressure was placed upon Li to appear; he agreed, backed off, and, ultimately, refused and decided to resist by arms.[38] With a record of flagrant irregularities in his administration, he surely feared that he would never return from court, while, on the other hand, he must have counted on the government's unwillingness to press the issue if he took a strong stand of his own.[39]

This turned out to be Hsien-tsung's easiest victory. Although troops in neighboring provinces were mobilized against Li Ch'i, no fighting ever took place. At the rebel leader's first move, his commanders turned on him, captured and surrendered him, and so put an and to the rebellion.[40] The fact that the province was militarily indefensible had doomed any separatist attempt from the beginning. However, the outcome was of considerable significance in showing that the government was again prepared to use force. This was, incidentally, the first and the last rebellion mounted by a Yangtse Valley governor until the very late T'ang.[41]

Hsien-tsung's first strategic error, like that of his grandfather Tetsung, was made in Hopei, the citadel of provincial autonomy. The Hopei provinces of Yu-chou, Wei-po, and Ch'eng-te had been entirely outside court control since the An Lu-shan Rebellion. While Tetsung's earlier attempts at recovery of central control had failed disastrously, a compromise peace between the court and these provinces had lasted, by Hsien-tsung's accession, for two decades, and the provinces themselves had remained relatively stable. In 809 a change of leadership took place in that region for the first time in the reign, in this instance in Ch'eng-te.[42] Such an occasion, as we have seen, offered the court its only real opportunity for exerting its ultimate authority over such a province: until he gained official court recognition, any new claimant to provincial leadership could not feel secure.

38. *TCTC* 237.7640–41.

39. For an unsuccessful attempt to interpret this revolt as an expression of the interests of new landed and mercantile groups, see Tanigawa Michio, "Tōdai no hanchin ni tsuite," *Shirin* 35 (1952): esp. 289–92. This is otherwise a useful article.

40. See his biographies and also *TFYK* 374.4b.

41. There was indeed here a very strong tradition of literati governors who were far less inclined to mount armed resistance to the central government than were military men (see Tanigawa, "Tōdai no hanchin ni tsuite," p. 288, note 2). In this light Li Ch'i's behavior is exceptional.

42. Eugène Feifel, *Po Chü-i as a Censor* (The Hague, 1961), has much material on this event. See pp. 114–55 and, for relevant documents from Po's hand, pp. 226–37.

There is no doubt that the emperor and his advisers were altogether at variance on how best to treat the claims of Wang Ch'eng-tsung to succeed his father to the Ch'eng-te governorship.[43] Nor is there any doubt as to where the real power of decision at court lay. Analysis of the lengthy debates recorded on the subject reveals a determined and willful monarch who disagreed with his advisers not only concerning the tactical approach to the issue at hand but also concerning the long-range prospects for the recovery of Hopei. In the end, despite the government's momentary triumph in that region upon the close of Hsien-tsung's reign, the advisers' assessment of the situation proved to be closer to the mark.

From the emperor's point of view, no lasting headway against the autonomous forces could be made until the practice of granting official post facto recognition to local decisions on succession to provincial leadership (i.e. so-called hereditary succession) had been firmly brought to an end. Moreover, to put off drawing the line at this time, when similar cases would soon be arising elsewhere (in other Hopei provinces particularly), would form a harmful precedent. Assuming the feasibility of the ultimate objective, the recovery of Hopei, this was an irrefutable argument.

From a less optimistic assessment of the situation, the advisers, especially Li Chiang, stressed the historical and geopolitical obstacles to any significant and enduring ascendancy over these provinces. The local leadership and administration after a half century of autonomy, had acquired genuine legitimacy in the eyes of the local populations and a considerable base of popular support. Second, the broad identity of interests among these provinces, together with their physical proximity, made it difficult for the central government to play off one against the other and, at the same time, made them a highly effective combination in any joint enterprise. If, Li argued, the emperor wished to move against an autonomous province, he would do well to aim at Huai-hsi (in southern Honan), which itself faced a change of leadership and lacked the strategic advantages of any of the northeastern provinces.

In the end a compromise was reached in these deliberations: in order to gain official recognition, Wang Ch'eng-tsung, like Li Shih-tao in P'ing-lu before him, would have to make concessions with respect to taxes and the selection of officials as well as give up two of his outlying prefectures.[44] These terms Wang did agree to accept—only to turn

---

43. On these debates see *TCTC* 237.7659–238.7664. For Li Chiang's able arguments see *CTW* 646.4a-6a. Wang has biographies in *CTS* 142 and *HTS* 211.

44. There is a history to the two prefectures in question, Te and Ti, which made the prov-

around, upon duly gaining his appointment as governor, and retake the prefectures.[45] This touched off a punitive campaign, which involved the mobilization of several armies (including that of the northernmost Hopei province of Yu-chou) and a grandly planned advance against Ch'eng-te from three sides. But less than a year later, in mid-810, the campaign was abandoned, the probable reasons being halfhearted fighting by the armies, poor direction of operations, and finally a serious shortage of funds.[46] The last factor is suggested, among other things, by Hsien-tsung's subsequent preoccupation with building up a financial reserve.[47] It is probable that another factor was the heavy pressure applied by officials at court to halt the campaign.[48] When the emperor eventually did abandon the campaign, little had been achieved. Wang, his original territory essentially intact, was pardoned and given back his credentials. While he agreed to contribute taxes and to accept centrally appointed officials, this was surely more a face-saving statement of principle than a commitment to practical action.[49] Moreover, as a consequence of this abortive attempt, the court found itself obliged to accede without resistance to changes of leadership in two other autonomous provinces, in Huai-hsi in early 810[50] and in Yu-chou in the autumn of that year.[51]

Yet the Ch'eng-te defeat cannot be called a major disaster, for it had no immediate negative repercussions either politically or militarily. Indeed, the campaign was an indirect factor in two distinct triumphs. In the southern Ho-tung province of Chao-i government agents were able to spirit away a volatile and menacing governor in the spring of 810 before the garrison could intervene, thus keeping this province within the central sphere of control.[52] Then, late in the year and certainly in response to the heightened prestige of the court, the governor of one of the minor Hopei provinces, I-wu, gave up the family claim to

ince vulnerable in their regard. An earlier court attempt to cut them off having failed, they were retained by the province only as special dependencies. See *CTS* 142 and *HTS* 211 under Wang Wu-chün.

45. *CTS* 14.15b; *TCTC* 238.7664; and Wang's biographies. This is the official account, which might well make matters too black and white.

46. *TCTC* 238 and passim. From the beginning Li Chiang had advanced the serious drought in the southeast as a reason for not undertaking the campaign.

47. *TCTC* 238.7682. Aslo significant is a statement made subsequently by Li Chiang that the campaign cost seven million *min* (*TCTC* 238.7693).

48. *CTW* 667.19a–23b; Feifel, *Po Chü-i as a Censor*, pp. 229–37.

49. *CTS* 14.17a; and Wang's biographies.

50. That is, in the third month of Yüan-ho 5, according to *CTS* 14.16b.

51. That is, in the ninth month, according to *CTS* 14.17b.

52. *CTS* 132.5b–6a; *TCTC* 238.7674. Credit is given to P'ei Chi, chief minister at this time, for this stratagem and its success. See also his biographies in *CTS* 148 and *HTS* 169.

the governorship and asked the government to appoint his successor.[53] Not having overcommitted itself against Ch'eng-te, the government could execute a tactical withdrawal.

Undeterred by this setback, the emperor frankly acknowledged that only a lack of funds held him back from pursuing his long-range goals more aggressively.[54] As we shall see, the fact that it was more than four years before the government initiated another military action in the interior in no way betokened a slackening of the overall effort to reassert central control. Furthermore, though the ability to call on powerful military forces was crucial, important results could be obtained without actual resort to arms.

One spectacular instance of this occurred, ironically, in Hopei itself, where direct military action had failed. Characteristically, it was a crisis surrounding a change of leadership which set the stage. Upon the death of the governor of Wei-po in the summer of 812, his young son tried with disastrous results to succeed him. Out of the ensuing local confusion one strong figure emerged, a popular and able general who extracted a remarkable concession from the garrison in return for assuming command. This was, namely, that the province would return to a normal, subordinate relationship with the court: remitting taxes, accepting central appointments, and heeding central directives.[55] The probable motivation of this new figure, T'ien Hsing (afterward T'ien Hung-cheng)—and this is not to deny him all those qualities of loyalty and dedication perceived by our sources—was to gain quick court confirmation of his governorship and to shore up his precarious local position with the power and prestige of the throne. Since he maintained control over Wei-po until he was transferred to another province eight years later, his move must be regarded as successful.

Essentially, all this occurred beyond the power of the central government, though it stirred considerable debate at court. News of the abortive succession attempt and ensuing dissension was met at first by a vigorous but finally dissuasive discussion of the idea of armed intervention. Hsien-tsung, however valid his image as a martial emperor, on this occasion ultimately rejected a military solution; and presumably the failure of the court promptly to confirm the accession of the former-governor's son was a factor in his being ousted.[56] The question then emerged of how to treat T'ien Hsing's assumption of power. After some

53. *CTS* 141.14b.
54. *TCTC* 238.7682.
55. On these developments see *CTS* 15.2a and 141.7a–8b; *TCTC* 238. 7692, 7694.
56. *TCTC* 238.7692–239.7696.

initial skepticism, it was decided that his offer to restore normal relations was made in good faith and that he should be quickly confirmed as governor.[57] The improbable phenomenon that a province such as this should fall into the hands of a loyalist usurper can only be explained by the prestige that the central government had by this time recovered. But, conscious of the disaffection that the sacrifice of fiscal autonomy might inspire, the court presented a bounty of 1.5 million *min* to the Wei-po army.[58] Such gratuities have not infrequently had the effect of awakening latent sentiments of loyalty.

The return of Wei-po to the fold had great impact on the subsequent course of events under Hsien-tsung. Politically, though doubts may be entertained regarding the extent to which the province ever became integrated into the central administrative structure,[59] and though the relationship was to end after T'ien's transfer to an even more critical position in 820, the loyalty of Wei-po effectively neutralized the remaining autonomous provinces in Hopei and thus allowed the government to direct its resources to the recovery of other critical provinces. More tangibly, Wei-po participated in subsequent campaigns against rebels, making it no exaggeration to say that Wei-po's adoption of a loyalist posture was a critical factor in the major military victories achieved thereafter by Hsien-tsung.

We observed previously that a primary concern of government strategy was to safeguard the canal system, vital link to the productive southeast. Virtually from the close of the An Lu-shan Rebellion the provinces of Huai-hsi and P'ing-lu, both of which had successfully defended their autonomous status in armed conflicts with the central government, had posed a threat to this link. Both were characterized by capable leadership—from a single family line in P'ing-lu and an apparently just as strong succession of individual leaders in Huai-hsi.[60] But, in comparison with the provinces of the Hopei group, both lay in relatively exposed positions. Indeed Huai-hsi was literally isolated among court-controlled provinces,[61] which makes its case of particular interest (see map).

57. This was Li Chiang's view as against Li Chi-fu's greater skepticism and desire to exploit this opportunity in a more active way.

58. *CTS* 141.8b, 15.2b.

59. *CTS* 141.8b and *HTS* 148.10b record far-reaching measures which T'ien committed himself to carrying out and which, if implemented, would have tied the province closely to the central government.

60. See the biographies of their governors in *CTS* 145 and *HTS* 214 and *CTS* 124 and *HTS* 213, respectively. Note that neither province lay directly on the canal but rather along the borders of provinces that did.

61. Li Chiang had stressed this very point some years before. See *CTW* 646.4a-b.

Though small (three prefectures) and not especially well endowed, the province of Huai-hsi had one of the toughest armies of its day.[62] The success of this army—which repulsed larger loyalist forces in 782–86 and again in 798–800 and which continued to hold out until overcome by a surprise attack in the campaign of 814–17—is a remarkable phenomenon and, given the data available to us, difficult to account for fully.

In any event Hsien-tsung approached the recovery of Huai-hsi, projected some years earlier, with considerable caution.[63] The first favorable occasion presented itself in 814 when the governor died and his son Wu Yüan-chi, as expected, sought the succession. Furthermore, Chief Minister Li Chi-fu, familiar with conditions in Huai-hsi as former governor of an adjoining province and always eager for action, was ascendant at court.[64] Li immediately initiated a mobilization of forces in the surrounding provinces and argued for a showdown by stressing both the feasibility and the desirability of subduing Huai-hsi.[65] Isolated, the province lacked such immediate allies as members of the Hopei block could usually count on; unsubdued, it required the costly garrisoning of 100,000 men on its borders.[66] The showdown came quickly with Wu himself launching operations.[67]

The war was to drag on for three years, partly because the Huai-hsi army put up a typically effective defense, but no doubt also because the government had to contend with a campaign of harassment by P'ing-lu in Shantung and eventually to open up hostilities with Ch'eng-te in Hopei as well. P'ing-lu's acts of harassment took such extreme forms as the destruction by fire of the huge tax entrepôt at Ho-yin (near Loyang), attempted guerrilla action in Loyang itself, and the assassination of an uncompromising chief minister.[68] Yet, as long as the

62. In fact, the populace, together with the army, came to be viewed as wild and as uncivilized as barbarians. See *CTS* 145.13b and *TCTC* 240.7745.

63. See above p. 162. Also note Li Chiang's remarks on maintaining peace with the Uighurs in order better to deal with Huai-hsi: *HTS* 217a.10b–11b; *TCTC* 239.7704.

64. *CTS* 15.6b, 145.11a; *TFYK* 374. 9a; *TCTC* 239.7705; *HTS* 146.5b.

65. See appointments of military leaders to governorships of adjoining provinces in *CTS* 15.6b and *TCTC* 239.7705–06. The mobilization included the withdrawal of an important army from the borders of the now trustworthy Wei-po, which province again received a sizable imperial grant—apparently as down payment for future services. See *CTS* 15.6b; *HTS* 146.6a errs here with *erh-ch'ien-wan* for *erh-shih-wan*.

66. *HTS* 146.6a; *CTS* 148.5b; *TCTC* 239.7706. Li died almost immediately afterward, though this does not seem to have had an impact on this policy.

67. *CTS* 145.11a; *TCTC* 239.7706–07. This was in the ninth lunar month of this year (814).

68. The burning of Ho-yin occurred in the fourth month of Yüan-ho 10 (815), with a very serious loss of government revenue and supplies. See Ch'üan, *T'ang-Sung ti-kuo yü yün-ho*, pp.

Huai-hsi campaign was unfinished, the government could not afford an open break with P'ing-lu, which would have entailed defense of the canal zone provinces from both front and rear.

The case of Ch'eng-te, still under the leadership of Wang Ch'eng-tsung, was significantly different in that the six bordering provinces, all possessing respectable armies, could be deputed to crush the Ch'eng-te force.[69] Nevertheless, reflecting the great wariness toward Ch'eng-te at court, two of the three highest ranking ministers protested vigorously against the perilous strategy of opening a second front.[70] According to the official accounts, Ch'eng-te's extraordinary provocations did not leave the government much choice.[71] Loyalist forces advanced, but, firm as his resolve to chastise this province seems to have been, Hsien-tsung let the campaign founder by failing to impose unified command on the several armies operating in Hopei, which the capable Ch'eng-te army could and did check one by one. After close to a year and a half of reverses, the government ceased hostilities in 817.[72]

Meanwhile, the inconclusive military situation in Huai-hsi had more than once brought the government to the point of calling off the effort.

81–82. The incident in Loyang took place in the eighth month of that year; see *TCTC* 239. 7715. The murder of Wu Yüan-heng occurred in the sixth month; Chao I, *Nien-erh-shih cha-chi*, chap. 20, has recreated the event very well by drawing on several different sources.

69. *TCTC* 239.7721. At the beginning of 816 the court ordered all provinces of Hopei and Ho-tung into action against Ch'eng-te, namely, Yu-chou, Wei-po, I-wu, Heng-hai, Chao-i, and Ho-tung.

70. Chang Hung-ching resigned as chief minister in protest against this second war, while his colleague Wei Kuan-chih took Hsien-tsung to task for failing to learn from Te-tsung's example that impetuosity in dealing with the Hopei problem led to disaster. Two other lesser but vocal critics were relieved of their functions as a warning to other critics at court. See *CTS* 15.9b and *TCTC* 239.7720–21. Ts'en, *Sui-T'ang shih*, p. 272, observes that Hsien-tsung retained or dismissed his ministers according to the sole criterion of their willingness to pursue action against the recalcitrant provinces. This instance supports such a view, but on the whole the question is not that clear-cut.

71. Even if these provocations have been exaggerated, it would surely have been in the long-range interest of any autonomous province to distract the government in its effort to eliminate another of its kind. If such a design lay behind Ch'eng-te's intervention, it failed in the end. On the increasing sources of conflict see *TCTC* 240.7713–14, 7719–20. There was clearly no lack of drama in the situation to begin with. What then served only to intensify feelings was the widespread belief at the capital that Wang was responsible for the assassination of Wu Yüan-heng. It is likely that Wang was somehow implicated, though *CTS* 142.10b and *HTS* 212.8b associate him in a blanket manner with all of Li Shih-tao's sixth-column work. However, when documents were seized upon the defeat of P'ing-lu in 819, it became clear that it had been Li's men who committed the murder. Not all questions, nevertheless, have been answered. See also Chao I's account cited in note 68.

72. There seems to be rather little material available on this campaign, possibly because of the relative inactivity that characterized most of the forces in the field. However, see *TCTC* 239.7721–240.7734 passim; *CTS* 15.9b–12a passim; and Wang's biographies in *CTS* 142 and *HTS* 211.

Only the energy and perseverance of the dominant chief minister P'ei Tu maintained the emperor's resolve to see this action through;[73] and, interestingly, success came only after P'ei, altogether civilian in background, personally assumed field direction of the campaign. P'ei was, however, at best only indirectly responsible for the brilliantly conceived final battle, a lightning seizure of the provincial capital that suddenly ended the long campaign in the fall of 817.[74] Huai-hsi's territories were apportioned to adjoining provinces, and the province was simply liquidated.[75]

However limited the military effectiveness of the loyalist armies in this campaign would appear to have been, the ability of the government to keep forces in the field at length and even to maintain sizable forces in two separate conflicts at once is notable, all the more in view of the imperfect system of military support employed. Campaigning provincial armies, normally dependent on local means of support, became eligible, once outside their home provinces, for so-called expeditionary rations *(ch'u-chieh liang)*,[76] that is, disbursements at specified rates per man from the central government. This system, to which there was probably no good alternative, bred abuse by the many provincial commanders who did not hesitate to cross a border to qualify for the subsidy while eluding tighter court control and pressure to produce commensurate military results.

That this system seriously inflated the costs of such campaigns goes without saying, and by the latter part of 816 the financial pinch had

73. See of course, P'ei's biographies in *CTS* 170 and *HTS* 173 and also Han Yü's "P'ing Huai-hsi pei," in *Han Ch'ang-li chi* (Kuo-hsüeh chi-pen ts'ung-shu ed.), *ch.* 30, pp. 50–55, which stresses P'ei's role (and which was subsequently officially rejected for that reason).

74. This attack was carried out by Li Su and is generally regarded as one of the outstanding exploits in Chinese military annals (cf. Chang Ch'i-yün, *Chung-kuo chan-shih lun-chi* [Taipei, 1954], vol. 1). Since the campaign as a whole is perhaps the best-documented military event in T'ang history and since it is of considerable intrinsic interest, I have done a study of it which will be published shortly in *Chinese Ways of Warfare: Eight Studies* under the editorship of J. K. Fairbank and F. A. Kierman, Jr. (in press). I indicate there the full range of sources available; however, the reader here is directed to substantial accounts which can be found in the biographies of Wu Yüan-chi and Li Su, *CTS* 145 and 133, *HTS* 214 and 154, respectively. *HTS* 214, incidentally, contains the full text of the Han Yü account mentioned in the preceding note, an instance of Ou-yang Hsiu's marked bias in the compilation of this work.

75. *TCTC* 240.7751; *HTS* 65.10b. The major act of grace issued in the last month of 818, a document infused with a sense of triumph and magnanimity, ordered an amnesty and humane treatment for the Huai-hsi populace. See the text in *TFYK* 89.27a–28b; its issuance only is recorded in *CTS* 15.14a and *TCTC* 240.7747.

76. See Hino, "Tōdai hanchin no bakko to chinshō," pp. 399–400, for a brief discussion of this system. A more recent piece by Sueda Shūichi, "Tōdai hanchin no shūkkai ryō ni tsuite," *Suzuki Shun Kyōju kanreki kinen Tōyōshi ronsō* (Tokyo, 1964), pp. 315-31, does not add greatly to our knowledge.

forced consideration of urgent measures. While tax quotas as such may generally have been increased at this time, there was a concurrent effort to put personnel regarded as especially effective tax collectors into posts where they could best exercise their talents.[77] Two such officials were made governors of Che-hsi and Hsüan-she late in 816 and performed altogether up to expectations.[78] At the same time the governor of the third vital lower Yangtse province, Huai-nan, was a major contributor of funds throughout the rebellion.[79]

The push for increased revenue found its fullest expression in Ch'eng I's mission into the Yangtse region, which took place in the first part of 817.[80] Recognized earlier in his career for his management of tax matters,[81] and at this point holding the number two post in the powerful Salt and Iron Commission, Ch'eng was now given, in effect, plenipotentiary powers to make a personal inspection of the several southern provinces and to exhaust every possible source of funds. He was to examine deficiencies, evaluate claims for tax relief, appropriate available surpluses, and dispatch posthaste to the armies whatever funds he could lay his hands on.[82] His biography disingenuously claims that he succeeded in his mission without imposing hardship.[83] This is, however, flatly contradicted by at least one source, which singles out for praise a governor who managed to raise the additional revenue demanded out of available administrative funds rather than through an increase in tax rates.[84] Ch'eng, on the other hand, appears to have been em-

77. As explicitly stated in *CTS* 162.2b.

78. Li Hsiao already enjoyed something of a mixed reputation as an effective financial manager when he was made governor of Che-hsi in 816. This reputation no doubt secured his elevation to that post. In the same year Wang Sui was appointed governor of Hsüan-she, bringing to this post considerable financial administrative experience. After carrying out his mission here successfully (see *TFYK* 485.7a), he was put in charge of logistics for the armies attacking P'ing-lu in 818-19 and handled that well too. Both men have biographies in *CTS* 162 and in *HTS* 206 and 116, respectively.

79. Li Yung, who served subsequently as chief minister for a brief time, had acquired a reputation as an effective local administrator, especially in financial matters. Throughout the campaign he provided both a military force, equipped with supplies, and funds. See his biographies in *CTS* 157 and *HTS* 146; also see *TFYK* 485.6b.

80. *TCTC* 240.7730 records this special assignment as being made in the first lunar month of Yüan-ho 12.

81. *THY* 84.1550, dating from 812.

82. *TFYK* 484.12a-13b contains the memorial submitted by Wang Po, Ch'eng's superior, outlining the proposed mission.

83. *CTS* 135.15b; *HTS* 168.12b.

84. This was Wei Kuan-chih, who had by now become governor of Hunan after having been a vigorous war critic at court. See *CTS* 158.10a-b and *HTS* 169.6b. On the other hand, Li Yung, who was mentioned in note 79, was one of the most cooperative. Somehow still in possession of large funds and stores, he opened up his treasury and storehouses to Ch'eng,

powered to authorize just such an increase in rates in the provinces throughout this region, either for a single collection or perhaps for the entire year. The result was a greater tax burden for the Yangtse Valley populace and crowning success for Ch'eng's mission. By the time of his return in early summer, central coffers were 1,850,000 *min* the richer.[85] It is highly probable that these funds were critical in permitting the campaign to be brought to a successful conclusion. The military success in Huai-hsi soon had a positive political fall-out in other provinces. Early in 818 the ruling line in the small Hopei province of Heng-hai voluntarily relinquished the governorship, thereby reducing the number of autonomous provinces in the empire to three, Yu-chou, Ch'eng-te, and P'ing-lu.[86] Though it would not be accurate to represent the government as the absolute master of all the provincial forces which had accepted its direction, there is little doubt that those still outside the pale were in a precarious position. Keenly aware of this, Ch'eng-te's governor Wang Ch'eng-tsung, who had not yet received formal pardon for his recent revolt, sought the mediation of T'ien Hung-cheng in Wei-po for a return to the good graces of the court. Wang offered what only a year or two earlier would have been regarded as startling concessions: to give up the much-coveted prefectures of Te and Ti, to contribute revenue to the central government, to accept central appointees, and to send his two sons as hostages to the capital.[87] Not to be overlooked is the fact that by doing this Wang in effect renounced the possibility of hereditary succession for his own sons. The court granted his request in the spring of that year (818).[88]

A parallel situation momentarily materialized in P'ing-lu where Li Shih-tao offered the court similar concessions. However, matters took a different course when Li subsequently bowed to heavy internal (especially family) pressures not to compromise and reneged on his promise to accept central officials in three of his prefectures.[89] The

---

presumably showing the way for others (*CTS* 157.4a and *TFYK* 485.6b). It was probably no accident that he became chief minister later in the same year.

85. *TFYK* 485.6b; *TCTC* 240.7736.

86. *CTS* 143.7a; *HTS* 213.5b; *TCTC* 240.7748.

87. *CTS* 142.11a-b; *HTS* 211.9a; *TCTC* 240.7748–49. In the latter source, Ssu-ma Kuang, by juxtaposing excerpts from a memorial by Han Yü calling for action against Ch'eng-te, attempts to suggest that this memorial had the effect of frightening Wang. That Han Yü had such influence is out of the question but, if one regards this as an example of the kind of demands officals were making at the time, then Wang might well have been made to feel concern.

88. *TCTC* 240.7749–50. *TTCLC* 122.650–51 and *CTS* 142.11a–b both contain the text of the edict.

89. *CTS* 124.9b; *HTS* 213.3b–4a; *TCTC* 240.7747 and 7750.

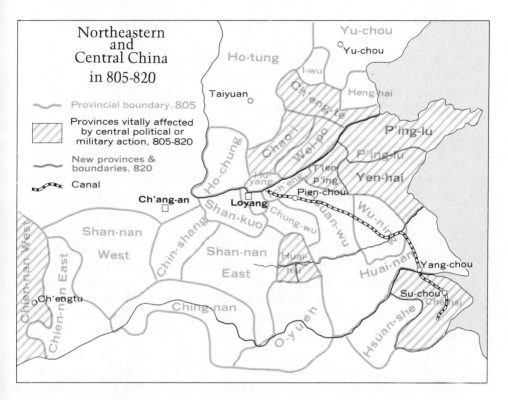

Northeastern
and
Central China
in 805-820

~~~ Provincial boundary, 805

▨ Provinces vitally affected
by central political or
military action, 805-820

〜 New provinces &
boundaries, 820

🝔 Canal

Yu-chou
o Yu-chou

Ho-tung
I-wu
Heng-hai
Taiyuan o
Ch'eng-te
P'ing-lu
Chao-i
Wei-po
P'ing-lu
Ho-chung
Yen-hai
Ho-
yang
Cheng
Tien-
p'ing
Ch'ang-an
Loyang
Pien-chou
Shan-
nan
Chung-wu
Hsuan-wu
Wu-ning
Shan-nan
West
Chin-shang
West
Chin-nan West
Shan-nan
East
Huai-
hsi
Huai-nan
Yang-chou
Chien-nan East
Ch'engtu
Ching-nan
Su-chou
Che-hsi
Hsüan-she
O-yüeh

court began making preparations for an attack at mid-year (818), but
no hostilities seem to have occurred till late in the year.[90] With able
generals and relatively disciplined armies to count on, Hsien-tsung
could afford to move with deliberation, to reduce risks by careful
preparation. Once underway, the campaign lasted but a few months,
moreover costing far less than anticipated.[91] With the assassination of
Li early in 819 by one of his own lieutenants, sixty years of domination
of the region by a single family line came to an end—as did the province itself. The emperor ordered a systematic study made of its population, geography, military potential, and financial resources, on the

90. See *TCTC* 240.7751 and *CTS* 15.14a, for appointments in pivotal provinces. The
latter source also mentions the transfer in the sixth month of 300,000 rolls of silk and 300,000
strings of cash from the emperor's personal treasury to the Department of Public Revenue
(*Tu-chih*) for the purpose of military expenditures. Some of these funds may have gone to the
support of armies elsewhere, but another entry (15b) records the withdrawal of 100,000 rolls
of silk from the emperor's treasury in the ninth month specifically to meet the needs of the
eastern armies. Once again the best overall synthesis with respect to this campaign is provided
by Ssu-ma Kuang. See *TCTC* 240.7751–241.7765 passim.

91. As head of logistics, Wang Sui was able to turn back to the central treasury some one
million *shih* of grain already provided for the campaign. *CTS* 162.2b; *HTS* 116.2b–3a.

basis of which P'ing-lu was carved up into three entirely new provinces.[92]

This concluded the military phase of efforts to eliminate separatism
in the provinces. Hsien-tsung had reestablished central control at least
over the highest echelons of provincial authority in all but two provinces, Ch'eng-te and Yu-chou; and few powerful regional satraps
remained anywhere.[93] (Note provinces affected by central action on
map.) Even these two provinces peacefully gave up their claims to full
autonomy and accepted court appointees as governors by early 821, in
other words within a year of Hsien-tsung's death. Within another year,
however, both of these provinces and Wei-po as well had thrown out
their court-appointed governors and successfully reasserted their nearly
complete independence from central control.[94] In light of this quick
reversal, it is clear that the government never really came to grips
with the central factors behind the autonomy of these provinces or
established its ascendancy over their basic power structure. Hsien-tsung
himself, indeed, hardly had the time to do so. Nevertheless, this need
not detract from his achievement in having put the entire remainder
of the empire on a stable political footing. He achieved this, it must
be remarked, without jeopardizing the throne, without damage to the
country's external position, and without the disaffection of any politically
prominent group. It is, on the other hand, doubtful that he did it
without significant cost to at least some segments of the population.

INSTITUTIONAL MEASURES

Initially installed in the interior during the An Lu-shan Rebellion to
provide a form of military command and government for the strife-
torn empire, the system of provincial governorships eventually became
the real center of executive power throughout the country. In the
immediate aftermath, there was no question of this system's being
dismantled or replaced, for no immediately viable alternative appeared.
In succeeding decades the governorship maintained the civil powers it

92. *CTS* 124.10a; *HTS* 213.4a; *TCTC* 241.7764-65; also *HTS* 65.10b.

93. One of the last of these, Han Hung, a loyal but perhaps irremovable figure as governor
of Hsüan-wu since 799, had become a veritable Croesus in this favored position on the Pien
Canal. In 819 he voluntarily gave up this position, putting it at the disposition of the court.
See his biographies in *CTS* 156 and *HTS* 158 and *TCTC* 214.7769-71.

94. These developments can be traced in the biographies of the following figures: Wang
Ch'eng-yüan and Wang T'ing-tsou (*CTS* 142 and *HTS* 212); Liu Tsung and Chu K'o-jung
(*CTS* 143 and 180 and *HTS* 212); T'ien Hung-cheng, T'ien Pu, and Shih Hsien-ch'eng
(*CTS* 141 and 181; *HTS* 148 and 212).

had acquired and, while some provinces were effectively demilitarized, it is fair to say that this office uniquely combined civil and military powers, and on a very significant scale.[95] The military and political consequences of this development emerged in the preceding discussion; here we wish to examine how the government under Hsien-tsung dealt with it in institutional terms. To the extent that the staffing of an office clearly has institutional implications, it is appropriate to begin with a consideration of Hsien-tsung's policy of appointments to provincial governorships.[96]

The series of confrontations over appointments in the autonomous provinces had something of a counterpart in the heavily garrisoned subordinate provinces, namely, those on the frontier and those along the canal. Under both Tai-tsung and Te-tsung such local garrisons did on occasion resist court appointees and put in charge men of military capacities, who then gained confirmation irrespective of how they obtained their posts. In the remaining provinces, probably the majority, there was no military problem. Here, considerations for the appointment of a governor ran more nearly along the lines of an individual's administrative skill and experience.

Te-tsung had quite bluntly adopted the policy of sounding out local garrisons on acceptable appointees and selecting men accordingly.[97] In both kinds of province, armed and otherwise, he did not, as we have seen, regularly transfer his governors but rather permitted them very lengthy tenures.[98] He is even accused of using an official's ability to raise revenue as the sole criterion in determining his further appointments and promotions.[99] Clearly, given this state of affairs, and in the interests of any genuine degree of central administrative control, two major changes had to come about. First, governors had to be uniformly and consistently selected and appointed by the central government; and, second, limitations had to be placed on tenure in office. It was

95. This aspect is the particular bane of Chinese historians. Cf. Wang Ming-sheng, *Shih-ch'i shih shang-ch'üeh*, chap. 78. Of course, on the frontier the system of military governorships had already largely taken this form by the time of the rebellion.

96. Since this was a high post, the names of appointees and their dates and places of appointments have been largely preserved. Wu T'ing-hsieh's "T'ang fang-chen nien-piao" (*Erh-shih-wu shih pu-pien*, vol. 6) is a splendid aid in this connection. By contrast it will never be possible to obtain any more than a thin sampling of prefectural appointments at any particular time.

97. See *TCTC* 234.7526.

98. During the reigns of Tai-tsung and Te-tsung, and leaving aside the Hopei provinces, over twenty individuals served upward of ten years as governor in a single province. See Wu, "T'ang fang-chen nien-piao."

99. *CTS* 48.2a; *TCTC* 235.7572.

deemed consonant with the first objective to foster the tendency, already some decades old, toward the greater employment of civil bureaucrats as distinguished from professional military men.[100]

A survey of the appointments to provincial governorships made during the reign of Hsien-tsung shows, in fact, that the government successfully established, with the exception of Hopei, full control in this sphere.[101] As detailed above, coercive measures were sometimes necessary to achieve this, and there were a few other cases of irregularities where the government subsequently reasserted its authority successfully.[102] But the pattern of continual local mutinies and usurpations that had persisted since the An Lu-shan Rebellion was largely brought to an end under Hsien-tsung.

In addition, the government in this period both adopted and successfully implemented a policy of limiting the tenure of its provincial governors, a policy entailing their regular transfer either to other provinces or to the central administration. There was, apparently, by contrast with prefects and county magistrates, no fixed period of service in one province, but six years seems to have been regarded as the absolute maximum. Hardly more than a half-dozen exceptions to this rule can be found in the ninth century down to the Huang Ch'ao Rebellion.[103]

Finally, a few words are necessary about the composition of the corps of officials selected to serve as governors.[104] There were, as we have noted, several provinces with direct military responsibilities, which only men of proven military competence could properly head. By the end of Hsien-tsung's reign this number had been rounded off at something over a dozen. Now we find that while military figures were appointed almost exclusively to these provinces, all other provinces were placed under civil, career bureaucrats. Moreover, as in the case of their civilian counterparts, the military men were drawn from the center, many

100. An examination of Wu T'ing-hsieh's tables reveals the gradual but steady replacement under Tai-tsung and Te-tsung of the military-officer types who held sway at the end of the rebellion. That literati types were not always, however, better gambles in positions of power is shown by the cases of Liu P'i and Li Ch'i.

101. I reported the results of this survey, covering about 150 individuals serving in governorships in the sample years of 763, 804, 820, and 845, in a paper (unpublished) presented to the Conference on Change in China, 750–1350, held in Chicago in September 1966. Wang Gungwu, *The Structure of Power in North China during the Five Dynasties* (Kuala Lumpur, 1963), pp. 12 f., has a relevant survey which covers late T'ang from 845.

102. As in Hsia-Sui in 806, Chen-wu in 813, and I-wu in 816.

103. Wu, "T'ang fang-chen nien-piao." This of course excludes the three autonomous provinces in Hopei.

104. These conclusions are based on the above-mentioned (note 101) survey and draw on Wu's tables, relevant biographies, and *CTW* materials where available.

from Palace Army units in and around the capital. With respect to the bureaucrats, it was during Hsien-tsung's reign that the practice developed of appointing outgoing chief ministers to provincial governorships.[105] Instances of total disgrace and harsh exile now became infrequent for the highest ranking officials.[106] Their appointment to lucrative provincial posts, compensating for the loss of influence and position at court, not only tended to provide an important link between central and provincial administration but also helped take the sting out of factional rivalries at the capital.

Central control over appointments to the governorships was important but still inconclusive. It made possible the installation of generally suitable men into these key positions, but except by the threat of ultimate dismissal, it provided no guarantee for their conduct once in office. For this purpose Hsien-tsung turned, like his predecessors, to the traditional instruments—and sometimes masters—of monarchy in China, the eunuchs.

The system of eunuch army supervisors *(chien-chün shih)*, already largely perfected by Te-tsung, had existed in the same basic form since the mid-eighth century. The importance it assumed after the An Lushan Rebellion clearly reflects the isolation which the throne felt from its own officialdom and from the provinces in general. In principle, these supervisors were attached to each provincial administration with the task of observing the manner in which the governor and his staff conducted affairs.[107] Their reports were submitted directly to the throne to supplement information received from the governor himself. This basic intelligence function remained, no doubt, the supervisors' major one, even after others were acquired and expanded. It is not hard to imagine how this latter development took place. As personal agents of the emperor, with a direct channel to him, the supervisors soon began interfering in the administration of provinces and armies and even assuming direct command of troops in battle. On the other hand, the throne itself made increasing use of them: to assume temporary control of a province upon the death of the governor; to undertake negotiations with a recalcitrant governor or garrison; to disburse grain in the event

105. Observe appointments made upon dismissal at court in *HTS* 62.

106. But not for lower ranking ones, as two famous writers serving in official capacities in this reign, Yüan Chen and Han Yü, unequivocally discovered.

107. This discussion is drawn largely from two studies by Yano Chikara, "Tōdai kangunshi-sei no kakuritsu ni tsuite," *Nishi-Nihon shigaku* 14 (1953): 16–32, and "Tōmatsu kangunshi-sei ni tsuite," *Shakai kagaku ronsō* 7 (1957): 17–25. Supervisors were present in most provinces, and certainly in the heavily garrisoned ones; but it has not, I think, been established whether they were uniformly placed in all provinces.

of famine. On most occasions eunuchs could most safely be entrusted with these functions, since they were entirely without status save by reference to the throne. It has been aptly observed that objections to the system first became vociferous under Te-tsung and that these objections must bespeak its increased effectiveness.[108] There is also explicit evidence for its growing use during his reign.

Specific innovations introduced into this system by Hsien-tsung are difficult to pinpoint, but the thrust of its operation took an unmistakably new direction under his reign. For Te-tsung the system had acted essentially as an intelligence arm; for Hsien-tsung, guiding a resurgence of central power, it functioned as an active centralizing agent. There were also, in the latter's reign, many complaints about this system's negative effects. On one occasion the emperor was even induced to withdraw the eunuch supervisors from armies in campaign—with decidedly favorable results. To be sure, a very strong bias is to be expected from our official sources, compiled by and for bureaucrats; but contemporary disparagement of eunuch activity was almost certainly also an attack on the attempts by the throne at achieving tight central control in the provinces.[109] In spite of its defects, inherent or otherwise, and the opposition that it raised, the system proved effective from the throne's point of view and was retained, with some subsequent modifications, throughout the remainder of the dynasty.

Naturally, measures going beyond the choice and supervision of personnel were necessary for any lasting improvement in central control over the provinces. Structural changes also had to be made. Hsien-tsung moved slowly on this front, but two major reforms he carried out were crucial in shaping the subsequent course of ninth-century history. For a proper appreciation of these reforms, it would be best to begin with a brief consideration of the principal components in the provincial structure at that time.

Forcibly imposed upon the hitherto viable administrative units of prefecture and county,[110] the provincial system was not a very tidy or uniform affair. Provinces could embrace anywhere from two to twelve prefectures differing vastly in resources and strategic importance. Counties persisted as the most basic administrative unit but were of

108. Remarked by Yano, "Tōmatsu kangunshi-sei ni tsuite."

109. See P'ei Tu's *CTS* biography (170); *TCTC* 240.7738; and Li Te-yü's comments in *TCTC* 248.8009.

110. No one has covered the early stages (i.e. An Lu-shan Rebellion and following decades) of this development very well, but I attempt to do so in my article for *The Cambridge History of China* (in progress).

insufficient size to play a significant political role. The relationship which emerged between province and prefecture, that is, between governor and prefect, never did achieve uniformity or proper definition. In theory, the governor was an administrative overseer, in the style of the pre-rebellion provincial inspectors. In practice, with an army to back him and either the approval or acquiescence of the court, he asserted varying but genuine degrees of direct control over the prefectures within his jurisdiction. The fact that the government itself made heavy use of these provincial administrations in the decades immediately following the rebellion would make it incorrect to see this development as entirely separatist in motivation. However, the essentials for separatism were, as the record shows, very much present.

The prefect was the pivotal figure in this situation: was he, leaving nuances aside, to be an agent of the central government or of the provincial governor?[111] Since the end of the rebellion, attempts had been made, until 777 only sporadically, to restore his position and to protect him from the governors' encroachments upon his authority.[112] In that year the government, showing faint new signs of determination under relatively stabilized conditions, launched an effort both partially to demilitarize the provinces and to reassert its authority over the prefects.[113] It tightened up procedures governing their movements, their official communications, and their replacement; at the same time it forbade the governors to remove prefects on their own authority or to name their own appointees to the post. While such measures probably gained some degree of compliance, progress in this direction was virtually brought to a standstill by the provincial revolts of 781–86.[114] Thus, by the early ninth century the prefect still remained very much under the shadow of his provincial superior. One reason for this, perhaps the principal one, was financial.

The financial relationship between province and prefecture, at the outset probably somewhat haphazard, was systematized in 780 upon

---

111. Since the governor always held the post of prefect concurrently in the home prefecture, the reference here is of course to prefects serving in the remaining prefectures of the province.

112. For example, see *THY* 75.1362 and *TFYK* 630.11a.

113. On this effort see the following sources: *THY* 68.1204, 69.1214, 78.1439, and 91.1658–59; *TFYK* 506.12b–13a; *TCTC* 225.7245; and *HTS* 142.1b–2a. Also, cf. R. des Rotours, *Traité des fonctionaires et traité de l'armée* (Leiden, 1947), pp. 671 and 715.

114. One reason that the 777 measures do not seem to have borne fruit was the short-lived character of the leadership that engineered them. Their principal proponent, Yang Wan, died within months of his appointment as chief minister (*HTS* 62.10a). An edict from 787 (*THY* 69.1214; *TFYK* 60.16a) is testimony at one and the same time that such past measures had not been particularly effective and that Te-tsung had not totally abandoned the effort.

the adoption of the two-tax reform *(liang-shui fa)*.[115] The more commonly noted aspects of this measure need not concern us, though they are most certainly related closely to the provincial problem.[116] What we must notice is the procedure adopted in this reform for the allocation of revenue in the provinces, conceivably a carry-over from previous practice.[117] For the central government, revenue from direct taxation issued from the county, the lowest central government organ. The county, after withdrawing a portion to sustain its own operation, sent the bulk of revenue collected up to the prefecture. On the prefectural level the major allocation of funds took place: portions were assigned to the prefecture *(liu-chou)*, the province *(liu-shih)*, and the central government *(shang-kung)*. The prefecture, like the county, retained its share and forwarded the remaining funds to their respective destinations. It is likely that revenue dispatched to the central government actually passed through the hands of the province.[118] If this was the case, it would obviously have given the province all the more fiscal latitude.

The provincial administration, by virtue of directly administering the prefecture which served as its seat, had itself a tax quota to meet vis-à-vis the central authorities. However, the total revenue at the disposal of the provincial administration was drawn from *all* the prefectures within its jurisdiction. At the origin of this arrangment lay the need to support the provincial army[119] and, as the system evolved, this helped to give the province a corporate character. Combined with the governors' wide powers of administrative supervision and the great latitude allowed them by the government until Hsien-tsung's time, the

115. See D. C. Twitchett, *Financial Administration under the T'ang Dynasty*, (Cambridge, 1963), pp. 39 ff., and his references.

116. This point is made, though overstated, by Hino in his articles "Ryozeihō no kihonteki yon gensoku, *Hōseishi kenkyū* 11 (1960): 40–77, and "Yō En no Ryōzeihō no kenkyo gensoku to sensū-sennō gensoku," *Shien* 84 (1960): 1–37.

117. What we know about this system of allocation comes from the Yüan-ho period; no contemporary material on it from the time of the reform has survived. See sources cited in note 122.

118. I have not come across evidence that shows this necessarily to have been the case: indeed, the fact that the threefold allocation took place on the prefectural level implies, on the contrary, that the revenue did not pass through the hands of the provincial government. However, Hino, *Shina chūsei no gunbatsu*, pp. 88–89, and in more recent articles, suggests as much, particularly in his depiction of a fiscal hierarchy of the sort: central government–province–prefecture–county. Others (e.g. Matsui Shūichi, see note 122) adopt a similar point of view, though precisely on the basis of what evidence I do not know. Naturally, in view of the power generally exercised over his province by a governor, one could plausibly argue that his office *must have* handled all revenue coming up from the prefectures.

119. Note that an alternate name for *sung-shih* was *kung-chün*, i.e. not simply "provincial allotment" but also "funds for the support of the army."

system tended to give the governor something approaching direct financial authority over the prefecture. This went well beyond normal tax quotas and frequently took the form of special impositions levied illegally on the sole authority of the governor.[120] Moreover, when full quotas for whatever reason were not forthcoming from the prefectures, it was the central government's share, not the province's, which probably took the cut.[121] The solution to this general problem, aimed both at increasing central revenue and limiting the financial resources of the province, clearly lay in weakening the link between province and prefecture.

The first major step, taken in the spring of 809 following a proposal by then Chief Minister P'ei Chi,[122] was enactment of a measure aimed at both restructuring the system of financial allocation in the provinces and relieving the even more pressing deflationary crisis. This crisis, while inflicting severe hardship on the populace, was being exploited for personal and political gain by provincial officials.[123] The changes effected in the system of allocation itself were as follows:

1. Provinces were henceforth to draw their necessary revenue from the home prefecture. Only in cases of insufficiency were they to draw on their subordinate prefectures, and then they must draw on all in equal proportion.

2. In consequence of this loss of revenue from the prefectures, the provinces were no longer obliged to make tax contributions to the central government.

3. The prefectures were now to pay into the central government all

---

120. The notorious case of Yen Li in Szechwan offers some specific examples of these. See *Yüan-shih Ch'ang-ch'ing chi*, chap. 37, as well as my forthcoming study of it in *Asia Major*.

121. See Twitchett, *Financial Administration,* pp. 46 and 259n203.

122. The text of this measure, or portions of it, can be found in the following sources: *THY* 83.1537–38; *TFYK* 488.3b–5a; *CTW* 61.6a; and P'ei's biographies in *CTS* 148 and *HTS* 169. Although it had been noted previously (cf. Ch'ü Ch'ing-yüan, *T'ang-tai ts'ai-cheng shih* [Shanghai, 1940, pp. 51 and 151], it is Hino who first perceived its true significance. See especially his "Hanchin jidai no shūzei sanbunsei ni tsuite," *Shigaku zasshi* 65 (1956): 646–66. More recently Matsui Shūichi has subjected the measure and the policy it puts forth to very intensive (and sometimes tortured) analysis. See his "Hai Ki no zeisei kaikaku ni tsuite," *Shigaku Zasshi* 76 (1967): 1039–61. This study adds considerably to our understanding of the subject, though it is questionable to what extent Matsui makes any major revision of Hino's view. Attention should be called here to two points which he convincingly argues: (1) that the *TFYK* text is without question more complete and accurate than that in the *THY*; (2) that the date of the edict implementing the measure was in fact the fifth month of Yüan-ho 4, not, as indicated by the *THY*, the twelfth month (see pp. 1045–49). In this regard, *TCTC* 237.7654–55 is seriously misleading, if not downright mistaken.

123. On this deflation see Twitchett, *Financial Administration,* pp. 46–47 and 77ff., and his references.

revenue except that which was authorized for local purposes. In other words, the provincial allotment here disappeared, being absorbed as central revenue. (Obviously, adjustments would be required in the event that a provincial levy became necessary.)

Thus, an attempt was initiated to eliminate the province as a distinct level of financial administration. Although it continued to enjoy a special status exempting it from the obligation of contributing any revenue from direct taxes to the central government, the scope of its fiscal operation was sharply reduced; and in this sense it ceased being different in kind from the regular prefecture. The political significance of these several provisions, if implemented, needs no elaboration.

With regard to the economic crisis, which threatened the social order itself, the new measure imposed important restrictions on both the medium and the conversion rates used in the collection of taxes. With money scarce and commodity prices severely depressed, real taxes had more than doubled since the 780s, when rates had last been fixed. When forced by local officials to pay in cash, taxpayers were handed an even heavier burden, and at the same time these officials enjoyed considerable latitude in fixing the rates for cash-goods conversion. By increasing the proportion of goods in which taxes could be collected, by requiring the use of rates fixed at the capital, and by forbidding the use of arbitrary rates, the measure aimed to relieve the beleaguered taxpayer and to strike a blow at a major source of profit for provincial officials. These particular provisions no doubt had the most immediate importance for the populace at the time. Surely referring to these changes, P'ei Chi's biography states, "Thereupon (the people) of the Huai and Yangtse provinces obtained a measure of relief."[124]

The most important question nevertheless bears on the degree to which the measure as a whole was ever implemented. The dearth of pertinent material, including figures on central and provincial income, certainly rules out any easy answer. Nor would it be fair to judge by the deflationary crisis which, related to but separate from the problem of provincial control, obeyed dynamics of its own and defied quick solution for a decade and more.[125] From an edict issued early in 811 it is clear

124. *CTS* 148.2b. This discussion makes no pretense at thoroughness, particularly in that the whole issue could receive adequate explanation only in the context of a substantial treatment of the economic history of the period. Though Hino has by no means neglected this aspect (see "Hanchin jidai no shūzei sanbunsei ni tsuite," pp. 661-63), Matsui makes his main contribution to the discussion on this point. See "Hai Ki no zeisei kaikaku ni tsuite," especially pp. 1049-51.

125. See *THY* 83–84.

that the prefectures were still paying in portions of their revenue to the provinces.[126] However, the edict also makes it clear that the government seriously intended to pursue its reform policy. In the relative absence of other hard information, the argument put forward by Hino Kaizaburō is worthy of notice.[127] He suggests that the measure was for the most part implemented, though probably neither all at once nor in rigorous fashion. As a procedure, it was largely accepted because it did not at the outset curtail anyone's revenues. The provinces' loss from the prefectures was compensated by their exemption from any contributions to the central government. By the same token central and prefectural revenues remained about at previous levels. However, by obtaining a reduction, if not total elimination, of the amounts contributed by prefectures to the province, the reform weakened the link between the two and in the long run diminished the total resources available to the province. This in turn, one can add, enabled the court gradually to effect increases in revenue directly from the individual prefectures. Subsequent developments themselves are perhaps most conclusive. Following the reallocation of resources (and Hsien-tsung's series of triumphs), the provinces, save for those in the northeast, simply do not exhibit the same capacity for independent action.

By 819, when Hsien-tsung had accomplished his immediate political objectives, he was prepared to make another major modification in the provincial structure. Ostensibly, the 819 reform grew out of the following report by Wu Ch'ung-yin, a loyalist governor of one of the Hopei splinter provinces:[128]

> The reason that the Hopei provinces have been able to resist the orders of the court over the last sixty years is that they place garrison commanders in charge of affairs in all the prefectures and counties, who, taking over the powers of the prefects and magistrates, usurp the supreme authority (i.e. that of the emperor). Were the prefects again to exercise their functions independently, it would be impossible for any governor, even if he had the perverse ability of an An Lu-shan or a Shih Ssu-ming, to revolt on the strength of

126. Ibid. 83.1538–39. Matsui, however, observes that this contribution of revenue from the prefecture to the province concerned only cash and thereby reflects the monetary crisis more than anything. See his "Hai Ki no zeisei kaikaku ni tsuite," pp. 1054–57.

127. Hino, "Hanchin jidai no shūzei sanbunsei ni tsuite," pp. 650–52. Matsui, "Hai Ki no zeisei kaikaku ni tsuite," pp. 1042–44, who is much more sanguine on the question of implementation, offers minor disagreement with Hino on these points, though without adducing further evidence.

128. *TCTC* 241.7768; *TFYK* 60.21b–22a; and see his biographies in *CTS* 161 and *HTS* 171.

the resources of a single prefecture. In the three prefectures of Te,
Ti, and Ching, which are under the direction of your servant,
I have issued orders that the proper functions be returned to the
prefects and also that they assume jurisdiction over the military
units in their areas.

This situation would apply most particularly to Hopei, but the device of
controlling a province by establishing garrisons in key locations, including administrative centers, was employed by governors throughout
the empire. Members of the governor's own staff were placed at the
head of these garrisons and functioned as a parallel administrative arm,
differing however from the regular one in being responsible exclusively
to the governor. In this capacity they took some part in the direct administration of their localities, but above all they kept a watchful eye
on the activities of the regular local officials.[129] It would hardly have
taken Wu's report to enlighten the court in this respect. What apparently did occur was that Wu found such a situation upon assuming his
post in Hopei and on his own initiative took corrective action. This
action then became a model for an empire-wide reform.

The reform measure had essentially two provisions: (1) it withdrew
authority from the governors over all military units *outside the home
prefecture;* and (2) it placed these units under the prefects, respectively,
in whose prefectures they were located. For this purpose the prefects
were given explicit military powers on a permanent basis for the first
time since the Six Dynasties period. Border and undeveloped areas
were, for obvious reasons, excluded from the measure.[130]

Like the reform of 809 this was an attempt at nothing less than a
restructuring of the provincial system. Fragmentation of the military
power in each province meant a reduction of the political and military
potential of the province as such and a significant reinforcement of the
prefect's position vis-à-vis the governor. Since by far the largest garrison
was invariably located at the provincial seat, this hardly reduced the
governor to impotence. It is important to observe, however, that
because the province-prefecture relationship had always been characterized by ambiguity, the ability to dispose subordinate garrisons
throughout the province, outside the effective control of the local
prefects, had afforded the governor considerable political leverage.
This was spectacularly demonstrated in the governors' frequent re-

129. See especially Hino, "Tōdai hanchin no bakko to chinshō," pp. 330–35; and Wang,
The Structure of Power in North China, p. 146.
    130. *THY* 78.1441–42; *TCTC* 241.7768.

calcitrance toward the court; Wu Ch'ung-yin's report revealed that it worked locally against lower administrative levels as well.

In addition, this reform almost certainly had financial implications. Although these are not spelled out in the legislation, it is difficult to see how a further reallocation of revenues, going beyond that established by the 809 reform, could have been avoided. The prefectures now bore a military burden that had not been at all foreseen under the old system, invalidating in large part the rationale for prefectural contributions to the province. Of course, the province could claim continued or occasional contributions on the grounds of maintaining a sizable garrison and a substantial administrative staff. But even if the prefectures were not always or not completely free from financial responsibilities toward the province, their ties to it were weakened still further.[131]

It is, again, difficult to establish irrefutably the implementation of this measure. We are also dealing with the Chinese Empire at a time when it was at least as heterogeneous as in later and better-known periods. One direct piece of evidence, which suggests that the Yangtse provinces were indeed heeding the order, comes within months of its issue. Another appears twenty-five years later and shows not only that the rule was still on the books but that it was actively being implemented.[132] On the whole, the empire remained peaceful for the four decades following this reform. Only one major provincial revolt occurred outside Hopei during this period and this, not fortuitously, in a province bordering that region.[133] It would seem hard to deny that provincial military capabilities had been sharply reduced.

Other measures, though of less moment, were taken to restrict the power and influence of the provincial governors. Like the late campaigns and the reform of 819, they testify not only to the emperor's determination but also to the confidence he and his administration felt as the reign progressed. From 818 comes a prohibition against any governor concurrently holding the office of commissioner of military colonies *(ying-t'ien shih)*.[134] A considerable development in state farms had taken place in the interior of the country since the end of the An

---

131. Hino, "Hanchin jidai no shūzei sanbunsei ni tsuite," p. 654, speculates that the contribution from the province to the central treasury was revived as a result of this reform. This would have been a noteworthy accomplishment, but there are in fact no real grounds to support such a contention.

132. *THY* 78.1442; *CTW* 702.11b.

133. This was in Chao-i (Tse-Lu) in 843–44. See the biographies of the figures in the governing Liu line there in *CTS* 161 and *HTS* 214, the single throwback to hereditary rule outside Hopei after Hsien-tsung's reign.

134. *THY* 78.1434; *TTCLC* 101.515.

Lu-shan Rebellion, generally under the sponsorship of provincial governors.[135] This new prohibition appears to have been designed to cut back this potentially rich source of revenue. Again, legislation seems to have been issued sometime late in the reign, perhaps in 819, limiting the governors' role in the appointment of county magistrates. The relevant document itself is not extant, but we do find that at this time governors could incur penalties for taking liberties in the appointment of magistrates.[136] In view of the fact that previous legislation forbidding prefectural appointments by the governors was still in effect and undoubtedly being enforced,[137] it was natural that the government should seek to recover control over the magistrates. In other respects, too, it attempted to strengthen the prefectural and county authorities, for example, by authorizing prefects to report directly to the throne regarding local matters and by authorizing local officials to take relief measures without specific approval.[138] There was probably no real expectation of returning to the level of centralization achieved in the first half of the dynasty, but there surely was a strong preoccupation with achieving a safe and working balance of authority in the provinces.

The question of the true effectiveness of Hsien-tsung's policies has already been touched upon. Given the nature and relative thinness of surviving materials, we cannot expect detailed answers. In broad terms, however, a strong case is to be made for vastly improved central control and much greater stability in the empire in the decades following Hsien-tsung than at any time in the post-rebellion period. One evidence of this is the virtual absence of provincial rebellions down to the eve of the Huang Ch'ao Rebellion—a fact not contradicted by

135. See D. C. Twitchett, "Lands under State Cultivation under the T'ang," *Journal of the Economic and Social History of the Orient* 2 (1959): esp. 181–97; and Aoyama Sadao, "Tōdai no tonden to eiden," *Shigaku Zasshi* 63 (1954): esp. 23–25 and 29 ff.

136. Notice of such a penalty dates from the second month of Yüan-ho 14 (819); see *CTS* 15.16b and *THY* 78.1442. Since only a violation of rules is mentioned, without reference to *which* rules, it is difficult to be precise in our interpretation. Hino, "Tōdai hanchin no bakko to chinshō," interprets this to reveal a recent prohibition against the appointment by governors of garrison commanders to fill the post of magistrate. He relates this to the 819 transfer of authority over such garrisons to the prefects. He may well be correct, but I find it at least as likely that the government sought to remove the counties from direct provincial control. That the provincial governors had been exercising nearly absolute power over magistrates within their jurisdiction should not be overlooked. See *Yüan-shih Ch'ang-ch'ing chi* 38 for a case of manslaughter perpetrated by a governor in inflicting punishment on one of his magistrates.

137. See *THY* 68.1204, for a document from 830 which refers to such a prohibition as being in force since 777.

138. *THY* 68.1203, a document from 817; *THY* 88.1616 and *TFYK* 502.27b, a document from 818.

the recalcitrance of some garrisons, which seldom took more elaborate form than local, short-lived mutinies. The major provinces of Hopei, again, did remain outside the pale after 822, but even there internal conditions became stabilized, and a satisfactory modus vivendi with the court was worked out. Second, there was a return to true bureaucratic control on all levels of administration in the provinces, a process touching on the appointment of officials, the character of personnel employed, and the regulation of administrative conduct and procedures. To a surprising degree the central government regained control over appointments; and the men it appointed, so far as the records show, were overwhelmingly civilian literati. Only in border regions and in those moderately few interior provinces which retained a military mission were military specialists employed. More subtly, the government found itself increasingly able to govern conduct and procedures among its administrative corps. Legislation was issued which would have been unthinkable in the years of feeble central authority. Quite possibly such measures did not gain full compliance; however, that they were issued at all shows some expectation that they could.[139]

Fortunately, one category of statistical information has come down to us which testifies to the increased effectiveness of the bureaucracy— as well as to the improved state of its finances. Figures for the registered population—not censuses as such but the registration of households liable to taxation—exist for the years 807 and 821, in other words, for nearly the beginning and for the end of Hsien-tsung's reign. In this interval the number of registered households increased from roughly two and a half to four million. Subsequently, the high for the second half of the dynasty was reached in 839 at nearly five million. This was still a far cry from pre-rebellion totals, but it is an impressive figure, and, above all, it demonstrates a progression quite the contrary from what we should expect in a period of "decline."[140]

In Hsien-tsung's own day, it was his vigorous military policy which evoked the praise and admiration of his contemporaries. In consequence of his successes, the idea of a "restoration" came to be very much in

139. This is an issue I develop in my article for *The Cambridge History of China,* but, for example, note the restrictions placed on the size, selection, and so on of the governors' staffs in *THY* 79.1446–52.

140. The precise totals are: 807, 2,440,254 (the *THY* figure); 821, 3,944,959; and 839, 4,996,752. See *THY* 84.1551–52; *TFYK* 486.19a,21a. The pre-rebellion high was 9,069,154 (*TFYK* 486.17b). However, it must not be overlooked that the loss of administrative control over the populace was so complete that only 1,2000,000 households were registered in the decade or so after the rebellion (*T'ung-tien* [Shih-t'ung ed.] 7.41c).

the air.[141] Li Ao's paean of praise—"of all restoration monarchs since antiquity none have come up to this"—may have been fulsome, but it betrays a new morale among at least his stratum of society.[142] This is all the more noteworthy in that no particular enthusiasm or spirit of hope appears to have been present at the outset of Hsien-tsung's reign, unlike, for example, upon Te-tsung's accession in 779. However, as these and other signs show, a sense of achievement developed as the long-awaited assertion of central authority over the provinces materialized. Viewed historically and particularly with reference to the totality of actions undertaken, the idea of a "restoration" need hardly strike us as hollow.

Hsien-tsung as Monarch

Even though our concern here has been with the most important accomplishments of Hsien-tsung's reign rather than with the reign in its entirety, some consideration of the nature of leadership at court is both feasible and necessary. Insights into the style of rule of the monarch himself would be most pertinent, but, as we find with virtually every Chinese emperor, little of Hsien-tsung's individuality and personal traits have been revealed by the Chinese historiographers.[143] Nevertheless, the records bear the imprint of an ambitious and forceful personality, a monarch who not only reigned but who also ruled. An examination of his employment of chief ministers confirms such a characterization. In the course of his nearly fifteen years on the throne he appointed no less than twenty officials to this supreme position.[144] Even allowing for the fact that two or three normally held this post simultaneously at any given time, the average tenure was clearly quite brief. Only Li Chi-fu served for substantially more than three years (though his overall total of five and a half years was the sum of two separate terms), and only three others served as long as three years.[145]

141. Note the use of the term *chung-hsing* by Tuan Wen-ch'ang in *CTW* 617.21a, and by Han Yü in *CTW* 548.4b.

142. *CTW* 634.6b. This and the reference cited in note 141 date from the years 817–18. Note also another piece from this period by Li Ao mentioned below as well as the issue of the adoption of a new honorary title by the emperor in 819.

143. Nevertheless, see the revealing analysis of T'ai-tsung made by Arthur F. Wright in the paper he has written for this volume.

144. See *HTS* 62. Note that the inclusion of Yü Ti on p. 15b of this source is incorrect; his chief ministership was only honorary. Sun Kuo-tung characterizes the chief ministership in its later phase, from Hsien-tsung forward, in his article "T'ang-tai san-sheng-chih chih fa-chan yen-chiu," *Hsin-ya hsüeh-pao* 3 (1957–58): 99–120.

145. These were P'ei Tu and Wu Yüan-heng, whom we have noted above, and Cheng Yin,

Under the circumstances Hsien-tsung could hardly have come to rely on a single chief minister for any length of time, nor could any have acquired lasting influence. The practice of assigning outgoing chief ministers to important provincial posts gave Hsien-tsung much greater flexibility in the use of this institution than it had possessed under previous monarchs.[146]

Some observers have made the point that Hsien-tsung appointed and kept as chief ministers only those who were prepared to support his war policies.[147] This is only partly true, or perhaps only true of the latter part of the reign. While some of those on whom he relied most heavily, such as Li Chi-fu, Wu Yüan-heng, and P'ei Tu, were consistent advocates of a policy of force, others such as Li Chiang held views which were far more tempered. Li won appointment in 811 after he had already established himself as a strong opponent of any military action in Hopei. Interestingly enough, his term in office (811–14) coincided with the most peaceful years of the reign, and it was, we recall, his successful counsel against military intervention in Wei-po in 812 which led to a peaceful resolution of that problem. Yet the long campaign against Huai-hsi took a serious toll in chief ministers; certainly Hsien-tsung brooked no opposition on this occasion.[148]

Rather more specific conclusions, however, can be reached regarding the emperor's use of his highest ministers, namely, that at least on occasion he sought to balance off one point of view with another and that, above all, he sought men who took firm positions and articulated them. In this first respect the case of Li Chiang is again instructive. Upon Li Chiang's elevation to the chief ministership, Li Chi-fu had already been serving in this capacity for the better part of a year. Hsien-tsung could not have helped knowing the extent to which the two disagreed.[149] Yet he appointed Li Chiang and kept both working in tandem for over two years. As we shall see, he was probably attempting to maintain a similar balance among his ministers in 818–19. Second, his insistence on having men who were strong advocates is revealed by the succession of strong personalities whom he placed at

---

a literatus nonentity who owed his appointment to his support for Hsien-tsung's accession during Shun-tsung's last critical days.

146. We need only recall, by contrast, the deaths of Yüan Tsai in 777 and Yang Yen in 782 and the virtually definitive exile of Lu Chih in 792.

147. See Ts'en, *Sui-T'ang shih*, p. 272, and also Lü, *Sui-T'ang-Wu-tai shih*, p. 351.

148. See note 73. Eventually, not only Chang Hung-ching but also Wei Kuan-chih and Li Feng-chi were dismissed because of their disapproval of the war, though the latter case is complicated by a personal rivalry. See *CTS* 158.9b–10a and *TCTC* 239.7738.

149. *CTS* 164.8a; *TCTC* 238.7687 and 239.7699.

the head of his administration. Furthermore, there are instances where he showed no patience with ministers who remained silent or who refused to take part in court debates.[150] Thus, while he no doubt jealously guarded his own prerogative as final arbiter, he evidently regarded the free expression of views on the part of his ministers as essential. To be sure, even strong advocates eventually outlived their immediate usefulness, but sometimes they themselves provided the initiative for their departure,[151] and on no occasion was a departing minister treated ignominiously.

In his final year on the throne Hsien-tsung may or may not have departed from his characteristic manner of rule. Certainly, the official historiographers believe he did.[152] He is said to have become avaricious and intolerant, preoccupied with the search for a true elixir, and no longer able to distinguish good ministers from bad. Huang-fu Po, a chief minister since 818, is cast as a willing tool to the emperor's selfish desires. But the accounts we have on this final phase are so tendentious as to discourage credence. Tentatively, two suggestions can be put forward. On the one hand a factional division most certainly occurred, occasioned by Hsien-tsung's appointment to high office of officials regarded as narrow, unscrupulous financial experts. Apparently appointed in order to obtain the means needed to execute his further designs, these officials were bitterly opposed by at least one segment of the literati group exemplified by P'ei Tu and Ts'ui Chün. Inevitably, historians have taken the part of the literati and left us the slanted accounts which have since held the field. In reality, Hsien-tsung, fully cognizant of the political infighting and of its potential dangers, attempted to maintain a balance among his ministers until the dogged partisanship of both P'ei and Ts'ui led to their dismissals.[153] In other words, it can by no means be categorically claimed that he departed from previous practice. On the other hand, however, it seems certain that the emperor for the first time allowed a serious gap to open up between officialdom and himself, but we shall return to this presently.

150. See *CTS* 159.2b, regarding the dismissal of Cheng Yin; and *TCTC* 239.7699, regarding that of Ch'üan Te-yü.

151. According to *TCTC* 240.7752, P'ei Tu and Ts'ui Ch'ün long sought to be relieved of their appointments. One wonders, too, whether ill health was a reason or a pretext for the withdrawal of P'ei Chi in 810 and of Li Chiang in 814.

152. See *CTS* 15.20b; *HTS* 7.16b–17a; *TCTC* 240.7752, and 241.7776. Also see the biographies of Huang-fu Po in *CTS* 135 and *HTS* 167.

153. For a somewhat integrated account of these developments see the *TCTC* references in the preceding note; however, my tentative interpretation departs markedly from that of Ssu-ma Kuang. Regarding Hsien-tsung's concern over factionalism see *CTS* 15.17a and *TCTC*

Another critical and even more difficult problem to sort out is the extent of eunuch influence under Hsien-tsung.[154] That eunuchs played a significant role throughout the reign is evident. We have seen that the emperor made heavy use of eunuch army supervisors in the provinces in order to maintain an instrument of intelligence and control separate from the regular bureaucracy. Eunuch power at court continued to be centered in the Palace Armies, to the supreme command of which they were appointed without exception. Though no crisis arose in this reign inducing the eunuchs to use this unique military advantage, such a time soon came.[155] Moreover, in addition to the influence they were able to exert through these offices and through their more orthodox functions in the imperial household, their direct participation in court counsels was becoming formalized during this period through the activities of the Bureau of Secret Documents *(Shu-mi-yüan)*, which they dominated.[156] Therefore, the complaints we find being raised about eunuchs at this time are by no means groundless. Nevertheless, there is every indication that under this emperor they remained no more than instruments, and Hsien-tsung had every confidence in his ability to control them.[157] On the whole, the weaknesses inherent in his conception of the permissible role and powers of this group were only to become apparent upon his own assassination and thereafter.[158] It surely seems that he underestimated the influence they could exert on the royal succession. And his wide use of eunuchs was predicated on the presence of an energetic, forceful autocrat such as himself. Without this the monarchy was only too vulnerable to these sometime domestics. In sum, whereas Hsien-tsung was personally able to manipulate the eu-

---

240.7756–57. Ch'en Yin-k'o's discussion of parties in this period in his *T'ang-tai cheng-chih shih shu- lun kao*, pp. 97–104, sheds little light on this particular issue.

154. There does not seem to be even a remotely adequate treatment of the eunuch question in late T'ang. Biographies of individual eunuchs can be found in *CTS* 184 and *HTS* 207. A traditional account of eunuch domination at the court in the ninth century is given by Franke, *Geschichte des chinesischen Reiches*, 2: 486 ff.

155. Most notably in the "sweet dew" incident of 835. See Franke, *Geschichte des chinesischen Reiches*, 2:488–89.

156. The origins and early development of this institution, which was to play a major political role later in the ninth century, is shrouded in obscurity. See *Wen-hsien t'ung-k'ao* (Shih-t'ung ed.) 58.528. In any case the commissioner for secret documents *(shu-mi-shih)* was already a figure of some influence under Hsien-tsung. See *TCTC* 239.7695 and 7699. Wang, *The Structure of Power in North China*, pp. 89–90n9, makes reference to this institution at a later date, but at this time it did not have the specifically military responsibilities it would have in Wu-tai and Sung (and therefore Wang's translation of *Shu-mi-yuan* as "Bureau of Military Affairs" is hardly suitable here).

157. See his remarks regarding T'u-t'u Ch'eng-ts'ui in *TCTC* 238.7686.

158. Hsien-tsung's death is attributed to eunuchs; see *CTS* 15.20a and *TCTC* 241.7777.

nuchs in a manner advantegeous to his own absolutist control, he failed
to maintain adequate institutional safeguards against their direct
exercise of power. Indeed, his style of rule might be said to have encouraged it.

There is a final aspect of Hsien-tsung's as role monarch and restorer
of T'ang fortunes that should be mentioned. In historical perspective
his policies toward the provinces must surely be judged sound in conception and successful in execution. However, they were costly:
campaigns were undertaken in ten of his fifteen years on the throne,
and even those that proved short-lived required extensive mobiliza-
tions. Financial difficulties inevitably ensued; and, though there was a
consistent effort to increase revenue through expanding the number of
taxpayers on the rolls,[159] the immediate income necessary could be
derived only from existing sources. Ch'eng I's mission of 817 is an
example of the kind of expedient which had to be taken. In a word,
the campaigns, the continued state of military preparedness, the
largesse paid out to guarantee the loyalty of potentially dangerous
armies, all of these must have substantially increased the burden on the
average taxpayer, a burden already grievously increased by the deflationary economic conditions which the regime, in fact, moved none
too quickly to alleviate. Thus, political necessity demanded no small
measure of ruthlessness on the part of the ruler, and Hsien-tsung did
not shrink from the demand. At the same time, however, his policies
could be justified in terms of potential long-range benefits, for populace
as well as state.[160]

Was ruthlessness also at the heart of the split that occurred between
the monarch and most of his officials in the final year of his reign? We
have seen a divergence of view develop at court in this period, but,
while on the surface criticism took the form of ad hominem attacks on
leading ministers, policy differences must surely have been involved.
Unfortunately, we have no real idea of the emperor's further political
intentions; we are told only that he maintained pressure to obtain
maximum revenue.[161] As for the bulk of officials at court, they felt that
with the defeat of P'ing-lu early in 819 it was time for peace and a slow-
down in tempo. Li Ao's call for a new era, one of "supreme peace"

---

159. See p. 185.

160. As the emperor in fact in 810 justified his assiduous attention to building up finances.
See *TCTC* 238.7682.

161. See *CTS* 159.6b; *TCTC* 241.7770; and also Twitchett, *Financial Administration*, pp. 56,
95, 268n58, and 316n88.

(t'ai-p'ing), probably typified this mood.[162] The time for the civil virtues had come, the time for the easing of burdens and a return to the old ways. The emperor's assumption of a new honorary title *(tsun-hao)* may be significant here.[163] If it were genuinely the product of the initiative of officials at court, this new title would have been intended to signify that a corner had been turned and a time for new policies was at hand.[164] But, even if the major act of grace issued on this occasion was also the result of their initiative, in fact its far-reaching amnesties and tax remissions hardly square with the image we are given otherwise of Hsien-tsung's regime in its final months.[165] Therefore, by noting deeds rather than words we find some solid ground for doubting this standard image. Perhaps in the final analysis the answer to the enigma posed by this last phase is neither that Hsien-tsung became despotic at the end nor that he had been victimized by the literati-bureaucratic class. Perhaps the answer will be found to lie in the teleology underlying Chinese historiography. Since Hsien-tsung, a good and effective monarch, met a bad end, an explanation consonant with a fundamentally moral conception of human existence had to be found. Obviously something had gone wrong between the time when the emperor was fully in command of his powers and his death. With the conviction that an explanation of this phenomenon was imperative, an editor and compiler could easily and sincerely have established the record of this final phase in such a way as to account for—justify?—the unfortunate outcome. If this were the case, it would surely not be unique in the annals of Chinese history.

162. In his "Lun-shih shu-piao," *CTW* 634.8a–11a, briefly summarized in *TCTC* 241. 7768–69.

163. *CTS* 15.8a; *TCTC* 241.7769.

164. The text of the memorial submitted to the emperor asking him to assume the new title can be found in *TTCLC* 7.46.

165. This document can be found in *TTCLC* 10.59–60 and *TFYK* 89.28b–31a.

6. The Middle Yangtse in T'ang Politics

Wang Gungwu

The political history of China has often been examined in terms of major strategic and economic regions. Comparisons have been made, for example, between the pastoral lands of Inner Mongolia and the agricultural lands of North China, the highlands and the alluvial plains of North China, the wheatlands of the north and ricelands of the south. Certainly, in the history of China proper, a tremendous influence has been exercised by the broad division between north and south, especially in periods of division, such as the Three Kingdoms, the Northern and Southern dynasties, the Five Dynasties, and the Southern Sung. There have also been finer divisions marking out political and economic regions, such as the Wei Valley in Shensi, the lower Huang Ho Valley or North China plain (mainly Hopei, Honan, and parts of Shantung), the lower Yangtse or Chiang-Huai region (parts of Kiangsu, Chekiang, and Anhwei), the upper Yangtse (Szechwan), and the area formerly called Ling-nan (Kwangtung and Kwangsi). These regions all have distinct geographical and cultural identities and have been the subject of many careful studies. Identifying them has helped us to understand shifts of political power, the spread of the Chinese people and their culture, and the problems of unification and division under different dynasties.

In any study of unification or division, one striking fact has been the perennial importance of the Huang Ho and Yangtse valley power bases. The two valleys have often been the bases for rival kingdoms and empires, as with Wei and Wu in the Three Kingdoms period (220–65), Eastern Chin and the Sixteen Kingdoms (fourth and fifth centuries), the Southern Dynasties (fifth and sixth centuries) and the T'oba Wei

For a discussion of source materials referred to, see the Bibliographical Note at the end of the chapter.

(386–534), the southern kingdoms and the Five Dynasties (tenth century), the Southern Sung and the Chin (twelfth and thirteenth centuries). But the regional centers of power were not the same in all these cases. The northern Huang Ho region had several loci of power, including southern Shensi (Ch'ang-an), northern Honan (Loyang), and northern Hopei (Peking). In the Yangtse Valley, however, the power base was invariably in the east, in the lower Yangtse region (the upper Yangtse in Szechwan was often independent, but so isolated and self-sufficient that it was never a serious contender for control of the empire). Because the southern power base was invariably in the lower Yangtse, the Huai Valley in the east has, in times of division, always been a historic and predictable boundary between north and south.

In central China, however, the division between north and south was less clearly demarcated. This was not for lack of natural features separating the two regions—the Ta Pieh Mountains, for example, are a formidable barrier between the North China plain and the central plains of the middle Yangtse region. But the area of the middle Yangtse, although possessing its own cultural identity (it had been the homeland of the ancient state of Ch'u), was not until the Ming and Ch'ing dynasties nearly as heavily settled and developed as the areas of North China and the lower Yangtse. There were even major physical differences, including a vast swamp area covering land later reclaimed for agriculture, which slowed the settlement of the area. Because it was relatively late in developing, the middle Yangtse region lacked great historic centers of wealth and culture which could draw together the resources of the region.

With no regional center capable of withstanding attacks from other areas of China, the middle Yangtse was often a major area of contention. The Three Kingdoms of Wu, Shu, and Wei fought back and forth to control it; it was greatly fragmented during the Five Dynasties period; the Southern Sung saw it as the weakest link in their defense against the Chin, and later, against the Mongols. Although vulnerable to attack, the middle Yangtse was never easy to hold and control, whether the effort was made from the Huang Ho region in the north or from the lower Yangtse area in the east. Control from the east, of course, meant only the political unification of a great area of southern China. Conquest from the north, however, seemed always to lead to the unification of China. Control of this region was therefore a critical factor in the balance between unification and division.

Such a picture may be too simple and is necessarily preliminary. This essay is an effort to examine the role of the middle Yangtse in one of the periods of division, the late ninth and early tenth centuries. This timespan includes the end of the T'ang, when the central government was weak, and the Five Dynasties, a period of territorial fragmentation (880–963).

First, the middle Yangtse must be defined more exactly. There has been no sharp and permanent natural boundary dividing the vast area of central and eastern China between the Yangtse gorges (the boundary between modern Szechwan and Hupei) and the sea into a middle and lower Yangtse. There had been an indistinct division in the pre-Ch'in period between the central state of Ch'u and the eastern states of Wu and Yüeh; and a sense of division, expressed in the conventional geographical regions of Ching and Yang respectively, remained from the Ch'in (221–06 B.C.) and Han (206 B.C.–A.D. 220) to the Sui dynasty (589–618). Thus, a long tradition existed of distinguishing between two halves of the Yangtse Valley east of the gorges.

This division became increasingly significant as imperial power and Chinese settlement expanded southward during the centuries from the Han to the beginnings of the Sui. Two major north-south routes developed linking the Yangtse Valley with the Huang Ho and the north. One of these followed the Han River Valley to its confluence with the Yangtse (in modern Hupei), and the other followed various canals across the Huai lowlands to the Yangtse delta. In times of unification, the political and economic importance of these two different routes linking north and south helped to confirm the division between the middle and lower Yangtse. Historical developments thus helped to distinguish a rough geographical division between the two areas. The middle Yangtse can be considered as the region centering on the Yangtse and stretching across the width of Hupei province. It includes the valley of the great tributary stream, the Han, and the area around the Tung-t'ing Lake (fed mainly by the two rivers Hsiang and Yüan) and thus comprises most of modern Hupei and Hunan provinces (see map 1).[1]

For this study of the late T'ang and Five Dynasties periods, however,

1. Sung Hsi-shang, *Ch'ang-chiang t'ung-k'ao* (Taipei, 1963), describes the middle section *(chung-liu)* of the Yangtse as stretching from I-ch'ang to Han-k'ou (Hankow). Strategic, political, and economic considerations point to a slightly longer area reaching further up the gorges to Wu Shan range and down to where the Ta-pieh and Mu-fou ranges almost meet just above Chiu-chiang (Chiang-chou in T'ang times).

It is perhaps arguable how far up the Han, Hsiang, and Yüan rivers should be included in the middle Yangtse region. To the north and west, the Wu-tang range forms a clear boundary; so also does the Fu-niu range in Honan, although the T'ung-pai range does even better by linking with the Ta-pieh. To the south, the Wu-ling, Hsüeh-feng, and Lo-hsiao ranges mark the limits of the region in the areas north of the great Nan Ling range separating Hunan from Kwangtung and Kwangsi.

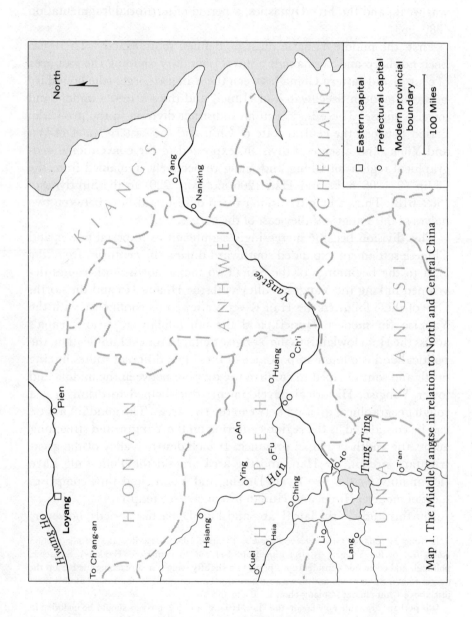

Map 1. The Middle Yangtse in relation to North and Central China

it is not appropriate to think simply in terms of these two modern provinces. The T'ang placed great emphasis on prefectures *(chou)*, which were the basic and comparatively permanent units of local administration; and it is more satisfactory to consider primarily those prefectures that were actually on the banks of the Yangtse and those on the key stretches of its tributaries. I have selected fourteen perfectures, the histories of which clearly illustrate the complexities of the problem of controlling the middle Yangtse.

This list includes all the prefectures in the area except Sui and Heng: the relevant features of Sui-chou and Heng-chou were the same as those of An-chou and T'an-chou, respectively. As for Mien-chou, this was absorbed into O-chou after 826, and we refer to it as O/Mien for the period before 826. The fourteen to be examined in detail are as follows (see map 2):[2]

Prefecture (chou)	Administrative Center (hsien)	Modern Name (hsien)
Hsiang	Hsiang-yang	Hsiang-yang
Ying	Ch'ang-shou	Chung-hsiang
Fu	Mien-yang	T'ien-men
An	An-lu	An-lu
Ching	Chiang-ling	Chiang-ling
Hsia	I-ling	I-ch'ang
Kuei	Tzu-kuei	Tzu-kuei
O	Chiang-hsia	Wu-ch'ang
Huang	Huang-kang	Huang-kang
Ch'i	Ch'i-ch'un	Ch'i-ch'un
Yo	Pa-ling	Yo-yang
T'an	Ch'ang-sha	Ch'ang-sha
Li	Li-yang	Li-hsien
Lang	Wu-ling	Ch'ang-te

These fourteen prefectures constitute the main parts of a major region. For the last three hundred years and down to the present day, the first ten have been found in Hupei and the remaining four in Hunan. During the Ming dynasty they were all part of Hu-kuang province, and it is easy to think that all of them have always been recognized as

2. Although the prefectures of Teng and T'ang in southern Honan had much in common with Hsiang-chou, they were really in a marginal area between the Yangtse and the Huang Ho and above the upper Huai (Huai-hsi). Similarly, there were the marginal prefectures in the south, Yung and Tao, which had less to do with the middle Yangtse than with the Lingnan region.

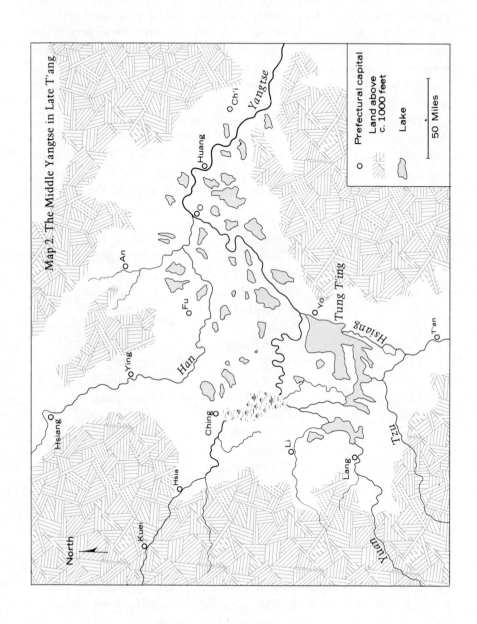

Map 2. The Middle Yangtse in Late T'ang

Yangtse

Ch'i

Huang

An

Fu

Ying

Han

Hsiang

Ching

Hsia

Kuei

North

Li

Lang

Yuan

Tzu

Hsiang

Tung T'ing

Yo

T'an

Prefectural capital

Land above
c. 1000 feet

Lake

50 Miles

belonging to a common regional administration.[3] But during the T'ang and Wu-tai periods they were not seen in that way at all. For about two hundred years, from 760 to 960, they were arranged in four or even five different regional groupings. This was most dramatically illustrated when the T'ang dynasty fell in 907 and the Yangtse Valley came under the control of several independent military organizations. The upper Yangtse was controlled by the former Shu, the lower Yangtse mainly by the state of Wu and partially by that of Wu Yüeh. In contrast to this the middle Yangtse was divided into five segments, each under a different political control, between 907 and 926, and four between 926 and 963. The extent of the fragmentation was astonishing, as can be seen below:[4]

Years	Polities	Groups of Prefectures
907	Liang	Hsiang, Ying, Fu, An, and Ching
	Shu	Hsia and Kuei
	Wu	O, Huang, and Ch'i
	Ch'u	Yo and T'an
	Wu-chen	Li and Lang
927	Later T'ang	Hsiang, Ying, Fu, and An
	Ching-nan	Ching, Hsia, and Kuei
	Wu	O, Huang, and Ch'i
	Ch'u	Yo, T'an, Li, and Lang
958	Later Chou	Hsiang, Ying, Fu, An, Huang, and Ch'i
	Ch'ing-nan	Ching, Hsia, and Kuei
	Nan T'ang	O
	Ch'u	Yo, T'an, Li, and Lang

The following questions are provoked by these facts: What was it in the middle Yangtse that led to such fragmentation for so long? How significant was this in late T'ang and Wu-tai history? In what ways does

3. Most of them were in Hu-Kuang province of the Yüan dynasty, but many were part of Honan. During the Sung, most of them were divided into Ching-hu North and Ching-hu South, but several were placed in Huai-nan West and Ching-hsi South. *Ch'ing shih kao*, Ti-li ch. 14–15; *Ming Shih*, ch. 44; *Yüan Shih*, ch. 59 and 63; *Sung Shih*, ch. 85. See also *Chia-ch'ing Ch'ung-hsiu i-t'ung chih*, ch. 334 and 353; Ku Tsu-yü, *Tu-shih fang-yü chi-yao*, ch. 75–82; Albert Herrmann, *An Historical Atlas of China*, new ed. (Edinburgh, 1966).

4. *CTS* 39–40; *HTS* 40–41; *CWTS* 133–34, 150; *HWTS* 60, 61–63, 66, 69. See also Tu Yu, *TT*, Shih T'ung ed., 177, 181, 183; Li Chi-fu, *Yüan-ho chün-hsien t'u-chih*, 21, 27, 29 (a key *chüan*, 20, unfortunately has been lost); Yo Shih, *T'ai-p'ing huan-yü chi*, 112–14, 118, 127, 131–32, 144–48,; *SKCC* 111–14.

it help us understand the issues of unification and division during this
period?

From the beginning of T'ang rule, mountains and rivers were used as
convenient boundaries. In 627 T'ai-tsung ordered the empire divided
into ten provinces *(tao)* according to these natural barriers. This seems
to have been inspired by military and strategic considerations more than
by administrative convenience or regard for regional differences. For
example, the division into ten provinces divided the fourteen prefectures
of the middle Yangtse into three parts. Two of the three parts belonged
to Huai-nan and Ching-nan provinces and were separated by the Yangtse, with the river forming a boundary. The third belonged to Shan-nan
province and comprised a large strategic area astride both the Yangtse
and the Han rivers, reaching southward to the western shores of Tung-
t'ing Lake. It was located so as to support the two capitals of Ch'ang-an
and Loyang from the south and was also the frontier province defending
the settled areas from the various Man tribesmen of Hunan, Szechwan,
and Kweichow.

The fourteen prefectures with which we are concerned were distributed among the provinces as follows: in Shan-nan, eight prefectures—
Hsiang, Ying, Fu Ching, Hsia, Kuei, Li, and Lang; in Huai-nan,
three—An, Huang, and Ch'i; and in Chiang-nan, three—O/Mien, Yo,
and T'an. In 733, during the reign of Hsüan-tsung, the arrangements for
the provinces were changed, but only to subdivide the two largest ones,
Shan-nan and Chiang-nan. At this point, the prefectural boundaries
remained the same; the first eight were in Shan-nan East, the next
three remained in Huai-nan, and the last three formed part of Chiang-
nan West.[5]

Another interesting grouping of prefectures was attempted in an
effort to define the size of the governments-general *(tu-tu-fu)*—strategic
and investigatory units each covering a number of prefectures. The
fourteen prefectures of the middle Yangtse were found in the governments-general listed on the facing page.[6]

A debate in 711 about the appointment of governors-general *(tu-tu)*,
however, had emphasized the dangers implicit in concentrating so much
territorial power in their hands, and it was successfully argued that

---

5. *TT* 172, 911–14; *CTS* 38.1b–2a; 39.30b–44b; 40.4b–6b, 20a–22b.
6. *THY*, Ts'ung-shu Chi-ch'eng ed., 68.1192–94; *TT* 32.185–86.

Province	Government-General (Grade)	Other Prefectures
Shan-nan East	Ching Chou (A)*	Ying, Hsia, O, Yo, Li, and Lang
	Hsiang Chou (C)	(six others in the upper Han Valley to the north and northwest)
	K'uei Chou (C)	Kuei (plus five others in Szechwan)
Huai-nan	An Chou (C)	Fu, Huang, and Ch'i (plus Mien and three others in Hupei and Honan)
Chiang-nan West	T'an Chou (C)	(six others in Hunan)

*It is noteworthy that the government-general at Ching Chou controlled both banks of the Yangtse and was one of only four Grade A governments-general in the empire.

direct communications between each prefect and the central government were essential. Thus, in practice, the governments-general were probably no more than superior prefectures, which did not really affect the internal functioning of the prefectures under their nominal control.[7] It is ironical that while this debate on the concentration of local power was going on, the first formal military commission *(chieh-tu-shih ssu)* was created along the northwestern border, a development that was to lead eventually to a system of powerful frontier governors each controlling several prefectures.[8] But, up to the outbreak of the An Lu-shan Rebellion in 755, it can be said that there were no meaningful groupings of prefectures into superior administrative units which could have presaged the later political divisions. What is clear from a comparison between the provincial and government-general divisions of the early T'ang and the divisions of 907 is that the middle Yangtse region did not divide easily and naturally and could be divided in several different ways.

One fact, however, does emerge. The middle Yangtse was strategically important, and Ching-chou was the center of the region. Ching-chou was a Grade A government-general from the start, and there were only three others of that grade in the whole empire in 711. The three others were the capitals of clearly defined regions and were all obviously more

7. *THY* 68.1194–96.

8. For a very thorough discussion on the origins of the *chieh-tu shih,* see E. G. Pulleyblank, *The Background of the Rebellion of An Lu-shan* (London, 1955), pp. 149–52.

populous, as can be seen from their household figures for 742, as follows:[9]

	Governments-General	Households
I	(Ch'eng-tu in Szechwan)	156,812
Ping	(Taiyuan in Shansi)	126,190
Yang	(Chiang-tu in Kiangsu)	73,381
Ching		28,932

This suggests that Ching-chou was given high status principally for strategic reasons. This assumption is further confirmed by comparing the government-general of Ching-chou with the three other governments-general in the middle Yangtse all of which were classified as Grade C:

Government-General (Grade)	Households
Ching (A)	28,932
Hsiang (C)	46,056
T'an (C)	32,226
An (C)	21,835

There can be little doubt that Ching would not have merited the A classification except for its key position on the middle Yangtse.

It is also interesting to compare the household figures of the fourteen prefectures of the T'ang as of 742 with those of the Sui as of 609:[10]

Prefecture	Sui (609)	T'ang (742)
Hsiang	99,577	46,056
Ying	53,385	13,720
Fu (with Mien)	?41,714	13,942
An	68,042	21,835
Ching	58,836	28,932
Hsia	5,179	7,317
Kuei	?21,370*	4,364
O	13,771	19,417
Huang	28,398	14,787
Ch'i	34,690	25,620
Yo	6,934	11,676
T'an	14,275	32,226

---

9. *TT* 32.186, 176.935, 179.952, 181.961; Ku Chieh-kang and Shih Nien-hai, *Chung-kuo chiang-yüeh yen-ke shih* (Ch'ang-sha, 1938), pp. 181–87. In 729, Lu-chou was added as the fifth Grade A *tu-tu-fu*, and it had 67,944 households, more than twice as many as Ching-chou; *TT* 179.952.

10. *Sui Shu* 29.16b; 31.5a, 15a–21b; *TT* 181.963, 183. 971–75.

Prefecture	Sui(609)	T'ang(742)
Li	8,906	16,190
Lang	3,416	7,722

*Includes K'uei-chou.

Two points should be noted. Although the two sets of figures are not strictly comparable because of differences in the boundaries of the prefectures, the relative size and importance of each prefecture is quite clear. For example, at both dates Hsiang, An, and Ching prefectures were larger and probably more prosperous than the other nine. Huang and Ch'i remained medium-sized prefectures. On the other hand, Ying and Fu (and Mien) declined considerably in their relative importance among the fourteen. As for O, Yo, T'an, Li, and Lang prefectures, it is noteworthy that their numbers of households increased while most others declined. It is obvious why—within fifteen years after 742, O and T'an joined Hsiang, An, and Ching as centers of larger administrative and military units.

The second point concerns the decline from Sui to T'ang in numbers of households in eight out of the fourteen prefectures. Although there may not have been as large a decrease in the population of the middle Yangtse as the figures suggest—certainly not the 45 percent decrease indicated by the two totals—there is a sharp contrast between these and comparable figures for the lower Yangtse prefectures, where the average *increase* in households between 609 and 742 was about 300 percent.[11] Even if we cannot prove that the middle Yangtse population drifted southeastward toward the lower Yangtse, it is clear that in terms of human and economic resources the middle Yangtse was relatively more important in the Sui and the early T'ang than in the late T'ang. Further, the continued importance of the middle Yangtse throughout the T'ang must have been determined more and more in terms of its strategic position as an alternate route to Ch'ang-an and Loyang and as the guardian of the upper Yangtse Basin in Szechwan. Finally, it is probable that, within the middle Yangtse region, there was a movement of population south and southwestward to the southern bank of the Yangtse.

The An Lu-shan Rebellion was the turning point in T'ang history. Among many things, it aggravated the problems of central administration and created many opportunities for regional developments. The consequences for Hopei and Shantung are well known. The effects on grain transportation from the lower Yangtse to the metropolitan cen-

11. *Sui Shu* 31.3a–8b; *TT* 182.965–68; see Pulleyblank, *Rebellion of An Lu-shan*, app. 2, pp. 172–77.

ters have also been closely studied.[12] The precarious position of the
Grand Canal running close to the frequently rebellious provinces of
the lower Huang Ho made an alternate route up to the capitals via
the middle Yangtse imperative; and this certainly increased the
strategic significance of the Han River route via O-chou and Hsiang-
chou. Thus during the dangerous years between 756 and 763, there
were strong military and financial reasons to restructure the middle
Yangtse administration. This was done hurriedly and under conditions
of great uncertainty. Four new military governorships *(chieh-tu shih)*
were created affecting the middle Yangtse prefectures:

Huai-nan	centered on Yang-chou on the Grand Canal.
Huai-hsi	the area around the Upper Huai Valley, with various centers in 756–79 and centered on Ts'ai-chou in 779–818.
Shan-nan East	centered on Hsiang-chou covering mainly the Han Valley.
Ching-nan	centered on Ching-chou, the traditional center of the middle Yangtse.

In addition, there was also considerable difficulty settling the composition of the civil governorship *(kuan-ch'a shih)* of O-yo, which was pivoted
on the junction of the Han and the Yangtse. This can be seen in the
table on the next page, showing to which province each of the
fourteen prefectures of the middle Yangtse was attached after 756.[13]
From this table, it can be seen that the three key prefectures on the
middle Yangtse and its tributaries, that is Ching, Hsiang, and T'an,
were fairly obvious centers for the new military and civil provincial
governors, and all three remained provincial administrative centers
until the end of the T'ang. What was less obvious was the situation
where the tributaries met the Yangtse—at Yo-chou for the Hsiang
River and at O-chou and Mien-chou for the Han River.

The most difficult principle involved here was whether larger administrative units formed at the junctions of the middle Yangtse and its
great tributaries should control both the north and south banks of the
Yangtse. Where prefectures were concerned, obviously each should be
confined to one bank of the Yangtse River; Yo-chou and O-chou were
on the south bank, while Mien-chou was on the north. At the same time,

12. Pulleyblank, *Rebellion of An Lu-shan*, chap. 6. A more recent study is D. C. Twitchett,
"Provincial Autonomy and Central Finance in Late T'ang," *Asia Major* 11 (1965): 211–32.
13. *HTS* 65 and 67–69; Wu T'ing-hsieh, *T'ang fang-chen nien-piao*, Er-shih-wu shih pu-pien
ed., vol. 6, chaps. 4–6 and 8.

Prefecture	Province	Prefecture	Province
Hsiang	Shan-nan East from 757	O/Mien	Huai-nan (Mien) 756–58
Ying and Fu	Ching-nan 757–85 Shan-nan East after 785		O-yo-mien 759 O-mien 761–65 O-yo after 765
An	Huai-nan 756–57 Shan-nan East 757–59 Huai-hsi 759–85 Shan-nan East 785–99 An-Huang 799–806 O-yo after 806	Huang and Ch'i	Huai-nan 756–59 Huai-hsi 759–65 O-yo after 765
		Yo	O-yo-mien 759–60 Ching-nan 761–65 O-yo after 765
Ching	Ching-nan from 757	T'an	Ching-nan 761–64 Hunan after 764
Hsia and Kuei*	Ching-nan 757 K'uei-hsia 757–58, 759–60 Ching-nan after 760	Li and Lang	Ching-nan 757–59 Li-lang (tu t'uan-lien shih) 759–60 Ching-nan after 760 or 766 (?)

*Information incomplete for Kuei; probably the same as Hsia.

it is interesting to note that Yo and Mien were astride both banks of the Yangtse tributaries, that is, the Hsiang and the Han respectively. O-chou was entirely on the south bank of the Yangtse until 826 when Mien-chou was absorbed into it. This brought O-chou not only astride the Yangtse but also astride the Han River and made it the biggest prefecture in the middle Yangtse.

Also of interest is the slight uncertainty over Hsia-chou and Kuei-chou and over Li-chou and Lang-chou—how far up the gorges or into Man tribal territory in western Hunan could an area be controlled from the middle Yangtse? There was uncertainty over Huang-chou and Ch'i-chou on the north bank of the Yangtse, which had long been part of the Huai-nan region. Should they still be controlled from the Huai Valley, or should they be administered from the Yangtse itself? And there was also the long-standing difficulty over Ying-chou and Fu-chou. These were both astride the Han River between Hsiang-chou and O/Mien-chou—was it not more efficient to control them from the up-river prefecture of Hsiang-chou than to have them supervised from Ching-chou across the low-lying marshlands between the Yangtse and the Han?

Finally, there was the major problem of An-chou. The prefecture barely reached the Yangtse near O/Mien-chou, but its strategic importance had long been recognized during the four centuries between the fall of the Later Han and the reunification of Sui. It was a prefecture that controlled several key passes into the Huai Valley and also provided access into the Yangtse Valley from Honan in the north. The T'ang imperial government seemed to have tried everything to ensure its firm control. An-chou was placed first in Huai-nan, then under the military governor of Shan-nan East, then briefly made the center of the military governor of Huai-hsi (761–72), and then put back under the control of Shan-nan. In 799, it seemed important enough to set up a new military governorship based on An-chou itself, and the prefect was given a measure of control over Huang-chou on the north bank of the Yangtse. By 806 a major decision was finally made, and An-chou was placed under the military governor of O-yo; in short, it finally came to be controlled from the middle Yangtse.

In summary, during the late eighth and early ninth centuries the fourteen prefectures of the middle Yangtse were distributed among provinces as follows:[14]

Province	Prefectures
	760
Shan-nan East	Hsiang (also included others in upper Han Valley and in Honan)
Ching-nan	Ching, Ying, Fu, Hsia, T'an (to 764), probably Kuei, Li, Lang, and others south of Yangtse in Hunan
Huai-hsi	An, Huang, Ch'i (and others north of the Ta Pieh range stretching toward the Grand Canal
O-yo-mien	O/Mien, Yo
Hunan	T'an (and others south of Yangtse; after 764)
	785
Shan-nan East	Hsiang, Ying, Fu, An (to 799 and after 806) and others in the upper Han Valley and Honan
Ching-nan	Ching, Hsia, Kuei, Li, Lang, and others west of the gorges in Szechwan.
O-Yo	O/Mien, Yo, Ch'i, Huang (to 799 and after 806)

---

14. Wu, *T'ang fang-chen nien-piao.*

Province	Prefectures
Hunan	T'an and others covering both Chinese and tribe territory in most of modern Hunan
799–806 only	
An-Huang	An, Huang
813	
Shan-nan East	Hsiang, Ying, Fu, and others in the upper Han Valley and Honan as in 785
Ching-nan	Ching, Hsia, Kuei, Li, Lang, and others west of the gorges as in 785
O/Yo	O/Mien, Yo, Ch'i, Huang, An, and Shen (after 818)
Hunan	T'an and others as in 785

The uncertainties of the years 756–63 were followed by the gradual hardening of the new administrative units, and the stabilization of the divisions that followed after 765 was welcomed for both military and financial reasons. The alternative route to the wealth of the lower Yangtse was better guaranteed during a period when the Grand Canal was constantly in danger, and the defenses against potential and actual revolt in the upper Huai Valley (Huai-hsi) from 762 to 817 were also better organized. And, indeed, for the forty years or so until the end of the reign of Emperor Hsüan-tsung (846–59) the middle Yangtse was largely undisturbed.

The preceding discussion has shown that while the T'ang empire recognized strategic regions, its policy was essentially that of centralization as expressed in the phrase "strong trunk and weak branches" *(ch'iang-kan jo-chih)*, and each prefect was responsisble to and had direct access to the court in Ch'ang-an. This was the ideal and was more effective among the richer and larger prefectures than among the smaller and poorer ones. Throughout the dynasty, it was frequently admitted that prefects of good quality were rare, and a high percentage of the prefectures in the empire were indifferently administered.[15]

We have noted that the An Lu-shan Rebellion precipitated many changes; among them were the creation of the provinces summarized in the preceding table and, when the rebellion was but five weeks old, the establishment of the first military governorship *(chieh-tu shih)* in the area, which was shortly followed by the creation of another. In 756 Prince Lin, younger half-brother of the new emperor Su-tsung, took control of the vital middle Yangtse. Unfortunately, the young prince

15. *THY* 68.1194–1208, 69.1209–12.

made an effort to seize the whole Yangtse Valley for himself. His effort failed, but it brings out clearly what a great prize the lower Yangtse was and how valuable it was to control the middle Yangtse routes to its wealth.[16]

An Lu-shan's forces failed to get beyond Nan-yang (southern Honan) to the Han River Valley. Lu Hui, a professional officer in the imperial army, saved the middle Yangtse in 756–57. He was succeeded at Hsiang-chou by another military careerist, Lai T'ien and then by three civilian officials, at least two of whom proved to be ineffectual.[17] One was driven out in 759 and chased to Ching-chou. There the Hsiang-chou mutineers captured the fortified town and caused the abandon-ment of three other prefectures in the middle Yangtse. Although the mutiny was quashed within three months, the next governor was killed five months later, and the court was forced to send the popular profes-sional soldier Lai T'ien back to govern Shan-nan province again.[18] From this time in 760 until 781 this section of the middle Yangtse re-mained under the control of military men whose loyalty to the empire was uncertain. In 763 the military commander Liang Ch'ung-i seized Hsiang-chou by force and held it for eighteen years. He rebelled unsuccessfully in 781, and the area was then recaptured by loyal troops.[19]

Although this part of the middle Yangtse eventually came under central control again, the neighboring prefectures, including the vital An-chou, which gave access to the Han-Yangtse junction, were in the hands of autonomous military governors in Huai-hsi, who frequently threatened both the Grand Canal and the Han River routes between the capital and the lower Yangtse. The fluid and unstable province of Huai-hsi was particularly dangerous. It was really beyond the control of the central government for some fifty-five years (762–817) and was governed successively by the arrogant Li Chung-ch'en (762–79), his

16. *TCTC* 217.6940, 6953; 218.6962–7000; 219.7009–10, 7019–20. There are many notable studies of the decades after 755. The recent studies that touch on the importance of the Yangtse are E. G. Pulleyblank, "Neo-Confucianism and Neo-Legalism in T'ang Intellectual Life, 755–805," in *The Confucian Persuasion*, ed. A. F. Wright (Stanford, Calif., 1960), pp. 77–114 and 322–34; D. C. Twitchett, "Lu Chih (754–805): Imperial Adviser and Court Official," in *Confucian Personalities*, ed. A. F. Wright and D. C. Twitchett (Stanford, Calif., 1962), pp. 84–122 and 336–45; Matsui Shūichi, "Tōdai Kōhanki no Kō-wai ni tsuite," *Shigaku Zasshi* 66, no. 2 (1957): 94–122.

17. *TCTC* 218.6962 and 219.7024–25; *HTS* 147.2a–3a and 144.1a–2b; *T'ang fang-chen nien-piao* 4.111.

18. *TCTC* 221.7080–81, 7088, 7091.

19. *HTS* 224A.6b–7b; also *HTS* 144.1a–2b; *TCTC* 222.7121, 7129, 7142; 226.7298–99; and 227.7307.

nephew the rebellious Li Hsi-lieh (779–86), and finally by Wu Shao-ch'eng, Wu Shao-yang, and by Shao-yang's son the rebel Yüan-chi (786–817).[20] During the active fighting of 783–86 and 799–800 between Huai-hsi and government forces, large numbers of middle Yangtse troops were involved, and both O-chou and An-chou were attacked by Li Hsi-lieh. Also, in the very long-drawn-out and exhausting rebellion of Wu Yüan-chi in 814–17, troops from the middle Yangtse were sent to fight to the north of the region.[21]

Military governors were appointed to Ching-nan and Shan-nan East throughout the late T'ang, but there were no military governors in Hunan and other provinces wholly south of the Yangtse, such as the neighboring Chiang-hsi and Hsuan-she. These were always under civil governors. The intermediate O-yo area, which changed its bound-aries three times and came to be astride the Yangtse by 780 and reached the foothills of Ta Pieh Mountains after 806, was made a province with a military governor at least three times, in 806–10, 825–31, and 847–53. This raises some doubts about the T'ang policy of appointing military governors only when an area was strategically significant. Nevertheless, it was surprising that O-Yo did not stay a military province after 810 or after 831 or even after 853.[22]

20. *HTS* 224B.1a–2b, 225B.1a–3a; *TCTC* 225.7255–56, 227.7336–37; *HTS* 214.2a–5b; *TCTC* 232.7470, 238.7668, 239.7706.

21. *TCTC* 229.7378–79, 7393–94; 231.7452; 232.7468–69; 239.7707–08; 240.7731–36.

22. The reasons why O-Yo was raised to *chieh-tu shih* status and then returned to *kuan-ch'a shih* are puzzling. In 805 Han Kao objected to serving under the ambitious Wang Shu-wen and was sent out to O-Yo as *kuan-ch'a shih*. When Wang Shu-wen was ousted at the beginning of 806, Han Kao was promoted to *chieh-tu shih*, which was more appropriate to his seniority at court; *CTS* 14.2b and 6b; *HTS* 126.16a–b; *TCTC* 237.7625. His successor Hsi Shih-mei was senior enough, having been metropolitan governor *(ching-chao yin)* at Ch'ang-an, but it is not certain that he was *chieh-tu shih* throughout his term, 808–10; *CTS* 157.2b–3a and *HTS* 143.10a–b say he was *kuan-ch'a shih*, while *HTS* 68.10b–11b asserts that O-Yo was Wu-ch'ang *chieh-tu shih* from 806 to 810. This is followed by *T'ang fang-chen nien-piao* 6. 161–62, which also quotes *Shun-tsung shih-lu* as saying that Han Kao was appointed *chieh-tu shih* in 805, but wrongly quotes *HTS* as saying 805; see also B. S. Solomon, *The Veritable Record of the T'ang Emperor Shun-tsung* (Cambridge, Mass., 1955), pp. 28 and 32, which notes the differences.

For the second period, 825–31, *CTS* 17A.5a explicitly says that O-Yo was raised to *chieh-tu shih* status in order to accommodate the former chief minister, Niu Seng-ju; and *CTS* 17B.1a and 5b say that his successor, another former chief minister, Yüan Chen, was also *chieh-tu shih* from 830 until his death in 831; see also Tu Mu, *Fan-ch'uan wen-chi*, 7.4b–11a; *CTS* 172. 7a–9b and 166.1a–8a; *HTS* 174.2b–7b and *TCTC* 243.7841–42.

For the third period, 847–48 and 850–53, the sources are fragmentary, and only the *HTS* 68.14b–15a clearly gives the dates. The *chieh-tu shih* in 847–49 was Lu Shang, who had just been an unsuccessful chief minister. Why the *chieh-tu shih* reverted back to *kuan-ch'a shih* in 848 is not clear; it is possible that *HTS* 68 was wrong and the third period was a continuous one from 847 to 853; *HTS* 182.6a; *TCTC* 248.8028; *CTS* 176.15a–b calls him a *kuan-ch'a shih*.

The actual appointments made to the governorships of the four middle Yangtse provinces show that senior appointments were consistently made to Ching-nan and Shan-nan East; while some of the appointments to O-Yo were of relatively obscure officials, and the bulk of the civil governors appointed to Hunan were very little known. Also, as can be seen in the following table of military and civil provincial governors (c. 756–880), a much higher percentage of Ching-nan and Shan-nan governors had been, or went on to become, chief ministers at the court as compared with those of O-Yo and Hunan.[23]

Prefecture	Total Governors	Number of Chief Ministers	Period	Total Years	Average Years of Tenure
Ching-nan	43	19	757–849	121	2.8
			851–80		
Shan-nan East	44	16	756–880	124	2.8
O-Yo	33	6	765–78	102	3.1
			783–842		
			845–60		
			865–80		
Hunan	58	11	764–800	114	2.0
			802–80		

A more careful examination of the various appointments further shows that there were important differences between the period before the death of Emperor Hsien-tsung in 820 and the following period, 820–80. Prior to 820, there were several long tenures of five or more years each,

Lu Shang's successor, Wei Shun, governor in 850–52, is obscure, and we have no biographical details about him. It is not clear why he was made *chieh-tu shih*, although he seems to have been senior enough to follow this appointment with a presidency of the ministry of justice and then another *chieh-tu shih* office; Shen Hsün in *CTW* 763.8b–9a, and *T'ang fang-chen nien-piao* 6.163. His successor, Wei Ch'üeh, was no less obscure, but his son, Pao-heng, became a chief minister, and the *HTS* 74A.1b and 184.3b–4a say that he was *chieh-tu shih;* also Shen Hsün in *CTW* 763.11b–12a notes that he was promoted from a *kuan-ch'a shih* post; see also *CTS* 177.15b.

Following each of the three periods, the appointment of *kuan-ch'a shih* again is unexplained. Lü Yüan-yin in 810 was a senior bureaucrat, and so was Ts'ui Yen in 831, and both were very successful administrators; *HTS* 162.5b–6a and 163.6b–7b; *TCTC* 238.7681–82 and 244.7877. As for the successor of Wei Ch'üeh in 853, we do not know his name. We merely know that he was followed in 855 by Ts'ui Yao, the son of the Ts'ui Yen, mentioned above, and a member of one of the most powerful and successful families of the late T'ang; he was certainly not a mere *kuan-ch'a shih; HTS* 73C.40b and 163.7b.

23. *T'ang fang-chen nien-piao* 4–6; *HTS* 61–63 and 70–75; and Wang Shou-nan, *T'ang-tai fan-chen yü chung-yang kuan-hsi chih yen-chiu* (Taipei, 1969), app. 1, pp. 730–64, 858–75.

while during the sixty years after 820, there was only one example of such long-term appointments, that of Wang Ch'ien at Ching-nan (821–29), and he was a senior member of the imperial family through his mother, the daughter of Emperor Hsüan-tsung.[24]

In Ching-nan, the two longest appointments were those of Wei Po-yü, who governed from 763 until just before his death in 776, and P'ei Chou (729–803), who governed from 792 until his death in 803. The two show a striking contrast in background, and their careers as governors reflect the changing situation. Wei Po-yü was an obscure soldier who came to prominence by fighting bravely against the An Lu-shan rebels. His appointment to Ching-nan was obviously a reward for past services. Furthermore, he was loyal during a period of grave uncertainty when the court saw fit to be especially indulgent toward military men. One of his predecessors, Lü Yin (712–62), was a *chin-shih* graduate who rose to become chief minister and brought great skills and experience to the administration. His prestige and influence made Ching-nan briefly into a subsidiary southern capital, and the province was expanded to cover seventeen prefectures, including most of what was to become Hunan. At least three thousand troops were stationed there, and, in three years, a select band of officers and administrators helped Lü Yin to become one of the great governors of Ching-nan. Thus Wei Po-yü inherited a rich and well-governed province and had no difficulty in doing his job. From the court's point of view, with Ching-nan so successfully organized by Lü Yin, it was a safe post for a military appointee. The court did take the precaution of reducing the province to about half its size but was indulgent toward Wei Po-yü's wish to stay on indefinitely as governor and did not try to move him for thirteen years.[25]

P'ei Chou, who stayed for eleven years, came from an aristocratic family with connections at the court and in several major provinces and was a skillful and experienced politician of sixty-three when he was promoted from Chiang-hsi civil governor to military governor of Ching-nan. Again, he was fortunate in having had two able predecessors—the imperial Prince Kao (733–92) and Fan Tse (742–98), both of whom performed successfully against the rebels of the upper Huai Valley in the bitter battles of 783–86. They had also successfully defended the middle Yangtse after the professional soldier Chang Po-i (Ching-nan governor, 782–85) was disastrously defeated by the rebels at An-chou. By the time P'ei Chou arrived, Prince Kao and Fan Tse had succes-

24. *HTS* 191.6a.
25. *HTS* 140.5–7a and 141.3a–b; also *TCTC* 221.7096; 222.7104.

sively pacified Ching-nan province and then Shan-nan East.[26] P'ei
Chou's length of appointment was mainly the result of an overall
T'ang policy at the end of the eighth century of allowing governors and
inspectors to stay on at their posts as long as they liked, and throughout
the Yangtse provinces of Shan-nan, O-Yo, Huai-nan, Chiang-hsi,
Hsuan-she, Che-hsi, and Che-tung, there were long-term appointments
up to the first years of the ninth century.[27]

In Shan-nan East, I have already mentioned the eighteen-year tenure
of Liang Ch'ung-i who finally rebelled and was killed in 781. In 784,
Fan Tse, a literate but obscure soldier, was personally selected for appointment by Emperor Te-tsung (779–805) and could well have stayed
in the post for a long time. He was transferred in 787 only because
Prince Kao, who had shown great brilliance as a field commander,
was thought a more suitable governor for a province bordering on the
rebellious Huai-hsi. Prince Kao remained governor until his death in
792, and Fan Tse was then brought back from Ching-nan and served
until his own death in 798. Significantly, for fourteen crucial years
these two men, both of unquestioned loyalty, played a vital defensive
role for the middle Yangtse, guarding the alternative grain and tribute
route to the capitals and the routes in and out of the Szechwan Basin.[28]

The next long-term appointment in Shan-nan East was Yü Chou,
who was governor for ten years from 798 to 808. With Yü Chou, an
aristocrat with eunuch connections, as with his successor P'ei Chün
(750–811), we see clearly the workings of the power combination of
aristocrats and eunuchs which was to dominate the politics of the T'ang
court and provinces down to the end of the dynasty. The power of the
eunuchs began to increase rapidly toward the end of the long reign of
Te-tsung, and their influence began to pervade many departments of
military and civil administration. As their power increased, both the
traditionally influential aristocrats and the newly risen literati-
bureaucrats were forced to deal with them, and many sought alliance
with them in increasingly complicated political intrigues.[29]

Yü Chou openly flaunted his influence at court and was confident
enough to defy the normal channels of authority and govern arbitrarily,

26. *HTS* 80.10a–12b and 159.2b–3a; also *HTS* 136.5b–6a; *TCTC* 229.7393–94.

27. *HTS* 130.3b–4a. See *T'ang fang-chen nien-piao* 4–6.

28. *HTS* 80.10a–12b and 159.2b–3a.

29. Ch'en, *T'ang-tai cheng-chih shih shu-lun kao*, 66–127; Lü Ssu-mien, *Sui T'ang Wu-tai shih*
(Peking, 1959), pp. 321–33; Chao I, *Nien-erh shih cha-chi*, 20; see also Pulleyblank, "Neo-
Confucianism and Neo-Legalism," pp. 78–82; Twitchett, "Lu Chih," p. 108. For the begin-
nings of eunuch influence, see J. K. Rideout, "The Rise of the Eunuchs in the T'ang Dynasty,"
Asia Major 1 (1949): 53–72.

particularly in his relations with the prefects under his supervision. He was remarkable in that he was not an illiterate soldier dependent on a personal army; there were many of those who defied the central government. Nor was he an obscure literatus carried away by exceptional favor like Ch'en Shao-yu, who had been poised for rebellion in Huai-nan earlier (773–84). Nor was he like his contemporary Li Ch'i, a minor member of the imperial family, who overestimated his privileges and power as governor of the province of Che-hsi at the southern end of the Grand Canal and thought it rich enough to form the basis of a successful rebellious regime.[30] Yü Chou was a discreet aristocrat who had married his son to a princess (the daughter of Emperor Hsien-tsung) and who kept powerful eunuch friends, but who also cultivated and gained the respect of prominent literati, including the great essayist Han Yü. His long tenure in Shan-nan East brought him great profit and ended only after Hsien-tsung offered him a post as chief minister. Even then he was not content and seems to have asked his son to intrigue with the eunuchs to have him sent out to a rich province again. Eventually, he did fall quickly from power, but not so much because of his arrogant conduct and corruption while in office in Shan-nan as because of his failure in the political infighting at court after his return to Ch'ang-an.[31]

His successor, P'ei Chün, died at his post in 811 after only three years, but P'ei Chün had spent five years in Ching-nan immediately before being sent to Shan-nan East and was thus very influential in the middle Yangtse area for some eight years. He too was a member of an aristocratic family working in alliance with the eunuchs, so much so that the other officials found his behavior disgraceful and successfully objected to his appointment as a chief minister.[32] Both Yü Chou and P'ei Chün belonged to the category of officials who played court politics, gained imperial favor by producing lavish revenue for the imperial treasury and for their court friends, and at the same time made fortunes for themselves. They seem to have been effective enough as provincial administrators, providing much-needed financial support for a harassed court, but they were better at short-term gains for the court and themselves than at maintaining Confucian ideals of benevolent government. It is a measure of the resilience of the T'ang dynasty that such men,

30. *HTS* 224A.9b–12a; *TCTC* 229.7378–79, 236.7596–97, and 237.7642.

31. *HTS* 172.1a–2a; *TCTC* 235.7588; 237.7647; and 239.7699; see Han Yü's letters, *CTW* 551.10b–11b and 552.14a–15b; 555.3a–4b. See also Po Chü-i, *Po-shih Ch'ang-ch'ing chi (SPTK* ed.) 14. 7b–10b, 16a–17a, 19b–21a.

32. *HTS* 108.7a–b; *TCTC* 237.7649–50. See also note 31.

and the many more who were to come after them, do not seem to have undermined the court's authority in the middle Yangtse at all. Thus when the Huai-hsi governor Wu Yüan-chi rebelled in 814, there was no real danger to imperial authority either in Shan-nan East or in Ching-nan although Yuan Tzu (748–818) and Yen Shou (c. 744–820), who alternated as governors of these provinces between 811 and 816, were both aged and ineffectual literati.[33]

The southern half of the middle Yangtse region, the provinces of O-Yo and Hunan, provided a similar picture in some respects. With a very few exceptions, such as Prince Kao who governed Hunan in 780–82, the two brilliant literati governors of O-Yo, Hsi Shih-mei in 808–10 and Liu Kung-cho in 813–16, and the ruthless Li Sun, governor of Hunan in 792–97, none of the civil governors were distinguished men. Even these four men made their reputations mainly after their governorships in these two provinces.[34] What is worth noting, however, is that before the accession of Hsien-tsung in 805, very obscure officials were appointed to O-Yo, while Hunan had governors at least as distinguished as Prince Kao, Li Sun, and two future chief ministers, Hsiao Fu and Chao Ching.[35] This contrast is also borne out by a comparison of the only two men who held long-term appointments during this period, Hsin Ching-kao, governor of Hunan from 770 to 779, and Ho Shih-kan, governor of O-Yo from 788 to 802. Hsin Ching-kao was a cousin of an outstanding general and had himself had a notable military career before his Hunan appointment, while Ho Shih-kan was a literatus so obscure that, despite fourteen years as inspector of O-Yo, we only know him by one slight "judgment" (p'an) of his own and through a shadowy picture of him as a friend of literary men by the minor essayist Fu Tsai (c. 785–804).[36]

The chief reason for the relative importance of Hunan as compared with O-Yo during the years 764–805 was that while Hunan was already a large and well-defined area almost coinciding with the modern province of Hunan, O-Yo had uncertain boundaries which were constantly being redefined to include or exclude prefectures *north* of the Yangtse like Huang, Ch'i, and An, and even for a while stretched eastward *south* of the river to include the prefecture of Chiang. This

33. HTS 151.3b–4b and 129.7b–8a; TCTC 239.7707–08.
34. HTS 80.10a–12b, 143.10a–b, 163.8a–10a, 149.8b–9a. For Liu Kung-cho, see Han Yü's letters in CTW 554.4a–6a.
35. HTS 101.4b–5b and 150.3a–4a.
36. Ibid. 147.3b–4a, no biography of Ho Shih-kan. Hsin Ching-kao was powerful enough to get rid of Prince (Li) Kao from Hunan; TCTC 226.7269. For Ho Shih-kan, see CTW 436. 11a–12a, and Fu Tsai's essays in CTW 688–91.

uncertainty was removed in 805 when Han Kao, grandson and son of two generations of chief ministers, was appointed to O-Yo as a result of political intrigues at court, and O-Yo briefly became a military governorship *(chieh-tu shih)* for five years. Although O-Yo reverted to a civil province after Han Kao's tenure and was not raised to military status again until 825–31 when two famous ex–chief ministers, Niu Seng-ju and Yüan Chen, were successively posted there, and then again in 848–53, it nevertheless became an increasingly important province once it had been finally established and expanded to control five prefectures astride the Yangtse.[37]

This did not mean that the province was always governed by able men. The majority of those who came after Han Kao (805–08) were distinguished more by the families they came from than by their own administrative records, and out of the twenty-four civil and military governors, seven were from the great Ts'ui family, three from the Wei family, and two from the imperial house. More significantly, all six of those who had been chief ministers or were to become chief ministers were appointed to O-Yo only after 818.[38]

While it can be seen that the importance of O-Yo was better recognized after Emperor Hsien-tsung came to the throne, the appointment as governors of aristocrats and others who were later to become chief ministers was not peculiar to O-Yo. In Shan-nan East and Ching-nan provinces after 805 we find this to an even more striking degree. Their governors were mainly powerful courtiers whose period of office in the province was either a preparation for higher political office or a temporary exile from the court after having been politically outmaneuvered.

It is interesting to note that military men were no longer appointed to these provinces after Hsien-tsung's reign, especially after the defeat of Wu Yüan-chi in 817. By this time the alliance of governors with various aristocrat-eunuch groups had been firmly established. From this time until the traumatic shock of the Huang Ch'ao Rebellion, 875–84, there was, in fact, a growing stability and complacency about the imperial system in the provinces, and the middle Yangtse probably encouraged this complacency more than any other region. The lower Yangtse was immensely wealthy, and the most favored officials were sent to

37. See note 22.
38. *T'ang fang-chen nien-piao* 6.160–64. The six were: Li Ch'eng (818–21), *HTS* 131.4a–b; Ts'ui Chih (823–24), *HTS* 142.4a–5a; Niu Seng-ju and Yüan Chen, who had been chief ministers (see note 22); Cheng Lang (845–47), *HTS* 165.5b; and Lu Shang, who had also just been a chief minister (see note 22).

Huai-nan and Che-hsi; but the middle Yangtse was, if anything, more crucial a center of stability. It had suffered no rebellion since 781, had survived all efforts to attack it, and had always ensured the court's access to the wealth of the lower Yangtse even when the Grand Canal was attacked and when the Hopei and Huai-hsi rebels had threatened Loyang.

In this context, it can be seen that the most important development for the Yangtse Valley in the ninth century was the growth into a major center of O-Yo. This was not immediately obvious because O-Yo was not made a military province in its own right and, as long as its territories were entirely south of the Yangtse, did not border the disputed territories in the upper Huai Valley. From the writings of Yüan Chieh (723–72), it can be seen how vital the north bank of the Yangtse was during the great rebellions after 755, and therefore how strategically important the military governorships established at Ching, Hsiang, Teng, and An really were—hence the great power given to Lü Yin and the seventeen prefectures of Ching-nan.[39]

In comparison, O-Yo remained insignificant in the eyes of the court until Emperor Hsien-tsung appointed first Han Kao and then Hsi Shih-mei to an enlarged province. With the appointment of Hsi Shih-mei, we have a lengthy account describing the efforts to make O-chou into a major administrative center. In the admiring words of the youthful scholar-politician, Shu Yüan-yü (died 835, in an abortive coup against the eunuchs), Hsi Shih-mei saw that "O-ch'eng was situated among many islets, where the land-forms rise and fall steeply. The high parts were precarious and the depressions liable to floods." Therefore, he ordered that the highlands be leveled to fill the depressions, that the streets be extended and widened and fine trees be grown, and that the marshes be drained and diseases kept under control. He also tore down the crowded housing, which demoralized even the officers and administrators, and planned and built a completely new center for the provincial government. The garrison had become, Shu Yüan-yü claimed, thirty thousand strong, and the camps were inferior and built on low-lying lands subject to annual flooding, so a new site was found for fifteen camps and three thousand buildings. Furthermore, this attention to detail was not limited to O-ch'eng itself but also extended to other prefectures in the province.[40]

Shu Yüan-yü's essay was probably overenthusiastic, and we must discount the idea that Hsi Shih-mei was responsible for all that was

39. *CTW* 380–83.
40. Ibid. 727.16b–19a.

successful in O-Yo. All the same, we have enough evidence to show that O-Yo was never again the backwater suggested in the writings of Fu Tsai from the latter part of Te-tsung's reign, but increasingly became a province of great trading and administrative activity.[41]

The growing importance of O-Yo can be brought out by a direct comparison of the appointments to the four areas of the middle Yangtse. There is a lack of source materials after 850, but the forty years 810–49 provide an adequate picture of the position of O-Yo in relation to the other three provinces. First, a comparison with Hunan: There were at least fourteen governors or inspectors of O-Yo and twenty-three of Hunan during this period. Of the fourteen at O-Yo, only four, or possibly five, were appointed to O-Yo as their first post as a civil governor, while out of the twenty-three at Hunan, nine are known certainly to have gone there as first appointments to governorships, and eight others were probably also sent out at that level for the first time.[42] On the other hand, we know that five of the O-Yo civil governors had had a tour in the same capacity elsewhere before being sent to O-Yo (two of them were promoted from Hunan), while only one person out of twenty-three at Hunan was definitely a second appointment to a civil governorship.[43] It is also of interest that while four chief ministers were removed from office and demoted to O-Yo and at least four others posted to Hunan, the demotion to O-Yo was not a serious setback, and the province was raised to military governorship status mainly to accommodate two of them; while all four demoted to Hunan were probably seriously disgraced.[44] Further, we have biographical details about

41. Fu Tsai, *CTW* 688–91; Tu, *Fan-ch'uan wen-chi*, 8–16, esp. 11.6a–10a and 14.9a–15a, on law and order problems in the middle and lower Yangtse.

42. At O-Yo, the following were first appointments: Lü Yüan-ying (810–13) (see note 22); Li Ch'eng (see note 38); Ts'ui Chih (see note 38); Kao K'ai (838–40), *HTS* 177.4a; Cheng Lang (see note 38); and Ts'ui Li (840–42), *HTS* 144.6a.

At Hunan, the following were first appointments: Liu Kung-cho (811–13) (see note 34); Chang Cheng-fu (813–16), *CTS* 162.8b–9a; Wei Kuan-chih (816–17), *HTS* 169.5a; Ts'ui Leng (818–19), *HTS* 142.5a–b; Ts'ui Ch'ün (819–20), *HTS* 165. 10b–11a; K'ung Chi (820–23), *HTS* 163.4b; Shen Ch'uan-shih (823–26), *HTS* 132.10a–b; Liu Tsun-ku (826–27); Wang Kung-liang (827–28); Wei Tz'u (829–30); Kao Ch'ung (830–33), *HTS* 95.3a–b; Li Jen-shu (834–35); Lu Hsing-shu (835–37); Li I (837–39); Lu Chien-tz'u (841–42), *HTS* 117.7a–b; Ts'ui Yuan-shih (842–43), *HTS* 160.6b–7a; and P'ei Shih (848–51), *HTS* 174.7a–b.

43. The five at O-Yo were Liu Kung-cho from Hunan (see notes 34 and 42); Li Tao-ku (816–18) from Ch'ien-chung, *HTS* 80.12a–b; Ts'ui Yuan-lüeh (822–23) also from Ch'ien-chung, *HTS* 160.5a–b; Ts'ui Yen from Shan-Kuo (see note 22); and Kao Ch'ung from Hunan after two years at Ch'ang-an (835–38, see note 42).

The second appointments at Hunan were Li Ao (833–34) from Kuei-kuan, *HTS* 177.6a–7a and P'ei Hsiu (843–47) from Chiang-hsi, *HTS* 182.8b–9a.

44. The four demotions to O-Yo were those of Ts'ui Chih (823–24), *HTS* 142.4a–5a; Niu

all fourteen O-Yo civil governors, while we have similar details for only sixteen out of the twenty-three at Hunan.

A comparison with the twenty-one Shan-nan East governors for the same period shows a somewhat different picture. Only two out of the twenty-one seem to have gone directly to Shan-nan East province from posts either of prefect or metropolitan governor *(yin)*; one of them was a member of the imperial house, and the other was appointed to a truncated province in 815 when the province was divided into two.[45] Normal appointments were mainly of two kinds. The majority of the governors, fifteen out of the twenty-one, started in appointments as either civil governors or military governors before being posted to Shan-nan East. Of these fifteen, seven had had long and distinguished careers both at court and in the provinces, had served in at least three other provinces, and had served as chief ministers in between provincial governorships.[46] The remaining four, Yüan Tzu, Li Feng-chi, P'ei Tu, and Niu Seng-ju, had had brilliant careers at court and had risen to chief minister before they went out to the provinces. Being appointed to Shan-nan East, unlike O-Yo and Hunan, after having been a chief minister was not normally regarded as a demotion.[47] Finally, three men who had been civil governors of O-Yo during this period later went on to became governors of Shan-nan East. They were Liu Kung-cho, Li Ch'eng, and Niu Seng-ju. Niu's case was exceptional in that he was sent to O-Yo in 825–30 after having been a chief minister, and O-Yo province was raised to *chieh-tu shih* status for his sake. The other two, however, illustrated the long steady careers of able administrators.

Seng-ju; Yüan Chen; and Lu Shang (for the last three, see note 22, O-Yo was raised to *chieh-tu shih* status).

The five to Hunan were Wei Kuan-chih (816–17), *HTS* 169.5a; Yüan Tzu (817–18, see note 33); Ts'ui Ch'ün (819–20), *HTS* 165.10b–11a; and Yang Ssu-fu (840–41), *HTS* 174.10b–13a; the fifth, Li Hui (848), was demoted first to Hsi-ch'uan *chieh-tu shih*, and then to Hunan, and then further to a lowly prefect.

45. Li I-chien (811–13), *HTS* 131.3b–4a, was the member of the imperial house; Cheng Ch'üan (815), *HTS* 159.5a–b, had been metropolitan governor of Loyang (Honan *yin*).

46. The seven with long and distinguished careers were: the three chief ministers, Tou I-chih (828–30), *HTS* 151.5b; Li Ch'eng (838–39, see notes 38 and 42); and Cheng Su (844–45), *HTS* 182.5b; the other four, Wang Ch'i (834–35), *HTS* 167.7b–8a; Yin Yu (836–37), *HTS* 164.10b–12a; Lu Chün (841–44), *HTS* 182.6a–7b; and Lu Chien-tz'u (847–48, see note 42).

The remaining nine were: Yen Shou (814–15, see note 33); Li Sun (815), *HTS* 162.9a–b; Li Su (816–18), *HTS* 154.6a–8a; Meng Chien (818–20), *HTS* 160.2a–3a; Niu Yüan-i (822–23), *HTS* 148.14a–15a; Liu Kung-cho (823–26, see notes 34, 42, and 43); Li Ao (835–36, see note 43); and Kao Yüan-yü (848–52), *HTS* 177.8b–9b.

47. Yüan Tzu (813–14, see notes 33 and 44); Li Feng-chi (820–22), *HTS* 174.1a–2a; P'ei Tu (830–34), *HTS* 173.1a–6a; Niu Seng-ju (839–41, see notes 22 and 44).

Liu Kung-cho took seven years to get from civil governor of O-Yo to governor of Shan-nan East; Li Ch'eng rose quickly to chief minister after 821, but did not go to Shan-nan East until sixteen years later.[48]

The appointments to Ching-nan were even more different from those at O-Yo. Between 810 and 849, there were thirteen governors, seven of whom had been chief ministers before going out to provincial appointments, a much higher proportion than in either O-Yo or Shan-nan East. The reasons for their being posted to Ching-nan, or indeed to other provinces, were not always the same. Some were victims of fierce political intrigues and factional struggles like the two aristocrats Li Shih and Li Te-yü (787–849). The others were merely continuing their careers of loyal service to the empire in another capacity.[49] The remaining six, however, who had not been chief ministers, had had careers similar to those of their counterparts in Shan-nan East. Three of them seem to have risen very swiftly because of special connections: Yen Shou was favored by the emperor Te-tsung (780–05) and appointed to govern a major province; Ts'ui Kuan was appointed because he was a protégé of the chief minister Li Te-yü; and Wang Ch'ien had the unusual position at court of being Emperor Hsüan-tsung's grandson through the princess Yung-mu and therefore three generations senior to Emperor Hsien-tsung, who gave him his first appointment as military governor.[50] The last three governors, curiously enough, have left almost no biographical details: they were P'ei Wu, Wei Ch'ang, and Cheng Yai. Their careers were conventional and undistinguished and their lineage impeccable, but it is surprising that we know so little about these three appointees to Ching-nan, on all counts one of the major provinces of the empire.[51] The above comparison does lead us, however, to suspect that the prestige of Ching-nan was traditional and convenient and not necessarily an index of its wealth of resources, its size and population, or even its continued strategic superiority.

One final point should be made in comparing O-Yo with the other three provinces. There were examples of direct promotions from Hunan

48. Liu Kung-cho, see note 34; Li Ch'eng, see note 38; Niu Seng-ju, see note 22.

49. The seven former chief ministers were Chao Tsung-ju (809–11), *HTS* 151.4b–5a; Yüan Tzu (814–16, see note 33); Ts'ui Ch'ün (829–30, see note 44); Tuan Wen-ch'ang (830–32), *HTS* 89.9a–b; Li Shih (838–43), *HTS* 131.5a–5b; Li Te-yü (846), *HTS* 180.1a–9a; and Cheng Su (846–49, see note 46).

50. The three who rose swiftly: Yen Shou (811–14, see note 33); Ts'ui Kuan (832–34), *HTS* 182.4b; and Wang Ch'ien (see note 24).

51. *T'ang fang-chen nien-piao* 5.124–25; Wang Shou-nan, *T'ang-tai fan-chen,* app., pp. 484, 508, 515, 560, 620, 651, 729, 737, 748, 758, 759. P'ei Wu had been metropolitan governor of Ch'ang-an and then chief censor and metropolitan governor of Loyang, while Cheng Yai went on to be governor of four provinces and also chief censor.

to O-Yo, and it was possible for officials who had administered O-Yo to become military governors of Shan-nan East after a series of promotions; but there were no examples of civil governors of O-Yo becoming governors of Ching-nan, nor was there any regular way to this governorship. Ching-nan appears to have been useful as a province to which imperial favorites could be appointed as a move in the game of the court politics.

Throughout the ninth century the four distinct segments of the middle Yangtse had been separately administered and supervised. Although they were unequal in size and resources and, despite the gradual rise of O-Yo, unequal in status, the important fact was that they were four independent segments and that the central government had no trouble in controlling them. There were very few notable clans with local power and political ambitions, and there was little incentive to build up local armed forces for each province. Each of the long line of civilian officials who administered the provinces did so mainly with the help of an outside garrison, most of whom were recruited from the north.[52] There were, right up to the decade of the Huang Ch'ao Rebellion, no indications that the four segments would separate to become four or five independent political entities. Only their long period of administrative separateness, their limited capacity to support themselves, and their distance from the potential centers of power can help us understand why the middle Yangtse became the most fragmented region of China for eighty years.

The traditional explanation of the fall of the T'ang dynasty was that it failed to contain the rebellions of Wang Hsien-chih and Huang Ch'ao, and that, when Ch'ang-an fell to Huang Ch'ao in 880, the end was near and inevitable. There have, however, been several efforts to trace the origins of fatal weakness to earlier uprisings and mutinies during the reigns of Hsüan-tsung (846–59) and I-tsung (859–73). The most important of these was the P'ang Hsün mutiny at Hsü-chou in 868–69 which combined with the consequences to South China of the

52. On the local middle Yangtse political and economic conditions, I have depended on scattered references in T'ang prose collections, especially those of Yüan Chieh (T'ang Yüan Tz'u-shan wen-chi), Han Yü (Chu Wen-kung chiao Ch'ang-li hsien-sheng wen-chi), Liu Tsung-yüan (Tseng-kuang chu-shih yin-pien T'ang Liu hsien-sheng chi), Po Chü-i, and Tu Mu, and other pieces found in Ch'üan T'ang-wen. Also helpful are HTS 71–75; Wang Hsiang-chih, Yü-ti chi-sheng (Taipei, photo reprint edition) 47, 49, 64–86; Hu-pei t'ung-chih; and Hu-nan t'ung-chih.

On local armed forces, see Tu, Fan-ch'uan wen-chi 11.6a–10a and 14.9a–15a; HTS 190.3a. Otherwise, the garrisons were mainly troops from the Honan region, especially the Chung-wu, the T'ien-p'ing, and the Wu-ning armies; see TCTC 226–53 passim.

Nan Chao invasion of Annam in 860. Attention has also been drawn to the fierce battles at the southern end of the Grand Canal following the rebellion of Ch'iu Fu in 859–60, and to the series of mutinies all over South China in 855, 857, and 858, notably those immediately south of the Yangtse in Hunan (858), Chiang-hsi (858), Hsüan-she (858), and in Che-tung (856) close to the Grand Canal terminus. It seems clear that the imperial treasury, full in 859, was exhausted fifteen years later just before the Huang Ch'ao Rebellion broke out.[53]

South China was certainly turbulent during the decade after 858, and the middle Yangtse region was deeply involved in its pacification. The garrisons of Ching-nan, Shan-nan East, O-Yo, and Hunan were drawn upon for help to put down several mutinies as well as tribal uprisings in the southwest and the full-scale invasion of Annam in the far south. But, significantly, except for a small unit in Hunan which mutinied and chased out its civil governor, the middle Yangtse remained fully under control. Thus each time the Grand Canal route was threatened or cut, the alternative route up the Han River always remained open. This remained true up to 877 when Wang Hsien-chih and Huang Ch'ao for a few weeks broke through into the ninety years' peace of the middle Yangtse.[54]

It would be unwise to suggest, from the events of the period 858–80, that control of the Ching-Hsiang-O-T'an provinces was in itself crucial to the survival of the T'ang dynasty. Certainly many other factors, such as the discontent in the provincial garrisons, the cupidity of most officials, the increasing inefficiency of revenue administration, and the complacency and corruption at the court, all contributed to the general disorder in the south and the lower Yangtse, which made the middle Yangtse provinces the chief buffer region as well as the main route for revenues to reach Ch'ang-an.[55] But it is noteworthy that once the central government lost control of the middle Yangtse, which it steadily did from 876 to 886, the emperor and his court, whether they were in Kuan-chung or in Szechwan, became impoverished, isolated, and impossible to save.

The chronology is interesting. The Wang Hsien-chih and Huang Ch'ao rebels started along the Grand Canal in 875, threatened the east-

53. *HTS* 222B.6a; *TCTC* 252.8174. See Matsui Shūichi, "Tōdai no Kō-wai"; Hori Toshikazu, "Tōmatsu shohanran no seikaku," *Tōyō Bunka* 7 (1951): 52–94, and "Kō Sō no hanran," *Tōyō Bunka Kenkyūsho Kiyō* 13 (1957): 1–108; and Hino Kaizaburō, "Tōmatsu Konran Shikō," *Tōyō Shigaku* 10 (1954): 1–94; and 11 (1954): 1–18.

54. *TCTC* 252.8187 and 253.8192–8202.

55. For a vivid contemporary statement of the reasons for T'ang failure, see Ku Yün's memorial on behalf of Kao P'ien, *CTS* 182.7a–8a; *TCTC* 255.8269–71.

ern capital Loyang a year later, and reached the middle Yangtse at the end of 876. Although capturing minor prefectures was relatively easy, and the rebels did not believe in defending what they captured, it is significant that they reached the Han Valley, took both Ying-chou and Fu-chou in Shan-nan East, and established that the middle Yangtse was vulnerable. They then confirmed this by attacking and looting Ch'i-chou in O-Yo and capturing O-chou itself in early 877. By this time, the rebels had been weakened by division, and Wang Hsien-chih's forces, which had captured O-chou, returned north of the Huai Valley to rejoin Huang Ch'ao. Toward the end of 877 the two returned to the middle Yangtse and were again successful in O-Yo and Shan-nan East. The climax of this attack was when Wang Hsien-chih breached the outer walls of Ching-chou (Chiang-ling), sacked the city, and, if Ssu-ma Kuang can be believed, killed 30 or 40 percent of Chiang-ling's 300,000 households. The rebels were driven off with the help of Chinese and Turkish troops sent from Shan-nan. As Wang Hsien-chih turned east into O-Yo, he was defeated in Ch'i-chou north of the Yangtse and killed. His remaining forces scattered in several directions. Most of them joined Huang Ch'ao near the Grand Canal, but many roving bands crossed south of the river and attacked both the middle and the lower Yangtse prefectures. Soon afterward, Huang Ch'ao himself brought the main armies across the Yangtse, having discovered that North China and the middle Yangtse were well defended, while South China was much weaker and easy prey.[56]

This was early in 878. For the next two years, Huang Ch'ao's troops freely roamed the length and breadth of South China, sacking Chiang-hsi, attacking Che-tung and Fu-chien, and then seizing Ling-nan. By the end of 879, the rebel armies were ready to go north again through Kuei-chou and down the Hsiang River to the middle Yangtse. T'an-chou was easily taken; Ching-chou was abandoned and looted even before Huang Ch'ao's troops arrived. Only the Shan-nan East forces under Governor Liu Chü-jung fought back, defeated the rebels, and blocked their route to the north. Once again the middle Yangtse was devastated, and this time the strategic province of Ching-nan was almost lost to imperial control. Its civilian governor, a senior chief minister sent there as chief commander against Huang Ch'ao, was a complete disaster. Fortunately, the soldier Liu Chü-jung did well in defending Shan-nan East, and the governor of O-Yo managed to hold

---

56. See note 54, also *CTS* 200B.4b–9a; *HTS* 225C.1a–9a; Howard S. Levy, trans., *Biography of Huang Ch'ao* (Berkeley and Los Angeles, 1955), pp. 10–16 and 50–57.

O-chou. By this success, Huang Ch'ao was diverted from the middle Yangtse and sought to cross the Yangtse further east.[57]

For the next eight months until August 880, the main strategy was to prevent Huang Ch'ao from crossing the Yangtse. The defenses on the north bank of the middle Yangtse were obviously still formidable, and Huang Ch'ao concentrated his efforts on crossing the lower Yangtse into the province of Huai-nan. The Huai-nan governor, Kao P'ien, first took the initiative and sent his troops south of the Yangtse in pursuit of the rebels. There was much false optimism at court when Kao P'ien reported successes; he was certainly overconfident in believing that Huang Ch'ao was ready and content to negotiate for a governorship for himself. The situation changed rapidly when Huang Ch'ao realized that Kao P'ien had turned back imperial reinforcements. The rebels found a weak link at Ts'ai-shih, crossed north of the Yangtse, and camped within striking distance of the Huai-nan provincial capital of Yang-chou.[58]

The importance of this crossing, the responsibility of Kao P'ien for the disasters to the T'ang empire which were to follow, and the rapidity with which the rebels reached Ch'ang-an have all been remarked on in many studies of this period and need not detain us here. From January 881 to May 883, Ch'ang-an was in rebel hands. The court had hurriedly departed for Szechwan and sent for help from the governors of the middle and lower Yangtse. At this point the middle Yangtse provided the court's only contact with southern and eastern China, and, for the first few months, it was uncertain how regularly tribute from these provinces could be expected to reach Szechwan either via Ching-nan and the Yangtse gorges or via O-Yo and Shan-nan up the Han River into northern Szechwan.[59]

The main contestants for power, for men and arms, and for provincial revenues were four groups. These were firstly the remnants of the imperial armies who protected and supported the few imperial officials still being appointed as well as the imperial army commanders who retained control of strategic provinces, like Kao P'ien in Huai-nan and Chou Pao in Che-hsi. The second group consisted of provincial armies and their officers who were thought better placed to defend their own provinces or who saw good opportunities to seize certain provinces for themselves. The third was a miscellaneous group of local militia and

57. *TCTC* 253.8217–19, 8224–25, and 8228–29; Levy, *Biography of Huang Ch'ao*, pp. 19–21.

58. *CTS* 182.5b–11b; *HTS* 224B.3a–11b; Levy, *Biography of Huang Ch'ao*, 21–22.

59. Chou Lien-k'uan, "T'ang Kao P'ien chen-Huai shih-chi k'ao," *Lingnan Hsüeh-pao* 11, no. 2 (1951): 11–45; *TCTC* 254.8251–58.

self-defense units and their officers and local adventurers and toughs who formed small bands to take over prefectures and occasionally whole provinces. Finally, there were the large number of scattered rebel armies, some broken off from Wang Hsien-chih's and Huang Ch'ao's units, and later from Ch'in Tsung-ch'üan's armies, and others that had started as local bandits and increased in strength as the larger armies were weakened by continuous fighting.[60]

The middle Yangtse survived not only the direct attack of Huang Ch'ao in 879 but also the second stage during the years when Huang Ch'ao occupied the capital and the court was reestablishing itself at Ch'eng-tu. During 881–83, both Shan-nan East and O-Yo remained under the control of loyalists. The cynical general who governed Shan-nan East, Liu Chü-jung, was from the second group of men whose loyalty was, in fact, doubtful, but who still valued the legitimacy conferred upon him by the court as long as he sent regular tribute and kept open the route to the west. Ts'ui Shao, who was civil governor of O-Yo, was probably a court-appointed bureaucrat and belonged to the first group. He seems to have had neither imperial troops nor a strong provincial army under his command and had to concentrate on organizing local militia in order to maintain law and order. Between these two men, the Han River route was kept open until the third stage of the great rebellion when Huang Ch'ao's armies came east again and joined forces with Ch'in Tsung-ch'üan and the rebels of the upper Huai and Honan.[61]

The same could not be said of Ching-nan where the imperial garrison and the various provincial troops left there experienced a very uneasy relationship. The key figures seem to have been the two successive eunuch army supervisors *(chien-chün)* with the garrison, Yang Fu-kuang in 880 and Chu Ching-mei in 880–85. Yang Fu-kuang was faced with Tuan Yen-mo, a provincial army officer from the Grand Canal area stationed at Ching-chou, who refused to accept either the court-appointed bureaucrat Cheng Shao-yeh as governor or the provincial army officer from the Honan region, Sung Hao, as garrison commander. The court was forced to recall Cheng Shao-yeh, and Tuan Yen-mo took over. In the middle of 882, the army supervisor Chu Ching-mei had the governor killed and then eventually put up his own protégé as governor, the local army commander and a native of Ching-chou called Ch'en Ju. Through Ch'en Ju, Chu Ching-mei probably remained

60. *HTS* 186–90 and 225C.
61. Ibid. 186.5a–b; 190.3a.

powerful in the province until the beginning of 885 (possibly even after he was replaced as army supervisor by another eunuch). But the relationship between the various troops at Ching-nan remained unstable throughout these years.[62]

The fourth province, Hunan, was the first to fall outside imperial control. The last civil governor, probably the last court-appointed bureaucrat, was Li Yü, who was unable to defend the chief prefecture at T'an-chou against the mixed Ching-hsi and Hunan provincial army led by Min Hsü at the end of 881 or very early in 882. Under Min Hsü, the middle Yangtse saw its first autonomous military province *(chieh-tu shih)* since 781.[63]

The recovery of Ch'ang-an by the imperial forces in 883 turned out to be a totally misleading event as far as the future of the T'ang dynasty was concerned. There was to be no real restoration, and the dynasty survived in name only until its formal end in 907. Possibly a major factor in the downfall of the dynasty was the loss first of the lower and then of the middle Yangtse. On the surface, the provinces of Shan-nan East and O-Yo remained loyal; so, also, to some extent, did Ching-nan. Farther east, the two imperial army commanders Kao P'ien in Huai-nan and Chou Pao in Che-hsi continued to be theoretically the emperor's men for several years after 883. But the rot had, in fact, set in earlier along the Yangtse. Not only had Hunan gone by 882, Kao P'ien himself had, in fact, severed relations with the court by mid-882 when his titles of Supreme Commander *(Chu-tao tu-t'ung)* and of Salt and Transport Commissioner *(Yen-t'ieh chuan-yün shih)* were successively taken away from him. By this time, Chiang-hsi was largely under the control of the local rebel leader Chung Ch'uan, and Kao P'ien soon sent his forces under the ex-Huang Ch'ao officer Ch'in Yen south of the Yangtse to take the province of Hsüan-she. By this move, Chou Pao in Che-hsi was effectively cut off from the middle Yangtse, and no revenues intended for the court could have reached O-Yo in any case.[64] Furthermore, Szechwan itself faced severe uprisings throughout 882, and the Yangtse route from east of the gorges was closed most of that year.[65] Thus, it would appear that in 882 the court completely lost the revenues of the lower Yangtse and much of the middle Yangtse tribute as well. It was in this same year 882, that Kao P'ien twice proposed, how cyni-

62. Ibid. 186.4b–5a; 190.2a–3a; *TCTC* 255.8271–72.

63. *HTS* 186. 3a–4a; *TCTC* 254.8260–61 and 255.8269–70.

64. *CTS* 182.7a–8a; *TCTC* 255.8269; *HTS* 190.4a–b on Chung Ch'uan, 224B.6a–11b, 186.1a–2a.

65. *TCTC* 254.8263–64.

cally it is not possible to know, that the court should move out of Szechwan and reestablish itself in the Chiang-Huai region.[66]

Shan-nan East remained in loyalist hands until 884; Ching-nan was under great pressure from local rebel leaders in 884 and was seized by a rebel officer from the lower Yangtse early in 885; and finally, O-Yo or, more accurately, O-chou itself, was abandoned by its loyalist civil governor in 886. But, with the lower Yangtse cut off by the end of 882, little was reaching the court even before Shan-nan East fell to the rebel forces of Ch'in Tsung-ch'üan who controlled the upper Huai. By early 885, when Ching-nan also fell into rebel hands, the middle Yangtse had become largely irrelevant to the politics of the court.[67] The main question that remains is how important the region was in the ensuing struggle between rival aspirants hoping to succeed the T'ang and to reunify the empire.

The T'ang empire was transformed during the three years in which Huang Ch'ao fought for Ch'ang-an (880–83); the middle Yangtse was gradually lost to imperial control over a slightly longer period, 876–86. No clear causal relationship can be established between the two sets of changes. Many other crucial events were taking place elsewhere in the empire as the mobile rebel armies disrupted imperial administration, and various sections of the imperial and provincial armies mutinied, became independent of their commanders, and even changed sides. What is significant for this study of the middle Yangtse is that the four provinces of the region shared common strategic and financial functions but, as was consistent with basic T'ang administrative and military policy, were never recognized as *one* military region and were never given sufficient strength to be defended as a coherent defense system. The policy was to keep the provinces weak if there had to be provinces at all. Nevertheless, the specific fragmentation of this region was remarkable. After eighty years of fairly constant provincial boundaries, two of the provinces experienced virtual dismemberment, one preserved itself more or less intact, and fourth expanded into a large, independent state. It is interesting to note that the provinces centered in the valleys of the two tributaries, the Han and the Hsiang rivers, were preserved or expanded, while the two astride the middle Yangtse proper, Ching-nan and O-Yo, were greatly reduced. All the same, during the last twenty years of the dynasty, O-Yo and Hunan also became provinces

66. Ch'oe Chi-won, *Kuei-yuan pi-keng chi (SPTK* ed.) 2.9a–12b.

67. Shan-nan East: taken in 884 by Chao Te-yin (884–93), *HTS* 186.6a–b. Ching-nan: taken in 885 by Chang Huai (885–88), *TCTC* 256.8326. O-Yo: taken in 886 by Tu Hung (886–905), *HTS* 190.3a–4a; *CWTS* 17.2b–4b.

with military governors. The four provincial centers of Hsiang, Ching, O, and T'an retained their status and provided their *chieh-tu shih–cum–prefects* with some authority and gave at least two of them, the Hsiang-chou and T'an-chou prefects, enough power to control their neighboring prefectures.

Thus, the basis for the division of the middle Yangtse into four segments persisted beyond the T'ang into the period of the Five Dynasties. These four areas were controlled as follows:[68]

1. *Shan-nan* (six prefectures)

Chao Te-yin (884–93)	Rebel officer under Ch'in Tsung-ch'üan of Huai-hsi. Attacked Ching-nan in 887, abandoned rebel cause in 888, and became supporter of Chu Wen, who controlled most of Honan.
Chao K'uang-ning (893–905)	Te-yin's son, lost the province to Chu Wen's troops in 905.

2. *Ching-nan* (three prefectures)

Chang Huai (885–88)	Rebel officer from Huai-nan in the lower Yangtse. Driven off by Chao Te-yin's troops.
Ch'eng Jui (888–903)	Former rebel officer of Huai-hsi, took over after driving off Shan-nan East troops. Drowned in river battle against Huai-nan troops attacking O-chou.
Chao K'uang-ming (903–05)	K'uang-ning's brother; the province was thus controlled from Shan-nan East. Lost province to Chu Wen's troops.

3. *O-Yo* (mainly one prefecture, O-chou)

Tu Hung (886–905)	Local actor, recruited into militia and rose to become army officer and prefect of Yo-chou, saved O-chou from rebels. Harassed by Huai-nan forces and finally absorbed into the Huai-nan state of Wu.

68. See note 67 for Ch'eng Jui, *HTS* 190.3a–4a; *CWTS* 17.1a–2b; for Chou Yo, Teng Ch'u-na, Liu Chien-feng, *HTS* 186.3a–4a and 190.1a–b. For Ma Yin, P'eng Yüan-jui's annotated edition of *HWTS* or *Wu-tai shih-chi chu* (Taipei photo reprint edition) 66.1a–14a.

4. *Hunan* (mainly three prefectures until after 898)

Chou Yo (886–93)	Local Hunan adventurer, killed by his predecessor's officer Teng Ch'u-na, another Hunanese.
Liu Chien-feng (894–96)	Rebel army officer of Huai-hsi, ravaged Chiang-hsi, then seized Hunan from Teng Ch'u-na.
Ma Yin (896–930)	Also rebel officer of Huai-hsi, succeeded Liu Chien-feng after his death, and founded the Ch'u state.

The prominence of ex–Huai-hsi rebels in these events is obvious. These forces were mainly those of Ch'in Tsung-ch'üan centered at Ts'ai-chou and probably included remnants of the Huang Ch'ao armies. Only O-Yo for twenty years and Hunan for eight were controlled by local men, but they, too, owed no loyalty to the T'ang dynasty.

During the twenty years before the end of T'ang, Chao Te-yin and his son appeared to have been in control of their province made up of at least six prefectures and thus succeeded in keeping Shan-nan East almost intact. In Ching-nan, the original eight prefectures were broken into three parts—the three beyond the gorges in Szechwan and later the two above Ching-chou were cut off by new governors in the west, while the two south of the Yangtse at Lang-chou and Li-chou were in the hands of local adventurers and tribal armies. Only Ching-chou survived under Ch'eng Jui. The earlier boundaries of O-Yo also proved indefensible. Tu Hung expended a great deal of effort trying to hold its five prefectures together, but was under constant pressure from Huai-nan in the east, Chu Wen's forces from the north, and later, from both Ch'eng Jui in the west and Ma Yin in the south. After 894, Tu Hung really only controlled O-chou itself. By 905, O, Huang, and Ch'i-chou became part of the Huai-nan state of Wu, while An-chou had fallen to Chu Wen, and Yo-chou became part of the Hunan state of Ch'u. Unlike O-Yo, which was steadily dismembered, Hunan grew from strength to strength. From the two or at most three prefectures under Chou Yo (886–93), the province was expanded into a large state embracing at least fifteen prefectures under the rule of Ma Yin.[69]

As we noted at the beginning of this essay, during the fifty-five years or so after 907, the middle Yangtse remained divided among different states. There were several attempts to bring the four segments under

69. See notes 67 and 68; *TCTC* 260.8485 ff. Also *SKCC* 1.21a–27b, 67.1a–4b, 100.1a–2b.

one empire, but the absence of one legitimate central authority made this sector of the Yangtse an unstable frontier region for the whole period of the Five Dynasties. A close examination shows that the struggles for the borders reflected not so much the classical Warring States situation, which the first half of the tenth century has often been said to resemble, but the continuation of the dual strands of T'ang provincial and prefectural administration. The following is a brief outline of the main border wars in the middle Yangtse.[70]

907–08	The four-cornered fight for Ching-chou, held by the Liang Empire and defended against two autonomous *chieh-tu shih* and against the Huai-nan state of Wu.
912–14	Autonomous Ching-chou made two attempts to expand and failed, while Wu and the Hunan state of Ch'u fought over O and Yo-chou.
919	Ching-chou called for help from Wu against Ch'u; officers attacked both Fu and An-chou of the Liang Empire.
923–26	Ching-chou acknowledged the Later T'ang of the Sha-t'o Turks and tried to expand westward up the gorges into Szechwan, while the T'ang conquered the Szechwan state of Shu.
927–29	T'ang effort to take Ching-nan (now three prefectures) with Ch'u help, while Ching-nan was aided by Wu. Ching-nan was than rejected by Wu and returned to T'ang.
934, 937, 940	An-chou provided border insecurity between Wu/Nan T'ang and Later T'ang and Later Chin.
942	Ching-nan effort to expand to Han Valley during rebellion at Shan-nan East (Hsiang-chou) failed.
947–48	Ching-nan's second effort to expand up the Han Valley following Khitan invasion and retreat also failed.
947–51	Ch'u civil war and the end of Ma family rule.
956–58	The empire of Chou invaded Nan T'ang and took *all* its territories north of the Yangtse.
963	The Sung empire captured the whole of the middle Yangtse except for O-chou (in Nan T'ang).

70. *TCTC* 266–94 passim; P'eng, *Wu-tai shih-chi chu*, 2.13a–20b (including rebellion at Shan-nan East); *SKCC* 100.2b–4a, 67.8b–9a, 100.4b, 2.20a–b. For the events of 923–29, P'eng *Wu-tai shih-chi chu*, 5B.18b to 6B.22a; *SKCC* 100.5a–10a and 101.1b. An-chou troubles, *TCTC* 278.9102; *CWTS* 97.10a–12a and 12a–13b. Ching-nan expansion efforts, *SKCC*

In my study of North China, I have shown how the northern dynasties of Liang, T'ang, Chin, and Han had steadily eroded the power of the military governors *(chieh-tu shih)* and, despite lapses of control, had prepared the ground for eventual reunification.[71] Thus the sector of the middle Yangtse controlled from the north—the four prefectures of Hsiang, Ying, Fu, and An—were never placed under a single governor. Both Hsiang and An were centers of military provinces—the well-established Shan-nan East province, which was reduced to at most four prefectures by 907, and the An-fu province which probably never exceeded two. After the successive troubles with An-fu governors in 934, 937, and 940, An-chou was reduced to a defense commission *(fang-yü shih)* comprising one prefecture, and after An Ts'ung-chin's rebellion in Shan-nan East in 941–42, Hsiang-chou was similarly reduced to a *fang-yü shih* prefecture. Also, by 943, it is certain that Fu-chou was raised from an ordinary prefecture to a defense commission prefecture, on a par with both An-chou and Hsiang-chou.[72]

In 947 both Hsiang-chou and An-chou were restored to their *chieh-tu shih* status, but there is no evidence that their governors were given back their military power. This is worth noting in the case of Hsiang-chou and the great Shan-nan East province of which it was the center. There were three long-term governors during fifty-five years—K'ung Ching (c. 909–24), An Ts'ung-chin (935–42), and An Shen-ch'i (947–58). All three owed their long tenure of office in Shan-nan East to periods of instability at the center—violent changes of emperors or of dynasties. But a comparison of the three clearly shows a striking difference. K'ung Ching was relatively powerful, almost autonomous; his position was strengthened by the usurpation at the Liang capital, by Liang's loss of the Hopei provinces after 915, and by the dynasty's fight for survival during the years 918–23. An Ts'ung-chin, too, was emboldened to rebel by the fall of Later T'ang in 936 and by Chin Kao-tsu's troubles with the Khitans, the T'u-yü-hun tribes, and a rebellious governor on the northern borders; but he realized he was not strong enough and sought support for his rebellion from the ruler of Shu and the autonomous governor of Ching-nan. Without their assistance, all he could do was to defend the city of Hsiang-yang. After

---

101.3b–5b; P'eng, *Wu-tai shih-chi chu,* 51.21a–24a. Ch'u civil war, *SKCC* 69.1a–11b; P'eng, *Wu-tai shih-chi-chu,* 66.26a–31b. Chou and Sung conquests, *SKCC* 16.15a to 17.12b; 70.5a–8b; 101.9b–12a.

71. Wang Gungwu, *The Structure of Power in North China during the Five Dynasties* (Kuala Lumpur, 1963), chaps. 5 and 7.

72. See note 70, also *CWTS* 98.5a, *HWTS* 51.15b–17b, *CWTS* 95. 8b–10a.

a siege of about nine months, the city fell, but in spite of this long resistance the outcome was never in doubt.[73]

An Shen-ch'i too probably benefited from the death of the first Han emperor and the insecurity of the second and certainly from the usurpation of the first Chou emperor in 951 and his death in 954, so that he was not moved from his post for nearly twelve years. But by this time, the imperial army was very strong, and its units did all the border fighting; and Shan-nan East, like many other northern provinces, had become a post with which to reward loyal generals—a province from which revenues could be raised for the central government.[74]

A similar development may be observed in Wu (later Nan T'ang) control of its three middle Yangtse prefectures of O, Huang, and Ch'i. O-chou was still the center of the Wu-ch'ang army and this remained a *chieh-tu shih* appointment. But all *chieh-tu shih* after the initial years of Wu were tightly controlled by Hsü Wen and his adopted son Li Sheng who became ruler in Nan T'ang in 937. Also, the creation of new *chieh-tu shih*, especially along the Huai River border with the Northern Dynasties, was most remarkable. Out of the five T'ang provinces that came under Wu control, at least fifteen new provinces were created, several with no more than two prefectures and each incomparably weaker than those of the past. Wu-ch'ang (no longer O-Yo after the loss of Yo-chou to Hunan in 907) province was important to Wu (Nan T'ang) throughout, but its forces were mainly naval and defensive, only capable of efforts at subverting An-chou to its north. The rulers of both Wu and Nan T'ang were threatened on never less than three sides at a time—especially by the Northern Dynasties, by Wu Yüeh to its southeast, and by Ch'u to its west; they were conscious of O-chou's distance from their capital and never intended the Wu-ch'ang army to be used for offensive purposes.[75]

The remaining two segments of the middle Yangtse were in the hands of dependent states, one of which continuously acknowledged the northern five dynasties and the other intermittently so. Neither had any pretensions, as had Wu/Nan T'ang, to rival the northern claim to legitimacy and the right to reunify China. The first, Ch'u, controlled two of the key prefectures of the middle Yangtse, Yo-chou and T'an-chou, and from the strategic and rich Hsiang River Valley established

73. K'ung Ching, *CWTS* 64.7b; An Ts'ung-chin, *CWTS* 98.5a.

74. *CWTS* 123.4a–6a.

75. *SKCC* 2–3 and 15–17, 5.10b–11a, 7.10b–11b, 9.4a–b, 22.2b–4a, 27.7b–8a. See Hsü Wen's arguments against taking the offensive in the Middle Yangtse beyond O-chou, *SKCC* 3.6b.

a strong and prosperous dependent state which lasted from 907 to 951.
Initially, it made several attempts to control a longer stretch of the
middle Yangtse Valley from Ching-chou to O-chou, but these failed.
Later, it concluded that Ching-nan was a useful buffer between itself
and its nominal suzerains in North China and concentrated its attention upon defending its lands from Wu/Nan T'ang to its east and Nan
Han to its south (in Kwangsi and Kwangtung).[76] Between 951 and
952, there was a brief interregnum when Nan T'ang was invited to take
over Hunan, but the local commanders of T'an-chou and Lang-chou
soon reestablished ties with North China, and the Hunan parts of the
middle Yangtse remained under autonomous *chieh-tu shih* of the Chou
and then the Sung dynasties until 963. The important fact about the
state of Ch'u was that its founder Ma Yin decided in 907 that it was
in the interest of Ch'u to acknowledge the legitimacy of any dynasty in
North China, and all his successors, with the exception Ma Hsi-o in
951, followed this policy.[77] This policy brought a relative stability to
the middle Yangtse which, as a region fragmented into so many parts,
it could hardly be expected to have had.

Finally, there was the very weak Ching-nan (sometimes referred to as
the state of Nan P'ing) which looked mainly to North China, but also,
after 926, simultaneously kept close relations with Wu/Nan T'ang and,
later, also with the kingdom of Shu in Szechwan. It consisted of only a
single prefecture, Ching-chou, from 907 to 926, and only three, with
the addition of Hsia-chou and Kuei-chou, from 926 to 963. Its founder,
Kao Chi-hsing, who governed it from 906 to 929, held it for the Liang
for nearly seven years (until 912) and then as a virtually independent
ruler until his death. He was able enough to hold one prefecture for
twenty years and was lucky to have gained two others about two and
half years before his death. His eldest son Ts'ung-hui, who held the three
prefectures for twenty years (929–48), had skillful advisers and concentrated on peace and developing trading facilities. His grandson Pao-
yung was fortunate in having an able younger brother Pao-hsü, and the
family continued to do well out of the strategic needs of Yangtse Valley.
Ching-nan survived two major attacks in 907–08 and in 927–29 and
numerous minor attacks from Ch'u in the south. It even tried, when the
opportunity arose, to expand into the Han Valley toward Ying-chou
(in 942 and 947–48). In between, it organized its defenses and its trade
and made itself useful to all its four neighbors. And as long as the
Northern Dynasties, the kingdoms of Shu and Wu/Nan T'ang, were

76. *SKCC* 67.12b–13a, 68.
77. *SKCC* 67.4a–6b, 69.7b–11a.

busy elsewhere and the state of Ch'u valued its survival as a buffer between itself and the Northern Dynasties, Ching-nan probably provided the key to the middle Yangtse equilibrium.[78]

This chapter began by asking why the middle Yangtse was so fragmented and whether it constituted a significant political region. I have suggested that its strategic importance in the center of China, between north and south and between the lower and upper Yangtse, led it to be administratively fragmented for many centuries, especially during the Three Kingdoms period, the Northern and Southern dynasties period, and during the T'ang. I have also suggested that throughout the T'ang the policy of prefectural government was maintained in the middle Yangtse, but that this had been steadily replaced by a form of military provincial government in the northern half and was being eroded by the civil provincial system in the south, just before the T'ang dynasty fell. Significantly, the strongest provincial governments in the region were established in Shan-nan East and Ching-nan, and these were obvious targets for the new centralizing forces that appeared during the last years of T'ang. They each had had at least nine prefectures under their control until 880, but were thereafter steadily reduced to about six in Shan-nan East and three in Ching-nan. Ching-nan was reduced to a single prefecture for over twenty years and never succeeded in recovering control over more than three prefectures. By the second half of the Five Dynasties, Shan-nan East also controlled, at most, four prefectures.

The two other segments followed a different course. O-Yo grew in importance after 810 and was, although briefly, twice raised to military provincial status. It controlled at least five large, rich, and relatively populous prefectures and seemed at times to have become a military province in all but name. But when the crisis came in 880, it was the first to disintegrate and, although control of Yo-chou was recovered and lost several times and An-chou wavered between northern and southern control, the province as an entity was never successfully put together again. Wu-ch'ang was a military governorship *(chieh-tu shih)*, which administered one of the largest single prefectures on the Yangtse, but after 880 its control north of the Yangtse was always precarious, and it is doubtful whether the Wu and Nan T'ang *chieh-tu shih* at O-chou were ever more than one-prefecture appointments. The southern centralizing forces based on Nanking did not appear to have had any

78. See note 70. *SKCC* 100–03; P'eng, *Wu-tai shih-chi chu*, 69.

difficulties in restoring prefectural (sometimes, as in North China, called defense commissions) rule.

On the other hand, Hunan was never really a military province until after 880 and never became really powerful until Ma Yin took over in 897. Then, in a series of skillful expeditions toward the south and the west, he created a province for himself mainly in the Hsiang River Valley. In 908, he took the two prefectures Li and Lang and was within easy striking distance of Chiang-ling. Viewed in terms of the ultimate reunification of China, it was an independent, powerful province, an obstacle to effective central government. But on the other hand, Ch'u was an example of successful centralization on a smaller, regional scale.

This study has shown that there was marked continuity in late T'ang and Five Dynasties political history. Any resemblance between the Five Dynasties and the Warring States periods is purely superficial and ignores the salient forces in the later period: the recurring pattern of province versus prefectures, large army-dominated provinces giving way to revived civilian prefectures backed by armies of would-be centralizers. All over the former T'ang empire, the same forces manifested themselves. All potential reunifiers were, whether deliberately or not, reducing the power of the military governors and the size of their satrapies. Each potential reunifier was therefore contributing toward that moment when one of them would bring the whole of China together again. Thus when the Chou emperor, Shih-tsung, conquered Huai-nan in 958, he did not simply conquer a unified province, but rather several very small "provinces," which could be readily reconverted into the prefectures from which they were formed. Thus, also, when Sung T'ai-tsu sent his armies to take Ching-nan and Hunan in 963, he was not adding two more provinces to his empire, but really so many more prefectures for his regular bureaucracy to administer. This was also true of the conquests of Shu, Nan Han, Nan T'ang, and Wu Yüeh during the following fifteen years.

Recentralization of the empire had been the goal of many since the An Lu-shan Rebellion. As the preceding essay by Charles A. Peterson shows, it had been seriously attempted by Hsien-tsung between 806 and 820, to be resumed by powerful contenders after the Huang Ch'ao Rebellion. As we have contemplated the middle Yangtse region during this period, we have noticed that it had no single magnetic center. Rather, under the pressure of outside centers of power, it devolved into smaller and smaller units, each less and less capable of resisting outside force and each contributing to the eventual emergence of a unifying central authority.

BIBLIOGRAPHICAL NOTE

I am indebted to a number of earlier studies, notably Chi Chao-ting's pioneer *Key Economic Areas in Chinese History* (London, 1926) and Ch'üan Han-sheng's detailed study of the Grand Canal, *T'ang Sung ti-kuo yü yün-ho* (Chungking, 1944; reprinted Shanghai, 1946). On the financial details, D. C. Twitchett's *Financial Administration under the T'ang Dynasty* (Cambridge, 1963) and Chü Ch'ing-yüan's *T'ang-tai ts'ai-cheng shih* (Changsha, 1940) have been valuable; on the political side, Ch'en Yin-k'o, *T'ang-tai cheng-chih shih shu-lun kao* (Chungking, 1944; Shanghai, 1947; Peking, 1956), has been particularly helpful.

The materials have been taken mainly from the old and new versions of the *T'ang Shu* and the *Wu-tai shih*, the *Tzu-chih t'ung chien*, the *Ch'üan T'ang-wen*, and the *Shih-kuo ch'un-ch'iu*. All quotations from the twenty-four Standard Histories are from the Ssu-pu ts'ung-k'an edition. For the *TCTC*, I have used the Peking 10 volume ed., 1956; for the *CTW*, the Taipei 20 volume photo reprint, 1965; and for the *SKCC*, the Taipei 4 volume photo reprint, 1962. Two valuable reference works have been the *Hu-pei t'ung-chih*, 3 vols., 1921, reprinted Shanghai, 1934; and the *Hu-nan t'ung-chih*, 5 vols., 1885, reprinted Shanghai, 1934.

Part II
Thought and Religion

7. T'ang T'ai-tsung and Buddhism

Arthur F. Wright

The reign of T'ang T'ai-tsung (627–49) has long been regarded as a golden age and the central figure of the emperor exalted as a paragon of princely virtue. While many aspects of his reign have been studied, T'ai-tsung's attitudes and policies toward Buddhism—the dominant faith of his subjects—have been ignored or treated in an oversimplified way. These oversimplifications are in general attributable to neglect or misunderstanding of three relevant orders of historical phenomena: (1) the cultural context in which T'ai-tsung lived; (2) the emperor as a person—his political and psychological biography; and (3) the great complexity of the ideological and policy choices he had to make vis-à-vis powerful clerical communities, influential Buddhist laymen, and his subjects generally. Someday perhaps these and other dimensions of the problem of T'ai-tsung and Buddhism will be definitively studied. For the present it may be useful first to explore these three orders of phenomena in an effort to bring the problem into better focus. In the second part of the chapter I shall analyze a few specific acts that seem to me to reveal something about the man and his outlook or something about his multivalent attitudes toward the prevailing religion of his people.

Cultural Context

Li Shih-min, born the second son of Li Yüan, had an upbringing not untypical of his time and class. His father was from a family of mixed stock that had weathered the political divisions and internecine wars of sixth-century North China. Shih-min's paternal grandmother had been of the great powerful Hsien-pei clan of Tu-ku. Such families had strong military traditions; horsemanship, archery, and the hunt figured more in a boy's training than book learning. The nobles all had fine horses, falcons, and hunting dogs. One of Li Shih-min's brothers remarked: "I would rather go three days without eating than one day without hunting."[1] The sons of great houses were given the rudiments of literacy and perhaps a brief exposure to a Confucian Classic. In the three hundred years preceding Shih-min's birth, one's genealogy and family connections had been decisive in gaining public office and wealth; the Sui, under which Li Yüan served, had attempted sweeping reforms designed to produce a more open elite, but the Li family was, in its culture, very much of the older northern governing elite, among whom descent, marriage alliances, and connections had long been vital for a family's survival. For all the efforts of dynasties from the Northern Wei through the Sui to encourage the individual taxpaying peasant household, the Li's, like others of their class, probably had extensive landholdings with semiservile dependents *(pu-ch'ü)* to work them and slaves for household and personal service.

The personal style of these northerners was, shall we say, "hearty." They were far more open and frank than cultivated southerners. Their rituals were simpler, and outward show was valued less than personal vigor. Concubinage was far less common in the north than in the south, and women had much more freedom to make contacts outside the house. Indeed, according to Yen Chih-t'ui (531–91), northern women went about attending to all manner of practical affairs.

> But in the city of Yeh it was the custom for women to handle all family business, to demand justice and to straighten out legal disputes, to make calls and curry favor with the powerful. They filled the streets with their carriages, occupied the government offices with their fancy dresses, begged official posts for their sons, and made complaints about injustice done to their husbands.[2]

Confucian biography naturally tells us little about domineering wives or henpecked husbands, but Sui Wen-ti (reigned 581–604), married to a typical northern woman—a member of the Tu-ku clan—stands out as the most henpecked emperor in Chinese history and was not even allowed by his jealous and strong-minded wife to keep a favorite concubine.

Southerners sneered at northern poetry and scholarship. Indeed

---

1. *CTS* (photolithographic edition, Shanghai, 1884) 64.8a.
2. For cultural contrasts, see Moriya Mitsuo, "Nanjin to Hokujin" [Southerner and northerner], *Tōa Ronsō* 6 (1948): 36–60. For the best contemporary observations on these contrasts, see Teng Ssu-yu, trans., *Yen-shih chia-hsün* [Family instructions for the Yen clan] (Leiden, 1968), passim; for the passage on women, p. 19.

northern traditions had become very thin during this period of rulers from the steppe and of a mixed-blood elite with genealogical and military claims to status. Confucian learning was largely neglected, and Yen Chih-t'ui has little but scorn for those who flaunted their scholarly attainments. He tells the story of the scholar of the city of Yeh who bought a donkey, wrote up three documents relating to the transaction, none of which contained the complicated character *lü*, donkey![3] It is suggestive of the ethos of North China in these times that the Sui founder initially had only *one* fully trained literatus among his high officials, and this man's advice was once dismissed by his master with the statement, "You bookworm! You are not fit to decide this matter."[4] Wei Cheng (580–643) in his preface to the "Literati" (*Ju-lin*) section of the Sui history comments on the state of traditional learning: "Since new year's days ceased being the same (i.e. since the onset of political division), nearly three hundred years have passed; the teachings of the ancient masters have become disordered, and there is no way of choosing what is right."[5]

The whole of northern society was suffused with Buddhism. Jacques Gernet has brilliantly described the ways in which it penetrated economic life and affected customs at all levels of society.[6] Its monasteries and shrines dotted the landscape; its clergy assumed many social roles; that of preacher and teacher, medical doctor and chanter of magic spells, performers of masses for the dead and guardians of temples that also served as family shrines. Elite families were for the most part Buddhist in belief. They made gifts to monasteries and shrines, used clergy for family and seasonal observances, had the lay vows administered to their sons, and so on. The Li family was very much a part of this world of belief. Several of their children had Buddhist childhood names; that of Li Yüan's eldest son was Pi-sha-men, Sanskrit Vaiśra-vaṇa.[7] Another son had taken Buddhist vows and, although only four-teen and probably still a novice, bore the monk's name Chih-yün. In the course of the uprising that established the T'ang, Chih-yün was seized and executed by Sui authorities; and one of the first acts of Li Yüan on taking the Sui capital was to establish a temple in his memory.[8]

3. Teng, *Yen-shih chia-hsün*, p. 64.

4. *Sui-shu* 42.8b.

5. Ibid. 75.2a.

6. Jacques Gernet, *Les aspects économiques du Bouddhisme dans la société chinoise du Vᵉ au Xᵉ siècle* (Saigon, 1956).

7. *HTS* 79.1b.

8. *CTS* 64.11b, and Hsü Sung, *T'ang liang-ching ch'eng-fang k'ao*, photolithographic ed. (Kyoto, 1956), 3.16b–17a.

There is an inscription which records that Li Yüan, while serving as a provincial official under the Sui, asked the mercy of the Buddha for his son Shih-min, who was ill. For the boy's recovery, Li Yüan "respectfully had a stone stele-image made, hoping that the merit of this act would bring benefits to the Buddha disciple, my son, and our whole family."[9] As archeology attests, such votive steles were very common expressions of Buddhist piety throughout North China.

Before concluding this brief sketch of the cultural context, we should note the extreme insecurity of life, the intensely predatory character of this society. In the half century before the rise of T'ang, there had been a high proportion of psychotic rulers (even when one discounts the moral clucking of Confucian historians). Blood feuds were common, and racial tension endemic. The lives of slaves, bondsmen, and corvée recruits were eminently expendable, as the vain Sui efforts to conquer Koguryō dramatically demonstrated. As a single example of the cruel social practices that had grown up in the long period of conflict and division, we should note that it had become customary, when the master of a house died, for his sons and grandsons immediately to sell off his women to other husbands. Sui Wen-ti issued an order forbidding this, but it applied only to the wives or concubines of officials of certain specified ranks.[10] This must suffice as a rough sketch of the culture into which Li Shih-min was born. It is meant to correct the usual bland picture that results in part from the bias of Confucian historians and in part from the tendency to project backward the culture of the long-gowned civil official of later dynasties.

Li Shih-min's Personality and the Politics of Buddhism

Li Shih-min was obviously a product of this culture. As we have noted, his paternal grandmother had been of the Hsien-pei clan of Tu-ku; his mother was of a leading northern family. *Her* mother was the elder sister of the Northern Chou emperor Wu (reigned 561–78) and was thus by birth a member of the Hsien-pei clan of Yü-wen. Li Shih-min's mother was, in her youth, a great pet of her uncle the emperor Wu (Yü-wen Yung) and was brought up at his court. Shortly after the emperor's death in 578 came the coup d'etat by the house of Yang; in the course of the next two years fifty-nine Yü-wen princes were

9. Lo Chen-yü believed this inscription to have been faked by Shih-min to "document" his father's early favor. For a summary of the controversy over this inscription, see Ts'en Chung-mien, *Sui-shu ch'iu-shih* (Peking, 1958), p. 364.

10. *Sui-shu* 66.1b. and 2.11a–b.

murdered, and the women of the last emperor forced, with two exceptions, to become Buddhist nuns. Shih-min's mother is said to have wept bitterly and to have cried out: "I regret that I was not born a man so I could come to the rescue of my uncle's family." Her parents quickly shut her up, asking if she wanted to bring annihilation upon their own clan.[11] She was married to Li Yüan, who is said to have won her in an archery contest, bore him several sons, and died before his seizure of power.

Two biographically significant observations may be made on this brief sketch of Shih-min's mother. One is that she was born and brought up in the upper level of the racially and culturally mixed elite of North China, where the women were strong and independent (as they are indeed in the nomadic cultures from which the leading families drew numerous cultural traits) and devout believers in Buddhism. The other is more tenuous: that the father-son rivalry so typical of Turko-Mongol ruling families[12] gave the women great influence over their sons and particularly their favorite sons. This is strikingly exemplified in the way the Tu-ku empress moved amid the jealousies and suspicions that characterized the Sui founder's relations with his sons to secure the succession for her favorite son Yang Kuang. Although Shih-min's mother died before the Li seizure of power, her influence upon him must have been great; we shall see that some of Shih-min's most conspicuous acts of Buddhist piety were in memory of his mother.

There is no need here to recapitulate the collapse of the Sui and the successful emergence of the Li's of Taiyuan from among the many contenders for power. Revisionist views developed over the last twenty years seem to me to prove that Li Shih-min, although no doubt precocious in military arts, was *not* the mastermind of the Li bid for power.[13] After his father became emperor of the new T'ang dynasty at the age of fifty-three—old for a Chinese of the time—the question of succession immediately arose. The eldest son, Chien-ch'eng, was duly made crown prince, and the obvious challenger was the second son Shih-min, then prince of Ch'in. During the T'ang consolidation of power, Shih-min had been in charge of many campaigns in the rich eastern plains, where he had assiduously cultivated the powerful families of the area and won over former rebel soldiers, as well as literati.

11. *CTS* 51.3a.

12. Peter Boodberg, "Marginalia to the Histories of the Northern Dynasties," *HJAS* 4 (1939): 266.

13. Woodbridge Bingham, *The Fall of Sui and the Rise of T'ang* (Baltimore, 1941); Li Shu-t'ung, *T'ang-shih k'ao-pien* (Taipei, 1965); and Howard Wechsler, draft chapter on early T'ang political history for the *Cambridge History of China*, 1968.

His brother the crown prince, though he could claim significant victories for the T'ang, may have been somewhat less successful in building a personal following. In 626 the aging Li Yüan, Emperor Kao-tsu, despairing of the rivalry between his sons, proposed to send Shih-min to be, in effect, viceroy of the eastern plain with headquarters at Loyang. The crown prince's party objected to Shih-min's leaving the capital, possibly thinking that he could be kept under closer watch (or perhaps disposed of) if he remained in Ch'ang-an. The plan was dropped; the prince of Ch'in remained in the capital where, we are told, his brothers attempted to poison him. Shih-min then planned and carried out the assassination of his brothers, the crown prince Chien-ch'eng and Yüan-chi, prince of Ch'i, in the famous incident of the Hsüan-wu Gate.[14] Shih-min became briefly crown prince and shortly thereafter forced his father to abdicate.

Evidence on Shih-min's personal attitude toward Buddhism during the struggle of the T'ang against its rivals is meager but significant; in his ultimate seizure of power, as I hope to show, the politics of Buddhism was an important factor. When, in 621, Li Shih-min was locked in a bitter struggle with Wang Shih-ch'ung, the city of Loyang was the focus of action. Nearby was Sung-shan, the "central peak" in Chinese cosmology and long the site of a great Buddhist monastery, the Shao-lin ssu. Li Shih-min appealed to the warrior-monks of this temple for support, and they rallied to his cause. Loyang was taken; Wang Shih-ch'ung was publicly executed, and Shao-lin ssu was rewarded with a gift of silk, while its senior clerics were given military titles (which they properly refused).[15]

Two further official acts related to our theme followed the capture of Loyang. The first was straightforward: the city, having been the last functioning capital of the Sui and the stronghold of Wang Shih-ch'ung, had to be stripped of some of the physical symbols of its status as an imperial capital; one of the Sui palaces, a gate tower, and a gate were duly destroyed.[16] The second was more complex. Included in

14. Cf. Woodbridge Bingham, "Wen Ta-ya: The First Recorder of T'ang History," *Journal of the American Oriental Society* 57 (1937): 368–74.

15. Paul Demiéville, "Le Bouddhisme et la guerre," *Mélanges Publiés par l'Institut des Hautes Études Chinoises* 1 (1957): 362–63. The key text analyzed by Demiéville is the stele inscription of 728 which recounts the relations of Li Shih-min with the Shao-lin ssu. Many rubbings and facsimiles exist. I have used the profusely annotated text in the *Chin-shih ts'ui-pien* photolithographic reprint of the edition of 1805 (Shanghai, 1921), 41.1–2b. In 625 he donated to the temple a sizable landed estate. In his last years T'ai-tsung retained a great affection for the temple on Sung-shan. See Hui-li and Yen-ts'ung, *Ta Tzu-en ssu San-tsang Fa-shih Chuan*, ch. 6; *T* 50.253.

16. *TCTC* (Peking punctuated edition, 1956), 189.5918.

one account of the "punishment" of Loyang is the statement that Shih-min ordered the destruction of all Buddhist temples in the city and the secularization of all but thirty monks and thirty nuns. In my view this was a local application of a measure (from which the monks of Shao-lin ssu sought and won exemption) ordered by Shih-min's father in 621 to be effective in all territories taken from their rivals by the T'ang. We should recall that the rooting out of dissidents was primary to winning territorial control and that one of the standard disguises of dissidents (or of others who wanted to stay out of trouble) was the habit of a Buddhist or Taoist cleric. Only a brief account survives: "There was an imperial order that since, because of the disorders, it was difficult to distinguish the true from the false among the local clergy *(ti-seng)*, there should be set up one Buddhist establishment in each prefecture with a complement of thirty monks. The rest should return to their lay pursuits."[17]

The battles in the provinces over, the scene of action shifted to Ch'ang-an, and in the power struggle between Shih-min and his brothers, Buddhism was again influential. In the fifth moon of 626 the emperor Kao-tsu proposed to order a purge *(sha-t'ai)* of Buddhist and Taoist clergies and a drastic reduction in the number of temples of both religions. In the capital the number was to be reduced (from about 130) to three Buddhist and one Taoist: the number to be allowed in each prefecture was one for each faith.[18] Kao-tsu's motivation for taking this step is difficult to establish. But there is some evidence that his government was in financial trouble after years of keeping armies in the field and paying lavish bounties to rival leaders who submitted to the T'ang.[19] The aged Fu I had just laid out for him the usual anti-Buddhist arguments, including references to the wealth of the church and the numbers and idleness of the clergy.[20] It is at least possible that the

17. *Hsü Kao-seng chuan*, ch. 24, *T* 50.633, biography of the monk Hui-ch'eng.
18. *FTTC* 39.363a. The estimate of number of Buddhist and Taoist temples, 120 and 10 respectively, in the capital is for c. 605. The source is Hsü, *T'ang liang-ching ch'eng-fang k'ao*, 2.2a.
19. *CTS* 57.11b–12a gives a vivid picture of the expedients to which he was reduced. The brief passage on his reign in the "Shih-huo chih," *CTS* 48.1b, is bland and implausible.
20. Cf. *TCTC* 191.6001–2 for this anti-Buddhist diatribe. I discussed Fu I in an article entitled "Fu I and the Rejection of Buddhism," *Journal of the History of Ideas* 12 (1951): 33–47, where his life under the T'ang was slighted. Fu I's biography, *CTS* 79.8a, says that in the fifth moon of 626 the old man memorialized that the stars foretold the prince of Ch'in's imminent seizure of power. Kao-tsu sent the memorial to the prince of Ch'in as a complaint (meaning: had he elicited the "prediction"?). It goes on to say that when the prince of Ch'in came to power, he made Fu I a gift of food and said, "What you memorialized a while back almost got me in trouble. But henceforward you should speak your mind fully. . . ." One

chance to relieve his financial stringency was what tempted Kao-tsu to make this politically hazardous move against the two organized religions.

We cannot be certain, but it seems clear that the prince of Ch'in's faction made political capital out of the proposed repression. Hsiao Yü, who was a powerful figure under Kao-tsu and one of the few such men to continue in the service of T'ai-tsung, spoke out strongly in court in favor of Buddhism. Yü Shih-nan, a high-ranking official on the prince of Ch'in's staff, wrote a laudatory preface to the most powerful of the pro-Buddhist polemics, the *P'o-hsieh lun* by the monk Fa-lin.[21] Li Shih-cheng, still another member of the prince of Ch'in's staff and a devout Buddhist layman, produced an extensive defense of the faith entitled *Nei-te lun*.[22] It seems clear that the prince of Ch'in's faction was bidding for the support of the Buddhists of the capital and the empire. His rival the crown prince appears to have taken no part in the controversy.[23] Whether the silence of the sources is significant or whether it reflects the general tendency of historical sources to drop references to "losers" we cannot know. The sequence of events seems to support my hypothesis. Kao-tsu, despite all opposition, issued his order against Buddhism and Taoism in the fifth moon (May 31–June 30) of 626. On July 4, 626, Li Shih-min murdered his brothers, and on July 7 he had his father issue an edict of amnesty applicable to the entourages of the two murdered princes; in the same edict it was decreed that the Buddhist and Taoist clergy were to revert to their status before the aboritive purge and that all military and political matters would be handled by the prince of Ch'in.[24] Thus at age thirty Li Shih-min, as both a fratricide and defender of the faith, assumed the central political role. Five months later, after the accomplishment of various

---

suspects that Fu I had intelligence as to what was about to happen and took steps to get on what looked like the winning side.

21. For a summary of the debate, see *FTTC* 39.362–63. For Yü's preface, see *T* 52.474–75.

22. Li's polemic is preserved in *Kuang Hung-ming chi* 14, *T* 52.187–95. There is no biography of him in a standard source; the fullest "biography" is in *Ta T'ang nei-tien lu* 5, *T* 55. 281–82, but this is mostly formulaic. Only the *FTTC* 39.363a identifies him with the prince of Ch'in's staff, and this is too late a work to merit full confidence; on the other hand, it is a serious and much respected work of Chinese Buddhist historiography.

23. T'ang Yung-t'ung, in his article "T'ang T'ai-tsung yü Fo-chiao," *Hsüeh-heng* 75 (1931): 3, argues that the crown prince was more favorable to the Buddhists. He cites in evidence two dedications of copies of the *P'o-hsieh lun* submitted to the two brothers and points out that only the dedication to the crown prince mentions Buddhist virtues specifically. I cannot locate the material he cites from *Fa-yüan chu-lin*, ch. 100, but I do not find the argument convincing.

24. *FTTC* 39.363a–b and *TCTC* 191.6002. A fuller text of the edict is found in *CTW* (imperial edition of 1814, photolithographic reprint, Taipei) 3.7b–8a.

formal steps, including the elevation of his father to the status of re-tired emperor *(T'ai-shang-huang)*, Shih-min ascended the throne to reign as T'ai-tsung.

There now begins a new phase in his life, a period in which he sought all manner of support in his efforts to consolidate the T'ang's hold on power and his own position as a legitimate and effective emperor of China. It is in this period, lasting until about 636 or 637, that T'ang T'ai-tsung appears in the sources as the learner, the listener, the military man of action now become the careful and patient pupil of a galaxy of avuncular civil officials. In choosing his high officials, he was at pains to appoint at least some who had followed other stars than his. One of his favorite counselors, for example, had been on the personal staff of the crown prince Chien-ch'eng.[25] In his central government appointments generally, T'ai-tsung took care to recognize the regions, families, and interest groups that could help in the consolidation of his power. His official acts relating to Buddhism in this period appear to have had a similar purpose: to please many, alarm no one, and heal the many social and political wounds of the period of civil war and his own rise to power. A sampling will suffice to suggest the tone and the purpose of these acts.

In the first moon of his reign he ordered the virtuous monks of the capital to come to the palace and hold services for seven days. In the same moon he ordered the ordination of three thousand clergy with standards to be enforced by the officials. Later in the same moon, he ordered the conversion of one of the Li family palaces into a Buddhist temple.[26] In the third moon of 628 he remarked in an edict that he had killed with his own hand more than three thousand men in the wars that had brought first the T'ang and then himself to power. He ordered vegetarian feasts offered to the monks and services of re-pentence held "in the hope that by these means, the torments of the three Buddhist hells may be escaped." In the fifth moon he ordered that the death anniversaries of rulers of the preceding dynasty should be collectively observed at the Chang-ching ssu in the capital with vegetar-ian feasts and services. He further specified that this should be carried out in perpetuity. In 629 and 630 he ordered the establishment of temples and reliquaries with appropriate inscriptions commemorating

---

25. I am indebted here and throughout this paper to the doctoral dissertation of Howard Wechsler, "Wei Cheng at the Court of T'ang T'ai-tsung" (Yale University, 1969).

26. For the sequence see *FTTC* 39.363b; for the text of his edict ordering ordinations, see *CTW* 5.17a–18a.

those who died in the various battles prior to his reign, with the income from certain fields *(fu-t'ien)* for their upkeep.[27]

None of these actions is particularly characteristic of T'ai-tsung. All of them could have been taken (and proclaimed in the same stately official prose) by most of the monarchs of the preceding three centuries. They do not give us a hint of his real feelings regarding Buddhism. Nevertheless, the building and dedication in 634 of the Hung-fu ssu in memory of his mother may have been more than a pro forma observance; we shall return to this in the second part of this paper. In 636 his empress, who had been given the lay vows in 634, and who had been his adviser and close companion, fell mortally ill. The doctors and their medicines having failed to bring improvement, the crown prince asked his mother if he might not memorialize the emperor, requesting an amnesty for prisoners throughout the empire and the ordination of a certain number of people in the Buddhist priesthood, in the hope that these measures would bring divine help. The dying empress responded with a speech urging the primacy of state concerns, casting aspersions on Buddhist clerics, and so on, which would come more plausibly from a Confucian historian than from a woman of her place and time. She ended with the question, "Is it for me, one poor woman, to disturb the emprie's laws?" T'ai-tsung duly proclaimed the amnesty; there is no evidence that he went through with the Buddhist ordinations. But despite all, the empress died, not before making a plea to the faithful minister Fang Hsüan-ling to protect the emperor from unscrupulous women and their families.[28] We can make little of this incident, but we may perhaps surmise that the empress had been—like other aristocratic women of her time—responsive to the appeal of Buddhism and that she would have been a restraining influence on any anti-Buddhist moves the emperor might have contemplated.

The year before the death of T'ai-tsung's wife, his father, the retired emperor, had died. These years mark a gradual change in the tone and style of T'ai-tsung's rule. He gradually cast aside the role of humble learner of the arts of government (so necessary when he was consolidating his power) and began to behave more and more as a "Grand Monarque," supreme autocrat of a rich and powerful empire, increasingly self-indulgent and impatient of criticism. The members of his immediate family who could have provided criticism and informal restraints were

27. *FTTC* 39.363b. Another version of one of these edicts appears in *CTW* 4.24b–25a and has different specifics, e.g. he donates articles of clothing and a quantity of sandalwood in support of services at the battlefield temples.

28. *CTS* 51.6a–7a.

dead.[29] T'ai-tsung became increasingly unresponsive to the moral strictures of his faithful counselor Wei Cheng and other officials. Wei Cheng, in a blunt and bitter memorial of 637, documents the change that had gradually come over T'ai-tsung: "For five or six years you happily accepted remonstrances. Since that time you have gradually come to hate frank speech."[30] In 638 Wei Cheng contrasted the early years of T'ai-tsung's reign with the later ones in these terms: "Long ago, when the empire had not yet been pacified, you always made righteousness and virtue your central concern. Now, thinking that the empire is without troubles, you have gradually become increasingly arrogant, wasteful, and self-satisfied."[31]

In these years the emperor enjoyed the hunt, his horses, dogs, and falcons as men of his background did and was taken to task by his civil officials for endangering his person, disrupting the life of the peasants, and neglecting his official duties. Despite the earnest deathbed strictures of his empress, he was not particularly restrained in adding to his female entourage. In 642, T'ai-tsung remarked, "I have already appointed my eldest son crown prince, but the fact that his brothers *and the sons of my concubines* number almost forty is a constant source of worry to me."[32] In his later years, T'ai-tsung was repeatedly admonished about his growing extravagance compared to his earlier frugality. One incident that illustrates both his extravagance and his capriciousness is his building in 640 and 641 of the Hsiang-ch'eng Palace in the mountains southwest of Loyang. T'ai-tsung had commissioned Yen Li-te, one of the most accomplished artists and architects of the age, to select a site and design a detached palace. It is said that the corvée labor employed amounted to nearly two million man-days, with other expenses in proportion. When the emperor arrived, the weather was very hot, and there turned out to be poisonous snakes at the site. In a rage he ordered Yen Li-te dismissed from office, the palace dismantled, and the building materials given to the local populace.[33]

In the political sphere, in domestic but particularly in foreign affairs, T'ai-tsung became increasingly flamboyant. The success of his armies against the Turks, the Tu-yü Hun, and still farther afield fed T'ai-tsung's already considerable self-esteem, and when he proposed more expeditions beyond the frontiers, he was increasingly impatient with

29. The empress, for example, on one occasion talked T'ai-tsung out of killing the groom he held responsible for the death of a favorite horse. See *Chen-kuan cheng-yao, SPPY* ed., ch. 2.29b.

30. Wechsler, "Wei Cheng," chap. 6, p. 14. He is translating from the *Wei Cheng-kung wen-chi.*

31. Quoted in Wechsler, "Wei Cheng," p. 16, from the same source.

32. *Chen-kuan cheng-yao* 4.3b–4a; italics mine.

the usual Confucian counsels of prudence and frugality. As early as 632, ministers of the court had urged T'ai-tsung to perform the *feng* and *shan* sacrifices at Mount T'ai, and thus to let August Heaven and his subjects know that his power was secure and his empire well governed. The tireless Wei Cheng argued that memories of the upheavals at the end of Sui and the civil war were too recent, that the preparations for the sacrifices would place an unnecessary burden on the people, and so on. T'ai-tsung desisted, but in 637 he appointed high-ranking officials to investigate the history of the rituals and recommend procedures. In 641 he announced his intention of performing the sacrifices. The imperial equipage was at Loyang on its way to Mount T'ai when the ill-omened appearance of a comet obliged the emperor to cancel the plan.[34] But his intent was clear: Let all know that T'ai-tsung of the Great T'ang has achieved preeminence in the Central Kingdom and in the known world. In this same year, 641, one of his officials rebuked him for boasting in court: "Yü (the Great) did not brag, yet none in the world could compare with him. Your Majesty has swept away disorder and returned the empire to rectitude. Your myriad officials truly are not up to contemplating such pure brilliance (irony?). But you need not come to court to tell us about it."[35] Had the heady wine of absolute power and many successes indeed done its work? Had the thoughtful, cautious T'ai-tsung of the early years become the vain capricious tyrant of his middle and later years? The answer is not a simple one.

We observe here a configuration of personality and behavior which, for Chinese history, we might call the Han Wu syndrome. Pan Ku, in his estimate of Han Wu-ti (ruled 140–87 B.C.), says, "If Emperor Wu, with his superior ability and his great plans, had not departed from the modesty and economy of Emperors Wen and Ching . . . among those heroes mentioned in the *Book of Songs* or the *Book of History*, who could have surpassed him?"[36] We may recall that when Sui Yang-ti's power was at its zenith and he was planning further conquests, the great historian Ssu-ma Kuang said of him, "Thereupon the emperor began ardently to emulate the accomplishments of Ch'in Shih-huang and *Han wu*."[37] It is the nature of supremely gifted autocrats to act boldly and imaginatively, to pursue distant or unreachable goals, and, in the

33. *THY* 30.560.

34. Edouard Chavannes, *Le T'ai Chan* (Paris, 1910), pp. 169–80. His translations are from *CTS* 23, "Essay on Ceremonial Impedimenta and Procedures."

35. *TCTC* 196.6173–74.

36. H. H. Dubs, trans., *History of the Former Han Dynasty* (Baltimore, 1944), 2: 120.

37. *TCTC* 180.5635; italics mine.

process, to ride roughshod over the claims of their people, the prudential counsels of their officials, and whatever combinations of circumstances may seem to block their path. T'ai-tsung in his middle and later years was still a gifted and careful administrator, a master strategist, and a shrewd politician, but the Han Wu syndrome is present too. This of course is a universal and not a Chinese phenomenon, and it may be relevant to quote here Gibbon's classic characterization of Constantine the Great.

> In the life of Constantine, we may contemplate a hero, who had so long inspired his subjects with love and his enemies with terror, degenerating into a cruel and dissolute monarch, corrupted by his fortunes, or raised by conquest beyond the necessity of dissimulation. The general peace which he maintained during the last fourteen years of his reign was a period of apparent splendor rather than of real prosperity; and the old age of Constantine was disgraced by the opposite yet reconcilable vices of rapaciousness and prodigality.[38]

It is not possible to provide a representative sample of the Buddhist activities of T'ai-tsung in the years 635 to about 647. These activities are too diverse and indeed contradictory to permit sampling, but we may mention a few of them. In 635 he sent the Crown Prince to participate in the funeral of the great Buddhist prelate Hsüan-yüan and ordered the appropriate officials to provide burial impedimenta—thus, it is said, setting a precedent for such imperial gifts. In the eleventh moon of the same year he ordered the ordination of three thousand monks, perhaps (though there is no textual evidence) as a measure for the repose of the soul of his father who had died five or six months before.[39]

In 637 he issued an edict ordering that Taoist adepts be given precedence over Buddhist monks. For this edict and the controversy surrounding it there are many texts and versions with greater or lesser detail. The Taoists had, one presumes, "got to" the emperor and persuaded him of several things: (1) that he and his house were descended from Lao-tzu; (2) that Taoist teaching was more basic, more ancient, more Chinese, and more conducive to public order and social discipline than

---

38. Edward Gibbon, *The History of the Decline and Fall of the Roman Empire*, ed. J. B. Bury (New York, 1946), 1: 497. This characterization is colored by Gibbon's casting of Constantine as a principal villain in his drama of the "triumph of barbarism and religion." For a more judicious view, see Ramsay MacMullen, *Constantine* (New York, 1969).

39. *FTTC* 39.364c.

Buddhism; and (3) that the emperor should say all these things in an edict which would have the ostensible but minor purpose of giving Taoist adepts precedence over Buddhist clergy at formal ceremonies. The Buddhists reacted by memorializing their protests in high polemical style, for example: "Present day Taoists do not follow their ancient practices (of withdrawal, contemplation, etc.). The clothes they wear are all residues of the Yellow Turban movement. Basically they are not followers of Lao-tzu but practitioners of the base techniques of the three Chang (Yellow Turban leaders)." The emperor rebuked them for their petition and sent a high official to tell the monks they must submit or be bastinadoed. The monk Chih-shih still resisted, was bastinadoed, and returned to lay life.[40]

Although the texts vary, it is clear that T'ai-tsung asserted at this time that the imperial house was descended from Lao-tzu. Why would he do this at this time and in a context that would be an affront to many if not the majority of his subjects? One reason may have been his almost obsessive concern (derived in part from his family and class background) with genealogy and with raising his own house and the houses of T'ang followers in the empire's prestige scale. This led in 638 to the official publication of the *Shih-tsu chih* [Treatise on Hereditary Clans]. T'ai-tsung insisted on final revisions that would upgrade his own house and downgrade the ancient and arrogant "four families of Shantung (the eastern plain)."[41] It is at least possible that claiming his family's descent from Lao-tzu—a national culture-hero—was related to this concern with genealogy. And once the claim was made, it was appropriate to place the living representatives of his teaching before Buddhist clergy on all formal occasions. Another reason might be found in the complexities of Taoist rebel messianism recently illuminated by Anna Seidel. She shows that the native place of the Li family (Kansu) and the mythology of the "Savior Li" links the T'ang ruling house to popular Taoist messianic movements originating in the second century A.D.[42] Li Yüan's revolt against the Sui was fueled in part by the residual power of this myth.

In 638 T'ai-tsung's long-time confidant and trusted adviser Yü Shih-nan died, and after his death the emperor saw him in a dream.

---

40. Basic text of the edict in *KHMC* 25.283. See also *CTW* 6.6b–7a. The earliest account of the incident may well be in the biography of Chih-shih, *Hsü Kao-seng chuan* 24, *T* 50. 635–36.

41. *THY* 36.664. The literature on this list, its predecessors, and sequels is voluminous.

42. Anna Seidel, "The Image of the Perfect Ruler in Early Taoist Messianism: Lao-tzu and Li Hung," *History of Religions* 9 (1969–70): 216–47.

Knowing that his old friend had been a devout Buddhist, T'ai-tsung praised him in an edict and ordered that a maigre feast for five hundred monks be held and a Buddha image made for the spiritual benefit of his old friend.[43] In 639 the emperor appears to have been taken in by a Taoist who claimed that the *P'o-hsieh lun,* written for the defense of Buddhism against Kao-tsu's threatened purge, contained slanders of the imperial lineage *(tsung).* We may doubt the source which says that T'ai-tsung immediately ordered a purge of the Buddhist clergy, but judicial proceedings were started against the monk Fa-lin, author of the *P'o-hsieh lun* and, naturally, of the offending passages.[44] The proceedings are interesting, and we shall return to them in the second part of this paper. The year 639 marked the promulgation of the *I-chiao ching,* which we shall also want to discuss in some detail. For now let us say that it takes a very "hard line" as regards monastic discipline and charges officialdom with enforcing the various prescriptions throughout the empire.

In 640 the conduct of the crown prince Ch'eng-ch'ien began to attract unfavorable notice. He was afflicted with a strange neurosis which is less strange if one recalls his family history on both his mother's and his father's side. He developed a passionate fondness for Turkish life, Turkish music, the rough customs of the steppe; and his pursuit of Turkish pleasures in the civilized capital of Ch'ang-an became a scandal. Of course there was intrigue, followed by an alleged plot to revolt, and in 643, the crown prince was deposed, reduced to the rank of commoner, and exiled. T'ai-tsung found that his favorite T'ai, prince of Wei, had not been blameless in the tense tangle of ambition and intrigue. So he was passed over, and the weak, young Li Chih, prince of Chin, was made crown prince. The tide of good fortune had begun to ebb. From about 643 until his death in 649, disappointments, defeats, and illness crowded in upon him.

In 644 T'ai-tsung planned and commanded an expedition meant to chastise the usurper who had seized power in northern Korea and eastern Manchuria. Despite careful planning and some striking victories, the T'ang army failed in the siege of An-shih ch'eng and failed also to capture the usurper. T'ai-tsung lifted the siege when winter approached and returned to Ch'ang-an with the unfamiliar

---

43. *FTTC* 39.364c; *CTW* 9.2b; *CTS* 72.7a–b adds that he had Yü's protrait added to those of his other ranking advisers in the Ling-yen ko. It unaccountably substitutes "T'ien-ts'un hsiang," image of a Heaven-honored one, a Taoist divinity, for the Buddha image of the other texts.

44. *Hsü Kao-seng chuan* 24.638a–c.

taste of defeat in his mouth. His health appears to have been undermined by this last period on campaign, and he was ill much of the time between his return and his death. In these last years he was chastened and saddened by experience, grieved by the successive deaths of his lifelong counselors and friends.

T'ai-tsung's fondness for his loyal but cantankerous Buddhist minister Hsiao Yü and the irritability brought on by age and illness are illustrated in the following sequence. After his return from the Korean campaign, during which Hsiao Yü had been in charge of the key city of Loyang, T'ai-tsung had made him presents of an embroidery depicting the Buddha with Hsiao Yü in an attitude of worship beside him, a copy of the *Mahā-prajñā-paramitā-sūtra,* and a robe for his Buddhist observances. These were surely not-so-subtle hints that Hsiao Yü, now past seventy, should retire and lead a life dedicated to religion. But old Yü was not so easily got rid of. He shortly accused a number of high officials from the great Fang Hsüan-ling down of forming a cabal *(p'eng-tang).* T'ai-tsung rebuked him severely. Shortly thereafter Hsiao Yü asked to leave lay life, and T'ai-tsung said (with what sense of relief we can imagine), "Knowing full well that you have long loved the śramanas, I cannot deny your wish." But Yü then petitioned that he had reconsidered. T'ai-tsung was furious and in his own hand wrote an order rebuking Hsiao Yü and decreeing appropriate punishment. According to one source this occurred in the tenth month of 646[45] or less than three years before his death. If it is authentic, it shows T'ai-tsung to have had toward the end of his life a set of rather standard anti-Buddhist biases which are not easily reconciled with his simultaneous patronage of Hsüan-tsang to be discussed below. Let us summarize his biases as they appear in this document.

Buddhism, he says, is not to his taste; while the state lays down moral constants, Buddhism encourages corrupt customs. Buddhism has not brought good fortune to those who have practiced it. And here T'ai-tsung swings with relish into an account of Hsiao Yü's ancestors, the emperors Wu and Chien-wen of the Liang dynasty. They used up treasure and manpower in the service of Buddhism, yet were swept away in violent disorders, their kingdom laid waste, their sons and grandsons destroyed. Now Yü proposes to continue the corrupt practices of a defunct dynasty. Yü has shown himself secular in body, religious in speech, failing to discriminate (in his accusations) between the upright and the vicious. T'ai-tsung then reviews Hsiao Yü's changes

45. The basic text on Hsiao Yü and T'ai-tsung is *CTS* 63.4a–10b. The date mentioned here is from *TCTC* 198.6240.

of mind, calling them an affront to the imperial person and the ministers of the highest rank. "Our suffering in patience continues down to now, while Yü is still totally unrepentant. It is appropriate straightway to expel him from this court and city and have him go out and take a small provincial post. Let it be prefect of Chang-chou. And let him be deprived of his fief!"[46] A year later Hsiao Yü, back in favor, died, and T'ai-tsung made munificent funerary gifts and awarded him the posthumous title "Duke True but Narrow."[47]

There is ample documentation on T'ai-tsung's relations with the great prelate and traveler Hsüan-tsang from the time of the latter's return from India in 645 to the emperor's death in 649. It is clear that T'ai-tsung was most interested in Hsüan-tsang's account of the lands through which he had passed on his pilgrimage to India and in evidence of the successes and failures of Chinese policies toward them. Hsüan-tsang was received, talked with the emperor on several occasions, and was given a temple and some assistance to carry on his translation work. Hsüan-tsang, on his part, flattered his imperial patron, sought to interest him in the solace of the Buddhist faith and to develop in T'ai-tsung an attitude that would be favorable to Buddhism, and particularly to the new Indianized variety that Hsüan-tsang had just imported. (See the following essay by Stanley Weinstein.) The Buddhist sources overstate both the intimacy of T'ai-tsung with the monk and the depth of his belated interest in Buddhism, while the secular sources, with equal if opposite bias, omit all references to either. In the fourth moon of 649, Hsüan-tsang (and the crown prince) accompanied the ailing emperor to his summer retreat. A month before he died, the emperor reputedly said to Hsüan-tsang: "Our meeting with the Master was too late to permit the spread and development of Buddhism (under imperial patronage)."[48] Whether T'ai-tsung ever made such a statement can never be known with certainty.

The life of T'ai-tsung as we have sketched it falls into four phases: (1) his youth as the son of a Sui official and as a participant in the T'ang seizure of power, through his own seizure of power by a coup d'etat in

46. *CTS* 63.9b–10a. Some minor details are added from *HTS* 101.

47. *CTS* 63.10a; the edict conferring funerary gifts is found in *CTW* 8.21a.

48. This quotation is from *Ta Tz'u-en ssu San-tsang Fa-shih chuan* by Yen-tsung and Hui-li, younger contemporaries of Hsüan-tsang; ch. 7, *T* 50.260a. This *pieh-chuan*, particularly chs. 6 and 7, provides the most detailed account of the relations between T'ai-tsung and Hsüan-tsang. For a briefer account, see *K'ai-yüan lu* 8 *T* 55.559–60. On this relationship and early T'ang Buddhism generally Yuki Reimon, "Shotō Bukkyō no shisōshiteki mujun to kokka kenryoku to no kōsaku" [Historical contradictions in early T'ang Buddhist thought and their interconnections with state power] *Tōyō Bunka Kenkyūjo kiyō* 25 (1961): 1–28, is excellent.

626; (2) the period of consolidation of power and increasing confidence, 627–c. 637; (3) the period of glory, success, and the onset of what I have called the "Han-wu syndrome," c. 637–c. 644; (4) the last years of personal sorrow, illness, and perhaps premature aging, 645–49. We must take account of these phases (or alternatives that may be proposed) if we are to make sense of any of the actions that T'ai-tsung took relating to Buddhism, or of any of the beliefs and attitudes behind those actions.[49]

The various events or clusters of events to be discussed below illustrate some of the complexities of T'ai-tsung's relations with Buddhism. We can make better sense of them by seeing them in relation to the phases of his life and the succession of life-styles discussed above, and also by recalling the habits of men of his time and background. This is the barest sampling, but perhaps each incident will contribute something to our understanding.

BUDDHIST OBSERVANCES IN MEMORY OF HIS MOTHER

In 631, a few years after his seizure of power, T'ai-tsung ordered the conversion of a palace into a Buddhist temple for the spiritual felicity of his mother.[50] In 634 he ordered a new temple "built" in the northernmost ward of the chain of wards just to the east of the imperial palace complex. This was the Hung-fu ssu, previously the mansion of a military notable who came over to the T'ang and was given high honors. Either in his lifetime on his own initiative or after his disgrace and death it had been converted into a temple called the Hsing-fu ssu. T'ai-tsung remodeled and elaborated the temple, and he attended in person the ceremonies of dedication.[51] This must have been impressive indeed, for he himself participated in the ancient ritual of "opening the eyes of the Buddha." We have no details on this particular performance, but in the dedication of the Great Buddha at Tōdaiji a century later, the abbot of the temple wielded the brush that painted in the eyes of the figure, and

49. We should remind ourselves that until very recently Western historians, like the Chinese, regarded the psychological makeup of the actors in history as given and as static, events as revealing more or less of the "true character." See the splendid article of David P. Jordan, "Gibbon's 'Age of Constantine' and the Fall of Rome," *History and Theory* 8 (1969): 71–96, esp. p. 82.

50. *FTTC* 39.364a. Neither the temple name nor the palace name appears in the usual sources on Ch'ang-an and Loyang or in Hiraoka Takeo's index to them.

51. *T'ang liang-ching ch'eng-fang k'ao* 4.8b.

his brush was connected by myriad strings to the crowds of participants who thus played their part in the ceremony.[52]

In 642 T'ai-tsung participated in a memorial service for his mother at the Hung-fu ssu. In the very formulaic Buddhist vow offering a vegetarian feast to the monks of the temple, he refers to himself as the "emperor, disciple under the Bodhisattva vows," recalls, in conventional terms, his mother's love which he can have remembered very dimly after thirty years. After mentioning his gifts to the monks, he closes with the vow itself:

> I vow that my mind will awaken to nonaction (wu-wei), that my spirit will change to a wonderful joyousness, that I will whip up my horse to enter the fragrant city, walk up the golden stairs and ascend to the jeweled palace hall, there to enjoy the delights of the dharma and wander happily (hsiao-yao!) in the Pure Land. May I be shaded forever by the dharma-clouds, always slaking my thirst on ambrosia. May I quickly attain Bodhi and early rise to Sambodhi. May the sentient beings at the six levels and the four varieties of living creatures all share in this vow.[53]

T'ai-tsung talked with the abbot and tried to explain the official favor shown the Taoists. T'ai-tsung said that since the imperial house descended from Lao-tzu, it was necessary to give Taoists preference over Buddhists, but he wondered whether the latter were not resentful. The abbot, supple and respectful, replied, "Your Majesty, in honoring an ancestor, is following an established practice. Who would dare harbor resentment?" T'ai-tsung, in response, repeated the genealogical basis for giving precedence to Lao-tzu. Yet, he went on to say, "Whenever it is a question of accumulating spiritual merit, we all turn toward the Buddhist way. In former days We erected Buddhist temples on the battlefields, and Our old mansion at Taiyuan was offered as a temple to the Buddha. We have never established Taoist temples(!). Since Our sentiments are like this, you people should be aware of them."[54] Here the great T'ai-tsung was in a quandary. The monks who were saying the masses for his mother in a temple that he himself had dedi-

52. The *Kissō Jigo* (Tokyo, 1801) as quoted in Oda Tokuno, *Bukkyō Daijiten*, rev. ed. (Tokyo, 1928), p. 163a. A recent performance of this ceremony in Ceylon is described in Richard Gombrich, "The Consecration of a Buddhist Image," *Journal of Asian Studies* 26 (1966): 23–36.

53. *CTW* 10.19b–20a. The colorful mixture of Taoist and Buddhist imagery is to be noted. I infer the date from the entry in *FTTC* 39.365b, which says that on this occasion, T'ai-tsung composed a prayer in which he styled himself as he does in the opening of this document.

54. *FTTC* 39.365b–c. I have not found an earlier account of this interchange.

cated and supported may well have been troubled by the signs of imperial favor going to their deadly rivals. His explanation is a rather
lame attempt to reassure them.

The last entry in this chain of events is in 645. Hsüan-tsang had just
returned from his long pilgrimage and was anxious to set up a place
where he could begin to translate the scriptures he had brought. The
Shao-lin ssu in the mountains east of Loyang (whose monks had long
before helped the young Li Shih-min to take that city) had been discussed. T'ai-tsung said, "There is no need to be in the mountains.
After the Master left on his journey to the western lands, We built,
on behalf of Mu T'ai-hou (Our Mother) the Hung-fu ssu. The temple
has a meditation hall which is very quiet. The Dharma Master should
start his translations there."[55]

According to the *Chen-kuan cheng-yao*, T'ai-tsung was often admonished by his ministers that he was failing in the proper show of
filial devotion to his father. They remarked on the infrequency of his
visits to Kao-tsu when the latter was living as retired emperor and on
the rather mean and remote palace which housed him. Then, after
Kao-tsu's death, they remarked on the inadequacy of the tomb which
T'ai-tsung provided for his father. All this contrasts sharply with T'ai-
tsung's lifelong devotion to the memory of his mother who must have
died when he was in his teens. That this contrast is to be explained by
the special Turko-Mongol sentiments between father and son, or by the
special relation of strong mixed-stock northern women to their sons is
one line of speculation. Another line would give more weight to the
special circumstances of T'ai-tsung's forcible rise to power and the
mutual antipathies this left between him and his father.

T'AI-TSUNG AND THE BUDDHIST-TAOIST RIVALRIES

Sharp clashes had occurred in 637 and 639 between T'ai-tsung and
the Buddhist clergy. The first of these was precipitated by the order
giving precedence to Taoist monks which we have referred to. The
monks Chih-shih and Fa-lin were given audience and laid out their
arguments against the order. Their protests were disallowed in an edict.
They followed the emperor's progress to Loyang and there renewed the
attack, accusing the Taoists of not being followers of Lao-tzu at all
(and thus having no legitimate connection with the imperial house)
but of carrying on the base traditions of the Yellow Turbans (which

55. *Ta T'ang Tz'u-en ssu San-tsang Fa-shih chuan*, ch. 6, *T* 50.253c.

would make them subversive of the imperial order). The emperor ordered the ranking minister Ts'en Wen-pen (who was himself a Buddhist) to issue an imperial edict reiterating the previous order. This should have been the final decision, since the emperor's edicts were binding on all his subjects, but Chih-shih and his associates stoutly refused to accept the edict. T'ai-tsung was furious, had Chih-shih flogged in the audience hall, ordered him to wear commoner's clothing, and sent him into exile where he died. Someone chided Chih-shih for not knowing when it was expedient to give way, and his reply is a rare fragment of Chinese Buddhist martyrology and one immediately understandable to the student of Western history. He said, "I knew full well that an edict already promulgated was not going to be reversed. The reason I fought it so strongly was to let posterity know that here was a monk!"[56]

Fa-lin was one of the monks associated with Chih-shih in this incident, but he seems to have escaped drastic punishment. Fa-lin, we should recall, was the leading clerical defender of the faith against Kao-tsu's anti-Buddhist proposal of 626, and at that time, we have suggested, was part of a pro-Buddhist group favorable to Li Shih-min. At that time he had written his famous *P'o-hsieh lun* in defense of Buddhism. Since that time he had written the *Pien-cheng lun,* a further polemic, for the same purpose. In the winter of 639 the Taoist adept Ch'in Shih-ying, a favorite in T'ai-tsung's household, brought charges that Fa-lin had, in his writings, slandered the imperial line, the descendants of Lao-tzu.[57] T'ai-tsung, in an order that, one suspects, was drafted by Ch'in Shih-ying, accuses Fa-lin of the unpardonable crime of defaming the imperial ancestors and *lèse majesté.*[58] T'ai-tsung "sent people to find Lin and to carry out an investigation according to law." The monk did not wait to be apprehended, but went on his own to the official bureau or courtroom *(kung-t'ing),* where he was bound and the imperial edict was read to him. Fa-lin presented a brief in his own defense. He adduced the authority of the ancients to show that when principles prevail over kinship, the empire is peaceful. He paid tactful tribute to Lao-tzu, extolled certain of the Classics, and praised Buddha's teaching for its universality and for its truth for time and eternity. He then defended his *Pien-cheng lun,* saying that it was written as a reply to the

---

56. *FTTC* 39.364c. Text of the edict in *CTW* 6.6a–7b and *KHMC* 25.283c.

57. *Ch'ang-an chih,* Kyoto facsimile ed., 10.10a records that Ch'in Shih-ying was called in by T'ai-tsung in 631 to assist in curing the crown prince of an illness; as a reward for his success, T'ai-tsung built for him the Lung-hsing kuan in the capital.

58. Text of the order in *Hsü Kao-seng chuan* by the seventh-century monk Tao-hsüan, ch. 24, *T* 50.638a–b; also *CTW* 6.14b–15a.

Taoists, that it consisted of historical accounts and earlier sayings, that it was not slanderous of the ruling house, and so on.

The court then transmitted an order citing section 8 of his *Pien-cheng lun,* which claimed invulnerability for those who invoked Kuan-yin.[59] Fa-lin was granted a seven-day reprieve during which he was to invoke Kuan-yin. At the end of this time, the order said, "we shall test whether, when the punishment of beheading is applied, you are invulnerable or not." Fa-lin's pious biographer describes his successive spiritual states as he lived out the reprieve. An imperial order arrived indicating that the allotted time was nearing an end and the test of his faith was imminent. Fa-lin, who seems, unlike most Chinese prisoners, to have had access to writing materials, took his brush and wrote a new appeal. In this he praised the virtue of the great T'ang for its victories over the forces of chaos, for its nurturing of the people, for its restoration of peace within and control over the barbarians without. Then he said that all this is attributable to the power of Kuan-yin.[60] We may wonder how much Fa-lin was knowingly but subtly evoking a moment in T'ai-tsung's early career. For in 622, when he had just triumphed over two deadly rivals of the T'ang, he halted his army for the night on the way back to the capital. At sunset, after a rain, the young prince saw a vision of Kuan-yin in the sky. He took this as a fortunate sign, an indication of supernatural assistance, and he ordered a temple built in honor of Kuan-yin and stone inscribed to record the happy occasion.[61]

But Fa-lin, if he was invoking this memory, did not rest his case there. He asserted that he had used the period of reprieve to invoke, not Kuan-yin, but T'ai-tsung himself! When asked by an official why he had not followed the imperial order to invoke Kuan-yin, he replied with further fulsome praise of the Great T'ang, and then said: "When His Majesty nurtures like sons the ordinary creatures according to the sutras, he is indeed Kuan-yin, and indeed their supernatural perceptions are in perfect accord. That is why I only invoked His Majesty." He was eventually given a sentence of exile instead of death, but died on the way to exile.[62] Fa-lin appears to have narrowly escaped a violent death and to have checkmated his Taoist rivals by outrageous flattery of T'ai-tsung—likening him to Kuan-yin—and possibly by evoking mem-

---

59. The section of the *Pien-cheng lun* cited in the indictment is found in ch. 6, *T* 52.537c.

60. *Hsü Kao-seng chuan* 24.638b.

61. *CTW* 146.25a–b.

62. *Hsü Kao-seng chuan* 24.638c. A variant text of the whole sequence with much pious embroidery is found in the *T'ang hu-fa sha-men Fa-lin pieh-chuan* by the seventh-century monk Yen-tsung, *T* 50.198–213. A variation on this passage appears on p. 211a.

ories of his youth. The incident fits in well with phase three of T'ai-tsung's biography as proposed in the first part of this chapter.

SETTING STANDARDS FOR THE BUDDHIST CLERGY

T'ai-tsung, like many rulers before him, was concerned with the perennial problem of clerical abuses: the use of the real or feigned status of monk or nun to indulge in what the emperor regarded as antisocial, corrupt, or subversive conduct. In 634 T'ai-tsung had specified such abuses in the second part of his edict for the ordination of three thousand monks, and there he had ordered that malefactors be punished by the appropriate officials in accordance with the rules of monastic discipline (*Vinaya*).[63]

In 639 he took measures against the same types of abuses. His move may have been linked to the quarrels between Taoists and Buddhists described briefly above. One source says that after Ch'in Shih-ying's indictment of Fa-lin, in the year 639, "The emperor suddenly issued an order for the purge (*sha-t'ai*) of monks and nuns, providing that such clerics as remained should adhere to the *I-chiao ching*."[64] There is no supporting evidence that the emperor intended a drastic reduction of legitimate clergy. He did, however, seek to set standards for clerical conduct and to eliminate the irregular clergy by promulgating the *I-chiao ching*. This is "the sutra of the testamentary teaching" alleged to have been given by the Buddha just before he entered Nirvana.[65] T'ai-tsung's edict of promulgation is interesting for its specification of secular rulers as surrogate defenders of the faith and for its characteristic attention to detail.

T'ai-tsung's edict of promulgation may well reflect his mood and his attitude toward the Buddhists at this time:

> Long ago, after the Buddha passed away, because of the demoralization accompanying the last age of the kalpa, it devolved upon princes and great ministers to protect and maintain the Buddha's teaching. Now, as to the monks and nuns who leave lay life, conduct according to their vows must be total and perfect. If they

63. *FTTC* 39.364c. Gernet, *Les aspects économigues du Bouddhisme*, p. 242 has translated the list of abuses.

64. *Hsü kao-seng chuan* 24.638a.

65. *T* no. 389, vol. 12.1110–1112. The Chinese text has neither Sanskrit nor Tibetan version; it may indeed be a collection of excerpts put together in China, or, in parts at least, a Chinese "original." The catalog of prohibitions quoted below is close to the list Chinese secular authority would draw up!

then give rein to their passions, indulge in lewdness and indolence
. . . this means violation of the canonical prescriptions *(vinaya)*
and the loss of the Tathagata's perfect and wonderful ideal. Moreover they will discredit the rightness of the ruler's having received
the trust. As to the *I-chiao ching,* it was pronounced by the Buddha
when he was about to enter Nirvana. Its warnings and exhortations to his followers are both detailed and fundamental. . . . Let
the offices assign ten copyists to make multiple copies of this
scripture, that it may be promulgated and carried out in practice.
Let the appropriate officials provide paper, brushes, and ink. Let
officials of the fifth rank and above and the governors of all the
prefectures *(chou)* be given a copy. If monks and nuns are observed
whose conduct does not accord with this scripture, let them be
admonished publicly and privately that they must carry out its
prescriptions obediently.[66]

When we turn to the scripture itself, we see at once why T'ai-tsung
wished to make it the standard. If such prescriptions were enforced, it
would guarantee him a tame, docile, and otherworldly clergy, with no
chance for such tough zealots as Chih-shih or Fa-lin, nor for monk-
entrepreneurs who had built wide circles of wealth and influence, nor
for the irregular monks who ministered to the peasantry's needs and had
a proven potential for subversion. Here are a few admonitions, in the
manner of the ancient Pratimoksa:

Ye Bretheren! . . . Those who would follow pure discipline ought
not to buy, sell, or exchange. They ought not covet fields and buildings, nor accumulate servants or attendants or animals. . . . You
ought not cut trees and grass, plow the soil, hoe the fields, mix
medicines, divine fortunes, study the stars' positions, cast horo-
scopes by the waxing and waning of the moon, nor reckon days of
good fortune. . . . You should not concern yourselves with
worldly affairs nor circulate rumors, nor recite incantations, nor
mix potions, nor bind yourselves to eminent people in friendship
nor become familiar with them that you can boast of it indecent-
ly.[67]

We know that neither this set of restrictions nor similar measures
before and after effectively limited the activities of the Buddhist clergy.

66. *CTW* 9.9a–b.
67. *T* 12.1110c. I have adapted the translation by Philipp Eidmann entitled *The Last
Word* (Kyoto, 1952).

It is of interest here as illustrative of T'ai-tsung's tough imperious "no nonsense" mood at the height of his power and the pinnacle of his career.

T'ai-tsung's total record of handling Buddhism seems to have been consonant with his background, his personal proclivities, and—most of all—with his astute political sense. Though markedly less devout than Sui Wen-ti, his policies toward Buddhism strike many of the same notes: the welfare of the state and dynasty is the first consideration; linked to this is concern for the morale of his people, and here Buddhist belief, if properly channeled and controlled could be a positive influence. If clergy and believers were not so controlled—he believed—corrupt and subversive practices would proliferate and have to be dealt with by drastic means. The imperial family, individually and collectively, stood to benefit from appropriate observances and acts of pious generosity, but never from excessive favor to the Buddhists or prodigal giving to their establishments; a measured patronage would reassure the mass of their subjects and enlist for the T'ang the benevolent assistance— present and future—of all the divinities and forces of the Buddhist universe.

8. Imperial Patronage in the Formation of T'ang Buddhism

Stanley Weinstein

It is customary to say that Buddhism in China reached its apogee under the T'ang dynasty. Despite the widespread acceptance of this generalization, when we reexamine the position of Buddhism under the T'ang, at least insofar as church-state relations are concerned, the T'ang was anything but an "apogee" or "golden age" in the history of Chinese Buddhism. Not only did Buddhism during the Hui-ch'ang period (841–46) suffer the harshest persecution that it had ever experienced, one so severe that its subsequent development was permanently affected, but throughout much of the T'ang the prevailing attitude in court circles was essentially negative.

Compared with the emperors of the Southern Dynasties, the early T'ang rulers generally took a lukewarm attitude toward the Buddhist religion. They felt a special affinity with Taoism because they bore the same family name, Li, as did Lao-tzu, its legendary founder whom they revered as their ancestor.[1] Kao-tsu, the first emperor of the T'ang, was sharply critical of the Buddhists and actively sought to restrict the power and wealth of the temples and monasteries. In the year 625, some seven years after ascending the throne, he issued an edict in which he declared that Taoism and Confucianism constituted the foundations of the empire, whereas Buddhism was of foreign origin. He decreed, therefore, that Taoism should be accorded first place in order of precedence; Confucianism, second place; and Buddhism, last place.[2] The following year he issued another decree in which he denounced

---

1. On the pro-Taoist sentiments of the T'ang emperors see Yūki Reimon, "Shotō bukkyō no shisōshiteki mujun to kokka kenryoku to no kōsaku" [Contradictions in the history of Buddhist thought the in early T'ang and ideological involvements with the state], *Tōyō Bunka Kenkyūjo kiyō* 25 (1961): 8–14.

2. Tao-hsüan, *Chi ku-chin fo-tao lun-heng* 3, 52.381a.

the corruption within the Buddhist church and called for a severe reduction in the number of temples. The capital region was to have no more than three temples, and each province, no more than one temple.[3]

This basically cautious attitude was continued by Kao-tsu's son, T'ai-tsung.[4] We find, for example, that in the year 637 T'ai-tsung issued an edict which, while recognizing that Taoism and Buddhism ultimately shared the same ideal, declared that the former was more suitable for China and hence its priests should be accorded precedence over Buddhist monks.[5] Elsewhere in the edict he repeated his father's view that the imperial family is descended from Lao-tzu. A Buddhist monk, Chih-shih, who repeatedly denounced the emperor's pro-Taoist stance, was ordered by T'ai-tsung to be publicly whipped at court and then exiled.[6]

The long-standing controversy as to whether monks should recognize their social obligations by paying homage to their parents as well as to the emperor was reopened in 662.[7] Some five years earlier Kao-tsung, the third T'ang emperor, had issued a decree forbidding parents from doing obeisance before a son who had become a monk.[8] Now Kao-tsung proposed taking the matter a step further by requiring monks and nuns to render homage both to their parents and to the ruler.[9] The clergy, which, especially in South China, had long been exempt from this requirement, reacted quickly to the threatened loss of one of its most cherished prerogatives and in a matter of days succeeded, with support from the mother of Empress Wu, in mobilizing the opinion of prominent laymen and monks against the new proposals,[10] thereby forcing the emperor to withdraw them.[11] But the Buddhist victory was short-lived, for fifty-two years later, in 714, Hsüan-tsung issued an

3. The text of the edict is given in *CTS* (K'ai-ming ed.) 1.3066a.

4. For an account of T'ai-tsung's changing attitudes toward Buddhism see the paper by Arthur F. Wright in this volume.

5. An abridged version of the edict is included in Tao-hsüan's *Kuang-hung-ming-chi* 25, 52.283c.

6. *FTTC* 39, 49.364c.

7. For a detailed study see Michihata Ryōshū, *Tōdai bukkyōshi no kenkyū* [Studies in the history of T'ang Buddhism] (Kyoto, 1957), pp. 335–57.

8. *FTTC* 39, 49.367a.

9. The text of the edict is included in Yen-tsung's *Chi sha-men pu ying pai su teng shih* 3, 52. 455a–b.

10. The *Chi sha-men pu ying pai su teng shih*, 52.455b–464c, contains thirty-two documents opposing Kao-tsung's proposal.

11. In an edict dated the eighth day of the sixth month of the year 662 Kao-tsung exempted monks from the obligation of doing obeisance to the emperor. He insisted, however, in the same edict that they must kneel before their parents as a token of respect. For the text of the

edict decreeing that Buddhist and Taoist monks and nuns would henceforth be required to do obeisance before their parents.[12]

If the word *apogee* is to be used with reference to Buddhism under the T'ang, it should be understood that it does not apply to the overall status of the church vis-à-vis the state. The church could claim more enthusiastic devotees among the rulers of the Northern Wei or the Southern Dynasties than it could show among the early T'ang emperors, none of whom could match the sincere piety and devotion of, say, Emperor Wu of the Liang. Although the T'ang rulers clearly established the supremacy of the state over the church and, in general, showed their preference for Taoism, they actively sought an accommodation with Buddhism on their own terms. Each of the early T'ang emperors, in spite of attempts to exercise control over the church, contributed to the founding of new temples, had sutras chanted at court, arranged for the ordination of monks, heard lectures on scripture, and sponsored masses for the dead. Such acts of piety were, of course, commonplace under the preceding dynasties, the rulers of which were usually devout Buddhists. With the early T'ang emperors, however, we get the impression that these public displays of devotion were carried out, not so much to satisfy their own religious yearnings in the direction of Buddhism, as for political expediency.[13]

As the popular reaction to the suppression of Buddhism by the Northern Chou in 574 had shown, Buddhism had gained devoted followers in the various strata of Chinese society and hence was a force to be reckoned with. Its power and organization were such that when Kao-tsung, as we have seen, prematurely attempted to withdraw some of the privileges of the church, he was forced to beat a hasty retreat. The early T'ang emperors were therefore circumspect in matters concerned with the church. That Buddhism eventually suffered the harshest persecution in its history toward the end of the T'ang is hardly coincidental. Things had been pointing in this direction since the establishment of the dynasty.[14]

---

edict see the *Kuang-hung-ming-chi* 25, 52.289c–290a. Clerical opposition to this latter requirement persisted, ultimately forcing Kao-tsung to retreat on this point as well (see the biography of Wei-hsiu in the *SKSC* 17, 50.812b.

12. *CTS* 8.3081b.

13. Yūki, "Shotō bukkyō," pp. 18–19; see also Tsukamoto Zenryū, *Nisshi bukkyō kōshōshi kenkyū* [Studies in the history of the relations between Chinese and Japanese Buddhism] (Tokyo, 1944), p. 23.

14. In the year 714 twelve thousand monks were said to have been laicized. Sometime later in the K'ai-yüan period another thirty thousand monks were defrocked. See Kenneth Ch'en, "The Hui-ch'ang Suppression of Buddhism," *Harvard Journal of Asiatic Studies* 19 (1956): 79.

Although the political position of the Buddhist church was unstable under the T'ang, on the doctrinal side Buddhism reached its highest level of development under this dynasty. During the 170-odd years between the founding of the Sui in 581 and the outbreak of the An Lu-shan Rebellion in 755, no less than eight schools of Buddhism appeared. Three of these—the T'ien-t'ai, the Fa-hsiang, and the Hua-yen—can be characterized as basically philosophical in their outlook, each with a highly complex metaphysical system. In addition to these three philosophical schools there arose four other schools—the Three Stages (San-chieh), the Pure Land (Ching-t'u), the Ch'an, and the Esoteric (Mi)—which may be loosely termed "religious schools," since they placed primary emphasis upon religious practices that led directly to the attainment of enlightenment, for example, the universal worship of all Buddhas in the Three Stages school, the invocation of the name of Amitābha Buddha (O-mi-t'o fo) in the Pure Land school, meditation in the Ch'an school, and the use of mystical hand signs and incantations in the Esoteric school. The Disciplinary school (Lü), which was systematized by Tao-hsüan (596–667) in the early T'ang, concerned itself primarily with ordination procedures, the interpretation of the rules governing the behavior of monks and the administration of monasteries and hence does not fit into either of the two categories given above.

Chinese Buddhism as it is practiced today by both monks and laymen represents a synthesis of the T'ang religious schools, exclusive of the Three Stages school, which was suppressed by the state during the T'ang. It is interesting to note that the founders of these popular schools, which assumed definitive shape under the T'ang and subsequently emerged as the mainstream of devotional Buddhism in China, received little support from the early T'ang emperors, whereas the founders of the philosophical schools all enjoyed imperial patronage, as we shall see below. Of the religious schools only the Esoteric school could claim any substantial degree of imperial sponsorship in its formative years. Emperor Hsüan-tsung, who showed great interest in Taoist magic, provided support for, and maintained close contact with, a number of Tāntric monks who arrived in Ch'ang-an and Loyang during his reign (712–56), presumably in the hope that the Esoteric texts that they were translating and expounding would provide additional knowledge that might be of use in the performance of Taoist magical rites.[15] Al-

15. For Hsüan-tsung's involvement with the Tāntric master Pu-k'ung, see Yamazaki Hiroshi, *Zuitō bukkyōshi no kenkyū* [Studies in the history of Buddhism under the Sui and T'ang] (Kyoto, 1967), pp. 239–50.

though Esoteric ritual ultimately became an integral part of Chinese Buddhist practice,[16] Esoteric Buddhism itself was never systematized in China as it had been in Japan. It might also be mentioned here that despite the fact that several Ch'an monks were invited to the court by Empress Wu, which might suggest some degree of imperial patronage, these monks all belonged to the branch of Ch'an technically known as "Northern Ch'an," which is different from that of the famous Ch'an masters who flourished during the T'ang and Sung dynasties. It is significant that even though contemporary Ch'an is divided into many branches, none claims descent from the imperially patronized Northern Ch'an.

Traditionally, the three T'ang philosophical schools have been regarded as the fruition of different exegetical lines that originated in the Nan-pei-ch'ao.[17] Thus the T'ien-t'ai school, which is based on Chih-i's interpretation of the *Lotus Sūtra,* is seen as an elaboration and systematization of the Nieh-p'an school (an exegetical school devoted to the study of the Mahāyānist *Mahāparinirvāṇa Sūtra*) which flourished during the fifth and sixth centuries; the Fa-hsiang school, which represents the Dharmapāla branch of Indian Yogācāra Buddhism, is viewed as a continuation of the She-lun school, which was based on Paramārtha's translation of the Yogācāra text, *Mahāyāna-saṃgraha,* completed in 563; and the Hua-yen (the school based on a systematic interpretation of the *Avataṃsaka Sūtra)* is held to be a successor to the Ti-lun, an early sixth-century school primarily concerned with the study of Vasubandhu's commentary (called *Ti-lun* in Chinese) on the *Daśabhūmika Sūtra.* It would indeed be a curious coincidence, however, if these three pre-T'ang schools had each reached maturity within the relatively short span of one hundred years after the establishment of the Sui. The reasons for the emergence of these three philosophical schools in such rapid succession cannot be properly understood as long as we limit ourselves to purely doctrinal considerations. From the orthodox point of view, Chih-i, the de facto founder of the T'ien-t'ai, Hsüan-tsang, the translator of the Fa-hsiang scripture, and Fa-tsang, the systematizer of the Hua-yen, each succeeded in formulating a major school of thought on the basis of his own religious intuition and philosophical insight. While in no way intending to minimize their originality,

16. See, for example, the account of the masses for the dead in Holmes Welch, *The Practice of Chinese Buddhism* (Cambridge, Mass., 1967), pp. 185–97.

17. From the standpoint of the history of Buddhist thought, the T'ien-t'ai school, which originated under the Sui, has all the characteristics of a "T'ang" school and hence must be so classified, as we shall explain below.

we hope to show that certain political factors influenced the doctrines formulated by these men and had a direct bearing upon the sequence in which their schools emerged as well as upon the subsequent vicissitudes of these schools.

The first of the philosophical schools to appear was the T'ien-t'ai, a distinctively Chinese-type school, which in many respects signified a great advance over the earlier, more Indian types of Buddhism in China. Yet despite the ardent patronage of the two Sui emperors and the enthusiastic support of many prominent courtiers and monks, the T'ien-t'ai dropped almost completely from view during the seventh century only to be resuscitated in the middle of the eighth century. What is surprising is that following the decline of the T'ien-t'ai at the beginning of the T'ang dynasty, the focus of Buddhist scholarship in the T'ang capitals, Ch'ang-an and Loyang, shifted to the rigidly Indian Fa-hsiang school. From a doctrinal point of view, T'ien-t'ai, with its advocacy of the ultimate enlightenment of all sentient beings, represented a far more developed type of Mahāyāna than did the Fa-hsiang with its doctrine of eternal damnation for one hapless group of sentient beings. Although Chinese monks in the T'ang already had sufficient understanding of Buddhism to realize that the Fa-hsiang, in purely doctrinal terms, constituted a step backward in the evolution of Buddhist thought, they were unable to prevent the Fa-hsiang from dominating the intellectual centers of Buddhist scholarship in the capitals during the second half of the seventh century. When the Fa-hsiang gave way to a more Chinese form of Buddhism, as was inevitable, it was not, as one might have expected, to the T'ien-t'ai which it had supplanted, but to the newly established Hua-yen, which, like the T'ien-t'ai and Fa-hsiang before it, enjoyed favor at the court until it too was superseded by a new school—the Esoteric Buddhism introduced by Śubhakarasiṃha and Vajrabodhi early in the reign of Hsüan-tsung.

Most of these Sui and T'ang schools had their precursors in the period that begins with the arrival of the great translator, Kumārajīva, in 401 and ends with the founding of the Sui in 581. This period saw the emergence of six exegetical schools: the San-lun, which expounded the philosophy of Nāgārjuna; the Ch'eng-shih, which was based on an obscure Indian treatise, possibly entitled *Tattvasiddhi* in Sanskrit; the P'i-t'an, which was devoted to the study of the Savrāstivāda Abhidharma; and the aforementioned Nieh-p'an, Ti-lun, and She-lun schools. Although each of these schools was based upon a different text or group of texts, they shared a number of characteristics that set them apart from the T'ang schools. First, each of the pre-T'ang schools bears the name of either a particular text or a closely related group of texts, while each of the T'ang schools either indicates in its name the central doctrine of the school, for example, Fa-hsiang ("Dharma aspect"), Ching-t'u ("Pure Land"), Ch'an ("Meditation"), Mi ("Esotericism"), or adopts a proper name associated with the founder, for example, T'ien-t'ai. The Hua-yen school, named after the *Hua-yen-ching*,[18] and the Disciplinary school (Lü-tsung), named after the Vinaya *(Lü)*, would seem to be the only exceptions. Yet even in these two cases we find alternate names in common use, the former being popularly called the Hsien-shou school, and the latter, the Nan-shan school.[19] Hsien-shou was the honorific name conferred by Empress Wu on Fa-tsang, the systematizer of the Hua-yen school, while Nan-shan, the alternate name of the Disciplinary school, is an abridgment of Chung-nan-shan, the mountains situated south of Ch'ang-an where Tao-hsüan, the de facto founder of the Disciplinary school, spent much of his life. It should be observed that none of the pre-T'ang schools has such an alternate "Chinese" name.

Another distinguishing feature of these pre-T'ang schools is that they all centered around the Chinese translation of a specific Indian text or group of texts and, furthermore, that with the exception of the Nieh-p'an school,[20] the text that served as the basic scripture always belonged to the division of the canon containing the philosophical treatises, that is, the so-called *lun-tsang,* and not to the sutra division *(ching-tsang),* which contrasts sharply with the practice of the T'ang schools. The T'ien-t'ai, for example, takes the *Lotus Sūtra*[21] as its fundamental scripture, the Pure Land bases itself upon three or four "Amitāyus" sutras, and the Esoteric school draws upon a variety of texts which, while classified as tantras in India and Tibet, are regarded as sutras in East Asian Buddhism. The Hua-yen school, as we have already seen, is based upon the sutra of the same name. Only the Disciplinary school does not have a sutra as its fundamental scripture.

The main scholarly concern of the monks of the six pre-T'ang schools

18. The full title of this sutra, which is traditionally believed to have been preached immediately after the enlightenment of the Buddha, is *Ta-fang-kuang fo hua-yen-ching (Buddhāvataṃsaka-mahāvaipulya-sūtra).* It exists in two Chinese translations (*TD* nos. 278 and 279), the former completed in the year 420 and the latter in 699.

19. See, for example, the treatment of these schools in the *FTTC* 29, 49.292c and 296c.

20. The Nieh-p'an school was based on a Mahāyāna sutra called *Ta-pan-nieh-p'an-ching (Mahāparinirvāṇa-sūtra),* *T* no. 374, translated into Chinese by Dharmakṣema in the year 421. This sutra, which claims to be the last discourse of the Buddha, is completely different in content from the Hīnayānist sutra with the same name and pretensions.

21. I.e. the *Miao-fa lien-hua-ching (Saddharma-puṇḍarīka-sūtra)* [Lotus of the True Law], which exists in three Chinese translations (*T* nos. 262, 263, and 264).

was directed toward the exegesis of a basic scripture. The *Kao-seng-chuan* [Biographies of eminent monks] and the *Hsü-kao-seng-chuan* [Supplement to the biographies of eminent monks] give us a comprehensive picture of the intense exegetical work carried on during the fifth and sixth centuries. Of the 257 biographies included in the former, no less than 101 biographies are those of exegetes *(i-chieh-seng)*. Although the overwhelming proportion of the commentaries produced during this period has been lost, a number of representative works of the fifth and sixth centuries fortunately survive, from which we can get a general idea of the type of exegesis undertaken at this time and how it differs from that of the T'ang schools. In general terms, the most distinctive feature of pre-T'ang exegesis, when compared with that of the T'ang schools, is the conscious effort of the Chinese commentator to interpret a text in a fashion which he believes to be faithful to the original intent of its author. When viewed from the standpoint of the Indian text, the commentary may be, and in fact often is, wide of the mark. Interpretations are frequently made which show that the commentator failed to grasp the meaning of the original. But the significant thing is that his intention was to interpret the text faithfully. That he often did not do so may be attributed to his inability to consult the text in the original language or to the linguistic ambiguity of the Chinese translation he was using. We get a very different impression, however, when we read the works of such leading Sui and T'ang commentators as Chih-i and Fa-tsang, who clearly felt themselves free to interpret the sutras of their schools on the basis of their own religious experience, often showing no concern whether a particular interpretation was at all feasible from the standpoint of the original text.

The T'ang schools, while nominally basing themselves on a particular Indian canonical work, in fact developed highly systematized dogmas that derived their authority from the writings of Chinese patriarchs *(tsu)*. The Indian canonical works, termed "fundamental scriptures" *(so-i ching)*, were often little more than pegs to which the patriarchs could attach their own ideas. A literal reading of the *Lotus Sūtra* or the *Hua-yen-ching* would hardly lead an impartial commentator to make the types of interpretations that are found in the writings of Chih-i and Fa-tsang. In the older schools of the fifth and sixth centuries the translator of the basic scripture occupied a prominent place in the patriarchal lineage, and his interpretations were treated with a respect bordering on veneration. In the case of the T'ang schools, however, translators were uniformly excluded from the list of patriarchs, which was limited to Chinese monks. Thus Kuan-ting (561–632), the editor of Chih-i's major works, recognized Hui-wen, who lived under the Northern Ch'i, as the first Chinese patriarch,[22] but omitted Kumāra-jīva, the translator of the *Lotus*, from the patriarchal succession. Similarly the Chinese monk Fa-shun (557–640) is held to be the first patriarch of the Hua-yen,[23] while the translator Buddhabhadra is excluded from the patriarchal lineage. Even in the case of so eminent a translator as Hsüan-tsang, we find that the Fa-hsiang school, whose treatises he rendered into Chinese, does not regard him as a patriarch. Rather it is his disciple, Tz'u-en, the author of two major commentaries on the *Ch'eng-wei-shih-lun*, who is venerated as the founder and first patriarch.[24] With the pre-T'ang schools there is not a single instance of a Chinese monk being raised to such an exalted status.

In the period of exegesis, that is to say, in the fifth and sixth centuries, the Buddhist church, despite the extensive support it received from devout imperial and aristocratic patrons, had not yet succeeded in transforming Indian Buddhism into a Chinese religion or in adapting it sufficiently to the Chinese situation. If in the fourth century Chinese monks had as yet failed to distinguish adequately between Buddhist concepts and the ideas of post-Han Neo-Taoism, in the fifth and sixth centuries they still had not been able to produce from the rapidly expanding corpus of Buddhist literature a religious and philosophical system that could satisfy the diverse and often conflicting needs of the different strata of Chinese society. In formal terms Buddhism was still primarily a monastic system that had little room for the layman who was unwilling or unable to break his ties with the mundane world. The primary role of the layman, at least insofar as the monastic community was concerned, was that of a *dānapati (shih-chu)* or lay supporter. Gifts of money, cloth, grain, or land were of course necessary for the sustenance of the monastic community, which assured its lay supporters that such acts of pious charity would generate great merit and lead to a blissful reward.

Although by the end of the sixth century hundreds of sutras and treatises had already been translated and a large number of commentaries written, there was a growing feeling among a number of leading monks that no real progress was being made toward the realization of the ultimate goal of Buddhism—the attainment of enlightenment. The church was rich in worldly goods and had a large following, but it was not succeeding in its own terms as a religion. One need only read the

22. *Mo-ho chih-kuan* 1, *T* 46.1b.
23. *FTTC* 29, *T* 49.292c.
24. Nien-ch'ang, *Fo-tsu li-tai t'ung-tsai* 12, *T* 49.583c.

Ssu Ta-shih li-shih yüan-wen [The vows of the master (Hui-) ssu],[25] an extremely interesting document written in 558, which speaks in detail of the wickedness of the monks and the general decline of religious morality. Hui-ssu was probably the first man to emphasize the concept of *mo-fa* ("the doctrine for the Final Period"), which asserted that the world had now entered the period of degeneration, a period in which the traditional Indian style morality of the exegetical schools would have no relevance. This idea, clearly enunciated by Hui-ssu, who was the teacher of Chih-i, the founder of the T'ien-t'ai school, became central to the Pure Land and Three Stages schools. Some monks began to feel that Buddhism could become meaningful to the Chinese of their day only if it took account of the degenerate conditions inevitably prevailing in the *mo-fa* period. As the monk Tao-ch'o (died 645) observed in his *An-lo-chi* [Anthology on Pure Land]: "In the period of degeneration in which we are now living countless sentient beings are devoting themselves to religious practices and cultivating the Way, and yet not a single one of them has attained enlightenment."[26] To Tao-ch'o the reasons for this anomaly were straightforward:

> When a particular teaching within Buddhism is in harmony with both the needs of the period and the intellectual capacity of the men for whom it is intended, it is easy both to practice this teaching and to attain enlightenment. When, however, the intellectual capacity of the devotee, the teaching of the Buddha, and the needs of the period are in conflict with each other, it is impossible either to practice the teaching or to attain enlightenment.[27]

The six exegetical schools, in their philosophical concepts, their monastic organization, and their religious practices, patterned themselves after what were conceived to be Indian models as revealed in the scriptures. It was only under the succeeding Sui and T'ang dynasties that Buddhism matured so as to become truly Chinese in both its philosophical expression and its religious aspirations.

The T'ien-t'ai School

As we have already noted, the first of the new, "Chinese" schools to appear was the T'ien-t'ai, founded by Chih-i (538–97). This school, which was characterized by a high degree of syncretism, embodied most

25. *T* 46.786b–792b.
26. *T* 47.13c.
27. *T* 47.4a.

of the features that have come to distinguish the "Chinese" Buddhism of the T'ang period from the Buddhism of the preceding period of exegesis: a Chinese patriarchate, emphasis on religious practice, recognition of the possibility of attaining enlightenment in this life, a belief in the ultimate salvation of all sentient beings, and, lastly, a free, openly subjective, interpretation of scripture. If the foundation of the Sui dynasty signified the reunion of a politically divided China, so the emergence of the T'ien-t'ai represented the synthesis of the many disparate tendencies that constituted the Buddhism of the fifth and sixth centuries.

Chih-i, whose lay name was Ch'en Wang-tao, was born in Hua-jung-hsien in Ching-chou (in present-day Hunan) in 538.[28] His father, Ch'en Ch'i-tsu, served as an adviser to Hsiao I, the seventh son of Emperor Wu of the Liang dynasty. When Hsiao I ascended the throne in 552 in Chiang-ling as Emperor Yüan, he confererrd a high title[29] on Ch'en Ch'i-tsu and enfeoffed him as K'ai-kuo Marquis of I-yang-hsien (in present-day Hunan). But Ch'en Ch'i-tsu's glory was short-lived. In the year 554 Chiang-ling was sacked by the Western Wei, who promptly murdered the emperor and many of his ranking officials. Chih-i's parents both died about this time, leaving him free to begin the religious life in which he had already professed great interest. The following year Chih-i, aged seventeen, began his religious training under Fa-hsü at the Kuo-yüan monastery in Hsiang-chou (in present-day Hunan). Wang Lin, a powerful general who had previously been in the service of Hsiao I along with Ch'en Ch'i-tsu, provided the necessary financial support for his late colleague's son. Chih-i was ordained as a novice (sha-mi) by Fa-hsü, with whom he stayed for about one year, before joining Hui-k'uang, a scholar versed in both Vinaya and Mahāyāna philosophy. After receiving his full ordination under Hui-k'uang in the year 558, Chih-i paid a visit to Mount Ta-hsien in Heng-chou (in present-day Hunan), where he spent twenty days chanting the Lotus and two related sutras, during which time he had a mystical experience that confirmed his faith in the Lotus. Two years later, aged twenty-two,[30] Chih-i moved to Mount Ta-su in Kuang-chou, where he became a disciple of Hui-ssu.

Although Hui-ssu, like Chih-i, was a southerner, he had been strong-

28. The earliest and most reliable biography of Chih-i is the Sui T'ien-t'ai Chih-che pieh-chuan (T no. 2050) compiled by his disciple Kuan-ting. See also the excellent study of Chih-i by Leon Hurvitz in Mélanges chinois et bouddhiques 12 (1963).

29. Shih-ch'ih-chieh san-chi-ch'ang-shih, CTP ,T 50.191b.

30. Chan-jan, Chih-kuan fu-hsing chuan-hung-chüeh 1, T 46.142c.

ly influenced by the Buddhism of North China, which placed great
emphasis on religious practice, particularly as manifested in meditation
and pietism.[31] Before proceeding to the north in search of new religious
ideas, Hui-ssu had become a devotee of the *Lotus Sūtra,* which had been
one of the most widely read scriptures in the south. His deep attachment
to the *Lotus,* with its message of an eternal Buddha and universal enlightenment, remained with him throughout his life. In the north
Hui-ssu studied under a number of scholars, from whom he learned
various meditative techniques. On the doctrinal side, he was introduced
to the *Ta-chih-tu-lun,* an encyclopedic commentary on the *Ta-p'in po-
jo-ching* [*Prajñāpāramitā Sūtra* in twenty-five thousand lines] purporting
to have been written by Nāgārjuna, the founder of the Mādhyamika
school. Although this voluminous work had been translated into
Chinese by Kumārajīva in 405, it had been virtually ignored until the
early sixth century when northern scholars discovered in it a synthesis
of meditational practices and the doctrine of nonsubstantiality. Hui-
ssu devoted himself to this northern meditative Buddhism for a number
of years before returning to the south in 553 to disseminate these new
doctrines.[32] Because of the long-standing southern prejudice against
the practice of meditation,[33] Hui-ssu encountered much hostility after
his return. Subjected to frequent harassment and at times even physically assaulted, Hui-ssu decided to retire to the Nan-yüeh mountains,
in present-day Hunan, but owing to the unsettled political situation, he
was unable to reach his destination until the year 568. In the interval,
between 554 and 568, Hui-ssu was active in Kuang-chou, where he
made Mount Ta-su his headquarters.

Under Hui-ssu's guidance Chih-i devoted himself to the practice
of meditation, which he now applied to the *Lotus.* Before Chih-i became
a pupil of Hui-ssu, his involvement with the *Lotus* had been, in typical
southern fashion, limited to textual exegesis. Hui-ssu enabled him to
add a new dimension to his religious life by teaching him, through the
techniques of meditation, how to go beyond a mere scholastic interpretation of the text in order to understand its inner meaning. When
Chih-i reported to Hui-ssu that he had at last grasped the true significance of the text, his master replied: "It is only you who could have

31. The most detailed biography of Hui-ssu is the one included in the *HKSC* 17, *T* 50.
562c–564a.

32. Mochizuki Shinkō, *Bukkyō daijiten* [Encyclopedia of Buddhism] (Tokyo, 1933), 1.274c.

33. Ōchō Enichi has written a fascinating study of the conflict between southern exegesis
and northern meditation entitled *Chūgoku nambokuchō jidai no bukkyō gakufū* [Attitudes toward
the study of Buddhism in the Nan-pei-ch'ao], which is included in his *Chūgoku bukkyō no
kenkyū* [Studies in Chinese Buddhism] (Kyoto, 1958), pp. 256–89.

attained such an enlightenment, and only I who could perceive
this. . . . Even though one thousand exegetes were to challenge you,
none could plumb the depth of your words."[34] Here we can already
detect the independent spirit that is to distinguish the "Chinese"
Buddhism of the T'ang from the earlier, India-centered Buddhism of
the Nan-pei-ch'ao. Hui-ssu was convinced that in Chih-i he had found
a true successor, one who would be able to propagate in the south the
meditative techniques that Hui-ssu had learned in the north. In 568
he instructed Chih-i to proceed to the capital of the Ch'en state, Chin-
ling (the modern Nanking), to proclaim the new doctrines. Hui-ssu
himself declined to go to the capital insisting that the time had come
for his long-awaited retreat to the Nan-yüeh mountains. That he dispatched his disciple Chih-i to carry out the important mission of propagating the Dharma in the acknowledged center of southern Buddhism
rather than undertaking this task himself shows his shrewd reading of
the situation, as indicated by his words to Chih-i: "If you establish
yourself in [the capital of] the state of Ch'en, our doctrine will surely
flourish because of your connections there!"[35]

When Chih-i arrived in Chin-ling in 568, his father had been dead
for some fourteen years, while his father's erstwhile colleague, the
founder of the Ch'en dynasty, Ch'en Pa-hsien, had been dead some
nine years. Yet many family friends, now in positions of authority, were
still around to give a sympathetic hearing to the new doctrines espoused
by the thirty-year-old Chih-i. During Chih-i's sojourn in Chin-ling
between 568 and 575, the throne was occupied by Emperor Hsüan
(reigned 568–82), a nephew of Ch'en Pa-hsien. Emperor Hsüan had
spent his youth in Chiang-ling in the service of Hsiao I,[36] and his son
and successor Shu-pao, posthumously called Hou-chu ("The Last
Ruler"), had been born there in 553. Thus the Ch'en imperial family,
whose surname Chih-i shared, all had close links with the group surrounding Hsiao I in Chiang-ling in the early 550s, the same group in
which Chih-i's father had held a prominent position. To the Ch'en
imperial family as well as to many powerful bureaucrats in Chin-ling,
Chih-i was no obscure purveyor of a new gospel, but the son of an esteemed, now deceased, colleague.

In Chin-ling Chih-i took up residence at the famous Wa-kuan
monastery, where he attracted a large following. It is recorded that
several southern monks who were impressed by his ideas promptly

34. *CTP*, *T* 50.192a.
35. *HKSC* 17, *T* 50.564b.
36. *Ch'en-shu* (K'ai-ming ed.) 5.1857a.

"renounced exegesis to devote themselves to meditation."[37] Sometime after his arrival in Chin-ling it seems likely that Chih-i administered the "bodhisattva precepts" to a number of prominent laymen, among whom was Shen Chün-li,[38] whose daughter had been chosen as a concubine for the crown prince in 570. Both Shen Chün-li and his father, Shen Hsün, had been in the entourage of Hsiao I in Chiang-ling and hence can be presumed to have been on friendly terms with Chih-i's father.

In response to a request from Shen Chün-li, Chih-i gave a series of lectures in 569 on the religious significance of the title of the *Lotus*,[39] which apparently had a great impact on the Chin-ling Buddhist community. These lectures were attended by some of the most eminent members of the Ch'en court,[40] which was recessed by imperial command for one day to mark the occasion. Since the text of these lectures has not been preserved, it is not possible to know what Chih-i's view of the *Lotus* was at this time; but judging from his early works, it is probably safe to assume that his position was still close to that of Hui-ssu, that is, primarily concerned with the practice of meditation. The three works that survive from this period of residence in Chin-ling are all concerned with meditative practices and contain none of the important points of doctrine that came to distinguish the T'ien-t'ai system.[41]

When, in the year 575, Chih-i announced his intention of leaving the Ch'en capital for the T'ien-t'ai mountains, his supporters were visibly shaken. Emperor Hsüan appealed to him not to ignore the salvation of his followers in the capital,[42] and Hsü Ling, a high-ranking official who had been a member of the Chiang-ling group with Chih-i's

37. *CTP*, *T* 50.192b.

38. This supposition is based upon Shen Chün-li's letter to Chih-i requesting him to lecture on the title of the *Lotus*, in which he describes himself as "your disciple in the bodhisattva precepts" (*KCPL* doc. no. 18, *T* 46.801a). Since Shen Chün-li died in 573, Chih-i must have administered the precepts before that date. Shen's biography is given in the *Ch'en-shu* 23. 1877c–d and the *Nan-shih* 68.2704d–2705a.

39. *FTTC* 6, *T* 49.181c. *CTP* does not specify the year.

40. In addition to Hsü Ling, Wang Ku, and Mao Hsi, whose biographies are summarized by Hurvitz, *Mélanges chinois et bouddhiques*, p. 111, two other ranking officials, K'ung Huan and Chou Hung-cheng, are listed in the *CTP*, *T* 50.192c as being present at the lectures. The biography of the latter is contained in the *Ch'en-shu* 24.1878b and the *Nan-shih* 34.2631a. Virtually all of the prominent men present at Chih-i's lectures had been with Hsiao I at Chiang-ling.

41. The three works that survive from his Chin-ling period are the *Shih ch'an-po-lo-mi tz'u-ti fa-men* (*T* no. 1916), the *Fang-teng san-mei hsing-fa* (*T* no. 1940), and the *Fa-hua san-mei ch'an-i* (*T* no. 1941). For a critical analysis of the works attributed to Chih-i, see Satō Tetsuei, *Tendai Daishi no kenkyū* [A study of the great master T'ien-t'ai] (Kyoto, 1961), especially pp. 49–50.

42. *KCPL* 1, doc. 8, *T* 46.799a.

father, pleaded tearfully with Chih-i to remain.[43] Chih-i would not be dissuaded and departed with a small group of close disciples for T'ien-t'ai, where he arrived later in the same year. Although there were no major temples in the T'ien-t'ai mountains at this time, a number of fairly well known monks who were themselves devotees of the Lotus had resided here in the past, which may be the reason why Chih-i chose this site. Shortly after reaching his destination, Chih-i ascended Hua-ting peak and here had the deep mystical experience that formed the basis of his subsequent religious life. The monastic community that he established on Fo-lung, another of the T'ien-t'ai peaks, at first was hard pressed financially, but its plight was soon alleviated, thanks to Chih-i's court connections, when, in the second month of the year 577, Emperor Hsüan ordered part of the taxes levied on Shih-feng-hsien (Chekiang) to be used for the support of the T'ien-t'ai community.[44] The following year Emperor Hsüan granted the name Hsiu-ch'an-ssu to the temple that Chih-i was then building. During Chih-i's first prolonged stay in the T'ien-t'ai mountains, which lasted from 575 to 585, he received donations from at least two laymen[45] and acquired a devout supporter in the person of Ch'en Po-chih, who was the twelfth son of Emperor Wen (reigned 559–66) and a nephew of Emperor Hsüan. Ch'en Po-chih's five surviving letters to Chih-i indicate that he received the bodhisattva precepts from Chih-i, to whom he was deeply attached.[46]

In 582 Ch'en Shu-pao, upon his father's death, ascended the Ch'en throne. Apparently anxious to show himself to be no less a patron of Buddhism than his father, Shu-pao made three appeals to Chih-i to return to Chin-ling,[47] but each time he was met with a refusal, Chih-i pleading illness. Only after Ch'en Po-chih, Chih-i's powerful benefactor, interceded at the request of Shu-pao did Chih-i reluctantly agree in 585 to return to the capital, where he received an enthusiastic welcome. We need not detail his activities there—suffice it to say that he once again played an extremely prominent role while maintaining his very close ties with the imperial family, as is evidenced by his administering of the bodhisattva precepts to the crown prince.[48] During his stay at the Kuang-che monastery in Chin-ling in 587, Chih-i gave his celebrated

43. CTP T 50.193a.
44. The text of Emperor Hsüan's edict is given in KCPL 1, doc. 9, T 46.799a.
45. CTP, T 50.193b.
46. KCPL 2, doc. 15–17, T 46.800a–801a.
47. The texts of these three appeals are included in KCPL 1, doc. 11, T 46.799b.
48. KCPL 2, doc. 14, T 46.800a.

series of lectures on the *Lotus,* which were posthumously edited by his disciple Kuan-ting under the title *Fa-hua wen-chü.*[49]

While Chih-i was renewing his contacts with the Ch'en court, important changes were taking place on the political scene. Yang Chien, after establishing himself as Emperor Wen of the Sui dynasty in North China in 581, gradually began to turn his attention southward. In 587 he destroyed the buffer state of Later Liang, and the following year he ordered an attack on the state of Ch'en, which was conquered and occupied in the first month of 589, when Yang Kuang, the second son of Emperor Wen, entered Chin-ling. Whatever Chih-i's personal feelings toward the Ch'en state might have been, he clearly felt no need to go down with the dynasty. As Chin-ling was being fought over by contending armies, Chih-i apparently decided that this would be an appropriate time to undertake some long-planned pilgrimages to the Nan-yüeh mountains, where his master had spent the last years of his life, and to Lu-shan, one of the great centers of Buddhism since the fourth century. At the beginning of the following year, however, Chih-i received a letter from the victorious Emperor Wen of the Sui, seeking to establish relations with him.[50] Although Emperor Wen was no doubt a sincere Buddhist, he was also well aware of the political advantages that would accrue from a close association with the leading cleric of South China. Emperor Wen had succeeded in unifying the empire by force of arms, but as a northerner he had encountered considerable resistance in the south. He no doubt felt that a strong endorsement by Chih-i, who was held in high esteem by the southern aristocracy and clergy, would facilitate the task of bringing about a real unification.

When Yang Kuang became governor of Yang-chou *(Yang-chou tsung-kuan)* toward the end of the year 590, he promptly dispatched a letter to Chih-i inviting him to visit Yang-chou.[51] After the customary refusal of three times, Chih-i finally journeyed to Yang-chou, where, in the eleventh month of 591, he formally administered the bodhisattva precepts to Yang Kuang in a splendid ceremony attended by a thousand monks.[52] Such was the beginning of the close relationship between Chih-i and his powerful patron, Yang Kuang, which continued until the former's death in 597. Chih-i stayed in Yang-chou only a few months, perhaps because he found this place too distracting for his religious life. By the summer of 592 Chih-i was once again back in Lu-

49. *T* no. 1718.

50. For a summary of the letter see Hurvitz, *Mélanges chinois et bouddhiques,* p. 140.

51. *KCPL* 2, doc. 24, *T* 46.803a.

52. For a description of the ceremony see Yang Kuang's letter to Chih-i dated the twenty-third day of the eleventh month of the year 591, *KCPL* 2, doc. 26, *T* 46.803a.

shan. He then seems to have revisited the Nan-yüeh mountains and other places associated with his deceased master, finally arriving in his native Ching-chou in the twelfth month of 592; there he stayed for two years, during which time he completed his famous systematization of Buddhist doctrine. Shortly after his arrival in Ching-chou, Chih-i undertook the construction of the Yü-ch'üan monastery, which was granted an imperial charter in the seventh month of the year 593 by Emperor Wen.[53] It was at this monastery that Chih-i gave his famous lectures on the inner meaning of the *Lotus*, which his disciple Kuan-ting subsequently edited under the title *Fa-hua hsüan-i*.[54] The following year he expounded his theories of meditation and religious practice, which were later edited to form the treatise called *Mo-ho chih-kuan*.[55] These two works, together with the *Fa-hua wen-chü* mentioned above, constitute the three major texts of the T'ien-t'ai school.

While Chih-i was in Ching-chou, Yang Kuang seems to have sent him a number of letters imploring him to return to Yang-chou. Chih-i reluctantly acceded to his patron's wish and took up residence at one of the larger monasteries in Yang-chou in the early part of 595. In the sixth month of that year Yang Kuang requested Chih-i to prepare a commentary on the *Wei-mo-ching (Vimalakīrti-nirdeśa-sūtra)*, a Mahā-yāna scripture that elevates a pious layman to a status virtually equal to that of the Buddha, a notion which, no doubt, appealed to Yang Kuang. In his reply Chih-i mentioned that it was his intention to return to the T'ien-t'ai region where he could practice the Way in the quiet of the mountain forests. Yang Kuang tried in vain to dissuade Chih-i from leaving, but Chih-i was so determined that Yang Kuang was finally compelled to allow his departure.[56] Once back in the T'ien-t'ai mountains, Chih-i devoted himself to the commentary on the *Wei-mo-ching*. Yang Kuang on several occasions sent envoys to T'ien-t'ai in an effort to persuade him to return to Yang-chou. Chih-i, who by 597 was ailing seriously, finally agreed to rejoin Yang Kuang and left for Yang-chou with the latter's envoy, who had arrived in the tenth month of that year. When the group reached Shih-ch'eng,[57] Chih-i announced that he was too ill to proceed any further. Sensing that his end was imminent, he divided up his possessions and undertook various religious

53. *KCPL* 2, doc. 44, *T* 46.806c.

54. *T* no. 1716.

55. *T* no. 1911.

56. *KCPL* 2, doc. 49, *T* 46.807b.; Ibid. 3, doc. 54, *T* 46.808b.

57. Situated thirty *li* to the northwest of the present-day Shao-hsing-hsien in Chekiang. See the *Chung-kuo ku-chin ti-ming ta-tz'u-tien* [Encyclopedia of ancient and modern Chinese place names] (Shanghai, 1930), p. 269b.

exercises. One of his last acts before his death on the twenty-fourth day of the eleventh month was to dictate a final letter to Yang Kuang entrusting the Dharma to his care.[58]

Chih-i's disciples were well aware of the necessity of maintaining the close contact with the Sui court that their master had established during the last eight years of his life. Within two months after the death of Chih-i, two leading disciples, Kuan-ting and P'u-ming, made the journey to Yang-chou to present Yang Kuang with a copy of their master's letter, his commentary on the *Wei-mo-ching* specially written for Yang Kuang, and various objects intimately associated with Chih-i's religious life. As might be expected, the meeting between Yang Kuang, the great T'ien-t'ai patron, and Chih-i's disciples was an emotional one, Kuang vowing his continued support for the T'ien-t'ai community. A high-ranking official was dispatched to the T'ien-t'ai mountains with instructions to arrange for the transfer of rich agricultural land to provide economic support for Chih-i's followers. Yang Kuang also promised to assist in the construction of the temple on the Fo-lung peak, which Chih-i had first proposed in 595.[59] Yang Kuang had originally agreed to act as patron, but little was actually accomplished during Chih-i's lifetime. When Chih-i reluctantly accepted the invitation from Yang Kuang to return to Yang-chou, he drew up a detailed layout of the proposed temple which, after his death, would serve as the headquarters for his school. When asked by his disciples how resources could be found for the establishment of such a grand temple in the wilderness of the Chekiang mountains, he replied that the temple that he had in mind could be constructed only through the support of the imperial family.[60] It is quite understandable, then, that Chih-i, in the last letter to Yang Kuang written on his deathbed, should have appealed for support for this temple, which was given unstintingly. Construction was completed in the year 601, and in 605 Yang Kuang, in accordance with a request from Chih-i's disciples, designated it the Kuo-ch'ing-ssu ("monastery for the purification of the empire"), the name it still bears.[61]

58. For a partial translation of this last letter see Hurvitz, *Mélanges chinois et bouddhiques*, pp. 166–69.

59. *KCPL* 3, doc. 66, *T* 46.810c; ibid., doc. 53, *T* 46.808a.

60. *CTP, T* 50.196a.

61. The name is indicative of the role the temple was supposed to play in the protection of the state. According to tradition, this name was chosen for the temple because of a vision that Chih-i had in which a deceased monk prophesied that the empire would become pure only when such a temple would be erected for Chih-i by a powerful ruler who had unified the empire. See *KCPL* 3, doc. 88, *T* 46.816a.

Yang Kuang continued to feel a deep sense of commitment toward the T'ien-t'ai community, as can be seen from the surviving correspondence in the *Kuo-ch'ing po-lu*. When Yang Kuang became crown prince in the year 600, two of Chih-i's leading disciples, Kuan-ting and Chih-tsao, were dispatched to convey the good wishes of the T'ien-t'ai community. At Yang Kuang's accession in 604 a letter of congratulations was sent to Ch'ang-an by Chih-yüeh, the head monk at T'ien-t'ai. The new emperor responded by sending various gifts to the T'ien-t'ai community.[62] There is little doubt that Yang Kuang remained a devoted patron of the T'ien-t'ai school for the remainder of his life. Thus we find him, as he is making preparations for his ill-fated Korean expeditions in 607, inviting Kuan-ting to visit him at his field headquarters to reminisce about his deceased master.[63]

Just as it might be said that the most significant accomplishment of the Sui dynasty was the unification of a China that had been politically divided for two and one half centuries, so also can it be asserted that the most outstanding achievement of Chih-i was his successful synthesis of two distinct, and often hostile, traditions: northern meditative Buddhism and southern exegetical Buddhism. It is not surprising that Chih-i should have effected in the religious sphere what his imperial patrons accomplished in the political one; the times seemed to demand unification, both political and cultural. The necessity of integrating northern meditation and southern exegesis must have already become apparent to Chih-i while he was studying under Hui-ssu, for there is evidence that he practiced both before moving to Chin-ling in 568.[64] Nevertheless, his early surviving works indicate that before the unification of China by the Sui, Chih-i had not yet formulated the fundamental principles on which his later synthesis was to be based, which strongly suggests that his harmonization of northern and southern Buddhism was influenced by political events.

Chih-i's efforts to achieve a new synthesis had to take account of the various schemes of classifying the scriptures according to the degree of spiritual truth they revealed. Such classifications, called *p'an-chiao*, varied with the individual scholar, since each scholar had his own view as to which text in the canon contained the ultimate doctrine of the Buddha. Although Chih-i himself mentions no less than ten such clas-

62. *KCPL* 3, doc. 72, *T* 46.812b; ibid., doc. 82, *T* 46.814c; ibid., doc. 83, *T* 46.815a.
63. *HKSC* 19, *T* 50.584c.
64. Besides practicing meditation Chih-i lectured on the *Po-jo-ching* and *Lotus*. See *HKSC* 17, *T* 50.563b and 564b; also *CTP, T* 50.192a.

sifications,[65] three of which are southern and seven northern, two classifications clearly predominate: that of the Nieh-p'an scholar, Hui-kuan (363–443), in the south and that of the Ti-lun scholar, Hui-kuang (468–537), in the north. Five of the remaining eight classifications can be considered minor variations of these two.

For Chih-i to achieve a real unification of Chinese Buddhism he would somehow have to reconcile not only the divergent approaches toward Buddhism manifested in the long-standing antithesis between northern meditation and southern exegesis, but also the conflicting classifications of doctrine, such as the northern claim that the *Hua-yen-ching* represented the highest teaching of the Buddha as opposed to the southern view that the *Nieh-p'an-ching* constituted his ultimate message. His task was rendered more difficult by his own conviction that in fact it was neither the *Hua-yen-ching* nor the *Nieh-p'an-ching* that embodied the quintessence of Buddhist doctrine but the *Lotus Sūtra*, which, despite its great popularity in the south, did not figure in any of the ten classifications as the highest revelation.

As was typical of the founders and systematizers of the T'ang schools, Chih-i read the scripture in the light of his own religious intuition and experience rather than in the literal fashion that had prevailed before his time. Whereas the traditional method of exegesis had been one of "literal interpretation" *(sui-wen chieh-shih)*, Chih-i perfected the method of searching out and expounding the "hidden meaning" *(hsüan-i)* of the text,[66] which was subsequently adopted by such eminent T'ang scholar-monks as Chi-tsang, Shan-tao, and Fa-tsang. It was Chih-i's discovery of the "hidden meaning" of the *Lotus* after the unification of China by the Sui that enabled him to integrate northern and southern Buddhism and, in the process, to establish the supremacy of the *Lotus* over all other scriptures.

After a critical study of the various existing systems of classifying the sacred books, it became apparent to Chih-i that in addition to the opposing theories regarding the ultimate teaching of the Buddha, there was also some inconsistency in the arrangement and the categories used. The northern classifications merely listed in ascending order five schools *(tsung)*, each identified by a particular doctrine *(chiao)*. The southern classifications, on the other hand, first arranged the Buddha's teachings into categories based on pedagogical methods described as "sudden,"

65. *Fa-hua hsüan-i* 10A, *T* 33.801a.

66. Compare, for example, the commentary by Seng-chao (384–414) on the *Wei-mo-ching* (*T* no. 1775) with Chih-i's commentary on this same sutra entitled *Wei-mo-ching hsüan-shu* (*T* no. 1777).

"gradual," and "indeterminate" and then proceeded to subdivide the "gradual teachings" into five ascending sets of doctrines, each represented by a particular sutra or class of sutras preached in one of the five periods into which the life of the Buddha had been divided. Such a classification, however, had serious shortcomings in Chih-i's view. The *Hua-yen-ching*, described simply as a "sudden teaching" by Hui-kuan, was neither characterized doctrinally nor assigned to one of the five periods in the life of the Buddha, since these periods came under the heading of "gradual teachings." Equally unsatisfactory was the identification of the five sets of doctrines with specific sutras or groups of sutras, since a particular doctrine, for example, nonsubstantiality, might be found in several different groups of sutras; or, conversely, a single sutra, for example, the *Nieh-p'an-ching*, might contain a variety of doctrines.

In his own synthesis Chih-i asserted that a proper classification *(p'an-chiao)* must treat three distinct elements: (1) the five periods *(wu-shih)* in the life of the Buddha, each corresponding to a sutra or group of sutras; (2) the four methods resorted to by the Buddha to teach sentient beings *(hua-i ssu-chiao)*; and (3) the four basic types of doctrines *(hua-fa ssu-chiao)* that the Buddha taught.[67] Like Hui-kuan, Chih-i divided the life of the Buddha into five periods, each bearing the name of a sutra or class of sutras: (1) *Hua-yen (Avataṃsaka)*; (2) *O-han (Āgama)*, the period of the Hīnayāna sutras; (3) *Fang-teng (Vaipulya)*, the period of the Mahāyāna sutras other than the *Hua-yen*, *Po-jo (Prajñāpāramitā)*, *Lotus*, and *Nieh-p'an (Mahāparinirvāṇa Sūtra)*; (4) *Po-jo*; and (5) the *Lotus* and *Nieh-p'an*. Chih-i modified Hui-kuan's classification of five periods by grouping the *Lotus* and the *Nieh-p'an* together in the last period in order to accommodate the *Hua-yen-ching*, which he placed in the first period. Thus the sutra that had been held in the highest esteem in the north was accorded the honor of being recognized as the first sermon of the Buddha; while the *Nieh-p'an-ching*, the most widely read text in the south, retained its position as the last discourse of the Buddha.

In his formulation of the pedagogical methods used by the Buddha Chih-i relied upon the terminology current in the south. He adopted without change the designations "sudden," "gradual," and "indeterminate," but subdivided the last category into "secret indeterminate teachings" *(pi-mi pu-ting-chiao)* and "manifest indeterminate teachings" *(hsien-lu pu-ting-chiao)*. Chih-i, however, reinterpreted the word *indeter-*

---

67. The following account is based on Ti-kuan, *T'ien-t'ai ssu-chiao-i*, *T* 46.774c–780a.

minate to apply to the type of spiritual benefit derived by a person who came in contact with a particular doctrine and not to a category of sutras, as his predecessors had done. Chih-i held that a person's religious attainments ultimately depended more upon his native intellect than upon the specific teachings to which he was exposed. Thus a man with a sharp mind could perceive a Mahāyāna doctrine even though he was reading a text which was ostensibly Hīnayānist, while a dull person would tend to reduce the most profound Mahāyāna ideas to Hīnayānist banalities. In Chih-i's view sutras were not exclusively Hīnayānist or Mahāyānist, since these terms referred to the state of mind of the reader rather than to the text itself. Chih-i applied the term *secret indeterminate teaching* to the method employed by the Buddha whereby he preaches to an assembly of people, each of whom is unaware, thanks to the Buddha's supernatural powers, that other persons are also present. This sort of discourse is called "indeterminate" because each person in the assembly interprets the meaning of the Buddha's words in his own way and hence achieves a different degree of spiritual insight. In the case of the "manifest indeterminate teachings" one sees that other persons are present at a discourse, but does not realize that each person is understanding the Buddha differently.

By far the most original element in Chih-i's synthesis is to be found in his categorization of the four types of Buddhist doctrine. The first of these, termed "Teaching of the Tripiṭaka" *(tsang-chiao)*, signified Hīnayāna and included the P'i-t'an (Abhidharma) and Ch'eng-shih *(Tattvasiddhi)* schools. The second type of doctrine, called "Common Teaching" *(t'ung-chiao)*, referred to the concept that all things are nonsubstantial. The designation "common" indicated that although this is essentially a Mahāyānist view, it also appears in certain Hīnayāna texts. The San-lun (Mādhyamika) school was regarded as the principal exponent of this view, although it was accepted by all other Mahāyānists. The third type of doctrine was designated "Separate Teaching" *(pieh-chiao)* because it embraced concepts unknown to the Hīnayāna—specifically, the view that each dharma (element) has three distinct aspects: one of nonsubstantiality *(k'ung)*, one of seeming substantiality *(chia)*, and one representing the middle position *(chung)* which combines both of the preceding aspects. The Ti-lun and She-lun schools (both Yogācāra schools) were held to be representative of this type of doctrine. Chih-i designated the fourth and highest doctrine "Perfect Teaching" *(yüan-chiao)*, which, in his view, found its fullest expression in the *Lotus*, although he recognized that it appeared fragmentarily in other Mahāyāna sutras as well. In contrast to the Separate

Teaching, which held that the world is made up of discrete elements *(dharmas)*, the Perfect Teaching of the *Lotus* stressed the essential harmony and interrelatedness *(yüan-jung)* of all phenomena. This type of doctrine was not restricted merely to a discussion of metaphysical questions, such as the nature of the three aspects of a given dharma, but was drawn upon by Chih-i to provide doctrinal justification for the reconciliation between the hitherto conflicting practices of meditation and exegesis, both of which received equal weight in Chih-i's new system.

Chih-i's classification had two clear goals. The first was to unify the Buddhist world, which had been divided both in its religious practices and its choice of scripture; the second was to establish the supremacy of the *Lotus* over all other sutras. Having determined that the hidden meaning of the *Lotus* was the doctrine of the interrelatedness of all dharmas, Chih-i was able to proclaim that there was no real opposition between the southern practice of exegesis and the northern practice of meditation. On the contrary, one complemented the other; either by itself was inadequate. The northerners who regarded the *Hua-yen-ching* as containing the highest doctrine were conciliated by having their sutra recognized as the first discourse of the Buddha after his enlightenment. Its teaching, like that of the *Lotus,* was classified as "perfect," differing from the latter only in that it was intended for great bodhisattvas rather than for ordinary men. Chih-i similarly took account of the followers of the Nieh-p'an school in the south by conceding that this sutra, in purely temporal terms, represented the last discourse of the Buddha before his death. Like the *Hua-yen-ching,* the *Nieh-p'an-ching,* too, was said to contain elements of the Perfect Teaching. Although Chih-i, in deference to its southern devotees, was forced to recognize that the *Nieh-p'an-ching* was the final message of the Buddha, he held that it was only in the *Lotus* that the Buddha revealed his ultimate teaching. To the obvious criticism that if this were the case, the Buddha would not have preached still one more sutra after the *Lotus,* that is, the *Nieh-p'an-ching,* Chih-i replied that the Buddha taught the latter sutra out of compassion for those people who were not present when the *Lotus* was preached, citing specifically the incident related in the *Lotus* in which some five thousand persons withdrew just as the Buddha was about to give a discourse on the concept of One Vehicle.[8]

Since it would be out of place here to attempt a comprehensive survey of T'ien-t'ai doctrines, we shall merely mention briefly those teachings

---

68. *Fa-hua-ching* 1, *T* 9.7a.

that might be viewed as fundamental to the Chinese Buddhism of the T'ang period. One of the principal ideas of the T'ien-t'ai school is the concept of universal enlightenment *(i-ch'ieh ch'eng-fo)*. This idea, which permeates the *Lotus* but is also found in many other Mahāyāna sutras, in essence rejects the exclusiveness of Hīnayāna, which would limit the attainment of enlightenment only to those people who were able to sustain a long, arduous course of various religious practices. At the root of the idea of universal enlightenment is the belief that since the Buddha is the embodiment of compassion, he would not proclaim a doctrine so difficult that only a few men could benefit from it. In the *Lotus* the Buddha declares that the real purpose of his coming into this world is to cause men to achieve an enlightenment that is in no way different from his own, and he solemnly prophesies that all sentient beings, male and female, wise and ignorant, will ultimately attain Buddhahood.[69]

Related to this ideal of universal enlightenment is the rejection of the concept of Three Vehicles *(san-ch'eng)* as real ultimate entities.[70] The Three Vehicles refer to the traditional threefold division of the Buddhist doctrine into Śrāvakayāna, Pratyekabuddhayāna, and Bodhisattvayāna, which for our purposes may be reduced to Hīnayāna (the first two vehicles)[71] and Mahāyāna (the third vehicle). Since Chih-i, basing himself on the *Lotus*, held that all men were ultimately destined to attain an enlightenment no different from that of the Buddha, he could not accept that Hīnayāna, which from his own Mahāyānist point of view offered an inferior reward, could ever have been taught by the Buddha as an independent spiritual goal. Rather he viewed Hīnayāna as an expedient doctrine devised to win over those men of limited intellectual capacity who would be unable to appreciate the subtleties of Mahāyāna at their first exposure to it. In place of Three Vehicles Chih-i taught that there was in fact only one *real* vehicle *(i-ch'eng)*, that of the Buddha, into which both the traditional Hīnayāna and Mahāyāna would coalesce—hence the celebrated T'ien-t'ai thesis that "the Three Vehicles are but a means, the One Vehicle being the ultimate truth."

The practical side of Chih-i's Buddhism can be seen in his formulation

69. Ibid., 7a, 8a–10b.

70. Ibid., 7b.

71. Strictly speaking, Śrāvakayāna ("Vehicle of the Disciples") refers to those people who follow the teachings of the Buddha as outlined in the *Āgamas* (the Hīnayāna sutras), whereas the Pratyekabuddhayāna("Vehicle of the Solitary Buddhas") is the name given to those persons who attempt to attain enlightenment on their own by meditating on the law of causality without ever coming into contact with the teachings of the Buddha. Since the Śrāvakayāna and the Pratyekabuddhayāna achieve similar results, they are customarily grouped together under the generic name of Hīnayāna.

of the principle that Buddhahood could be rapidly attained in the present life.[72] In traditional Indian Buddhism the status of the Buddha was so exalted that some select individuals might ultimately reach his level, but only after countless kalpas (eons) of religious practice. Even in the case of the historical Buddha, Śākyamuni, it was thought that his religious life did not begin in this world at the age of twenty-nine, but in fact commenced many millennia ago so that his attainment of enlightenment at the age of thirty-five represented the culmination of an effort sustained over many lives.[73] Although such a view might be acceptable to the Indians with their own peculiar concept of time, it clearly was not to the Chinese, who sought a more tangible reward for their religious efforts. Even though Chih-i formulated a highly complex system of meditations, each of which brought the devotee to a higher stage of awareness, he opened up the way, at least in principle, for the rapid attainment of Buddhahood in this life. In taking this position he drew inspiration from the well-known story in the *Lotus* of an eight-year-old girl who, through simple acts of piety, was promptly transformed into a man and attained Buddhahood.[74] It was probably for this reason that Chih-i set up the category of indeterminate teachings, which makes it possible for people exposed only to Hīnayāna texts to derive a Mahāyāna-type reward. Similarly, despite his intricate schema of fifty-two stages for the aspirant to Buddhahood, Chih-i recognized the possibility of jumping over whole groups of these stages.[75]

Although the T'ien-t'ai doctrines were formulated under the Sui dynasty and reflect the cultural and political exigencies of the day, they have nevertheless come to be recognized as an embodiment of the most cherished ideals of Chinese Mahāyāna and as such are found to a greater or lesser degree in all of the T'ang schools except the Fa-hsiang school. From the standpoint of the Buddhist historian, it would be futile to attempt to distinguish, on the basis of doctrine, between the T'ien-t'ai Buddhism of the Sui and the various T'ang schools, since they share common ideals. Yet despite the "T'ang" character of the

72. See, for example, his *Fa-hua wen-chü* 8B, *T* 34.117a.

73. Theravādin tradition holds that the historic Buddha began his religious quest "four asankheyyas ('incalculably long eons') and a hundred thousand cycles ago" (T. W. Rhys Davids, *Buddhist Birth-Stories* [English translation of the *Jātaka-nidāna*] [London, n.d.], p. 82). For a similar view in the Mahāyānist literature see the *Shen-mi chieh-t'o-ching (Samdhinirmocana-sūtra)* 5, *T* 16.684c.

74. *Fa-hua-ching* 4, *T* 9.35b–c. When the *Lotus* was compiled c. first century A.D., it was not considered possible for a woman to attain enlightenment without first being reborn as a man.

75. This process of "jumping over," which occupies an important place in the T'ien-t'ai dogma, is technically termed *pei-chieh*. For a brief account see Ti-kuan, *T'ien-t'ai ssu-chiao-i*, *T* 46.778a.

T'ien-t'ai school, it entered an almost total eclipse during the first half of the T'ang dynasty. It is difficult to accept the explanation offered by some contemporary scholars that this sudden decline was due to a lack of suitable successors to Chih-i and Kuan-ting,[76] since they had a very large number of disciples who could carry on their work.[77] Furthermore, we have abundant evidence that the patriarchate was maintained at the Kuo-ch'ing-ssu. The compiler of the *Hsü-kao-seng-chuan*, completed in 664, demonstrated by his detailed biographies of Hui-ssu, Chih-i, Kuan-ting, and other T'ien-t'ai figures that he was familiar with the T'ien-t'ai tradition, as did Fa-tsang (643–712), the de facto founder of the Hua-yen school, who cited Chih-i's writings.[78] The fact that T'ien-t'ai texts were brought to Japan in 754 by the Vinaya master Chien-chen[79] indicates that despite the apparent waning of interest in T'ien-t'ai among the clerical elite during the first half of the T'ang, its literature was still circulating and its ideas were respected.

Since T'ien-t'ai is doctrinally inseparable from the T'ang schools, its decline throughout the first half of the T'ang ought not to be ascribed to a dogmatic bias on the part of prominent T'ang monks. Rather it would seem that the T'ang imperial family declined to give support to the T'ien-t'ai, as did those monks whom the state was patronizing, because of the extraordinarily close connections that existed between the T'ien-t'ai school and the Sui imperial house of Yang, now supplanted by the T'ang. Chih-i, in his last letter to Yang Kuang, repeatedly spoke of his "three obligations": to the Buddhist religion, to the state, and to all sentient beings, vowing that even after his death he would protect the territory of Prince Kuang. He gave advice to Yang Kuang on how to cope with economic problems arising from the shipment of tax grain and affirmed that both the land and its inhabitants belong to the prince.[80] We have noted that Yang Kuang—first as Crown Prince and then as Emperor—continued his support for the T'ien-t'ai community after Chih-i's death in 597. It is hardly surprising, then, that the newly estab-

76. Michihata Ryōshū, *Chūgoku bukkyōshi* [A History of Chinese Buddhism], 4th ed. (Kyoto, 1969), p. 131.

77. *CTP,T* 50.197c, credits him with having personally ordained more than fourteen thousand monks and states further that he had thirty-two disciples to whom he transmitted his teachings.

78. Shimaji Daitō, *Tendai kyōgakushi* [A history of T'ien-t'ai doctrine] (Tokyo, 1929), p. 118.

79. Genkai (fl. late eighth century), *Tō Daiwajō tōseiden* [A record of the journey to the East by the great T'ang monk (Chien-chen)], *Dainihon bukkyō zensho* 113.120a.

80. *KCPL* 3, doc. 65, *T* 46.810a–c.

lished T'ang ruling family did not look upon the T'ien-t'ai community with much enthusiasm.

THE FA-HSIANG SCHOOL

We observed earlier that the first three T'ang emperors could not be regarded as pious Buddhists in the same sense that the emperors of the southern dynasties were and that their concessions to the Buddhist church were based on political rather than religious considerations. Such considerations led T'ai-tsung and Kao-tsung to patronize the Fa-hsiang school, which completely dominated the scene in the capitals from the time of Hsüan-tsang's return from India in 645 to the usurpation of the T'ang throne by Empress Wu in 690, after which date the Fa-hsiang gradually began to lose influence among clerical scholars in Ch'ang-an and Loyang, until its lineage came to an end in the middle of the eighth century.[81] Judged by the sophisticated standards of Chinese Mahāyāna set by the T'ien-t'ai and acknowledged by the other T'ang schools, the Fa-hsiang can be regarded only as an anomaly in the development of Buddhist thought in China. The great, albeit short-lived, success that it scored under the reigns of T'ai-tsung and Kao-tsung can be understood only if we consider the personal relations between Hsüan-tsang and the T'ang rulers. Without these connections, the Fa-hsiang school, arriving from India when it did, would hardly have had so profound an impact on the Buddhist scholars in the great monasteries of seventh-century Ch'ang-an and Loyang.

The rise of the Fa-hsiang school is of course intimately connected with Hsüan-tsang (600–64), the prodigious translator who first introduced its ideas into China.[82] Even before his ordination in Ch'eng-tu at the age of twenty-two, Hsüan-tsang showed great interest in the *She-ta-ch'eng-lun* (*Mahāyāna-saṃgraha*),[83] a treatise belonging to the Yogācāra school of Indian Mahāyāna. His fascination with this text continued unabated during his subsequent studies under various masters

---

81. The last orthodox Fa-hsiang commentator was Chih-chou who died in 733 (*Bokuyō-kō hyōhaku-mon*, quoted in Fukihara Shōshin, *Nihon yuishiki shisōshi* [A history of Vijñaptimātratā thought in Japan] [Tokyo, 1944], p. 121).

82. The most detailed biography of Hsüan-tsang is the *Ta-tz'u-en-ssu San-tsang Fa-shih chuan* (*T* no. 2053), compiled by two of his disciples, Hui-li and Yen-tsung. There are two incomplete English translations: Samuel Beal, *The Life of Hiuen-Tsiang* (London, 1911), and Li Yung-hsi, *The Life of Hsüan-tsang* (Peking, 1959).

83. *T* nos. 1592, 1593, 1594, and 1596 (which includes the commentary by Vasubandhu). This treatise is the basic scripture of the She-lun school, the designation She-lun being an abbreviation of *She-ta-ch'eng-lun*.

in different parts of China. Convinced that this work could be properly understood only when the encyclopedic *Yogācāra-bhūmi*[84]—the fundamental treatise of the Yogācāra school—became available in Chinese, Hsüan-tsang resolved to go to India to procure a copy. In the year 629 he applied to the authorities for permission to journey abroad but was forbidden to leave the country. Since T'ai-tsung was at this time completing the process of consolidating the empire, his bureaucrats no doubt felt it too risky to allow one of his subjects to travel to foreign lands for such a dubious purpose as collecting Buddhist scriptures. Hsüan-tsang was nevertheless determined to pay a visit to India and left China surreptitiously, occasionally aided en route by highly placed Chinese officials who were well disposed toward Buddhism. In India, where he spent some fifteen years, Hsüan-tsang concentrated on the Yogācāra and Abhidharma doctrines. His principal teacher, under whom he studied for five years, was Śīlabhadra, an elder at Nālandā, the greatest center of Buddhist learning in India.

Śīlabhadra had been a disciple of Dharmapāla (died c. 560), a brilliant but highly unorthodox Mahāyāna thinker, whose views Śīlabhadra subsequently transmitted to Hsüan-tsang. Although East Asian Buddhists have traditionally regarded Dharmapāla as the authoritative interpreter of Vasubandhu, one of the most important Yogācāra philosophers, modern critical research based upon Indian and Tibetan sources unknown in China and Japan has established that Dharmapāla, for all his prominence in East Asian Buddhism, was a relatively minor figure in Indian Yogācāra who did not faithfully represent Vasubandhu's ideas in his commentaries.[85] Although firmly committed to such fundamental Mahāyāna teachings as the non-substantiality of all dharmas, the bodhisattva ideal, and the theory of the four bodies of the Buddha,[86] Dharmapāla, perhaps as a reflection of the frustrations encountered by the Buddhist community in India of his day, challenged a number of widely held Mahāyāna assumptions. He rejected, for example, the view found in the *Lotus* that the Three Vehicles are merely an expedient device designed to lead all men to the ideal of Buddhahood. The gap between Hīnayāna and Mahāyāna,

84. This work was translated by Hsüan-tsang in 648 under the title *Yü-chia shih-ti-lun* (*T* no. 1579).

85. Dharmapāla's position in the history of Indian Buddhism was first reappraised by Ui Hakuju in his monumental *Indo tetsugaku kenkyū* [Studies in Indian philosophy] (Tokyo, 1929 and 1930), vols. 5 and 6.

86. The body of the Buddha as he appears to unenlightened beings in this world, as he appears to bodhisattvas in the upper regions, as he appears to himself, and as an embodiment of the Absolute.

in his view, could not be bridged—each had its unique practices and each led to a different result, the former of course, being inferior to the latter. Dharmapāla argued that the man with a Hīnayāna mentality was constitutionally incapable of appreciating Mahāyāna, so absolute was the distinction between the two.[87] He also held firmly to the traditional view that enlightenment could be achieved only after undergoing complex meditations for a period of "three kalpas of incalculable length."[88] His highly scholastic conception of Buddhist religious practices had little sympathy for the pietism expressed in the *Lotus* that allowed an eight-year-old girl to attain Buddhahood.

Dharmapāla's sharpest break with orthodox Mahāyāna thinking is to be found in his repudiation of the doctrine of universal enlightenment. He did not maintain simply that some persons might not reach enlightenment, but argued that there was one category of people for whom the attainment of Buddhahood was impossible. Such beings, through no fault of their own, inherently lack what Dharmapāla termed "untainted seeds" and hence are eternally excluded from salvation.[89] The best that the unfortunate beings in this category might hope for is a round of favorable rebirths, which could be achieved by an accumulation of merit.

Such were some of the unconventional ideas that Hsüan-tsang picked up during his sojourn in India. The concept of three distinct vehicles and the view that Buddhahood was realizable only after a lengthy period of religious practice, although vehemently rejected by T'ien-t'ai, at least represented views that had been held by some monks belonging to the exegetical schools of the Nan-pei-ch'ao. However, the notion that one group of sentient beings was to be permanently excluded from salvation ran counter to the most cherished ideal of Chinese Buddhism. As far back as the beginning of the fifth century Tao-sheng had argued on the basis of an incomplete version of the *Nieh-p'an-ching* that even the most corrupt man was eligible for, and indeed would ultimately attain, enlightenment.[90] In view of this background, it seems strange at first glance that Hsüan-tsang should have accepted such doctrines during his stay in India. That he did so, however, is probably attributable to his deep personal attachment to his Indian master, Śīlabhadra, whom he regarded as the most authoritative spokesman of the Yogācāra school.

87. *Ch'eng-wei-shih-lun* 2, *T* 31.8a–b.
88. Tz'u-en, *Ch'eng-wei-shih-lun shu-chi* 9B, *T* 43.555c.
89. *Ch'eng-wei-shih-lun* 2, *T* 31.9a.
90. *Kao-seng-chuan* 7, *T* 50.366c.

If his biographies are to be believed, Hsüan-tsang won great fame in India. It is reported that he expounded the Dharma before kings, gave lectures on the scripture to monks and laymen, defeated heretics in debate, and composed a number of Sanskrit polemics. When he arrived in Turfan in 644 en route back to China, he took the precaution of sending T'ai-tsung a letter which, in addition to offering an apology for having left the country without authorization, contained a tantalizing description of his travels abroad. Hsüan-tsang did not fail to point out that while in India he "proclaimed the virtue of His Majesty so as to win the respect and admiration of the foreign people."[91] T'ai-tsung, not slow to sense that Hsüan-tsang with his unique firsthand knowledge of foreign lands could prove to be a valuable asset to the state, promptly replied that he was overjoyed that Hsüan-tsang was now returning and urged him to proceed to Ch'ang-an with all possible haste. Envoys were dispatched to make contact with him in Sha-chou whence he was to be conducted to the capital to receive an official welcome. Hsüan-tsang arrived at Ch'ang-an on the twenty-third day of the first month in the year 645 only to find that T'ai-tsung was in Loyang making preparations for his forthcoming campaign against Koguryŏ.

The first meeting between the two men, which was apparently a brief one, took place in Loyang on the first day of the second month. Their second meeting, of which we are fortunate to have a detailed account,[92] occurred on the twenty-third day of the same month. At this meeting Hsüan-tsang thought it prudent to apologize once again for his illegal flight abroad, while at the same time he took care to flatter T'ai-tsung by telling him that he (Hsüan-tsang) was able to complete safely his seventeen-year journey through foreign lands only because of the protection afforded by his being a subject of the emperor of China. T'ai-tsung then proceeded to question Hsüan-tsang in detail, needless to say, not about the latest trends of Buddhist thought in India, but about the "climate, products, and customs of the countries to the west of the Snowy Peaks." Apparently overwhelmed by Hsüan-tsang's thorough knowledge of conditions in foreign lands, T'ai-tsung requested that he present the throne with a written account of the countries that he had visited, which Hsüan-tsang did by the middle of the following year. There is no indication that T'ai-tsung at this point had any real interest in the new variety of Buddhism that Hsüan-tsang brought back, nor did he display any particular curiosity toward it. That he valued Hsüan-tsang primarily for his firsthand knowledge of foreign

91. Li, *The Life of Hsüan-tsang*, p. 203.
92. *Ta-tz'u-en-ssu San-tsang Fa-shih-chuan* 6, *T* 50.253a–c.

countries and not for his devotion to Buddhism can be seen from T'ai-tsung's exhortation to Hsüan-tsang that he abandon the religious life so that he might advise the emperor on political matters. Although Hsüan-tsang no doubt realized the benefits accruing from imperial support, he was not prepared to renounce his life's work for a political appointment. Rebuffed by Hsüan-tsang's refusal to return to lay life, T'ai-tsung sought to persuade him at least to travel with the imperial train during the Koguryŏ campaign, but Hsüan-tsang remained firm, protesting that this would be a violation of the precepts that he had vowed to uphold.

Thus faced with Hsüan-tsang's intransigence, T'ai-tsung decided to draw what advantage he could from this monk who, because of his unique experience and qualifications, had already attracted such great interest in the capitals. When Hsüan-tsang declared that it was his wish to serve the empire by translating the six hundred-odd texts that he had brought back from India and therefore sought permission from T'ai-tsung to take up residence at the Shao-lin monastery on Mount Shao-shih, southeast of Loyang, T'ai-tsung responded by offering to install Hsüan-tsang in the Hung-fu monastery, which had been built in Ch'ang-an some eleven years earlier in honor of T'ai–tsung's deceased mother. The emperor instructed the ranking minister, Fang Hsüan-ling, to give whatever material assistance Hsüan-tsang might require. As soon as Hsüan-tsang arrived at the Hung-fu monastery in the third month of 645, he requested Fang Hsüan-ling to make the necessary arrangements so that he might enlist services of "verifiers, stylists, secretaries, copyists, and so on."[93] By the sixth month no less than twenty-three monks, drawn from monasteries throughout China, had been brought to Ch'ang-an to collaborate with Hsüan-tsang. Among these early assistants were such distinguished monks as Tao-hsüan, Hsüan-ying, and Ch'ing-mai. When, in 648, Hsüan-tsang completed his translation of the *Yogācāra-bhūmi*, the text that had originally led him to India, T'ai-tsung honored him with a preface and had copies of the treatise distributed throughout the empire,[94] thereby helping to disseminate Fa-hsiang ideas. T'ai-tsung's son and successor, Kao-tsung, who ascended the throne in 649, continued his father's policy of supporting the translation projects of Hsüan-tsang, even inviting him on occasion to work within the imperial palaces.

From the time of his return to China in 645 until his death in 664

93. Ibid., 253c.
94. Ibid., 256a.

Hsüan-tsang devoted all his energies to translating the texts that he had brought back from India. Although his translations include texts belonging to most of the major traditions of Indian Buddhism, his primary concern, of course, was with the Yogācāra school, which in China came to be called the Fa-hsiang school. To him goes the credit for having made available in Chinese virtually all of the important works of this school. Backed by a large staff of able assistants, Hsüan-tsang translated a total of seventy-six different texts in 1,347 fascicles,[95] which was equivalent in size to almost one-quarter of the entire Chinese Buddhist canon as it existed in his day. In all, his output was more than three times greater than that of Kumārajīva, the next most productive translator. The support provided by T'ai-tsung and Kao-tsung enabled him to maintain a large group of disciples who systematically studied each of the newly translated Yogācāra texts and produced commentaries on them. The thoroughness with which each of the Yogācāra texts was examined was unprecedented in the history of Chinese Buddhism.[96] Yet the Fa-hsiang school, whose foundations Hsüan-tsang had so carefully laid, barely survived his death by seventy years. The reason for this sudden decline is not difficult to find.

Hsüan-tsang had introduced a form of Buddhism from India which, as we have noted above, ran counter to the ideals of Chinese Buddhism so recently given systematic expression by the T'ien-t'ai school. There is no doubt that many ideas of the Fa-hsiang school, such as its elaborate theories regarding the mind, its epistemology, its detailed analysis of the nature and varieties of illusion, its conception of the subconscious, and so on, aroused great interest in the world of Buddhist learning. But ultimately its exclusion of one group of sentient beings from even the possibility of attaining enlightenment and its rejection of the ideal of One Vehicle doomed this school to oblivion. Although imperial patronage assured Hsüan-tsang of a prominent position in the two capitals, with a large captive audience, he nevertheless encountered resistance from various monks, including his own associates. One of his earliest collaborators, Ling-jun, wrote a sharp denunciation of the new ideas introduced by Hsüan-tsang, pointing out fourteen differences between his "new" texts and the older versions translated by Paramārtha.[97] And even so close a disciple as Fa-pao, who wrote one of the two stan-

95. K'ai-yüan-lu 8, T 55.557b.

96. For a list of the commentaries produced by Hsüan-tsang's associates on each of the Yogācāra texts see Yūki Reimon, Genjō to sono gakuha no seiritsu [Hsüan-tsang and the formation of his school] Tōyō Bunka Kenkyūjo kiyō 11 (1956): 357–64.

97. Ling-jun's essay is quoted by the Japanese monk Saichō (767–822) in his Hokke shūku 2A, Nihon daizōkyō, Tendaishū kengyō shōsho 1.554a.

dard commentaries on Hsüan-tsang's translation of the *Abhidharma-kośa*,[98] took issue with his master on the question of whether some beings were doomed to endless transmigration.[99]

It should come as no surprise, then, that when Hsüan-tsang died in 664 and his collaborators scattered, often to join other translators, the Fa-hsiang school fell on hard days. Hsüan-tsang's mantle was inherited by Tz'u-en (632–82),[100] who had been personally ordained by Hsüan-tsang and had been charged by him with the task of propagating the Fa-hsiang doctrine.[101] Despite Tz'u-en's enormous literary output—twenty-eight works attributed to him still survive[102]—and the vital role he played in systematizing the Fa-hsiang teaching, he was not successful in attracting a large following of his own, probably because of the limited appeal of the Fa-hsiang doctrine. After the death of his master, Tz'u-en stayed on at the Ta-tz'u-en-ssu, the great monastery built in 648 by Kao-tsung while still crown prince for the repose of his mother's soul. Kao-tsung held Tz'u-en in high esteem and after the latter's death wrote a eulogy of him.[103]

THE HUA-YEN SCHOOL

After Kao-tsung became ill in 660, Empress Wu gradually began to concentrate political power in her own hands despite the opposition of her ailing husband and of some powerful figures at the court. When Kao-tsung died in 683, she put their twenty-seven-year-old son, Li Hsien (known as Emperor Chung-tsung), on the throne but promptly deposed him two months later in favor of his younger brother, Li Tan (Emperor Jui-tsung). It was probably about this time that Wu Chao began actively scheming to occupy the throne in her own right. Since the Confucian tradition did not allow a woman to govern the empire, Wu Chao obviously needed some authoritative statement that would lend legitimacy to her plans. A group of unscrupulous monks headed by Huai-i, who enjoyed entrée into the imperial palace and who is reputed to have been her lover at this time, conveniently discovered some

---

98. *Chü-she-lun-shu* (*T* no. 1822).

99. See his *I-ch'eng fo-hsing chiu-ching-lun* 3, *Dainihon zokuzōkyō* 1.95.4.377 recto b.

100. Tz'u-en's biography is given in later sources under the misnomer K'uei-chi. See my "Biographical Study of Tz'u-en," *Monumenta Nipponica* 15 (1959): 119–49.

101. *SKSC* 4, *T* 50.726a.

102. Four or five of these are dubious ascriptions. For a discussion of one such doubtful work see my "Authorship of the *Hsi-fang yao-chüeh*," *Transactions of the International Conference of Orientalists in Japan* 4 (1959): 12–25.

103. *SKSC* 4, *T* 50.726b.

passages in a sutra called the *Ta-yün-ching (Mahāmegha-sūtra)* which prophesied that seven hundred years after the passing away of the Buddha a pious woman would emerge as the ruler of an empire to which all countries would submit.[104] Not only was the woman in the prophesy identified with Wu Chao,[105] but it was also asserted that Wu Chao was an incarnation of Maitreya, the future Buddha.[106] In 690, the year in which Wu Chao replaced the T'ang dynasty with her own Chou dynasty, of which she was the first and only ruler, Huai-i was rewarded for his services with the title of Duke of O-kuo. Copies of the *Ta-yün-ching* with appropriate commentaries were ordered to be distributed throughout the empire. In the twelfth month of 690 it was decreed that a monastery designated Ta-yün-ssu should be constructed in each of the provinces as well as in the two capitals. The following year T'ai-tsung's rescript of 637, which gave precedence to Taoism over Buddhism, was formally rescinded.[107]

While there can be no doubt that Wu Chao used Buddhism for her own ends, she nevertheless appears to have had a sincere attachment to it. Her maternal grandfather was a member of the strongly pro-Buddhist Sui imperial family, and her mother is reputed to have been a pious Buddhist.[108] After the death of T'ai-tsung, whose concubine Wu Chao had been, she retired to a convent, the Kan-yeh-ssu, where she lived as a tonsured nun until being called into Kao-tsung's service. She showed herself as a patron of Buddhism as far back as 670 when, as the empress of Kao-tsung, she commissioned the construction of the T'ai-yüan-ssu in Ch'ang-an to commemorate her recently deceased mother.[109] The period of greatest activity at the Lung-men cave temples, it should be noted, coincides almost exactly with the years of Wu Chao's ascendancy in Ch'ang-an.[110] After the death of Kao-tsung she ordered the construction of the Ta-chien-fu-ssu in his memory.[111]

104. *T* 12.1107a.

105. *Wu-hou teng-chi ch'en-shu* [Prophesies concerning Empress Wu's accession to the throne], Stein MS no. 2658, reprinted in Yabuki Keiki, *Sangaikyō no kenkyū* [Studies relating to the Three Stages school] (Tokyo, 1926), pp. 686–94, esp. p. 686.

106. *CTS* 183.3554c. In the ninth month of 693 Empress Wu formally assumed the title "Universal Monarch" *(Chin-lun sheng-shen huang-ti)*. In 695 she added to this title the appellation "Maitreya," but dropped the latter one month later, after a sudden fire destroyed the Ming-t'ang (*CTS* 6.3076b).

107. *CTS* 6.3076a.

108. Kenneth Ch'en, *Buddhism in China* (Princeton, 1964), p. 220.

109. Ts'ui Chih-yüan, *T'ang Ta-chien-fu-ssu ku-ssu-chu fan-ching-ta-te Fa-tsang Ho-shang-chuan, T* 50.281b.

110. Tsukamoto Zenryū, *Shina bukkyōshi kenkyū* [Studies in the history of Chinese Buddhism] (Tokyo, 1942), p. 372.

111. Mochizuki Shinkō, *Bukkyō daijiten*, 4.3302a.

The Fo-shou-chi-ssu in Loyang, where I-ching did much of his translation, was another great temple sponsored by her.[112]

Like the pious rulers of earlier dynasties, Wu Chao enthusiastically
supported translation activities. She encouraged the work of Divākara,
an Indian monk who arrived in China in 676, by permitting him to
reside in such imperially sponsored temples as the T'ai-yüan-ssu and the
Hung-fu-ssu, where he was provided with a large staff of assistants.
Before his death in 687, Divākara managed to translate eighteen different Buddhist texts and was honored for his contributions to the canon
with an imperial preface composed by Wu Chao.[113] After becoming
interested in Hua-yen thought, about which we shall have more to say
below, Wu Chao dispatched an emissary to Khotan specifically to
invite Śikṣānanda to come to China. He arrived in 695 and promptly
began work on a new translation of the *Hua-yen-ching*, which he completed four years later at the Fo-shou-chi-ssu. Wu Chao herself attended
the lectures on the text as it was being translated and wrote a preface
for it that still survives.[114] When I-ching returned to China in 695 after
a stay of twenty-four years abroad, Wu Chao personally welcomed him
back at the gates of Loyang. Largely under her sponsorship I-ching
translated fifty-six texts in 230 fascicles and was granted an imperial
preface, as were the other translators supported by Wu Chao.[115]
Another literary enterprise which she encouraged was the compilation
of a new catalogue of the canon entitled *Ta-Chou-k'an-ting chung-ching
mu-lu*, completed in 695. The editor-in-chief, Ming-ch'üan, in his
preface to the catalogue, likened his imperial patroness to a universal
monarch who descends into this world to save all sentient beings.[116]

We have seen that when Wu Chao was scheming to usurp the T'ang
throne, she was not loath to use corrupt monks who would distort
texts and produce spurious commentaries as long as she could derive
some political advantage from them. Her decrees calling for the dis-
semination of the relatively unimportant *Ta-yün-ching* throughout the
empire and the construction of a Ta-yün-ssu in each province were
likewise clearly motivated by political considerations. Once she was
firmly established in power, however, she rid herself of these corrupt
monks; Huai-i, the most influential of them, was put to death in 695.
After this date she began to establish close relations with a number

112. Ibid. 5.4454b.
113. *K'ai-yüan-lu* 9, *T* 55.564a.
114. Ibid. 566a.
115. *SKSC* 1, *T* 50.710b–711a.
116. *T* 55.372c.

of respected Ch'an masters. A late eighth-century Ch'an text discovered at Tunhuang, called the *Li-tai fa-pao-chi*, mentions that in 697 Empress Wu summoned Chih-hsien, a disciple of the fifth patriarch of the Ch'an school, to the court.[117] Three years later she invited another disciple of the fifth patriarch, the famous Ch'an master Shen-hsiu, who was then ninety-five. When he presented himself the following year, he was treated with the utmost respect by Empress Wu, who excused him from the obligation of doing obeisance before the sovereign. He was given the title "Master of the Dharma in the Two Capitals and Teacher of the Three Rulers"[118] and honored accordingly.[119] So great was her respect for Shen-hsiu that she is said to have knelt before him when inquiring about the Dharma.[120] Another monk whom she summoned to the court at this time was Heng-ching (634–712), who belonged to the T'ien-t'ai school.[121] The *Sung-kao-seng-chuan*, which records this event, does not offer any explanation why a representative of the T'ien-t'ai school, which had been out of favor for some seventy years, should have been suddenly chosen to serve as Precepts Master *(shou-chieh-shih)* at the court. It seems likely that Wu Chao's decision to accord some degree of recognition to T'ien-t'ai at the imperial court was motivated by a desire to dissociate her newly established dynasty from the Fa-hsiang school, which had been receiving lavish support from the preceding T'ang emperors T'ai-tsung and Kao-tsung. Her partiality toward T'ien-t'ai was no doubt also influenced by her family ties to the Sui imperial household, the great benefactor of the T'ien-t'ai.

From the standpoint of the history of Buddhist thought in China, the most significant development during the reign of Empress Wu was the emergence of the Hua-yen school, which soon achieved prominence among the clerical elite, thanks to her support for its brilliant systematizer, Fa-tsang.[122] The Hua-yen school, as its name indicates, is based upon the *Hua-yen-ching*, a massive sutra,[123] which is a composite work consisting of a number of texts that had been circulating independently

117. Ibid. 51.184a.

118. A reference to Empress Wu and her two ex-emperor sons, Chung-tsung and Jui-tsung.

119. See Chang Yüeh's biographical notice of him in *CTW* 231. 1a–4b.

120. *SKSC* 8, *T* 50.756a.

121. Ibid. 6, *T* 50.732b–c.

122. For Empress Wu's involvement with the Hua-yen school see Kamata Shigeo, "Chūtō no bukkyō no hendō to kokka kenryoku" [Shifts in Buddhism during the "Middle T'ang" and state authority], *Tōyō Bunka Kenkyūjo kiyō* 25 (1961): 201–45; idem, *Chūgoku Kegon shisōshi no kenkyū* [Studies in the history of Hua-yen thought in China] (Tokyo, 1965), pp. 107–28.

123. In the *T* edition, the Buddhabhadra version covers 394 pages. The *Nieh-p'an-ching*, by comparison, covers 238 pages; the *Lotus*, 60 pages; and the major Pure Land scripture, the *Kuan-wu-liang-shou-fo-ching* (*T* no. 365), not quite 6 pages.

in India. Some portions of the *Hua-yen* are as early as the first century A.D., while other sections are considerably later. Although the *Hua-yen* has many ideas in common with the *Lotus,* such as the concept of One Vehicle, universal salvation, and the transcendental Buddha, it is in many ways a more sophisticated work philosophically, since it is, at least in part, a product of a later period. One of the most distinctive concepts in the *Hua-yen* is its view that the universe does not consist of a number of discrete elements, but rather is one perfectly integrated whole, each part being organically connected with every other part. From this standpoint the sutra teaches that there cannot be any ultimate distinction between the unenlightened man and the Buddha or between the Hīnayānist and the Mahāyānist. That such differences do exist in the empirical world the *Hua-yen* does not deny, but it ascribes them to illusions. This position led to an idealistic tendency in the *Hua-yen,* which can be seen in such well-known lines as "Just as paintings are produced by a master, so are all the worlds created by the artist in one's own mind"[124] and "The mind is like a skillful artist. . . . In all of the worlds there is not a single thing which it has not made."[125] Another feature of particular interest in the *Hua-yen* is its cosmology, which depicts a Pure Land presided over by Vairocana Buddha situated in the center of an infinite universe. Surrounding Vairocana's Pure Land in the ten directions are countless other worlds, each with its own Buddha, which reflect perfectly the central Pure Land of Vairocana in accordance with the *Hua-yen* principle of the interpenetration of all phenomena.

Although the *Hua-yen-ching* was translated in 420, the actual study of the text did not begin until the last decades of the fifth century. In its basic religious ideas, the *Hua-yen,* as we have observed, was similar to the *Lotus;* but it differed from the *Lotus* in that it contained a far more elaborate philosophical apparatus to justify these positions. The partisans of the *Hua-yen* naturally took pride in its doctrinal subtleties, while the devotees of the *Lotus* viewed these refinements in the *Hua-yen* as more of a hindrance than a help on the path to enlightenment. Although such noteworthy *Hua-yen* scholars as Fa-shun (557–640) and Chih-yen (602–68) were active during the reigns of T'ai-tsung and Kao-tsung, they were not given any significant support by the throne for the propagation of their ideas.[126] Chih-yen, who was the author of

---

124. *Hua-yen-ching* (Śikṣānanda version) 10, *T* 10.51c.
125. Ibid. (Buddhabhadra version) 10, *T* 9.465c.
126. Fa-shun's biography indicates that he was, in fact, esteemed by many prominent

fourteen works, five of which still survive, was one of the most able Buddhist scholars of his day. Yet we do not find in his biography[127] any indication that he was ever invited by T'ai-tsung or Kao-tsung to the court or that he was requested to lecture at any of the great imperial temples in the capital. T'ai-tsung, and Kao-tsung after him, were both committed to the support of Hsüan-tsang and the Fa-hsiang doctrines that he was disseminating.

As we have already seen, a new situation arose with the usurpation of the T'ang throne by Wu Chao in 690. Buddhism was again accorded precedence over Taoism and placed in a favored position. To justify her seizure of the throne, Wu Chao identified herself with the Buddhist ideal of the universal monarch who proclaims the Dharma for the benefit of all beings throughout the world. Because of the close connection between the Fa-hsiang school and the T'ang rulers whose dynastic line she was now attempting to replace, Wu Chao felt the need to associate herself with a different school of Buddhism, one which would glorify her reign. This she found in the Hua-yen, which, although representing the loftiest Mahāyāna ideals, was as yet untainted by an earlier, discredited imperial patronage. Seeing herself as a universal monarch, she must have been attracted by the Hua-yen with its well-ordered universe presided over by Vairocana Buddha, whose every act was reflected throughout the countless worlds. The analogy with the highly centralized imperial state that she ruled no doubt suggested itself to her.[128]

Wu Chao's connection with the Hua-yen school can be traced back at least to the year 670, when she ordered that Fa-tsang, an erstwhile disciple of Chih-yen be tonsured and appointed abbot of the T'ai-yüan-ssu, which she had just established in memory of her deceased mother.[129] Wu Chao apparently was very much impressed with Fa-tsang, for in 674 she instructed the ten senior monks *(ta-te)* in the capital to give him the highest ordination *(man-fen-chieh)*. To commemorate the occasion, Wu Chao granted Fa-tsang the honorific appellation

people at the court, not for his knowledge of the *Hua-yen-ching*, but for his alleged magical skills. See *HKSC* 25, *T* 50.653b–654a.

127. The earliest biography of Chih-yen is the one written by Fa-tsang in his *Hua-yen-ching-chuan-chi* 3, *T* 51.163b.

128. It might be mentioned here in passing that the *Hua-yen-ching* was viewed in a similar fashion in Japan during the reign of Emperor Shōmu (724–49). See Hashikawa Tadashi, *Sōgō Nihon Bukkyōshi* [A comprehensive history of Japanese Buddhism] (Tokyo, 1932), pp. 141–43.

129. The chronology of Fa-tsang's life is based on Hsü-fa, *Fa-chieh-tsung wu-tsu lüeh-chi* (*Dainihon zokuzōkyō* 1.2B.7.3.273 recto a–275 recto b).

Hsien-shou ("wise and preeminent"), by which he is still known. When shortly afterward he lectured on the *Hua-yen* at the T'ai-yüan-ssu, he was sent various gifts by the empress. From 680 onward Fa-tsang frequently consulted the translator Divākara on questions concerning the Sanskrit text of the *Hua-yen,* which probably led him to the conclusion that a new translation was needed. Wu Chao, as we have already noted, subsequently invited the Khotanese *Hua-yen* scholar, Śikṣānanda, to come to China for this purpose, and in 695, under her sponsorship, the second translation of this huge text was begun. The method of translation was similar to that employed by Hsüan-tsang, some of whose assistants were invited to take part in the project. Fa-tsang served as Śikṣānanda's secretary, and Empress Wu, in the fashion of the pious rulers of the preceding dynasties, personally participated in the editorial work.[130] When, in 697, rebellion broke out in border areas, Fa-tsang was requested to pray for victory of the imperial forces and was eulogized in an imperial edict when the issue was favorably resolved. Upon the completion of the translation of the *Hua-yen-ching* in 699, Empress Wu invited Fa-tsang to lecture on the text at the Ch'ang-sheng Palace. Since the empress had difficulty following the abstract ideas in the *Hua-yen-ching,* Fa-tsang resourcefully used a golden image of a lion in the palace to summarize in concrete terms the abstruse Hua-yen doctrines.[131] The outline of that celebrated lecture to Empress Wu survives under the title *Chin-shih-tzu-chang* [Essay on the golden lion].[132]

After Empress Wu died in 705, her son, the emperor Chung-tsung, who was restored to the T'ang throne, continued to support Fa-tsang as enthusiastically as his mother had done.[133] He commissioned an artist to paint a portrait of the distinguished monk and had a lengthy eulogy of him written. On the initiative of Fa-tsang, Chung-tsung ordered the construction of five Hua-yen monasteries, which were to serve as centers of Hua-yen learning and repositories for the writings of the patriarchs of this school. When Fa-tsang died in 712, he was honored with a state funeral and posthumously given the title of *Hung-lu-ch'ing.*

During the thirty-five years that Fa-tsang enjoyed the patronage of Wu Chao, he developed and systematized the Hua-yen doctrines and succeeded in establishing his school as one of the major lines within Chinese Buddhism. Appearing at a time when a new tradition of Buddhism was called for by prevailing political conditions, Fa-tsang,

130. Ibid., 274 recto a.
131. *SKSC* 5, *T* 50.732a.
132. *T* no. 1881.
133. *Fa-chieh-tsung wu-tsu lüeh-chi,* p. 274 verso a.

like Chih-i before him, rose to the occasion. Just as the latter was influenced by the Sui ideology to harmonize the disparate trends in the Buddhism of the Nan-pei-ch'ao, so Fa-tsang, as the formulator of a new school that was to be identified with the Chou dynasty, was led to synthesize the major lines of thought that had emerged during the preceding hundred years: the T'ien-t'ai of the Sui dynasty, the Fa-hsiang of the early T'ang, and the Hua-yen of the newly arisen Chou.

Fa-tsang accomplished this synthesis by devising a fivefold classification of Buddhist doctrine *(wu-chiao)*.[134] The first, and lowest, category for him, as well as for Chih-i, consisted of the Hīnayāna schools *(hsiao-ch'eng-chiao)*. The second category, designated "Elementary Teaching of Mahāyāna" *(ta-ch'eng shih-chiao)*, was divided into two parts: the first corresponding to the moribund San-lun school and the second, to the Fa-hsiang school. The third category, termed "Advanced Teaching of Mahāyāna" *(ta-ch'eng chung-chiao)*, referred to the Yogācāra doctrines as taught by the defunct Ti-lun and She-lun schools, which had been introduced into China before the time of Hsüan-tsang. The fourth category, called "Sudden Teachings" *(tun-chiao)*, encompassed the doctrines found in the *Wei-mo-ching (Vimalakīrti Sūtra)*, namely, the ineffable character of all religious experience and the suddenness of the attainment of enlightenment, which are both fundamental to Ch'an Buddhism. The fifth, and highest, category, termed "Perfect Teaching" *(yüan-chiao)*, embraced the concept of One Vehicle with its implicit promise of salvation for all beings. The category of Perfect Teaching was subdivided into two types: (a) that of the *Lotus*, that is, the T'ien-t'ai school, which was relatively inferior because it was based upon the negative concept of rejection, in that it repudiated the notion of Three Vehicles in favor of One Vehicle; and (b) that of the *Hua-yen*, which was relatively superior because it was based upon the direct revelation of the doctrine of One Vehicle in accordance with the principle of the interpenetration of all phenomena.

It is interesting to note here how neatly Fa-tsang's classification of the major schools of Buddhism corresponds to the political alignments of the founders of these schools. The Fa-hsiang school, for example, which was so closely identified with the T'ang dynasty, is placed in the second from the lowest category of teachings, behind even the Ti-lun and She-lun schools which it superseded. On the other hand, the Ch'an school, as yet still in its formative stage, is put in the second from the highest category, perhaps in deference to the great esteem in which Wu

134. Fa-tsang, *Hua-yen i-ch'eng chiao-i fen-ch'i-chang* 1, *T* 45.481b–482b.

Chao held various Ch'an monks whom she brought to the capital. The T'ien-t'ai school, which lost its stigma with the temporary eclipse of the T'ang, is suddenly elevated to the status of "Perfect Teaching" after having been ignored for close to a century.

In the foregoing dicussion we have endeavored to show that imperial patronage played a decisive role in the formation of the three philosophical schools of T'ang Buddhism. That each of these schools came to the forefront among the Buddhist elite at the time that it did was attributable not so much to the momentum of its own inner doctrinal development as to the close connection that existed between the de facto founder of the school and the imperial family. Although the T'ien-t'ai, Fa-hsiang, and Hua-yen schools each had highly complex metaphysical systems, each, in fact, also served a clearly definable political end. Hence abrupt changes in the political situation immediately affected the standing of these schools. There has been a tendency to regard the philosophical schools as having an independent existence of their own, totally unrelated to the society in which they developed. In this respect they have usually been contrasted with the "popular" schools of Pure Land and Ch'an. The truth is, however, that the philosophical schools were not formulated by monks who were immured in remote monasteries, but rather reflected, to a considerable degree, albeit in the recondite terminology of Buddhism, the political needs of their imperial patrons.

We cannot trace here the subsequent development of the T'ang schools in the eighth and ninth centuries, but we should note that imperial patronage—and after the An Lu-shan Rebellion, patronage by regional commanders and local magnates—continued to play a crucial role in the development of Buddhist thought. We have already mentioned that the sudden rise of Esoteric Buddhism *(mi-chiao)* during the reign of Hsüan-tsung was related to that emperor's interest in Taoist magic. Similarly, the infusion of Ch'an ideas into Hua-yen by Ch'eng-kuan (737–838) and Tsung-mi (780–841), the fourth and fifth patriarchs of this school, can be attributed to the support that these two monks received from military men, among whom Ch'an ideas had great appeal. The An Lu-shan Rebellion led to a decline in the emperor's authority, thus compelling monks to seek other, more reliable, sources of support, which in turn affected the future evolution of Buddhism. Pure Land and Ch'an, which had been steadily gaining adherents among the common people, lesser bureaucrats, and military men now had lay supporters who were emerging as patrons of leading monks, with the result that Pure Land and Ch'an ideas were incorporated into the once aristocratic schools. The decline in imperial authority following the An Lu-shan Rebellion marked the end of an era of unprecedented originality and creativity in the history of Chinese Buddhism, one which was distinguished by the appearance of new, highly syncretic schools that demonstrated beyond any doubt the extent to which the Chinese had grasped the intricacies of Buddhist thought.

9. Historical and Literary Theory in the Mid-Eighth Century

David McMullen

The outbreak of the An Lu-shan Rebellion in the late autumn of 755 is recognized as a turning point in the history of T'ang thought. The sudden disruption of over a century of internal peace stimulated the interest of intellectuals in social and political problems and forced them to reexamine their own tradition. A fresh critical spirit grew up. New emphasis was given to history and literature as disciplines relevant to the contemporary situation. Most modern accounts suggest, however, that this reawakening was a gradual process and portray the two decades after the rebellion as a time of delayed rather than immediate reaction, a period of preparation for the fuller flowering of intellectual life that occurred during the late eighth and early ninth centuries.[1] Only recently has it been pointed out that a lot of thinking and writing went on among those who actually lived through the rebellion.[2]

For the purposes of this chapter, I have studied five of the leading prose writers who were active during the rebellion period—Li Hua (c. 710–c. 767),[3] Hsiao Ying-shih (706–58),[4] Yüan Chieh (719–72),[5]

1. E.g., Aoki Masaru, *Shina bungaku shisōshi* (Tokyo, 1943), p. 98; Lo Ken-tse, *Chung-kuo wen-hsüeh p'i-p'ing shih* (Shanghai, 1957), vol. 1, pp. 122–27; Ch'ien Tung-fu, *T'ang Sung ku-wen yün-tung* (Shanghai, 1962), pp. 11–14. All these accounts treat this period as one of preparation for the ninth-century *ku-wen* movement.

2. E. G. Pulleyblank, "Neo-Confucianism and Neo-Legalism in T'ang Intellectual Life, 755-805," in *The Confucian Persuasion*, ed. A. F. Wright (Stanford, Calif., 1960), pp. 84–88. My debt to this article will be apparent in the following pages.

3. Li Hua, biographies in *CTS* (*Po-na* edition) 190C.1a–b and *HTS* (*Po-na* edition) 203.1a–b; prose works in *CTW* (Taipei, 1965 reprint) 315.1a–321.19a and *T'ang wen shih-i* (Taipei, 1962 reprint) 19.13a–b; poems in *CTShih* (Peking, 1960), vol. 3, pp. 1585–90. Li's approximate dates may be inferred from his *HTS* biography, his collected works, and the fact that he was about the same age as Hsiao Ying-shih, having studied with him in the T'ai-hsüeh before coming of age; see *T'ang wen-ts'ui* (*SPTK* edition) 15B.5b. Li was alive but sick in 766; see *CTW* 315.10a and note 138 below.

Tu-ku Chi (725–77),[6] and Yen Chen-ch'ing (709–84).[7] Before analyzing their remarks on history and literature, I have sketched their family backgrounds and described briefly the intellectual world in which they grew up. This may yield some understanding of their motives in writing, and perhaps also of their thought.

These five men were, their writings tell us, closely connected with one another. They knew each other at various times in their lives and often dedicated works to one another. They had much in common in background and attitudes, since all five came from cadet branches of long-established aristocratic clans that had intermarried in T'ang times. Hsiao Ying-shih gave an informal account of his own origins in a long letter to Wei Shu, a leading official historian, written before the rebellion. Hsiao was descended from one of the princes of the Liang royal house. His ancestors had served the Sui and T'ang in some numbers and with considerable distinction, but since the late seventh century, he had had no forebear of rank.[8] This combination of an illustrious pedigree with immediate ancestors of no great eminence was typical of the intellectuals in the group.

Less is known of Li Hua's immediate descent. But from remarks made in commemorative works for members of his clan and from independent genealogical sources, it is clear that he was from the Li clan of Chao-chün. This was the nonimperial Li family, distinct from the Lung-hsi Li clan, the T'ang royal house, from which they gained a certain amount of reflected luster.[9]

4. Hsiao Ying-shih, biographies in *CTS* 190C.1b–2a and *HTS* 202.12a–13b; prose works in *CTW* 322.1a–323.24a; poems in *CTShih*, vol. 3, pp. 1591–98, and vol. 12, p. 9970. T'ang Cheng-pi puts Hsiao's death at 768; see *Chung-kuo wen-hsüeh-chia ta tz'u-tien* (Taipei, 1962 reprint), vol. 1, p. 292. This date, which is accepted by Pulleyblank ("Neo-Confucianism and Neo-Legalism," p. 86), is almost certainly wrong. Li Hua, Hsiao's lifelong friend, offered him a sacrificial graveside prayer in 760 (*CTW* 321.16b–17a). He also grouped him with Yüan Te-hsiu, who died in 754 (*CTW* 383.21b) and Liu Hsün, who died c. 761 (*HTS* 132.3a), in his "Essay on the Three Sages" (*CTW* 317.3b–7a). *CTS* 202.14b moreover says that Hsiao died "at the start of Ch'ien-yüan (c. 758)."

5. Yüan Chieh, biography in *HTS* 143.2a–5a; prose works in *CTW* 380.1a–383.27b; poems in *CTShih*, vol. 4, pp. 2690–717, vol. 12, p. 10052, and *Ch'üan T'ang shih-i*, in *CTShih*, vol. 12, pp. 10214–17; on the identification of these poems, see Ōta Shōjirō, "Kaiyō sen chō kō," *Rekishi chiri* 86, no. 2 (1955): 31–54. I accept the dating argued by Sun Wang, *Yüan Tzu-shan nien-p'u* (Shanghai, 1962), p. 1.

6. Tu-ku Chi, biography in *CTS* 162.1b–3a; prose works in *CTW* 384.1a–393.26a and *T'ang wen shih-i* 22.7b; poems in *CTShih*, vol. 4, pp. 2760–79.

7. Yen Chen-ch'ing, biographies in *CTS* 128.5a–9b and *HTS* 153.5a–9b; prose works in *CTW* 336.1a–344.25a and *T'ang wen shih-i* 19.22b–20.1a; poems in *CTShih*, vol. 3, pp. 1582–84, vol. 11, pp. 8880–86.

8. *CTW* 323.11a–b.

9. *CTW* 388.11b; *Yüan-ho hsing tsuan* (1802 edition) 1.1a; Li Chao, *Kuo-shih pu* (Shanghai,

Yüan Chieh was descended from the ruling house of the Toba Wei dynasty.[10] Collateral members of his clan, like the historian and canonical scholar Yüan Hsing-ch'ung, had distinguished themselves in the early eighth century, but Yüan's own grandfather and father had not held high office, and he spoke of "two generations of impoverishment."[11] Such claims of deprivation in early life by writers of this period should be treated with reserve, since poverty, after all, was highly honorable and part of the topos for the virtuous scholar. But in Yüan's case the facts about illustrious remoter origins and immediate forebears of no great distinction are unassailable.

Tu-ku Chi came from what must have been the most illustrious Turkic clan not to have claimed full imperial honors, one which had provided consorts for the emperors of Sui and T'ang. His writings for relatives prove that he was very conscious of his origins, but again, his father had not held high rank.[12]

Finally Yen Chen-ch'ing came from a Chinese gentry family with the strongest traditions of scholarship and bureaucratic service, dating back to the end of the Han period. He too was interested in his clan history and wrote on the subject.[13]

Families with such a glorious but remote history and a more obscure record in recent times might well be expected to be conservative. It is not surprising to find them interested in those periods of the past when their own clans had flourished. Hsiao Ying-shih, for example, showed special interest in the Liang period, writing several works on it;[14] and Yüan Hsing-ch'ung, a collateral cousin of Yüan Chieh active in the K'ai-yüan period (713–41), wrote a history of the Wei dynasty.[15]

1957), p. 20. Li Hua composed commemorative texts for both clans, e.g., *CTW* 321.5a–7a and 11b–12a for the Chao-chün clan, ibid., 321.9b–11b for the Lung-hsi clan.

10. *HTS* 143.2a and *CTW* 344.16a.

11. *CTW* 381.12b.

12. For remarks on the Tu-ku family in Sui and early T'ang times, see Woodbridge Bingham, *The Fall of Sui and Rise of T'ang* (Baltimore, 1941), p. 5. The emperor T'ai-tsung also took a concubine from the clan; see Chao Lin, *Yin-hua lu* (Shanghai, 1957), p. 69. For Tu-ku Chi's immediate ancestry and family, see Ts'en Chung-mien, *T'ang chi chih-i*, in *T'ang jen hang-ti lu* (Peking, 1962), p. 361; also *CTW* 522.3a.

13. *CTW* 337.10a–b.

14. *HTS* 202.12b lists a "Genealogy for the Liang Hsiao Clan" and an essay on the question of dynastic legitimacy as it involved the Liang, "Essay on the Fact that the Liang Did Not Abdicate for the Ch'en." See also Pulleyblank, "Neo-Confucianism and Neo-Legalism," p. 86, and Hiraoka Takeo, *Keisho no dentō* (Tokyo, 1951), pp. 107–10. Hsiao's interest in the Liang was not consistent with his sweeping dismissal of the entire Period of Disunion, for which see below.

15. The *Wei tien*, in 30 *chüan*, by Yüan Hsing-ch'ung a chronicle style history for the Later Wei rather than a compendium; see *CTS* 102.9b and *HTS* 48.5b.

But these men, though of aristocratic descent, were no longer courtiers, nor did they have significant local power. They depended for their own advancement on the examination system, the civil service, and the bureaucratic state. Though they often had an ambivalent attitude toward those in power, they were deeply committed to the T'ang and to the idea of a great, united, and long-lived dynasty. Their loyalty to the T'ang modified their clan ties, leading them, as we shall see, to prefer the Han empire to the Period of Disunion, when their ancestors had been preeminent.

The record of the five men in the examination system testifies to their cohesion as a group. Two examiners were responsible for admitting all five to their degrees. Hsiao Ying-shih, Li Hua, Yen Chen-ch'ing, and also Yüan Chieh's cousin and teacher Yüan Te-hsiu all passed under Sun Ti in the late K'ai-yüan period.[16] Tu-ku Chi and Yüan Chieh passed in late T'ien-pao (742–56), during the brief interlude between the dictatorship of Li Lin-fu and the outbreak of war. Their examiner was Yang Chün, who in his selection reportedly took the advice of Hsiao Ying-shih, ten or more of whose disciples were successful.[17] It is highly likely that Yüan Chieh, whose cousin Hsiao admired,[18] and Tu-ku Chi, whom Li Hua thought highly of,[19] were helped on the way by Hsiao Ying-shih.[20]

Four of the five men were teachers and had disciples following them both before and after the rebellion. Hsiao Ying-shih, whose pupils were so successful in the examinations of the late T'ien-pao, was particularly influential in this role. When some of them gathered to feast him in 754, they gratefully likened him to Confucius himself: "The subtle words of the First Teacher came to an end over a thousand years ago. Only after the advent of our Master has their immeasurable beauty been restored.[21]" In reply Hsiao dwelt on the great responsibili-

16. Yüan Te-hsiu, Yüan Chieh's cousin, graduated *chin-shih* in 733, see Hsü Sung, comp., *Teng-k'o chi-k'ao (Nan-ching shu-yüan ts'ung-shu* edition) 8.3a; Yen Chen-ch'ing in 734 (ibid., 8.4a); Li Hua, Hsiao Ying-shih, and also the historian Liu Fang (see note 86) in 735 (ibid., 8.11a–12b). Yen Chen-ch'ing (*CTW* 337.12a–b) and Hsiao Ying-shih (*CTW* 323.9a) paid tribute to Sun Ti.

17. Yüan Chieh gained his *chin-shih* in 754 (*Teng-k'o chi-k'ao* 9.27b). Tu-ku Chi was successful in a Taoist degree examination in the same year (ibid., 9.28a). For Hsiao Ying-shih's part in the selection of graduates, see *CTW* 317.6b and *CTShih*, vol. 3, p. 1594.

18. *HTS* 202.12a; *CTShih*, vol. 3, p. 1595.

19. *CTW* 522.4a.

20. For the friendship between Yen Chen-ch'ing, Li Hua, and Hsiao Ying-shih before the rebellion, see *CTW* 317.7a. Some of this circle had met before coming of age, at the T'ai-hsüeh; see *T'ang wen-ts'ui* 15B.5b, *HTS* 202.13b and 151.4b.

21. *CTW* 395.5a.

ties of the teacher in the four branches of instruction traditional to Confucianism—virtuous conduct, ability in speaking, administrative service, and literature and scholarship.[22] He evidently made a great impression on his pupils, for they remembered him years after his death.[23]

Li Hua was involved in educational writing. His letter to two maternal granddaughters about to be married is the only surviving example of the *chia-hsün* ("family injunctions") type of literature written by any of the five men studied here.[24] A preface to the educational handbook *Meng-ch'iu* is also ascribed to him[25]. He too might have been a teacher had he not been captured by the An Lu-shan rebels and forced to collaborate. Though a prospective pupil later came from afar to visit him, he did not feel qualified to give instruction.[26]

Yüan Chieh's cousin Yüan Te-hsiu had had disciples, Li Hua and Hsiao Ying-shih among them;[27] and Yüan Chieh himself followed suit. When still a young man he called his pupils "little ones" in the manner of the *Analects*.[28] After the rebellion, as governor of Tao-chou in the far south, he too attracted pupils from a distance.[29]

Tu-ku Chi as a governor in the southeast after the rebellion was also interested in education and personally appointed a lecturer to his prefectural school. A visitor there testified to the way in which Tu-ku "governed by virtuous conduct, learning, and literature, so that within a year Confucianism had spread widely."[30]

Their roles as public exemplars and teachers may help to explain the highly serious and moral positions these men took on most issues and the dry tone of much of their writings. This may also have been a secondary factor legitimizing their intellectual conservatism, since the Confucian Classics tended to advocate a conservative outlook and led students to look back to a better past.

One area in which these five intellectuals differed was religion.

22. *CTShih*, vol. 3, p. 1594; *Analects* (*HYISIS* edition) 11.3.

23. *HTS* 203.14a. Several of Hsiao's disciples composed an "Essay on the Collected Works of Hsiao Ying-shih," since lost; see also *CTW* 395.3b. Hsiao's disciples gave him the posthumous name of Wen-yüan hsien-sheng (*HTS* 202.13b). He was also invited to go to Japan or Korea (*CTW* 395.5a).

24. *CTW* 315.3a-4b.

25. *T'ang wen shih-i* 19.13a-b.

26. *CTW* 315.15a.

27. *HTS* 202.12a and 194.1b. Li Hua gave Yüan Te-hsiu the posthumous name of Wen-hsing hsien-sheng.

28. *CTW* 383.4b; *Analects* 3.24, 7.24.

29. *CTW* 381.19b; *CTS* 185B.14a.

30. *CTW* 518.24a.

Under Hsüan-tsung there had been a state-sponsored revival of intellectual Taoism,[31] and for a time in the T'ien-pao period knowledge of Taoism considerably helped a man's examination and career prospects. This and a family tradition of interest in Huang-Lao may account for the Taoist orientation of much of Yüan Chieh's early thinking.[32] Toward Buddhism, in his one recorded encounter with it, Yüan expressed only a good-humored sense of mystification.[33]

Tu-ku Chi's early interest in Taoism seems to parallel that of Yüan Chieh. He was successful in a Taoist decree examination of 753.[34] After the rebellion, when they both held governorships in the south, Taoism offered Yüan and Tu-ku psychological solace in times of stress.[35] But, unlike Yüan, Tu-ku had also become interested in Buddhism, which he studied with dedication. He clearly derived comfort from it, for he told his friends to do likewise,[36] and he was familiar with the history of the Buddhist monasteries he visited and with certain Buddhist texts and their doctrines.[37]

Buddhism seems to have been a diversion, or perhaps a consolation, to Hsiao Ying-shih, who wrote that he had fond memories of "sitting together with good friends, being served with tea from time to time, criticizing the sages of antiquity, and discussing Buddhist scriptures."[38] He is known to have read and studied sutras with his lifelong friend Li Hua.[39]

Li, at least in later life, had an active interest in Buddhism, which led him to compose commemorative texts for foreign Tantric priests[40] and to be connected with the eighth and ninth partriarchs of the T'ien-tai sect.[41] Although his thought elsewhere suggests skepticism,[42] he accepted the claims of Buddhist thaumaturgy. Li seems to have looked to Buddhism also as a means of escape from an oppressive personal situation, from the guilt he felt over his collaboration. The long

31. Hsiao Kung-ch'üan, *Chung-kuo cheng-chih ssu-hsiang shih* (Taipei, 1954 reprint), pp. 423 and 439n1–3.

32. *CTW* 383.10b, 11b, and 18a.

33. *CTW* 383.24a.

34. *Teng-k'o chi-k'ao* 9.28a.

35. *CTW* 386.11a and *CTShih*, vol. 4, p. 2704, both instances relating to times when they were prefectural governors threatened with heavy tax demands on exhausted populations.

36. *CTShih*, vol. 4, p. 2771.

37. E.g., *CTW* 389.20a and 24b.

38. *CTW* 323.11b.

39. *CTS* 190C.1a; *HTS* 203.1b.

40. Chou I-liang, "Tantrism in China," *HJAS* 8 (1945): 250–51.

41. *FTTC* 188b, 189a, in *T* (Tokyo, 1924–32), vol. 49.

42. *CTW* 317.10a. Li was not as systematic a skeptic as was, for example, Lü Ts'ai (*CTW* 160.10a–15b) at the start of the dynasty.

poems he wrote toward the end of his life reflecting on his predicament end with expressions of dedication to Buddhism.[43] Tu-ku Chi testified to his colleague's devotion to the faith when he wrote of him in his final years that "he looked upon rank and salary and his own body as if they were merely his remains in the soil."[44]

Yen Chen-ch'ing's religious interests were possibly the most unusual of the group. He was a believer in the Taoist pantheon and in the miracles and apparitions of its tradition.[45] But he also had extensive social contacts with Buddhism and knew the history of the monasteries he visited.[46]

Such diversity in religious interests among so homogeneous a group need cause no surprise. It is well known that in T'ang China there was, within predictable limits, no interference in private beliefs. Buddhism and Taoism generally affected only the private areas of a lay follower's conduct and provided little in the way of active social values. It is true that Yüan Chieh, before taking an examination in 747, had written an essay suggesting that Taoism had once offered a social ideal, but he did so probably with an eye to the emperor's interest in the subject and before he had had administrative experience.[47] In areas where society was involved, such as historical and literary theory, members of the group in their maturity all turned to the Confucian tradition, endorsing it with a unanimity that stands in contrast to the diversity of their interests in religion.

The scholarly careers of the five men were greatly affected by the rebellion. Late T'ang tradition was to look back on the reign of Hsüan-tsung, the age in which they started their careers and which shaped their expectations, as one of the great periods of the dynasty and indeed of all time.[48] But even in the two decades after the outbreak of rebellion, before distance in time had lent them charm, intellectuals felt nostalgia for the years of security and prosperity. Thus Yen Chen-ch'ing wrote of the good government of the Chen-kuan (627–49) and K'ai-yüan

---

43. *CTShih*, vol. 3, pp. 1587, 1589.

44. *CTW* 388.11b.

45. *CTW* 338.25a.

46. E.g., *CTW* 339.2a, 2b. The work professing nonbelief in Buddhism ascribed to Yen in *CTW* 337.18b–19a which opens, "I do not believe in the Buddhist Law, but like staying in Buddhist monastaries . . . ," is very reasonably rejected as spurious by the commentator in *Yen Lu-kung chi* (*SPPY* edition) 5.5b–6a. Ou-yang Hsiu strongly disapproved of Yen's Buddhist and Taoist leanings; see *Ou-yang Yung-shu chi* (*Kuo-hsüeh chi-pen ts'ung-shu* edition), ch. 16, p. 3.

47. *CTW* 383.12a; see also Hsiao Kung-ch'üan, *Chung-kuo cheng-chih ssu-hsiang shih*, p. 425.

48. Chang Yen-yüan, *Li-tai ming-hua chi,* translated by W. R. B. Acker, *Some T'ang and Pre-T'ang Texts on Chinese Painting* (Leiden, 1965), p. 203; see also *CTW* 555.18a.

periods,[49] and Yüan Chieh reminisced about the "great peace" in which he had grown up.[50] Li Hua recalled it as a time when "the world was at peace, and the gentleman *(chün tzu)* was able to take his leisure with learning, so that in the field of letters men of great ability abounded."[51]

In history and literature, the particular concerns of this paper, the volume of production in the first half of the eighth century had been considerable. Many of the intellectuals of the time had led secure working lives in the academies, the imperial library, or the history office and had had exceptionally long careers in scholarship, particularly in the field of history. Thus Wu Ching, who died in 749, had held posts as a historian for nearly thirty years[52] and had had a hand in some twenty-two works.[53] Wei Shu, who died in 757, had had a scholarly life spanning forty years, twenty of which were spent as an official historian working on almost all the types of historical writing then practiced.[54] Yet these are only two examples of a type of scholar active in Hsüan-tsung's reign, and there were many others like them.[55] The *New T'ang History*'s bibliography indicates the range of their work: official histories, chronicle form histories, informal historical works, collections of anecdotes and biographies, works on institutions, ritual, law, bibliography, genealogy, and geography.[56]

Nor should it be thought that this activity was all purely mechanical and uncritical or that the state was the only initiator of large-scale scholarly projects. Liu Chih-chi (661–721) is perhaps the best-known critic of state-sponsored scholarship in all Chinese history, and his *Shih-t'ung* is one of the most systematic works of intellect to have come to us from the first half of the eighth century.[57] But there were other scholars showing independence and a critical sense. Even an official historian like Wu Ching could disapprove of the imperially sanctioned

49. *CTW* 336.13a–b.

50. *CTShih*, vol. 4, pp. 2704–05.

51. *CTW* 315.9a.

52. Wu Ching, biographies in *CTS* 102.12a–b and *HTS* 132.3b–5a.

53. These are listed in *I-wen chih erh-shih chung tsung-ho yin-te* (Peking, 1933), p. 35.

54. Wei Shu, biographies in *CTS* 102.13a–14a and *HTS* 132.5a–6a; works listed in *I-wen chih erh-shih chung tsung-ho yin-te*, p. 172.

55. E.g., Hsü Chien, biographies in *CTS* 102.8a–9a and *HTS* 199.2a–3a, works listed in *I-wen chih erh-shih chung tsung-ho yin-te*, p. 188; Yüan Hsing-ch'ung, known as Yüan Tan, biographies in *CTS* 102.9a–12a and *HTS* 200.2a–3b, works listed in *I-wen chih erh-shih chung tsung-ho yin-te*, p. 62; T'ang Ying, for whose works see *HTS* 58.5b.

56. *HTS* 58.1a.

57. See E. G. Pulleyblank, "Chinese Historical Criticism: Liu Chih-chi and Ssu-ma Kuang," in *Historians of China and Japan* (London, 1961), pp. 135–51, and William Hung, "A T'ang Historiographer's Letter of Resignation," *HJAS* 29 (1969): 5–52.

histories of earlier dynasties and revise them for his own purposes.[58] There was criticism of the authorized canonical commentaries,[59] at least one lively bibliographical controversy on the Classics,[60] and debate on the best form for writing histories.[61] Hsiao Ying-shih took part in this dispute not long before the rebellion, advocating, as we shall see, the chronicle form, and planning a long chronicle-style history himself.

Literature had flourished in the pre-rebellion period as never before. Some ten thousand poems survive from the first half of the century. Early in Hsüan-tsung's reign the regulated styles of verse had commanded most prestige, but in late K'ai-yüan and T'ien-pao freer forms were also popular. Themes varied from the fantasy journeys of Li Po to the frontier campaign verse of Ts'en Shen and Kao Shih, from the quietist nature poems of Wang Wei to the poetry of social criticism that Yüan Chieh had begun to write as a young man.[62] This was an age of great self-confidence, when the compiler of a comprehensive anthology of verse just before the rebellion could claim in a preface addressed to the emperor that "after K'ai-yüan 15 (727), both tonal regulations and vigorous style attained perfection for the first time."[63]

Literary criticism had also flourished, though it could not rival historical criticism in producing any long or systematic treatises. The ability to write verse was taken for granted among the educated, but for the technically more exacting forms, like the *chüeh-chü* or *lü-shih*, handbooks of rules and examples were written. Indeed this prescriptive criticism was the kind most typical of the late seventh and early eighth centuries,[64] when, as writers of the rebellion period remind us, the regulated styles attained their final form.[65] Throughout Hsüan-tsung's

58. *CTS* 102.12b.

59. *CTW* 272.2a, and K. P. Kramers, "Conservatism and the Transmission of the Confucian Canon: A T'ang Scholar's Complaint," *Journal of the Oriental Society* 2 (1955): 118–32

60. William Hung, "A Bibliographical Controversy at the T'ang Court, A.D. 719," *HJAS* 20 (1957): 74–134.

61. Liu Chih-chi's comments on this controversy are given in *Shih-t'ung t'ung-shih* (*SPPY* edition) 2.1a–3a; see also below at note 129.

62. For this fourfold characterization compare Liu Ta-chieh, *Chung-kuo wen-hsüeh fa-chan shih* (Shanghai, 1949), pp. 333–80. For Yüan's "social realist" verse see *CTShih*, vol. 4, pp. 2696–98 and 2703.

63. *CTW* 436.20b.

64. *HTS* 60.15a lists five works of prescriptive criticism likely to have been written between early T'ang and the An Lu-shan Rebellion. Some of these were incorporated in Kūkai's *Bunkyō hifuron* and preserved in Japan; see *Bunkyō hifuron*, annotated and indexed by Konishi Jinichi (Tokyo, 1953).

65. This judgment was made very early, for example by Tu-ku Chi (*CTW* 388.1a). Cf. note 64; and the modern critic Wang Yün-hsi, in "Shih *Ho-yüeh ying-ling chi* hsü lun sheng T'ang shih-ko," *T'ang shih yen-chiu lun-wen chi* (Peking, 1959), p. 28, who gives the same judgment.

reign anthologies were compiled, and their prefaces, setting out the criteria for the selection of the poems they contained, were an important vehicle for criticism. Critical remarks are also to be found scattered in the verse of the period. This was a kind of "work-shop criticism," to borrow T. S. Eliot's phrase,[66] and though random and unsystematic, sometimes offers clues to the attitudes of writers who did not otherwise commit themselves.[67]

The security and wealth of the intellectual world in which the five men grew up is also suggested by its libraries; this was a period of great collections. The imperial library itself had an establishment of a director, two vice-directors, and some seventeen staff;[68] before the rebellion both Yen Chen-ch'ing[69] and Hsiao Ying-shing[70] held posts in it. The imperial collection contained over fifty thousand *chüan*.[71] And there were large private libraries as well—Wu Ching, the historian, had a collection large enough to need its own catalog,[72] and Wei Shu one of some two thousand *chüan*.[73] There were also many valuable collections of paintings.[74]

The sack of Ch'ang-an in 756 destroyed forever the security that had fostered this learning and wealth. Many intellectuals fled south to the lower Yangtse or attempted to join the loyalist forces at the temporary capital in the west. But a significant number, like Li Hua and Wei Shu the historian, were forced to collaborate with the rebels.[75] The cause of intellectuals was further discredited when Fang Kuan, one of the intellectual leaders before the rebellion, offered the emperor disastrously bookish advice during the military crisis of 756.[76] During the next decade or so, power belonged with military men, and intellectuals were, by comparison with pre-rebellion days, in the wilderness.

66. T. S. Eliot, "The Frontiers of Criticism," in *On Poetry and Poets* (London, 1957), pp. 106–07.

67. See the two articles by Itō Masafumi, "Sei Tō shijin to zendai no shijin—jō," *Chūgoku bungaku hō* 8 (1958): 93–135, and "Sei Tō shijin to zendai no shijin—ge," *Chūgoku bungaku hō* 10 (1959): 17–51.

68. R. des Rotours, *Traité des fonctionnaires* (Leiden, 1947), pp. 204–08.

69. *CTW* 514.10a.

70. *HTS* 202.12b.

71. *CTS* 46.1b; cf. *HTS* 57.1a–b.

72. *CTS* 102.2b.

73. *CTS* 102.13a.

74. Acker, *Some T'ang and Pre-T'ang Texts on Chinese Painting*, pp. 204–05, 207–08.

75. *TCTC* (Peking, 1956), ch. 220, p. 7042, mentions a figure of three hundred officials. Apart from Wei Shu, Li Hua, Chao Hua, and Shao Chen were among the intellectuals forced to collaborate; see *CTShih*, vol. 3, p. 1588. Also, for Ch'u Kuang-hsi, see Hsin Wen-fang, *T'ang ts'ai-tzu chuan* (Shanghai, 1957), p. 18.

76. *TCTC*, ch. 219, p. 7004. For this episode and its background, see Pulleyblank, "Neo-Confucianism and Neo-Legalism," pp. 98–99.

All the five men under review were much affected by the war. Tu-ku Chi was a junior official of a county near the capital when he was forced to flee to the southeast. He took up local office there, and this service led to his reappointment to the region in later life. Yüan Chieh, though a *chin-shih* of 754, held no office at the outbreak of war. He fled to the Yangtse Valley, and his official career started only in late 757 when he was summoned north to give advice to the emperor. He later claimed that he had originally wanted "some leisurely appointment in an office to do with letters,"[77] but he was soon involved in mustering troops in Honan. Almost all his later serving career was spent in the south, sometimes under dangerous and isolated conditions. He was finally summoned to Ch'ang-an in 772 but died before reappointment.

Of all the group Hsiao Ying-shih had advanced his scholarly career furthest by the outbreak of war. He had established himself as a teacher, had held an appointment in the imperial library, sought the patronage of Wei Shu the historian, and had written a number of works on history. He might have continued to work on larger projects if the rebellion had not denied him the opportunity. When the war broke out, he fled to Hsiang-yang in Honan and then took up minor office with a military governor in the southeast. In 758, however, he died in Honan while trying to move his father's coffin south for reburial.

Li Hua fared worst of the group, for he was taken by the rebels while trying to rescue his mother and was forced to collaborate. He was later pardoned and in 758 summoned to court. But he felt that his service with the rebels permanently disqualified him from office and, in his own words, "made bold to disobey the order of the court and follow my private wishes,"[78] by remaining in retirement in the lower Yangtse area.

Yen Chen-ch'ing was governor of P'ing-yüan in Hopei just before the rebellion, and in his leisure he had been working on a large dictionary project there.[79] When An Lu-shan swept down from Yu-chou toward Loyang, he was forced to marshal all available military resources and organize resistance behind the rebel lines. Later he held numerous commissionerships and posts in the metropolitan bureaucracy. He was able to resume his scholarly activities only in 773, when a governorship in the southeast gave him the leisure to do so.[80]

The catastrophe of 755 and its sequel therefore meant that none of

---

77. *CTW* 381.12b.
78. *CTShih*, vol. 3, pp. 1587–88.
79. *CTW* 514.21a–b.
80. *CTW* 339.6b.

the five men enjoyed secure tenure in the metropolitan bureaucracy or worked in the imperial library as their predecessors had done in the days of peace. Instead, those who took up office suffered all the vicissitudes of bureaucratic service away from the capital, at the mercy of a temporizing court, and of increasingly insecure provincial conditions. Those who retired to the south, like Li Hua, and later on two occasions Yüan Chieh, paid for their security by their isolation. They managed to keep up only occasional contact with one another. We know only that Li Hua and Tu-ku Chi met in the southeast after the rebellion,[81] and that Yen Chen-ch'ing communicated with Yüan Chieh[82] and enlisted the help of Hsiao Ying-shih's son when he resumed work on his dictionary project in 773.[83]

Yet it would be a mistake to attribute the pattern of their careers solely to the rebellion. Isolated service in the remote south had been a possibility in days of peace as well. Retirement, too, was a path often taken before the rebellion. And though the capital had been sacked in 756, was evacuated before the Tibetans in 763,[84] and was to prove more and more difficult to administer,[85] the former institutions continued to operate. The *Old T'ang History* claims that at the time of the rebellion, "the old books were almost all lost or dispersed,"[86] but when the capital was recovered, prompt efforts were made to retrieve them.[87] The history office was reestablished, and though there was a drop in the number of large projects, work went on. At least one historian, a fellow graduate of the intellectuals under review and a colleague of the pre-rebellion historian Wei Shu, managed a long career there.[88] Private libraries too were apparently soon built up again.[89] Yüan Chieh and

81. *CTW* 388.11b.

82. *CTW* 380.7a. Yüan Chieh's "Eulogy for the Revival of the Great T'ang," composed in 761, was written out by Yen Chen-ch'ing and carved in rock at Wu-ch'i, Hunan, in 771; see Sun Wang, *Yüan Tzu-shan nien-p'u*, p. 99.

83. *CTW* 339.7a; cf. *CTS* 48.8b, biography of Ch'üan Kao. Ch'üan was known to both Yen and Li Hua after the rebellion.

84. *TCTC*, ch. 223, p. 7151.

85. *CTW* 384.21a–b.

86. *CTS* 46.1b.

87. *HTS* 57.2a; *CTS* 149.1b.

88. Liu Fang, biographies in *CTS* 149.14a–b and *HTS* 132.8a.

89. K. T. Wu, "Libraries and Book Collecting in China before the Invention of Printing," *T'ien-hsia Monthly* 5, no. 3 (October, 1937): 259–60, lists large private collections in the T'ang. In the post-rebellion period, Li Pi, who died in 789, and Su Pien, brother of the author of the *T'ang hui-yao*, both had large collections. Acker, *Some T'ang and Pre-T'ang Texts on Chinese Painting*, pp. 205–06, notes that collecting and trading in pictures and manuscripts went on after the rebellion.

Yen Chen-ch'ing had collections with them in the south in the 770s,[90] but it may be that, though forced to flee before the rebels, they had never lost their original libraries.

But official service in dangerous conditions, or retirement and sometimes poverty, did mean that no member of the group was able to settle down to any work of major length for the two decades after the rebellion. Instead their later collections consist of shorter length *san-wen* ("miscellaneous prose") pieces, memorials, biographical and commemorative works, inscriptions, essays, letters, prefaces, casual notes, and verse. The composition of their collected works is important to a student of their ideas. The mid-T'ang tradition of *san-wen* writing was, as Ch'en Yin-k'o noted,[91] a highly stereotyped one. The genre a writer used often imposed narrow restrictions on the content of his writing. Most of the extant remarks on literature and history by the five men occur in short essays and prefaces, as the T'ang tradition of *san-wen* writing demanded. But what is new in these writings, when compared to early eighth-century *san-wen*, is their sharper critical spirit and stronger convictions. The five men felt keenly about the climate of the late T'ien-pao and the post-rebellion world. It was this that led them to reexplore and update traditional ideas on history and literature.

Finally, it should be stressed that although these five men have the largest collections extant from their period, they do not represent completely the intellectual developments of their time. Others were writing sometimes in quite different ways, advocating, for example, legalist or quasi-legalist solutions to political problems or adhering to a more aesthetic approach toward literature.

Yet it is not entirely fortuitous that the works of these five men should have been relatively well preserved, while others have been lost. Although unselective forces have destroyed large numbers of works from this period, preservation has not been wholly impartial. A somewhat sinister force is discernible in the selection process, namely, the power of the editor silently to reject what is not in his view sufficiently orthodox, exemplary, or consonant with the Confucian reading of history, and to keep what is. It is no accident, therefore, that those mid-eighth-century figures whom Confucian historiography condemns, whether intellectuals or not, have almost no writings preserved. The villains of

90. Yüan was visited during his final retirement in the years 769–72 at Wu-ch'i in Hunan by Wang Yung, a fellow graduate, who remarked that "there were many books in the house"; see *CTW* 356.18b. Yen Chen-ch'ing needed a comprehensive library of classics to compile his dictionary; see *CTW* 339.6b.

91. Ch'en Yin-k'o, *Yüan Po shih chien-cheng-kao* (Shanghai, 1958), pp. 2–3.

the era—Yang Kuo-chung, Li Fu-kuo, and others—were not illiterate; it was just that their works stood little chance of survival. In less clear cases the same forces must also have operated. Thus Fang Kuan, the intellectual who advised the emperor so disastrously in the campaign of 756, was severely censured by the histories; virtually none of his writing survives today. Yet he must have been a productive and stimulating thinker in his own time. Even selective editing has not quite managed to excise the fact that he had friends and admirers among men who were judged respectable—Tu Fu, Li Hua, and Tu-ku Chi, for example.[92]

The same forces that made the survival of works by Yang Kuo-chung or Li Fu-kuo unlikely, and that lessened the chances for the works of men like Fang Kuan, worked the other way for the writings of the men under review. They were all loyalists, or at least if they strayed, they showed due penitence. None was closely identified with any party or individual whom history subsequently condemned. Two, in particular, had moments of greatness—Yüan Chieh, when as governor of Tao-chou he repelled successive Man incursions and protected his populace from the depredations of visiting tax collectors,[93] and Yen Chen-ch'ing, when in 784, after three decades of tireless service under four emperors, he was finally martyred to the loyalist cause.[94]

Historians were also interested in these men because of their connection with the emergence of exclusive Confucianism in the ninth century. The vital role here was played by Han Yü. Han had a link with Tu-ku Chi,[95] who in turn had a strong connection with Li Hua and Hsiao Ying-shih.[96] Han Yü and other ninth-century figures also commended Yüan Chieh.[97] Thus a line of transmission was established. In the early Sung, when Han Yü was virtually canonized, the interest in his intellectual forebears intensified. From then on the chances of having their works preserved further increased. Their biographies in the official histories were also affected by Sung Neo-Confucian interest in them. Hsiao Ying-shih and Li Hua were given expanded biographies in the *New T'ang History*, and Tu-ku Chi and Yüan Chieh, who had been

92. See Pulleyblank, "Neo-Confucianism and Neo-Legalism," pp. 99 and 330n96, 99. Also *CTW* 522.4a, 317.3b, and 318.7a; and *CTShih*, vol. 4, p. 2478. In *CTW* 588.1a–2a, Liu Tsung-yüan praised Fang Kuan very highly and noted that Li Hua had composed an inscription for him that was not erected because of the rebellion. See also Li Chao, *Kuo-shih pu*, pp. 18, 22, and 49.

93. Sun Wang, *Yüan Tzu-shan nien-p'u*, pp. 66–67, 75.

94. *TCTC*, ch. 229, p. 7393 and ch. 231, p. 7443, and the sources cited in note 7.

95. *CTS* 160.1a; Pulleyblank, "Neo-Confucianism and Neo-Legalism," p. 95.

96. *CTW* 388.11b, 518.6a.

97. For Han Yü's commendation of Yüan Chieh, see *CTW* 555.3a; for that of Lü Wen, ibid., 628.11b; and that of P'ei Ching, ibid., 764.17a–b.

omitted in the older history, were now included. Only Yen Chen-ch'ing had so high a standing in the older history that his biography needed no expansion in the new.[98]

HISTORICAL CRITICISM

The writings of the five intellectuals under review show three main approaches to history. There were, first, general reviews of history as an impersonal process susceptible to periodization or demonstrating certain long-term trends. Second there was historical criticism in the specific sense of criticism of existing histories and the procedures for writing them. Finally, the five men analyzed the roles of certain figures in history, critically evaluating in moral terms.

The general reviews of history by Hsiao Ying-shih, Li Hua, and other contemporaries open by referring to a concept of long standing in the Confucian historical and literary tradition, that of *wen*. Like other Confucian concepts, this idea was rooted in laconic statements in the Classics, the *Tso chüan*, the *Analects*, and the *I ching*.[99] It had been elaborated in the Han period in the *Li chi*, in Tung Chung-shu's *Ch'un-ch'iu fan-lu*, and in the *Mao shih ta-hsü*, where it had attained essentially its full range as an idea.[100] Ever since Hsiao T'ung had alluded to it in his preface to the *Wen-hsüan*,[101] writers had had the habit of starting their prefaces and introductions to works of history and literature alike by referring to it. Thus in early T'ang it is to be found in introductions by the historians Li Yen-shou[102] and Wei Cheng[103] and in prefaces by the poets Yang Chiung[104] and Wang Po.[105] In K'ai-yüan it appears in the writing of Han Hsiu,[106] Chang Yüeh,[107] and Liu Chih-chi.[108]

Wen meant primarily pattern, the rhythmic repetition of a shape. The *I ching* had spoken of two kinds, *t'ien-wen*—the pattern of the

---

98. For Hsiao Ying-shih and Li Hua, see *HTS* 202.12a and 203.11a; for Tu-ku Chi and Yüan Chieh, see ibid., 162.1b and 143.2a; for Yen Chen-ch'ing see note 46 above.

99. *Tso chuan*, in *Ch'un-ch'iu ching chuan (HYISIS* edition), Hsiang 25, p. 307; *Analects* 3.14, 6.18; *I ching (SPTK* edition), hexagram 22 (*fen*), 3.2a–b.

100. *Li chi (SPTK* edition) 11.6a–b, 17.6a; *Ch'un-ch'iu fan-lu (SPTK* edition) 7.3b; *Mao shih (SPTK* edition) 1.1b–2a.

101. J. R. Hightower, "The *Wen-hsüan* and Genre Theory," *HJAS* 20 (1957): 518.

102. *Pei shih (Po-na* edition) 83.1a.

103. *Sui shu (Po-na* edition) 76.1a.

104. *CTW* 191.9b.

105. *CTW* 182.15b.

106. *CTW* 295.4b.

107. *CTW* 225.17b.

108. *Shih-t'ung t'ung-shih* 6.12a, 6.16b.

heavenly bodies and the pattern of the topography of China herself[109] —and *jen-wen*— human pattern, which denoted the three media of music, ritual, and the written word. *Wen* was hypostatized, that is, held to exist of itself, not merely to be the attribute of anything patterned. The concept of *wen* shares features with the early medieval European idea of musical harmony—the music of the universe, *musica mundana*, is parallel to *t'ien-wen*, while the music of man, *musica humana*, and instrumental music, *musica instrumentalis*, correspond to *jen-wen*.[110] Both notions stress in different ways—the Chinese humanistically and the European theistically—man's intimate connections with the universe.

The ways in which the five intellectuals approached this concept fall into a polarity. At one extreme *wen* was considered as an objective phenomenon in the natural world or in society, to be observed and analyzed. Irregularities in heavenly pattern, according to this well-known theory, indicated irregularities in the human world below, and specifically in the moral conduct of government. *Jen-wen* was also an index of the condition of the state and, especially in the case of the written word, of the workings of the government. At the other extreme, *wen* was treated as a component in the traditional psychology of literary creation. This was an expressionistic concept: *wen* was the patterning of the inner feelings of man, mainly in literature, but also in music and ritual. Writers in the eighth century were conscious of the breadth of the idea. Thus Hsiao Ying-shih, referring at the start of a preface to *t'ien-wen* and *jen-wen*, the latter especially in the sense of the written word, remarked: "How perfect is *wen!* It is a great unifying principle to which heaven and man unite in responding, and through which the purpose of names and schedules is preserved."[111]

Such an allusion to the *wen* concept at the start of a preface was conventional, but some of the men under review explored the idea more fully. They considered *jen-wen*, in the sense of ritual, music, or the written word, as an indication of the condition of the state in any period, which offered them a measure for analyzing the historical process itself.[112] Li Hua made this his theme in his "Essay on Substance and Pattern,"[113] one of the most important works by any of the group.

109. For the clearest expression of this idea by a contemporary of the men under review, see *CTW* 443.16a.

110. E. de Bruyne, *Études d'ésthetique médiévale* (Bruges, 1946), vol. 1, p. 12.

111. *CTW* 322.15a–b.

112. This idea is explored earliest in *Ch'un-ch'iu fan-lu* 7.3b; see Feng Yu-lan, *A History of Chinese Philosophy* (Princeton, N.J., 1953), vol. 2, pp. 58–71.

113. *CTW* 317.1a–b. *Chou shu* (*Po-na* edition) 38.7a and *Pei shih* 64.20a mention an essay with a similar title, "Essay on Pattern and Substance," by Liu Ch'iu. This is no longer extant,

Li opened his essay by discussing an extension of the *wen* concept as a phenomenon in society. *Wen,* pattern, he explained, was antithetical to the value *chih,* substance. *Chih* was to be identified with austerity, tending to coarseness and then crudeness. *Wen* here had the extended meanings of refinement and extravagance, leading to falsehood. In this sense it took on its most extreme meaning, a negative one in contrast to its generally positive value. A balance between *wen* and *chih* was ideal, as Confucius had said.[114] But if this could not be effected, then an excess of substance was preferable to an excess of pattern. The latter state was a dangerous one: "If when extravagance prevails, an attempt at reform is made, stability will be sought for but not secured." Li was here alluding to the essential premise of all Chinese historical writing, that though the cycles and trends of history might be impersonal and mechanistic, yet men, and specifically the ruler, could intervene and arrest these processes by acting on a moral level. As long as the situation had not reached an extreme, Li implied, it was within the power of the ruler to redress the balance between *wen* and *chih.*

Li went on to give historical examples of the way in which an imbalance toward *chih* could provide a basis for reform, while an imbalance toward *wen* made recovery difficult. His main example of *chih* was from the early Han. At the start of the dynasty, the royal house had been threatened by rebellion from the relatives of the empress Kao, and, a little later, in 154 B.C., from the princes of Wu and Ch'u. This period, he argued, had been a time of austerity and frugality, when the harsh and complex laws of the Ch'in and the burdensome ritual of the later Chou had been abolished and simplicity had returned to administration. It was precisely this frugality that had enabled the Han house to overcome the threats it faced. An example of the opposite situation was to be found in the later Hsia dynasty, when rulers had tampered with the perfect and sufficient decrees of Yü. As a result, *wen* had succeeded *chih,* and the dynasty had easily been overthrown. Li's third example was that of the Chou, which after the reign of King K'ang (traditionally 1078–53 B.C.) had allowed its ritual and its administration to grow in complexity, making eventual disaster inevitable.

Finally Li indicted his own times for an excess of *wen* over *chih.* In doing so he again made it clear that *wen,* though susceptible of control by the ruler, was an impersonal factor of great breadth. Punishments

---

but to judge from the brief résumé in his biographies, it dealt only with literature; see Lo Ken-tse, *Chung-kuo wen-hsüeh p'i-p'ing shih,* vol. 1, p. 251. Li's essay is datable on the evidence of *CTW* 388.15b to between 752 and 762.

114. *Analects* 6.18.

had become too involved, ritual too complex, divination and superstition rampant. The learned world was divided, a hundred schools existed where one would have been enough: "The empire is inundated like a lake, or flows along like a great flood. And even if the divine Yü were born again, neither he nor anyone else would be able to save it." Unity and restraint must be restored where now there was plurality and extravagance. The idea of an orthodoxy, which was to appeal so strongly in the ninth century, is evident here: "I am of the humble opinion that any further search to bring about good order should start with the study and application of the Classics and histories. Works such as the *Tso-chüan, Kuo-yü, Erh-ya, Hsün-tzu,* and *Mencius* are support for the Classics. . . . The theories of the remaining hundred philosophers . . . should be preserved but not used."

Of the other intellectuals in the group, Tu-ku Chi is said to have expounded *wen* and *chih* as they applied to early history.[115] Yen Chench'ing also alluded to the *wen-chih* polarity as it applied to one of his chief concerns, ritual. He was, like Li Hua, criticizing current practice. "They have done away with the *chih* of the ancients and set value on extravagant ornamentation," he wrote; "substance is closer to antiquity, pattern to the present day. . . . When *wen* deteriorates, it should be rescued by *chih*."[116] His use of the concept, though an incidental one, is similar to Li's.

The *wen-chih* polarity was not, however, the only way in which these intellectuals viewed history. One of the fullest of the extant reviews, by Hsiao Ying-shih, written before the rebellion, started by alluding to the *wen* idea, but did not make it central, as Li had done in his essay. Rather, Hsiao used it throughout only in its positive sense: patterned, cultured, pertaining to the written word.[117]

A striking feature of Hsiao's review is that he commends exactly those periods in history Li had praised and condemns those Li had criticized. A common historical perspective may therefore be abstracted from the writings of the two men. Hsiao's review is the more explicit, however, and supplies the details. Hsiao saw history not as the repetition of a strictly dynastic process, but as a thousand-year cycle involving first prosperity and good government and then disorder. There had been

---

115. *CTW* 522.4a.

116. *CTW* 336.14b–16b; Yen's knowledge of ritual was recognized when, in 779, he was appointed to a ritual commissionership.

117. *CTW* 322.15a–19a. There is a difference between the views Hsiao expressed here on behalf of Ch'en Cheng-ch'ing and those he put forward for his own projected history, described below. Hsiao himself was clearly prepared to pay more attention to the Period of Disunion than he suggests here.

three great periods in history, the age of Yao and Shun in antiquity, the Han, and the T'ang itself.

The reigns of Yao and Shun, described in the *Book of History*, had been praised by Confucius himself, Yao for his *wen-ssu*, culture and thought, and Shun for his *wen-te*, culture and virtue.[118] During their reigns, the moral record had been perfect. Deterioration had set in with the Hsia, and even the early Chou had been short of perfection. Thereafter, "there was decline, usurpation, and disorder until the tyrannical Ch'in." Ritual and music had declined, vertical alliances were linked, horizontal ones joined. But, Hsiao quoted the *Analects*, "Heaven does not let the cause of *ssu-wen*, culture, perish."[119] The Han arose, and there was a restoration of the ritual and laws of the period of Shun. The Han's great achievements, reviving a simple ritual and the calendar, putting down the revolts of the Wu and Ch'u princes, and expanding its influence abroad, made it equal to the exemplary period of antiquity.

After the Han, the record again was one of failure. China was sadly divided. "It was a matter of splitting into four or cracking into five, of success in the morning and defeat in the evening." The Sui dynasty, lasting two generations, precisely the duration of the Ch'in, had prepared the way for the T'ang, and this parallelism was clear evidence of Heaven's purpose. The Han and the T'ang were thus fully comparable. "What need is there to speak of Eastern Chin, Later Wei, Liang, Ch'en, Chou, or Ch'i?"

Reviewing the T'ang itself, and particularly the period through which they lived, Hsiao Ying-shih and the other members of the group tended to have two standards. Their intense loyalty to the dynasty infuses many of their public writings, memorials, inscriptions, and so on, but their private writings bear more closely the stamp of their own experience. Before the rebellion they spoke of a rise in the level of culture and learning, leading to unseemly competition for office. Thus in 753 Yüan Chieh, who then still had to pass an examination, remarked of Hsüan-tsung's reign that its ritual and music had reached as far as the outlying barbarians and that "even the slave classes can recite the works of the Duke of Chou and Confucius, or discourse on the way of T'ao T'ang and Yü Hsia."[120] Under such conditions, he continued, the scramble for office was degrading. Hsiao Ying-shih also protested before the rebellion about the unseemly competition for posts.[121] There

118. *Shang shu* (*SPTK* edition) 1.1a, 2.6a.
119. *Analects* 9.5.
120. *CTW* 383.19a–b.
121. *CTW* 323.8a.

is an echo in these remarks of Li Hua's plea for a more restricted and more austere learned world. *Wen* had exceeded *chih*. After the rebellion, as we have seen, the five men felt nostalgia for the age of peace, their regret at its passing given edge by resentment against those who had hastened its end.[122] The evidence of their prose works proves that they were well aware of the changes in power structure which were taking place, both at court and in the increasingly independent provinces,[123] but there is little to suggest that they had concrete, technical proposals for reform.[124] Those who were active as civil servants—Tu-ku Chi, Yüan Chieh, and Yen Chen-ch'ing—restricted their roles to education, ritual, and public morality. They appear in fact to be true Confucians in their emphasis on the *wen* aspects of statecraft rather than on technical, institutional, or financial problems, on the moral role of the individual rather than on his special skills as an administrator.

The five intellectuals found the *wen* concept and the *wen-chih* polarity useful not only in analyzing history in broad terms, but also in the second kind of history they practiced, the discussion of historical writing itself. Histories, like anything written, were *wen*, both in the objective sense of being a written record of the past and in the expressionistic sense as historians' judgments on events. Viewed as such they had solemn functions indeed: "For effecting the transformation of the world, nothing is of greater importance than *wen*. The great institution of *wen* is the dynastic history, which has the office of giving praise and blame, reproof and exhortation, of separating the light from the dark."[125]

The writing of full-length histories needed settled conditions. Only Hsiao Ying-shih, the member of the group most active before the rebellion, showed an interest in the technical problems of history writing. Hsiao's ambition before the rebellion had been to compile a history of the period from the start of Han until the end of Sui, a *Li-tai t'ung-tien* in one hundred *chüan*.[126] His main objection to existing accounts was formal. He held that the proper organization for a history was the

122. E.g., *CTW* 336.14a, 315.9a.

123. E.g., *CTW* 380.8b, 336.12a.

124. A possible exception to this was Yen Chen-ch'ing, who was said to have rediscovered in discussion the idea of the salt monopoly while governor of P'ing-yüan in Hopei, in 756; see ibid., 514.18b and D. C. Twitchett, *Financial Administration under the T'ang Dynasty* (Cambridge, 1963), p. 263*n*13. Yet even here Yen did not act promptly on the idea, for Ti-wu Chi is said to have stolen it and memorialized it to Su-tsung before him.

125. *CTW* 316.5a, datable to 748. See William Hung, "The T'ang Bureau of Historiography before 708," *HJAS* 23 (1960–61): 95.

126. *CTW* 323.15a–b; see also Hiraoka Takeo, *Keisho no dentō*, pp. 101–04.

chronicle, with entries made chronologically and by region. The annals-biography model introduced by the Han historians was, he claimed, a presumption and a departure from the practice of antiquity as enshrined in the *Book of History* and the *Ch'un-ch'iu*. Ssu-ma Ch'ien and Pan Ku were therefore to be condemned. The structure of their works was repetitious, and they used inconsistent language to describe the same event in different sections of their works. The resulting lack of precision defeated the main purpose of historical writing, and would, Hsiao said, "be inadequate to promote the basic principles of government."

Later historians had followed the Han models, Hsiao complained, but had lacked the talent of Ssu-ma Ch'ien or Pan Ku. However, the chronicle style had not by any means died out. Hsiao mentioned ten writers of chronicle histories for the Period of Disunion and implied that he knew of several more. "But to the end they were unable to blunt the speartip of the Han historians' presumption or continue even by a thread the Lu style of discussing events." It had been Hsiao's ambition to correct this situation, but he had failed to secure a post at the history office and had withdrawn to the southeast some years before the rebellion. An observer later recalled that he had been writing busily,[127] but we know that he had abandoned his project before the rebellion broke out.[128]

This dispute about the ideal form for histories was a lively and long-standing one in T'ang times. At least four chronicle histories had been written in the late K'ai-yüan and T'ien-pao periods.[129] The catalog to the imperial library which Wei Shu, a friend and correspondent of Hsiao Ying-shih, had compiled listed no fewer than fifty-five chronicles.[130] Yet Hsiao regrettably left no detailed reasons for his preference, other than the canonical status of his model, the *Ch'un-ch'iu*, and his insistence on the utmost brevity in narrative. Perhaps in implying that the chronicle, because it is closer to the *Ch'un-ch'iu*, is more efficient at dispensing praise and blame, he gives some clue to his position. Hsiao seems to have seen historical writing as fulfilling a narrowly moral task.

127. *CTW* 395.3b.

128. *CTW* 323.16a–b, 317.4b.

129. Yüan Hsing-ch'ung's *Wei tien* (*HTS* 58.5b); Ch'en Cheng-ch'ing's *Hsü Shang shu* (for which see *CTW* 322.15a and *HTS* 57.3b); Wu Ching's *T'ang Ch'un-ch'iu* and Wei Shu's work of the same name (*HTS* 58.3b).

130. This figure, quoted from *CTS* 46.17b, assumes that the *CTS I-wen chih* derives from the *Ku-chin shu-lu* of Wu Ching, itself a condensation of the catalog in 200 *chüan* compiled by Wei Shu and others and submitted in 721 (*CTS* 46.1b); see *CTS* 46.4a and Piet van der Loon, "On the Transmission of the *Kuan tzu*," *T'oung Pao* 41, nos. 4–5 (1952), p. 368 and n. 3.

The *pien-nien*, or chronicle, form perhaps performed this function better because it concentrated on showing men in action. It combined in one comprehensive yet concise narrative the essential matter of both the *pen-chi* and *lieh-chüan* sections of the conventional *chi-chüan* histories. Moreover, it avoided the specialist technical issues to which the treatise sections of conventional histories were devoted. If Hsiao thought along these lines, stressing moral action over technical information, then he was adopting, even before the rebellion, a position generally characteristic of the intellectuals under review.

The third and most typical kind of history the five men wrote reflects precisely this greater interest in men than in processes or in technical knowledge. It involved the evaluation of historical figures and their moral roles. This was again a traditional activity; essays rating the respective merits of groups of figures may be found as far back as the early Six Dynasties.[131] The appreciation, or *tsan*, essays of the early T'ang dynastic histories provided more recent models.[132] As Hsiao Ying-shih suggests, criticism of this kind seems to have enjoyed a vogue in mid-T'ang times, even before the rebellion.[133]

The two best surviving examples of this form are essays by Yüan Chieh and Tu-ku Chi. Yüan's *Essay on Kuan Chung*, written in 757, was an attempt to correct what its author thought an excessive respect for this figure among contemporaries.[134] It is not difficult to imagine why Kuan Chung should have appealed to many T'ang thinkers and to see why Yüan should have been anxious to redress the balance.[135] The *Kuan tzu* combined, as no other work did, an acceptable moral position with a frank discussion of the techniques of control and administration. Kuan Chung had been a very successful practitioner of his own ideas and had been commended, though in less than fulsome terms, by Confucius himself.[136] But Yüan Chieh, perhaps most of all the group, analyzed political problems relentlessly in moral terms. There were parallels, he suggested, between Kuan Chung's era and the situation in which

131. E.g., Ts'ao Chih, "Essay on the Respective Merits of the Two Han Founding Emperors," in Yen K'o-chün, *Ch'üan Wei wen* (Canton, 1887–93) 18.1b.

132. E.g., *Sui shu* 75.21b, 76.20a.

133. *CTW* 323.13b

134. *CTW* 382.9b–12a.

135. The *Kuan tzu* had had two commentaries written for it during the early eighth century; see W. Allyn Rickett, *Kuan tzu, a Repository of Early Chinese Thought* (Hong Kong, 1965), pp. 16–20. Li Han, a cousin of Li Hua, had written an essay very similar to Yüan's, evaluating Chu-ko Liang's claim to be the equal of Kuan Chung and Yüeh I; see *CTW* 431.2b–5a.

136. *Analects* 14.16, 3.22.

China found herself after the rebellion—both were times when the central authority had lost power. But to Yüan it was wrong that Kuan Chung should be admired or that it should be thought that his example was relevant to the present situation. He had in fact failed morally because he had not devoted his energy to the weakening Chou dynasty; instead, he had dedicated his powers solely to the interests of the state of Ch'i. This failure, Yüan argued, had been a disservice to China. For had Kuan Chung put his able leadership behind the Chou feudal organization, then, despite their weakness, "the Chou emperors would never become slaves, nor would the states of the feudal lords have been destroyed, nor would Ch'in's position in the empire have advanced as far as it did."

A second essay, which demonstrates even more clearly a wish to revise conventionally accepted evaluations of historical figures, is Tu-ku Chi's *Essay on Chi Cha of Wu*.[137] Chi Cha was an exemplar of the Ch'un-ch'iu period, primarily known for his ability to predict the fate of states by listening to their music. Like Kuan Chung, he seems to have been discussed in the mid-eighth century.[138] Tu-ku Chi, however, was not interested in Chi Cha for the role in which he was best known, but rather for his conduct in refusing three times to accept the throne of the state of Wu.[139] The principle of declining or abdicating a throne was, he showed, to be thought of as relative. The only overriding, absolute consideration involved was that the best possible ruler be on the throne. "Hence for the sake of a man's wisdom one should disregard his age, for the sake of his right conduct one should disregard auguries against him, and for the sake of his ruler's commands one should disregard the requirements of ritual in his case."

It was wrong, Tu-ku considered, when Chi Cha was the ablest of his family, for him to disobey his father and brothers and refuse the throne. He had "preserved his own integrity," withdrawing in a way that was usually praiseworthy, but had neglected the demands of this

137. *CTW* 389.10a–11a.

138. Yüan Te-hsiu, Yüan Chieh's cousin, had written an essay on him, since lost, but quoted by title by Li Hua (*CTW* 320.16b). Li mentioned him and, probably in 766, visited and left an inscription in his honor at one of the temples that stood to him in the area of Jun-chou and Ch'ang-chou; see *CTW* 315.10a and the Sung dynasty geographical handbook *Yü-ti chi-sheng* (Taipei, 1962 reprint) 7.17b; this text is not included in Li's works in *CTW* and *CTShih*. Tu-ku Chi held his final post, the governorship of Ch'ang-chou, in the area where Chi Cha had lived, and where his tomb still stood.

139. He had also been alluded to in this context by Ts'ao Chih; see Huang Chieh, ed., *Ts'ao Tzu-chien shih chu* (Peking, 1957), p. 32. Li Hua's inscription, cited above, read, in part, "Chi tzu declined the throne of Wu, but by his writing perpetuated the *Kuo-feng* [section of the *Odes*]."

particular situation. If he had accepted the throne, "he would certainly have been able to bring luster to the Chou and to hold hegemony over the Ching and Man barbarians. Thus the great heritage would have been secure and many difficulties would have been avoided." The parallels with Yüan Chieh's essay are evident. Yet Tu-ku is the more incisive, since he revised the implicit judgments on Chi Cha of the *Ch'un-ch'iu*, *Tso chuan*, and *Shih-chi*.[140]

Both essays discuss moral problems in history. Kuan Chung's conduct is analyzed in terms of its consequences, as well as by the absolute requirement of loyalty to the ruling house. In Tu-ku's essay the results of Chi Cha's action are considered, but they are secondary to the insight that moral principles may be relative rather than absolute. Yet these essays also show a characteristic limitation. In the West such factors as the results of an action and the absolute or relative nature of moral precepts are recognized as general ideas. Ethics, the science of morals, which supplies these ideas, has been a subject in its own right, with its own body of theory. But here there is no comparable tradition of ethics to draw on, and the level of generalization is low. In Yüan's essay the general principles have to be inferred from the particular case under review. In Tu-ku's they are enunciated, but placed crudely at the start of the essay as normative rules, rather than as its final deduction.

The approach of these essays to moral problems in history may therefore be characterized as personal and individual, in the sense of always requiring a specific figure as the principal object of inquiry. Without their specific examples before them, Tu-ku and Yüan would not have been able to argue as they did, for they could not have given their warning messages in generalized abstract form. This approach to historical analysis stands in contrast to the other main approach we have described, that of seeing history as an impersonal process susceptible to periodization, or of analysis in terms of *wen* and *chih*. The personal approach was evidently very natural to the intellectuals under review, since a similar concern for the moral role of the individual is to be seen in many of their random remarks on history, remote and recent. The same kind of moralism underlay the biographical and commemorative works they produced for their contemporaries with such great facility

140. The *Ch'un-ch'iu* itself only once mentions Chi Cha by name, stating merely that he paid a ritual visit to Lu; see *Ch'un-ch'iu ching chuan*, Hsiang 29, p. 326. The praise (*pao*) Tu-ku mentions is presumably that implicit in the *Kung-yang chuan*, *Ku-liang chuan*, and *Tso chuan* commentaries on this passage; see ibid.,pp. 326–27. There is an account of the whole epis ode in *Shih-chi* (*Po-na* edition) 31.3b–13a; Ssu-ma Ch'ien's opinion of Chi Cha is given in *Shih-chi* 31.20a.

and in such great numbers; and the same approach was, we shall see, integral to their literary theory as well.

Literary Criticism

The high level of knowledge and keen sense of historical perspective that informed the historical criticism of these five men is present also in the second aspect of their thought which is the concern of this chapter, literary criticism. The two fields moreover shared some key concepts and had a few important differences, which throw interesting light on the way they looked at their literary heritage.

Literary criticism may be divided broadly into three types: the prescriptive, which formulates rules for genres, prosodic models, and so on; the descriptive, which concentrates on the exposition of existing works of literature; and the theoretical, which discusses such questions as the nature of literature, its psychological origins, and its functions.[141]

Prescriptive criticism, the formulating of prosodic rules, was more typical of the early eighth century, when the regulated styles of verse were being perfected, than of the rebellion period. Only one of the five men under review, Yen Chen-ch'ing, seems to have been even marginally involved in this kind of criticism. When he resumed work on his rhyming dictionary, nearly twenty years after the outbreak of war, he had as a companion a monk who wrote a work of prescriptive criticism.[142] Together, Yen, the monk, and others composed *lien-chü*, one of the most technically exacting of verse forms.[143] But other members of the group disapproved of excessive concern for the intricate requirements of the regulated styles and gave little hint of interest in this sort of criticism.

Descriptive criticism, the exposition in detail of existing works of literature, is not a feature of T'ang critical writing. There was no parallel in literature to the detailed treatment of historical figures like Chi Cha or Kuan Chung. But in their prefaces, the men under review did pass epigrammatic comments on past literature and on each others' works. These remarks, though laconic, are useful, for they set an author in his literary historical context and suggest, for example, whether he was appreciated for moral or for aesthetic reasons.[144]

141. George Watson, *The Literary Critics* (London, 1962), pp. 9–18.

142. *CTW* 339.7b; and Lo Ken-tse, *Chung-kuo wen-hsüeh p'i-p'ing shih*, vol. 2, pp. 39–45.

143. *CTShih*, vol. 11, pp. 8880 ff.

144. E.g., *CTW* 388.11b and especially Yin Fan in *Ho-yüeh ying-ling chi*, in *T'ang-jen hsüan T'ang shih* (Peking, 1958), pp. 40–124.

Finally, there is theoretical criticism, which is concerned with the nature and function of literature, the psychology of composition, and so on. This is perhaps the characteristic critical activity for the two decades after the rebellion and for the intellectuals under review. Here they reformulated some of the most striking insights of the Chinese literary critical tradition, focusing on the relation of literature to society and the psychological genesis of literature.

The cornerstone for their position on the theoretical aspects of literature was again the versatile concept of *wen*. The breadth of this idea has already been suggested. First, it was an objective phenomenon in society, morally determined, to be noted as an index of the condition of the state. And second, it was a component in an expressionistic psychology, the patterning of the inner feelings through the media of music, ritual, or the written word. *Wen* in the first sense was the concept Li Hua had treated in his "Essay on Substance and Pattern." But though *wen* could apply to ritual and music, as it did in this essay, it had always had special reference to the written word. The very term had a specific substantival meaning, translatable by "literature" in the wide sense, marking it off from ritual and music. And the most influential account, the *Mao shih ta-hsü*, shows that literature, most of all the three media to which the *wen* concept referred, was envisaged as reflecting the state of the government and the feelings of the people.[145] The condition of the government and the populace, moreover, changed with time, and literature reflected these changes. In modern terms, this amounts to a primitive literary historicism: the nature of literature is related to the condition of the society that produced it.

The intellectuals under review endorsed this traditional idea, though they never made very direct statements about it. They followed early T'ang writers in upholding a distinction between the literature of "those above," that is the emperor, government, and themselves, and that of "those below," meaning broadly the people. The former was thought of as an expression of the rulers' moral desires, and as having a transforming effect on the society that received it. The latter was the spontaneous response of the people to government.[146] It was naturally the latter, the literature of the governed, which best illustrated the traditional concept of literature as socially and politically determined. But the literature of those who ruled, as an instrument for the moral

145. *Mao shih* 1.1b–2a.

146. *Sui shu* 76.1a makes this distinction very clearly. An earlier source for the same idea is Pan Ku, *Wen hsüan (SPTK* edition), 1.3a, quoted by Chu Tzu-ch'ing, *Shih yen chih pien* (Peking, 1956), p. 76.

transformation of society, was also thought of as closely related to the age in which it was produced.

Yen Chen-ch'ing, for example, held that in high antiquity the emperors, that is "those above," had illustrated their great virtue as rulers through their *wen*, compositions, and that these in turn had had a profound effect on society. "When Shun composed his song, prince and subject changed their demeanor. When the royal grace expired, reform of customs did not proceed. The flourishing or decline of government is in truth bound up with this."[147] Yen went on, rather brazenly, to introduce a brief survey of past literature by taking up the *wen* concept in its descriptive rather than substantival sense and restating the idea of a *wen-chih* polarity as a means of analyzing literature. A balance was ideal, but "age has followed age, and none has been able to find the mean."

Li Hua referred to the historicist idea in slightly clearer terms when he stated that two factors, the character of the author and the mood of the age, were determining forces in literature. "Literature has its origin in the author, but the joy or sorrow it expresses are bound up with the times. . . . It reflects rejoicing over kings Wen and Wu, and grief over kings Yu and Li."[148]

The five men were especially interested in the figure of Chi Cha, who, as we have seen, had used the literature of "those below" to diagnose the condition of the states in the Ch'iu-ch'iu period.[149] They referred also to the *kuo-feng* principle, by which popular songs were to be collected and studied as indications of the attitude of the people to the government. This idea was beginning, in the mid-eighth century, to be taken seriously again on the creative level. Yüan Chieh, who led this development, wrote a series of imitation ballads and collected folk songs in the lower Huai Basin before the rebellion.[150]

This literary historicism, rudimentary though it appears, was unparalleled in the post-classical West until the eighteenth century, when Vico related Homer's *Iliad* and *Odyssey* to the changing society that had produced them.[151] The theory, however, was never worked out in detail. It is not clear whether the five writers took it at the most primitive level and thought literature good only to the extent that it reflected

147. *CTW* 337.10b–11a.

148. *CTW* 315.4b. The clearest statement of this idea comes slightly later, ibid., 518.2b, 3b.

149. See above, note 138.

150. *CTShih,* vol. 4, pp. 2696–98, 2703. Yüan also suggested that his own verse describing popular conditions should be presented to the central authority (ibid., vol. 4, pp. 2697, 2704).

151. Edmund Wilson, *The Triple Thinkers* (London, 1952), pp. 244–45.

good government; or whether their historicism was more developed, and they thought that only a good political age allows the production of good literature—in other words, that literature has features of its own, to be judged independently of its social base, but that a good social base is prerequisite for literature of any excellence. Confronted with this vagueness, it may be helpful for us to compare the remarks the five writers made on past literature with those they made on history itself.

It was a long-established practice in prefaces to collected works or anthologies to review past literature and to set the author in his literary historical context. Reviews of this kind are to be found in prefaces by Li Hua,[152] who also recorded Hsiao Ying-shih's position,[153] Yen Chen-ch'ing,[154] and Tu-ku Chi.[155] Their scheme for literature was indeed parallel to their scheme for history itself. Just as they considered the canonical age one of social and moral near-perfection, so they insisted that canonical literature was uniquely authoritative and that the process of decline started thereafter. "Confucius's writings were transmitted by Yen and Shang. When they had died, K'ung Chi and Meng K'o wrote, and may be said to have handed on the six canons. But Ch'u P'ing and Sung Yü were mournful and distressed, and extravagant beyond recovery. The way of the six canons lapsed."[156]

None of the men under review provided an elaboration of this well-known judgment or described in detail why the canons had such great authority. We may infer that they appreciated the *Odes* at least partly for literary reasons because so much of the technical critical vocabulary they used, words like *feng-ya* and *pi-hsing*, stemmed from them. But it is clear that Li Hua, who wrote most about this, was more concerned with the connection between the *Odes* and the society that produced them than with their technical quality as literature: "When the kings of old neglected the mandate of Heaven, the Grand Master expounded poems for them to observe the feelings of the people. Emphatically these were not about 'pines and snow on distant peaks,' or 'cloud and moonlight over limpid rivers.' "[157] Li saw some of the *Odes* as reflections of a perfect administration and society, and others of a period when the ancient rulers "neglected the mandate of Heaven," that is, of a government that fell short of perfection but of a populace that still produced

152. *CTW* 315.4b–5a.
153. *CTW* 315.8a–b; another slightly different review by Hsiao Ying-shih is included in his *HTS* biography (*HTS* 202.13b).
154. *CTW* 337.10b.
155. *CTW* 388.1a.
156. *CTW* 315.4b.
157. *CTW* 315.14a.

exemplary poems of criticism. Moral factors in the society of early China, implied Li, were essential to the excellence of the *Odes*.

Ch'ü Yuan and Sung Yü, the principal authors of the *Ch'u tz'u* tradition, marked the start of the age of decline. Though their writing was, in Hsiao Ying-shih's words, "very virile and robust," it "could not be counted as canonical."[158] It was, as Li Hua remarked in the quotation above, "mournful and distressed," in contrast to the *Odes*, which Confucius had commended for being "mournful but not distressed."[159] The later Chou was, we saw in Li and Hsiao's reviews of history, a period of general decline. History and literature ran parallel.

The Ch'in was barren as far as literature was concerned and was not discussed. But the Han was another matter. We have seen how Li Hua had characterized it as an age when *chih* had exceeded *wen*, and Hsiao Ying-shih considered it one of the three great ages of history. We would expect, then, that its literature should reflect its general excellence, and we do indeed find the intellectuals under review praising Han authors. But their commendation is typically less enthusiastic for Han writers than for the *Ch'u tz'u* authors, as if they represent a further stage in a continuous process of decline from the canonical age. Thus Hsiao Ying-shih, having stressed that their writing "does not approach the *Feng* and the *Ya* [sections of the *Odes*]," singled out Han writers and commended them briefly on technical points, while Tu-ku Chi was said to have imitated the Han writers Tung Chung-shu (c. 179–c. 104 B.C.) and Yang Hsiung (53 B.C.–A.D. 18).[160]

After the Han dynasty, the five men might be expected to run into some sort of conflict if they held to a primitive historicist theory of literature. For it would not seem reasonable for them to dismiss all the literature of the post-Han and pre-T'ang period as contemptuously as Hsiao Ying-shih had dismissed its history. They all knew that major technical developments had taken place since the Han and that the verse of the Wei and Chin, disastrous periods politically, was particularly vigorous. Here then literature and history must have seemed to part company, in a way that would challenge any simple historicist theory.

In fact, the writers under review seem to have dodged this problem by considering the Wei and early Chin as an extension, from the point of view of periodization, of the Han. They may have seen political unity—the existence, however precarious, of one nominal government

158. *CTW* 315.8a.
159. *Analects* 3.20.
160. For Hsiao Ying-shih, see *CTW* 315.8a–b; for Tu-ku Chi, see *CTS* 160.1a.

for all China under the Chin until the loss of the north in 317—as their justification for this position. At any rate they commended the Wei and Chin in general terms and praised the poets of the late Han, like Wang Ts'an (died 217); of the Wei, like Ts'ao Chih (died 232); and of the early Chin, like Chang Hua (died 300), Tso Ssu (died 306), and P'an Ni (died 310). Significantly perhaps, the last names to receive commendation were Liu K'un, who died in 317, and Kan Pao, who was also writing just at the time when the northern homeland was lost to barbarian invaders and China became divided.[161]

In their treatment of the Period of Disunion itself, the five men consistently dismissed its literature as emphatically as they had its history. Hsiao Ying-shih, breaking off after mentioning Kan Pao, remarked, "Beyond these the remainder are far behind and without renown."[162] And he noted elsewhere that he "never let his attention be detained by any literature since Wei and Chin."[163] Yen Chen-ch'ing censured the verse of the Liang and Ch'i and the *Kung-t'i*, or Palace style, for its triviality.[164] Only Tu-ku Chi implicitly admitted the positive technical developments of the Period of Disunion. He did this grudgingly, merely pointing out that mid-T'ang verse owed its special excellence to its fusion of ancient qualities with more recent tonal rules. His review of five-word verse, "passing over a thousand years," jumped from Han and Wei to the seventh century.[165]

Since these writers viewed the T'ang as a great dynasty, and the seventh century as a time of order and prosperity, we would expect them to praise the literature of that time as well. But here they seem to have operated the same sort of double standard that they used in interpreting history itself. Before the rebellion Yüan Chieh and Hsiao Ying-shih had noted the high level of literature Hsüan-tsung's reign had brought about, and Li Hua too recalled that this had been a time when "in the field of letters, men of great ability abounded." But after the rebellion the members of the group were on the whole reluctant to praise any early T'ang literature.

Perhaps this reluctance to bestow approval on seventh- and early eighth-century literature is to be explained partly by the idea that there was a time lag between the establishment of the T'ang and the creation of a T'ang style of writing to reflect the improved conditions.

---

161. *CTW* 315.8b; *HTS* 202.13b. The one exception to this scheme is Hsiao's praise for the Liang dynasty historian P'ei Tzu-yeh as being a "good writer" (*HTS* 202.13b).

162. *CTW* 315.8b.

163. *CTW* 323.12a.

164. *CTW* 337.11a.

165. *CTW* 388.1a–b.

This explanation had been used by early T'ang historians reviewing the literature of the Sui period.[166] Yüan Chieh hinted at it when he remarked after the rebellion, "Writers of recent generations have adhered to inherited practice."[167] But whatever their reason for so negative an attitude toward early T'ang literature, the men under review show striking agreement in singling out one figure in the seventh century for commendation. This was Ch'en Tzu-ang, the official and writer of the empress Wu's reign. Shortly after his death, a contemporary had claimed that through him, *"wen* and *chih* had undergone a change."[168] This praise was reiterated by Hsiao Ying-shih,[169] Tu-ku Chi,[170] Yen Chen-ch'ing,[171] and, implicitly, Yüan Chieh,[172] besides a number of other eighth-century writers.[173] This impressive consensus highlights a paradox in the attitudes these men had toward literature. Up to this point in their reviews they had treated it as a general phenomenon running more or less parallel to history itself. But now this broad characterization is abandoned, and a single, exceptional author is selected for commendation in contrast to his age.

The key to this paradox is almost certainly to be found in the two ways these writers looked at history and, indeed, at the *wen* concept itself. History, it will be recalled, was both considered as an impersonal, cyclic process and also analyzed in terms of specific individuals involved in it and in terms of their actions. These two approaches to history seem to have been paralleled exactly in literary criticism. There was the broad historical review of literature, when the writing of successive ages was implicitly related to its historical background. And there was the more detailed consideration of individual authors, often in contrast to the age that had produced them. But this more detailed approach occurred only in prefaces, which were usually reserved, by convention, for the collected works of the recently deceased. The parallels in historical writing are the biographies and other tributes to dead colleagues that these intellectuals wrote in such quantity.

166. *Sui shu* 76.2a.
167. This idea was more clearly expressed slightly later (*CTW* 518.3b).
168. *CTW* 238.4a.
169. *CTW* 315.8b.
170. *CTW* 388.12a.
171. *CTW* 337.11a.
172. *CTW* 381.15b; *CTShih,* vol. 4, p. 2711. Yüan Chieh's remarks echo Ch'en Tzu-ang's and are probably modeled on them.
173. Li Yang-ping, writing on Li Po (*CTW* 437.13b); Li Chou (ibid., 443.16a); Liang Su (ibid., 522.6b). Li Po modeled his *Ku-feng* series of poems (*CTShih,* vol. 3, p. 1670) on Ch'en's *Kan-yü shih* (ibid., vol. 2, p. 889). Also Liang Su (*CTW* 522.6b) and Chao Tan (ibid., 732.1a).

The desire to comment on the collections of their contemporaries and on their own creative experience led these men to pay attention to an aspect of Confucian literary theory distinct from the question of literature's social origins and effect on society. They turned to reexplore a second area in which the Chinese tradition had shown great insight, that of the psychological genesis of literature. Their position is the expressionistic one mentioned earlier in connection with the *wen* concept. Tu-ku Chi formulated their position in greatest detail: "When emotion overflows it finds expression in words. When words overflow they find form as *wen*. The feelings move within and take form in sounds. This is an aspect of *wen* which is still intangible. They [i.e. words] are made to blaze forth as song or hymn, spread abroad as deed or act. This is the aspect of *wen* which is fully apparent." Li Hua wrote similarly, "Emotion that is declared forth is called words; words that are ornamentally wrought are termed *wen*."[174] Literature to members of the group was thus the patterning, *wen,* of the inner feelings, first in the medium of sound, and then in writing itself. The terminology here stemmed from brief statements in the Classics, the *Book of History,* the *Tso chuan,* and the *I ching.*[175] These had been brought together in the influential *Mao shih ta-hsü,* to which, in effect, Li and Tu-ku were alluding. The *Mao shih ta-hsü* had said, "Poetry is concerned with the movement of emotion. When in the mind, it is emotion; when expressed as words, it is poetry." This was a well-known graphic pun; the character *shih,* "poem," consisted of the speech radical and the word *chih,* "emotion," which in turn was divisible into the heart radical and a verb meaning to go. Poetry, and indeed all literature, *wen,* in the passages by Tu-ku and Li cited above, was therefore the verbal expression of movement in the heart or mind, or of emotion.

The word *chih,* "emotion," or "earnest thought" in Legge's translation,[176] which figured in these early definitions of poetry, had in the *Analects* and other early sources a strongly positive moral connotation. Tu-ku Chi, Li Hua, and other T'ang writers preferred it and the definitions of poetry and literature in which it occurred to rival terminology from a later definition of the *shih.* In the Chin period, the

174. *CTW* 388.2b, 315.4b. The word *tsu,* strictly meaning to fill up, is here translated freely as to overflow.

175. *Shang shu* 1.11a; *Tso chuan,* Hsiang 25, p. 307; *I ching,* hexagram 2 *(k'un),* 1.6b–7b. Wilson, *The Triple Thinkers,* p. 254, has a remarkably similar definition of lyric poetry, "A lyric gives us nothing but a pattern imposed on the expression of feeling."

176. James Legge, *The Chinese Classics,* vol. 3 (Hong Kong, 1865), p. 48, and vol. 4 (Hong Kong, 1871), prolegomena, p. 34.

critic Lu Chi (261–303) had said, "Poetry traces feelings gracefully."[177] It was felt that "tracing feelings" *(yüan ch'ing)* in the context of poetry had less force than "expressing emotion" *(yen chih)*. Lu Chi's definition was almost certainly linked in the minds of Tu-ku Chi and others with the excesses of the verse of the Period of Disunion, and with the aesthetic approach to poetry associated with the regulated styles. Tu-ku noted of the latter that they "perfected the task of tracing feelings gracefully" but insisted that they were "very far removed from the *Ya* [section of the *Odes*]."[178] He and Li Hua preferred the canonical terminology, therefore, because of its strongly moral implications. Their position, since it implied that writing which results from the true expression of the inner feelings would be good, is optimistic about human nature, and therefore truly Confucian.

This expressionistic account of the origins of literature is to be seen as a concomitant of the individual and personal approach of these writers to the authors whose collected works they prefaced. For, as in the West. an expressionistic emphasis in criticism went with an interest in the character and biography of the author. It seems to have been assumed that good people would produce excellent writing.[179] This assumption justified the many fulsome tributes these men paid one another in prefaces whose formal function was to introduce the written works rather than their authors. It also lay behind their belief that literature was a legitimate means of self-advancement, of, in Li Hua's words, "establishing one's person and promoting one's name."[180] The literature of the gentleman *(chün tzu)* was thus, Tu-ku Chi observed, a fitting bequest to posterity, and a permissible way to win everlasting fame.[181]

The five writers under review all insisted on what amounts to the

---

177. Lu Chi, *Wen fu,* in *Wen hsüan* 17.6a; cf. Achilles Fang, "Rhymeprose on Literature— the *Wen-fu* of Lu Chi (A.D. 261–303)," *HJAS* 14 (1951): 536.

178. See Chu Tzu-ch'ing, *Shih yen chih pien,* pp. 1–42, for a discussion of the distinction between *shih yen chih* and *shih yüan ch'ing,* especially in the Period of Disunion. In early T'ang times, the *yüan-ch'ing* definition of the *shih* was disapproved of by Wang Po (*CTW* 182.15b); in mid-T'ang times implicitly by Jui T'ing-ch'ang (ibid., 356.23b), Shang Heng (ibid., 394.20a), Tu-ku Chi (ibid., 388.1a) and Li Hua (ibid., 315.4b, 9b and 13b).

179. Confucius had in fact made a distinction between the man and his words; see *Analects* 15.23. This is quoted wryly by Wei Cheng (*Sui shu* 76.2b), conceding that Sui Yang-ti, though an evil man, wrote good literature. Such a position is not to be found in the writers under review. Li Hua, for example, wrote in a preface (*CTW* 315.7a), "When you see his writings, you will know his life," and Tu-ku Chi (ibid., 388.2a), "When you see his compositions, you will know his values."

180. *CTW* 315.4b.

181. *CTW* 388.4b.

essence of their position, that literature had to be explicitly monitory, didactic, or exhortatory. Even Yüan Chieh, the most adventurous *san-wen* writer of the group, insisted on this, in a preface to his own collection: "My purpose has always been to encourage loyalty and filial piety, to urge fairness and uprightness, to induce charity and compassion, and to lead people to preserve integrity and accept their lot in life."[182] This same austerity of purpose also informed their demands for style. Simplicity and plainness were required both before the rebellion and, with greater insistence, after it. Tu-ku Chi spoke metaphorically of this requirement in a well-known passage. To indulge obsessively in ornate or intricate stylistic devices was "like having an orchid as a boat and a kingfisher feather as an oar. One may toy with them on dry land, but they cannot be used for crossing rivers."[183] Yüan Chieh,[184] Hsiao Ying-shih,[185] Li Hua,[186] and Tu-ku Chi condemned writing that merely demonstrated powers of description or technical dexterity. Tu-ku spoke against those who "take the eight faults [to be avoided] and four tones as if they were manacles and observe them as if they were honoring laws or commands."[187]

Their seriousness of purpose led these writers to disdain one of the major literary developments of their day, the growing tradition of fiction. Perhaps their attitude was influenced by their interest in historical criticism, and they felt, as Liu Chih-chi had, that tales of the exotic and supernatural (later called *ch'üan-ch'i*) were not to be classified with the works of serious historians.[188] They may also have wished to observe the traditional Confucian injunction against interest in "extraordinary things, feats of strength, disorder, and spiritual beings."[189] But it is interesting that a theoretical justification for recording exotic or supernatural occurrences, the sort of material basic to many stories of the period, was available to them. This apology is used by Ku K'uang, a late contemporary of the group. Exotic happenings were evidence of disturbance in the pattern of heaven, *t'ien-wen* and were therefore to be collected and studied just as *jen-wen* was in the human sphere.[190] But this idea is never mentioned by any

182. *CTW* 381.15b.
183. *CTW* 388.11b.
184. *CTW* 381.16b.
185. *CTShih*, vol. 3, p. 1594.
186. *CTW* 315.4b, 7a.
187. *CTW* 388.12a.
188. *Shih-t'ung t'ung-shih* 18.3b.
189. *Analects* 7.21, quoted by Aoki Masaru, *Shina bungaku shisō shi*, p.17.
190. *CTW* 528.13b.

of the men under review. Probably if they had any justification for fiction of any kind, it would have relied on the concept of indirect protest, of giving admonition through fable or allegory. The fable occurred often in *Chuang tzu* and other pre-Ch'in texts and therefore commanded literary prestige. Satirical animal fables by Li Hua are the nearest any of the group came to writing fiction.[191]

Conclusion

This chapter has explored the historical and literary ideas of a small group of intellectuals active over the An Lu-shan Rebellion period. These men came from aristocratic backgrounds and lived in a time of decline for aristocratic power and of sudden military crisis. Their intellectual outlook was conservative. It could be said that there were few new elements in their thought, for most of their theoretical ideas may be traced back through early T'ang to roots in the Han dynasty or earlier. But they wrote more freely and personally than their predecessors about their literary experience, and more critically about the past. One result was that the *wen* concept in its full range, which lay behind much of their historical and literary theory, was as prominent in their writings as in any since Han times.

We have seen that *wen* in the writings of the men under review could refer to a phenomenon in the universe, a value in society, literature itself, or a value in literature. A modern critic may perhaps feel disappointment that this versatility was not more analytically explored. We should be on our guard, however, against making anachronistic demands of these writers. Their main aims in writing were to express disapproval of the contemporary political world and of current literary practice and to praise one another for their efforts to put things right. In effect they were invoking the authority of traditional ideas rather than subjecting them to critical analysis. They would not have felt the need to provide a more systematic description of *wen*.

The *wen* concept was, nonetheless, the main Confucian theoretical idea about which they wrote, and it would be difficult to illustrate any other philosophical term from their collected works in such detail. This is first and foremost an indication of the importance of literature and history to these men. Since their identity depended so much on these activities, it was natural that they should have discussed them as

---

191. *CTW* 316.20a, 318.5b. There are also some brief examples of historical fiction, set in the pre-Ch'in period, by Li Hua (ibid., 318.1a–4a) and Yüan Chieh (ibid., 380.1a–7a). These are likely to have been acceptable for similar reasons.

they did. But secondly, and more tentatively, their liking for *wen* reflects the character of the concept itself and the intellectual milieu to which it appealed. We have seen that *wen* was either substantival, meaning culture or the written word, or a hypostatized descriptive term, meaning the patterned,cultured, or refined. In none of these senses did it present the analytical problems that arose in the more metaphysical or psychological ideas of Confucianism, or in the increasingly important common ground between Confucianism and Buddhism. *Wen* did not, moreover, unlike much Confucian psychological terminology, have to be reconciled to other closely connected but conflicting terms. Its moral value was clear. It had a descriptive, objective, almost tangible quality. Its prominence in the writings of the men under review thus suggests the corollary that other, more involved Confucian ideas were less immediate to them. They could endorse the idea of *wen* and make keen observations on literature and history. But they did not yet feel the need to discuss the complex and introspective philosophical ideas that exercised Confucians so much from the late eighth century on. To this extent it is right to describe their writings and the post-rebellion decades through which they lived as preparatory for the expansion of intellectual life that followed.

Despite these reservations, the account of *wen* abstracted from the writings of the men under review is detailed enough to provide a specific example of a well-known generalization often applied to the Confucian speculative tradition. It was, like its medieval European counterpart, predisposed to make elaborate correlations between man's immediate experience and the universe and between the moral and physical worlds. The concepts by which it did this were flexible. The intellectuals discussed here referred to *wen* in different senses according to context and quoted as their authority the brief and scattered canonical sayings from which these senses derived. But we know that they were aware that in the background all senses of the term were related. It was indeed as "a great unifying principle" that Hsiao Ying-shih extolled the perfection of *wen*.

Part III
Literature

10. The Contemplation of the Past
in T'ang Poetry

Hans H. Frankel

One feature that sets the Chinese literati apart from other cultural traditions is their sense of history. They studied it intensely as part of their training for the civil service examinations; when they became officials, they used argument from history as a standard device of policy debate; and it was they who kept the records and wrote the voluminous histories. It is therefore not surprising that when they wrote poetry—mostly for each other—they frequently evoked historical events, situations, and personalities. Such evocations of the past tended to fall into definite patterns. The purpose of this essay is to identify and discuss some of those patterns as they appear in the poetry of the T'ang, by which time they had become established as poetic conventions.

In the following poem by Meng Hao-jan (689?–740) we find a number of elements whose relationship is not immediately apparent.

Ascending Mount Hsien with Several Gentlemen

Human lives succeed each other and decay,
2   They come and go, becoming past and present.
Rivers and mountains keep their vestiges,
4   We in turn ascend to have a look.
The water level sinks, the fishing sluice is shallow,
6   The weather is cold, Lake Meng-tse is deep.
Lord Yang's stele is still here,
8   After we read it tears moisten our robes.[1]

1. Hsiao Chi-tsung, ed., *Meng Hao-jan shih shuo* (Taichung, 1961), pp. 65–66. Previous translations: Witter Bynner and Kiang Kang-hu, eds. and trans., *The Jade Mountain* (New York, 1929), p. 109; Ambros Rust, *Meng Hao-jan (691–740): Sein Leben und religiöses Denken nach seinen Gedichten* (Ingenbohl, Switzerland, 1960), p. 2.

The complexity of this poem results in part from its moving on two different time scales. On the one hand, it records a momentary experience: the poet and his companions ascend Mount Hsien, take in the view from the top, and are moved by the reading of the stele commemorating Yang Hu. On the other hand, the poet, his friends, and Yang Hu are seen as links in the long chain of history, subject to its eternal laws of succession and disintegration. The transition from the larger to the smaller scale is achieved near the middle of the poem, in the fourth line, which is ambiguously worded so as to fit both scales. "We in turn" means, on the wider scale, that the poet and his contemporaries have their turn in the succession of generations. On the lesser scale, it means that they come on this day to visit the scenic spot, like others before them. "Ascend to have a look," in the narrative context, means climbing to the mountain top and looking down. On the contemplative level, it means rising above the here-and-now and looking into the past. The topical association of *ascent* and *contemplation* of the past will become clear later in this essay. The simultaneous employment of two time scales enables the poet to place the mountain in a double perspective: it is the goal of the present excursion, but it also represents nature's constancy in the face of human transience (lines 1–3) and serves the function of handing down the vestiges of the past to the present (line 3).

A further complexity is introduced into the poem by the allusion to Yang Hu (221–78), a model official who made his mark at the court and also became popular as a local administrator. Two passages from his official biography should be quoted here because they are relevant to our poem:

> Hu loved natural scenery. Whenever the weather was fine, he would visit Mount Hsien, where he had wine served and poetry recited, without tiring all day long. Once he heaved a deep sigh, looked at his followers—Tsou Chan and others—and said to them: "From the beginning of the world, this mountain has always been here. All along, worthy and outstanding men have climbed up here to enjoy the distant view. There have been many like you and me, who have perished without leaving a reputation behind. This makes one sad. If a hundred years from now there are conscious souls, they are still bound to climb up here." Chan said: "Your virtue caps all within the four seas, in your conduct you are the heir of former sages. Your noble reputation, your noble

fame will surely be preserved together with this mountain. As for the rest of us, it will be as you have said."

On Mount Hsien, at the place where Hu used to go for recreation, the people of Hsiang-yang erected a stele and built a shrine. At the time of the seasonal festivals they offered sacrifices there. No one could look at the stele without weeping. Tu Yü therefore named it the "stele of dropping tears."[2]

We can see now that Meng Hao-jan's poem is in large part a rephrasing of five ideas taken from those two passages: the continuous succession of sightseers climbing Mount Hsien; the beauty of the surrounding scenery; the permanence of the mountain in contrast with man's ephemeral existence; the singularity of Yang Hu, whose memory lives on while other men are forgotten; and the tears that invariably accompany a perusal of the inscription, anticipated by Yang Hu's "deep sigh." But all five ideas take on fresh significance in the poem because they are enlivened with actuality: Meng and his friends are themselves experiencing the pleasures enjoyed by Yang and his associates; they are themselves reading the inscription; and their tears are not merely a perfunctory act traditionally associated with the occasion but a genuine realization of their limitations when measured against a paragon of virtue such as Yang Hu.

Before leaving Meng Hao-jan's poem, it will be useful to recapitulate six topoi which, as we shall see, are associated with the evocation of the past in other T'ang poems as well: ascent to a high place; looking into the distance in conjunction with viewing the past; the permanence of rivers and mountains in contrast to human transience; reference to historical personalities and extant relics of the past; description of a landscape devoid of historical association (lines 5–6 of Meng's poem); and tears.

The following poem by Wang Ch'ang-ling (698–765?) exemplifies all of these topoi, omitting only reference to a specific historical figure.

The Myriad-Year Tower

Lofty above the River, the Myriad-Year Tower,
2   Uncounted thousands of autumns it has braved.
Year after year there's joy in seeing the mountains always endure,

---

2. *Chin shu,* Po-na ed., 34.5a, 6b, cited by Hsiao, *Meng Hao-jan shih shuo,* pp. 65–66. Tu Yü was a friend of Yang Hu's.

4   Day after day there's grief in watching the water just flow.
     Why did the monkeys leave the evening mountains?
6   The cormorants aimlessly by themselves drift around the
         cold island.
     Who can bear to climb and look out among the clouds and
         mist?
8   Toward evening the vast expanse stirs the traveler's grief.[3]

We note here a refinement in the topos of mountains and rivers. While both are images of nature's constancy, as already observed in the preceding poem, Wang contrasts the immutable firmness of the mountains with the river's ceaseless flow. The poem further expresses man's emotional response to this dual aspect of his natural environment: he rejoices in its permanency but is troubled by the relentless progression of time, which moves in one direction only, without any possibility of return.

We encounter in this poem two more topoi that are frequently associated with the passage of time: "autumn" and "evening," being the season and the time of day that bring to mind termination and decline. The correspondence between the passing of years and of days is further emphasized by the juxtaposition of "year after year" and "day after day" (lines 3–4).

The spectacle of sunset is the starting point of the following poem by Li Ho (791–817), which is devoted to the leveling and destructive force of time.

Song of the Endless Past

     The bright sun goes back to the western mountains,
2   The azure splendor stretches high and far.
     Present and past—where do they end?
4   A thousand years drift with the wind.
     The ocean's sand changes to rock,
6   The fish's froth blows down the bridge of Ch'in.
     Empty brightness floats far on the waves,
8   The bronze pillars melt in the course of the years.[4]

The "bridge of Ch'in" (line 6) refers to a stone bridge which the

3. Kanno Dōmei, ed., *Tōshi sen shōsetsu* (Tokyo, 1966 [first publ. 1929]), pp. 624–25. The tower was at modern Chen-chiang in Kiangsu province; the river is the Yangtse.

4. *Li Ch'ang-chi ko shih Wang Ch'i hui chieh*, in *San chia p'ing-chu Li Ch'ang-chi ko shih* (Shanghai, 1959), p. 67; Saitō Shō, ed., *Ri Ga* (Tokyo, 1967), p. 106. Previous translations: A. C. Graham, *Poems of the Late T'ang* (Harmondsworth, Middx., 1965), p. 96.

first emperor of Ch'in is supposed to have built at Green Wall Mountain, extending out into the sea for a distance of thirty *li*. The "bronze pillars" (line 8) were erected by Emperor Wu of Han near Ch'ang-an to support bronze statues of immortals who held basins to catch the dew of immortality coming down from heaven. Li Ho is saying, then, that even Emperor Wu's instruments of immortality are subject to the decaying force of time, just as another mighty emperor's stone bridge was rendered so fragile by the ravages of time that the flimsiest of substances—the froth of fish—could bring it down. It is worth noting that Li Ho renders the immensity of time in spatial terms: "Present and past—*where* do they end?" In the same vein, he visualizes the passage of time as physical motion: "A thousand years drift with the wind."

The passage of time, without any reference to a definite point in history, is also the concern of a poem by Liu Hsi-i (651–after 671).

Imitation of the Whitehead's Song

East of the Loyang city walls, peach and plum blossoms
2   Fly back and forth: at whose house will they drop?
The girls of Loyang worry about their looks.
4   Strolling and meeting the falling blossoms, they heave long sighs:
As the blossoms fall this year, attractive looks change;
6   When the blossoms open next year, who will be around?
You've seen pines and cypresses cut to make fuel,
8   You've also heard of the mulberry orchards that became an ocean.
The people of old are no more east of Loyang's walls,
10   The people now still face the falling blossoms and the wind.
Year after year, age after age, the blossoms are alike;
12   Age after age, year after year, the people are not the same.
This message is for the young in their full rosy bloom:
14   You should pity the half-dead old whitehead.
This whiteheaded old man is surely to be pitied.
16   Once he was a handsome youth, in full rosy bloom,
With nobles and princes beneath fragrant trees,
18   Fresh songs and exquisite dances in front of falling blossoms,
Splendid moats and terraces, figured embroideries,
20   Generals, storeyed mansions, painted immortals—
One morning down with illness, no longer recognizable.

22   At whose side can he pass the joys of spring?
      How long can moth-antenna eyebrows keep their charm?
24   In a short while hoary hair is tangled like silk.
      You only see the old singing and dancing places,
26   There's nothing but the mournful cries of birds at dusk.[5]

Here, as so often in Chinese lyric poetry, the human condition is compared to and contrasted with flowering trees. The common element is the inevitable decay of beauty; the contrast lies in the trees' ability to renew themselves each year, while man is doomed to progressive decline. The blossoms, then, in conjunction with reflections on passing time, are an image comprising change and permanency, decay and renewal:

    Year after year, age after age, the blossoms are alike;
    Age after age, year after year, the people are not the same.

The contrast between past and present is also visualized in the anonymous figure of the whitehead. ("The Whitehead's Song" was a traditional *yüeh-fu* title.) The poem furthermore brings out the contrast between places that remain intact ("the Loyang city walls," lines 1 and 9; "the old singing and dancing places," line 25) and human beings who grow old (lines 3, 5, 21–24) and die (lines 6, 12). The evocation of past splendor (lines 16–20) is followed by stock formulas speaking of melancholy, isolated vestiges and reminders of bygone pleasures: "you only see . . ." (line 25), "there's nothing but . . ." (line 26).

Such visible remains of past glory may become the focal point of an entire poem, as in the following example, written by Tu Fu (712–70).

Jade Flower Palace

      The stream twists, the wind goes on among the pines,
2   Grey rats scurry on ancient tiles.
      I don't know who was the king
4   Whose palace remains here below the sheer cliff.
      In dark chambers, ghost lights are green;
6   On decayed roads, melancholy streams flow.
      The myriad sounds are truly mouth organs and pipes,
8   The appearance of autumn is at its most somber.
      The beautiful women have become brown earth,
10   As have the powdered and painted burial figures.

5. Kanno, *Tōshi sen shōsetsu,* pp. 93–98. The authorship of this poem is not quite certain; it has also been attributed to Sung Chih-wen (c. 663–712?).

Formerly they accompanied the emperor's golden sedan-chair,
12 Now only stone horses remain.
Full of grief, I sit down on the grass.
14 Loud I sing, tears fill my hands.
Continually on the road,
16 How can one expect to live long?[6]

The Jade Flower Palace (Yü-hua Kung) was erected in 646 for T'ai-tsung, the second emperor of the T'ang. Tu Fu's professed ignorance of its history (line 3) is likely to be a pose, assumed in order to emphasize the universality of human decline and decay, as suggested by William Hung.[7] The sight of the ruins is linked in this poem to the somber atmosphere of autumn (a topos that we observed in Wang Ch'ang-ling's poem above), and, at the end, to the personal fate of the poet and others who, like him, find themselves torn away from their roots.

While Tu Fu here takes pains to ignore the identity of the historical site to which his poem is devoted, the more usual procedure is to re-create the past associated with the place being visited and then to contrast the past glory with the present state of decay. Such a juxtaposition is found in a poem by Wang Ling-jan (chin-shih of 717).

The Willows of the Pien River

The Son of Heaven of the house of Sui longed for Yang
    province,
2 He tired of residing deep in the palace and wished to be near
    the sea.
Boring through the earth and tunneling through mountains, he
    opened a royal passageway.
4 With sounding pipes and rolling drums he floated on clear
    water,
Floating from northern Kung, where the rivers divide,
6 Straight to Huai-nan, with willows planted by the state.
The work was done, strength was exhausted, men died in turn,
8 Generations perished, years shifted, the trees exist in vain.
At that time, gaily dressed women served the sovereign ruler,
10 Embroidered tents and gates with insignia faced the rows of
    willows.

6. Ch'iu Chao-ao, ed., Tu shih hsiang chu (Shanghai, 1915), 5.26a–27b. Previous translations: Erwin von Zach, trans., Tu Fu's Gedichte, Harvard-Yenching Institute Studies, no. 8 (Cambridge, Mass., 1952), 3:47; Robert Payne, ed., The White Pony (New York, 1947), pp. 236–37; William Hung, Tu Fu: China's Greatest Poet (Cambridge, Mass., 1952), p. 114.

7. Hung, Tu Fu, p. 110.

Green leaves hanging together joined with colorful curtains,
12 White blossoms wafting across became decorations on fragrant
    clothes.
Today, decline and decay—no need to speak of it.
14 For many miles not a single tree is fine.
Among postal couriers and sailboats the losses are even greater,
16 Mountain spirits and field ghosts must have been hiding long.
A cold wind in the eighth month, dew turns to frost,
18 Day and night lone sailboats enter the imperial domain.
At the river bank from time to time are heard falling leaves,
20 Among the travelers there's none whose tears don't moisten his
    robes.[8]

The poet's attitude toward the past that he recreates is ambivalent. He sympathizes with the pleasure-seeking Sui emperor (Emperor Yang, reigned 604–17) but also condemns him for the cruel hardships that his gigantic canal-building project imposed on the laborers (lines 7–8). The "decline and decay" (line 13) that characterize the present scene are not only the inevitable result of the ravages of time but more particularly the consequence of Emperor Yang's wickedness. The general deterioration extends even to the willow trees (line 14), which had been planted on the emperor's orders (line 6); they somehow share his guilt and now "exist in vain" (line 8). The season is appropriately autumn (line 17), and the sadness of the scene is felt most keenly by homesick travelers (line 20)—a melancholy reversal of Emperor Yang's pleasure trips that had been evoked earlier (lines 3–6, 9–12).

In the next few poems, the evocation of particular segments of the past is occasioned by visits to historic sites. The first example is by Ts'en Shen (715?–70).

Ascending to the Ancient Site of the City of Yeh

I get off my horse and ascend to the site of the city of Yeh.
2   The city is empty, what is there to see?
The east wind blows on the wild fire,
4   In the evening it used to enter Flying Cloud Palace.
The city wall's south corner faces the Terrace Overlooking
    the Tomb.
6   The Chang River flows east without returning.
In Emperor Wu's palace all inhabitants are gone.

---

8. *T'ang-jen hsüan T'ang-shih* (Shanghai, 1958), p. 520.

8   For whom does spring's splendor come year after year?[9]

Yeh (in modern Honan) was Ts'ao Ts'ao's (155–220) fief, and after his death the city became one of the capitals of the Wei dynasty. "Emperor Wu" was the title posthumously given to Ts'ao Ts'ao when his son Ts'ao P'ei founded the Wei dynasty in 220.

We note in this poem several topoi that are already familiar from previous examples: the poem opens with an ascent (line 1); the river flows east without returning (line 6); the city is empty (line 2); the landscape is wild (line 3); the people of the past are gone (line 7); there is little left to see (line 2). One of the extant sights is a tomb (line 5), which in this case is Ts'ao Ts'ao's. The recurring splendor of spring is wasted because the place is no longer inhabited (line 8). The wind (lines 3–4) has a multiple function: It is one of nature's constants, like spring. It is also in perpetual motion, like the river, and brings out the contrast between the present (line 3) and the past (line 4), representing the change and destruction brought about by the passage of time. We may recall Li Ho's line, "A thousand years drift with the wind."

In the following poem by Li Po (701–63), more than one historical period is evoked by a single sight.

Ascending Phoenix Terrace at Chin-ling

On Phoenix Terrace phoenixes used to roam.
2   The phoenixes are gone, the terrace is empty, the river just
      flows.
The flowers and grasses of the palaces of Wu are buried among
      neglected paths,
4   The robes and caps of the Chin court have become old tombs.
Triple Mountain is half submerged beyond the blue sky,
6   Double River is split in the middle by White Egret Island.
As drifting clouds manage to cover the sun,
8   Ch'ang-an is invisible, how sad![10]

Chin–ling (modern Nanking) was the capital of the Southern Dynasties, of which our poem mentions the first two, Wu and Chin. Besides, the opening line refers to an auspicious event reported to have occurred on this spot during the Yüan-chia era (424–54) of Sung (the third of the Southern Dynasties), namely, the gathering of phoenixes.

Just as in Meng Hao-jan's poem cited at the beginning of this essay,

9. Kanno, Tōshi sen shōsetsu, pp. 158–60.
10. Ibid., pp. 550–54; Aoki Masaru, ed., Ri Haku (Tokyo, 1965), pp. 164–65.

the penultimate couplet (lines 5–6) describes the landscape as seen from above. But while in Meng's poem the description was devoid of historical association, Li Po in the present poem has thoroughly fused the visible scene with the evocations of the past. Witness the consistent sequence of predicates in every line, beginning with line 2: "are gone . . . is empty . . . just flows . . . are buried . . . have become old tombs . . . is half submerged . . . is split in the middle . . . manage to cover . . . is invisible . . . how sad!" The lament for things invisible, made explicit in the last line, informs the whole poem. It applies to the phoenixes, the vegetation of the Wu palaces, the Chin courtiers, half of Triple Mountain, the sun, and the present capital, Ch'ang-an. They are invisible for diverse reasons, some having to do with time, others with distance, others with permanent or temporary obstructions. We are reminded again that distance in time is commensurate with distance in space.

Our final examples will be two cycles of poems, the first one by Ch'en Tzu-ang (661–702).

Contemplating Antiquities at Thistle Hill, Presented to Hermit Lu Ts'ang-yung

Preface

In the year *ting-yu* (697) I went on the northern campaign. Going out from Thirstle Gate, I got a comprehensive view of the old capital of Yen. Its walls and moats, the traces of its might, were overgrown with weeds. Deeply moved, I looked up and sighed. My thoughts turned back to the time when worthies such as Lord Yüeh and Sage Tsou roamed and flourished there. Thereupon I ascended Thistle Hill and composed seven poems to commemorate them. I sent the poems to Recluse Lu in the Chung-nan Mountains. There were also vestiges of Hsüan-yüan.

1. The Terrace of Hsüan-yüan

In the north I ascend Thistle Hill and look,
2   Seeking out the ancient terrace of Hsüan-yüan.
The winged dragon is seen no more,
4   Horses graze in vain in yellow dust.
I also think of Kuang-ch'eng Tzu.
6   Their vestiges—a bay of white clouds.

2. King Chao of Yen

In the south I ascend to Upright Rock Hall,

2   In the distance I see Yellow Gold Terrace.
    On hills and mounds nothing but tall trees,
4   King Chao—where is he?
    His plan for hegemony failed, alas!
6   Spurring my horse I go back again.

3. Lord Yüeh

    The Royal Way was ruined and obscured,
2   The Warring States competed for fighters.
    Lord Yüeh, how loyal!
4   Devoted to duty he downed the walls of Ch'i.
    Heroic plans in the end brought him calamity,
6   Leaving behind a sigh addressed to the ministers of kings.

4. The Heir Apparent of Yen

    The king of Ch'in grew daily more immoral,
2   The heir apparent's hate of him grew ever stronger.
    The sudden news of T'ien Kuang's devotion—
4   The dagger—the gift of a thousand gold.
    The enterprise, though unsuccessful,
6   Has stirred men's hearts a thousand years.

5. Master T'ien Kuang

    From ancient times there has been death for all,
2   But such loyal rectitude is rare.
    How could the heir apparent of Yen
4   Doubt Master T'ien Kuang?
    He fell on his sword to end his life in honor,
6   Moving me to moisten my robe with tears.

6. Sage Tsou

    Fortune declined during the Three Dynasties,
2   Heavenly men became a rare sight.
    Sage Tsou, how extraordinary!
4   His art of suasion spanned the Nine Seas.
    Since his rise and fall a thousand years have passed,
6   Nowadays he has no equal.

7. Kuo Wei

    Only when he was met his worth was realized,
2   It's not that there's no talent through the ages,
    Lord Wei, how very fortunate!

4   As a result, Yellow Gold Terrace arose.[11]

The historical matters invoked in these seven poems are related to Ch'en Tzu-ang's personal situation at the time, which was, in short, as follows. He was holding the position of Omissioner of the Right *(yu-shih-i)* in the eastern capital, Loyang, when in 696 he was appointed military adviser *(ts'an-mou)* to General Wu Yu-i, prince of Chien-an, who was commanding one of the imperial armies defending the northern frontier against a Khitan attack. In the spring of 697 another imperial army was defeated by the Khitan. General Wu, stationed at Yü-yang (northeast of modern Peking), cautiously kept his troops in place without engaging the enemy. Ch'en Tzu-ang then submitted to him a plan for a more aggressive strategy, suggesting stricter military discipline and a new offensive, but General Wu rejected his proposal. When Ch'en presented his plan again in a new form, Wu angrily transferred him to the post of assistant military administrator *(chün-ts'ao)*. This "transfer" *(hsi)* was both a promotion and a demotion: it gave him a higher rank but less responsibility.[12] In the summer of 697 the campaign against the Khitan was victoriously concluded, and Ch'en Tzu-ang returned to his former post in the eastern capital.[13]

The seven poems, then, were written at a dark moment in the poet's life when he had lost his superior's confidence and favor; they are an attempt to work off his frustration by contemplating comparable and contrasting situations in history. In the first poem he recalls a mythological ruler of the Golden Age, the Yellow Emperor, whose name was Hsüan-yüan, and a recluse, Kuang-ch'eng Tzu, who is known for having been consulted by the Yellow Emperor regarding the Way.[14] Thus the poet evokes the ideal situation of a perfect ruler who willingly accepts the advice of his sage counselor. It is worth noting that both Hsüan-yüan and Kuang-ch'eng Tzu were considered to be Taoist sages and that Ch'en Tzu-ang and his friend Lu Ts'ang-yung, to whom

11. Hsü P'eng, ed., *Ch'en Tzu-ang chi* (Shanghai, 1960), pp. 22–23; *Ch'en Po-yü wen chi* (ed. in *Ssu-pu ts'ung-k'an*), 2.2a–3a. In the latter text, the preface says "six poems" in place of "seven poems," and the last poem ("Kuo Wei") is printed separately, not as part of the cycle. If it was part of the original cycle, it seems to have remained incomplete, being two lines shorter than the other poems. No. 2 is also in Kanno, *Tōshi sen shōsetsu*, pp. 15–18.

12. This sense of *hsi* is explained by Yen Keng-wang, *T'ang p'u shang ch'eng lang piao*, Academia Sinica, Institute of History and Philology, Monographs, no. 36 (Nankang, 1956), "Fan li," p. 1.

13. Lu Ts'ang-yung, *Ch'en shih pieh-chuan* [Unofficial biography of Ch'eng Tzu-ang], in Hsü, *Chen Tzu-ang chi*, pp. 253–54; Lo Yung, *Ch'en Tzu-ang nien-p'u* [Chronological biography of Ch'en Tzu-ang], ibid., pp. 346–55.

14. See *Chuang Tzu*, sec. 11, "Tsai yu."

the poems are addressed, were adherents of Taoism. The poet dwells on the fact that those two paragons are no more, that is, he sublimates his acute personal disappointment by rising to a more general, historical view: a wise leader should listen to his adviser, as Hsüan-yüan did, but even such a perfect relationship eventually becomes nonexistent with the passage of time.

The other six poems deal with two periods in the history of the feudal state of Yen (around modern Peking), one centering on King Chao (poems 2, 3, 6, 7) and the other on Heir Apparent Tan (poems 4 and 5). The poet focuses on certain figures and events that can be related to his own situation. King Chao (reigned 312–279 B.C.) greatly strengthened the state of Yen but failed in his attempt to win the hegemony over the other feudal states (2.5). He succeeded in defeating the state of Ch'i with the help of his minister and general Yüeh I ("Lord Yüeh," poem 3). After King Chao's death, Yüeh I fell out of favor—like the poet, Ch'en Tzu-ang—and fled from Yen to Chao to escape persecution by the new king, Hui (reigned 279–72). Tsou Yen ("Sage Tsou," poem 6) was also favored by King Chao and imprisoned by his successor, Hui. He was a master in the art of persuasion (6.4)—the art in which Ch'en Tzu-ang had just experienced failure.

Kuo Wei (poem 7) was honored by King Chao as his personal tutor, and attracted other sages to the court of Yen, including Yüeh I from Wei and Tsou Yen from Ch'i. They were housed in the Upright Rock Hall (2.1) and in the nearby Yellow Gold Terrace (2.1 and 7.4). King Chao frequently went to those two buildings in person to receive their instruction. Yellow Gold Terrace was so named because King Chao placed a thousand pieces of gold there in order to lure scholars from neighboring states.[15] King Chao in these poems is an idealization of the poet's superior, General Wu Yu-i, prince of Chien-an. (Note that both bore the same title, *wang*, "king" or "prince.") The contrast is striking: King Chao surrounded himself with learned men and revered them as teachers, while General Wu rejected Ch'en's proposals and transferred him to a different post. King Chao, furthermore, fought a victorious campaign against the enemy of his state, while Wu refused to have his troops advance.

Poems 4 and 5 deal with the feud between Prince Tan, heir apparent of Yen (died 226 B.C.), and King Cheng of Ch'in (reigned 247–210 B.C., took the title "First Emperor" when he unified China in 221). This conflict was often treated in Chinese literature. The salient facts to

15. *Shih chi*, Po-na ed., 34.7a–8a; Kanno, *Tōshi sen shōsetsu*, pp. 16–17.

which our poems allude are these: Prince Tan bore a grudge against King Cheng from the time when the prince was humiliated by the king while living as a hostage at the court of Ch'in. Prince Tan realized, furthermore, that the aggressive power of Ch'in threatened the existence of Yen and all the other feudal states. He sought advice from T'ien Kuang, who introduced him to Ching K'o, an expert swordsman. T'ien Kuang killed himself after his interview with Prince Tan, partly out of loyalty to the prince—to make sure that their secret deliberations would not leak out—and partly out of shame because Prince Tan, by cautioning him not to mention their discussion to others, had seemed to consider him capable of betraying the secret. Later Prince Tan sent Ching K'o on an abortive mission to assassinate King Cheng of Ch'in. The weapon intended for the murder was a dagger (4.4), concealed in a map which Ching K'o presented to the king. To gain access to the royal presence, Ching K'o presented gifts worth a thousand catties of gold (4.4) to Meng Chia, an influential minister at the Ch'in court, but he died in the unsuccessful assassination attempt.[16]

Why were Prince Tan, Ching K'o, and T'ien Kuang admired so much by Ch'en Tzu-ang and many others before and after him? Partly because they took action against King Cheng of Ch'in, whom the Chinese literati detested for his efforts to impose thought control and to destroy some of their most highly prized values. A deeper reason is that these men were tragic heroes, motivated by sublime idealism, fighting against overwhelming odds and laying down their lives for a noble cause. When he was writing these poems, Ch'en Tzu-ang must have envied those men for their selfless though unsuccessful actions, while he himself was condemned to frustrating inaction; he must have contrasted in his mind their patriotism and courage with General Wu's unwillingness to attack the Khitan; and he must have seen in Ching K'o's and T'ien Kuang's self-sacrificing loyalty to Prince Tan a more honorable relationship than existed between himself and his own prince, General Wu.

Ch'en Tzu-ang's seven poems, though dealing with different historical personalities, are unified by their association with a single site. In the following cycle by Tu Fu (712–70), on the other hand, each poem evokes a different place and describes a different man.

---

16. For a thorough study of Ching K'o as a historical and legendary figure, see Herbert Franke, "Die Geschichte des Prinzen Tan von Yen," *Zeitschrift der Deutschen Morgenländischen Gesellschaft* 107 (1956): 412–58.

Poetic Thoughts on Ancient Sites

1

Forlorn in the northeast among wind and dust,
2 Drifting in the southwest between heaven and earth,
Lingering for days and months in towers and terraces at the
Three Gorges,
4 Sharing clouds and mountains with the costumes of the Five
Streams.
The barbarian serving the ruler in the end was unreliable.
6 The wandering poet lamenting the times had no chance to return.
Yü Hsin throughout his life was most miserable,
8 In his waning years his poetry stirred the land of rivers and
passes.

2

"Decay and decline": deep knowledge have I of Sung Yü's
grief.
2 Romantic and refined, he too is my teacher.
Sadly looking across a thousand autumns, one shower of tears,
4 Melancholy in different epochs, not at the same time.
Among rivers and mountains his old abode—empty his writings;
6 Deserted terrace of cloud and rain—surely not just imagined
in a dream?
Utterly the palaces of Ch'u are all destroyed and ruined,
8 The fishermen pointing them out today are unsure.

3

Groups of mountains and myriads of streams run to Ching-men.
2 It's still there, the village where Ming-fei was born and bred.
No sooner had she left the crimson terraces than she was linked
to the northern desert,
4 Alone there remains the green tomb facing the yellow dusk.
The painting made known incompletely her spring-wind face,
6 With tinkling pendants, her soul comes back empty in the
moonlit night.
For a thousand years the lute, with words in barbarian language,

8   Has made clear her sorrow in the lyrics of the song.

4

The ruler of Shu had his eyes on Wu and progressed as far as
    the Three Gorges.
2   In the year of his demise, too, he was in the Palace of Eternal
    Peace.
The blue-green banners can be imagined on the empty moun-
    tain,
4   The jade palace is a void in the deserted temple.
In the pines of the ancient shrine aquatic cranes nest;
6   At summer and winter festivals the comers are village elders.
The Martial Marquis's memorial shrine is ever nearby;
8   In union, sovereign and minister share the sacrifices together.

5

Chu-ko's great name hangs across the world,
2   The honored minister's likeness awes with noble purity.
Triple division and separate states twisted his plans,
4   A single feather in a sky of a myriad ages.
Neither better nor worse was he than Yi and Lü;
6   Had his direction succeeded, he would have bested Hsiao and
    Ts'ao.
As revolving fate shifted the fortunes of Han, they were hard to
    restore;
8   His purpose was cut off and his body destroyed as with the
    army he toiled.[17]

The assignment of separate sites and personalities to each of the
five poems is not so simple. The persons stand out more clearly than the
places: in poem 1, it is Yü Hsin (513–81); in poem 2, Sung Yü (third
century B.C.); in poem 3, Wang Ch'iang, known as Ming-fei (first
century B.C.); in poem 4, Liu Pei, the first ruler of Shu (161–223,
reigned 221–23); and in poem 5, Chu-ko Liang (181–234). But it
cannot be said that each poem is exclusively concerned with a single
person. In poem 1, Yü Hsin is not mentioned until the penultimate
line. In poem 2, the word "too" (2.2) indicates that this poem is not an

---

17. Ch'iu, *Tu shih hsiang chu*, 17.29b–36a. A useful commentary to poems 1–3 can be found
in Hsiao Ti-fei, *Tu Fu yen-chiu* (Tsinan, 1957), 2:179–82. Previous translations: von Zach,
Tu Fu's Gedichte, 15:55–59; poems 1 and 3: Hung, *Tu Fu*, p. 236; poems 3 and 5: Bynner and
Kiang, *The Jade Mountain*, p. 157, and David Hawkes, *A Little Primer of Tu Fu* (Oxford, 1967),
nos. 27 and 28; poem 3: Payne, *The White Pony*, p. 227.

independent entity but the continuation of poem 1. The word "too" also implies that Sung Yü, the hero of poem 2, belongs to a sequence of masters to whom Tu Fu feels indebted, including presumably Yü Hsin. Poem 4, though primarily devoted to Liu Pei, also mentions Chu-ko Liang ("the Martial Marquis," 4.7, Chu-ko Liang's posthumous title), anticipating the theme of poem 5.

The situation is even more complex when we examine the localities to which the poems refer. Supposedly, the poems were "each inspired by Tu Fu's visit as a sightseer to some place of interest associated with a famous historical personage."[18] This may be the case in poems 3, 4, and 5. But in respect to poem 1, William Hung, an expert on the biographical background of Tu Fu's poems, first states that "the subject of the poem was the site of Yü Hsin's house in Chiang-ling" and then goes on to point out that "Tu Fu, when he wrote the poem, had not yet been to Chiang-ling, and therefore, had not seen the site of Yü Hsin's early home."[19] In regard to poem 3, too, Hung doubts that Tu Fu actually visited Wang Ch'iang's native village.[20]

While the village is expressly mentioned in 3.2, there is no reference in poem 1 to Yü Hsin's dwelling in Chiang-ling. In fact, it is not necessary to assume that Tu Fu personally visited any of the sites of which he speaks in these poems. In this respect the cycle differs from the other poems discussed in this essay. Tu Fu's visits to the past are *spiritual* journeys rather than records of travels to historic sites. On the other hand, he identifies more closely than most other poets with the historical figures whom he evokes.

With these considerations in mind, we are now ready to take a closer look at the cycle. In poem 1, the name of the poet Yü Hsin is not introduced until line 7, as mentioned earlier. Consequently, it is possible to read the first six lines without any thought of Yü Hsin, and the wording is appropriately ambivalent. Line 1 can be taken to refer to the outbreak of the An Lu-shan Rebellion in northeast China in 755, and line 2, to Tu Fu's travels in the southwest in the 760s. But the first two lines can also be read as a reference to the disorders in Yü Hsin's time and to *his* travels. In this reading, the juxtaposition of "northeast" and "southwest" would not be taken literally but as an instance of reciprocal phrasing *(hu-wen)*, and the couplet would amount to saying that there was strife all over China—north, east, south, and west—and a man was wandering from one part of China to another. Similarly,

18. Hawkes, *A Little Primer of Tu Fu*, p. 175.
19. Hung, *Tu Fu*, pp. 228, 229.
20. Ibid., p. 229.

"the barbarian" of line 5 can be identified with Hou Ching of Yü Hsin's time as well as with An Lu-shan, and "the wandering poet" (line 6) is both Yü Hsin and Tu Fu.

In poem 2, Tu Fu's involvement with the historical figure he invokes—Sung Yü, in this case—is even more explicit. In the first half of the poem, he adopts as his own certain sentiments voiced in Sung Yü's poetry, identifying with the ancient poet across the abyss of time. (The phrase "thousand autumns" had already been used by Wang Ch'ang-ling in the poem cited above.) The merger is marked in line 1 by three words ("decay and decline," "grief") taken verbatim from the opening couplet of Sung Yü's "Nine Arguments." Also, the phrase "cloud and rain" (line 6) alludes to a passage in the description of the goddess in the "Kao-t'ang fu," attributed to Sung Yü: "In the morning I am the dawn cloud, in the evening I am the driving rain." The evocation of the poet Sung Yü in this poem is combined with reflections on the transience of the glory of Ch'u in the now familiar manner of this poetic convention. In line 5 the topical adjective *k'ung* ("empty") is placed in such a way as to allow for two alternative readings. (Such ambiguity is characteristic of Tu Fu's later poems, beginning in 766, when this cycle was written.)[21] The adjective may either be taken as the predicate of the noun preceding it: his old abode is empty, that is, Sung Yü is gone; or it may be read as modifying the following noun: empty writings, that is, Sung Yü's works are his only remains.

In poem 3 the fate of the Chinese palace lady who had to leave her homeland to become the wife of a nomad ruler obviously engaged Tu Fu's sympathy because he, too, at the time of writing this cycle found himself far from home and from the imperial court—namely, in K'uei-chou (in modern Szechwan).[22] Poem 3 is thus closely connected with poem 1. According to a legend told in the *Hsi-ching tsa-chi,* Ming-fei, unlike all the other palace ladies, refused to bribe the court painter, Mao Yen-shou, who then made her portrait ugly, so that Emperor Yüan was unaware of her beauty and allowed her to be married to the Hsiung-nu ruler.[23] The tinkling pendants (line 6) that remain after her death are "empty" in the same sense as Sung Yü's house and writings (2.5): they make visible the loss of the distinguished person to whom they formerly belonged.

Liu Pei and Chu-ko Liang, the heroes commemorated in poems 4 and 5, are fitting subjects for this kind of evocation because they both

21. See Graham, *Poems of the Late T'ang,* pp. 20–22.
22. Hung, *Tu Fu,* pp. 222, 228–29.
23. *Hsi-ching tsa-chi, SPTK* ed., 2.1a.

failed in their noble endeavors. From other poems by Tu Fu we know of his great admiration for both men, as well as for Sung Yü and Yü Hsin. The conventional topic of the transience of human grandeur is forcefully expressed in 4.5–6: the only visitors to the former imperial palace are the cranes that nest there and a few village elders who come to the semiannual festivals. The concept of "void" (4.4), encountered several times previously, is very apt here next to "the empty mountain" (4.3) and "the deserted temple" (4.4); besides, it assumes an additional meaning in its application to a Buddhist temple.

The twenty poems discussed in these pages have a sufficient number of features in common to justify our considering them as belonging to a distinct category. Yet they do not seem to have been so considered in T'ang times, since they did not receive a generic name comparable to other recognized categories of T'ang poetry, such as "palace poems" and "frontier poems," which, like our poems, share among themselves a common thematic imagery. Yet some of the poems belonging to our category do have recurring titles referring to the past or to history. Typical titles are *huai ku*, "cherishing the past"; *lan ku*, "contemplating antiquity (or antiquities)," implying both a physical and a spiritual view; *ku i*, which may be rendered "evoking the past," "turning to the past," or sometimes "in ancient style"; *yung-huai ku i*, "a poem evoking the past"; *yung-huai ku chi*, "a poem cherishing vestiges of the past"; *yung shih*, "a poem on a historical theme"; and *hsi hsi*, "lament for the past." Many poems belonging to our category have in the title the word *teng*, "ascending," since ascent is, as we have seen, a favorite topos in this type of poem. Still others bear titles that give no indication of their having anything to do with the past.

In general, the T'ang poets confront history differently from the way a historian or a writer of historical fiction would handle it. They are not interested in the past for its own sake but in its relations to the present and to the problem of time in general. The past, in their view, is similar to the present—and at the same time dissimilar. Because of the similarities, contemplation of the past helps to clarify the problems of the present, showing them in a broader perspective. Because of the differences, the past may be recalled to show what the present might have been like but unfortunately is not. History is viewed as a constant process of deterioration, a steady decline from a remote golden age down to the degenerate present. That is one reason why all our poems are laments: the poet regrets living in an age worse than the one he is evoking. Another reason for the inevitable sighs and tears is the fact that the past is dead and gone, hence the contemplation of history is a

painful reminder of man's transience. A third reason is that a close look
at the past shows it to have been just as replete with misery and misfor-
tunes as the present. Or, to put it more precisely, one of the conventions
of our category is to focus on historic failures rather than successes. The
heroes of these poems are men like Ching K'o and Chu-ko Liang.

Since the past is generally superior to the present, the evocation of
noble deeds and egregious men of old serves as *inspiration,* and since the
great men of history suffered the same disappointments as the poets,
their memory becomes a *consolation.* As a third function of the use of
history we may consider *deviation,* which has recently been shown to
be a basic strategy of all poetry.[24] Rather than proceeding in a straightforward manner, poetry works largely by indirection. It uses detours,
circumlocutions, and metaphors. The past is a convenient counterpart
of the present. Exploiting the analogies and contrasts between past and
present situations, the poet can exhibit, through history, a more perfect state than exists in actuality; at the same time, he can hold up the
past as a mirror to the present, demonstrating the unchanging character of the human condition.

The contrast between the past and the present is sometimes rendered
as a juxtaposition of time and place: the situation has changed, but
the local frame is the same, as at the end of Liu Hsi-i's poem:

> You only see the old singing and dancing places,
> There's nothing but the mournful cries of birds at dusk.

But time and place are not always in juxtaposition. The passage of
time may be transposed into spatial terms, as in the favorite image of
the river flowing forever eastward, without returning. Other tropes
that transform the progress of time into physical motion are wind,
falling blossoms, and falling leaves.

These and other images from the natural world are commonly used
to contrast time's destructive effect on man and his works with nature's
constancy and self-renewal. In particular, trees and mountains are used
as representatives of permanency through the ages. The falling blossoms of flowering trees are, at the same time, an established metaphor
for the transience of youth and beauty. Mountains, besides being
symbols of durability, are also the sites where history is recorded and
remembered, and climbing a mountain is one of the topoi conventionally associated with our category. This is another instance of the merging
of time and space: the ascent enables the poet to rise above the limitations of his momentary situation and to peer into temporal as well as

24. See Jean Cohen, *Structure du langage poétique* (Paris, 1966).

spatial distance. It follows naturally that the contemplation of the past is frequently coupled with a description of the landscape. The physical scene often contains visible remainders of the past, such as ruins, tombs, or inscriptions. At other times, the natural setting harmonizes with the theme of passing time by exhibiting a sunset, falling leaves, or growing weeds. The descriptive passages tend to operate with the contrast between what is visible and what for various reasons remains invisible, and this contrast becomes another reason for lamenting the general law of decay: the remaining vestiges of the past are characterized as "few," "empty," and "vain."

Both the description of the scene and the evocation of the past are invariably selective. The poet focuses on the features most relevant to the situation at hand and to the purposes of the poem. The tone of every description, evocation, and reflection tends to be highly emotional and predominantly melancholy. It is generally a combination of yearning, admiration, regret, and lament.

11. On Li Po

ELLING O. EIDE

Although Sinology is a field crowded with men and issues still untouched by the hand of modern scholarship, even Sinologists are often astonished to discover how little work has been done on the T'ang poet Li Po. He and his contemporary, Tu Fu, are so closely associated, now so universally famous, that one tends to assume that these two, at least, have surely been "done" adequately for the present time. Yet, the abundance of rather careful Tu Fu scholarship is matched by a striking absence of serious Li Po material, and I suspect that no one in world literature has been so much read and so little analyzed. The fact is that since the commentary by Wang Ch'i (1696–1774), we have only a handful of significant contributions to Li Po studies: Arthur Waley's short and rather unsympathetic biography, Erwin von Zach's admirable but now dated translations, the invaluable though somewhat clumsy Kyoto concordance, the two useful volumes of essays and research material by Chan Ying published in Peking in 1957 and 1958, and now Kuo Mo-jo's fresh and imaginative *Li Po yü Tu Fu* [Li Po and Tu Fu], the first scholarly book published in China since the Cultural Revolution.

It is nice, of course, to have a writer whose appeal can survive the centuries without a mulch of annotation, and the critical neglect of Li Po does tell much about Chinese attitudes toward criticism and the man. In the little that has been written we find, for example, a kind of "homeopathic" critical approach that treats the subject matter in a fashion as carefree and bizarre as Li Po's presumed personality, to give us a certain unlooked for measure of the poet in the critics' eyes.[1] Again,

For further discussion of the above and other works on Li Po, see the Bibliographical Note at the end of the chapter.

1. There is a measure of Li Po's originality in the *Li shih pien-i* by the Ming scholar Chu

367

in what is written—and in the critics' failure to write more—there is reflected the Confucian, and now Marxist, moral judgment that while Tu Fu is good for you, Li Po, in all probability, is not. Yet important questions have been neither answered nor asked, and although Wang Ch'i and his two predecessors have identified most of the place-names and allusions, the appreciation of Li Po, as man or poet, is no deeper or more firmly grounded today than it was at the close of the T'ang dynasty.

One of the questions that has long intrigued me—a basic question about the nature of Li Po's accomplishment—is, simply, what was it about Li Po that so excited Tu Fu's admiration? Why, indeed, was he one of the very few Chinese poets to be widely and immediately recognized as a genius by his contemporaries? Needless to say, the traditional view that they admired him because he was a genius and that he was a genius because he was supernaturally inspired is no more helpful than the explanation that his poems seem powerful and spontaneous because he was a passionate man who wrote spontaneously. This, clearly, is mistaking effect for cause, and I am fond of pointing out that "spontaneous" poetry is not written spontaneously any more than fast music is written in a hurry. The publication of Dylan Thomas's workbooks nicely checked our own tendency to make a similar mistake about a Western poet, and Yeats made the point well in "Adam's Curse":

> We sat together at one summer's end,
> That beautiful mild woman, your close friend,
> And you and I, and talked of poetry.
> I said, 'A line will take us hours maybe;
> Yet if it does not seem a moment's thought,
> Our stitching and unstitching has been naught.'

To probe the question of how Li Po achieved effects worthy of Tu Fu's admiration and, further, to identify those effects more clearly, I have been reading Li Po's poems, attempting to use a rigorous philological method while employing the same sensors and permitting myself the same reactions that I would allow when reading English poems.

Chien, who dismisses many of the best poems, most often finding them deficient in the very respects in which they are most excellent and original. The extent to which he seemed exotic can be judged by another essay, which argues that Li Po must have been a Nestorian Christian because he named one son "P'o-li" ("rock crystal") and there is mention of a rock-crystal goblet in a Nestorian inscription. Similarly, admiration for the poem "The Road to Shu Is Hard" can be measured by the fact that two respected modern scholars, Yü P'ing-po and Li Ch'ang-chih, continue to insist that it must have been written to dissuade the emperor from flight to Shu. A great poem should mark a great occasion.

That is to say, I start with my own somewhat simplistic definition of poetry as "the art of putting language under tension to make the pieces vibrate so that the whole will say more than one has any right to expect," and I then look to see what Li Po is doing to get maximum vibration from his language.

Thus far, I am satisfied with the results, for the analysis has in no way fragmented the poems or killed the poetry. On the contrary, it has shown them to be extremely well knit, meaningful, and often moving. Here, I should like to discuss three of the poems that are, I believe, considerably better, more complex, and more meaningful than has generally been supposed. When we see what is said and something of *how* it is said, I think we can also begin to see just what it was that so dazzled Tu Fu and his contemporaries. The transcription that accompanies the Chinese texts is Karlgren's reconstructed T'ang dynasty pronunciation, which contributes to an appreciation of the poems by revealing a great deal about their structure. The translations, Chinese texts, and tone-pattern schematizations are divided into stanzas according to the rhyme changes revealed by that transcription: a new rhyme, a new stanza. In what follows I shall not explain every allusion and term; rather, I shall concentrate almost entirely on techniques, relationships, facts, and *speculations* that have not previously been touched upon by the commentators. In the notes Li Po's compositions will be identified by their numbers in the Kyoto concordance, and for my basic text I use the facsimile of the unique Sung edition, also found in the Kyoto index series. For the transcription of ancient Turkish, I follow V. M. Nadeljaev et al., *Drevnetjurkskij slovar'* (Leningrad: Nauka, 1969).

"My Trip in a Dream to the Lady of Heaven Mountain" is a good starting point because it is the easiest of the three poems, and because it provides examples of some half-dozen of Li Po's most characteristic devices for getting the most out of his language. David Hawkes has already called attention to the way he enriches the texture of his poem by drawing on Taoist mysticism and other shamanistic or supernatural elements found in earlier poetry.[2] Indeed, with its flight through space theme, it belongs to one of the most venerable traditions in Chinese

2. David Hawkes, "The Supernatural in Chinese Poetry," *The Far East: China and Japan* (Toronto: University of Toronto Press, 1961), pp. 311–24. Many of the images in this poem correspond with shamanistic techniques and symbols analyzed by Mircea Eliade in *Shamanism: Archaic Techniques of Ecstasy*, Bollingen Series, no. 76 (New York: Pantheon, 1964), e.g. dream, flight through space, ascending a ladder, entering trance and awakening, journey to the center of the earth, music, confluence of spirits, and the world tree (the Rooster of Heaven perches in a kind of world tree).

literature. Most interesting, however, is the way Li Po weaves the supernatural, natural, philosophical, and literary elements into a net that involves the reader in the act of creativity—reflecting that a line can be taken in this way or in that and savoring the embellishments of sound and allusion, he becomes a participant in the performance of the poem.

夢	遊	天	姥	山	別	東	魯	諸	公
mi̯ung-	i̯ə̯u	tʻien	muo:	ṣăn	bʻi̯ät	tung	luo:	tśi̯wo	kung

	海	客	談	瀛	洲		
1	χậi:	kʻɐk	dʻâm	i̯äng	tśi̯ə̯u		
	煙	濤	微	茫	信	難	求
2	·ien	dʻâu	mjwe̯i	mwâng	si̯ĕn-	nân	gʻi̯ə̯u
	越	人	語	天	姥		
3	ji̯wɐt	ńźi̯ĕn	ngi̯wo:	tʻien	muo:		
	雲	霓	明	滅	或	可	覩
4	ji̯uən	ngiei	mi̯wɐng	mi̯ät	ɣwək	kʻâ:	tuo:
	天	姥	連	天	向	天	橫
5	tʻien	muo:	li̯än	tʻien	χi̯ang-	tʻien	ɣwɐng
	勢	拔	五	岳	掩	赤	城
6	śi̯äi-	bʻuât	nguo:	ngåk	·i̯äm:	tśʻi̯äk	źi̯äng
	天	台	四	萬	八	千	丈
7	tʻien	tʻậi	si-	mi̯wɐn-	pwăt	tsʻien	d̂ʻi̯ang:
	對	此	欲	倒	東	南	傾
8	tuậi-	tsʻie̯:	i̯wok	tâu-	tung	nậm	kʻi̯äng
	我	欲	冥	搜	夢	吳	越
9	ngâ:	i̯wok	mieng	ṣi̯ə̯u	mi̯ung-	nguo	ji̯wɐt
	一	夜	飛	度	鏡	湖	月
10	·i̯ĕt	i̯a-	pjwe̯i	dʻuo-	ki̯ɐng-	ɣuo	ngi̯wɐt
	湖	月	照	我	影		
11	ɣuo	ngi̯wɐt	tśi̯äu-	ngâ:	·i̯ɐng:		
	送	我	至	剡	谿		
12	sung-	ngâ:	tśi-	źi̯äm:	kʻiei		
	謝	公	宿	處	今	尙	在
13	zi̯a-	kung	si̯uk	tśʻi̯wo-	ki̯əm	źi̯ang-	dzʻâi:
	淥	水	蕩	漾	清	猿	啼
14	luk	świ:	dʻâng:	i̯ang-	tsʻi̯äng	ji̯wɐn	dʻiei
	脚	著	謝	公	屐		
15	ki̯ak	d̂ʻi̯ak	zi̯a-	kung	gʻi̯ɐk		
	身	登	青	雲	梯		
16	śi̯ĕn	təng	tsʻieng	ji̯uən	tʻiei		

[no break]

牛	壁	見	海	日		
17 puân-	piek	kien-	χậi:	ńźi̯ĕt		
空	中	聞	天	雞		
18 kʻung	tʻi̯ung	mi̯uən	tʻien	kiei		

千	巌	萬	轉	路	不	定
19 tsʻien	ngam	mi̯wɐn-	tʻi̯wän:	luo-	puət	dʻieng-
迷	花	倚	石	忽	已	瞑
20 miei	χwa	·i̯e:	źi̯äk	χuət	i:	mieng-

熊	咆	龍	吟	殷	巌	泉
21 ji̯ung	bʻau	li̯wong	ngi̯əm	·i̯ən:	ngam	dzʻi̯wän
慄	深	林	兮	驚	層	巓
22 li̯ĕt	śi̯əm	li̯əm	γiei	ki̯ɐng	dzʻəng	tien
楓	青	青	兮	欲	雨	
23 pi̯ung	tsʻieng	tsʻieng	γiei	i̯wok	ji̯u:	
水	澹	澹	兮	生	煙	
24 świ:	dʻâm-	dʻâm-	γiei	ṣeng	·ien	

列	缺	霹	靂	
25 li̯ät	kʻi̯wät	pʻiek	liek	
丘	巒	崩	摧	
26 kʻi̯ə̯u	luân	pəng	dzʻuậi	
洞	天	石	扇	
27 dʻung-	tʻien	źi̯äk	śi̯än-	
訇	然	中	開	
28 χwɛng	ńźi̯än	tʻi̯ung	kʻậi	

青	冥	浩	蕩	不	見	底
29 tsʻieng	mieng	γâu:	dʻâng:	puət	kien-	tiei:
日	月	照	耀	金	銀	臺
30 ńźi̯ĕt	ngi̯wɐt	tśi̯äu-	i̯äu-	ki̯əm	ngi̯ĕn	dʻậi

霓	爲	衣	兮	風	爲	馬
31 ngiei	jwi̯e	·i̯ei	γiei	pi̯ung	jwi̯e	ma:
雲	之	君	兮			
32 ji̯uən	tśi	ki̯uən	γiei			
		紛	紛	而	來	下
		pʻi̯uən	pʻi̯uən	ńźi	lậi	γa:

虎	鼓	瑟	兮	鸞	回	車
33 χuo:	kuo:	ṣi̯ɛt	γiei	luân	γuậi	tśʻi̯a
仙	之	人	兮	列	如	麻
34 śi̯än	tśi	ńźi̯ĕn	γiei	li̯ät	ńźi̯wo	ma
忽	魂	悸	以	魄	動	嗟
35 χuət	γuən	gʻjwi-	i:	pʻɐk	dʻung:	tsi̯a
恍	驚	起	而	長		
36 χwâng:	ki̯ɐng	kʻji:	ńźi	dʻi̯ang		

[no break]

	惟	覺	時	之	枕	席	
37	i̯wi	kâk	źi	tśi	tśi̯əm:	zi̯äk	
	失	向	來	之	煙	霞	
38	śi̯ět	χi̯ang-	lậi	tśi	·ien	γa	

	世	間	行	樂	亦	如	此
39	śi̯äi-	kǎn	γeng	lâk	i̯äk	ńźi̯wo	tsʻi̯e:
	古	來	萬	事	東	流	水
40	kuo:	lậi	mi̯wɐn-	dzʻi-	tung	li̯ậu	świ:

	別	君	去	兮	何	時	還
41	bʻi̯ät	ki̯uən	kʻi̯wo-	γiei	γâ	źi	γwan
	且	放	白	鹿	青	崖	間
42	tsʻi̯a:	pi̯wang-	bʻɐk	luk	tsʻieng	ngai	kǎn
	須	行	即	騎	訪	名	山
43	si̯u	γeng	tsi̯ək	gʻi̯ię	pʻi̯wang-	mi̯äng	șǎn
	安	能	摧	眉			
44	·ân	nəng	dzʻuậi	mji			
			折	腰	事	權	貴
			tśi̯ät	·i̯äu	dzʻi-	gʻi̯wän	kjwei-
	暫	樂	酒	色	凋	朱	顏
45	dzʻâm-	lâk	tsi̯ậu:	și̯ək	tieu	tśi̯u	ngan

My Trip in a Dream to the Lady of Heaven Mountain
A Farewell to Several Gentlemen of Eastern Lu

1 Seafarers tell of a magic island,
2 Hard to find in the vague expanse of mist and towering waves.

3 In Yüeh men talk of the Lady of Heaven,
4 Glimpsed by chance, dissolving and glowing, amid the rainbows and clouds.

5 The Lady of Heaven, joining the heavens, faces the Heavenly Span,
6 Her majesty tops the Five Summits and shadows Vermilion Wall.
7 Heavenly Terrace rises up forty-eight thousand staves,
8 Yet tips southeast beside her as if it wanted to fall.

9 Wanting to probe the mystery in a dream of Wu and Yüeh,
10 Through a night I flew across the moon on Mirror Lake.

[stanza break]

11 The moon on the lake projected my shadow,
12 Escorting me to the River Shan.
13 The place where Duke Hsieh once retired stands to the present
      day;
14 The lucent waters swiftly purl and shrill-voiced monkeys cry.
15 Duke Hsieh's cleated clogs on my feet,
16 I climbed the ladder of blue clouds.
17 From the slope I could see the sun in the ocean;
18 From space I could hear the Rooster of Heaven.

19 A thousand cliffs, ten thousand turns, a road I cannot define;
20 Dazzled by flowers, I rest on a stone and darkness suddenly falls.

21 Bears grumbling, dragons humming, fountains rumbling on the
      mountainside.
22 Quaking before a deep forest. Frightened by impending spires.
23 Green, green the gum trees. On the verge of rain.
24 Rough, rough the river. Breaking in spray.

25 Flashing, cracking, roaring, clapping,
26 Hills and ridges crumble and fall.
27 The stone gates of the Grotto Heavens
28 Boom and crash as they open wide.
29 The Blue Dark is a rolling surge where bottom cannot be seen,
30 Where sun and moon throw glittering light on platforms of
      silver and gold.

31 Rainbows are his clothing. His horses are the wind.
32 The Lord Within the Clouds appears. All things swirl as he
      descends.

33 Tigers strumming zithers. Coaches phoenix drawn.
34 The immortals now assemble. Arrayed like rows of hemp.
35 With the sudden excitement of my soul, my vital force is
      roused;
36 I rise distraught and startled, long and drawn my sighs.
37 There is only the pillow and mat on waking;
38 Gone are the mists of a moment ago.

39 The pleasures found within the world are also just this way;
                        [no break]

40   Ten thousand affairs out of the past are an easterly flowing
          stream.

41   Parting now I leave you. When shall I return?
42   A white deer will soon be loosed within the blue-green shores;
43   When I must go, I shall ride away to visit the peaks of renown.
44   How could I ever furrow my brow and bend my back in service
          of rank and power?
45   To hurry the pleasures of love and wine wilts man's youth away.

How shall the poem be read? On how many levels? Li Po delights in
playing with levels of meaning, and the technique is particularly appropriate here, where he is also playing with real and unreal worlds.
The poem is a technicolor dream and a rhapsody about a real mountain; a frolic with allusions and word magic and an exercise in rejuven-
ating an ancient theme; a discourse on timeless eternity and the carefully clocked narration of a single day. It is also an essay in Taoist
metaphysics, a statement of personal belief, and a magnificent description of a mountain thunderstorm. Probably no one will miss the
progression from night to day that parallels Li Po's progress up the
mountain. But note also the progression of the storm: sunlight, gathering clouds, wind, rain, thunder and lightning, and finally clearing
with rainbows and the reemergence of the animals and birds. The
darkening of trees before the storm is nicely observed, and earlier usage
gives gum trees special association with rain; just as dragons and tigers
have associations with gathering clouds and rising wind. In all, this
description of a thunderstorm seems to compare very well with the
highly praised storm in the *mu'allaqa* of Imr al-Qays (fl. c. 530), who
was apparently also a wanderer addicted to wine, women, and poetry
in the Li Po manner.[3]

This blending of levels and blurring of distinctions between real and
unreal worlds makes for effective poetry and must have been one of the
characteristics to excite Tu Fu's admiration. It is also a reminder that
the poem is no mere exuberant outburst of song. Indeed, it is somewhat surprising to discover that Li Po, from whom we might expect and
accept almost any fantasy, is so careful to maintain a balance between
the real and unreal. As if he were providing his reader with justifications
for the suspension of disbelief, he often reconciles poetic license with
rationality—as he does here by setting his fantasy within a dream and

3. See A. J. Arberry, *The Seven Odes: The First Chapter in Arabic Literature* (London: Allen
and Unwin, 1957), p. 66.

permitting us to explain the flight through space as the water-reflected moon's projection of his shadow.[4] A better appreciation of this characteristic feature may have been one reason that Tu Fu and other good Confucians of the T'ang could accept Li Po more wholeheartedly than could the scholars of later dynasties.

With the main features of the poem in mind, we might look back at the contribution made by literary allusion. (For a general analysis of this device, see chapter 12.) The two opening couplets are the first blocks in a structure full of echoes and a sly reminder of an important precedent for one of the dominant themes: the exploration of worlds. Like this poem, "The Rhymeprose on a Trip to the Heavenly Terrace Mountains" by Sun Ch'o (c. 310–97) also opens with reference to mysteries on land and sea:

> Across the sea there are [the islands] of Fang-chang and
>   P'eng-lai,
> On land [the ranges] Ssu-ming and T'ien-t'ai.
> Both these are where the mystic sages roamed and taught,
> Where ghostly sylphs, encaverned, dwelt.[5]

From this, Sun Ch'o proceeds with an exploration of mountains that is at the same time an exploration of Buddhist-flavored Neo-Taoist metaphysics. In the present poem we find Li Po improving upon Sun's lines to introduce his own geometaphysical explorations; and any suspicion that it is all coincidence is removed by line 9, where he again borrows from Sun Ch'o, using the rare and rather technical term *ming-sou*, which I have translated as "to probe the mystery."[6]

Farther along in the poem, the T'ang reader must have been pleased to note the echoes of the poet Hsieh Ling-yün (385–433) and the click-clack consonance *(kiak d'iak zia- kung g'iuk)* in line 15 that underscores the reference to Hsieh's mountain-climbing shoes. He might also have paused over line 6 to remember the opening of Hsiang Yü's famous poem: "My strength could topple mountains, my energy covered the

---

4. Cf. the Kyoto concordance, nos. 502, 578, and 636.

5. Quoted from Richard B. Mather, "The Mystical Ascent of the T'ien-t'ai Mountains: Sun Ch'o's *Yu-t'ien-t'ai-shan fu*," *Monumenta Serica* 20 (1961): 234–35.

6. Here, I follow the *Ho-yüeh ying-ling chi*, hereafter *Ho-yüeh*, notable for its interesting variants, as I do also for the last line of this poem. All other texts I have seen ignore that variant and write, "It would mean that my heart and face would never be able to smile" *(shih wo pu te k'ai hsin yen)*. To my knowledge the *Ho-yüeh* variant is the only instance in polite Chinese literature where the pleasures of wine and sex are mentioned *together* without some sort of reproving noise.

world." But lines 5 and 8 contain the features most characteristic of Li Po and most deserving of our attention here.

I sometimes detect in his poetry what, for want of a better word, might be called a "trigger"—a pun, a bit of strange syntax, or an unexpected word which, when recognized and "activated," sets off a chain of associations alerting the reader to new levels of meaning and camouflaged allusions elsewhere in the poem. Line 5, as usually construed, is taken to say, "The Lady of Heaven, joining the heavens, stretches across the heavens." But this reading requires a syntactic construction that is atypical of Li Po, and I suspect that we have, instead, one of his "triggers." Slowing down to decide whether he likes the line's three repetitions of "heaven," the reader might recall the rather obscure constellation "Heavenly Span," a group of eight stars in Cassiopoeia that is thought of as a bridge across the Milky Way. Just such a bridge would be necessary to reach the magic islands, located, as the *Lieh-tzu* tells us, in a ravine filled with the waters of the earth and the Milky Way.[7] At the same time, the obscurity of this asterism is just what is needed to alert the reader so that he will give proper attention to what follows.

Sun Ch'o's high estimation of those mountains notwithstanding, the Heavenly Terrace reels back and tips southeast before the greater magic of the Lady of Heaven. We are, however, being asked to sense more than magic, for there is also cosmology and allusion here. The "T'ang wen" section of the *Lieh-tzu*, which tells us about the magic islands cut off by the waters of the Milky Way, also tells us about Kung-kung breaking the Pillars of Heaven, the celestial counterpart of the Heavenly Terrace, causing the earth and sky to tilt, with the result that, ever after, heavenly bodies have rolled toward the west, while the waters of the earth flow southeastward into the sea. The reader need not, of course, recall this *Lieh-tzu* story in order to follow the poem on at least one level, but he probably will recall it if he has proceeded with all his sensors out, seeking confirmation of his suspicions about the "Heavenly Span." The recollection, then, will tend to confirm those suspicions, while simultaneously tightening the poem by setting up resonant associations between outwardly unrelated lines. It is, at the same time, noteworthy—and characteristic of Li Po—that these associations should be established by knotting together threads of allusion and reference in a common external source which itself has some more general relevance to the poem.[8] In this case, recollection of the *Lieh-tzu* chapter adds depth to

7. See A. C. Graham, *The Book of Lieh-tzŭ* (London: John Murray, 1960), p. 97.

8. Cf. "The Road to Shu Is Hard" (no. 062), where the totemism of ancient Shu (Sze-

the poem, since, like the poem on one level, it too is concerned with the concept of worlds within worlds. One might note, incidentally, that this cosmology also anticipates and "explains" line 40, thereby pumping a bit of juice back into that tired cliché about life being like an easterly flowing stream. Anticipation is only one of the ways Li Po revives clichés. He does it with parallelism in lines 14 and 15 of the next poem, balancing "green shadows" against "birds flying" to remind us that *this* "green" is "*kingfisher* green." As if informed of Roman Jakobson's observation that everything sequent is simile, he does it with juxtaposition in line 4 of the third poem, where the proximity of "orchid-strong jaw sinew"[9] reactivates the sense of "cheeks" in *ch'üan-ch'i*, which is usually regarded simply as a mysterious term meaning "a fast horse."

A final noteworthy aspect of Li Po's craft displayed in this poem is his manipulation of meter, tone, and rhyme to tighten the structure and reinforce the imagery and literary allusion. The usual observation that Tu Fu was a great master of regulated verse, while Li Po preferred a freer and less rigorous style seems to have led to a critical consensus that Li Po did not do anything particularly worthy of analysis in this area. But look at what is happening here:

Immediately obvious are the six two-line stanzas punctuating the poem—all but one of which rhyme in the oblique tones. One also quickly notices lines like 22–24 and 31–34, recalling the patterns (and the word magic) of the "Nine Songs," and others like 25–28 and 35–38, which are reminiscent of, and sometimes actually borrowed from, Han dynasty rhyme prose. At closer inspection, one then discovers the unusual tonic features of the poem, set forth here with "o" for the even tones and "x" for the oblique ones, while the rhyming lines are marked by "R."

| 1 | XX OOO | R |
| 2 | OOOO XOO | R |

[stanza break]

---

chwan) and the snake and cuckoo symbolism all come to life after one is led back to the *Hua-yang kuo chih* and the lore of that area.

9. Although jaw sinews could easily be likened to the tough, flat leaves of the orchid (an *Epidendrum*), it is by no means certain that *lan* did mean "orchid" at the time this term was coined. If *lan* does denote a plant and is not simply a phonetic borrowing, it might be better to translate it as "boneset" *(Eupatorium perfoliatum)*, or "agrimony" *(E. cannabinum)*. It is clear that in many *early* texts *lan* is often a member of the genus *Eupatorium*, perhaps *E. Lindleyanum* (= *E. Chinense* and *E. Kirilowii?*). Still, as Bretschneider notes, the occasional emphasis on great fragrance suggests than *lan* may have sometimes denoted "orchid" even in the Classics.

3	XO XOX	R
4	OOOX XXX	R
5	OXOO XOO	R
6	XXXX XXO	R
7	OOXX XOX	
8	XXXX OOO	R
9	XXOO XOX	R
10	XXOX XOX	R
11	OX XXX	
12	XX XXO	R
13	XOXX OXX	
14	XXXX OOO	R
15	XX XOX	
16	OO OOO	R
17	XX XXX	
18	OO OOO	R
19	OOXX XXX	R
20	OOXX XXX	R
21	OOOO XOO	R
22	XOOO OOO	R
23	OOOO XX	
24	XXXO OO	R
25	XXXX	
26	OOOO	R
27	XOXX	
28	OOOO	R
29	OOXX XXX	
30	XXXX OOO	R
31	OOOO OOX	R
32	OOOO OOOOX	R
33	XXXO OOO	R
34	OOOO XOO	R
35	XOXX XX	
36	XOXO OO	R
37	OXOO XX	
38	XXOO OO	R

[stanza break]

39	XOOX XOX	R
40	XOXX OOX	R
41	XOXO OOO	R
42	XXXX OOO	R
43	OOXO XOO	R
44	OOOOXO XOX	
45	XXXX OOO	R

In tonic poetry, as in music, monotony produces a tension that one seeks to resolve, perhaps unconsciously, by getting on to a contrasting or "resolving" tone as quickly as possible. Here, in lines 6–8, 11–15, and 31–32, for example, the long sequences of words in the same tonic category—particularly those in the less easily sustained oblique tones— are quite extraordinary, and one can hardly doubt that they contribute to the poem's breathless pace, which seems so appropriate to the narration of events in a dream. Neither can one doubt that the effect was intentional, for even and oblique tones would be much more evenly dispersed in a random text, and we shall see Li Po using tones to achieve special but very different effects in the next poem.

	廬	山	謠	寄	盧	侍	御	虛	舟
	liwo	ṣân	i̯äu	kjie̯-	luo	źi-	ngi̯wo-	χi̯wo	tśi̯ə̯u

	我	本	楚	狂	人			
1	ngâ:	puən:	tṣʻi̯wo:	gʻi̯wang	ńźi̯ĕn			
	鳳	歌	笑	孔	丘			
2	bʻi̯ung-	kâ	si̯äu-	kʻung:	kʻi̯ə̯u			
	手	持	綠	玉	杖			
3	śi̯ə̯u:	dʻi	liwok	ngiwok	dʻi̯ang:			
	朝	別	黃	鶴	樓			
4	ti̯äu	bʻi̯ät	ɣwâng	ɣâk	lə̯u			
	五	嶽	尋	仙	不	辭	遠	
5	nguo:	ngåk	zi̯əm	si̯än	puət	zi	ji̯wɐn:	
	一	生	好	入	名	山	遊	
6	·i̯ĕt	ṣɐng	χâu-	ńźi̯əp	mi̯äng	ṣân	i̯ə̯u	
	廬	山	秀	出	南	斗	傍	
7	liwo	ṣân	si̯ə̯u-	tśʻi̯uĕt	nậm	tə̯u:	bʻwâng	
	屏	風	九	疊	雲	錦	張	
8	bʻieng	pi̯ung	ki̯ə̯u:	dʻiep	ji̯uən	ki̯əm:	ti̯ang	
	影	落	明	湖	青	黛	光	
9	·i̯eng:	lâk	mi̯wɐng	ɣuo	tsʻieng	dʻậi-	kwâng	
	金	闕	前	開	二	峯	帳	
10	ki̯əm	kʻi̯wɐt	dzʻien	kʻậi	ńźi-	pʻi̯wong	ti̯ang-	

[no break]

	銀	河	倒	挂	三	石	梁
11	ngiěn	γâ	tâu-	kwai-	sâm	źiäk	liang
	香	爐	瀑	布	遙	相	望
12	χiang	luo	b'uk	puo-	iäu	siang	miwang-
	廻	崖	沓	嶂	崚	蒼	蒼
13	γuậi	ngai	d'âp	tsiang-	liəng	ts'âng	ts'âng
	翠	影	紅	霞	映	朝	日
14	ts'wi-	·iɐng:	γung	γa	·iɐng-	t̂iäu	ńźiĕt
	鳥	飛	不	到	吳	天	長
15	tieu:	pjwęi	puət	tâu-	nguo	t'ien	d'iang
	登	高	壯	觀	天	地	間
16	təng	kâu	tsiang-	kuân	t'ien	d'i-	kǎn
	大	江	茫	茫	去	不	還
17	d'âi-	kâng	mwâng	mwâng	k'iwo-	puət	γwan
	黃	雲	萬	里	動	風	色
18	γwâng	jiuən	miwɐn-	lji:	d'ung:	piung	siək
	白	波	九	道	流	雪	山
19	b'ɐk	puâ	kięu:	d'âu:	liəu	siwät	șǎn
	好	爲	盧	山	謠		
20	χâu-	jwię	liwo	șǎn	iäu		
	興	因	盧	山	發		
21	χiəng-	·ien	liwo	șǎn	piwɐt		
	閑	窺	石	鏡	清	我	心
22	γǎn	k'jwię	źiäk	kiɐng-	ts'iäng	ngâ:	siəm
	謝	公	行	處	蒼	苔	沒
23	zia-	kung	γɐng	tś'iwo-	ts'âng	d'ậi	muət
	早	服	還	丹	無	世	情
24	tsâu:	b'iuk	γwan	tân	miu	śiäi-	dz'iäng
	琴	心	三	疊	道	初	成
25	g'iəm	siəm	sâm(-)	d'iep	d'âu:	tșiwo	źiäng
	遙	見	仙	人	綵	雲	裏
26	iäu	kien-	siän	ńźiĕn	ts'ậi:	jiuən	lji:
	手	把	芙	蓉	朝	玉	京
27	śięu:	pa:	b'iu	iwong	d'iäu	ngiwok	kiɐng
	先	期	汗	漫	九	垓	上
28	sien	g'ji	γân-	muân-	kięu:	kậi	źiang-
	願	接	盧	敖	遊	太	清
29	ngiwɐn-	tsiäp	luo	ngâu	iəu	t'âi-	ts'iäng

A Lu Mountain Song for the Palace Censor Empty-Boat Lu

1   I am, in fact, the Madman of Ch'u,
2   Making fun of Confucius with a Phoenix Song.
3   In my hand I carry a green jade cane
                    [no break]

4 And set forth at dawn from Yellow Crane Hall.

5 When I search for immortals on the Five Summits, I never com-
     plain how far,

6 For all my life I have liked to roam in the mountains of renown.

7 Lu Mountain bursts in splendor at the side of Southern
     Dipper;

8 The nine panels of Folding Screen covered in cloud brocade;

9 And shadows fall on the shining lake to grow like indigo eye-
     brow paint.

10 The Golden Gates before me open with a curtain between two
     spires,

11 The Silver River upside down hangs across three beams of stone.

12 The Incense Burner and the waterfall look to each other from
     far away,

13 The winding cliffs and huddled peaks rise in the blue on blue.

14 Green kingfisher shadows and red clouds intensify in the
     morning sun,

15 And birds fly on but never arrive, and the skies of Wu are long.

16 Climbing the height gives a splendid view of all of heaven and
     earth;

17 The mighty Yangtse in endless flow departs and never returns.

18 Yellow clouds for ten thousand miles have colored the driving
     wind,

19 White waves on the nine circuits are flowing mountains of snow.

20 I like to sing about Lu Mountain,

21 With inspiration from Lu Mountain.

22 At rest, I gaze in Stoney Mirror to purify my heart;

23 Green moss obscures the tracks that Duke Hsieh left behind.

24 Sublimed cinnabar, taken soon, will throw off worldly care;

25 When the heart is a lute thrice tuned, the Way can be
     attained.

26 Far above I see the immortals in the midst of luminous clouds,

27 Proceeding to court in the Palace of Jade with lotuses in their
     hands.

28 I made a promise long ago to meet Boundless above the nine
     spheres;

29 I wish I could take Lu Drifting along to visit Transcendently
     Pure.

As we turn now to "A Lu Mountain Song for the Palace Censor Empty-Boat Lu," it might be best to stay with the discussion of tonic features, for in this poem, which is also superficially about a mountain, we have an equally lush vocabulary, but a totally different disposition of tones. The striking thing in "Lu Mountain Song" is that sequences in the same tonic category are regularly *avoided*—so much so, in fact, that a balance of even and oblique tones before the caesura becomes a dominant pattern throughout the poem:

1	XX XOO	
2	XO XXO	R
3	XO XXX	
4	OX OXO	R
5	XXOO XOX	
6	XOXX OOO	R
7	OOXX OXO	R
8	OOXX OXO	R
9	XXOO OXO	R
10	OXOO XOX	
11	OOXX OXO	R
12	OOXX OOX	
13	OOXX OOO	R
14	XXOO XOX	
15	XOXX OOO	R
16	OOXO OXO	R
17	XOOO XXO	R
18	OOXX XOX	
19	XOXX OXO	R
20	XO OOO	
21	XO OOX	R
22	OOXX OXO	
23	XOOX OOX	R
24	XXOO OXO	R
25	OOXX XOO	R (*and* OOOX XOO R)
26	OXOO XOX	
27	XXOO OXO	R
28	OOXX XOX	
29	XXOO OXO	R

As can be seen, eight of the lines (1, 6, 10, 15, 16, 17, 19, and 26) do not have the balance or "resolution" before the caesura, but the pattern is sufficiently well established by the others so that these departures from that pattern can themselves make a contribution to the effectiveness of the poem. It is hard to be sure how much of this was intentional on Li Po's part, but it is interesting to observe that in several cases (lines 1, 6, 10, and 15) any weakening of the caesura that one might feel as a result of the imbalance would not be inappropriate to the sense of the line. It is also interesting, and probably more significant, that irregular lines predominate in the third stanza (lines 16–19), setting it off tonically from what precedes, just as it is set off by its shift of focus, anticlimactic imagery, and the double meanings which will be discussed below. It would seem very possible that Li Po counted on this tonic variation to serve as a "trigger" alerting the reader to the special significance of the lines. The peculiar nine-line second stanza,[10] which has always given commentators so much difficulty, may be similarly served by the irregularity of line 10 which tends to "set off" the three opening lines. This slight variation of the pattern (together with the perfect tonic identity of lines 7 and 8 and some balanced expressions in the later couplets) may have made it easier for the T'ang reader to guess that the stanza was, as it turns out, Li Po's own "Phoenix Song," to be construed as a tercet with three rhyming refrains. In any event, the tonic features of this poem like those of the first, must have made an impression on Tu Fu even though he preferred to use tones very differently in his own poetry.

And just as these tonic features stand in sharp contrast to those of the first poem, so does the experience of "Lu Mountain Song" proceed in a somewhat different order. In the first poem, the primary intent was conveyed rather quickly through vivid description and fairly obvious multiple levels of meaning, leaving the reader to work out his appreciation of details at leisure. Here, though one is again struck by a rich description of a mountain, the numerous details must sink in first before the poem can burst open to reveal the full range of its intention. (And it is, of course, appropriate that the more difficult poem should have the more regular tonic pattern to sustain the poetry and guide the reader through its compiexities.)

On a first reading, one notices a variety of little excellences: the consonance and alliteration of *liwok ngiwok d'iang:* and *γwâng γâk lẹu* in lines 3 and 4 to underscore the rightness of these phrases in a Taoist-

10. I may be alone in accepting the Sung text without emendation. Most critics substitute *d'iang,* "long," for *liang-,* "curtain" in line 10 and explain that *miwang-* in line 12 must be given the special, even-tone reading *miwang.* One wonders how they felt about the parallelisms in the couplets made up of lines 10–11, 12–13, and 14–15.

flavored poem; the survey of the landscape with lines echoing Hsieh Ling-yün (385–433) followed by contemplation in a mirror (also echoing Hsieh), where one may survey the past and future;[11] and the evocation of the *Huai-nan tzu* which features "Lu Drifting" (Lu Ao) and such personified abstractions as "Boundless" and "Transcendently Pure." One might also pause over line 9 to think of Cho Wen-chün, famous for "eyebrows like distant mountains," and wonder if she, too, were not hiding behind a brocade screen[12] when she listened to Ssu-ma Hsiang-ju play the second famous "Phoenix Song."[13]

Gradually, as one rereads, still other random elements begin to make an impression. How like Li Po to write a "Lu Mountain Song" for a Mr. Lu—Wallace Stevens would have made it "A Jamaica Song for Mr. James"— and does not the man-mountain association make it all the more reasonable to associate Li Po with the waterfall, and the Incense Burner Peak ("lu" again) with Mr. Lu, the authority on throne room protocol?[14] Then one pictures Li Po at the mountain top discovering that his elevation so minimizes ground distance that the birds, seen as far-off specks, seem to fly endlessly without getting anywhere. And it is, of course, a "mountain of renown"—one where elixirs can be brewed most satisfactorily. Thus, green shadows and red clouds, the food of would-be immortals who would themselves learn to fly, seem all the more nicely to anticipate the more elaborate elixir, sublimed cinnabar, mentioned in line 24.

From this point, one begins to struggle a bit, especially with the difficulties of line 25; the immediate context suggests the Taoistic

11. "Stony Mirror" was a round rock formation on the east side of Lu Mountain—perhaps composed of mica which abounds in the area. The magic of mirrors is frequently mentioned, as in the *Ōkagami:* "When I look upon a shining mirror, both those things already past and those still in the future do I see," quoted from Reischauer and Yamagiwa, *Translations from Early Japanese Literature* (Cambridge: Harvard University Press, 1951), p. 291.

12. The eyebrows of Cho Wen-chün are described in the *Hsi-ching tsa-chi (SPTK)* 2.2b. I have no early text saying that she was behind a screen, but that picture seems to suggest itself naturally. See, for example, *Ming jen tsa-chü hsüan* (Peking: Jen-min Wen-hsüeh, 1962), p. 121.

13. The seduction of Cho Wen-chün by Ssu-ma Hsiang-ju is given in the *Shih chi* (Po-na-pen) 117.2a. The text of what purports to be his irresistible "Phoenix Song" can be found in the *Yüeh-fu shih chi (SPTK)* 60.9a. The original "Phoenix Song" was, of course, that sung to (or at) Confucius by the madman Chieh-yü to urge him to get out of political affairs. See Legge, *Analects* 18.5.

14. Perhaps one could work out a typology of plays on words in Chinese. Here we have a near identity of both sound and characters; in the last line of this poem something that is more of a pun and nonce kenning; and something else again in poem no. 702, where Li Po says, "T'ai-po Mountain talks with me." Yet another type might be represented by the word *tieh* when used to mean "the three cinnabar fields," as here in line 25; there is even the remote possibility of an interlingual pun in line 24 of the third poem.

interpretation, "making one's heart pure as lute music through breath control concentrated on the three cinnabar fields of the body,"[15] but it is hard to forget that the phrase "lute heart" occurs first and most memorably in the *Shih chi* biography of Ssu-ma Hsiang-ju, where it is recorded that Ssu-ma seduced the young widow Cho Wen-chün by "luting his heart"—that is, conveying his feelings in lute music—as he played his "Phoenix Song." If this is to be the interpretation, then the words *san-tieh,* previously construed as "the three cinnabar fields," may be taken in their more usual sense of "three repetitions or refrains,"[16] and one is thereupon drawn back to the second stanza, where Li Po seems to have written his own "Phoenix Song" consisting of a tercet with three refrains. He says he is making fun of Confucius (and therewith the establishment), but he is writing to Mr. Lu. Could it be that when he says "Confucius" *(kʻung: kʻiau),* he is also punningly pulling the leg of his friend "Empty-Boat" *(kʻung tśiau)?*

Suddenly it all seems too much, for we have complexity without sufficient form and direction. Everything resonates, but there is no progression. And we may even note that we seem to be left with a very limp stanza in lines 16–19, coming as an anticlimax after the exuberance of what went before.

The answer is that Li Po is trying to make his reader see something more—something that would have been more readily appreciated by Empty-Boat, Tu Fu, or any of their contemporaries. Fortunately, we have the keys to the mystery. Empty-Boat, a native of unreliable Fan-yang—which had become the more unreliable since An Lu-shan established his base of power there—was appointed to the post of palace censor sometime shortly after 756, at the height of the An Lu-shan Rebellion.[17] When news of the appointment reached Li Po in 759 or 760, he was no doubt quick to see that a Fan-yang man at court was

15. I am indebted to Professor Nathan Sivin for help with the Taoist interpretation of this line.

16. The most famous "three refrains" are the so-called "Yang-kuan san-tieh" evolved from a poem by Wang Wei (699?–761?). That poem in no way resembles this, but it suggests that songs with three "refrains" or "repetitions" were popular in the T'ang. I am grateful to Professor Laurence Picken for calling to my attention the *Chʻin-hsüeh ju-men* (Shanghai: Chung-hua T'u-shu-kuan, 1881?), B.16a–19a, where the compiler Chang Ho (fl. c. 1850) gives a score for the "Yang-kuan san-tieh" and shows how, at a late period at least, the words were associated with the music. Professor Ogawa Tamaki discusses the "Yang-kuan san-tieh" briefly in "The Song of Ch'ih-le: Chinese Translations of Turkic Folk Songs and Their Influence on Chinese Poetry," *Acta Asiatica* 1 (1960): 54n1.

17. The edict promoting Empty-Boat to the post of palace censor may be found in the *CTW* 367.2a. We know it cannot have been drafted until after its author Chia Chih (718–72) was appointed editor of imperial edicts and proclamations in 756.

in a precarious position—especially quick to see it, perhaps, because news of the appointment was probably brought to him by Chia Chih, drafter of Empty-Boat's appointment, a man of considerable influence who had himself fallen from favor and had stopped to visit with Li Po on his way into exile.[18]

With this in mind, we need only the "trigger" of the poem's last line to be convinced of what Li Po is up to here. When he says he would like to take Lu Drifting (Lu Ao) along, we know that he means Empty-Boat Lu, not only because of the general sense of the poem and the identity of the surnames, but also because a palace censor, an authority on protocol, would be precisely the man to take if you were planning to have an audience with the immortals. We can be still the more certain because Empty-Boat's name comes from the *Chuang-tzu*, where the ideal man is likened to an untied boat, both *empty* and *drifting along*.[19] Thus, Li Po has constructed his line so that Lu Ao's name plus the next word become a pun or kenning for Empty-Boat Lu. The ploy is just outrageous enough to send the reader back through the poem to confirm and reorganize his initial impressions.

There is no doubt now that Li Po is having fun, that the dual interpretations and innuendoes are really there, and that this is, indeed, his "Phoenix Song." In fact, two "Phoenix Songs." One, like the original sung for Confucius, to warn Empty-Boat of political dangers; the other, like Ssu-ma Hsiang-ju's, to seduce Empty-Boat with the attractions of Lu Mountain so that he, too, will run away. And if the warning seems weak in comparison with the praise of the mountain, we need only reexamine the third stanza with an expectant eye. Surveying the world from his lofty perch, Li Po can contemplate the "yellow wind" from the West, stirred up by the Sogdian An Lu-shan. That same height would make it hard to see waves on the "nine rivers" of Kiukiang at the foot of Lu Mountain even if one could conceive of them as "flowing mountains of snow,"[20] but the impossibility is the magic of the line, for it forces us to see instead the social order of the T'ang flowing away like water to the sea. The use of the word *circuit* instead of *channel* or *river* is, then, no accident here as some have assumed. Li Po is reminding us that he is thinking of China's plight by recalling the Nine Circuits into which China was divided by Emperor

18. For that visit, see Li Po's poem no. 378.

19. *Chuang-tzu* 32.1.

20. Kiukiang supposedly derives its name ("Nine Rivers") from the "nine channels" Emperor Yü dug to control the floods. It is improbable that there were nine obvious channels, not even commemorative ones, in Li Po's day, so there is all the more reason to see something else in this line.

Yü after he had dug the nine rivers to control the flood. The symbolism is heightened by the evocation of lines from Hsieh Ling-yün:

> But a thousand thoughts torment me day and night,
> Ten thousand passions harass me, dawn till dusk.
> I climbed the cliffs to watch the Stone Mirror shining.
> I pushed through the forest and entered the Gates of Pine.
> Tales of the Three Rivers are mostly forgotten by now,
> Only the names of the Nine Streams still remain.
> The magic things rarely display their marvels,
> The weird people hide their subtle souls.[21]

In his contribution to the present volume, Hans H. Frankel has proposed six *topoi* as characteristic of poems concerned with the contemplation of history: (1) ascent to a high place; (2) looking into the distance in conjunction with viewing the past; (3) the durability of rivers and mountains as a contrast to human transience; (4) reference to historical personalities and extant relics of the past; (5) description of a landscape devoid of historical association; and (6) tears. It is probably no mere coincidence that we can find something of at least five of the *topoi* in this one stanza, where Li Po is contemplating China's past, present, and future.

Admittedly, Tu Fu or a contemporary would have responded to all of this much more readily than we do today. But I suggest that his response would have proceeded more or less in the order I have described, causing him to marvel at the skill and wit with which Li Po had woven his lines together to create a dense and beautiful poem that is also an effective statement about himself and his society. An appreciation of this skill in making statements about himself and his society depends, of course, on knowing as much as possible about Li Po and the T'ang—but properly applying what we do know can also enable us to learn still more. The last poem provides a case in point, for we can see there that the T'ang reader's familiarity with the facts of Li Po's life must have greatly reinforced the impact made by the poem. At the same time, we today can, by careful correlation of the facts at hand, see that Li Po may be telling us more than we have previously known about what it was like to live in the T'ang and to be Li Po.

Before considering the poem itself, I will have to digress to summarize my own position on various questions relating to Li Po's background and ancestry. This is necessary when proposing a correlation of Li Po's

---

21. Quoted from J. D. Frodsham, *The Murmuring Stream: The Life and Works of Hsieh Ling-yün (385–433), Duke of K'ang-lo* (Kuala Lumpur: University of Malaya Press, 1967), 1:154.

life and poetry because one never knows to which group of believers his readers happen to belong: those who feel that Li Po was so surely of foreign origin that there is nothing to discuss; those who feel that he was so thoroughly Chinese that there is nothing to discuss; or those, like Herbert Franke, who feel that the question is meaningless because "Li Po belongs to Chinese literature just as Chamisso does to the German and Joseph Conrad to English."[22] The trouble is that for Franke's analogy to work, we would have to have a Conrad *suspected* by some of Polish birth, protesting his English origin, but often writing about Poland and sometimes composing in Polish at the court of an English king who was uneasy about his own Slavic ancestry and suspicious of all foreigners including Poles.

To draw only the most reasonable conclusions from the most reliable sources—Li Po himself; the writings of Li Yang-ping, Wei Hao, and Liu Ch'üan-po, who knew Li Po; and the inscription by Fan Ch'uan-cheng, who knew Li Po's granddaughters—we ought to be able to agree on the following general propositions, which are sufficient to support the present analysis of his poetry:

1. Li Po was born in 701, somewhere in Central Asia, where his family had been living for a century or more. In a letter datable to 757, Li Po wrote that he was fifty-six years old—thus born in 701.[23] Li Yang-ping and Fan Ch'uan-cheng indicate that the family returned to China no earlier than 705. (He probably died in late 762 or early 763, but we cannot use the Li Yang-ping preface to establish the year of his death as virtually all recent writers have been inclined to do. That preface, dated November 30, 762, says only that Li Po was sick and nothing about his having died.)

2. There is no reason not to accept the claims that while "in exile" the Lis lived in Suyab, now Tokmak in the Kirghiz S.S.R., *and* near T'iao-chih in what is now northern Afghanistan.[24] Both spots were on the trade routes, and it scarcely matters whether the areas were under Chinese control at any given time. Once exiled, the Lis might have gone secretly where they pleased (it is said that they changed their name), and we cannot, for that matter, even be positive that the family was Chinese to begin with. In any event, we know that there were upheavals in the Lis' claimed ancestral home area (near T'ien-shui in

22. Herbert Franke, *Sinologie* (Bern: A. Francke, 1953), p. 169.

23. No. 1008 in the Kyoto concordance.

24. Waley objects that the T'iao-chih in Afghanistan, which slipped from Chinese control around 680, would have been forgotten by most people in the eighth century. Perhaps so, but people who had lived there would not have forgotten the old name, and Li Yang-ping is probably only recording what he heard from Li Po.

Kansu) during the late Sui, when they are said to have fled, and we know that an embassy from northern Afghanistan was able to reach China without difficulty in 705.[25]

3. Much more likely than not, the Li family was engaged in trade both before and after their return to China. That would have been the most usual way to make a living along the trade route, and when they returned to China, the Lis returned to Szechwan, known for its foreign merchant community, rather than to their claimed ancestral home. A merchant background would also account for the fact that Li Po seems always to have had plenty of money without holding land or office; and the double stigma of being a "foreign merchant" might be added to "drink" and "indifference" on the list of possible explanations for his failure to enjoy the usual civil service career. China's ethnocentrism and Confucian disdain of merchants are well known. In fact, Li Po does *not* seem to have been indifferent to a career, and it is questionable whether he really drank more than some successful officeholders.[26]

4. There is no reason not to believe Liu Ch'üan-po and Fan Ch'uan-cheng when they imply that Li Po could compose in a foreign language, and there is at least one poem (no. 945) by Li Po himself with a similar suggestion. It would be strange if the Lis did *not* know Turkish or some other foreign language after living for a century in Central Asia; and many people, including members of the T'ang royal family, are said to have known Turkish. Naturally if they were merchants, there would have been all the more reason to keep the language alive even after their return to China.

5. Regardless of whether he was born to it or whether it was acquired, Li Po shows the marked influence of Central Asian culture. We know, of course, that he writes about Central Asian subjects, as in the poem we are about to consider. We might also note that his elder son Po-ch'in (<*ppk g'iəm*, a Chinese name that might yet transcribe *begim*, the

---

25. See Edouard Chavannes, *Documents sur les Tou-kiue (Turcs) Occidentaux* (Saint Petersbourg, 1903; reprint Paris: Adrien-Maisonneuve, n.d.), p. 157.

26. Kuo Mo-jo is one of the few to defend Li Po against the charge of alcoholism. On page 196 of the paperback edition of his new book (see Bibliographical Note) he observes that Tu Fu has 300 compositions (21 percent of the total) with references to drinking, while Li Po has only 170 (sixteen percent of his total). One could, however, still come away with the impression that Li Po was the greater drinker. He uses the word "wine" some 210 times in his poems, while for Tu Fu the count is only 176 occurrences. Of course, if Li Po did not drink inordinately, the talk about his drinking could have been a disingenuous way of calling attention to his foreign background. Foreigners, Turks in particular, were generally presumed to be heavy drinkers. There is also some evidence that Li Po may have mocked China's ethnocentrism by caricaturing the popular image of barbarians both in his poetry and in his personal life. See, for example, poem no. 084.

Turkish for "My Prince") had a second and very un-Chinese name, "Moon Slave," which is a typically Turkish name for an *eldest* son.[27] His younger son had the equally exotic name P'o-li,[28] a transcription of a foreign word for "rock crystal," which evokes the culture of Central Asia in several ways. During the T'ang dynasty rock crystal most often came to China from that area in northern Afghanistan where the Lis are said to have lived, and P'o-li was also the name of the mountain in that same area containing the cave said to produce the "heavenly horses."[29] We might further observe that P'o-li, taken word for word, means "quite black" and is, therefore, just the opposite of Li Po's courtesy name T'ai-po, meaning "very white," which happens, of course, to be the name of a mountain in China, as well as a perfect translation of the well-attested Turkish personal name "Appaq." We know that black and white mountains held special significance for the Turks, and this suggestion of Turkish cultural influence seems the more compelling when we consider the name of Li Po's father. It has been argued before that he acquired his name K'o, meaning "stranger," when he returned to China. And quite possibly so. But what was he called "back home," and why did he choose to stick with this none too flattering name? Very possibly it was a compromise, for K'o, pronounced *k'vk* in the T'ang, sounds very much like *kök,* the Turkish word for "blue." We know that blue, white, and black were three colors of special significance to the Turks,[30] and it is curious to find them so easily associated with three successive generations of Lis. Curious also that among close blood relatives for whom names are preserved, it is only his daughter P'ing-yang (< *b'iwvng iang)* whose name suggests no immediate association with Turkish culture—and even here it is perhaps not impossible to see a transcription of the Turkish for "thousand echoes." A preoccupation with black and white mountains, a

27. V. V. Radlov (W. Radloff), *Opyt" slovarja tjurkskix" narěčij,* reprint (Moscow: Izdatel'-stvo Vostočnoj Literatury, 1963), vol. 1, part 1, pp. 5–6, under *ai,* gives a long list of epic and folk heroes with "moon" in their names: Moon Khan, Moon Wing, Moon Marksman, etc.

28. Lest Turcologists think I have nodded, let me note that I am still brooding over the possibility that the name P'o-li (*p'uâ liei*) was the more pleasing to Li Po because of its similarity to *böri,* "wolf." The wolf was important to the Turks, of course, but I do not like *p'uâ.* Where "wolf" seems certain we get *b'iu- ljie.* See Chavannes, *Documents,* p. 220.

29. *HTS* (Po-na-pen) 221b.6a.

30. Interestingly, Li Po wanted to be buried on a *blue* mountain (Ch'ing-shan southeast of Tang-t'u in Anhwei). Of course, it may have been, as generally presumed, simply because the poet Hsieh T'iao (464–99), whom he greatly admired, had once built a villa there. There is data on Turkish color preferences scattered throughout René Giraud's *L'Empire des Turcs Célestes* (Paris: Adrien-Maisonneuve, 1960) and Ilse Laude-Cirtautas's *Der Gebrauch der Farbbezeichnungen in den Turkdialekten,* Ural-altaische Bibliothek, no. 10 (Wiesbaden: Harrassowitz, 1961).

great weakness for wine, and a passion for the moon are reported or detectable characteristics of the Turkish people throughout much of history.[31] We have just spoken of the mountains, and Li Po's love of wine is well known. It only remains to be noted that Li Po mentions the moon approximately 403 times, exclusive of date-time references, in some 1,000 poems. Tu Fu has 167 moons in 1,457 poems; and Yeats, our own most moonstruck poet, refers to the moon 176 times in 448 poems with a total length roughly equal to the Li Po corpus.

The significance of many of these points will, I hope, become more evident when we consider our final poem:

	天	馬	歌				
	t'ien	ma:	kâ				
	天	馬	來	出	月	支	窟
1	t'ien	ma:	lâi	tś'iuĕt	ngiwɐt	tśiẹ	k'uət
	背	爲	虎	文	龍	翼	骨
2	puậi-	jwiẹ	χuo:	miuən	liwong	iək	kuət
	嘶	青	雲		振	綠	髮
3	siei	ts'ieng	jiuən		tśiẹn-	liwok	piwɐt
	蘭	筋	權	奇	走	滅	沒
4	lân	kiən	g'iwän	g'jiẹ	tsəu:	miät	muət
	騰	崑	崙		歷	西	極
5	d'əng	kuən	luən		liek	siei	g'iək
	四	足	無	一	蹴		
6	si-	tsiwok	miu	·iĕt	kiwɐt		
	雞	鳴	刷	燕	晡	秣	越
7	kiei	miwɐng	ṣwat	·ien	puo	muât	jiwɐt
	神	行	電	邁	躡	恍	惚
8	dź'iɛn	γɐng	d'ien-	mwai-	ńiäp	χwâng:	χuət
	天	馬	呼		飛	龍	趨
9	t'ien	ma:	χuo		pjwẹi	liwong	tś'iu
	目	明	長	庚	臆	雙	鳧
10	miuk	miwɐng	d'iang	kɐng	·iək	ṣâng	b'iu
	尾	如	流	星	首	渴	烏
11	mjwẹi:	ńźiwo	liəu	sieng	śiẹu:	k'ât	·uo
	口	噴	紅	光	汗	溝	珠
12	k'əu:	p'uən	γung	kwâng	γân-	kəu	tśiu

[no break]

31. I am indebted to Joseph Fletcher for help on many problems relating to Central Asia. Otto Maenchen-Helfen has notes on the moon in Central Asian culture in "The Yüeh-chih Problem Re-examined," *Journal of the American Oriental Society* 65 (1945): 80. Translations of a few dozen Li Po moon passages are provided by Ch'en Ch'in-jen, "The Moon and Li Po's Poems," *Tamkang Journal* 3 (1964): 215–22.

13	曾	陪	時	龍	躍	天	衢
	dz'əng	b'uâi	źi	li̯wong	i̯ak	t'ien	g'i̯u
14	羈	金	絡	月	照	星	都
	kjie̞	ki̯əm	lâk	ngi̯wet	tśi̯ɐu-	sieng	tuo
15	逸	氣	稜	稜	凌	九	區
	i̯ĕt	k'jei-	ləng	ləng	li̯əng	ki̯ə̣u:	k'i̯u
16	白	璧	如	山	誰	敢	沽
	b'ɐk	pi̯äk	ńźi̯wo	ṣăn	źwi	kâm:	kuo
17	回	頭	笑	紫	燕		
	ɣuâi	d'ə̣u	si̯äu-	tsi̯e:	·ien-		
18	但	覺	爾	輩	愚		
	d'ân:	kâk	ńźi̯e̞:	puâi-	ngi̯u		

19	天	馬	奔		戀	君	軒
	t'ien	ma:	puən		li̯wän-	ki̯uən	χi̯ɐn
20	騋	躍	驚	矯	浮	雲	翻
	si̯wong:	i̯ak	ki̯ɐng	ki̯äu:	b'i̯ə̣u	ji̯uən	p'i̯wɐn
21	萬	里	足	躑	躅		
	mi̯wɐn-	lji:	tsi̯wok	d̂i̯äk	d̂'i̯wok		
22	遙	瞻	閶	闔	門		
	i̯äu	tśi̯äm	tś'i̯ang	ɣâp	muən		
23	不	逢	寒	風	子		
	puət	b'i̯wong	ɣân	pi̯ung	tsi:		
24	誰	探	逸	景	孫		
	źwi	ts'ậi:	i̯ĕt	ki̯ɐng:	suən		

25	白	雲	在	青	天		
	b'ɐk	ji̯uən	dz'ậi:	ts'ieng	t'ien		
26	丘	陵	遠				
	k'i̯ə̣u	li̯əng	ji̯wɐn:				
27	崔	嵬	鹽	車	峻	坂	
	dz'uâi	nguâi	i̯äm	tś'i̯a	źi̯äng:	si̯uĕn-	pi̯wɐn:
28	倒	行	逆	施	畏	日	晚
	tâu-	ɣɐng	ngi̯ɐk	śi̯e	·jwə̣i-	ńźi̯ĕt	mi̯wɐn:

29	伯	樂	剪	拂	中	道	遺
	pɐk	lâk	tsi̯än:	p'i̯uət	t̂i̯ung	d'âu:	i̯wi
30	少	盡	其	力	老	棄	之
	śi̯äu-	tsi̯ĕn:	g'ji	li̯ək	lâu:	k'ji-	tśi
31	願	逢	田	子	方		
	ngi̯wɐn-	b'i̯wong	d'ien	tsi:	pi̯wang		
32	惻	然	爲	我	思		
	tṣ'i̯ək	ńźi̯än	jwi̯e-	ngâ:	si		
33	雖	有	玉	山	禾		
	swi	ji̯ə̣u:	ngi̯wok	ṣăn	ɣuâ		

[no break]

不	能	療	苦	肌		
34 puət	nəng	li̯äu-	k'uo:	kji		
嚴	霜	五	月	凋	桂	枝
35 ngi̯ɐm	și̯ang	nguo:	ngi̯wɐt	tieu	kiwei-	tśi̯e
伏	櫪	銜	冤	摧	兩	盾
36 b'i̯uk	liek	γam	·i̯won	dz'u̯âi	li̯ang:	mji
請	君	贖	獻	穆	天	子
37 ts'i̯äng:	ki̯uən	dź'i̯wok	χi̯ɐn-	mi̯uk	t'ien	tsi:
猶	堪	弄	影	舞	瑤	池
38 i̯ʌu | k'ậm | lung- | ·i̯ɐng: | mi̯u: | i̯äu | d'i̯e |

Song of the Heavenly Horse

1 From a Scythian cave came the heavenly horse,
2 With tiger-stripe back and dragon-wing bones.
3 Neighing to the blue clouds. Shaking a green mane.
4 Orchid-strong jaw sinew, speed-tokened cheeks, he vanished
   when he ran.
5 Over the Kunlun. To the West Edge of Earth.
6 His four feet never stumbled.
7 At cockcrow groomed in Yen, at dusk he was foddered in Yüeh,
8 The path of a spirit, a lightning flash, galloping past as a blur.

9 A heavenly horse summons. A flying dragon response.
10 Eyes bright as the Evening Star, his breast a brace of ducks,
11 His tail was like a comet, his neck a sprinkler cock;
12 Red light spewed from his mouth, in his sweat canals were
    pearls.
13 He once accompanied the Timely Dragon to leap in the
    heavenly streets,
14 Haltered gold and bridled moon that shone in the City of
    Stars.
15 A spirit apart, proud and assured, he vaulted the nine
    domains,
16 A white jade like a mountain that nobody dared to buy.
17 Soon they laughed at this Purple Swallow,
18 Thought to themselves, "How dumb your kind."

19 The heavenly horse dashed forward. He longed for the
    sovereign's coach.
20 With reins let out he could leap and rear to tumble the
    passing clouds,

[no break]

21 But his feet moved in check for ten thousand miles,
22 And he gazed from afar at the gates to the throne.
23 He met no horseman like Master Cold Wind
24 To employ the scion of vanishing light.

25 White clouds in a blue sky,
26 The hills are far away.
27 The salt wagon piled high must climb the precipitous grade,
28 Counter to custom, unmindful of right, fearing the close of day.

29 Po-le's art to curry and clip was lost along the way;
30 In my youth they used my strength, they cast me off in age.
31 I would like to meet a T'ien Tzu-fang
32 That he, in pity, might care for me,
33 But though he had Jade Mountain grain,
34 My flesh could not be healed.
35 A hard frost in the Fifth Month withered the buds on the
        cinnamon tree;
36 Now in the stall I furrow my brow, the bit of injustice in my
        teeth.
37 I beg the sovereign to redeem me, send me off to Emperor Mu,
38 That I may yet play with my shadow and dance by the
        Jasper Pool.

If the reader has, however tentatively, accepted my arguments concerning Li Po's background, it should be evident that this poem is far more autobiographical than has been supposed. Look, for example, at the number of terms and references that Li Po has used to underscore his identity with the heavenly horse: the Scythian cave (located in P'o-li Mountain); the Evening Star (also "T'ai-po" in Chinese); and the "white jade like a mountain" (since "Po" means "white," and "T'ai-po" is also the name of a mountain). Thus alerted, one might further note that "haltered gold" is a similar identity, since "gold" (or "metal") is the element associated with the West and with T'ai-po or "whiteness," be it the man, the mountain, or the star. "Bridled moon" in the same line is perhaps even more productive. First, it tightens the poem by "resonating" with the numerous astronomical references; then one might relate it to the other anatomical terms by thinking of the "moon" or "moons" of the horse's forehead and cheeks. But, of course, in this context, the phrase tends, above all, to make us think of Li Po and his passion for the moon. T'ang readers acquainted with Li Po might also have thought of his elder son "Moon Slave," who sometimes traveled with his father and was known to his friends. Finally, we probably need to consider "scion of vanishing light" in line 24 as yet another identity, since "vanishing light" suggests both speed and the West where the light goes when it disappears. At the same time, it is easy to think of T'ai-po, the Evening Star, as scion of the setting sun.[32] It would probably have to have been a rather private joke, but it is just conceivable that Li Po is also suggesting "scion of I Khan," King of the Turks.[33] This khan, whose personal name seems to have been Qara or "Black," would be relevant in a "horse context" because he sent an impressive gift of fifty-thousand horses to China in 553. But regardless of how we construe this identity, there is a nice irony in the fact that this allusion to a "son of the West," who is being badly used in China, is immediately followed by an allusion to a Chinese, the legendary Emperor Mu, who was graciously received in the Western world.

These various identities and affinities do not, of course, make a good poem or even an autobiographical poem in and of themselves. It is important, therefore, to note how well elements of the poem correspond with what we know about Li Po's career: exotic origin (lines 1–8); early evidence of great talent (also 1–8); pride, self-confidence, and ambition (especially lines 6–12, 15–16, 19–20); overnight fame and success at the capital plus association with the emperor and high officials (lines 9–16); rather inexplicable rejection (lines 17–18); desperate efforts to return to service (lines 19–28); disgrace, jail, and exile (lines 31–38); and an old age spent far removed from the splendors he had once known (lines 25–38). In many of his poems Li Po uses "blue clouds" and "cinnamon twigs" as symbols of honors and aspiration to

32. Professor Yang Lien-sheng, who has helped in countless ways, has some useful remarks on T'ang denotations of the word *ching* ('sun', etc.) in *Ch'ing-hua hsüeh-pao*, n.s. 7, pt. 2 (1969): 262.

33. Parallelism with the preceding line and the rhyme change and irregular meter in what follows put the language under such tension at this point that one might well expect some pun or other outrageous ploy. J. R. Hamilton, *Les Ouïghours à l'époque des Cinq Dynasties d'après les documents chinois* (Paris: Presses Universitaires, 1955), p. 154, speculates that *ching-ch'iung* (*kïvng: g'iwäng*) might transcribe *qaγan*. If he is right, then *ching (kïvng:)* would certainly do for "khan," and, in our horse context, *i ching* (iět kïeng:) could recall "I Khan," the shortened name of I-hsi-chi Qaγan (*ˑiět siək kji- kʿa: γan-*). We have a name of this type in Ko-shu Han, Khan of the Ko-shu Tribe. Since the "Hou" of Hou Ching's name represents Qojïn, it is tempting to speculate that he, analogously, was Khan of the Qojïn or Sheep Tribe and that we *do* have evidence of *ching* used to suggest "khan." I Khan and his gift are mentioned in the *Chou shu* (Po-na-pen) 50.3b–4a and the *TCTC* (Peking: Ku-chi Ch'u-pan-she 1956), pp. 5097–98. For his name shortened to "I" see the *Sui shu* (Po-na-pen) 84.1b. For speculation on the original Turkish form of "Ko-shu," see W. Eberhard, "Remarks on Širalγa," *Oriens* 1 (1948): 220n2.

high office.[34] In this poem the progression of this career from youthful ambition to an old age of rejection and neglect seems emphasized by the "neighing to the blue clouds" in line 3 and the "withered buds on the cinnamon tree" in line 35.

It is hard to guess how much this poem may have told a T'ang reader about the reasons for Li Po's frustration, but even now we can pick out a few suggestions. The repeated references to the West and the final couplet with its plea that he be sent back to the West may be a hint that his origins and China's ethnocentrism were, indeed, one source of his discontent. Then, just from the tone of the poem alone, we might suspect that an excess of pride and ambition was another factor. But interestingly, that may be what Li Po is consciously trying to tell us— particularly in line 28. The words which I translate as "counter to custom, unmindful of right" are still used in modern speech as a cliché for "acting irrationally," and it is assumed that the source is the *Shih chi* biography of Wu Tzu-hsü, who beat the corpse of a king who had killed his father and brother.[35] There is, however, another occurrence of the phrase in the *Han shu* biography of Chu-fu Yen (died 127 B.C.).[36] Accused of being overly ambitious and overly familiar with the emperor, Chu-fu Yen replied:

> From youth, I traveled and studied for more than forty years and never enjoyed success. My parents did not regard me as a son, my brothers would not receive me, my colleagues rejected me, my days of distress were long. But if a man cannot dine from five pots in life, then let him be boiled in five pots to die. My day is coming to a close. Thus, I act counter to custom and unmindful of right [i.e. careless about formalities].

It is not impossible that Li Po was aware that his personality could offend as well as charm, and read in the light of the Chu-fu Yen biography, line 28 could be both an apology and a hint of his desperation. Of course, the line might simultaneously evoke the Wu Tzu-hsü biography, so it is also possible to read in a criticism of officialdom for having acted irrationally. Perhaps Li Po meant to leave this point in question.

Thus far, I have talked primarily about *what* Li Po is saying in this poem without having said much about *how well* he is saying it. To some extent, an understanding of what is said is, of course, prerequisite to

34. E.g., no. 427.
35. *Shih chi* (Po-na-pen) 66.6a.
36. *Han shu* (Po-na-pen) 64A.20a.

judging how well it is being said, and we have already noted sufficient correspondences between Li Po's life and the poem to guess that it must have seemed a powerful personal statement, especially to the T'ang readers who knew Li Po. But before concluding, we might note a few additional features that reinforce the statement and strengthen the poem.

Most obvious among the "strengthening" devices is the elaborate blending of horse imagery, astronomy, anatomy, and references to himself and the West, which fills the poem with echoes and anticipations. And, as noted in the discussion of "bridled moon," the words sometimes cross over to resonate with terms and references in different categories. A similar case is that of Po-le, the great judge of horses, for Po-le is also the star that governs horses, and it was Po-le, the man, who came to the aid of the old horse relegated to pulling the original salt wagon. Still more strengthening or tightening of the poem is provided by lines 25 and 26 which anticipate the final couplet with its references to Emperor Mu and the Jasper Pool. "White clouds in a blue sky, The hills are far away" is a revision of lines from the song for Emperor Mu sung by the Queen Mother of the West when he visited her at the Jasper Pool.[37] Appropriately, a note of despair ("the hills are far away") has been substituted for the optimism of the original song.

By now, any reader familiar with Chinese literature will probably have noticed the numerous echoes of earlier "horse poetry" which serve as another strengthening device. In the Han dynasty sacrificial ode of identical title and in the "Rhymeprose on a Red and White Horse" (*Che-po mǎ fu*) by Yen Yen-chih (384–456) we have the source of many terms and phrases adapted here: the tiger's double spine, speed-tokened cheeks, the West Edge of Earth, exhaustion of strength in youth, the grooming in Yen and feeding in Yüeh, the gates to the throne, and the nine domains.[38] These special echoes would, I think, help to make an exotic poem seem at the same time familiar to a Chinese reader; and in that, their contribution is not unlike the one made by tone, rhyme, and meter, or other patterning devices which help to bind a complex of imagery so that it will hold a reader until he can work out his personal response.

It is, finally, the contribution of tone, rhyme, and meter that deserves our attention, for in this poem, as in the two previously discussed, Li Po has done more in this area than has been heretofore supposed. This

---

37. See *Mu T'ien-tzu chuan (SPTK)* 3.15ab.
38. See respectively *Yüeh-fu shih-chi (SPTK)* 1.6b and *Wen hsüan (SPTK)* 14.1a–10a.

time there is no tonic patterning of any importance, but something rather special has been done with the meter and the rhymes:

1	OXOX XOX	R
2	XOXO OXX	R
3	OOO XXX	R
4	OOOO XXX	R
5	OOO XOX	
6	XX OXX	R
7	OOXO XXX	R
8	OOXX XXX	R
9	OXO OOO	R RR
10	XOOO XOO	RR
11	XOOO XXO	R
12	XOOO XOO	R
13	OOOO XOO	R
14	OOXX XOO	R
15	XXOO OXO	R
16	XXOO OXO	R
17	OO XXX	
18	XX XXO	R
19	OXO XOO	R RR
20	XXOX OOO	RR
21	XX XXX	
22	OO OXO	R
23	XO OOX	
24	OX XXO	R
25	XO XOO	
26	OOX	R
27	OOOO XXX	R
28	XOXO XXX	R
29	XXXX OXO	R
30	XXOX XXO	R
31	XO OXO	
32	XO XXO	R
33	OX XOO	
34	XO XXO	R
35	OOXX OXO	R

[no break]

36	XXOO OXO	R
37	XOXX XOX	
38	OOXX XOO	R

Although I have attempted to indicate the internal rhymes only for lines 9 and 10 and 19 and 20, where they reinforce the final rhymes, the superfluity of rhyme is immediately evident from a glance at the above schematization. For a T'ang reader the effect may have been still more striking, since, with the exception of line 37, the nonrhyming lines are always the shorter lines. An equally striking feature of the poem is the irregular meter—in particular, the six-word lines that break into two units of three words with a caesura in the middle. It is easy to speculate that Li Po was striving for a special effect with this manipulation of meter and rhyme, but not so easy to guess what the effect was supposed to be. The abruptness of line 26, which is just three words, seems appropriate to emphasize the gloomy revision of the song by the Queen Mother of the West. And it is true that the Han sacrificial ode "Song of the Heavenly Horse" consists entirely of three-word lines. But one is left with the feeling that for the T'ang reader there was something more.

That "something" was, I think, Li Po's further evocation of the West by elaboration of some hitherto unrecognized verse form that was, in T'ang times, popularly associated with the music and culture of Central Asia—a verse form evolved, perhaps, to suit the requirements of music of Central Asian origin.[39] I suspect that identification of the basic form and a proper understanding of what Li Po has done with it will have to await the future studies of Laurence Picken, whose performance of T'ang music was a highlight of the conference that produced this volume. Nevertheless, I believe we can even now establish that superfluous rhyme and irregular meter were associated with music and Central Asia during the T'ang dynasty. Although it may not be the basic verse form behind "Song of the Heavenly Horse," we do find *one* basic unit of verse with those features that seems to have been so associated. It appears to be a seven-word verse of six lines, characterized by rhyme in all lines but the fifth and by the optional use of a "broken six-word meter" in one or two of the lines.[40] The following poem, also by Li Po, may be a significant example:

39. Professor Ogawa Tamaki is on the trail of this kind of influence in the article cited in note 16. For more material in ancient Turkish see Reşid Rahmeti Arat, *Eski Türk şiiri* (Ankara: Türk Tarih Kurumu Basımevi, 1965).

40. I regard it as a "basic" unit because *special* end-rhyme patterning would be impossible in a shorter verse. For two more examples, see "After a Party with the Governor of Wine

對　　酒
tuậi-　tsi̯ə̯u:

	蒲	萄	酒			金	叵	羅
1	b'uo	d'âu	tsi̯ə̯u:			ki̯əm	p'uâ:	lâ
	吳	姬	十	五		細	馬	馱
2	nguo	kji	źi̯əp	nguo:		siei-	ma:	d'â
	青	黛	畫	眉	紅	錦		靴
3	ts'ieng	d'ậi-	ɣwai-	mji	ɣung	ki̯əm		χuâ
	道	字	不	正	嬌	唱		歌
4	d'âu-	dz'i-	puət	tśi̯äng-	ki̯äu	tś'i̯ang		kâ
	玳	瑁	筵	中	懷	裏		醉
5	d'ậi-	muâi-	i̯än	t̂i̯ung	ɣwǎi	lji:		tswi-
	芙	蓉	帳	底	奈	君		何
6	b'i̯u	i̯wong	t̂i̯ang-	tiei:	nâi-	ki̯uən		ɣâ

Take Wine

1 Grape Wine.   Golden bowls.
2 A girl from Wu, just fifteen, bundled on a blooded horse.
3 Indigo blue she paints her brows, red brocade are her shoes;
4 She speaks her words a little askew to tempt when she sings her
   songs.
5 At the feast on tortoise-shell mats, she gets drunk in your arms,
6 In bed beneath the lotus curtains, what will she do to you?

1	oox	oxo	R
2	ooxx	xxo	R
3	oxxo	ooo	R
4	xxxx	ooo	R
5	xxoo	oxx	
6	ooxx	xoo	R

It would require a separate essay to make the case that this poem represents a distinct verse form and, moreover, a form associated with music and the culture of Central Asia. The main points of that argument can, however, be briefly raised if the interested reader will compare this poem with the two examples by Ts'en Shen (715–70) and T'ang Yen-ch'ien (fl. c. 885), cited in note 40. As one scans lines 1–6 of the three poems, three things are immediately obvious: (1) all three poems have the same rhyme pattern—and, in fact, the same rhyme;

Spring" (Chiu-ch'üan t'ai-shou hsi-shang tsui-hou tso) by Ts'en Shen, and "Farewell to Finance Minister Hsü" (Sung Hsü hu-ts'ao) by T'ang Yen-ch'ien, *CTShih* (Shanghai: T'ung-wen, 1887), 7.49b and 25.18a.

(2) all three poems are concerned with music and parties; and (3) all three poems refer in some way to the culture of Central Asia. (At a glance, only the Ts'en Shen poem is *specifically* concerned with Central Asia—written at a military encampment in Chiu-ch'üan ["Wine Spring"], it makes reference to *p'i-p'a* music, barbarian singers, and fricassee of wild camel—but all three use the foreign word *p'o-lo* when referring to "golden wine cups.")[41] The suspicion that three poems so peculiarly similar *do* represent a *distinct* verse form tends to be confirmed when we scrutinize the poem by T'ang Yen-ch'ien. It has, in fact, eight rather than six lines and would therefore seem to upset the argument—until one notices that the last two lines are simply a congratulatory couplet tacked onto the basic form. Such a tacked-on couplet could hardly be effective, unless it were being tacked onto something with an identity of its own. One might argue, of course, that T'ang Yen-ch'ien has merely written a bad poem that collapses at the end, but, happily for T'ang, the Li Ch'i poem that David Lattimore discusses in the next chapter shows another poet making similar use of this basic form. If one detaches the *clearly detachable* first and last couplets of that ten-line poem, he is again left with a six-line verse rhyming in all lines but the fifth. Again it is a poem about a party and music—indeed, it is even called a "zither song"—and again there is an evocation of Central Asia, for the poet is apparently contrasting frontier hardship with comfortable loneliness back home, and the crows are almost surely the carrion crows of the *frontier* wall.[42]

Regardless of whether I have successfully isolated a significant basic verse form behind Li Po's "Song of the Heavenly Horse," one can, I think, safely assume that the poem would, in any event, have seemed easily associable with *some* special music of the day. The soon to evolve *tz'u* or "lyric" poetry, also distinguished by irregular meter and "superfluous" rhyme, was unquestionably related to music, and it would be strange if Li Po were not epually as much influenced by music as his

41. There is still no consensus on the "*p'o-lo (p'uâ: lâ)* problem." Professor E. H. Schafer leaves it as *pala* in *The Golden Peaches of Samarkand* (Berkeley: University of California Press, 1963), p. 256. The dates and geographical contexts of the occurrences suggest to me an association with the Persian *piyāla*, "wine cup," perhaps cognate with Greek *phialē*. The T'ang *p'o-lo* often are of Tibetan provenance. For a suggestive cultural link see the silver bowl reproduced on page 256 of David Snellgrove and Hugh Richardson's *A Cultural History of Tibet* (London: Wiedenfeld and Nicolson, 1968). It is the right size and shape for a *p'o-lo* and has an unmistakable Greco-Bactrian design. My thanks to Professors Herbert Bloch and G. L. Tikku for help with Greek and Persian problems respectively.

42. For another very similar contrast see "Song of the Water-Clock at Night" by Wen T'ing-yün (812?-70?). James J. Y. Liu, *The Art of Chinese Poetry* (Chicago: University of Chicago Press, 1962), p. 44, and the *Hua-chien chi (SPTK)* 1.6a.

402 ELLING O. EIDE

immediate successors. He writes frequently about parties, dancing, and song, and Wei Hao even thought it relevant to record that "The Waves of Kokonor" *(Ch'ing-hai po)* was one of Li Po's favorite songs. Interestingly, the tune of that title which Picken has reconstructed from the Japanese Tōgaku (T'ang music) repertory, sounds astonishingly similar to the Central Asian music that we know today.[43] This all points, then, to another aspect of Li Po's craftsmanship, another simple, but often overlooked reason for his fame and popularity among his contemporaries: the ability to write dense and evocative yet very singable poems that were exceptionally well suited to the new music of the eighth century.

43. Laurence Picken, "Central Asian Tunes in the *Gagaku* Tradition," *Festschrift Walter Wiora* (Kassel: Bärenreiter, 1967), p. 550. Two of the poems in which Li Po mentions Kokonor (nos. 234 and 619) have quite unusual rhyme and meter patterns, and in one (no. 234) Li Po speaks of improvising a "Kokonor dance."

BIBLIOGRAPHICAL NOTE

Wang Ch'i's dates can be worked out from statements in his biography, "Cho-yai kung chuan," and surrounding text in *ts'e* 3 of the *Hsiu-shui Wang-shih chia-ts'ang chi* (n.p., preface dated 1856), a copy of which is preserved in the Harvard-Yenching Library. The thirty-two *chüan* version of his annotated Li Po was first published in 1758; the thirty-six *chüan* version in 1759. Among other problems, Waley's *The Poetry and Career of Li Po* (New York: Macmillan, 1950), like most works, sees little complexity in Li Po's verse and makes a hash out of the data concerning his background, wives (two wives, two mistresses), and children. Von Zach's virtually complete translation of Li Po's poetry appeared in *Asia Major, Chineesche Revue,* and *Deutsche Wacht.* For the specific references see Alfred Hoffmann, "Dr. Erwin Ritter von Zach (1872–1942) in memoriam," *Oriens Extremus* 10 (1963): 1–60. The Kyoto concordance, *Ri Haku kashi sakuin* (Kyoto: Jimbunkagaku Kenkyusho, 1957), suffers most from the foolish, albeit traditional, exclusion of Li Po's rhymeprose. Chan Ying (1916–) received an A.B. from Peking University in 1938, and an Ed. D. from Columbia Teachers College in 1953; at last report he was teaching psychology at Tientsin Normal College. His two splendid books are *Li Po shih lun ts'ung* (Peking: Tso-chia, 1957) and *Li Po shih-wen hsi-nien* (Peking: Tso-chia, 1958). Chan states that he did most of the work for his books during the war years in southwest China, where he benefited from the notes and advice of Lo Yung (1900–55?) and Wen I-to (1899–1946). Kuo Mo-jo (1892–) too frequently resorts to unacceptable emendations when the text is difficult, but his *Li Po yü Tu Fu* (Peking: Jen-min Wen-hsüeh, 1971) does go straight to most of the major issues with insight and imagination. It is probably the best of all the Li Po-Tu Fu studies. For one chapter in English see "Li Po and Tu Fu as Friends," *Chinese Literature,* 1972 no. 4, pp. 61–94.

Surprisingly, there are few useful Japanese contributions to the study of Li Po, apart from the Kyoto concordance. The best work—182 poems well annotated—is *Ri Haku,* Kanshi taikei, no. 8 (Tokyo: Shūeisha, 1965) by Aoki Masaru (1887–1964).

The most recent work, *Ri Haku*, Sekai koten bungaku zenshū, no. 27 (Tokyo: Chi-kuma Shobō, 1972) by Takebe Toshio (1925–) contains a much larger selection of poems, conveniently numbered as in the concordance, but the translations are un-punctuated and the work as a whole does not contain much new information. Mori Kainan (Mori Taijirō, 1863–1911), Ernest Fenollosa's tutor, does deserve some credit for his *Ri shi kōgi* (Tokyo: Bunkaidō Shoten, 1913), where it is pointed out, apparently for the first time, that "The Road to Shu Is Hard" cannot possibly be concerned with Emperor Hsüan-tsung's flight to Shu, since it appears in the *Ho-yüeh ying-ling chi*, which predates the An Lu-shan Rebellion.

12. Allusion and T'ang Poetry

David Lattimore

Any attentive reader of T'ang poems knows that they abound with allusions, some easy and trite, some difficult and recondite. Every allusion, I shall argue, has somewhat the character of an inside joke; but where T'ang times are concerned, we are all more or less outsiders. The allusions in T'ang poetry were meant in the first place as a sort of puzzle which you solve when you remember something that you know. The same device, of course, appears in Western poetry. In a modern dramatic monologue—one of Randall Jarrell's last poems—a mother-haunted man wants to tell his wife a dream he has dreamt:

> And had she not resembled
> My mother as she slept, I had done it[1]

—and we remember, with a shudder, perhaps after a surprised pause: Lady Macbeth.[2] But when it comes to T'ang poems, we do not always remember. The very presence of an allusion may escape us. Or we may have to comb through books seeking the object of an allusion, sometimes to conclude that it has passed beyond mortal memory. Successful or not, research of this kind mars for us the pleasure which is normal to allusion, the pleasure, Freud said, of recognition, of discovering "something familiar where one expects to find something new instead."[3]

For a discussion of source materials referred to, see the Bibliographical Note at the end of this chapter.

1. "Hope," in Randall Jarrell, *The Lost World: New Poems* (New York and London, 1965), p. 35.

2. William Shakespeare, *The Tragedie of Macbeth* 2.2.662–63:
> Had he not resembled
> My Father as he slept, I had don't.

The Norton Facsimile: The First Folio of Shakespeare, prepared by Charlton Hinman (New York, 1968), p. 744.

3. Sigmund Freud, *Wit and Its Relation to the Unconscious*, in *The Basic Writings of Sigmund Freud*, ed. A. A. Brill (New York, 1938), p. 714. See also I. A. Richards, *Principles of Literary Criticism* (New York, 1925), ch. 28, "The Allusiveness of Modern Poetry."

The difficulty of allusion for the scholar from another place and time is compounded for the translator. Whatever view one takes of the translatability of poetry, one must admit that allusions belong to its least translatable part. Translators from Chinese have not done well by allusions. Arthur Waley avoided allusive poems on principle because "by the time the reader has coped with the necessary explanations he is likely to have lost the mood in which one reads a poem as a poem, rather than as a document."[4] Many lesser translators simply miss the allusions, or wish them away. This is dangerous, for as I shall try to show, allusions like metaphors need not merely decorate a poem; they can be crucial to its meaning; they can even, joined in a series, supply its main thread of meaning.

The Latin verb *alludere* means "*To play* or *sport with* any thing, *to joke, jest, to do* a thing *sportively*" (Lewis and Short). From this come the Romance and English words for "allude" and "allusion," and also, by loan-translation, the German *anspielen* and *Anspielung*. In the sixteenth century allusion meant all sorts of fanciful and punning references (the sense of punning survives in the heraldic term *allusive arms,* arms exhibiting a rebus of the bearer's name). A little later the sense of the word narrowed; rather than playful references in general, it came to mean references in which the playful element is, specifically, the masking of the object of reference. Allusion in this still-current sense is, in the words of the OED, "a covert, implied, or indirect reference." When I speak of allusion in this chapter, I mean it in this sense. It is true that *allusion,* having been narrowed to the sense of indirect reference, subsequently broadened out again, at least in popular usage, to mean *any* reference. As the OED says of the verb *allude,* it is often "used ignorantly as = *refer* in its general sense." But in order to have a manageable subject rather than for puristic reasons, I have chosen to retain the limitation of allusion to indirect or concealed references.

One may object that the term lacks correspondence to traditional Chinese notions, although the modern expression *an-chih* comes close (as does, in some instances, *tien-ku*). But while Chinese also lacks an exact counterpart of our word *poetry,* we do not scruple to speak of Chinese poetry, on the well-founded assumption that poetry is a human universal—as Roman Jakobson says, "Apparently no human culture ignores versemaking."[5] I presume that allusion is also a human universal, and probably, at least in certain of its forms, a universal of poet-

4. Arthur Waley, *Yuan Mei: Eighteenth Century Chinese Poet* (New York, 1956), p. 105.

5. Roman Jakobson, "Closing Statement: Linguistics and Poetics," in *Style in Language,* ed. Thomas A. Sebeok (Cambridge, Mass., 1960), p. 359.

ry, so I shall not hesitate to apply the English word to the Chinese phenomenon.

One may further object that I am riding an etymology too hard in stressing the heritage of wit in allusion; allusions in Chinese, it may be held, are often enough a solemn affair, a rank-pulling self-identification with the cultural powers that be. Perhaps; but many serious things in literature originate as a kind of play and retain a playful tinge. That allusion can be turned to serious uses (like the quibbles and jingles at intense moments in Shakespeare) may be just a further twist of wit, a reminder that in literature the route between the sublime and the ridiculous runs both ways. I do not want to parlay an etymology into a genetic theory, but I do want to urge the enduring wittiness of allusion. In ancient China knights and nobles knew the *Shih-ching* poems by heart and often alluded to them, according to the testimony of the *Tso-chuan* and other books. As Waley and others have pointed out,[6] such allusions seem to have been traded both as a test of wit and as a means of indirect, face-saving discourse in admonishing a superior, or in diplomatic challenge and concession. We may see in this a combination of wit and deadly earnest, reminiscent of the Western tradition of riddling competitions for high stakes, a tradition which goes back to the riddles which Samson propounded to the Philistines.[7] In these situations, war was a continuation, by other means, of a war of wits.

One can most readily locate the wittiness of allusion in its feature of indirection or disguise, since disguise is a form of fooling. Moreover, allusion, because it omits direct reference, may be reckoned a kind of condensation, and brevity is the soul of wit; Freud saw in all forms of verbal wit a "condensation with substitute formation,"[8] which fairly describes allusion.

Indirection alone, however, does not explain the wittiness of the allusions that appear in poetry. Here the more elemental character of allusion, its character as a form of reference, itself adds to the wit, for reference is basically foreign to poetry; the incongruity, in poetry, of references makes them potentially witty. This statement will seem less odd if we observe the distinction that modern investigators draw between meaning and reference. In the sequence word-concept-thing, meaning concerns only word and concept, reference only concept and thing. We often speak meaningfully, less often referentially; ref-

6. See Arthur Waley, *The Book of Songs* (Boston and New York, 1937), Appendix I, "The Allegorical Interpretation," pp. 335–37.

7. Judges 14.12–14.

8. Freud, *Wit*, pp. 641, 686.

erences come into play only where speech, besides making general
statements ("children like oranges"), is applied to particular people,
things, and so on ("I'll take that one"). Poetry, as a kind of permanent
statement, largely abstracts itself from such practical, referential situations. It exaggerates the usual imbalance between meaning and reference, multiplying meanings and replacing references with fictions,
which are a sort of quasi reference cut loose from actuality. Even the
references that do appear in poetry, such as the names of real places
(the Forest of Arden, the deserts of Bohemia), become glamorized and
fictionalized. But allusions do refer, although indirectly, to particular
things that we know from our worldly or literary prior experience. They
break through the magic circle of fiction, as a clown does in his asides
to the audience. This explains the difficulty of translating allusions. It
is hard enough to translate a poem; harder to translate—within stylistic
bounds, and for an audience lacking the right prior experience—references to things outside the poem.

To define allusion as a kind of reference, as distinct from meaning,
might seem to contradict my earlier statement that allusions can be
crucial to the meaning of a poem. Yet everything submitted to the
organizing powers of the poet enters into the structure, including the
meaning-structure, of the poem. Allusive references, although themselves nonconceptual and thus meaningless, can be employed metaphorically, or in parallel with other elements in a poem (including other
allusions), forming pairs and sets with meaningful common properties.
In other words, allusions come to reflect and magnify a meaning from
their poetic context. In this their behavior resembles that of proper
names in poetry. Proper names in themselves, even if composed from
still-meaningful morphemes, have been held since John Stuart Mill
to possess reference but no meaning.[9] But the wordplay of poetry tends
to revive the meaning dormant in proper names; hence the exaggerated-
ly significant names of characters in the tradition of English comedy,
reflected also in serious novels through the time of Dickens. The poet
Mayakovsky suggested that, in a poem, the element *great* in the constel-
lation-name *Great Bear* would regain its full significance; Jakobson
points out the revival, through wordplay, of the senses "new" and
"haven" in Wallace Stevens's poem "An Ordinary Evening in New
Haven."[10] The city of Hsienyang ("all-*yang*") supposedly owes its name
to its location on the *yang* (sunny, versus *yin*, shady) side both of the
Chiu-tsung Mountains (the south side) and of the Wei River (the north

9. See Stephen Ullmann, *The Principles of Semantics* (Glasgow, 1951), p. 73.
10. Jakobson, "Closing Statement," pp. 376–77.

side). In ordinary usage the name evokes no such meaning; it merely *refers* to the city. But in a poem by Tu Fu (712–70), the well-known ballad "Ping-chü Hsing,"[11] the name Hsienyang fits the semantic structure of the poem, and consequently, although this is not an outright Shakespearean quibble, seems to regain at least a tinge of its original meaning. A theme of the poem is the perverse dominance of *yin* phenomena over *yang*: dark, damp, violence, reversal of sex-roles, and the prizing of women over men. Tu Fu specifically speaks of the dark sky as *yin*, and the poem also contains the line "There is so much dust that you cannot see the Hsienyang Bridge." Not only does *yin* obscure, but in the line quoted *yang* seems to be represented as obscured. The same poem contains a more obvious example of a resemanticized name. Tu Fu alludes to the contemporary emperor Hsüan-tsung (reigned 713–55) by the designation Wu-huang, thus likening him, as other T'ang poets do also, to the Han emperor Wu-ti (reigned 140–87 B.C.); but since the poem speaks of the ruthless military expansionism of "Wu-huang," the element *wu*, "military," clearly regains its meaning. In this case an allusion takes the form of a quasi name, but allusions in general relate closely to proper names. To grasp an allusion, one must often recall to mind a proper name, such as the name of the person alluded to, or of the text quoted. An allusion, like the normally meaningless proper name, acquires contextual meaning when it fits into a poetic pattern.

There are, I propose, two kinds of allusions in literature: topical and textual. A topical allusion is an indirect *denotation* of a current topic, for example, by a key word associated with it, or of a person, place, and so on, for example, by an epithet. A textual allusion is an indirect, that is, an unacknowledged, *quotation* of a well-known remark, proverb, or literary work, so that the reference points, first of all, not to a thing but to a text; although textual allusions may embrace topical allusions.

Purely topical allusions are by no means scarce in the literature of great periods of civilization, such as the T'ang, since in such periods there is often a widespread confidence that the topics of the day will continue to be memorable; it is, rather, the provincial and epigonic literatures that are too "literary," too academic, to accomodate topical allusions. Yet, in general, topical allusions belong more to conversation and to ephemeral literature than to poetry. Allusions to current topics are the more difficult sort to understand once the topics have passed from currency. Such allusions have, so to speak, a "horizontal" ex-

11. Vulgo "Ping-ch'e Hsing," *Tu Shao-ling Chi Hsiang-chu*, ed. Ch'iu Chao-ao (1638–1717), 2 (Peking, 1955), *ts'e* 2, p. 64.

tension; they may be widely understood at a certain time, but are little understood in subsequent times.

Textual allusions, too, are made in conversation and ephemeral literature. The family joke is often a rudimentary textual allusion, the "text" being some remark which, with its original context, is remembered in the family, although the connotations are lost upon others. The prerequisite for textual allusions is not literacy but memory, and a tradition of what is remembered. The ancient Chinese who alluded to the *Shih-ching* were not all literate. Our own highly literate society is not generally good at textual allusion; we read too many books, too seldom the same books. Ulli Beier has documented the extremely subtle use of allusions to proverbs in the Yoruba language of Nigeria; in Yoruba poetry, the point of a passage which quotes the first half of a proverb will reach the hearer only if he remembers the second half.[12] Textual allusion, Wolfgang Kayser points out, flourishes in proportion as there exists a homogeneous public.[13] Even the Yoruba are no longer such a public: "Few secondary school leavers nowadays will be able to follow when the drummers recite the praise-names of a line of some forty-odd kings," Beier says.[14] In a literate society the public at large lacks homogeneity; any "public" which enjoys allusions to written texts will comprise a small, self-perpetuating group of elite education, in a word, the "mandarins" of that society. In such a group, allusions lose their character of contemporary topicality, and will more likely refer to the past. Textual allusions thus have a "vertical" extension or endurance in time but are not widely understood at any particular time. Textual allusions in literature, legible to the elite, are more effectively concealed from other people. Their wit is an in-group wit.

Parody is a common form of textual allusion. But in a mandarin class the textual allusion undergoes a further transformation. It not only loses contemporaneity but becomes more serious because it converges with another device, the citation from authority *(tien-ku)*, familiar to us from legal and theological argument. Allusive citations, that is, learned textual allusions, may concern serious topics, but quite apart from this their habitual use may serve a serious, if unstated, social purpose. Any allusion gives a sort of conspiratorial pleasure by reinforcing the feeling that the speakers, or the author and reader, are in on the joke, hip, "in the know." In a learned group, legitimated by its ties to the past, the use of learned allusions will reinforce this feeling in the special

---

12. Ulli Beier, "Poetry of the Yoruba," *Delos: A Journal on and of Translation* 2 (1968): 8–9.
13. Wolfgang Kayser, *Das Sprachliche Kunstwerk*, 14th ed. (Bern and Munich, 1969), p. 111.
14. Beier, "Poetry of the Yoruba," 6.

form which it takes in such a group, a sense of corporate legitimacy based in great part on shared, exclusive knowledge of the past. In such a group, reading an allusive poem is something like taking part in a ritual. One takes part when one's memory contributes to the aesthetic experience the necessary recollection of the reference, exemplifying what E. H. Gombrich, in *Art and Illusion*, calls the "beholder's share" in artistic creation.[15]

In his recent study of poems on the Double Ninth festival, A. R. Davis discusses the traditional "furniture" of such poems, including allusions; he suggests, perceptively, that the poet used this furniture "to link his particular poem to the general stream of Chinese poetry."[16] This linkage of oneself to a continuing stream answers, I believe, a deep psychological need, the need which Robert J. Lifton calls "symbolic immortality": "man's need, in the face of inevitable biological death, to maintain an inner sense of continuity with what has gone on before and what will go on after his own individual existence."[17] J. B. Leishman has documented in detail the occidental impulse, from Pindar to Shakespeare, to erect a *monumentum aere perennius* in verse and thus to achieve symbolic immortality through letters.[18] We have evidence that by the Age of Disunion (317–589) Chinese poets, too, sought symbolic immortality not only through immersion in nature and the perennial "return" of the daily, seasonal, and life cycles (a central theme of T'ao Ch'ien), and not only through the endurance of family, class, and society, or through attachment to enduring classical texts or ancient moral exemplars, but also through the survival of their own literary works, believing these would continue to move the men of later generations. Indeed the sense of the historical past, a well-recognized distinguishing feature of the Chinese among Asian peoples, easily extends itself into a sense of the future, a sense that one's own experiences will survive as history (or literature) in an equally past-conscious future. Wang Hsi-chih (303–79) thus concludes his famous "Lan-t'ing Hsü" (A.D. 353): "Men in after time will look back upon

15. E. H. Gombrich, *Art and Illusion: A Study in the Psychology of Pictorial Representation*, 2nd ed., Bollingen Series, no. 35.5 (Princeton, N.J., 1961), Part III, "The Beholder's Share," and passim.

16. A. R. Davis, "The Double Ninth Festival in Chinese Poetry: A Study of Variations upon a Theme," in *Wen-lin: Studies in the Chinese Humanities*, ed. Chow Tse-tsung (Madison, Milwaukee, and London, 1968), p. 53.

17. Robert Jay Lifton, *Revolutionary Immortality: Mao Tse-tung and the Chinese Cultural Revolution* (New York, 1968), p. 7.

18. J. B. Leishman, *Themes and Variations in Shakespeare's Sonnets* (New York, 1963), Part I, "Poetry as Immortalisation from Pindar to Shakespeare."

us as we look back upon those who have gone before us, alas! . . . Though times and happenings alter and differ, may men in what moves them be brought together. They who regard us from the future will also be touched by these writings."[19]

One can argue, to be sure, that the kinds of literary immortality sought by occidentals and by Chinese were weighted differently: that Roman and Renaissance poets envisaged chiefly the immortality of their own literary "monuments" (which would, in turn, confer immortality on the subjects of the monuments), whereas the Chinese envisaged chiefly a corporate immortality, devolving upon the individual poet from his participation, as Davis suggests, in a continuing tradition. The allusion, in referring to something outside the poem, refers frequently (as in textual allusion) to *another* poem, or else to a recognizably "literary" subject; in so doing, it provides a sort of chemical bond within the "eternal" tradition. Although not itself a poem but rather a prose preface to a group of poems, Wang Hsi-chih's "Lant'ing Hsü" not only describes but illustrates this, for its concluding passage turns on an allusion. Wang's evocation of the enduring poetic experience is his answer to the question, itself immortal, of man's mortality: "Whether short or long our lives follow fate and at last must end. The ancients said: 'Great indeed are death and life.' Is this not painful? Whenever I ponder the men of old their sources of feeling agree with ours."[20] The allusion is to *Chuang-tzu,* where two passages mildly denigrating Confucius represent him as saying, "Great indeed are death and life, but they are all the same to him" (i.e., to Wang T'ai in one passage, and in the other to Sun-shu Ao).[21] Confucius, as often in *Chuang-tzu,* appears as a willful, conventional man, set in his ways, and therefore pained or awed by those natural or fated changes which do not abide man's wishes or his habits—the greatest such changes being, of course, birth and death. Confucius has vision enough, however, to concede the superiority to himself, and to other ordinary people, of those sages (such as Wang T'ai and Sun-shu Ao) who have learned to "roll with the punches" and who regard with indifference even questions of life and death. Wang Hsi-chih apparently likens himself to Confucius in being vulnerable to the pathos of mortality, but he finds release through a sense of transtemporal community with others similarly afflicted, and, especially, others similarly *aware* of brotherhood with those so afflicted; as he alludes to *Chuang-tzu,* so others will allude

19. In biography of Wang Hsi-chih, *Chin-shu* 80.4a.
20. Ibid.
21. Chuang-tzu, *Nan-hua Chen-ching,* 5 and 21, *SPTK,* 2.31a and 7.40a.

to Wang Hsi-chih. It is indeed a paradox that a means to symbolic immortality, and to the deep feelings associated with it, should for Chinese poets be found in the characteristically ephemeral and jocose device of allusion. But this paradox merely reflects another more essential: that men should erect enduring monuments in language, which owes its ordinary utility as a communicative medium to its property, as a linguist says, of "rapid fading"[22]—the fact that speech-bearing sound waves die quickly on the air, making room for more of their kind.

Textual allusions to the *Shih-ching,* of the type reported in the *Tso-chuan* and other ancient books, were allusions *to* poetry. Textual allusions *in* poetry are identifiable in any great quantity only from a later period; a period when poetry itself had become bookish enough to catch the craze for citation that permeates Chinese book learning. But by the time of the great medieval literary theorists, learning had been made a universal requisite of imaginative writers second only to talent or to inspired responsiveness to nature. This appears nowhere more strikingly than in the great "Rhymeprose on Literature" of Lu Chi (261–303), the opening distich of which reads, in Shih-hsiang Chen's translation:

Erect in the Central Realm the poet views the expanse of the
    whole universe,
And in tomes of ancient wisdom his spirit rejoices and finds
    nurture.

The first line suggests receptive personal vision piercing through nature, through space, to mysterious outermost regions; the second, a like penetration of time, by means of arduous learning, delving back to the era of the sages. Incidentally the first line alludes to the *Tao Te Ching,* the second to the *Tso-chuan,* a neat antithesis of Taoist and Confucian Classics, as well as of the terms "mystery" and "canon," respectively Taoist and Confucian in ambience.[23] Lu Chi expounds further the linked growth of the knowledge of nature and of books; the two coalesce in a single image when the poet "wanders through treasuries and *forests of literary works.*" The passage calls to mind the conclusion of Reuben A. Brower's *Alexander Pope: The Poetry of Allusion:*[24] "For Pope at the beginning of his career, as at the end, the imitation of life is also the imitation of literature." In third-century China as in eighteenth-

22. Charles F. Hockett, "The Problem of Universals in Language," in *Universals of Language,* ed. Joseph Greenberg (Cambridge, Mass., 1963), pp. 9, 14.

23. Shih-hsiang Chen, *Essay on Literature by the Third Century Poet Lu Chi* (Portland, Maine, 1952), p. 20. For "mystery" and "canon," see the text: *Lu Shih-heng Wen-chi, SPTK,* 1.1b.

24. Reuben A. Brower *Alexander Pope: The Poetry of Allusion* (Oxford, 1959), p. 361.

century England there existed fully developed the conditions necessary for the exploitation of textual allusion in poetry.

Outside of the lyric, allusion in China had indeed established itself earlier. Liu Hsieh (465–522) in his *Lettered Heart and Sculptured Dragon* says that "Before Ssu-ma Hsiang-ju (179–117 B.C.) and Wang Pao, poets mostly plied their talents and did not pursue learning; after Yang Hsiung (53 B.C.–A.D. 18) and Liu Hsiang (77–6 B.C.), they tended to draw from books as an aid in writing; here lay the great divide between 'taking' and 'giving,' a distinction such as one ought not to confound."[25] Liu Hsieh does not, however, condemn the "takers." Elsewhere in the *Lettered Heart* he praises the ability fully to assimilate an allusion into one's work. For this, however, deep learning is required: "To use the words of others as your own, the past must offer you no opacities."[26]

The question of the assimilation of a textual allusion into the texture of a new work is an interesting one because it raises the further question of how an allusion so assimilated can be recognized as an allusion. We recognize certain expressions as allusions because we can make sense of them no other way, but in these cases there is no assimilation: the allusion remains anomalous within the poem. I shall illustrate such an unassimilated allusion not from a T'ang poem but from a prose tomb inscription *(mu chih ming)* in which one great T'ang poet eulogizes another: the inscription on the grave of Tu Fu composed by Yüan Chen (779–831) at the request of Tu Fu's grandson.[27]

The inscription is in fact a notable piece of literary criticism. Like many such works, it begins with a miniature history of poetry, serving to place the poet eulogized in a lofty succession. The history in this case is not merely a hyperbolic exercise; Yüan Chen is making the valid, and probably at that time original, point that Tu Fu had been an unprecedentedly *comprehensive* poet, bringing together in his work the best of two ideals: the morally serious ideal of popular self-expression and protest, rooted in ancient balladry, and the courtly ideal of sensuous formalistic elegance. Yüan Chen, like his intimate friend Po Chü-i (772–846), himself subscribed to the former or Confucian ideal. It is not surprising, then, that in his capsule literary history Yüan Chen makes several rather condensed allusions to Confucian Classics. One of these occurs in his discussion of the period, about 100 B.C., when traditionally verse in lines of five syllables had arisen. Yüan describes the vigor of folk poetry in that period. He allows that the refined tradi-

25. Liu Hsieh, *Wen-hsin Tiao-lung, SPTK,* 10.4b.
26. Ibid. 8.6b.
27. In Tu Fu, ed. Ch'iu, 25, *ts'e* 10, pp. 23–24.

tion descending from some of the early *Odes (Ya)* had commingled with
a more licentious poetry (the "sounds of Cheng"). Yet, on the whole,
style remained simple, and thought profound. Then comes a cryptic
sentence, literally: "naturally not-be possess do and do" *(tzu fei yu wei
erh wei)*. Since this yields no particular likely sense, we infer the presence of an unassimilated allusion. The sentence becomes clear if we
recognize in it an allusion to a dictum of Mencius:"When men have
things that they wouldn't do, then afterwards they can have things that
they would do"[28]—that is, first decide what (on grounds of conscience)
you *won't* do; anything else you will then be free to do. The meaning
of Yüan's sentence then becomes "the poets were not people (such as
those Mencius hoped for) having certain things which they would do
(in consequence of having certain other things which they would not
do); they just did things spontaneously." In context, I think Yüan
means that while poets at this time no longer wrote on the basis of
considered moral judgments, traditions not yet badly decayed sustained
them, for the most part, in doing (or saying) the right thing. The im-
plication is the Mencian one that even when things are going downhill,
good traditions die hard, as does the Heavenly Mandate.[29]

Let me review this allusion briefly. The verbal congruity of Mencius's
text and Yüan's is slight, being restricted to the once-repeated pair of
syllables *yu wei;* beyond this, we have only the feature in both texts of a
pair of phrases contrasting as positive and negative. *Mencius* as a text
bears no special relationship to the period or situation which Yüan
describes, although it does fit the category of texts that he alludes to.
The marker of allusiveness is carried simply by the fact that Yüan's
sentence cannot be otherwise explained; it is unassimilated. The passage in *Mencius,* and no other traceable source-passage, explains the
passage in Yüan. Nonassimilation marks allusiveness; the unique
explanatory value of the *Mencius* passage verifies the particular allusion.

In the absence of nonassimilation, the presence of textual allusion is
unmarked and will go unrecognized without stronger evidence of congruity between source-passage and allusion. The presence of an allusion
will, however, be *suggested* if there is a *pattern* and hence an expectation
of allusion in the poem, supported perhaps by other patterns.

As I have cited the opening distich of the "Rhymeprose on Literature," perhaps as a final pre-T'ang example I may be allowed to cite
the closing distich of that work, illustrating both the congruity of source

28. *Mencius* 4B.8, *Meng-tzu Shih-ssu Chüan, SPTK,* 8.4a: "Meng-tzu yüeh: jen yu pu wei
yeh, erh hou k'o i yu wei."
29. Ibid. 2a.1, 3.2a-b.

with allusion and the patterned set of allusions.[30] The distich—let us
remember that this is Lu Chi's final word on literature—says that
literature

> Decks bronze and marble to broadcast virtue,
> Flows through pipes and strings, each day to renew.

Perhaps the first thing to note about this passage is the typical linkage,
or partial identification, of literature with music, rooted in the classical
doctrine that one's volition, to express itself, requires not only words
but also sighs, groans, and so on, and ultimately music (including meter
as well as melody). Conversely, music/poetry exerts a regulatory effect
on the volition. Thus the lines each express the idea that an artistic
work produces a result (virtue, self-renewal) which is morally good.
Beyond this, the lines strike us at first as strongly contrasting. In the
first line, the inscription-covered metal and stone suggest the permanence of literature. But the distich quite properly presents this feature of
permanence in a paradoxical context. The permanent literary work
results from a moment, itself transient, of spontaneous inspiration. In
the performer and reader it produces other transient moments of
inspiration. The poetic work, then, is a permanent link between
transient moments. The second line presents the aspect of transience:
music/poetry "flowing" through perishable bamboo and silk produces
a result not fixed but cyclical (daily renewal).

This would seem to exhaust the surface meanings of the distich, which
moreover presents no grammatical or semantic anomaly that would
itself alert us to an allusion. Yet the distich contains allusive elements,
which will be seen to amplify and further unify the patterning already
described. One allusion would certainly strike readers of Ezra Pound,
author of *Make It New*. The final two syllables allude to the slogan "If
each day you make it new, day by day make it new, yet another day
make new," supposed to have been inscribed upon the bathtub of
King T'ang, founder of the Shang state (c. 1751 B.C.); the inscription
having been preserved in the familiar *Great Learning*, the forty-second
chapter of the classical ritual-book *Li Chi*.[31] This bathtub, the instrument of daily lustrations, was itself an inscribed permanent object.
Thus our intuition of this allusion fits a pattern within the distich:

> inscribed permanent object/ human process (virtue)
> human process (music, song)/ inscribed permanent object

---

30. *Lu Shih-heng Wen-chi, SPTK,* 1.5b–6a.
31. *Tsuan-t'u Hu-chu Li Chi* 42, *Ta-hsüeh, SPTK,* 19.9a.

There is also another allusion. So far we have considered the contrast of metal, stone, media of permanent graphic inscriptions, as opposed to pipes, silken strings, media of transient musical sounds. There is, however, an underlying unity, for metal and stone are also themselves materials of musical instruments. In fact bronze (bells), stone (chimes, drums), bamboo (pipes), and silk (strings) are the four sound-sources of the classical orchestra, according to the same ritual-book, the *Li Chi*, which preserves King T'ang's bathtub motto.[32]

The two lists differ with respect to wording at two points and exhibit one reversal of word order, which is very important in the identification of allusion. Thus we have:

Li Chi:	*chin* (metal)	*shih* (stone)	*ssu* (silk)	*chu* (bamboo)
Lu:	*chin* (metal)	*shih* (stone)	*kuan* (pipes)	*hsien* (strings)

But there remains, I would claim, congruity of terminology and of order sufficient to confirm the allusion tolerably well, provided that we throw into the equation the scriptural authority of the proposed *Li Chi* source and the lack of a more congruous source-passage elsewhere. Indeed, the three differences—two of terminology and one of word order—can be reduced to a single difference of terminology (word choice)—the replacement of the unitary lexical item *ssu-chu* by the synonymous and equally idiomatic *kuan-hsien*, which can be explained semantically as the substitution of one sort of synecdoche for another, part-for-whole replacing material-for-whole.

Taking the alternate binomes *ssu-chu* and *kuan-hsien* as lexical items on a par with a repeating binome *chin-shih*, we have then a 50 percent lexical congruence between the *Li Chi* passage and the rhymeprose passage, a basic congruence of significance once the synecdoches are interpreted, and a full congruence of order. There is still very little verbal matter involved in the congruence, and there is not the partial nonassimilation and the conspicuousness of source evident in the "daily renewal" allusion, so that the argument for allusion made thus far is not strong. It gains strength, however, from the structural unity which the allusion, if accepted, adds to the poem, bringing the topic of music into the first line in a position paralleling the one that it certainly occupies in the second line and thus making the whole distich signify at once the allied topics of music, literature (*wen*, the grammatical subject carried over from a previous distich), and ritual (from the nature of the source). The *Analects* confirms the relationship: "Be

32. Ibid. 19 *Yüeh Chi* 11.13b.

aroused by poetry, firmed by ritual, perfected by music." Moreover, this allusion to *Li Chi*, if allowed, enters into a *pattern* with the "daily renewal" allusion, also from *Li Chi*. It may be argued that two allusions do not make a pattern, since it takes three trees to make a row. But two items in a complex context can indeed make a pattern—for instance, two trees flanking a doorway or two rhymewords in a couplet.

The perception of allusion in a passage—allusion (a part of verbal reference) as distinct from borrowing (a part of literary history)—is a complex intuitive process, a conclusion drawn from the simultaneous weighing of many minute probabilities, typical of many processes which "the great averager," as Sir Charles Sherrington called the human brain, can perform much more easily than it can define. A similar problem is that of the latent metaphor. For instance, in the following lines from "Bereft" (Robert Frost):

> Leaves got up in a coil and hissed
> Blindly struck at my knee and missed[33]

—is there or is there not the latent metaphor of a snake? A. A. Hill has devised a rough quantitative method for judging from sets and sequential orders of features (such as *coil, hissed, struck, missed*) the likelihood of latent metaphor being a part of the meaning in such cases.[34] Textual allusion is a much more complex phenomenon, depending not only upon the relation of message to code (e.g. to the concept "snake") but upon a relation of message to prior message—a prior message that must be judged not only with respect to its congruity but also with respect to its availability and uniqueness as the possible object of allusion. Often we feel surer of allusions if they come in related groups that include at least one highly probable case and thus an escape from *petitio principii*. I shall now discuss a T'ang poem which presents such a group of allusions.

The poem is a work of a talented minor poet, Li Ch'i *(chin-shih, 725)*, entitled "Lute Song" ("Ch'in Ko"), the "lute" (really a zither) being of course the archaic and austerely expressive instrument of sages, scholars, poets, and hermits.[35] The poem mentions the region of the River Huai as a place of official service; Li Ch'i at some time was a comptroller *(wei)*, that is, one of the several superintendants of employees and taxes in the subprefectural government of Hsin-hsiang near

33. *Collected Poems of Robert Frost* (Garden City, N. Y., 1942), p. 317.

34. Archibald A. Hill, "A Program for the Definition of Literature," University of Texas Studies in English no. 37 (1958), pp. 46–52.

35. Li Ch'i, "Ch'in Ko," in *Ch'üan T'ang Shih*, ch. 133 (Peking, 1960), 2.1349.

the Huai in what is now Honan, an area where Li Ch'i's family had lived for some time. We cannot be sure that the poem places him en route to this particular post, nor even that we are meant to take the work as autobiographical. There are, however, vague indications of a journey at the beginning and end of the poem. I shall try to show that a set of allusions in the poem greatly clarifies the sense of the poem; and that, in particular, the allusions give a significance to the journey resumed at the end of the poem different from that of the initial journey. Something happens during the brief overnight sojourn that the poem depicts, and this seems to alter the direction of the putative speaker of the poem. His voyage, originally connected with the mandarin's re- peated changes of office, turns into a voyage of opposite import: a voyage altogether out of public life and into some sort of eremitic retreat—a rejection of society and a return to nature. It does not seem likely that Li Ch'i is disclosing an actual conversion experience, a crucial event of his personal life; more likely, he is dramatizing a mere wistful longing, or complimenting a lutanist on the persuasive powers of his music. But that is beside the point. All that concerns us is the drama depicted. In this, I claim, there is indeed such a conversion experience. But this meaning is carried for the most part by allusion; it scarcely emerges into the surface meaning of the sentences.

There exists at least one rather slight piece of evidence that Li Ch'i had dabbled in practices associated with eremitism:[36] a poem, frivo- lous in tone, addressed to him by Wang Wei (701–61), which begins:

> I hear, sir, you've been nibbling cinnabar powder;
> You've certainly gotten a fine color!
> I suppose any day now
> You'll be sprouting wings!

Cinnabar, or crystalline mercuric sulphide, from which elixirs of longevity were concocted, gave its vermilion color to the eater's face, according to the alchemist Ko Hung.[37] The aerial flight of the adept- turned-immortal was, of course, the ultimate extension of the hermit's flight from the world. One must recall that, for the Chinese, retiring from the world was a matter of degrees along a scale. There was always a further degree in the background, an "India beyond India," just as in Wordsworth's "Tintern Abbey" the valley of the Wye impresses

36. Wang Wei, "Tseng Li Ch'i," *Hsü-hsi Hsien-sheng Chiao Pen T'ang Wang Yu-ch'eng Chi,* *SPTK,* 3.3a–b.

37. Ko Hung (284–363), *Pao-p'u-tzu Nei-wai-p'ien, SPTK, Nei-p'ien,* 4, "Chin Tan" [Gold and Cinnabar], 13a.

"thoughts of more deep seclusion," the smoke of cottage chimneys suggests "vagrant dwellers in the houseless woods" or the "hermit's cave, where by his fire/ The hermit sits alone."[38] At the near end of the scale was the comfortably jobless gentleman pursuing some sort of self-cultivation in his garden or villa. Much further out were the Taoist alchemist-adept and ultimately the "mountain man" or *hsien* who had transmuted his body, thus achieving longevity and powers of flight. On another scale—Confucian, rather than Taoist—were hermits who took to the wilderness not because of its attractions for them but because of some grievance against society, and who in their extreme form sought not longevity but death: culminating this scale were Po-i and Shu-ch'i, who "would not eat the grain of Chou" and, protesting the founding of the Chou kingdom (? 1111 B.C.), ate ferns upon the slope of Mount Shou-yang until they starved.[39] In poetry the various scales and degrees of eremitism often get mixed up; but there is a tendency to describe, or to express a wish for, some more extreme kind of eremitism than that which, we feel, the poet or his persona "really" wants.

Li Ch'i's poem reads:

> Our host has wine to cheer the evening,
> He bids the Kuang-ling visitor to pluck and sound the lute.
> Moonlight atop the city wall, crows half-flying.
> Frost grips a myriad trees, wind pierces my coat.
> Bronze braziers, colored candles, brightening each other—
> At first he strums the "Clear Stream," then the "Concubine of
>   Ch'u."
> The first note in motion, all things fall still.
> On four sides, all speechless till the stars grow few.
> Sent a thousand miles and more to a post on the Ch'ing and
>   Huai
> I presume to declare: mists, mountains, from this begin!

Notable in this, as in many poems, is a particular sort of departure from the norms of written (or memorized) discourse. Written discourse, with a few exceptions, exemplifies what the linguist Leonard Bloomfield called "displaced speech,"[40] that is, speech exchanged at a remove

---

38. William Wordsworth, "Lines Composed a Few Miles above Tintern Abbey, on Re-visiting the Banks of the Wye during a Tour. July 13, 1798," *Poetical Works*, ed. Thomas Hutchinson, rev. Ernest de Selincourt (Oxford, 1969), pp. 163–65.

39. Ssu-ma Ch'ien, *Shih-chi* 61.8a.

40. Leonard Bloomfield, *Language* (New York, 1933), p. 141.

from the objects of reference, if any. In displaced speech one must ordinarily specify any objects of reference, or of fictional quasi reference, more carefully than if the objects were physically present or otherwise known as familiar to particular interlocutors. In "Lute Song," however, the speaker is made to feign the manner of undisplaced speech, as if addressing not a displaced reader but rather his own friends or himself. The result is a sense of physical immediacy, of intimacy, and, to a degree, of natural speech, despite the use of rhymed verse and of literary language. But, in consequence, the narration and description appear fragmentary by the usual written-language standards. The place, time, and dramatis personae remain vague. A Chinese storyteller, paraphrasing the poem, would have named the town, the month, the year, and he would have identified the speaker, the host, and the "Kuang-ling visitor." The poem exhibits what Jean Cohen describes as contextual or situational ellipsis, gaps not of syntax, but in the continuity of representation.[41]

Modern criticism, reacting against Victorian vagueness, has stressed the "hard" qualities of poetry, its clarity, incisiveness, and structural design; less attention has been paid to these "soft," mysterious, sfumato effects, which can nevertheless play an important part in the economy of poetry. Effects of vagueness doubtless characterize some sorts of poetry more than others. I suspect them to be neither especially primitive nor especially sophisticated, but typical, rather, of poetry, such as Chinese lyric poetry, where the main underlying tradition is not epic or dramatic or forensic, but instead that of the song or ballad, with its characteristic reduction of action and description to a few high points and suggestive details, leaving out connections and context. In a ballad, the words themselves are usually graphic, not vague; vagueness enters through our sense of what has been left out, what happens between the stanzas. Vagueness in poetry can serve several artistic purposes. The indeterminate areas of a poetic narrative, as of a painting, being interpretable in various ways, make the total effect less mechanical than it would be if derived wholly from prominent compositional elements. Free zones, which Gombrich calls "screens,"[42] are left for the reader's imaginative elaboration and thus for participation in the aesthetic experience by one's faculty of projection, as when one pictures for oneself the characters and scenes of a story. This is not quite the same, Gombrich points out, as the kind of knowledgeable inference, although this too is a form of participation, which allows us

41. Jean Cohen, *Structure du langage poétique* (Paris, 1966), pp. 155–56.
42. Gombrich, *Art and Illusion*, p. 208.

to make sense of a partly hidden figure in a painting (or, we might add, allusions in poetry).[43] A vague feature often encountered in Chinese and other poems is that which Hans H. Frankel has called "open-endedness," that is, indeterminacy of the beginning and ending of an action, of which only some intermediate portion is represented.[44] "Lute Song" is open-ended in this sense.

Contextual vagueness, the absence of localizing background, can also impart a sense of typicality, even universality, to the particulars of a representation. The particulars become what W. K. Wimsatt, Jr., following a Hegelian tradition, has called "concrete universals."[45] Thus they help the poem to do what good poems often do, that is, suggest a general truth through details. "Curious power of a device fashioned of mere omissions," says Jean Cohen; "it possesses the gift of turning existence to essence and relative to absolute."[46] From its vague ambience the concrete universal obtrudes itself as a symbol, for instance the penetrating wind in Li Ch'i's poem, or as an omen, such as the crows. It then enters readily into symbolic contrasts of the kind which Harold G. Henderson, discussing haiku, has called "internal comparison";[47] for example, Li Ch'i's contrast of the cold, black-and-white, inimical outdoors to the warm, colorful, friendly indoors. The symbolic value of these details far outweighs any possible verisimilitude. In poetry, vagueness and symbolism are interdependent. The contrasting contextual vagueness accentuates the represented object, lets it be a symbol. But any symbol reverberates incalculably. It exerts its power of suggestion over the way we project our fantasies on the vague areas, which now serve as "screens." Arthur Symons meant something like this when he said that in symbolist writings "description is banished that beautiful things may be evoked, magically."[48]

But it is not only representational elements that poetic vagueness

43. Ibid., p. 212.

44. Personal communications. Also Frankel, "Time and Self in Chinese Poetry" (Paper read at meeting of the Association of Asian Studies, Chicago, March 28, 1961). Cf. Frankel, "Fifteen Poems by Ts'ao Chih: An Attempt at a New Approach," *Journal of the American Oriental Society* 84 (1964): 3, discussion of "Men Yu Wan-li K'o" by Ts'ao Chih (192–232): "The warm human encounter lasts only a moment, but this moment is presented as a segment of a continuing process. The brief meeting is seen as a stage in a long journey. Thus the lyric moment is linked to the eternal flow of time. It is, to borrow a line from Robert Browning, 'the instant made eternity.'"

45. W. K. Wimsatt, Jr., *The Verbal Icon* (New York, 1962), "The Concrete Universal," pp. 69–83.

46. Jean Cohen, *Structure du langage poétique*, p. 161.

47. Harold G. Henderson, *An Introduction to Haiku* (New York, 1958), p. 18.

48. Arthur Symons, *The Symbolist Movement in Literature*, rev. ed. (New York, 1958), p. 5.

throws into relief. The poet can make vague, that is, partially suppress, any normal form of order and continuity—grammar, logic, representation—and can thereby thrust to the fore or, to use the structuralist term, "foreground"[49] any form of *poetic* organization that pleases him: rhyme and meter, as well as more complex forms of parallelism and contrast, including parallelism and contrast of allusions.

It is my contention that Li Ch'i, in his "Lute Song," has foregrounded a set of three parallel textual allusions and that this set of allusions is a main structural member of the poem. It seems, furthermore, that the allusions have greater coherence, in more than one sense, than does the poem taken simply as a narrative-descriptive representation, that is, the way a reader ignorant of the allusions might take it—thus foredooming any approach to the poem via an "innocent eye" theory of poetry. And, in addition, the allusions, if understood, serve, in linguistic jargon, to "disambiguate" the representation and also to clarify the point of view of the poem.

In my translation of "Lute Song" I have indicated a point of view, specifically that of narrator, by the pronouns *our* in the first line and *I* in the last. Neither pronoun appears in the Chinese, since the poet gives no modifier of "host" in the first line, while in the last he exercises the Chinese privilege of omitting a grammatical subject. That is, no "I" appears before "presume" and "declare"; whether "mists" and "mountains" are subjects of what follows, objects of what precedes, or both, is unclear—a grammatical vagueness typical of T'ang poetry. Vagueness about pronouns occurs widely in poetry; this is the feature which Lewis Carroll parodied in the lines that begin

> They told me you had been to her
> And mentioned me to him. . . .[50]

In particular, the character which "I" denotes in poetry may be kept unclear, that the reader may more readily project himself into the part. The "I" which, constrained by the English requirement of grammatical subjects, I have introduced into the last line, represents the speaker according to my interpretation. I could have said not "I" but "he,"

49. "Foregrounding" is Paul L. Garvin's translation of the Czech term *aktualisace;* see Garvin, *A Prague School Reader on Esthetics, Literary Structure, and Style* (Washington, D. C., 1964), p. viii; also Josef Vachek, *The Linguistic School of Prague* (Bloomington, Ind., 1964), pp. 99–100. The Russian formalist notion of the "laying bare of the device" *(obnaženie priěma),* due originally to Roman Jakobson, represents a more primitive stage in the same formalist-structuralist tradition.

50. Verses read by the White Rabbit: Lewis Carroll, *Alice's Adventures in Wonderland,* chap. 12, *The Annotated Alice,* ed. Martin Gardner (New York, 1960), p. 158.

referring to the "Kuang-ling visitor," and making that person, the hypnotic musician of the poem, also its speaker.

The first allusion, in the group of three that I shall discuss, attaches to the expression that I translate as "Kuang-ling visitor" (line 2). The innocent reader, either of the Chinese text or of my translation, will at first take the expression to mean a guest from Kuang-ling. *Kuang-ling* ("Broad Mound") is an old place-name. Witter Bynner translates: "guest from Yang-chou,"[51] and Yang-chou had indeed been called Kuang-ling after 742, probably late in Li Ch'i's lifetime. We shall miss the basic meaning of the expression, however, unless we realize that there had been an air for the lute, called "Kuang-ling Melody" ("Kuang-ling san"), a piece with lofty literary associations. Like the "Clear Stream" and "Royal Concubine of Ch'u" named in line 6, the "Kuang-ling Melody" is mentioned in the greatest of works on the lute, the "Rhymeprose on the Lute" ("Ch'in-fu") by Hsi K'ang (223–62), an important poet and a leading spirit among that most celebrated group of aristocratic, Taoist free spirits, the Seven Sages of the Bamboo Grove. R. H. van Gulik declares that "next to being the author of the *Ch'in-fu*, Hsi K'ang's fame as a lute player rests on his connection with a melody of legendary fame, the *Kuang-ling-san*."[52]

The official biography of Hsi K'ang *(Chin-shu 49)*, a very late (seventh-century) but familiar source, preserves a story about the origin of this piece.

> In his early days K'ang once roamed west of Loyang. At dusk he stopped for the night at the Hua-yang Pavilion, and began playing his lute. In the middle of the night there was suddenly present a visitor who addressed himself to K'ang, identifying himself as "a person of ancient times." Conversing with K'ang on the rules of music, his words evinced the clearest discernment. Drawing the lute to himself, he played the "Kuang-ling Melody." The music was altogether extraordinary. Having taught the piece to K'ang, he exacted an oath that it would pass no further; nor would he tell his name and surname.[53]

In the same source we find another relevant story.

> When Hsi K'ang was soon to be executed in the East Market,

---

51. *The Jade Mountain: A Chinese Anthology, Being Three Hundred Poems of the T'ang Dynasty, 618–906*, trans. Witter Bynner from the texts of Kiang Kang-hu (New York, 1929), p. 48.

52. R. H. van Gulik, *Hsi K'ang and His Poetical Essay on the Lute*, Monumenta Nipponica monograph (Tokyo, 1941), p. 31.

53. *Chin-shu* 49.9a.

his spirit remained unperturbed. Drawing the lute close and finger-
ing it, he played the "Kuang-ling Melody." When the piece was
finished, he said "Yüan Chun once asked to learn this melody, but
I firmly refused to give it to him. Now the 'Kuang-ling Melody'
has perished."[54]

The latter story has made the "Kuang-ling Melody" a symbol of vanished glory too fine for our day and for the touch of ordinary mortals.
The story shows a poetic delicacy. Not only does Hsi K'ang, as one of
his final gestures, draw the lute to himself, exemplifying his intimate
and proverbial association with the instrument; but in the last sentence
we can hardly help observing that it is Hsi K'ang, as well as the melody, whose doom is sealed. Hsi K'ang uses the "Kuang-ling Melody"
as virtually a metaphor for himself. In the finality of the particle i,
he suggests his own acceptance of the end now all but accomplished.
Longevity—the finite-minded Chinese counterpart of immortality—
eluded Hsi K'ang's pursuit of it, for he died, the victim of political
intrigues, at the age of thirty-nine (A.D. 262).

But it is the former story to which, I think, Li Ch'i more particularly
alludes. The key is the word "visitor" (k'o). The occasion that Li
Ch'i's poem represents, in which several people take part and in which
(against the strictest provisions for lute-gatherings) wine is drunk, is
certainly not the occasion referred to in the story from Hsi K'ang's
biography, although that too represents a night scene; that is why I
suppose that Li Ch'i means us to take his poem as autobiographical,
rather than entirely an allusion to the earlier event. But should the
"Kuang-ling Melody" ever reappear in the world, it would no doubt
come to us once again in the intimacy of the night and from the fingers
of a nameless otherwordly visitor, Hsi K'ang's own spirit or that of his
teacher. It would be preposterously bad-mannered for Li Ch'i to depict
himself as such a spirit; that is why we cannot identify the "Kuang-
ling visitor" with the speaker of the poem. But there is in the depiction
some unnamed lutanist to whom poet and host wish to accord this
profound flattery.

The "Clear Stream" and "Concubine of Ch'u," like the "Kuang-
ling Melody," are mentioned in Hsi K'ang's "Rhymeprose on the
Lute," and it is the first of these—the first piece represented as *played* at
Li Ch'i's gathering—that I propose to take as the second instance of
allusion, this time to the great "Rhymeprose" itself. Hsi K'ang, in the
relevant passage of the "Rhymeprose," like Li Ch'i, speaks of lute-

54. Ibid.; also *Shih-shuo Hsin-yü, SPTK,* 2A.24a-b.

playing on a winter night and names the "Clear Stream" as the first melody that ought to be played. I translate the passage as follows:

> Now suppose a high gallery or soaring tower or a wide, spacious, quiet room, when the winter night is awesomely clear and the bright moon sheds its glitter, when new clothers rustle and tasseled waistbands drift perfume; then the instrument will be cold, its strings attuned, the heart at ease, and the hand clever, the touch will follow the will, responding as your thought determines. Now first you will ford the "Clear Stream."[55]

The third allusion occurs in, and explains, the last line of the poem. (Since the line needs explaining in this way, the allusion, unlike the first two in the group, is unassimilated.) The allusion is made in the three small words *ts'ung tz'u shih,* "from this begin." It may seem strange that a cluster of words so commonplace in meaning should comprise an allusion, and commentators have therefore ignored them. But the words in their setting do need explaining. The concordances suggest no possible source other than the one that I shall name (the use of *ts'ung* rather than *tzu* meaning "from" argues for a post-classical origin). The source-identification, as I shall show, receives strong support from features of meaning and of what phonologists call "pattern congruity."

Before naming the source-passage, I should like to point out that another allusion to it, under comparable circumstances, seems to occur in the work of Li Ch'i's contemporary Tu Fu. Tu Fu's poem ("Feng-hsien Liu Shao-fu Hsin-hua Shan-shui Chang Ko")[56] almost certainly postdates Li's. Whereas Li's poem concerns music, Tu Fu's concerns painting: it describes a gate-screen at Feng-hsien with landscapes newly executed by a certain Liu of the imperial ateliers *(shao-fu).* The poem, not one of Tu Fu's great works, is a rambling, friendly tribute to Liu and to Liu's sons, also painters. The younger son has painted a mountain-dwelling Buddhist priest attended by a servant lad, and this reminds the poet of a mountain stream and temple in Chekiang which he must have visited in his youthful wanderings. He regrets his worldly life and concludes, "Plain shoes and cloth stockings from this begin." As in Li Ch'i's poem, the words "from this begin" terminate the poem. This positional congruence, together with the congruence of theme, encourages me to feel that the recurrences of "from this begin" are not coincidental; I am curious to know whether the tradition will yield further instances.

55. *Hsi Chung-san Chi, SPTK,* 2.3a.
56. Tu Fu, ed. Ch'iu, 4, *ts'e* 3, pp. 12–14.

Now for the source. It is, I suggest, a poem universally familiar to T'ang poets from the *Wen-hsüan* anthology: the third of the eighty-two "Songs of Care" ("Yung Huai") by Juan Chi (210–63), known as a bibulous, eccentric poet-musician, and as the other leading spirit, besides Hsi K'ang, of the Seven Sages:

> Beneath good trees, paths come together.
> In the east garden are peach and plum.
> Autumn winds drive the flying bean-leaves;
> Our scattering, our fall, from this begin.
>
> Clustered flowers, even, must burn or languish.
> In the high hall grow bramble and thorn.
> I'll lash my horse and I'll be gone,
> I'll go and climb the Western Mountain.
>
> Since I cannot keep my single body
> How can I cherish wife and child?
> —A hard frost mantles the grasses of the wild,
> The year reaches evening; all is said and done.[57]

The eremitic tendency of this poem in its turn is "disambiguated" by allusion ("Western Mountain") to the archaic verses ascribed in *Shih-chi* to the martyr-hermits whom I have mentioned, Po-I and Shu-ch'i:

> Climb that Western Mountain, *hsi!*
> Pick its ferns, *i.*
> A tyrant traded for a tyrant, *hsi!*
> Not knowing the evil of it, *i.*
> Shen-nung, Yü [-shun] and Hsia [-yü] are forgotten.
>   If they are passed away, *hsi,*
> Where shall we betake ourselves, *i?*
> We are going, alas, we depart, *hsi,*
> Our destiny is decayed, *i.*[58]

Let me return to Juan Chi's poem. Not the poem but rather its first quatrain ends, as Li Ch'i's and Tu Fu's poems end, with "from this begin." Juan Chi's poem is more symbolistic, and even less verisimilar than Li Ch'i's. The time-scale is not that of an evening but of a whole season from the ripening of fruit at harvest time to (as in Li Ch'i) late autumn or winter. But Juan Chi's first quatrain resembles the Li Ch'i

57. *Liu-ch'en-chu Wen-hsüan, SPTK,* 23.2b.
58. *Shih-chi* 61.8a.

poem in more than one way. In Li Ch'i's poem there is a gathering of
guests, the sharing of an experience, followed by implied dispersal,
the speaker's thought now turning to journeys in connection with official
duty, and also to some apparently alternative journey among mists and
mountains. In Juan Chi's quatrain we find a similar dual movement,
first gathering, then scattering. In the first quatrain there is a coming
together of paths, and by inference of people, when the fruit-trees ripen;
then, as the season turns, there is a scattering of leaves which imparts
to the observer a sense of loss, an impulse to be gone. In Juan Chi's
poem the second quatrain projects the seasonal scale onto that of the
civilization, the dynasty, which also seems to be decaying; a justification to be off, with the flying leaves, to one's own "Western Mountain."
In Li Ch'i's poem, as in Juan Chi's and in Tu Fu's as well, there occurs
an aesthetic experience—for Li Ch'i of music, for Tu Fu of painting,
for Juan Chi of nature—which imparts a religious impulse. And in
Li Ch'i and Juan Chi there is a sense of a beginning which comes out of
an ending, the ending of a night, a season, a kingdom.

We have, then, three allusions, each of which adds something to Li
Ch'i's poem not only by itself but in concert with the other allusions.
These are *convergent* allusions. They join in calling to mind a particular
time, almost five centuries earlier than Li Ch'i, and a particular milieu,
that of the Seven Sages of the Bamboo Grove, led by Hsi K'ang and
Juan Chi. The analogy of the Seven Sages suggests that Li Ch'i's
friends, too, commune closely with each other and with nature, that
they share an unworldly persuasion, that for them music is not just
music but a mysteriously enduring and beneficent force which springs
from and influences the harmony of heaven and earth.

"Lute Song," read in the light of its allusions, suggests the following
interpretation: The speaker seems to have passed by or through a
wintry wood and a city wall. Perhaps he is a wanderer like the semi-
migratory crows that winter at this latitude. All is penetrating cold and
clashing black-and-white: frost in the trees, crows in the moonlight,
moonlight touching just the *top* of the wall. The crows half-fly (or half
of them fly) because it is the transitional hour of dusk and they are
desultorily settling to roost, or because the traveler has disturbed them.
There is thus a sense of instability and unease. This may extend to a
doubt about the crows as omens—usually they are bad omens, but
unexpected behavior from crows can augur well, and the reader might
remember a story from the *Tso-chuan* in which "crows atop the city
wall" had evidenced the abandonment of a city by the enemy force

defending it.[59] Another unsettling effect is the presentation of the scene as a flashback.

The next part of the representation (but the first in its unfolding, lines 1–2) introduces a sharply contrasting scene of good cheer, in which the speaker seems to have stopped as a guest at a musical gathering. Whereas the host offers the physical comfort of wine, another guest, likened to Hsi K'ang or Hsi K'ang's mysterious visitor, brings the gift of rare and unearthly music. In lines 5–6 the warmth, brightness, and color of the interior scene contrast sharply to the cold, half-lit *grisaille* outside. The musician begins to play pieces associated with Hsi K'ang and the Seven Sages; the first-named piece, also played first by Hsi K'ang according to his "Rhymeprose on the Lute," takes us back to a passage in that work describing lute-playing on a similar night and stressing the perfect establishment of mood necessary to the success of such music.

At this point I shall go back and point out a feature of the poem which repeats and develops. The poem names or suggests many situations of cause and effect. Frost freezes the trees, wind enters the traveler's coat to chill him, he perhaps alarms the crows (and—as omens—they him), wine cheers. We will overinterpret if we insist that the effect of crows and man upon each other is a part of what the poem definitely signifies; yet as part of an aesthetic experience of the poem this might be an allowable free inference. I mention it only because this would be a case of *reciprocal* causation. In line 2 the lutanist does not simply play the lute; he plucks it, the lute sounds, answers, so to speak—again, a hint of reciprocity. Then in line 5 we have a very strong reciprocity of cause and effect. As I understand the line, each brazier and candle glows in the light of the others, multiplying the brilliance—clearly symbolizing the warm rapport among host and guests. (The "Clear Stream" allusion, concerning the establishing of a mood, reinforces this.)

Lines 7 and 8 bring a further development in this direction. We must remember that lute music is chiefly solo music; of those present perhaps

---

59. In the winter of 554 B.C. the forces of Chin, with those of Lu and other allies, invaded Ch'i and inflicted an initial defeat on that state. The Duke of Ch'i climbed a mountain to view the attacking armies. The latter raised flags in strategic spots for which they could spare no troops, placed dummies in some of their chariots, and dragged branches to raise dust, so as to create the appearance of a greater force than they in fact possessed. Frightened, the Duke of Ch'i struck his standards and fled in the night, abandoning the city of P'ing-yin. It was announced to the Marquis of Chin that "there are crows on the city wall. The army of Ch'i must have retreated!" See *Tso-chuan Chu-shu, Ssu-pu Pei-yao* ed., 33.7. Presumably the cautious crows would have avoided the walls when these were defended, but there is more to the omen, since we are told that the sound of the crows was joyful.

only the "Kuang-ling visitor" performs. On the analogy of line 5, with its image of reciprocity, we might expect that the music would effect an answering music in the listeners' souls. But what happens is something less and perhaps more than this. The response to the music is a *silence* beyond words, beyond music. Measured music produces a *suspension* of time-sense. The dawn steals upon the listeners unawares; the music, perhaps, reaches a final pianissimo with the fading stars.

In a poem about music it is interesting that the experience of silence should assume such prominence. Moreover the syllable that I translate "fall still" *(ching)*, alone among line-terminating syllables in the poem, stands outside the rhyme-scheme; all the other lines, and the poem is unusual in this respect, are rhyming lines. Thus the word "still" itself momentarily stills the flow of rhymes—a good example of rhyme (or its lack) abetting the sense. The silence itself involves a reciprocity. The music causes all things to fall still; it charms them to silence or at least it seizes the attention, rendering all else inaudible (line 7). Reciprocal to this (line 8) is a *cessation of speech,* ordinary (or even philosophical) chatter about ordinary things.

What has been produced is a state of abnormally lucid calm and rapport in which repressed insight or self-awareness rises to consciousness. The silence need not be its own end. What matters is the self-discovery permitted when the jangling of the world gives way to something more harmonious, and this self-discovery finds expression, I believe, in the last distich. The speaker of the poem achieves a new consciousness of the journey, literal or figurative, upon which he has embarked. There is an official career, which always for the mandarin involves many changes of post, many journeys; there is or has been a call to a post in the region of the Ch'ing and Huai (or of the "clear Huai"). But in the final line the speaker has decided, at least momentarily, either to *imagine* that his journey (career) has a different sense or to turn it in fact in a different direction, not toward a subprefectural yamen but toward the mists and mountains, the death place of martyrs and the dwelling place of hermits and supernatural beings. This is not, I repeat, to say that Li Ch'i as a person had undergone a conversion experience, any more than Tu Fu had seriously resolved to become a Buddhist. What happened to Li Ch'i we cannot know. But we *can* recognize in the last line, through the allusion to Juan Chi's poem— which, in turn, alludes to Po-i and Shu-ch'i—a definite notion of rejecting a decaying society and taking to the wilderness. Through a strongly linked set of allusions, Li Ch'i evokes the mocking disdain for convention, the longings for a purer life-style, expressed by the Seven

Sages. And behind those aristocratic pseudo-hermits, far off in the direction of substantial sagehood, we descry the purer types of Hsi K'ang's mysterious visitor, and of Po-i and Shu-ch'i.

The result is not unambiguous; we still feel some of the uncertainty with which the poem opens. On the one hand the speaker declares that for him a life of mists and mountains is to begin. On the other hand he makes his announcement, curiously, in the archaic bit of officialese with which an inferior concludes an announcement to a superior: "I presume to declare" *(Kan kao)*. Yet there is, I think, a further significance to this "declaration." Line 8 tells us particularly that the group is speechless. Yet just as the flying leaves sweep Juan Chi into thoughts of decline and departure, just as the young painter's picture of a hermit is reflected in a graphic imagining by Tu Fu of the poet himself wearing rustic clothes and resolved to abandon the world, so also the lute music in Li Ch'i's poem at last echoes in a voice breaking the stillness: the speaker's *declaration* of intent. In this connection, it is interesting that, according to van Gulik, a surviving piece of early lute music purporting to be the lost "Kuang-ling Melody" indicates by the titles of its sections that its motif is the "magic journey" of the hermit-immortal—the ultimate, airborne flight from society.[60] On balance, it would seem that the speaker has resolved to leave the world; a meaning which, however, is carried not by the poem's surface sense, but almost entirely by allusion.

A final note on Li Ch'i's "Lute Song": if we want to understand a poem fully, we must of course study not only "the poem itself," but also the poem as situated in a larger tradition which in a sense is a larger work of art. And that tradition has not only its "vertical" dimension through time, linked among other ways by textual allusion; it has also a "horizontal" dimension, embracing, for example, the author's contrasting works. Several of Li Ch'i's best-known poems concern the barbarous, warlike northern frontier and the music, so popular in T'ang times, of that frontier. For instance, his poem "Ku I" mentions both the three-holed Tibetan flute, and the p'i-p'a which, unlike the ch'in of "Lute Song," is a true lute derived from Western Asia.[61] "Lute Song," which concerns the most conservative and characteristically Chinese of instruments, customarily forbidden to barbarian ears, and which depicts a journey, not across the border, but into the heart of the central plain, and likewise, through allusion, into the heart

60. Van Gulik, *Hsi K'ang*, p. 33.
61. *Ch'üan T'ang Shih* 133.1355.

of a peaceable, unworldly tradition, must in a larger view be seen as
contrasting with these other poems.

Li Ch'i's "Lute Song" illustrates the great artfulness achieved in
China by a kind of poetry nevertheless essentially occasional; "Lute
Song" might well have been improvised and chanted on the occasion
it describes. In such poetry, nearly an oral poetry, allusions might have
provided a kind of ready-made filler material functionally similar to
Homeric formulas, but lacking such convenient fixity. That allusions
nonetheless play the part they do in "spontaneous" and emotionally
vivid lyrics testifies, of course, to the liveliness of the learned tradition
that produced them.

We have also observed allusions in a more labored medium, the
highly condensed prose of a commemorative inscription by Yüan
Chen. I should like to conclude my examples with three passages from
a poem by Yüan's friend Po Chü-i, likewise a work of *limae labor et
mora*: the celebrated "Everlasting Remorse" ("Ch'ang Hen Ko")
which recounts the infatuation of the T'ang emperor Hsüan-tsung
for his concubine Yang Kuei-fei. Po Chü-i composed his poem in 806,
just fifty years after Yang Kuei-fei had been strangled, during the
An Lu-shan Rebellion, in order to placate the loyalist troops who hated
and feared the Yang clan.[62] The poem is a familiar one and is too long
to quote in full, but for convenience' sake I give here the three allusive
passages that I shall discuss:

> The Han emperor, bent upon "color" (=beauty, sex), thought
>   of shaking the state.
>
> > [Line 1]
>
> In the golden chamber, her adornment completed, she tenderly
>   *(chiao)* serves for the night.
>
> > [Line 21]
>
> Accordingly [the success of the consort clan] caused the hearts of
>   fathers and mothers under heaven
> Not to value the birth of boys, but to value the birth of girls.
>
> > [Lines 25 to 26]

As we have seen, "Lute Song" lays down a layer of allusions to the
third-century milieu of the Seven Sages of the Bamboo Grove, implying
an analogy between the unnamed actors in the poem and the Taoist
poet "sages." Yüan Chen's inscription alludes to the Confucian *Analects*,
Mencius, and other texts of the classical period, implying an analogy

62. *Po Shih Ch'ang-ch'ing Chi, SPTK,* 12.12b–20b.

between Tu Fu and the Confucian sages of the pre-Ch'in era, the same analogy later made explicit in a common epithet for Tu Fu: "Sage of Poetry" *(Shih-sheng)*. The men of T'ang were, however, much more conscious of an analogy between themselves and the men of Han, the one previous era in which China, as under the T'ang, had enjoyed prolonged centralized rule at home and imperial sway abroad. In particular, an analogy was felt to hold, as we have seen in Tu Fu's poem, between the Han emperor Wu-ti and Hsüan-tsung of the T'ang, both of them notable for their length of reign, their economically and socially taxing imperialistic successes, their patronage of the arts and of poet-cronies or buffoons, and their thralldom late in life to Taoist magicians, to beautiful women, and to the unscrupulous relatives of beautiful women. So marked was the analogy that poets regularly said Wu-ti when they meant Hsüan-tsung.

In "Everlasting Remorse" Po Chü-i names certain T'ang names, including Yang, the surname of Hsüan-tsung's concubine; but when being more specific than this, that is, when indicating specific people, he maintains the fiction that he is writing of the Han, not the T'ang. He does not, however, *name* Han Wu-ti, any more than he names T'ang Hsüan-tsung. He is subtler than this. Instead of naming Wu-ti as a cover for Hsüan-tsung, he indicates Wu-ti only by referring to three of the *women* of Wu-ti. Even these, however, are not referred to directly. Their identity is suggested, rather, by textual allusion. It is interesting to note the contrasting lack of allusion in the prose narrative "Ch'ang Hen Ko Chuan" by Ch'en Hung, which parallels the "Everlasting Remorse" and often accompanies it as an explanatory preface. Ch'en unabashedly refers to the T'ang dramatis personae by their true names and without allusion. When he draws a Han analogy, he does so by explicit comparison: thus Yang Kuei-fei "in her languid allure from first to last resembles Han Wu-ti's Li Fu-jen."[63] Ch'en's work occupies a middle ground between fiction and history, belonging to the literature of anecdote. But like Chinese fiction it makes a great pretense of historicity. By convention, the prose version pretends to be more historical than it is; the verse version, less historical than it is.

The first allusion in "Everlasting Remorse" occurs in line 1:

The Han emperor, bent upon "color" (= beauty, sex), thought
of shaking the state.

In context, the syllables translated as "shaking the state" *(ch'ing kuo)* scarcely make sense; they comprise an unassimilated (and truncated)

63. Ibid. 12.13a.

allusion to the following well-known lines, preserved in the *Former-Han History* chapter on consort clans:

> In the north there is a beautiful woman;
> The *ne plus ultra* of the age, she stands alone.
> One look would shake the cities of men,
> Another look would shake the states of men.[64]

The *History* attributes this bit of doggerel to Li Yen-nien, eunuch kennel-keeper of Han Wu-ti, who became a favorite singer and dancer of the court and who is supposed to have used these lines to draw the emperor's attention to his younger sister, who became Li Fu-jen.[65] Like Yang Kuei-fei, Li Fu-jen could dance; she caused the founding of a powerful consort clan, which, proving to be a nuisance, was virtually exterminated after her death; she died young; her death caused the emperor to pine and to place confidence in a Taoist magician who undertook to find or summon her spirit.

The second allusion occurs in line 21 of "Everlasting Remorse":

> In the golden chamber, her adornment completed, she tenderly
> (*chiao*) serves for the night.

This alludes to the tale, preserved in the *Han Wu Stories*, traditionally attributed to Pan Ku (32–92), that the future emperor Wu-ti as a small child had picked out his first bride, née Ch'en and called as a child A-chiao, saying: "If I could have A-chiao for my wife, I would build a golden chamber in which to treasure her."[66] In view of this reference, the second part of Po's line 21 would seem genuinely ambiguous but only marginally a covert allusion, for, allowing the omission of the proper-name prefix *A-*, we could also read it:

> Chiao serves for the night.

The third allusion occupies lines 25–26 of "Everlasting Remorse":

> Accordingly [the success of the consort clan] caused the hearts of
> fathers and mothers under heaven
> Not to value the birth of boys, but to value the birth of girls.

The lines allude to yet another of Han Wu-ti's consorts, the empress née Wei, who followed the empress Ch'en as a favorite and preceded Li

---

64. *Han-shu* 67A.13b–14a.
65. *Shih-chi* 125.3b–4a.
66. *Han Wu Ku-shih*, in *Han Wei Liu-ch'ao Wen-hsüeh Tso-p'in Hsüan-tu* (Hong Kong, 1961), p. 255.

Fu-jen. Her story, like Li Fu-jen's, displays remarkable similarities to that of Yang Kuei-fei, similarities certainly not lost upon the men of T'ang. Wei Tzu-fu, singing-girl and daughter of a slave, had like the others come to the emperor's notice through an incident worthy of anecdote: she had waited upon the emperor as he "changed his dress" (visited the latrines) and, being smitten with her, he had "favored" her almost on the spot (in a nearby covered carriage, probably his traveling wardrobe-carriage). After some years, having produced an heir as well as daughters, she supplanted Madame Ch'en as empress (128 B.C.). Five of her male relatives became marquises, one of these having been her younger half-brother Wei Ch'ing (died 106 B.C.), a distinguished general and commander-in-chief against the Hsiung-nu. As in the case of the Li family, clever members of the consort clan, unqualified to compete as literati, made their mark in frontier warfare, exemplifying most concretely the relationship, clear to poets such as Tu Fu, between *yin*-as-sex and *yin*-as-force.

The verses to which lines 25–26 of "Everlasting Remorse" allude are an example of the "Boys' Song," that is, an anonymous children's ditty regarded as a portent (along with other disturbances of the elements, these were normally recorded in the "Five Elements" treatises of the Standard Histories). The "Boys' Song" in question refers to the disturbed balance of *yin* and *yang* caused by the rise to power of the Wei consort clan. It said:

> In bearing sons there is nothing joyful
> In bearing daughters there is nothing to be despised.[67]

Pretty daughters, in other words, will gain your family imperial favor when the masculine virtues and accomplishments are no longer prized. Later poets, including Ch'en Lin (died A.D. 217) and Tu Fu, repeat this motif primarily in a reversed sense: frontier wars—in part fomented by consort clans or by emperors grown irresponsible under the influence of these—are taking the lives of so many boys that one might better beget daughters. This makes the negative value of boys the primary *yin-yang* disturbance, rather than the enhanced value of girls.

The men of T'ang had occasion more than once to remember Empress Wei as well as her lord and master. In 684 the dowager empress Wu (625–705, posthumously called Tse-t'ien Huang-hou), Hsüan-tsung's grandmother, was trying to usurp the throne. Her enemies were constantly comparing the empress Wu to various Han empresses, especially to the dowager empress née Lü, widow of the Han founder.

67. *Shih-chi* 49.13b.

Indeed, these comparisons are among the most striking examples of the proud but anxious consciousness of Han analogies in the minds of T'ang literati—and of the willingness of these men to risk drawing such analogies openly (or at least allusively). The crimes alleged against the Han empress Lü had never included sexual ones. The empress Wu, on the other hand, had entered the court as a concubine of Emperor T'ai-tsung (reigned 626–49). We do not know whether T'ai-tsung slept with her; but since she reentered the court to become empress of his son, Emperor Kao-tsung (reigned 649–83), she had at least technically committed incest. Moreover, rumor held that she had gained favor with the future Kao-tsung, during his father's lifetime, in the same manner in which Wei Tzu-fu had gained favor with Wu-ti, that is, when attending him at the latrines. This parallel clearly suggested itself to the poet Lo Pin-wang (died 684) who, in an elegantly worded diatribe against the empress Wu written for the party that took arms against her in 684, accused her of "having taken advantage of 'changing dress' in order to enter service."[68]

This last digression will serve to remind us of the notable role that allusion played not only in Chinese literature but in Chinese political life. Let us return, however, to the set of imperial beauties that Po Chü-i presents to us through poetic allusion. What is the basis of the analogies made among them?

The principal basis is, I think, the topos of seduction, seduction of man (the "sole man," man par excellence, the emperor) by or through woman, *yin* dramatically overmastering *yang*. Wei Tzu-fu and Wu Chao played the seductress in their own interests, acting swiftly as occasion offered, overpowering the male in the latrine. A-chiao (the empress Ch'en) and Li Fu-jen baited traps set by others: the first having been the creature of her mother, the princess Ch'ang, the second of her brother, the eunuch Li Yen-nien. In these cases the real seducer, the primary agent of *yin*, was another: a scheming older woman, a castrated felon turned court pet. Yang Kuei-fei appears, too, as something of an innocent, hardly past puberty in Po's poem, languorously yielding in love and in death; the infatuated emperor's plaything, then a tool of her cousin Kuo-chung, who became chief minister and died with her in 756. Arthur F. Wright likens the historical type of the imperial femme fatale to the folklore type of the "fox woman" who ruins men through sexual exhaustion.[69] This is decidedly apt in the cases of the

68. *Tzu-chih T'ung-chien* (Peking, 1956), 203.6423.
69. Arthur Wright, "Sui Yang-Ti: Personality and Stereotype," in *The Confucian Persuasion*, ed. Arthur F. Wright (Stanford, 1960), p. 63.

empresses Wei and Wu, perhaps less so in our other instances. The *wu-ku* sorcery of which Wu-ti at the last accused Empress Wei involved potions made from noxious insects which had devoured each other until only one remained; these were supposed to weaken the victim through sexual debauchery.

But there are many features besides the role of seductress that these femmes fatales share in common. Some of these topoi we may summarize as follows:

	Wei	Li	Yang
low origin	x	x	x
talent for music, dance	x	x	x
relatives who gain power	x	x	x
a bad end	x		x
emperor seeks magic contact after death		x	x

This diagram may help to explain the special prominence of Yang Kuei-fei in literature: she is the femme fatale who exemplifies *all* the principal topoi.

These examples of allusion have covered a wide range of experience, from tumbles in the palace latrines to the heights of mystical-aesthetic communion. Yet I have not tried to illustrate one very common kind of pattern that allusions in a Chinese poem may exhibit: the *divergent* set, in which allusions, although they may possess a common ground, are deployed across a wide historical or geographic range, implying the message, "This is always, or everywhere, true." I have, however, given examples of *convergent* patterns, where the allusions meet each other in referring to a particular context other than, but likened to, that of some layer of depiction or narrative more proximate in time. Thus Po Chü-i's three allusions converge at about 100 B.C., Li Ch'i's three at about A.D. 250. Diversity is preserved, however, in that each member of each set of allusions points to a different source. In Po, these are the *Former-Han History*, the *Han Wu Stories*, and the *Historical Records;* in Li, the *Chin History*, the "Rhymeprose on the Lute" by Hsi K'ang, and a poem by Juan Chi.

Aside from these similarities there is a notable difference between Li Ch'i's use of allusion and Po Chü-i's. I concluded that Li Ch'i's representation was of the quasi-autobiographical type. From the point of view of representation, the analogy presented by allusions to a past time was thus "out of the picture" and secondary. In Po's poem, on the other hand, the represented scene is by a somewhat diaphanous fiction actually ascribed, in the first instance, to the earlier time alluded to; so that in a sort of preliminary stage of understanding it is a conflation of three Han consorts who are "in the picture" while Yang Kuei-fei is analogous but outside. It will be seen that Po's method here is precisely that of parable or allegory, a *consistently maintained* metaphor, in which the "more real" depiction must as a whole be seen through the transparent screen of a more immediate but "less real" depiction; the Hsüan-tsung story must be seen through the Wu-ti story. However, both methods, Li's and Po's, partake of the nature of metaphor, one form of words standing for another normally more apposite one that must be simultaneously inferred. This is the art, in a broad sense, of metaphor, the art of introducing effects of simultaneity, and, through this means, effects of implied equation, into the linguistic medium.

All poetry draws analogies; as Wallace Stevens said, "Poetry is a satisfying of the desire for resemblance,"[70] by which means it intensifies our sense of reality. Metaphor is one way of satisfying this desire; it is moreover a natural part of language, one which accounts for many vocabulary innovations. Metaphor occurs early in Chinese literature: Confucius said, "At seventy I followed my heart's desire without overstepping the carpenter's square."[71] Metaphor has appeared in this chapter in Hsi K'ang's "Rhymeprose on the Lute": "Now first you will ford the 'Clear Stream.' " The word *ford,* meaning, as we might say, "wade through" or "embark upon," is a figurative substitute for some more natural expression meaning "play through" or "start playing." How do we know? From context: to disambiguate the sense of *ford,* the context offers us, after the manner of poetry, the resemanticized name "Clear Stream." One fords a stream—here the *meaning* of the name comes into play; but one plays a piece—and we know the reference of the name "Clear Stream" to a musical piece. So the context, generously in this case, both justifies the figurative expression "ford" and suggests the supplanted normal expression meaning "to play through a piece." Nevertheless, the senses of these expressions attach *simultaneously* to the one word *ford.* As in all "live" metaphor, a resemblance is suggested between the meaning of the normal expression ("play through" or the like) and of the substituted figurative expression.

Chinese poetry is unlike the prose of Confucius or the "rhymeprose" of Hsi K'ang, and it is conspicuously unlike occidental poetry, in that

---

70. Wallace Stevens, "Three Academic Pieces," *The Necessary Angel* (New York, 1965), p. 77.

71. *Analects* 2.4, *Lun-yü Chi-chieh, SPTK,* 1.10a-b.

it avoids metaphors of this simple and familiar kind, but instead draws analogies in a quite different way—by a process of combination, not selection; a process which is nonsimultaneous and does not contrast something said with something that normally *would* have been said but is not. Chinese poetry, for the most part, draws analogies through the process of internal comparison—the implicit comparison to each other of things which actually are said, sequentially, at different places in the same poem. In Chinese poetry, the combinatory device of internal comparison largely supplants the selective device of metaphor.

But not entirely. When the poet alludes to the "Kuang-ling visitor" but really intends a reference to a musician of his acquaintance, or when he alludes to Li Fu-jen but intends a reference to Yang Kuei-fei, or even when he simply says "The Sage of Poetry" in order to indicate Tu Fu, he is using changed words, metaphor or a close analogue of metaphor. He is playing a game with selection, using one choice of terms to imply another from the same box in the type-case, although he happens to do this with respect to reference, not meaning. Reuben S. Brower says that "for Dryden and for Pope allusion . . . is a resource equivalent to symbolic metaphor and elaborate imagery in other poets."[72] The same insight applies to T'ang poets. Without the fanciful comparisons of a Hafiz or a Shakespeare, they had hit upon an equally potent means of eliciting the likenesses and harmonies of things, with the same flashing rapidity of effect and the same heady, "hallucinatory" reliance on inference.

72. Brower, *Alexander Pope*, p. viii.

Bibliographical Note

Standard Histories are cited in the Po-na-pen editions. Other Chinese texts marked *SPTK* are editions reprinted in the *Ssu-pu Ts'ung-k'an*, first series, revised edition (Shanghai, Commercial Press, 1929). Where characters have variant readings, my romanizations follow the pronunciations indicated in the *Gwoyeu Tsyrdean [Kuo-yü Tz'u-tien]* (Ch'ang-sha, Commercial Press, 1947).

Contributors

ELLING O. EIDE, a Junior Fellow at Harvard, is now Assistant Professor of Chinese Language and Literature at the University of Illinois. He is currently at work on a complete translation of Li Po's prose and poetry.

HANS H. FRANKEL was educated at the Gymnasium in Göttingen, at Stanford University, and at the University of California, Berkeley, where he received his Ph.D. in 1942. He has taught at California, Stanford, and Peking universities and is now Professor of Chinese Literature at Yale. His field of interest is Chinese poetry from the second century B.C. to the thirteenth century A.D. He is the author of *Biographies of Meng Hao-jan*, "Fifteen Poems by Ts'ao Chih" (*Journal of the American Oriental Society* 84 [1964]), and other articles on Chinese literature and cultural history. He is now completing a book on coordination in Chinese poetry.

WANG GUNGWU is Professor and Head of the Department of Far Eastern History, Institute of Advanced Studies, The Australian National University, Canberra, and was formerly Professor of History at the University of Malaya, Kuala Lumpur. He studied at National Central University, Nanking, and the University of Malaya, Singapore, before doing his doctoral research at the University of London. His main work on premodern Chinese history has been his book on North China during the Five Dynasties and a monograph and several articles on Chinese relations with Southeast Asia.

DAVID LATTIMORE had his graduate training at Cornell and Yale universities and is currently Associate Professor of Linguistics, Brown University. He has published translations and critical essays in the field of Chinese literature, particularly poetry, and is engaged on a major study of Tu Fu.

DAVID MCMULLEN is Lecturer in Chinese Studies at Cambridge University. He received his doctorate at Cambridge in 1968, with a thesis on Yüan Chieh (A.D. 719–72). He is at present working on T'ang Confucianism and on a bibliography of concordances and indexes for Chinese texts.

IKEDA ON had his training at Tokyo University in East Asian history. He was for some years Associate Professor at Hokkaido University. In 1971 he joined the faculty of the Institute of Oriental Culture, Tokyo University. His interests and his publications center on T'ang social and institutional history, especially as documented by the Tunhuang finds.

CHARLES A. PETERSON took both his B.A. and Ph.D. at the University of Washington, Seattle; in addition, he studied in Paris, 1957–58, and in Kyoto, 1962–65, where he was a Fulbright Fellow. Following the year 1965–66, when he was associated with the Sung project in Paris, he joined the faculty at Cornell University where he is now Associate Professor of Chinese History. His research has focused on late T'ang

441

history, and he has contributed studies relating to the political, administrative, and military aspects of central government–provincial relations. He is a contributor to *The Cambridge History of China*.

DENIS TWITCHETT, F.B.A., studied at London and Cambridge universities and received his doctorate from Cambridge. After further study in Tokyo he taught at London University. He is now Professor of Chinese at Cambridge. His primary interest is in economic and institutional history. In addition to numerous articles, he has published *Financial Administration under the T'ang Dynasty*, and he is principal editor of *The Cambridge History of China*, which is now being prepared for the press.

HOWARD J. WECHSLER took his B.A. at Brooklyn College and his M.A. and Ph.D. at Yale University, where he wrote his dissertation on the early T'ang statesman Wei Cheng (580–643). He studied a year at Academia Sinica and a year at the Research Institute for Humanistic Studies, Kyoto University. He is now Assistant Professor of History and Asian Studies at the University of Illinois at Urbana-Champaign. His research interests are in T'ang political history, and he is a contributor to *The Cambridge History of China*, vol. 3.

STANLEY WEINSTEIN has a B.A. from Kamazawa University (Tokyo), an M.A. from Tokyo University, and a Ph.D. from Harvard. He is now Associate Professor of Buddhist Studies at Yale. His training and interests have been focused on the history of Buddhist thought in China and Japan. He has published numerous articles and reviews and is the author of a chapter on Buddhism under the T'ang for *The Cambridge History of China*, vol. 3.

ARTHUR F. WRIGHT had his training at Stanford, Oxford, and Harvard universities and in Kyoto and Peking. He taught for twelve years at Stanford and since 1959 has been at Yale where he is Charles Seymour Professor of History. His major interests are in the intellectual history of the middle dynasties. He is the author of numerous articles and of *Buddhism in Chinese History* (1959); he edited five volumes of studies in Chinese thought published by the University of Chicago Press and Stanford University Press between 1953 and 1962.

Glossary-Index